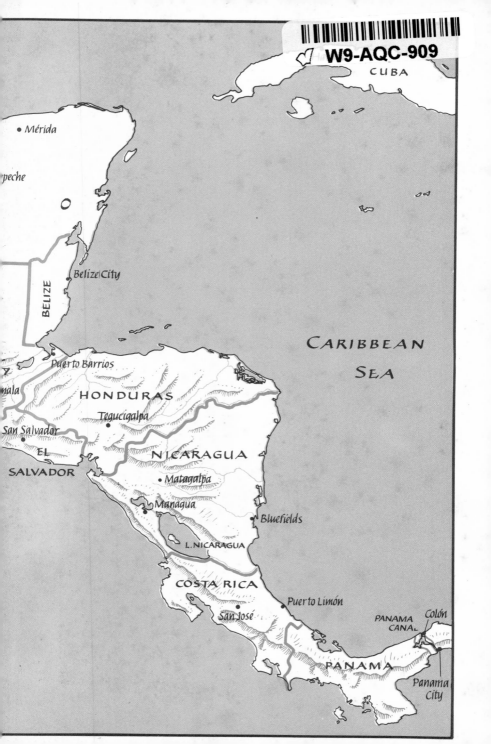

CUBA

Mérida

peche

O

Belize City

BELIZE

Puerto Barrios

CARIBBEAN

SEA

mala

HONDURAS

San Salvador

Tegucigalpa

EL

NICARAGUA

SALVADOR

Matagalpa

Managua

Bluefields

L. NICARAGUA

COSTA RICA

Puerto Limón

San José

PANAMA
CANAL

Colón

PANAMA

Panama
City

CRY OF THE PEOPLE

PENNY LERNOUX

CRY
OF THE PEOPLE

United States Involvement in the Rise of Fascism, Torture,
and Murder and the Persecution of the Catholic Church
in Latin America

Doubleday & Company, Inc., Garden City, New York; 1980

Library of Congress Cataloging in Publication Data

Lernoux, Penny, 1940–
Cry of the people.

Includes index.
1. Catholic Church in Latin America.
2. Persecution—Latin America. 3. United States—
Foreign relations—Latin America. 4. Latin America—
Foreign relations—United States. I. Title.
BX1426.2.L43   261.8
ISBN 0-385-13150-X
Library of Congress Catalog Card Number 78-55841

No copyright is claimed for the material quoted from the following publications of the
United States Government:
Congressional Record, p. S9891, U. S. Senate, June 15, 1977.
"Quality of Life in the Americas—Report of a Presidential Mission for the Western
Hemisphere," Department of State Bulletin, December 8, 1969, p. 18.
"The Recent Presidential Elections in El Salvador: Implications for U. S. Foreign Policy,"
Hearings before the Subcommittee on International Organizations and on Inter-American
Affairs of the Committee on International Relations, House of Representatives, p. 50.
"Human Rights in Nicaragua, Guatemala, and El Salvador," Hearings before the Sub-
committee on International Organizations of the Committee on International Relations,
House of Representatives, June 8 and 9, 1976, p. 73.
"Guatemala and the Dominican Republic," A Staff Memorandum prepared for the Use of
the Subcommittee on Western Hemisphere Affairs of the Committee on Foreign Relations,
U. S. Senate, December 30, 1971, pp. 1–6.
"Quality of Life in the Americas—Report of a Presidential Mission for the Western
Hemisphere," Department of State Bulletin, December 8, 1969, pp. 502–15.
AID, Proposal, Economic Assistance Program, FY 1967.
"Human Rights in Argentina," Hearings before the Committee on International Organiza-
tions of the Committee on International Relations, House of Representatives, 1976, p. 5.
Foreign Assistance 1965, p. 82.
Maxwell D. Taylor, Address at Graduation Exercises, International Police Academy, Wash-
ington, D.C., U. S. Department of State press release, December 17, 1965.
Institute of International Education, Military Assistance Training Programs of the U. S.
Government, Committee on Educational Interchange Policy, Statement No. 18, July 1964.
U. S. House of Representatives, Committee of Appropriations, Foreign Operations Appro-
priations for 1963, Hearings, 87th Congress, 2nd sess., Part I, p. 359.
U. S. House of Representatives, Committee on International Relations, Subcommittee on
International Assistance, Mutual Security Assistance Hearings, 1976.

Grateful acknowledgment is made for permission to include the following copyrighted
material:

"Arms," by M. J. Arce, from *Guatemala,* edited by Susanne Jones and David Tobis. Reprinted by permission of North American Congress on Latin America.

"Basic Christian Communities." Reprinted by permission of *Latin America Documentation.*

Excerpt from *The CIA and the Cult of Intelligence,* by Victor L. Marchetti and John D.
Marks. Copyright © 1974 by Victor L. Marchetti and John D. Marks. Reprinted by permission of Alfred A. Knopf, Inc.

MAPS BY RAFAEL PALACIOS

TO THE POOR PEOPLE OF LATIN AMERICA

ACKNOWLEDGMENTS

First acknowledgment must go to the Alicia Patterson Foundation, which enabled me, through a grant in 1976, to study the
complex changes in the Catholic Church in Latin America. I am
also indebted to Carey McWilliams, for many years the editor of
The Nation, who encouraged me to apply for the grant and to
write this book; to Blair Clark, his successor at *The Nation;* and
to Robert Hatch, *The Nation*'s film critic, who was responsible for
the editing.

Equal individual thanks must go to the people who have read
and commented on the work, chief among them my husband,
Denis, for his penetrating criticisms and insights. I am also grateful to Father Darryl Hunt, social communications director for
Maryknoll; his assistant Elaine Williams; and James Goff, editor
of the Lima-based ecumenical news service *Latinamerica Press,*
for their criticisms, corrections, and suggestions, and for providing material and documents included in this book.

Special thanks are also due Brita Engels, a Dutch lady with a
profound concern for the poor children of Colombia; Moises Sandoval, editor of *Maryknoll* magazine, who introduced me to the
book's subject; and José Ignacio Torres, director of the Bogotá-
based Indo American Press Service, who patiently guided me
through the labyrinth of Church politics. I am also indebted to
María Cristina Pérez, for helping to prepare the manuscript; the
Latin American Confederation of Religious; and the Capuchin
Fathers in Nicaragua.

The list would be incomplete without mention of the many
bishops, priests, nuns, and lay Latin Americans who have contrib-

uted to this work with their insights and, especially, their example.

And finally, events are moving so quickly in Latin America that each day brings more changes. Therefore, with few exceptions, the period covered by the book ends in mid-1979.

CONTENTS

MAPS

From the heart of Latin America, a cry rises to the heavens ever louder and more imperative. It is the cry of a people who suffer and who demand justice, freedom, and respect for the fundamental rights of man.

III General Conference
of Latin-American Bishops,
Puebla, Mexico,
February 13, 1979

INTRODUCTION

There are three truths, says an old Chinese proverb: your truth, my truth, and the truth. The following account of the Catholic Church's struggle against military dictatorship in Latin America is based on documented facts. Among the principal sources are the U. S. Congress, Amnesty International, and the Catholic Church, including the *Latin America Documentation* service of the U. S. Catholic Conference, such Catholic publications as the Jesuit magazine *Mensaje* in Chile, and pastoral letters from Latin-American bishops. But the facts are presented from the viewpoint of the poor people, who make up two thirds of the Latin-American population. The stories of repression and violence, of torture and murder, these are their truth.

The central issue in the ongoing religious war between Church and state in Latin America is human rights. One aspect of this struggle is the persecution of bishops, priests, and laity who have challenged a right-wing totalitarian ideology that has engulfed the area. The other, integral part of the story is the verified role of the U. S. Defense Department, the CIA, and corporate industry in the rise of this totalitarianism. Thus, on many occasions, Catholic bishops and priests, including U.S. citizens, have been tortured or murdered by organizations funded and trained by the U. S. Government, sometimes with the direct connivance of U.S. agencies. Because of this involvement, important sectors of the traditionally conservative Latin-American Catholic Church now oppose U.S. capitalism.

Much of the narrative of the book is composed of stories of the Church's martyrs, people who were murdered because they supported a farmers' cooperative or the construction of a sewer system in a slum or because they repeated God's commandment "You shall not kill." These courageous people have given new testimony to the essential character of the Gospel, which is the story of poor people, and of the Gospel message of human rights.

CRY OF THE PEOPLE

PART ONE

RETURN TO THE CATACOMBS

CHAPTER I

TORTURE—the Rise of Fascism—the Agony of the Church

> In Germany they first came for the communists; I did not
> speak because I was not a communist. Then they came for the
> Jews; I did not speak because I was not a Jew. Then they
> came to fetch the workers, members of trade unions; I did not
> speak because I was not a trade unionist. Afterward, they
> came for the Catholics; I did not say anything because I was
> a Protestant. Eventually they came for me, and there was no
> one left to speak. . . .
>
> Pastor Martin Niemöller,
> a Protestant minister imprisoned
> by the Third Reich

One warm spring evening in Villa Soldati, Father Patrick Rice and Fátima Cabrera left the shantytown's small chapel for her home a few blocks away. The slum was in darkness, with no lights anywhere. As Rice and Fátima picked their way around the piles of garbage, an old Jeep crept out of a side street and followed them. Neither saw the vehicle until it was upon them. "Stop or I'll shoot," shouted a man in civilian clothes, leaping from the car and waving a pistol.

"We didn't know what to do," said Rice. "He fired a shot in the ground. He pointed his gun at us and asked for our identity papers. He seemed nervous. He fired another shot in the air. Another man came around the corner, also carrying a gun. They bundled the two of us into the back of the Jeep. At no time did they identify themselves. We didn't know who they were or where they were taking us."

The experiences of Father Rice and Fátima Cabrera when the Jeep roared out of the Buenos Aires slum on that night in October 1976 were not uncommon: At least twenty thousand people have suffered the same fate since a police state was imposed on Argentina in 1974.[1] Nor has it been just an Argentine phenomenon. Tens of thousands of Latin Americans living under other military regimes have been similarly abused in a reign of terror unequaled in the continent's history. Unlike Rice, an Irish priest, many did not live to tell a tale of horror that often surpassed the inhumanity of the Nazi concentration camps.

"They took us to Police Station 36," said Father Rice. "I was taken into a room and my shirt was pulled up over my head and face. They asked my name and where I lived. When I identified myself as a priest, they first demanded that I recite the Lord's Prayer in Latin, then they told me, 'Now you'll find out that the Romans were very civilized toward the early Christians compared with what's going to happen to you.' After this, they beat me, although I was not asked any questions.

"Later that night I was put in the trunk of a car, my hands were tied behind my back, my head hooded. Fátima was put in the back seat. We were taken to what I thought was a barracks [probably the Guemes Brigade near Buenos Aires' Ricchieri Freeway]. The hood made of rags was removed and replaced by a yellow canvas hood with string around the neck. The man changing the hood said, 'Don't look at me! If you do you're dead!' I was beaten again. By this time I was in a bad state.

"They started with water torture. My nose was held and water was poured in my mouth. You swallow a lot of water and it has a drowning effect. My interrogators told me that they belonged to the AAA [a parapolice organization called the Argentine Anti-Communist Alliance]. The beatings and drenching with water continued throughout Tuesday, October 12, at three- or four-hour intervals.

"On Tuesday night they came and walked me to another room. Electric shocks were applied systematically to various parts of my body. They were also giving electric shock treatment to Fátima in the same room. All day Wednesday, October 13, they tortured Fátima—I could hear her screaming. I was told that I was accused of putting up propaganda slogans against the Army in Villa Soldati, which was a lie. They kept throwing water on us and increasing the shock and demanded that we give them the names of everyone we knew in the *villa*. They told me that I was stronger than Fátima and because of me they were going to destroy her. While denying their charges, I refused to give names, believing that anyone I knew would probably get the same treatment. This only increased their suspicion, but I think in the end they realized we didn't know anything. I was told by one of my interrogators, 'I am also against violence and for that reason I won't kill you.'

"At one point I was able to lift the hood on my head and see the rest of the room. There were seven other prisoners there, all with yellow hoods, chained to the wall, and two or three torturers were working in a torture chamber nearby. When they saw me moving the hood, they nearly lynched me with a cord around my neck. All day and night they kept torturing Fátima . . . her desperate screams drove me crazy.

"Finally on Thursday, October 14, I was given a little water and allowed to go to the bathroom for the first time. Then I was brought to the person in charge and told, 'You have been in detention for eight hours.' I was again bundled into the trunk of a car and taken to the Coordinación Federal [police headquarters for Buenos Aires, 1550 Moreno Street, Buenos Aires]. When I entered they asked me my name, but I couldn't answer because I could hardly speak. They beat me in the ribs and I fell down. Eventually I was taken to a small cell, given something to eat, and allowed to take a shower. I was horrified by all the marks on my body.

"The following day Fátima was brought in and put in a cell near me. She told me that during the electric shock torture, they had stripped her and applied electric shocks to her mouth to stop her screaming. One of the officials took off the bandage covering her eyes and told her to take a good look at him because it was his life or hers. She said she prayed to God that she would die to end her suffering, and then she fell into a coma.

"At police headquarters I was told to say that my black eye, a badly cut foot, and other signs of torture had been caused by my falling down some stairs. 'If you say anything else, you'll be found in the river,' they told me. Life at police headquarters is one continuous hell, with Swastika crosses painted on the passages, confinement for months without ever seeing the sun, terrible food, constant threats by the interrogators, and abuse by the guards, particularly of women prisoners.

"A week after my arrest I was washed, shaved, and brought before the Irish ambassador. I was quite disoriented and the ambassador realized that it wasn't in my interests to talk about ill treatment. Later I signed a document that apparently cleared me of the charges. I thought therefore that I would be released in a few days, but I was transferred to Villa Devoto Prison and then to La Plata Prison [in the province of Buenos Aires], where I was held for five weeks until my deportation. I was not tortured anymore."

Rice was taken to the airport on December 3, bound for London and freedom, but those terrible nights and days left a profound mark on the thirty-two-year-old priest, who spent two weeks recovering in a psychiatric ward. "My Christian faith became very real to me," he said. "In such suffering Christ is almost physically present, and one's prayer is a despairing plea to God to save one, as indeed Christ's own cry on the cross was. At times the proximity of death filled me with fear and dread, and my whole being wanted to cling to life, but then it seemed as though I had been rescued by Christ, that I was able to resist this evil, irrespective of my well-being or even life itself."[2]

An Ongoing Nightmare

Compared to others who were arrested or kidnapped, Father Rice was lucky—he had been born in Ireland, and most Europeans and North Americans picked up by the Argentine police can look for help from their embassies. Not so the Argentines or the fourteen thousand Chilean, Uruguayan, Bolivian, Brazilian, and Paraguayan political refugees living in Argentina.[3] They either languished in jail or died in the torture chambers. Fátima Cabrera, for example, was not released from prison until December 1977, when she was placed under house arrest.

What was Rice's crime or Fátima Cabrera's? Like most of those arrested, they never really knew. A worker-priest from County Cork who had lived six years in Argentina, Rice divided his time between earning a small wage as a carpenter on construction sites and organizing evening and weekend prayer meetings in Villa Soldati.

One of fifty shantytowns, or *villas,* that encircle Buenos Aires, Villa Soldati was built on the city garbage dump, where forty thousand impoverished people from the Argentine provinces and neighboring Paraguay were crowded into cardboard shacks. Some worked as street cleaners or garbage collectors, others as unskilled laborers in the construction industry. Before Rice was abducted, a number of the slum's garbage scavengers had been arrested and tortured; some were killed. The bloody corpses of two Uruguayan senators were found in a car that had been abandoned in the rotting refuse. The men, one of whom had been twice president of the Uruguayan Congress, had sought refuge in Buenos Aires from the military dictatorship in their own country, only to be kidnapped, tortured, and murdered by Argentine police working with the Uruguayan secret police.[4] The people in Villa Soldati thus lived in a state of terror, aggravated by nightly shootings by drunken policemen who used the slum's few streetlights for target practice.

In short, Rice was arrested simply because he was working and living with the poor. "Any Christian who defends the poor can expect to be persecuted and mistreated by the security police," he said. As for Fátima Cabrera, her crime was to have walked down the street with the priest. A part-time maid who earned five dollars a week, she was the sole support of a younger brother and sister. When her sister became ill with a serious nervous disorder, Fátima had sought out Rice for medicine. She was twenty-one at the time of her arrest. "In their barbarity they destroyed an innocent young girl just to put pressure on me," Rice said.

For those who survive, life is often worse than death. It is an ongoing nightmare of torture, of not knowing the fate of loved ones or when one's body will give out, of terrible memories and the thought of what might have been—for example, an aborted child. Isabel Gamba de Negrotti had such memories.

The twenty-seven-year-old nursery school teacher and her husband were seized in their home and taken to Police Station 39 in

Villa Urquiza, Buenos Aires. At the time of her abduction Mrs. Negrotti was four months pregnant. When she begged mercy for the unborn child, she was punched and beaten by eight men, her hair was pulled, and she was threatened with death. Her torturers also threatened to arrest her younger sister and her mother. Later that first evening, she began to have cramps; she could hear her husband screaming.

The next morning she was taken to police headquarters in Buenos Aires, where the torment continued: "The [police] took me to another room where they kicked me and punched me in the head. Then they undressed me and beat me on the legs, buttocks, and shoulders with something made of rubber. This lasted a long time; I fell down several times and they made me get up and stand by supporting myself on a table. The police continued to beat me. While all this was going on they talked to me, insulted me, and asked me about people I didn't know and things I didn't understand. I pleaded with them to leave me alone, or else I would lose my baby. I hadn't the strength to speak, the pain was so bad.

"They started to give me electric shocks on my breasts, the side of my body, and under my arms, all the time asking me questions. I was given electric shocks in the vagina and a pillow was placed over my mouth to stop me screaming. Someone they called the 'colonel' came and said they were going to increase the voltage until I talked. They kept throwing water over my body and applying electric shocks all over."[5]

Two days later she miscarried. When last seen, Mrs. Negrotti was in detention in Villa Devoto Prison.[6] As with Rice, no charges were made against her, nor was there any trial. Yet Mrs. Negrotti was fortunate in one respect: she was officially recognized as a political prisoner. Hundreds of other Argentines disappeared without a trace, nonpersons of whom the police denied any knowledge, dead or alive.

The scope of the terror is such that anyone can be caught in its net, even those who have nothing to do with social work in the slums, or with politics, unions, schools, newspapers, or a law practice, all hazardous professions in Argentina, where they are regarded as subversive. "Everyone has had a personal experience of the repression," said the head of a large U.S. subsidiary in Buenos Aires. Three of his workers had "disappeared"—that is, they were abducted by the police or by right-wing paramilitary squads. The seventeen-year-old daughter of a jeweler he knew was dragged screaming from the family's apartment while the police ransacked the rooms for money and jewelry. ("Stealing is officially approved as a means of encouraging these thugs," he said.) Other friends were imprisoned because a map with directions to their ranch had been found in the apartment of another person who was arrested. "It has reached the point," he said, "where you can leave your apartment for a minute to buy something at the corner grocery and end up in jail, as happened to another friend of mine." Trapped by one of the periodic police roundups in which everyone in the block is jailed, the man left his dinner burning on the stove. When his girl friend arrived for supper, she immediately guessed what had happened, and went to the local jail to protest. She, too, was arrested. Torture is automatic for anyone imprisoned.[7]

That such things happen in the most literate, best-fed nation of Latin America is not really surprising. Beneath the surface of Buenos Aires' opulence, behind the steak houses, nightclubs, theaters, and opera houses, are the same malignant forces responsible for still-cruder forms of repression in Bolivia, Paraguay, and a dozen other, poorer Latin-American countries. Though Latin America looks to be the most industrialized of the Third World areas, two thirds of its 320 million people still live in a Dark Ages, ruled by petty warlords ambitious only for power and money. The medieval torture chamber has been updated with sophisticated technology, though Uruguay and other countries still rely on such ancient methods as burning at the stake.*

As under Hitler, organizations that might have protested the brutality have been eliminated, one by one. The communists were the first to go; then the liberal and conservative political parties. Student federations and unions were banned, their leaders imprisoned or killed. Congress was abolished, civil courts were replaced

* According to a report by Amnesty International, one of seventeen commonly used torture methods in Uruguay included burning the prisoner alive in a barbecue pit or grill. "When the smell of roasting meat is emitted, the victim is taken away," reported Amnesty International. (*Human Rights in Uruguay and Paraguay*, Hearings before the Subcommittee on International Organizations of the Committee on International Relations, U. S. House of Representatives, [June 17, July 27 and 28, and Aug. 4, 1976], p. 50.)

by military tribunals, newspapers were closed or severely censored. Even lawyers' and doctors' organizations have been disbanded. On this wreckage of civil association has arisen a vast network of government spies, secret police, and para-police operations with their attendant torture chambers and death squads. Teachers are ordered to indoctrinate the young in a totalitarian ideology and to encourage them to denounce any critic of the state, including their parents.[8] By 1978 all but three countries† in South America were governed by military dictatorships. Most of Central America marched in the same direction.

As totalitarianism swept the hemisphere, courageous voices were raised in protest. Union leaders, politicians, and student representatives spoke out, often at the risk of their lives, and countless acts of heroism were performed by individual Latin Americans. But in time only one voice was left, that of the Catholic Church.

A Purifying Experience

Viewed historically, the Latin-American Catholic Church would seem the least likely institution to oppose the military regimes. From the moment Columbus set foot in the New World, cross and sword had been indistinguishable. Priests and conquistadors divided the plunder in people and land—it was a toss-up which was the greedier. And long before Latin America's military regimes installed their torture chambers, the Inquisition was at work with whip and rack. By the time of the wars of independence at the beginning of the nineteenth century, the Church was the largest landowner in Latin America. It was also the most conservative political force on the continent.

Because of its political and economic importance and its monopoly of education, the Catholic Church was the arbiter of Latin-American society. It taught the Indian and African slaves to embrace fatalism on the promise of a better hereafter. It planted the seeds of machismo brought from Spain and Portugal. It encouraged a deep strain of cynicism among the upper classes, who learned that they might do anything, including slaughter innocent peasants, as long as they went to Mass, contributed land and

† Colombia, Venezuela, and Guyana.

money to the Church's aggrandizement, and baptized their children. These were the "good Christians" honored by the Latin-American bishops. Their descendants run the military regimes that today govern two thirds of the area's people. Look behind a dictator; there stands a bishop. You can see the inevitable pair in colonial and nineteenth-century paintings, the bishop next to the commanding general. Or in the modern art of Colombia's Fernando Botero—vacuous-looking generals staring at enormous, puffed-up bishops. But though many Latin Americans still see the Church that way, the picture is changing.

It began to change, almost imperceptibly, in the early 1960s, when Rome convened the groundbreaking Second Ecumenical Council, or Vatican II. The council sparked reforms throughout the universal Church, but nowhere were they as profound or wide-reaching as in Latin America, the largest underdeveloped part of the Catholic world. For the first time in memory, important groups of bishops spoke of the need for social and economic change. And the more these men searched out the causes of social injustice, the more critical they became of Latin-American society and the Church's traditional role in its perpetuation. By a historical coincidence, their concern for the poor and the oppressed began to crystallize in new pastoral and theological work just when Latin America was engulfed in another wave of military dictatorship. Because of the unprecedented repression imposed by these regimes, many of those in the Church who had been merely critical found themselves forced into a position of open conflict. In any number of cases bishops who started out by mildly scolding the regime for failing to respect human rights ended up at war with the military. This was notably so in Brazil. The more the bishops and clergy protested, the harsher was the repression against the Church; and the fiercer the repression, the more the Church protested. It was a vicious circle, but also a purifying experience: out of adversity was emerging a socially conscious Church.

The military dictatorships could gag the labor unions and political parties, but they had never had the power to silence the Church, for, with the military and the landowning and industrial elites, it is one of the three institutions that preside over Latin America. In addition to its temporal wealth and political power, the Church has a hemisphere-wide base and, in the Vatican, an international forum. More important, it still has the authority and organization to command the loyalty of a majority of Latin Americans. (Even today, 90 percent of the people are baptized Catholics.) Like the Spanish and Portuguese languages, Catholicism is so deeply embedded in the Latin-American cultures that a government can no more ignore or destroy it than an Arab ruler can outlaw Islam. Thus the Catholic Church was and is the only body in Latin America powerful enough both to criticize dictatorship and to sustain a formal dialogue with the military leaders in government. It is also the only organization able to encourage alternatives to totalitarianism in the ongoing atmosphere of terror. Unions, student groups, political parties, all seek the protection of the Church: it alone can withstand the repression.

However, not everyone in the Catholic Church agrees that a commitment to social causes is necessary or desirable. There are serious divisions between traditionalists who want to preserve the old ways and progressives who envision a new Latin-American Church similar in spirit and organization to the primitive Christian communities. The split cuts right across the Church, from cardinal to layperson. But the trend clearly favors the progressives, at least in the concept of Vatican II.

One of the most important contributions of Vatican II was its image of the Church as a community of equals instead of a hierarchy of laity, clergy, and bishops. This concept of a "People of God" found quick acceptance in Latin America, where the mass of the people were starved for the Word of God. Although hitherto the Church had dealt with the poor as an afterthought, these Latin Americans cling to a deep sense of religiosity. Indeed, in many cultures it is the only means whereby the poor can express themselves. Unlike the secular societies of industrialized countries, community life in Latin America is still deeply colored by religion. Wherever bishops and clergy have reached out to these people, they have found an immediate response. But this is no longer the traditional Catholicism of pomp and circumstance, of rigid divisions separating the princes of the Church from the people. Bishops, priests, and nuns have come to look upon themselves as brothers and sisters of the people, at the service of the poor. And because almost everyone is poor in Latin America, this

Church will endure, even as the Church of the wealthy and middle classes is succumbing to the same materialism that has infected religious institutions in the United States and Europe.

By any historical measure the price of commitment to the poor has been enormous. Persecution of the Catholic Church in Latin America, and of the Protestants, too, is unparalleled in modern history, even in Hitler's Germany and Stalin's Soviet Union. Since 1968, when Latin America's Catholic Church began to question the miserable conditions in which two thirds of the people live, over 850 priests, nuns, and bishops have been arrested, tortured, murdered, or expelled, and thousands of the Catholic laity have been jailed and killed.‡ "Nowadays it is dangerous . . . and practically illegal to be an authentic Christian in Latin America," said Salvadoran Jesuit Rutilio Grande a month before he was shot dead by right-wing assassins in El Salvador. Two months later, in May 1977, a second Salvadoran priest, Alfonso Navarro Oviedo, was murdered in his home by a right-wing vigilante group that threatened to massacre all the Jesuits in the country. But unlike the Catholic churches in Franco's Spain and Hitler's Germany, Latin America's bishops and priests will not be cowed. "We will eat dirt before we betray our people," said Paraguay's Bishop Aníbal Maricevich.

On the contrary, persecution only stiffens the Church's resolve. "We thank our Lord for the privilege of having personally experienced the same sufferings of so many others who cannot defend themselves as well as a bishop," announced the Chilean hierarchy after three of its members were manhandled at Santiago's international airport by agents of the National Department of Intelligence (DINA), the Chilean secret police. Similar words have been spoken elsewhere—by Venezuelan Bishop Mariano Parra León, who suffered a heart attack when he and forty-seven bishops and priests were imprisoned in Ecuador during an inter-American pastoral meeting; by the bishops of northeastern Brazil, whom the military government has jailed and interrogated; and by

‡ See Appendix for a chart of Latin-American martyrs. The only comparable persecution against a religious body in recent times occurred in the Soviet Union after the Revolution (1918–20) when twenty-eight bishops of the Russian Orthodox Church and several thousand Orthodox priests and monks were murdered.

Brazilian Bishop Adriano Hipólito, who was kidnapped and beaten by the right-wing Anti-Communist Alliance.

"Why should the Church be surprised that it is persecuted?" wonders Dom Helder Cámara, the gentle, much-persecuted archbishop of Recife, Brazil. "Did the Lord's warnings refer only to the first centuries of the Church?" Many Latin-American Christians think not, pointing to the similarities between their sufferings and those of the primitive Church. In Brazil, they call themselves the "Church of the Catacombs."

CHAPTER II

REPRESSION—the Recognition of Human Rights

The Spirit of the Lord is upon me, because He has anointed me to announce the good news to the poor. He has sent me to proclaim release to the captives and recovery of sight to the blind, to set at liberty those who are oppressed, to proclaim the year of the Lord's favor. [Luke 4:18–19]

> Jesus Christ announcing his mission at the beginning of his public life, in a synagogue in Nazareth

One of the jokes repeated everywhere in Latin America, despite cultural and language differences, tells of how the Angel Gabriel complained to God about his excessive generosity to Argentina (or Brazil or Venezuela, depending on the nationality of the storyteller). Why, demanded Gabriel, had God given this country so many natural resources, so many lakes and rivers, such fertile land and fine weather, when other nations did not get half so much? Ah, said God, but wait till you see the kind of people I'm going to put there!

The idea that the people's shortcomings somehow balance nature's generosity almost always comes up in conversation with foreigners when comparisons are made between the development of the United States and that of Latin America. Educated Latin Americans are forever bemoaning their past: "If only our ancestors had been white Europeans," they will say, "we would be just as developed as you Americans." Yet the facts tell another story. Argentina, the "whitest," most European nation in Latin America, with many cultural characteristics similar to those of the United States, wiped out its Indian and black population in the nineteenth century. But observe Argentina today—three decades of military dictatorship, a perpetually unstable economy, public services that make New York City look like a model of efficiency, and the largest concentration camps in Latin America. So what ails these white Europeans?

Actually, there's nothing ethnically wrong with any of the Latin-American people, Andean Indians, Brazilian blacks, or white Argentines. The problem was created not by God but by the Spanish and Portuguese empires, with their methods of colonization and land settlement and a legal code twisted to venality and corruption. And neither land tenure nor the legal system has changed much since the eighteenth century.

Unlike the United States and "white" Argentina, much of Latin America was already occupied by culturally advanced Indian civilizations when the Spanish and Portuguese conquerors arrived. Although the Europeans managed to slaughter several million Indians, enough survived to provide the manual labor and the women for the basis of a colonial society. Many of Latin America's cities are built on the ruins of Indian settlements. Where the aboriginal source died out, as in coastal Brazil, the Europeans imported African slave labor.

From the very beginning, Latin-American society was constructed like a pyramid, with a few European settlers enjoying all the privileges of empire and a mass of Indians, blacks, and half-castes having no rights at all. The pyramid survived because the mass at the bottom was repeatedly told that it was stupid, lazy, and inferior. Foreign missionaries helped drum these ideas into the natives' heads by claiming that it was God's will that they should be poor and ignorant. As the archbishop of Lima told his Indians, "Poverty is the most certain road to felicity."[1] Any Indian or African who had the temerity to doubt such wisdom by rebelling against the system was promptly killed.

The law, to be sure, was written in a way to protect the poor and the Indians, but it never worked that way, for Spanish and

Portuguese legislation could be enforced only on the rare occasions when the Crown threatened to send troops to discipline the settlers. "The law is to be observed but not obeyed," claims an old Spanish saying still in vogue today. Put another way, the only law respected was—and is—the law of the fist.

Latin America's independence movement from Spain in the first part of the nineteenth century did not in the least alter the social pyramid, nor did twentieth-century industrialization. The only difference is that those at the top are now white Latin Americans instead of white Europeans and can count industries as well as ranches in their inheritance. The overwhelming majority of the people remains uneducated and fatalistic. All initiative was stamped out of the people's collective conscience over the centuries because it was not intended that they should think or react. "*¿Para qué?*" (Why bother?) has been the universal response in Latin America, whether in a Caribbean black community or an Indian village in the Bolivian highlands.

As anthropologists have amply proved, there is an enormous difference between a culture that is poor and a culture of poverty. In the former the people may have only a rudimentary economy and learning but they are proud of their traditions. In the latter the people are ashamed of their color and origins because they have been taught to feel inferior. That is the culture of poverty studied by Oscar Lewis in Mexico and Puerto Rico, and the culture of two thirds of the Latin-American population. They are the "kind of people" God put on the continent to balance the Angel Gabriel's uneven score.

The Catholic Church must accept a lot of the blame for this situation. Like the conquistadors, most of the European missionaries who came to Latin America saw themselves as bearers of cultures vastly superior to those of the natives. The missionaries were less interested in integrating the Indians or Africans than in subjugating them to the European religious structures. Little attempt was made to understand or appreciate the cultural heritage of the people, and most of the missionaries remained a group apart, European colonists on the American continent, right up to the twentieth century. Although the mass of the people accepted the white man's God, either under physical duress or because he seemed more powerful than their own gods, they never really assimilated the ideas of Christianity, but merely changed the names of their gods and rites for those of the Europeans. (The *orixas,* or deities of the Brazilian Africans' Macumba religion, for example, took on the names and characteristics of Christian saints.) Baptism, which in its biblical sense is a sign of conversion and hope, became a rite to ward off evil spirits, and in some countries, such as Brazil, a ceremony of the dying.

Blinded by their own cultural limitations, the missionaries never saw how superficial was the religious conversion. Nor did they think it strange that two cultures should coexist—one belonging to the masses with their syncretic religion, the other to the rich, educated elites. The Indian artisans who built the churches of marble and gold were not expected to understand the mysteries of the faith; it was enough that they submitted to its superiority. If there was any doubt about their ethnic inferiority in this religious hierarchy, they had only to observe the statues and pictures they were ordered to carve and paint—not one of these light-colored effigies looked like them.

At its best, Catholicism was a benevolent paternalism that protected the Indians and the Africans from the settlers' atrocities while it reinforced the colonial system through praise of patience, obedience, and the virtue of suffering. The people believed the missionaries when they said that it was God's will, or destiny, that they should be poor, wealth and poverty being conditions of birth and color. As Brazilian theologian Eduardo Hoornaert points out, "Colonizers show the colonized that there is wealth to be had, and even luxury, but they don't show them how to obtain it. Obviously, they tell them that wealth comes from work, but the people aren't convinced, because they can see it isn't so: a 'good' situation in society comes from a diploma, from position, from education, ultimately from belonging to the dominant culture."[2]

The Jesuit reductions, or missions, in Paraguay, southern Brazil, and northern Argentina are often cited by Church historians as examples of the good done by the colonial Church, and it is true that for 150 years these missions protected and sustained some 150,000 Guaraní Indians. When they were closed by order of the Spanish Crown in 1767, there was a dramatic decrease in the Guaraní population, which was slaughtered or enslaved by the settlers. Many of the Jesuits gave their lives for the Indians, caring for them during smallpox plagues and physically interposing themselves between the bloodthirsty settlers and the natives. The weather was hot and unhealthy. The woods and swamps were places of mosquito swarms, brackish waters, floods, jaguars, reptiles, and vermin. Frequently living alone or with a single companion, the typical Jesuit missionary was carpenter, farmer, physician, nurse, and one-man defense of the stockade. There is no doubt that these men were heroes, but to what avail?

Contrary to the claim that they were an advanced form of religious socialism, an Arcadian democracy in which the Indians enjoyed equal rights, the reductions were medieval estates where everyone lived under the grip of the Jesuits, a caste apart. The priests decided when and what the Indians should eat, how they should organize the workday, who should be punished or rewarded, where they should live, everything down to the last detail. True, this was a vast improvement over the wretched treatment meted out on the Spanish haciendas, but it was nevertheless a form of slavery. Even the Jesuits realized that they were destroying a millenary culture, but they could do no better because of the language block, the cultural gap, and the colonial mentality itself. Thus they continued to treat "those people" as children. Except for a few churches and religious carvings, nothing survived of this Jesuit empire of thirty cities and towns, for when Spain removed the Jesuits there was no one to lead or even think.

As an experiment in benevolent paternalism, the reductions were an example of the best aspects of the colonial Church—and the worst. When the Guaraní Indians were dispersed, they carried with them two centuries of fatalism. They had lost many of their cultural traditions and could find none to replace them in a white society whose name for Indian to this day is *chancho,* or "pig." Their descendants live in the festering slums of Asunción or on the large Paraguayan cattle ranches where, says a Paraguayan bishop, "they have less value than a horse or a cow."

"No one listens to the cry of the poor. . . ."

Over the past decade the Latin-American Catholic Church has consciously tried to rid itself of such paternalistic traditions and colonial attitudes in order to rebuild Christianity on the cultural heritage of the people and to encourage the emergence of a more mature and democratic Church. By doing so, it moves in direct opposition to the ruling classes and their governments, still mired in the prejudices of the eighteenth century. Whether the country is Brazil or Guatemala, more or less industrialized, in South or Central America, the statistics are always the same: a tiny minority, usually 1 to 4 percent of the population, owns the majority of the arable land and takes an overwhelming share of the nation's agricultural and industrial wealth. The great majority, in the slums or impoverished rural villages, owns little or no land, is undernourished, illiterate or semiliterate, and unemployed or underemployed. One third of Latin America's 320 million people earn less in a year than a U.S. housewife spends on groceries in a week. Conversely, the well-to-do in Latin America usually live better than do the upper classes in the United States; they have platoons of servants, enormous estates, limousines, private airplanes, and yachts, and pay practically no taxes.

This baronial style of life is still possible because the cornerstone of the colonial system remains intact—the law of the strongest. Typical of conditions in much of rural Latin America are the cattle haciendas of Paraguay. Enormous spreads that stretch for miles over the undulating red hills, with a few head of cattle here and there, they look like something out of the wild West, with a cluster of shacks for the peon cowboys, a slightly better house for the ranch administrator, and almost no evidence of agricultural machinery. Because manual labor is plentiful and cheap, less than fifty cents per worker per day, the large landowners are under no pressure to modernize. As a result only 1 percent of the country's arable land is efficiently cultivated.

Few of the peasants who serve these primitive estates ever learn to read or write, see a doctor, or know the luxury of running water or electricity. Malnutrition causes nine tenths of the deaths. Submissive, with intense feelings of inferiority, these peasants explain their tragedy by quoting an old Guaraní Indian saying: "No one listens to the cry of the poor or the sound of a wooden bell." Three fifths of Paraguay's 2.6 million people live this way.

Such conditions would be impossible if Paraguay's farm labor were sufficiently organized to demand better wages and a more equitable distribution of land, but whenever an attempt is made to establish cooperatives or unions, the government suddenly discovers a "communist conspiracy" and sends troops into the countryside to destroy the cooperatives, burn the peasants' huts, rape the women, and kill or imprison the men. During the last outbreak of terror, in 1976 in southeastern Paraguay, some three thousand people were arrested and several cooperative leaders murdered. The Catholic Church was also severely punished for sponsoring some of the cooperatives: twenty-four priests were jailed, tortured, and expelled.[3]

Like many of the largest landowners, Otello Carpinelli is also a general, head of the II Military Region headquartered in Villarrica in southeastern Paraguay. Carpinelli evicted two hundred peasants from twenty-five hundred acres of farmland so that it could be sold to a land development company from neighboring Brazil, which has absorbed large blocks of Paraguayan frontier land in its drive for Manifest Destiny.[4] Contrary to what might be expected, Paraguay's generals do not scruple to sell border land to their powerful neighbors, because often it's not their land and they can make huge profits on such transactions. An instance of the real estate speculation that goes on in Paraguay was the eviction of five hundred peasant families in the region of the Upper Paraná River by the Paraguayan Rural Welfare [sic] Institute, which claimed that the land was needed to provide military security for the giant Itaipu hydroelectrical complex under construction by the two countries. The institute sold the land for fifty dollars an acre, payable over ten years, to Paraguayan military commanders, who resold it to Brazilian businessmen for fifteen times that much. Altogether, nearly a million acres were transferred to the Brazilians, who now own 30 percent of Paraguay's arable land, the major source of the people's income and jobs.*[5]

Governed by the longest-ruling dictator in the hemisphere,

* The same sort of thing is happening in the Brazilian Amazon, except that there the land development companies are owned by Americans and Europeans instead of Brazilians. Rural conditions are the same as those in Paraguay; so, too, are the methods of eviction. The numbers, however, are larger: *more than 7 million Brazilian peasants* have been forced off the land since the 1950s. (*Marginación de un Pueblo*, Document of the Bishops of Central and Western Brazil, Spanish translation of Portuguese by Jesuits' *Revista del Centro de Investigación y Acción Social* [Buenos Aires, June 1974], p. 16.)

General Alfredo Stroessner, Paraguay is dismissed by the more-advanced Latin-American countries as a cowboy backwater, its President a crude throwback to the nineteenth-century caudillo. But whatever may be said of Stroessner, he has the courage of his convictions. Unlike the military regimes in Chile and Brazil, which dressed up dictatorship with ideological or technological trimmings, Stroessner has never pretended that there is any reason for power except corruption. Brazil's wealthy generals might talk about technology and efficiency in government, while privately enjoying such perquisites of office as butlers, lakeside chalets, and unlimited expense accounts. Paraguay's military and police make no such excuses: they support Stroessner for what they can get, and in addition to land, which is the foundation of Paraguayan wealth, this includes government graft, contraband, and revenue from narcotics and prostitution.

Dominated by military men and a few privileged civilians, the contraband trade in luxury consumer goods and cattle is regarded as a socially acceptable profession. Indeed, many shops in the capital city of Asunción openly display smuggled goods: the ones a tourist sees, such as the liquor and cigarette emporiums that surround Asunción's leading hotel, the Guaraní, on the city's principal plaza. Cabbies take visitors for a drive through Asunción's wealthy suburbs to see the new mansions built by contraband. One of the impressive homes belongs to a Cabinet minister who, from a position of modest means, in less than a year became the owner of a palace costing several hundred thousand dollars.

Most contraband comes from the United States in large transport planes crammed with cigarettes, whiskey, liqueurs, perfumes, and other expensive items that land at the Asunción International Airport in the special contraband section. (One of the smaller countries in Latin America, Paraguay is the world's largest importer of American cigarettes.) The goods are reshipped to neighboring South American countries, either in Paraguayan Air Force planes or on Navy landing ships that cross the Paraguay and Paraná rivers.[6]

Narcotics are almost totally controlled by the secret police in charge of the torture centers and Stroessner's spy network. The coca paste to make cocaine comes from neighboring Bolivia, run by another right-wing general; heroin is brought in from Europe.

The drugs are reshipped through Buenos Aires or flown direct to the United States. As a State Department report wryly notes, "It seems to have been difficult for some officials of Paraguay to understand the importance of the effort of the United States to terminate the illegal drug traffic into our country."[7] One of the more obtuse officials by all accounts is Pastor Coronel, head of the country's Criminal Investigations [read Torture] Department and a prominent organizer of the heroin trade. Coronel was a key contact of Auguste-Joseph Ricord, the Asunción-based Corsican kingpin of Latin America's United States–bound heroin traffic. (In 1972 Ricord was extradited to the United States on drug charges, after seventeen months of arm-twisting, including the threat to cut off all U.S. aid.)[8]

Stroessner encourages these illegal activities in the belief that the more people are compromised and corrupted, the more beholden they will be to his system of government. On the basis of this simple logic, his undoubted machismo, and shrewd understanding of the weaknesses of potential rivals, whether they be drugs or little girls, the burly, red-haired general has ruled unchallenged since 1954.

Stroessner's Paraguay is only an extreme example of what prevails in Latin America. The same sort of police thugs who terrorize people in Asunción work the streets of Buenos Aires, São Paulo, and Rio de Janeiro, where witch-hunts for communists are the excuse for blackmail, torture, and murder. José Alves da Silva, for example, was the assistant director of São Paulo's notorious Tiradentes Prison for political prisoners despite fourteen indictments for murder, robbery, torture, white slavery, and narcotics trafficking! Sergio Fleury, head of the secret police in São Paulo and a well-known drug trafficker, was accused of eleven murders, including those of two Brazilian drug traffickers who threatened to reveal what they knew of police involvement in narcotics. He was never convicted of any crime, because the Brazilian attorney general, the commander in chief of Brazil's Second Army, and other high-ranking officers all publicly testified to his good character.[9]

While considerably less savage than the military dictatorships, Latin America's few formal democracies are hardly models of good government. Corruption and government graft are as widespread in Mexico and Colombia as in Paraguay. Mexico's rural poor are as oppressed as the peasants on Paraguay's cattle ranches, and the entire Caribbean coast of Colombia is dominated by the local cocaine and marijuana Mafia.[10]

For years the Catholic Church, though supposedly the moral teacher and guardian of virtually all the Latin-American people, chose to ignore this lawless situation. Often it publicly collaborated with corrupt dictatorships for what it could extract in power and material privilege, and even as late as the 1940s churchmen were identified with the most reactionary sectors in Latin America, particularly the large landowners. In Colombia, for example, the Church sided with the country's Conservative Party in a civil war that lasted from 1948 until the early 1960s, parish priests and bishops encouraging and even personally leading the Conservatives in their slaughter of peasants.[11]

Why did the Church suddenly regret and reject its traditional alliance with the conservative rich? In the beginning, at least, it was fear of communism, and for this Fidel Castro must be thanked. The Catholic Church's experience in Cuba after Castro took power, when 70 percent of the clergy fled the island, profoundly shocked Latin America's bishops, many of whom were jolted out of their complacency to see clearly for the first time the extremes of Latin America's poverty and wealth. The seeds of violent revolution lay everywhere, they came to believe—in the teeming slums, the impoverished countryside, the universities. Religion no longer served as the opium of the people, and the upper-class youth who had once formed the Church's intellectual backbone were rallying to Marxism. Church leaders had only to look at the sharp decline in religious vocations and church attendance to realize that Latin-American Catholicism was in trouble. So the Church launched a great anti-communist crusade.

Like the Kennedy administration with its Alliance for Progress, the Catholic Church believed that the only way to stop the spread of communism in Latin America was to reform its social and economic structures. The Church had a ready-made vehicle to promote such programs in the Catholic Action groups that had been organized in various countries during the 1930s and 1940s. Originally formed to spread the Church's social teachings in Latin America, Catholic Action spawned numerous youth organizations, the Confederation of Christian Trade Unions, and the Christian Democratic parties of Chile, Venezuela, Peru, and Central America. In addition, it sponsored such innovative Church programs as radio schools and agrarian reform of diocese lands. In the early 1960s these programs were greatly expanded and modernized with foreign personnel and money, following the Vatican's worldwide appeal for aid to shore up the Latin-American Church.

But these reforms were badly timed, coming as they did at the end of the cold war and the beginning of the conflict in Vietnam when success was still measured in simplistic military and political terms with no consideration for complex social issues (that is, anyone who did not agree with U.S. foreign policy obviously had to be a Red). Both the Church and the U. S. Government saw the primary goal of reform as the defeat of left-wing political movements and guerrilla groups. Reform was a means, not an end, and therefore it failed. Everybody was so busy devising strategies to defeat communism that all completely overlooked the real cause of the people's misery: nearly five centuries of social and economic oppression. As long as the dictators, Stroessner and the others, proclaimed their fealty to the United States and their abhorrence of communism, Washington was prepared to support them with military and economic aid. Unions, political parties, housing developments, and agrarian reform were all designed to advance the anti-communist crusade; as a result they soon became political tools instead of vehicles for genuine reform. In Chile the reformers came full circle, promoting the take-over of the government by a right-wing military regime whose totalitarian ideas and brutal repression were the communists' best possible argument for a Marxist revolution.

The epitome of the Church reformer in Latin America during the 1960s was Belgian Jesuit Roger Vekemans, a brilliant and energetic man who was sufficiently liberal to favor labor unions and agrarian reform but who was, above all, a rabid anti-communist. A tall, broad-shouldered priest with the physical build to match a formidable intellect—and back up his outspoken opinions— Vekemans was just the crusader the Church had been seeking to lead its campaign against the Red Menace. A member of the Belgian underground during World War II, Vekemans had distinguished himself at the universities of Louvain, Belgium, and Nijmegen, Holland, two of Europe's most important Catholic centers of liberal theological and social thought. He was teaching sociology at the Gregorian University in Rome when the Jesuits' Belgian superior general, Jean Baptiste Janssens, tapped him for an emergency mission to Chile. That was in 1957, two years before Castro seized Havana, but the Chilean bishops already saw the handwriting on the wall, as more and more Chileans left the Church to join Marxist political parties.

Vekemans' job was to train Jesuit specialists in sociology, psychology, theology, economics, philosophy, and business administration, so that they in turn might advise and influence the country's intellectuals and social reformers, particularly the budding politicians of the Christian Democratic Party. To this end, he founded the Center for Research and Social Action, later to be known as the Centro Bellarmino, and the School of Sociology at the Catholic University of Santiago. But Centro Bellarmino was more than a training ground, since Vekemans early converted it into a laboratory for social projects, such as housing programs and workers' cooperatives, in order to further the political cause of the Christian Democrats in Chile and elsewhere in Latin America. With his fluency in six languages, talent for organization, and contacts on three continents, he quickly obtained money for these programs: first from the West German bishops and government, who were contributing $25 million a year by 1963; then from AID and the CIA—AID producing at least $1.8 million; the CIA, anything up to $5 million. (According to his Washington friend and fellow Jesuit, James Vizzard, Vekemans boasted after a meeting with John and Robert Kennedy in 1961, "I got $10 million bucks today—$5 million covert from the CIA and $5 [million] overt from AID.")[12]

Vekemans was assiduously courted by the U. S. Embassy in Santiago during the early 1960s, not only as a mine of information about possible AID projects, but also because he was the *éminence grise* of the old man in Chile who could stop the Marxists, the Christian Democrats' Eduardo Frei. Vekemans was particularly useful to Frei at the White House, according to Joseph John Jova, U.S. deputy chief of mission to Santiago,[13] arranging a clandestine Oval Office meeting between Frei and President Kennedy in the spring of 1963, to lay the groundwork for the following year's presidential election in Chile.

A man who has always privately claimed that the end justifies the means, Vekemans saw nothing wrong with using CIA money to promote the National Association of Farm Workers, the Union of Christian Peasants, and the Institute for Union and Christian Training, among others. "I'd take money from the devil himself if it were necessary to stop the communists," he once said.[14] Thus the Church, and specifically Centro Bellarmino, became a conduit for the CIA, which contributed $2.6 million to Frei's successful bid for the presidency in 1964, or more than half Frei's total campaign budget and twice as much per voter as Johnson and Goldwater together spent in their presidential campaigns that year.[15]

In the end, of course, Frei, with such backing, could not deliver on the promised reforms and simply paved the way for Socialist Salvador Allende. "The Frei government passed a series of laws to benefit the people, but it never put them into effect," said a Chilean metallurgical worker who deserted the Christian Democrats to support Allende. "What good were minimum wages when my boss refused to pay them? 'Go find another job,' he'd say."

Eventually discarded by the Christian Democrats as a political liability, the disillusioned Vekemans left Chile shortly before Allende's inauguration in 1970 for Bogotá, where he formed another Centro Bellarmino known as the Research Center for the Development and Integration of Latin America (CEDIAL). In the cold Andean highlands of this conservative Colombian city, he became increasingly right-wing and dogmatic. A bitterness underlay the abrasiveness, and the man who had once initiated so many ideas and projects seemed stuck in a rut of complaint— against the Christian Democrats, the Chilean Church, the Marxists, and the U. S. Government. For all his brilliance, Vekemans failed to grasp what had gone wrong in Chile, why the housing programs and cooperatives did not pay off in political success. But then the Americans made the same mistake in Vietnam, where neither money nor helicopter gunships could alter the fundamental weakness of a corrupt government in which the people had no real participation. The AID projects, the CIA-founded institutes and unions, and all the other strategies for Latin America in the 1960s were simply attempts to put a modern veneer on an outdated society in order to protect it from communism, without attacking its fundamental defects. Vekemans' strategy failed because it was based, not on Christian values, but on political advantage.

"People with no reasons for living will not find causes to die for."

By the end of the 1960s the Catholic Church found itself stalled. Religious vocations were still dropping, popular agitation had not abated, and the social and economic conditions of the majority of the people were even worse than they had been at the beginning of the decade. Nor could Washington show better results. For all the millions in aid that it pumped into the Latin-American economies during the 1960s, the average growth rate of the region's gross national product was actually lower than during the previous decade.

All this caused the more reflective members of the Church to wonder if they had miscalculated, not only by tying Catholicism's fortunes to a pseudopopulist party like the Christian Democrats, with its unworkable theories of reform, but also by believing that any reform was possible in the existing context. To expect Latin America's small, wealthy elite willingly to renounce centuries of privilege, even to forestall a communist revolution, was, they decided, as realistic as trying to level a mountain with a trowel, which was all that the literacy programs, agricultural cooperatives, and other reform projects amounted to. Reforms without revolution can be plausible, but only in a society such as those in Western Europe or that of the United States, where the majority of the people are at least moderately educated, have some idea of their civic rights and responsibilities, and are prepared to defend them. In a region like Latin America, where none of these conditions obtains, the informed pressure groups that normally support reforms do not exist. Or as U.S. writer Thomas Sanders put it: "Latin America is underdeveloped not just because it does not produce enough but because the people do not participate in national life."

A revolution would of course sweep away the political cobwebs, along with much else, but it is questionable whether this is desirable in the social context of Latin America. In any case, and contrary to the doomsday predicted by political seers who see revolution around every corner in Latin America, the probability of such an upheaval is remote: "People with no reasons for living will not find causes to die for," as Brazil's Archbishop Helder Cámara said.

Roger Vekemans' alma mater, the Catholic University of Louvain in Belgium, had a lot to do with the change of clerical thinking, though not always in ways that Louvain's professors could have foreseen. While Vekemans was off tilting with Marxists in Chile, Louvain experienced an intellectual flowering, caused by the crossbreeding of the social sciences and theology, that had far-reaching consequences for Louvain's Latin-American students, including Camilo Torres and Gustavo Gutiérrez.

A Colombian priest from a well-to-do family, Torres was revolutionized by his study of sociology at Louvain. Sociology not only gave him a scientific tool with which to measure the degree of Christian commitment in his country (he found it sadly wanting) but also allowed him to see Latin America's economic and political predicament without the rose-colored glasses supplied by Alliance for Progress salesmen. Unlike his classmate Gutiérrez, Torres was a doer, not a thinker, and when all his attempts at peaceful persuasion failed, he shed his cassock to take up arms with the Colombian guerrillas. He died in his first encounter with the Army, on February 15, 1966, in the central Colombian Andes.

Camilo Torres' death sent tremors through the Latin-American Church, which was unprepared for the phenomenon of the guerrilla-priest, and of all places in conservative Colombia, supposedly the continent's most Catholic country. The thirty-seven-year-old priest instantly became a martyr for the Latin-American Left, particularly high school and university students, and bishops everywhere worried about his influence on their own young clergy. In retrospect, however, it can be seen that Torres was less a model for the future than a symptom of the frustrated times. For while it is true that a few priests, mostly in Colombia, followed his path, the vast majority rejected the idea that, in order to love, it is necessary to kill. One such was Gustavo Gutiérrez, a Peruvian intellectual who has emerged as Latin America's principal spokesman for a Third World theology. Although the two men shared similar viewpoints on basic social problems, Gutiérrez did not support Torres' decision to join the guerrillas.

Like other young religious who were disappointed in Christian Democracy, Gutiérrez turned to Marxism as an analytical guide to the causes of economic and social underdevelopment. These Latin Americans believed that Christian theology had grown stagnant from its emphasis on the Greek deductive process of thought, because "deductive theology imposes its own, prior idea of God on Christ, and if he does not fit it, he is twisted and deformed to achieve that purpose." The inductive process, on the other hand, moves from reality to idea, from experience to theory. And it was one of the original tenets of the Judeo-Christian tradition. Thus "the whole Bible, Old and New Testament, is really the history of Israel and of Jesus, set forth in the most varied literary genres. The Event always preceded the Word."[16]

Although the language of the gospels has changed little since Christ's death, cultural interpretations have tended to alter its significance. Encumbered by bureaucracies and traditions that grew out of different historical circumstances, Roman Catholicism evolved over the centuries into a conservative institution that lost touch with the poor. It also became Church-centered instead of Christ-centered, bound up in rituals and rules that have little, if anything, to do with the original tenets of Christianity. By emphasizing an inductive process of thought, by starting from the reality of poverty and injustice in Latin America, the new theologians hoped to bring the Church back to earth, to face the facts and to do something about them. Nine out of ten Latin Americans are baptized Catholics, and eight of those ten are poor. Not only are they still deprived of the liberation promised by Christ, they don't even know of his promise.

What the Latin-American theologians find particularly attractive in Marx is his suggestion of the relationship between experience and theory—that if man has sufficient understanding of his reality he can improve that reality and himself, and that this new situation in turn influences, changes, and educates him. The study of Marxism nourished the seeds that had been planted in Louvain: namely, that scientific knowledge is necessary to interpret reality. Sociology, in its own area, was given importance equal to that of theology. Thus equipped, Gutiérrez and other theologians

developed a series of new religious and sociological insights based on Latin America's historical condition as an economically and politically dependent continent. Appropriately, their work was called the theology of liberation.

It is not surprising that Marxism was used to decipher capitalism in Latin America, since Marx, a respected sociologist in many parts of the developing world, makes sense to a people who have suffered both imperialism and colonialism. But an acceptance of Marx the sociologist need not imply support for a Marxist ideology, much less communism, which the liberation theologians reject as a political system incompatible with Christianity.

Although many of their conclusions are now taken for granted by Latin-American economists and sociologists, these theologians were pioneers, for they used the social sciences as guides to theological development. Moreover, it was a development based on the realities of Latin America and not on the Church's traditional colonial mentality or the political rationalizations of men like Vekemans.

Vatican II

The formulation of so radical a theology would have been impossible in Latin America without the Vatican's Second Ecumenical Council (1962–65), which sought to modify institutional rigidity and anachronistic liturgy. But even before Vatican II had announced its conclusions, Pope John XXIII had set the Church on a new path with his encyclicals *Mater et Magistra* (1961) and *Pacem in Terris* (1963), which emphasized the human right to a decent standard of living, education, and political participation. John also questioned the absolute right to private property and the Church's unswerving allegiance to capitalist individualism in the cold war against socialist collectivism. Vatican II widened the floodgates by establishing two radically new principles: that the Church is of and with this world, not composed of some otherworldly body of celestial advocates, and that it is a community of equals, whether they be laity, priest, or bishop, each with some gift to contribute and responsibility to share.

Among the participants at Vatican II was a highly vocal minority of Third World bishops who lobbied for a "Church of the

Poor." This idea was further developed in a 1966 declaration by fifteen bishops from the developing countries that went far beyond Vatican II in committing the Church to the Third World poor. The majority of the signers came from the impoverished northeast of Brazil; their leader was Dom Helder Cámara.

A slight, soft-spoken Brazilian with an iron will, Dom Helder was one of a small group of men responsible for carrying the ideas of Vatican II to Latin America. Although John XXIII had placed the Church firmly on the side of human rights, it fell to Cámara to put words into action in Latin America by denouncing the torture, imprisonment, and murder of political dissidents in Brazil in 1967. For daring to speak out, Cámara "was treated by the authorities and the media as no bishop has been treated in the Western world in this century," said Father José Comblin, a Belgian theologian who worked with the archbishop. "Only he knows the details of the round-the-clock persecution that went on for two years. The assassination of his associate, Father Enrique Pereira Neto, on May 26, 1969, was part of the campaign."[17]

Back in Rome, meanwhile, Pope Paul VI was writing *Populorum Progressio,* by far the most advanced of his encyclicals, with its emphasis on the economic, social, and political rights of mankind. Directed specifically at Latin America, *Populorum Progressio* encouraged the Latin-American bishops to hold a hemispheric conference to examine the conclusions of Vatican II in light of Latin America's own particular situation.

Cámara might have been a voice crying in the wilderness and Paül a wishful thinker had it not been for a third prophet, and superb organizer, Manuel Larraín, the bishop of Talca, Chile. Larraín was always an advanced thinker even in as politically advanced a nation as Chile. As early as the 1950s, when everyone else was worrying about communism, he was warning the Church that it would lose the masses if Catholicism remained a minority religion of the wealthy elites.

Larraín was instrumental in founding the Latin-American Episcopal Conference (CELAM), which in 1955 brought together the region's highly heterogeneous national bishops' conferences into a single organization. Not only did CELAM provide the first regular means of communication throughout the Latin-American hierarchy; Larraín and a like-minded minority of progressive bishops also saw to it that CELAM spread the conciliar word of Vatican II through a series of CELAM-sponsored institutes, which were really think tanks for the theologians of liberation and sociologists and economists trained at Louvain and other European and U.S. universities.

Many factors influenced these young Latin Americans' thinking, including Camilo Torres' desertion to the guerrillas, but the most decisive were Chile's sorry experiment in Christian Democracy and the overthrow of the populist administration of President João Goulart by the Brazilian military in 1964. Both experiences pointed to the same conclusion: whether you called it a populist government or a third way between capitalism and communism (the claim of Chile's Christian Democrats), such reformist governments were halfway measures that would never succeed because they started from the wrong base, namely capitalist "development."

While a number of prominent U.S. and Latin-American historians and economists are gradually coming to understand and accept the "dependency" theory of underdevelopment, Goulart's Planning Minister, Celso Furtado, was among the first to put his finger on the problem by insisting that "development" was a myth invented by the industrialized nations to con the Third World into footing the bill for the American (and European) way of life. He based his assertion on Latin America's experience in the 1960s, when development meant essentially a series of foreign, mostly U.S., loans for industrial infrastructure and large inputs of foreign investment. The loans have so burdened the Latin-American countries that many are now spending an average 25 percent of their foreign earnings just to service the debt![18] As for foreign investment, far from creating the millions of new jobs promised by the advance publicity, nearly half this money went to take over existing Latin-American industries. By the end of the "decade of development," *99 percent* of the loans made by AID to Latin-American countries were being spent in the United States for products costing 30 to 40 percent more than the going world price.[19]

True, U.S. loans also supported educational programs, low-cost housing, and the like, but these were politically oriented and in any case peripheral to the main thrust of development: foreign control of the most dynamic Latin-American industries and co-optation of the small upper and middle classes that wield the economic and political power and can afford the consumer goods produced by the foreign subsidiaries. Even the "green revolution," which promised such lavish grain yields for the small farmer, was part of the myth of development; it soon became a technological device whereby the large landowners might "agroindustrialize" the small, inefficient plots of the peasants, who were forced off their land in the name of progress to swell the cities' slums.

Naturally enough, development programs like the Alliance for Progress were not presented in this light. American taxpayers were told that foreign aid would help their poorer neighbors. The Latins were sold the idea that U.S. loans and private investment were essential for economic takeoff. Neither allegation was true, and the fact is that Latin America would have been better off had the United States left it alone. In contrast to its poor economic performance during the 1960s, when U. S. Government and business interests became deeply involved in the region's economies, Latin America did better during the depression and World War II when the export of U.S. goods and capital was sharply curtailed. In those earlier years Brazil and some of the other countries began to produce their own capital equipment instead of importing it. Had they continued to do so, the Latin-American economies might have taken off; but once the war was over, Latin America reverted to the old patterns of dependency—the habit was too old and too strong.

Long before the Americans appeared on the scene, Latin America was an economic colony of Europe, specifically of Victorian Britain. Before the British, it had been a colony of the Spaniards and the Portuguese. For three centuries after Columbus, it had served primarily to enrich the Iberian states through the export of precious metals, taxes, the import of European goods, and the African slave trade. After the wars of independence, outright imperialism was replaced by a more sophisticated arrangement when the British introduced mercantile capitalism, trading manufactured goods for raw materials. The United States followed a similar pattern at the beginning of this century, its interest being primarily minerals, and U.S. investors gradually replaced the British as the most important foreign influence in the region. The dependency relationship also changed, for now Latin America was no longer the Indian come to barter his skins at the trading post. It was an important source of income for corporations in the United States, of cheap labor for U.S. export subsidiaries, and of small but extremely lucrative markets, particularly for arms and capital equipment.

During these centuries economic colonialism ran in tandem with political dependence, first on the Spanish and Portuguese crowns, then on the nineteenth-century European powers, and finally on Washington. Even Latin-American leaders who wanted to take an independent course—and they were few—found themselves boxed in by an international economic system and the terms of trade. Though more sophisticated than the nineteenth-century European rulers who sent gunboats to collect money from Latin-American governments, the International Monetary Fund serves substantially the same purpose today. Any Latin-American government that ignores its dictates does so at the risk of bankruptcy, as Peru's nationalistic generals learned to their cost in 1977. Not that many countries want to object—most Latin Americans in government belong to a wealthy minority, often the *nouveau riche* military, and such people are perfectly content with their junior partnership in U.S. corporate industry. (Brazil's military regime has even invented a political doctrine to rationalize its satellite relationship with the United States—see Chapter VI.)

But the region's increasing economic dependence on the United States has paid no social dividends, propaganda notwithstanding. The rich got richer; the middle class got poorer; and the poor, that unregarded majority, got nothing. There was no trickle-down of wealth, but rather a substantial upward redistribution. Those who suffered most from this "trickle-up" process were the workers, whose real wages plummeted during the sixties and seventies. That was the second stage of "development"; not only were the people deprived of the benefits of economic progress, they also lost many of their earlier gains.

Workers whose buying power is sharply reduced can be counted on to protest, so the next and final step had to be military dictatorship. Without repression, it is impossible for the rich to increase their income indefinitely at the expense of the mass of the people who, for all their ignorance and lack of political organization, have the advantage in numbers. These millions will not stay quietly on the farms or in the slums unless they are terribly afraid. As in Stroessner's Paraguay, the rich get richer only because they have the guns.

A child born in the United States will consume thirty to fifty times more goods of all descriptions in his or her lifetime than one born in the impoverished highlands of Bolivia. A child born to wealthy parents in the Bolivian capital of La Paz will equal the consumption of the American. Consciously or not, both owe their life-styles in some degree to the poverty of the highland peasant child. A similar relationship exists between the economies of Latin America and the United States. And that is what the "dependency" theory of underdevelopment is all about—a mass of poor peasants and slum dwellers supply the wants of a few rich people, and they in turn satisfy the U.S. demand for raw materials and profit remittances.

As Panama's Archbishop Marcos McGrath points out, "Great doubt has been cast on the possibility of achieving the necessary reforms for the integral development of our people within the capitalist structure of the international, and particularly the inter-American economy," when the terms of trade and foreign investment are still colonialist in structure and thus contribute "to the continuing impoverishment of the poorer nations." "Ironically," adds McGrath, "the efforts of the prime producers—for instance, of crude oil—to exact a higher price from buyers to the north have roused pious cries of protest: 'Extortion!' Suddenly Northerners fear that they may have to 'depend' on foreign producers. Do they ignore the extortion and economic dependence they exercise upon the poorer lands? This is 'an eye for an eye and a tooth for a tooth' in international economics. But who set the rules for the game? The Christian nations to the north."[20]

A Magna Carta

Whatever their thoughts about socialism, by the end of the 1960s a good many Latin-American bishops were prepared to agree with McGrath's criticisms of capitalism. In fact it began to appear that U.S. capitalism, not Karl Marx, was Public Enemy No. 1. Unlike the theologians, sociologists, and economists in CELAM's think tanks, few bishops had sufficient training to define capitalism's failings in scientific terms, but they could see ample moral reasons to condemn the obsession with profit as selfishness, particularly in the repressive, right-wing military regimes spreading across the continent.

Thus Latin America was approaching a religious-political turning point, where the ideas of the theologians of liberation, of Cámara, Larraín, and Pope Paul, would be approved by the Latin-American hierarchy. The name of that turning point was Medellín, the Colombian city where in 1963 the bishops of Latin America met in an extraordinary assembly for the second time in their history.† Medellín produced the Magna Carta of today's persecuted, socially committed Church, and as such rates as one of the major political events of the century: it shattered the centuries-old alliance of Church, military, and the rich elites.

Paul himself traveled to Colombia to inaugurate the meeting, the first Pope in history to visit Latin America. He set the tone of the conference by telling a huge crowd in Bogotá, "We wish to personify the Christ of a poor and hungry people." But he also appealed to the rich:

> What can I say to you, men of the ruling class? What is required of you is generosity. This means the ability to detach yourselves from the stability of your position which is, or seems to be, a position of privilege, in order to serve those who need your wealth, your culture, your authority. . . . You, lords of this world and sons of the Church, you must have the genius for virtue that society needs. Your ears and your hearts must be sensitive to the voices crying out for bread, concern, justice, and a more active participation in the direction of society.[21]

The CELAM technicians who prepared the documents for Medellín came armed with statistical surveys, theological treatises, and sociological arguments, but the bishops had already seen the proof in the poverty outside their palace windows. Vatican II, the failures of the Alliance for Progress and the reformist

† The first assembly, held in Rio de Janeiro in 1955, dealt primarily with ecclesiastical matters.

governments, the upsurge of military dictatorships, and the growing misery of the Latin-American people all combined to open the bishops' eyes to "the design of God in the signs of the times."

"The design of God," as the bishops interpreted it, was radically opposed to the prevailing lawlessness, corruption, and repression of Latin America. According to the Medellín documents, the mass of the people were oppressed by the "institutionalized violence" of internal and external colonial structures that, "seeking unbounded profits, foment an economic dictatorship and the international imperialism of money." Capitalism was as bad as communism; both "systems are affronts to the dignity of the human being." The bishops scored the technocrats and "developmentalists" for "placing more emphasis on economic progress than on the social well-being of the people" and for failing to encourage popular participation in government. The common man should not be looked upon as a mere statistic, the bishops said, but should become an active agent for change.[22]

Recognizing the potential for class conflict, the document laid stress on the polarization between rich and poor and warned of the growing frustration—and anger—of the masses. The bishops placed the blame for social and economic injustice squarely on those with the "greater share of wealth, culture, and power" who "jealously retain their privileges," thus "provoking explosive revolutions of despair." Where there is injustice, they warned, there is no peace and God is rejected.[23]

Two key words emerged at Medellín: liberation and participation. Liberation was, and is, understood in the biblical sense of physical and spiritual salvation, the Exodus of the Old Testament and the Good News promised by Christ in his first public pronouncement. Of course, no one will be liberated from fear, hunger, and disease just by someone declaring it must be so. A human being must first understand what freedom means. That is why the Medellín documents placed so much emphasis on "liberating education."

Most Latin-American schools teach by the time-honored rote method in which the student parrots the professor, usually without understanding the words. The results are bad enough in the high schools and the universities; down at the primary level, which is as far as most Latin Americans ever get, they are disastrous. Millions of semiliterates pour forth, barely able to write their names, add two and two, or read a first-grade comic book, having learned neither to think nor to practice a skill. You can see them on the street corners of every Latin-American city, hawking cigarettes, oranges, and stolen watches, and in the countryside, on the large ranches, where from birth to death they follow the *patrón*'s orders unquestioningly, never understanding why. You can put such people on an earthly paradise, some coconut island in the Caribbean surrounded by lobster banks and schools of fish, and they will nearly starve to death—not only because they don't know how to fish but also because they don't know why they should fish. And the coconuts rot on the ground. How, one wonders, can these people be expected to choose a government or participate in a democracy?

It isn't that Latin Americans are naturally stupid or that they do not want to learn. No matter how backward or remote the community, the people inevitably ask for two things: a church and a school. Nor is it their fault that the level of education is so awful. Underpaid and poorly trained, most Latin-American schoolteachers quickly lose any enthusiasm for their work. If the schools are in rural areas or city slums, odds are that the teacher will show up one week out of four, if that. Even the conscientious ones despair of trying to educate undernourished, inattentive children when there are no blackboards, no books, no chairs, no toilet facilities, nothing but the teacher's own rapidly dwindling determination. Not surprisingly, two out of ten Latin-American children must repeat the first grade; only three out of ten finish primary school.

These abysmal standards are often cited by Latin-American administrations to defend government by a minority of the educated. What they fail to admit is that there is no financial or educational justification for the low levels of literacy. The real cause is political: as long as people remain uneducated, they cannot wish or hope to participate in a democracy. Many members of the radical Right in Latin America will point out, candidly enough, that educated people expect higher wages and more efficient public services, so it's better to keep the masses in darkness. Government officials are not nearly that blunt, but it is easy to surmise their opinion by looking at the national budget: in most cases education is at the bottom of the list, along with public health. The largest outlays are earmarked for the armed forces and internal security. One of the few exceptions is Costa Rica, where there are more teachers than policemen. Costa Rica is also a Central American rarity—an established democracy.

Like the governments, the Catholic Church used to disregard the poor. Most of its schools were oriented to children of the wealthy upper classes. The Jesuits specialized in universities for the rich. The values and structures on which Latin America's society of privilege was built were reinforced in the Catholic schoolroom.

Medellín recognized these failings by advocating for the illiterate and semiliterate masses radically new educational programs based on the pioneer work of Brazil's educational philosopher, Paulo Freire, who invented the technique of "conscientization," or consciousness-raising. In contrast to the rote method, conscientization encourages the student, whether child or adult, to understand the meaning of words, particularly such key words as "hungry," "barefoot," "land," and "rich." The aim is to make people aware of themselves and their environment, to learn to think. And once people begin to think, they ask questions. They want to know why their village has no running water, for example, and what they can do about it. That is the seed of civic participation, making Latin Americans reflective agents for change instead of "objects to be rescued from a burning building," as Freire phrases it. (Like the theologians of liberation, Freire has no time for left-wing guerrillas who would first seize power and then attempt to establish a dialogue with the masses, since that is but another form of paternalism.)

Consciousness-raising is closely related to participation in Christian grass-roots communities (*comunidades de base*), Medellín's second important goal. Unlike parish structures that encompass a heterogeneous population with different outlooks and life-styles, Christian communities are small (on average, twelve to fifteen members), tightly knit groups of people with similar incomes, jobs, education, problems, and aspirations. Everyone in the group knows everyone else on a first-name basis and is probably a godparent of one or more of the community's children. In contrast to Europe or the United States, the godparent relationship is socially binding in Latin America, and anyone who is a *compadre* or *comadre* at baptism or confirmation is virtually a member of the family, with all the pursuant obligations. The sacraments therefore reinforce the social ties of neighbors.

Christian communities in Latin America normally begin as spin-offs from the local parish churches, with the laity assuming many of the responsibilities of the priest for catechism classes and religious meetings. But because the orientation is a liberating one based on the techniques of consciousness-raising, particularly in the reading of the Bible, these groups develop a dynamic of their own. They soon add appendages such as schools, cooperatives, and health units. The fundamental difference between these organizations and the reforms of the 1960s is that these later groups come from the bottom, from the poor people themselves, and not from some well-meaning university graduate who knows a lot about statistics and organizational charts but cannot begin to communicate with the people.

Members of Christian communities pray, work, and live together, sharing their material and spiritual resources much as the first Christians did. (They call themselves the "People of God.") Their most important commandment is "Love Thy Neighbor," for "If a [man] does not love the brother whom he has seen, it cannot be that he loves God, Whom he has not seen." (1 John 4:20) Love is not just an attitude, however, but an active commitment. Community members share a sense of responsibility for their neighbors, feeding a family when the father is out of a job or helping them rethatch the roof on their hut. Each is his brother's keeper.

There are many thousands of such communities in Latin America today—80,000 in Brazil alone.

Revolution in the Ranks

The emphasis of the Medellín documents on Christian rather than political values was fundamental to the Church's declaration of independence from the state. Although frequently in the past Christianity has appeared in ideological guises, it is essentially a critical discipline, a constant call for justice. By denouncing poverty and social injustice at the cost of political influence and privilege, the Latin-American Church could claim, for the first time in its history, that it was the conscience of *all* Latin-American Catholics, not just a rich minority.

As events soon proved, however, few of the bishops present at Medellín recognized what this declaration of independence meant. No one will argue (though some may privately believe) that hunger and illiteracy are good things; thus the bishops were easily persuaded to denounce such injustices, having already been primed by Vatican II, Pope Paul's *Populorum Progressio,* and their own experiences. In any organization the most intelligent, dynamic sectors tend to dominate; at Medellín these were the progressive bishops like Larraín and Cámara and the young technicians of CELAM. The majority of the prelates merely followed their lead, unable to sense any contradiction between their own ideas and the documents they signed. Most missed the heart of the matter: that the Medellín documents were a revolutionary call to work for social justice, placing the Church in open conflict with the moneyed classes that for centuries had been its political and economic mainstay. There were no platitudes or concessions—the gates were wide open.

The first shock to hit the hierarchy was revolution in the religious ranks. Throughout the 1960s there had been a confused, sterile debate over the efficacy of violence and guerrilla warfare among young Latin-American leftists in universities, high schools, and trade unions, who mistakenly believed that Fidel Castro's guerrilla tactics could be successfully repeated in the rest of the hemisphere. The leftists' theory was quickly disproved in Venezuela and Peru, where rural guerrillas were destroyed by the military in, respectively, 1962 and 1963. Venezuelan guerrilla leaders privately admitted that they were defeated primarily because they could not elicit the support of suspicious, conservative peasants who had not the slightest idea what the university-educated guerrillas were talking about. Although the odds were heavily against guerrilla ventures, Latin-American university students remained unconvinced during most of the decade; so, too, did the Pentagon, which based its Latin-American military training on counterinsurgency techniques, to the lasting grief of the civilian population.

Many of the best-educated priests either worked on university campuses or were involved in programs that included students, and because of this association they became infected by the idea of violent revolution. When the student guerrillas were wiped out in country after country, the priests began to fill the gap. Very few actually joined the guerrillas, but a well-publicized minority openly upheld partisan positions in favor of socialist organizations, frequently participating in vociferous confrontations with the local authorities and with other members of the Church. Medellín was like a red flag waving them into action, although its documents deliberately skirted any suggestion of a political solution and certainly could not be considered a manifesto for violent revolution.

These combative young religious could put their own interpretation on Medellín, no matter what the bishops said, because of the institutional reforms of Vatican II. In an attempt to achieve more democracy within the Church, the council had thrown out many of the old canonical traditions of clerical obedience, and once those were gone, priests and nuns in growing numbers chose their own ideas and type of work. In Latin America, where there is only one priest for every 5,891 Catholics (in the United States the ratio is one to every 827) there are many more jobs than clergy. So, as a left-wing Peruvian priest put it, "Any bishop who doesn't like what we are doing can lump it, because there is always another bishop who will be glad to have our services."

Bereft of the old disciplinary rules and confronted by secularism and socialism, Latin-American priests and nuns went through a painful period of confusion and upheaval. During the late sixties more of them left the Church to marry than did the religious of any other continent.

Priests formed left-wing organizations in seven countries, some doing so in open support of radical parties or governments, as in Argentina, Chile, and Bolivia. And in several dioceses there were ugly, sometimes violent clashes between priests and bishops. Thirty diocesan priests in Mexico demanded the resignation of Bishop Leonardo Viera Contreras, and in Maracaibo, Venezuela, twenty-two pastors called on Archbishop Domingo Roa to resign. Several hundred priests and laymen petitioned the Guatemalan Congress to expel Archbishop Mario Casariego, cardinal of Guatemala City; in Argentina a group of priests from Córdoba and Rosario demanded the dismissal of Bishop Victorio Bonamín, chief military chaplain. Similarly, activist priests in Rio de Janeiro and Peru insisted on their right to elect the local archbishop. Chile's left-wing religious movement, Christians for Socialism, attacked Santiago's Cardinal Raul Silva, while in Rosario, Argentina, Archbishop Guillermo Bolatti and thirty priests belonging to the Third World movement engaged in a mud-slinging match that lasted three months. Dissident priests also demanded the removal of the papal nuncio in Bolivia; in Peru they actually prevailed on the hierarchy to blackball Papal Nuncio Rómulo Carboni. Although the majority of the militants were leftists, there were also cases, as in El Salvador, where conservative priests demanded the removal of a progressive archbishop.

With the exception of Peru, none of these radical groups achieved its aims, religious or political, and that was because many of the "new utopians," long on theory but short on political savvy, tilted with adversaries whose intelligence and resources they greatly underestimated. Moreover, they were "arrogant and narrow-minded," said a progressive U.S. missionary, who argues that the militants' insulting attacks on the hierarchy and their know-it-all attitude toward religion and politics alienated not only the bishops but the majority of priests and nuns as well.

The religious rebellion gave the bishops a sharp jolt, and, under the influence of the conservatives among them (particularly the Colombians, who had raised the lone dissenting voice at Medellín), they began to worry about what they had wrought. The idea that Marxist analysis had been used by CELAM theologians and sociologists to reach some of the Medellín Conclusions was particularly galling—and confusing. While by now the bishops had no love for capitalism, instinct and tradition made them wary of anything with socialist connotations. And then, of course, everyone could see what trouble poor Cardinal Silva was having in Chile with Christians for Socialism. There was no telling where the Church would find itself if such shenanigans were allowed to continue.

By 1972 many of the bishops were in hurried retreat. The progressive prelates who had engineered Medellín were voted out of their CELAM posts, and the think tanks that had nourished the theology of liberation were either closed or restaffed. The retreat might easily have become a rout had the region's armed forces not intervened in the nick of time, swinging the balance back in favor of Church progressives by unleashing a reign of terror unequaled in Latin-American history.

While terror had long been an instrument of repression in such old-fashioned military regimes as Stroessner's Paraguay and the Somoza dynasty of Nicaragua, it was not scientifically applied until the late 1960s when Brazil developed sophisticated systems of surveillance and torture and a geopolitical doctrine to rationalize the imprisonment, murder, and exile of political dissidents. This was the other side of Brazil's "economic miracle," which supplied the money and technology to computerize repression.

The Nixon administration and corporate business hailed Brazil as a model for development in the Third World, but Church leaders were not convinced. On the contrary, progressive prelates in Brazil, Paraguay, and Mexico warned their colleagues that Orwell's *1984* was almost upon them. But because these men had been the architects of Medellín, their warnings went unheeded. Few Latin-American bishops had experienced the sort of "round-the-clock persecution" Helder Cámara suffered in Brazil; most had other, more pressing diocesan problems, including rebellious priests. As far as these bishops were concerned, the "fascist menace" in Brazil was a figment of the communists' imagination. Then too, Brazil was far away, both physically and culturally, and what happened there seemed unlikely to influence some small parish in the Andes or Central America.

Nor was there any reason to perceive the threat. Despite its influence on Latin America, Vatican II was essentially a European event, and very few Europeans seriously believed that fascism could rise again. Council delegates took Western Europe's mix of liberalism and social democracy as their political reference and applied it to the developing countries. Despite their criticism of social injustice in Latin America, neither *Populorum Progressio* nor Medellín attempted to analyze the economic and political background responsible for such conditions.

This view prevailed until September 1973, when Chilean President Salvador Allende was overthrown in one of the bloodiest coups in living memory. His downfall was a milestone in Latin-American history, the ultimate proof of the fallacy of peaceful revolution. The Chilean experience also forced the Catholic

Church in Latin America to take a good look at what was happening in its midst.

Unlike Helder Cámara and the other bishops of northeastern Brazil who made no secret of their radical leanings, Chile's Cardinal Silva has always opposed Marxism. During the Allende administration, Church-state relations were correct but cool, with Silva steadfastly refusing to condone the partisan politics of Christians for Socialism, even though his support would have improved the Curia's standing with the government. The cardinal's unwillingness to compromise with either Left or Right greatly enhanced his prestige within the Latin-American Church and in Chile itself, where in the last, tense months before Allende's death, he became the chief intermediary between the hostile Christian Democrats and the ruling Socialists. That Silva failed to avert a coup in no way diminished his reputation as a diplomat of intelligence and integrity. Thus Chile's military junta committed a terrible blunder when it launched a smear campaign against this aging but resolute man.

The suggestion that Silva was unpatriotic and a fellow traveler merely because he defended human rights focused the Latin-American Church's attention on political realities as no amount of persecution of Helder Cámara had done. Cámara was the "Red Bishop" of Brazil; Silva, a man of the middle. By attacking the political center of the Church, the military forced the moderates back into the ranks of the progressives—only now there was no doubt of what was at stake.

As history has repeatedly shown, totalitarian regimes soon treat all critics as enemies of the state, even those who supported the regime's rise to power against a real or imagined threat, such as Marxism. Thus many of Chile's Christian Democrats came to rue the day they had encouraged the generals to overthrow Allende, since, contrary to their expectations, they suffered as much repression as did the Socialists and the Communists. The experience of repression, like the experience of living in a slum or a backward village, almost always provides a radical political education. Things that were taken for granted, such as food or freedom, no longer exist, and inevitably one is forced to ask, Why? In the Church's case, the bishops asked themselves why laity, priests, and nuns were being imprisoned and tortured and murdered in

Chile, and a dozen other Latin-American countries, merely because they objected to the lack of such political freedoms as the right to organize a union, or because they were trying to improve the living standards of the masses. And by studying the reasons for this repression, many bishops came to the conclusion that they had been right after all to take a hard line at Medellín; only it now appeared that the Medellín documents had not been tough enough.

Cross and Sword

Chile's aping of Brazil, and the emergence of a similarly repressive government in the once-proud democracy of Uruguay, gave credence to the earlier warnings of the bishops of northeastern Brazil, and the Church seriously began to question capitalism's model of development in Brazil, with its anti-Christian "Doctrine of National Security." A mixture of creole militarism, European fascism, and U.S. McCarthyism, the doctrine is a compendium of complex arguments that, when closely examined, turn out to be an excuse for Manifest Destiny and a colonial society embellished with the technological trimmings of an Orwellian state. Thomas Hobbes, the seventeenth-century English philosopher, is generally cited as the inventor of the doctrine's model of an all-powerful state that guarantees national security in exchange for the people's freedom. But Hitler's Nazism and Mussolini's corporate state, modern refinements of Hobbes's theory, also contributed to the doctrine's development, as did cold-war politics and the Pentagon's promotion of the Latin-American military as "nation builders."

Developed at the Brazilian Advanced War College in the 1950s, these ideas stemmed from the "science" of geopolitics, which, as its name implies, studies the interrelationship of geography and politics. Brazilian geopolitics start from the political premise of a permanent world war between the forces of communism and the West. Because by size and geographical position Brazil dominates the South Atlantic, it has a duty to keep that part of the world "safe for democracy and free enterprise." A corollary of this assertion is that Bolivia, Paraguay, and Uruguay should become satellites of their much larger neighbor, and that relationship has been achieved by economic imperialism and "living frontiers"—that is, by Brazilian colonists invading poorly protected border lands in areas like the Upper Paraná River basin of Paraguay. "Democracy," one realizes, is a relative term, like the word "Christian," which the generals so frequently invoke to describe their regimes. Along with "science," they are the necessary, if merely verbal, symbols of Western civilization.

Once the permanence of world warfare is assumed, national security becomes the first priority of geopolitics. Individual rights are sacrificed to the power of the state, since only it can defend and develop the nation. Critics of government policy are considered traitors because in wartime opinions are weapons and everyone is either a friend or a foe. Civilian politicians having proved inept in government, only the military can run the state and press the war against international communism.

This view of the world, which could be straight out of a Nazi primer, is shared by the governments of Brazil, Uruguay, Paraguay, Chile, Bolivia, Argentina, and, to a lesser extent, Colombia and Peru. (The Central-American dictatorships did not bother to dress up repression in such pseudoscientific frills.) Brazil has provided the chief ideologists, the most famous of whom is General Golbery do Couto e Silva, but Chile's General Augusto Pinochet, a professor of geopolitics before he assumed the presidency, is also known to be expert in the subject.

Inevitably, the formation of these military states has followed a pattern. Usually an all-powerful national security council is drawn from the chiefs of the armed forces; it then names the President and his Cabinet and sets national policy. The council is served by a national intelligence network answerable only to the President. All independent political parties, labor unions, and student federations are outlawed, and anyone critical of the regime is persecuted as a "communist subversive." Punishment ranges from imprisonment or exile to loss of job and/or smear campaigns by the government-controlled media. Following Argentina's example, several of the regimes have dispensed with the complications of police arrest, and "enemies of the state" are now kidnapped and disposed of by groups of unidentified men. Attempts by family or friends to trace the victims are futile, since the police deny all knowledge of their existence. (According to diplomatic sources, an average of thirty persons a day "disappear" in Argentina;

Chile's Catholic Church has calculated that some two thousand Chileans were thus swallowed up in the four years following the 1973 coup.)

Catholicism plays a crucial role in this new military order, not only because of its influence among the masses, but also because the Church has provided the moral legitimacy for authority in Latin America ever since the Conquest. Hence the archbishop must be present at the dictator's inauguration, a High Mass marks the regime's first year in power, and other such symbols of Church-state collaboration are scrupulously observed. Like the Spanish conquistadors, Latin America's generals feel that the Church should be an active agent for their regimes, not because they necessarily believe in Catholicism or any other religion, but because Christianity is part of Western civilization, the defense of which is their reason for being.

Like France's schismatic Bishop Marcel Lefebvre, who wanted to undo the reforms of Vatican II, this cross-and-sword Christianity places heavy emphasis on rituals and individual piety at the expense of Christian solidarity and a commitment to social and economic justice. It is also an extremely political concept of religion, empowering the military regimes, in the name of Christianity, to ostracize any Christian who expresses or supports popular aspirations within the Church, since these aspirations undermine national security and, again, Western civilization. This repression is accompanied by a great deal of flag-waving, nationalism serving as a convenient pretext to censor or ban critical Church publications supported by European and North American religious groups and to expel foreign priests, who comprise one third of the Latin-American clergy.

But despite promises of government protection and financial aid in exchange for religious support, the mainstream of the Church has refused to adopt this view of Catholicism, not only because it is basically un-Christian but also because, after Vatican II and Medellín, it is outdated. Even if the bishops had been willing to turn back the clock, to do so would have lost them a majority of their communicants and their religious base. After two decades of decline—in vocations, Mass attendance, and lay participation in Catholic organizations—the Church in Latin America is at last experiencing a renaissance that is directly related to its commitment to social justice. To renounce that commitment would be akin to institutional suicide, particularly since so many priests and nuns—those responsible for the day-to-day functioning of the Church—have chosen to work with the poor.

At first glance, this alliance with the people might seem unrealistic because, under the Doctrine of National Security, individuals do not count in the all-powerful state and therefore a people's Church would seem to have neither prestige nor power. But, says Chilean theologian Segundo Galilea, the crucial point missed in all the geopolitical double-talk is that "in the long run no government can survive without some measure of popular support." By taking the people's side, bishops and priests were following the example of the primitive Church, whose popular roots allowed it to survive the persecutions, calumnies, and ideological threats of the Roman Empire and eventually to absorb its very enemies.

Many churchmen also felt that, given the model of capitalist development, there was no alternative. José Comblin, the Church's foremost authority on national security, maintains with considerable statistical support that "development" as demonstrated in Brazil is "anti-people" and therefore "anti-Church," because "without people there can be no Church." Contrary to the claims of its rulers, there has been very little "trickle-down" from the country's so-called economic miracle, except to the *nouveau riche* military caste. According to São Paulo's prestigious pro-business daily *O Estado,* the military's standards of luxury have reached the point where the principal status symbol is not a house or a car but a butler. During the seven-year economic miracle, which collapsed in 1976, the richest 1 percent of the population increased its share of the nation's wealth from 11.7 to 17.8 percent. Almost half the country's 38 million workers earn less than the minimum monthly wage of $70, according to the government's own statistics. And for all the razzmatazz about Brazilian nationalism, the economy is actually more dependent on foreign markets and foreign corporations than it was when the military took power. The government has run up a $50 billion foreign debt, the highest in the developing world.‡

The Brazilian Church, scorning to endorse such a model of development, is "demanding a fair distribution of the [nation's]

‡ 1979 figure. Source: Brazilian Finance Ministry.

wealth." "Why is it that only a few people can eat well while the majority go to bed hungry?" the bishops asked in their October 1976 pastoral letter. "Why is it that some people, including foreigners, are able to amass millions of acres of land for cattle and the export of meat, while our poor people are not even allowed to continue cultivating the tiny piece of land on which they were born and grew up? Why is it that only a few people have the power of decision? The organized forces of evil do not want to share anything with the poor and the humble, who constitute the majority of the people. Only the great and powerful have rights. The humble are allowed to possess only what is strictly necessary to survive in order to continue serving the powerful. To mistreat these poor people is to mistreat Christ."

That sort of plain speaking is what has caused the Church so many problems in Latin America. "Oppressive regimes are afraid of a conspiracy against the established order, and we are questioning that order," said Cardinal Aloisio Lorscheider, president of both the Brazilian Bishops' Conference and CELAM. "The rationale of security is not acceptable when it means destroying human beings. This is the socially critical and prophetic position that the Church takes in light of the Gospel and in its fight against sin. We also believe that the [capitalist] economic system does not take sufficient account of the need for respect and development of the human being but emphasizes money and profits instead."[24] According to Lorscheider, many Latin-American bishops are prepared to act on the Medellín Conclusions, now that there is "widespread regret" for the Church's historical role as an ally of the rich. Like other churchmen, he believes this change is due primarily to external events.

Even the most conservative hierarchies, including Argentina's bishops, have been forced to protest a reign of terror that has converted South America into a giant concentration camp with some thirty thousand political prisoners, and thousands more murdered or exiled. In previous times of military dictatorship, there was at least somewhere to hide. Argentines could find safety in Uruguay; Bolivians and Brazilians could flee to Chile. But now, when all these countries are marching in step, with a central pool of computerized data on political exiles and open collaboration among the region's secret police, repression is standardized and ubiquitous. Brazilian military officers taught Chile's secret police the techniques of modern torture in the weeks following the 1973 coup. Several hundred Chileans and Uruguayans who fled to Argentina for fear of arrest were murdered by Chilean and Uruguayan police with the Argentine Government's collaboration.[25] Over fourteen thousand refugees live in Argentina in daily terror of arrest, torture, and assassination. They can run no farther because there is no longer any sanctuary in the neighboring countries. Frequently it is impossible to obtain a passport and visa to emigrate, not to mention the cost to these penniless people of passage to the nearest refuge, in Venezuela. Nor is there any suggestion of immediate relief. In earlier swings between democracy and dictatorship the latter rarely lasted longer than a decade, but most of the new Latin-American military regimes have fortified themselves to stay in power for several generations, the better to wipe out any vestige of liberal political traditions.

A New Exodus

In the hour of adversity, bishops and priests have closed ranks, forgetting old feuds in their need for solidarity, seeking new contacts with other religious groups and with the people. "Today is being born a Church with a visage similar to that perceived by the Indians [who saw the Church] as their defender during the Conquest," said the Chilean Segundo Galilea. "Its condition is the same: in one way or another bishops and priests 'lose their lives.' They risk ostracism and persecution, and the poor feel this."[26]

Divisions still exist within national churches and individual dioceses, to be sure, but in many countries the stridency of the late sixties and early seventies is gone and there is a stronger call for dialogue. In part, this has come about because some of the most militant priests left the religious life. But by far the most important factor is the solidarity of the Church's political mainstream with the suffering people. Chile's Cardinal Silva, for example, gained the respect and gratitude of the Left when he extended his personal protection to the ecumenical Committee of Cooperation for Peace and its Catholic successor, the Vicariate of Solidarity, the only organizations in Chile that defended and aided the thousands of people arrested after the coup. Many politically moderate bishops in other Latin-American countries have similarly used their offices to intervene on behalf of political prisoners, often at the risk of their reputations and lives.

Meanwhile, most priests and nuns had come to the conclusion that they impaired their effectiveness as religious leaders by supporting any political party. "They refuse to be carried away by political slogans anymore," said Jesuit Carlos Palmes, president of the Latin-American Confederation of Religious (CLAR), representing 160,000 men and women in 457 religious orders. Admitting that "this is no time for the faint-hearted," Palmes nevertheless reported an "exodus" to the slums and impoverished rural areas by such important orders as the Jesuits, Salesians, Oblates, Dominicans, and Sacred Heart. Forty percent of the priests and nuns in Latin America were working with the poor in 1978, whereas only 21 percent had been so engaged a decade earlier. And the trend is irreversible, said Palmes.[27] Most of these socially concerned men and women are younger than forty-four, and most are better educated than were their predecessors (40 percent have taken specialized courses or attended a university).

Unlike the first wave of militants, many of whom felt so frustrated that they left the Church, today's priests and nuns repeatedly testify to Palmes' assertion that "the religious life has never been richer." Such traditional vows as poverty and chastity, for example, have taken on a new and deeper meaning through contact with the poor. Poverty in this new concept means living with the poor, sharing their aspirations and frustrations and their cultural traditions; chastity is seen as a sign of love, not a sacrifice.

And, as Segundo Galilea points out, "The more the Church identifies with the people, the more the people identify with the Church." Examples of the people's sacrifice to help their priests and nuns, even to the point of giving their own lives, are countless, and in many countries the Church has become the center of national life. When Paraguay's Bishop Ramón Bogarín died in September 1976, over five thousand peasants broke through a military cordon to attend his funeral. A tall, stooped aristocrat who lived in a bare three-room house in rural Paraguay, Bogarín spent most of his life defending peasants and slum dwellers from the Stroessner dictatorship. Similar testimonies of faith and gratitude were given Church martyrs in mass demonstrations in Mexico, Honduras, El Salvador, Brazil, and Chile.

There is considerable physical risk in such commitment. Native-born clergy have frequently been arrested, tortured, or murdered; foreign priests and nuns have been expelled from the country. The vast majority of these victims took no part in politics; they were punished for their work with peasants and slum dwellers. Yet, however severe the persecution, they refused to give up, compromise, or retaliate. As the Roman emperors discovered, such men and women are far more dangerous adversaries than vengeful, violent revolutionaries.

Nevertheless, both Moscow and Washington tended to sneer at the Church's nonviolent tactics: the Soviet Union because it believed they were a subterfuge to diffuse violent revolution, the United States because it thought the Church politically naïve. The Church, however, had good reason to think otherwise. For one thing, there was practically no support for violent revolution within the religious base, notwithstanding the military regimes' frequent claims that "priests and nuns are inciting the people to revolt." According to a CELAM study, the overwhelming majority of Latin-American priests rejected violence, a conclusion supported by CLAR surveys of its members. But even had the Church been willing to condone violent tactics, the fact is that they do not work in the present Latin-American context. As Dom Helder Cámara pointed out, "The claim that armed violence is a politically realistic solution is not true. What can weapons stolen from Army barracks or bought with money obtained by holding up banks do against an enemy whose allies are the manufacturers of the most modern and powerful weapons of extermination?" (The "allies" being the United States and Western Europe, which supply most of the arms used in Latin America.)

Added theologian José Comblin:

> We must start by discarding such pseudo-solutions as the faith in rebel commando groups held by Che Guevara and Régis Debray: to believe that a band of guerrillas can seize power and exercise it through the magic of violence transformed into a sacred sword is sheer romanticism. It might be possible in a tiny republic, but it is quite unthinkable in Bra-

zil, and no serious person could possibly see any hope in it. And it is too simple, as well: obviously if it were possible, no method would be easier or more economical. The Church would merely have to arm a group (which would cost a great deal less than supporting all its present charitable institutions) and everyone would live happily ever after. It would not just be legitimate to do this, but positively obligatory, because it would be the cheapest and most certain method of success. Unfortunately the solution is not quite so simple.[28]

Nor was the Church necessarily naïve in believing that it could bring about new political solutions by encouraging the people to reflect on their situation and then to change it. The consciousness-raising techniques used in the development of Christian communities are far more subversive of the established order than the literature of any communist organization, because the former instill in the poor a sense of class solidarity, not at the urging of a university-educated guerrilla, but from within themselves. (The Brazilian military so feared the Christian communities that they were one of three issues raised in a government investigation of the ideology of Brazil's bishops.)

Everywhere the message is the same: "Speak up!" "The Church is not a supermarket for the sale of sacraments," announces one of a series of comic books produced by the Chilean hierarchy for the Santiago slums. "Get to know your neighbor in church; ask his name. We are all part of the same family and must feel responsibility for that family. Praying all the time won't help much if Christians don't assume responsibility for the difficulties of the people, just as Jesus did."

To teach the people to speak without fear, bishops in Latin America are doing so themselves. There is nothing theoretical or other-worldly about the pastoral letters coming out of El Salvador, Brazil, Chile, Peru, and Paraguay, where the bishops name names, cite statistics, and demand answers in their frequent denunciations of the land-tenure system, unjust wages, high unemployment rates, torture, and repression. They are also prepared to seek help from the Vatican and their colleagues in Europe and North America, to awaken world opinion, and, if need be, to endure jail themselves.

In talking back to government, bishops and priests show the cowed, insecure Latin American that there is nothing supernatural about power and nothing preordained about the death of children from malnutrition or a lifetime of semislavery. When Christ exhorted his followers to "render to Caesar the things that are Caesar's," he was in no way implying that Caesar had a divine mandate to rule, and neither are Latin America's generals picked by God to govern their countrypeople.

"The Americans are killing us."

Latin America's war lords are not the only targets of the bishops' campaign; increasing numbers of churchmen are denouncing U.S. capitalism and militarism for abetting the repression. "The Americans are killing us" is a cry repeated throughout Latin America, often by once-loyal friends of the United States who were brought up to believe that U.S. democracy is a "shining beacon for the Free World."[29] Between 1950 and 1975 the United States trained 71,651 Latin-American military personnel, including 8 of the region's current dictators, and in addition supplied $2.5 billion worth of armaments. Such collaboration is the lifeblood of the Doctrine of National Security.

Determined to play the role of world policeman, particularly in their own backyard, Washington's postwar administrations interpreted any popular manifestation, like the peasant-supported Arbenz government in Guatemala, as a tentacle of the "Red Menace." (President Jacobo Arbenz was overthrown in 1954 with the direct support of Secretary of State John Foster Dulles, after Arbenz's government expropriated 234,000 acres of banana lands belonging to United Fruit.) Then, when the Kennedy administration found it could not dislodge Castro from Cuba with a military invasion, two alternative strategies were devised: the Alliance for Progress and counterinsurgency training for the Latin-American military.

While détente has tended to blunt cold-war excesses in other areas of foreign policy, the political narrow-mindedness of the McCarthy era remains to this day a consistent feature of U.S. courses in counterinsurgency: "good guys" and "bad guys" and nothing in between. Moreover, all these courses have been directed to the same end—U.S. national security. The idea that what is good for the United States is good for Latin America is fairly beaten into Latin-American heads. "A major goal of most —if not all—American-sponsored training is to contribute to actively anti-communist and openly pro-American attitudes," explained Luigi R. Einaudi, Latin-American military expert of the California-based RAND Corporation, one of Washington's think tanks.[30] But what is perceived by the Pentagon or the State Department as "good for the United States" may run exactly counter to the interests of the Latin-American people. As one former State Department official concedes, the "word 'communist' has been applied so liberally and so loosely to revolutionary or radical regimes that any government risks being so characterized if it adopts one or more of the following policies that the State Department finds distasteful: nationalization of private industry, particularly foreign-owned corporations; radical land reform; autarchic trade policies; acceptance of Soviet or Chinese aid; insistence upon following an anti-American or nonaligned foreign policy, among others."[31] Or as theologian José Comblin said: "Almost everything that happens in the rest of the world is somehow made to appear related to U.S. national security, whether it occurs in the heart of Africa or in Paraguay or Bolivia. In such a concept, the American citizen is prompted to feel threatened by economic, political, and even cultural changes in the rest of the world."

Since there is no serious evidence to support the claim that Latin America is threatened by an external enemy, the next-best excuse for spending billions of dollars on arms is internal "subversion." While few of the guerrilla groups that emerged in the sixties were a serious menace to established governments, the phantom of "communist revolution" gave U.S. governments an excellent pretext to mold the political attitudes of two generations of military men. These men learned the lessons so well that they now see communists lurking in every doorway. Most of the techniques of counterinsurgency, such as intelligence gathering, police work, propaganda, and the skills to operate sophisticated equipment, have since been turned against the civilian population, and long after the last guerrilla has died, the bloodletting continues. Many of the victims of this repression charge, with good reason, that the nation that led the fight against fascism in Europe has contributed to its resurrection in Latin America.

That this could happen is due in large part to the United States' historically contemptuous attitude toward Latin America, which it has always looked upon as a purely business venture. Whereas the atrocities committed by Hitler and Mussolini outraged the American people, similar repression in Latin America elicits little more than a yawn. And yet Latin America supplies many of the United States' strategic materials, is its second most important trading partner, and is the ethnic root of 10 percent of its population. So, by default, business dominates U.S. foreign policy. And business as practiced in Latin America cannot live with the sort of checks that democracies impose through the media of a free press, elected Congress, and labor unions. Were U.S. companies to behave in the United States as they do in Latin America, with their bribes, double sets of books, tax evasion, monopolies, and failure to observe even the minimum standards for consumer protection, many of their executives would be behind bars. In Latin America such matters are considered standard business practice. After all these years, foreign companies are still selling thalidomide in Brazil and dumping DDT in Colombia.

For every dollar that U.S. companies invest in Latin America, three dollars come back to the United States in profits, according to the U. S. Department of Commerce. Between 1950 and 1965, this meant a drain on the region's economy of $7.5 billion.[32] Most of this burden has been loaded onto the shoulders of the poorer classes, and with it has come increasing repression. In taking up the issue of human rights, therefore, the Catholic Church necessarily finds itself in opposition to such business practices; yet every time it dares to question the ethics of the foreign companies it is immediately accused of "communist subversion," with the usual threats of repression. But the more abuse the Church suffers for such criticism, the more critical it becomes of capitalism's alliance with dictatorships.

Nelson Rockefeller foresaw such a possibility, though not precisely in these terms. After his 1969 tour of Latin America on President Nixon's behalf, he warned the U.S. business community of the anti-imperialist nature of the Medellín documents. The Rockefeller Report, which became the basis of Nixon's Latin-

American policy, also foresaw—indeed, looked forward to—the emergence of military regimes. Though not specifically stated, the logical conclusion was that Washington had better keep an eye on the region's Catholic Church, since it was "vulnerable to subversive penetration."[33] At least, that was the conclusion reached by the CIA, which had both used and abused the confidence of U.S. missionaries in the 1960s, and in 1975 concocted a master plan for the persecution of Church liberals that was adopted by ten Latin-American countries.* Just as the Pentagon encouraged the Latin-American military's phobias, the CIA used extreme right-wing Catholic organizations to harass political reformers and outspoken bishops and priests. Some of the military regimes' most knowledgeable religious inquisitors were trained by the CIA. They are not only versed in the fine points of theology but also so well educated in the science of intelligence that they have files on every nun, priest, and bishop in the country, including place of birth, education, ideological convictions, and personal weaknesses. Thus when bishops and priests criticize U.S. militarism and capitalism, they speak from personal experience: many of the Latin-American Church's recent martyrs were killed by people trained and armed by the United States.

* See Chapter V, pp. 142–46.

CHAPTER III

BE A PATRIOT (IN EL SALVADOR) AND KILL A PRIEST!

We will stay until we fulfill our duty or are liquidated.

Father César Jerez,
Jesuit Provincial for
Central America,
June 1977

"It was a Dantesque dawn in Aguilares. The Army had surrounded the town and besieged the church, a tank at the very door. There were six of us inside, three priests and three peasants. We were nervously ringing the bells to call for help from the people when soldiers with rifles burst into the bell tower and shot one of the peasants. We were tied up and forced to descend the stairs, all this accompanied by shouts, shots, and the breaking of windows. Hosts were scattered everywhere; bullets sprayed the altar. In the patio we were thrown to the ground, half-nude, face down. We knew nothing more of the wounded man. . . . Terror had engulfed the city."

Thus began the May 1977 siege of Aguilares, as related by Father Salvador Carranza. The Spanish Jesuit was one of three priests in Aguilares, an agricultural community of thirty thousand people north of San Salvador, the capital of El Salvador. A fourth priest, Rutilio Grande, had been murdered by right-wing assassins two months before.

"When they took us to a Jeep outside the church, I counted forty-five soldiers with machine guns," Carranza continued. "There were tanks and helicopters, too. The whole city was under siege. Shots here and there, soldiers ransacking the houses, breaking down the doors if there was any resistance. We three priests were taken to a police station in San Salvador, where we soon heard the beatings and cries of peasants as they were thrown into the jail. Although we were blindfolded, we knew they were bringing in all the furniture and belongings of our parish house. We later learned that they destroyed everything and that the church is now a barracks."[1]

"Operation Rutilio," as the military called the May 1977 siege, was swift and brutal. Within an hour of the dawn attack two thousand government troops had cut off the town's electricity and occupied the school, the railroad, the gas station, and the church. Then the killing began. The armed forces and the police, using tanks, aircraft, and tear gas, sealed off a five-hundred-square-mile area, and every house was searched. The exact death toll is not known, but Church sources estimate that three hundred and fifty to four hundred people were gunned down, most of them unarmed peasants. Carranza and the other priests were taken to the Guatemalan border and expelled, their crime being that they had supported landless people in their efforts to organize a union, the worst offense that can be committed in El Salvador, or so think the military regime and the large landowners who control the government. Peasants are not supposed to talk back in a feudal society, and in El Salvador "the peasants live like serfs in Europe four hundred years ago," said a Salvadoran priest.

The most densely populated, most undernourished country in Central America, with nearly five million people in an area the size of Massachusetts, El Salvador is a microcosm of Latin America's social and political ills. Ninety percent of the peasants have no land, and they comprise two thirds of the population. Two percent of the people own 58 percent of the arable land. The average monthly income of the peasant families, 50 percent of them illiterate, is twelve dollars. Four fifths of the children are ill-nourished. Unemployment and underemployment total 45 percent.

Ever since commercial coffee growing came to the country in

the nineteenth century, the large growers have been progressively squeezing the peasants off their communal lands. With no virgin land to exploit and an annual birth rate of 3.5 percent, El Salvador's desperate peasant population rose up—and was slaughtered—time and again; in 1932 President Maximiliano Hernández' government killed thirty thousand of them. The "green revolution's" agricultural advances hastened the land accumulation, and thousands more were driven from their tiny plots by large cotton, sugar, and coffee estates. "Coffee eats men!" became the anguished cry of the starving peasants.

In 1969 a "soccer war" erupted between El Salvador and neighboring Honduras. The pretext was a dispute on the playing field, but the real cause of the gunfire that killed two thousand was the invasion of Honduran territory by three hundred thousand land-hungry Salvadoran peasants, an exodus actively encouraged by the military regime to free farmland for such export crops as coffee and cotton. El Salvador's export earnings dramatically increased during the 1960s, but local food production and consumption plummeted, and the price in human suffering was enormous. Several thousand Salvadoran peasants were herded back over the border by Honduran troops in 1969, only to be met by more repression on their own side of the frontier. And though it lasted only two weeks, the "soccer war" permanently soured relations between the two countries, so disrupting the Central American Common Market that it has never recovered.

None of this mattered to the country's coffee oligarchy, supreme in its assurance of power and wealth. The "fourteen families," sons and grandsons of earlier dictators who had confiscated the communal lands of the peasants, continue to live in splendor, with mansions in San Salvador, lakeside chalets in the mountains, and colonial ranch houses on their haciendas, each with a permanent staff of six or seven servants. San Benito, the rich, new residential suburb of northern San Salvador, is a tropical Beverly Hills with acres of manicured lawn, orchid gardens, swimming pools, and marble palaces stuffed with crystal chandeliers, European art, and imported luxuries. At the other end of the social scale, in the southern part of the city where thousands of poor Salvadorans crowd the adobe tenement mazes, luxury means a pair of shoes or a small piece of white cheese to relieve the daily monotony of black beans and tortillas. Dirty, barefoot urchins beg through the narrow streets. The crush, the noise, and the smell are asphyxiating, said a rich Salvadoran, who cannot understand "how they live that way." He added that it is worse in the countryside because "the people are like pigs. This friend of mine, who says he has a social conscience, built some houses for his plantation workers. They were small but adequate and they had indoor plumbing, but would you believe, those people were so uneducated that they didn't even know how to use a toilet! What's the good of trying to help people like that?"

However they treat their peasants, San Salvador's rich can hardly be described as ungracious hosts: it is not uncommon for dinner guests at a San Benito mansion to receive such small party favors as diamond rings. Drinking, gambling, and whoring are favorite pastimes of the men, most of whom keep mistresses in apartments in the less-fashionable downtown area. Sports cars and an annual gambling tour of Europe also figure high on the list of pleasures. According to an American who married into one of the families, these rich playboys "are not all that bright," but neither are they stupid enough to share the good life with outsiders. Most marry within their own class, although a foreigner can occasionally penetrate this society if he is a white, Christian, European or American professional—marriage to a Jew or a slightly darker Salvadoran from the lower classes is taboo.

While many wealthy Salvadorans have been educated abroad, few will challenge the attitude of their fathers and grandfathers: "It's our land and we've got a gun to prove it." The idea that lucrative coffee-growing land should be converted to beans for local consumption is politically unacceptable; it raises the specter of agrarian reform. Besides, they say, it makes no economic sense, since El Salvador prospers more by importing foodstuffs with the foreign exchange it earns from export crops. What they really mean is that they prosper more: San Benito housewives can well afford the fresh vegetables and meat daily trucked in from Guatemala; most Salvadorans cannot.

A spurious republic with sham elections and a sham Constitution, El Salvador has always been governed by a privileged clique. (There have been only nine months of real democratic rule since 1931.) The current landowning-military coalition, known as the National Conciliation Party (PCN), dates from 1961, when a reform-minded junta was overthrown by military hard-liners with the blessing of the U.S. military mission.[2] The PCN has maintained itself in power by repression and blatant fraud, so strewing the path of the opposition parties with obstacles that they gave up any attempt to participate in the 1976 municipal elections. Typical of the regime's heavy-handed tactics were threats by a paramilitary organization, the Falange, against the life of Mrs. Alicia Cañizales, who was running for mayor of the city of Sonsonate. Mrs. Cañizales dropped out of the race only when the Falange threatened to kill her children as well.[3]

Under the enlightened leadership of San Salvador's elderly Archbishop Luis Chávez y González, the Church began gradually to take an interest in rural affairs—and was immediately attacked for its interference. Father José Inocencio Alas, the archdiocese's delegate in 1970 to El Salvador's first agrarian-reform congress, was kidnapped on his way to the congress by four men who seized him in front of San Salvador's cathedral. He was found the next day on a lonely road, his head shaved, and still suffering from the effects of the drugs and liquor his kidnappers had forced him to take. On January 2, 1972, Father Nicolás Rodríguez, the parish priest of Chalatenango, was arrested by agents of the National Guard, which has both police and military functions. His brutally dismembered body was found a few days later on the outskirts of the city.[4] Father Fabián Amaya, news commentator for the Catholic radio station YSAZ, received a series of death threats because he had disclosed, among other charges, the intimidation of workers and peasants during the 1972 presidential campaign. Despite strong pressure from the government, the hierarchy refused to silence Amaya or water down its charges of election fraud. What is more, a number of prominent bishops refused to attend President Arturo Armando Molina's inauguration; Bishop Pedro Arnoldo Aparicio telegraphed his refusal, saying he had "a more important appointment with the people." In reprisal for this obstinancy, the Catholic bookshop on the first floor of the YSAZ building was gutted by fire, the radio station on the second floor narrowly escaping the same fate.

These events were merely a warm-up for the nationwide repression that began in November 1974, at San Vicente in central El

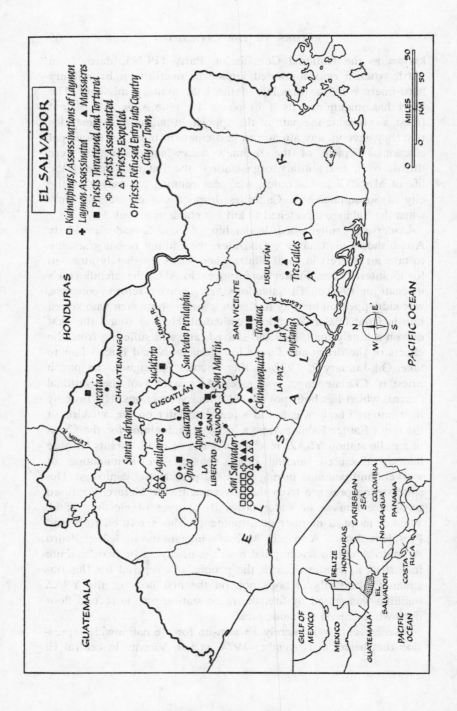

EL SALVADOR

- □ Kidnappings/Assassinations of Laymen
- ✚ Laymen Assassinated
- ▲ Massacres
- ■ Priests Threatened and Tortured
- ✠ Priests Assassinated
- △ Priests Expelled
- ○ Priests Refused Entry into Country
- ● City or Town

GUATEMALA

HONDURAS

PACIFIC OCEAN

Chalatenango
Arcatao
Santa Bárbara
Suchitoto
Aguilares
San Pedro Perulapán
Opico
Guazapa
San Martín
La Libertad
SAN SALVADOR
Apopa
CUSCATLÁN
San Salvador
Chinamequita
LA PAZ
La Cayetana
SAN VICENTE
Tres Calles
USULUTÁN
Ticoluca
LEMPA R.

MILES
0   50
KM
0   50

N E S W

MEXICO
GULF OF MEXICO
BELIZE
GUATEMALA
HONDURAS
EL SALVADOR
NICARAGUA
CARIBBEAN SEA
COSTA RICA
PANAMA
COLOMBIA
PACIFIC OCEAN

Salvador, the rural diocese of Bishop Aparicio, when police and Army troops arrested thirteen peasants who were involved in a rent dispute with the landowners. The soldiers raided the nearby homes, from which they stole food and money, and so badly mistreated a pregnant young woman that she miscarried. The arrested men were forced to walk naked several miles on the main road until they reached a local church, where they were ordered to lie on the floor while the soldiers kicked them and shouted profanities against the Catholic religion. The troops then moved into the fields, where they encountered six peasants returning from work. Four of the men died instantly when the soldiers opened fire. The two wounded peasants, José Morataya and Diego Hernández, were tracked to their huts, where the soldiers again shot them as they lay dying in their wives' arms.[5]

"The whole neighborhood is in terror, and many of us are in hiding and don't dare return home," was the desperate message received by Bishop Aparicio. In response, he called for funeral services and the tolling of the church bells in all thirty-five parishes of the diocese of five hundred thousand Catholics. The Bishops' Conference of El Salvador joined the prelate in denouncing such "deplorable actions which are symptoms of a decadent society, alienated from the Gospel." But the thirteen peasants were never seen again, and the violence continued.

There was a definite pattern behind the repression, said San Salvador's former mayor, Antonio Morales. "Frequently hundreds of armed security personnel will occupy a given city, village, or agricultural area, searching all houses and taking into custody hundreds of innocent persons. The majority of those arrested are freed within a few days, sometimes paying a small fine, or no fine at all. The purpose of these operations is not crime prevention but rather to instill terror in the population as a whole. In this way people come to accept the violation of their human rights as something inevitable, a force that cannot be resisted. When the people are released from jail, the authorities act as if they were giving them a gift by restoring their freedom."[6]

Similar tactics were employed against the Catholic clergy. In May 1975 Father Rafael Barahona, a San Vicente parish priest, was arrested and taken to National Guard headquarters in San Salvador, where he was handcuffed, hooded, and beaten on the stomach, chest, back, and legs. "All the while," said Father Barahona, "they used profanity to insult me as a priest. One of them struck me and said mockingly: 'I am excommunicated, I am excommunicated.' "[7] And so he was, along with all the other government officials responsible for Barahona's arrest. "The torturer who clamored for excommunication now has it," said the angry Bishop Aparicio in a letter to the national government in which he demanded to know whether "the Constitution of El Salvador has two interpretations, one for the authorities and the other for the people? We would like a response, if it would not annoy you, Honorable Authorities, so as not to teach our students a mistaken concept."

Aparicio got his answer in July 1975, when the Army attacked a peaceful student demonstration against the government expenditure of $3.5 million for a Miss Universe beauty pageant. When the marchers came to a bridge spanning a sunken roadway next to the Social Security Hospital in downtown San Salvador, they were blocked off by troops and five riot tanks. As the soldiers opened fire, the students jumped or fell in panic from the bridge to the highway below, where National Guardsmen were waiting. Police armed with pistols and machetes pursued fleeing students into a nearby slum. When nurses and social workers from the hospital tried to rescue the wounded and attend to the dying, the police attacked them. At the end of the carnage, twelve students were dead, eighty were wounded, and twenty-four had "disappeared," never to be seen again.[8]

Temporarily sated with bloodletting, President Molina next tried persuasion. In mid-1976 he decreed a mild agrarian reform supported by AID and the Inter-American Development Bank. Had it ever got off the ground, the 1.4-million-acre project would have benefitted 12,000 landless peasants. Although the 250 families that owned the land were to have received $53 million in compensation, the estate owners immediately denounced the project as "communist subversion"—just as, a decade earlier, they had denounced the Alliance for Progress and the then U.S. ambassador as "communist-inspired." In the face of determined opposition from the Association of Private Enterprise and the Planters' and Cattlemen's Front, President Molina quickly dropped his agrarian reform, but by then the landowners were clamoring for blood, particularly the Church's blood, since El Salvador's priests and bishops were held responsible for "inciting the people to revolt." Promising to "clear the country of rebellious priests," Molina and his Defense Minister, General Carlos Humberto Romero, though they claimed to be themselves "profoundly Catholic," ordered the arrest of five priests, expelled eighteen, and contributed to the deaths of two others.[9] But then ethics have never been a serious obstacle to power or personal gain in El Salvador. More typical of the government's morality was the behavior of the third man in the military hierarchy, Army Chief of Staff Manuel Alfonso Rodríguez, who was arrested and in late 1976 convicted in New York for trying to sell 10,000 machine guns to East Coast gangsters on behalf of the Salvadoran Defense Ministry.[10]

"The peasants began to open their ears."

Like most of rural Salvador, the sugar-growing region of Aguilares is divided among a few large estates and mills that occupy the most fertile land, along the Lempa River, and some thirty thousand peasants, who are squeezed onto tiny plots or have no land at all. The peasants grow a little corn and beans on two-acre parcels on the barren hillsides or rent small plots in the valleys, when they can afford the rent, which continues to climb as the large estates demand more land. They earn wages only during the four-month harvest season, when the plantations need extra labor. There is no electricity or running water in their one-room, thatch-roofed huts. Meat is an unheard-of luxury, and hunger is so severe that El Salvador rates as one of the five most undernourished countries in the world. "The dogs of the rich eat better than the poor," said a former newspaper publisher. If the peasant sees a doctor, it is only once in two years. A woman who has three changes of clothing—or three children who have survived to adulthood—thanks God for her good fortune.

Such were the extremes that defined the pastoral work of a team of four Jesuits who arrived in Aguilares in 1972. Three were foreigners. The fourth, their leader, was a middle-aged Salvadoran, Rutilio Grande, a sturdy, square-faced priest with the peasant features of his people; an outspoken man, fearless, and much loved by the poor. Following Medellín's guidelines for education and community development, these priests encouraged the formation of small Christian communities in Aguilares, the neighboring town of El Paisnal, and twenty-eight surrounding villages. They did so by eating and sleeping with the impoverished villagers two weeks out of four, making the rounds of the rural huts by Jeep but more often on foot or by mule. This sharing in the life of the poor began gradually to pay off, and, with the support of village lay leaders known as "Delegates of the Word," the priests stimulated the peasants to become, in Grande's words, "active agents of change and to seek such fundamental conquests as unions and the defense of labor rights." Said the Jesuits: "The peasants began to open their ears to the 'Good News' [which is what the word "Gospel" means] that God is the Father of all people, that all people are brothers and sisters, and that they must not live in conditions of such tremendous inequality that the very Fatherhood of God is denied. At the same time they received the message that the goodness of God does not make man any less responsible for building a more just world. That is why Jesus called us 'the salt of the earth' and the 'leaven in the meal.'" (Matt. 5:13 and 13:33)

Though nonviolent and nonpartisan, the Christian communities were strongly opposed by local landowners, who claimed the Church was "instigating class warfare." The landlords also objected to the priests' support of community members who joined the Christian Federation of Salvadoran Peasants (FECCAS). Grande was singled out from the others because of his influence among the peasants and his refusal to attend official ceremonies honoring President Molina during his visit to Aguilares in 1972.

As a result of the priests' work and FECCAS' presence in the region, the peasants began to demand better wages, agrarian reform, and lower prices for seeds and fertilizer. "Little by little the peasants were overcoming fatalism," explained the priests. "They were gradually beginning to understand that their situation of hunger and sickness, the premature death of many of their children, their unemployment, the verbal contracts for work that were never respected, that all these disasters are not due to the will of God but to the lust for profit of a few Salvadorans and to the peasants' passivity."

Grande repeatedly defended the peasants' right to organize and was repeatedly attacked by the landowners' associations and their phantom "Conservative Religious Front," which described FECCAS as "subversive" and the priests as "false prophets of hate." But as the Jesuits pointed out, "The Salvadoran Constitution in Article 160 recognizes the right of all Salvadoran citizens to assemble and to form associations. The constitutionality of this fundamental right of every Salvadoran cannot be arbitrarily denied to the peasants." Unless, of course, the Constitution is a worthless piece of paper.

Just how worthless such paper rights are in El Salvador was demonstrated by the landowners' government-supported campaign against the people of Aguilares, including the harassment, imprisonment, and torture of FECCAS members. In February 1975 a group of students was jailed and tortured for having organized literacy classes among the peasants. According to the priests, "The administrators of haciendas refused jobs to people who were organized; informers denounced them to foremen and officials; the authorities did not recognize their unions. This crude reality taught them that the defense of their human rights was going to be a long, hard struggle. Those who cause this struggle have vested interests and they are unmoved by the plight of the peasant."

Unable to obtain any recognition of their labor rights, the peasants suffered yet another blow when many of their small parcels of land were flooded by the Cerrón Grande hydroelectric project. In response to pleas for help, FECCAS organized a demonstration at a local hacienda in December 1976, to protest the peasants' loss of land, and during the meeting one of the estate owners was killed. Although there were conflicting reports of the shooting, the landowners' associations, not waiting for a judicial inquiry, seized on the man's death to launch a vitriolic campaign against the local priests and missionaries and the Jesuit order in general, including full-page advertisements in the national press accusing the priests of communist subversion and of inciting the peasant "hordes" to rebel. Some of the advertisements mentioned priests by name, including Grande and Father David Rodríguez, who went into hiding when his life was threatened. Archbishop Chávez y González denied the landowners' charges and defended the priests, demanding a government investigation of the man's death. Instead, the government staged a display of force, sending troops into Aguilares and the surrounding countryside. Two ex-Jesuit seminarians working with the Aguilares peasants were expelled, as was a Colombian parish priest; a former Jesuit, Juan José Ramírez, was interrogated, beaten, and tortured with electric shocks for ten days. The government also expelled two foreign missionaries working in the San Salvador slums, Belgian Willbrord Denaux and U.S. Maryknoll missioner Bernard Survil. Before being deported, Denaux was shackled to the metal springs of a bed during twenty hours of interrogation.[11]

Meanwhile, the government was preparing yet another fraudulent election to put Defense Minister Carlos Humberto Romero in power. An outspoken supporter of El Salvador's landed aristocracy, Romero had been instrumental in scuttling President Molina's timid efforts at agrarian reform. As Defense Minister from 1972 to 1976, Romero gained a reputation for ruthless repression of any popular opposition and was personally responsible for the San Vicente peasant massacres and the smashing of the 1975 student march.[12] He was also a good friend of the then Nicaraguan dictator Anastasio Somoza, who publicly endorsed him for the presidency.

General Romero was elected President in February 1977. Like Molina, he relied for his dirty work on a local Brownshirt organization known as ORDEN (Spanish for "order"). An extralegal instrument of repression with fifty thousand armed members, ORDEN controls the once-independent San Salvador police force and has groups at all levels of society, including committees in every city block and rural hamlet, to serve as shock troops against political opposition.[13] It keeps tabs on peasant and slum dwellers' associations, denounces noncomformist groups to the state security forces, and handles "disappearances" of community leaders. Such a one was Carlos Mauricio Carballo, a San Salvador slum leader, whom ORDEN abducted in August 1975.

Carballo was the elected community leader of the "Twenty-Second of April" colony, a shantytown housing some one thousand families on the capital's outskirts, and had been negotiating with the city administration to allow slum dwellers to buy land. On August 13 he left the community for the mayor's office to discuss the land purchase and never returned. The week before his disappearance, agents of ORDEN had visited his home. Despite a writ of habeas corpus, Carballo's family was unable to locate him in any place of detention.[14]

Romero won the presidency by a two-to-one margin over the reformist opposition candidate, Ernesto Claramount, although earlier election polls had indicated a neck-and-neck finish. Among tactics used to ensure Romero's victory were massive ballot stuffing and the registration of 150,000 phantom voters. On election day, government radio stations instructed their supporters to "stuff tamales in the tanks," or to stuff the ballot boxes. Spokesmen for the four opposition parties reported at least thirty instances of fraud.[15] In protest against such blatant manipulations, Claramount led six thousand supporters to San Salvador's Plaza Libertad for a peaceful demonstration that has since been named the "Monday Massacre." Shortly after midnight, on February 28, Army troops and police surrounded the plaza with water-throwing tanks and some fifty anti-riot squad cars. After a brief round of shooting, during which four people were injured, an officer announced that the demonstrators had ten minutes to leave the plaza peacefully. Claramount and some one thousand people took refuge in the church of El Rosario, next to the plaza, which the troops immediately sprayed with tear gas. About 4 A.M. a truce was finally arranged by the Red Cross and Archbishop Chávez y González. Of the approximately five thousand people who could not enter the church and who fled the plaza through the cordon of troops, one hundred were killed, two hundred wounded, and five hundred arrested. Claramount was put on a plane for exile in Costa Rica, and that evening the government declared a state of siege to facilitate further repression of the regime's critics.[16]

One of the first victims of government reprisals was Father Rutilio Grande, who was shot to death, along with a teenager and a seventy-two-year-old peasant, while on his way to Mass at El Paisnal, a town north of Aguilares. According to a Church autopsy, the bullets that riddled Grande and the others were of the same 9 mm caliber as the Manzer guns used by the police. By "coincidence" all telephone communications in the area were cut off within an hour of the triple assassination. Police patrols normally active in the region mysteriously disappeared.[17]

The forty-nine-year-old priest had predicted his martyrdom a month earlier during a peasant march to protest the expulsion of a

Colombian priest who had worked in the region. "The real issue facing us today is how to be authentic Christians in our country and in this continent that is suffering its hour of martyrdom," he told the crowds of peasants. "In this country a poor priest or a poor catechist from our community will be lied about and threatened; they will kidnap him under cover of darkness and they might even kill him.

"I greatly fear that very soon the Bible and the Gospel will not be allowed within the confines of our country. Only the bindings will arrive, nothing else, because all the pages are subversive—they are against sin. And if Jesus were to cross the border . . . they would arrest him. They would take him to many courts and accuse him of being unconstitutional and subversive, a revolutionary, a foreign Jew, a concocter of strange and bizarre ideas contrary to democracy, that is to say, against the minority. They would crucify him again, because they prefer a Christ of the sacristy or the cemetery, a silent Christ with a muzzle on his mouth, a Christ made to our image and according to our selfish interests. This is not the Christ of the Gospels! This is not the young Christ who at thirty-three years of age died for the most noble cause of humanity.

"Beware, you hypocrites with clenched teeth who call yourselves Catholics and are full of evil. You are Cains and crucify the Lord. . . . You have no right to say, 'I have bought half of El Salvador with my money' because this is a denial of God. The material world is for all without exception.

"Yet remember that we are not here because of hatred. We did not come with machetes. We even love those Cains, for the Christian does not have enemies. What we have is a moral force, the Word of God . . . which unites us and brings us together even if they beat us with sticks."[18]

A prophet in life, Rutilio Grande became a national hero in death. Over one hundred thousand people ignored the government's state of siege to attend his funeral at the San Salvador cathedral, where eight bishops, including the archbishop, and four hundred priests held the only Mass in the country that Sunday. The Church declared three days of mourning, and all the bells in the country tolled for this priest of the people. "Father Rutilio worked to achieve a profound evangelization of the people, and he was killed by representatives of Salvadoran groups that are try-ing to prevent the continuation of such work," said Bishop Arturo Rivera Damas, of San Salvador. But the work does continue—today there are more than sixty thousand pictures of Father Rutilio Grande in Salvadoran peasant homes.

"Violence begets more violence," the Catholic Church had warned, and now there was more killing, this time by the extreme Left. Two months after Grande's assassination, the Popular Forces of Liberation, one of four guerrilla groups to have emerged in El Salvador since 1971, kidnapped and murdered the country's Foreign Minister, Mauricio Borgonovo, a businessman belonging to the "fourteen families." Although the Church strongly condemned Borgonovo's kidnapping and the archbishop publicly pleaded for his release, the Church, particularly the Jesuits, was once again held responsible for the violence.

Rutilio Grande was a Jesuit; Father Alfonso Navarro Oviedo, thirty-five, was a parish priest; but both preached the same mes-sage of social justice and were active in rural parish work. Like Grande, Navarro told the peasants that God had made all men equal, including priests, peasants, and landowners. This "came as quite a shock," admitted a local Church official, who said that in the beginning "the peasants didn't know what to think." And the idea that peasants should think at all disturbed many of the coun-try's landowners, who, like other privileged minorities in Latin America, live in fear that hordes of machete-wielding peasants will one day descend on them, demanding their rights. That this nightmare is of their own making does not lessen the landowners' fears. Any hint of change is seized upon as a certain sign of the coming storm, which naturally is "communist-inspired." Such is the atmosphere in these tropical Dark Ages that long hair and peasant clothes and sandals of the sort worn by Navarro and other rural priests are taken as overt signs of communism, and any talk of equality is interpreted as an invitation to revolution.[19]

Navarro was therefore singled out to pay for the Foreign Minister's death—a right-wing vigilante organization calling itself the White Warriors Union killed him and a fifteen-year-old boy in the priest's home in San Salvador, using the same ammunition and guns as those issued to government troops. The assassins also an-nounced that they would murder all the country's forty-seven remaining Jesuits if they did not leave the country by July 21, 1977. "Be a patriot! Kill a priest!" urged a series of anonymous pamphlets that circulated after Navarro's death. San Salvador's auxiliary bishop, Arturo Rivera Damas, was forced to go into hiding because of threats to his life, and several priests had to leave their parishes, taking refuge in the archbishop's offices or fleeing the country. The Jesuit university in San Salvador was bombed six times, and the union warned parents that any student attending the city's five Jesuit schools might be killed. All this because the Jesuits had supported former President Molina's half-hearted attempts at agrarian reform.

Priests were not the only targets: hundreds of lay people were persecuted for their Church work. Felipe Salinas, a lay deacon in the parish of Comasagua, near San Salvador, was forced to re-enact Christ's agony on the way to the cross. After dragging him out of his house in his underwear, agents of the National Guard took Salinas to a nearby coffee grove to interrogate him about the religious services he had organized and his meetings with the parish priest. They then beat him up, dressed him in a red cape and a crown, and forced him to carry a cross for two miles between the towns of Comasagua and Shila. Salinas was eventually found by peasants who took off the terrible costume, but a little over a week later the same police agents again arrested and interrogated him in the coffee grove: Who took off the robe, crown, and cross we put on you the other day? Who are the peasant leaders? Who is helping you in your religious work? When Salinas refused to answer these questions, the police threatened to kill him by hacking him into little pieces. They slashed both his arms, filled his mouth with mud mixed with urine, then dragged him over the ground and stamped on his chest with their boots. He was left tied up with the promise: "The next time we're going to kill you for sure."[20]

The siege of Aguilares and the expulsion of the three foreign Jesuits was yet another warning to the Church to abandon its work with the peasants. " 'Operation Rutilio' attempted to destroy in a few days all the slow labor of these past years among extremely needy people," said Father Carranza. "The real issue is not whether the Jesuits directed or didn't direct peasant organizations. What worries [the government] is that these autonomous peasant organizations exist, truly free of the tutelage of the state, independent of the pressures of the special interests of the large landowners."

If Salvador's landowners thought to frighten or divide the Church by such tactics, they miscalculated. "They may end up as martyrs, but my priests are not going to leave [El Salvador], because they are with the people," warned the Jesuits' superior general in Rome, Father Pedro Arrupe. "If we have to die for the truth, to defend the poor, human rights, and justice, we believe that our Lord will give us sufficient strength to accept any consequence," added Father Víctor Guevara, press secretary for the San Salvador archdiocese. Nor was the Church taken in by the White Warriors' claim that no harm would come to "good priests." There are no "good" priests or "bad" priests, announced the archbishop, and "any attack against a priest of any congregation is an attack against the entire Church." Hope for a more malleable archdiocese after Chávez y González retired was similarly dashed when his successor, Archbishop Oscar Romero, blasted the government immediately upon taking office, then flew off to Rome to complain to the Pope. Former Archbishop Chávez y González meanwhile left for the town of Suchitoto, where he had been appointed parish priest at his own request. The seventy-six-year-old prelate's move was yet another slap in the regime's face, since the two Salvadoran priests stationed in Suchitoto had had to flee the country after receiving death threats from the White Warriors.

Nor did the siege of Aguilares destroy the people's solidarity or the Church's commitment to the people, as Father Carranza had feared. A month after the Jesuits' expulsion, several thousand peasants and two hundred nuns descended on Aguilares to hear Archbishop Romero, eight Jesuits, and two parish priests celebrate the first Mass since the massacre. The benches in the Church had been removed to make room for the people, but the crowd was so large that some two thousand peasants spilled out into the street and the church patio. Yet advance publicity for the Mass had been entirely by word of mouth.

In his sermon, Archbishop Romero told the people that "we suffer with those who have disappeared, those who have had to flee their homes . . . and those who have been tortured. We know that many homes are undergoing pain and humiliation. But I want you to know, brothers, that violence of any sort, particularly of the armed forces, is condemned by our Lord. Anyone who kills, persecutes, or beats another should remember the terrible warning of our Lord: 'He who lives by the sword shall die by the sword.'

"Here in Aguilares there have been priests and catechists who literally gave their souls to our Lord; they were not afraid of martyrdom and suffering. The testimony given by the people of Aguilares is an example to all the parishes in the country. Aguilares is simply wonderful. It is an outpost of the Church with a people prepared to fulfill the most dangerous part of the Church's doctrine, the Gospel's commitment to the crucified Christ. For this reason I say to you, courage! Our Lord will always enlighten us on this journey . . . to a genuine Christian liberation, especially in this continent where we have the Medellín documents to guide us. These documents are the real doctrine of the Church, and no one should be afraid to live them."[21]

There was no applause at the end of the sermon, because most of the people were crying.

To demonstrate the Church's commitment to the Aguilares peasantry, Romero presented the people with a new parish priest during the offertory. He also announced that three sisters of the Sacred Heart would leave their school in San Salvador to live and work in Aguilares. When Mass was over, an enormous procession followed the archbishop as he left the church carrying the consecrated Host, winding around the central plaza of Aguilares, the peasants laughing and singing. Vendors were selling food and drink, toys and candles, as if at a fair. It added to the colorful atmosphere that the houses on the plaza had been newly painted by the National Guard to cover up anti-government slogans. Aguilares' city hall, also recently repainted and now headquarters of the National Guard, was the only building to display fresh anti-government slogans and the letters FECCAS, standing for the Christian Federation of Salvadoran Peasants.

As the procession neared the city hall, eleven soldiers sprang in front of the archbishop, blocking his path. The procession stopped; so did the laughing and singing. In the tense silence a small boy approached the archbishop and, pointing at the soldiers, asked him what he was going to do. "Go forward," announced the archbishop. "Carefully, as if they were walking on elephants' eggs, the people slowly moved forward toward the soldiers, who were standing with legs apart ready to shoot," said one of the Jesuits present. "It was a tense situation. The Guardsmen retreated a few steps and then entered the porch of the city hall. They pointed their guns at us as we passed in front of them. They weren't the young, ignorant soldiers we usually see in the Army but hardened men of thirty or more, with a challenging look and an aggressive attitude full of rancor. It was frightening. But the people stared right back.

"Suddenly, one of the guards pointed to a peasant in the procession, shouting for his chief who was inside the building. When the soldiers began to surround the peasant, he and I called for help and instantly we were encircled by two hundred people, the man quickly lost in the crowd. We thought they were going to arrest him, but if that had happened, I don't think I would be here to tell the story. Two of the peasants told me: 'If they touch one of us, there won't be any soldiers or city hall left.' As the people passed in front of the guards, they sang: 'But where, where, where is our Lord? He is with the humble and the persecuted.' "22

"Be Not Afraid"

Contrary to the course of earlier repression in El Salvador, when a few bloody massacres had been sufficient to restore order, the government found that tangling with the Church only stirred the political fire. Although the offices of the Church's weekly newspaper *Orientación* were bombed several times, it kept reappearing and growing (circulation nearly tripled in the first six months of 1977). And whereas most of the earlier pastoral letters from the National Bishops' Conference were nothing more than mild scoldings, later pronouncements left no doubt that the Church held the military and the large landowners personally responsible for the massacre of peasants and the terrible misery in which most of the people live. As for the imprisonment, expulsion, and murder of priests, the bishops informed the regime, "We consider these acts to be clear proof that the government is engaged in operations to deprive the Salvadoran Catholic people of priests committed to serve them."

The attack on the Church also provoked a deluge of unfavorable international publicity and pressure. Church groups provided the U. S. Congress with information on human rights violations in El Salvador, and both the National Council of Churches and the U.S. National Federation of Priests' Councils lobbied for a cutoff in military aid. (Foreseeing what was to come, the Salvadoran Government rejected the $2.5 million in military aid before the 1977 congressional hearings on human rights were completed.) Protestant and Catholic leaders also met with Secretary of State Cyrus Vance to ask for stronger U. S. Government action to protect the human rights of Church leaders in El Salvador. (To show its displeasure, Washington refused to send a special representative to President Romero's inauguration or to fill the empty post of ambassador. El Salvador's bishops also boycotted the ceremony.) But perhaps the most effective threat came from Rome, where the Jesuits' second-in-command, Father Vincent O'Keefe, warned Salvadoran officials that they would all be excommunicated if they did not cease their persecution of the Church. As if by magic, President Romero was suddenly stricken with concern for the country's Jesuits, and on the day set by the White Warriors for them to leave the country government troops were on hand to protect the Jesuit seminary and schools. It was an unusual day— not a single priest was arrested, beaten, or killed.

Temporary lulls in the storm there may be, but the Salvadoran Church has no illusions about the cost of its continuing struggle against the large landowners and the military. Predicted the bishops: "Whenever Christians and the Church are faithful to their prophetic mission to denounce sin and to collaborate in the construction of a more just society for the dispossessed, be they peasants, workers, Indians, or slum dwellers, the reaction is always the same, not just in our country but in all of Latin America; those in power turn on these Christians, and there are deaths, disappearances, expulsions, and threats. But 'be not afraid,' we say to you with the Pope; 'for the Church this is an hour of encouragement and trust in the Lord.' "[23]

CHAPTER IV

MULTINATIONAL SKULDUGGERY IN CENTRAL AMERICA—
Nicaragua, Honduras, and Panama

Somoza may be a son-of-a-bitch, but he's our son-of-a-bitch.

Franklin D. Roosevelt

The conflict between Church and state in El Salvador was but one of several campaigns in the ongoing religious war in Central America. In Nicaragua, for example, the archdiocese of Managua denounced a death squad set up under the aegis of President Anastasio Somoza after Managua's Archbishop Miguel Obando y Bravo and a number of prominent Nicaraguan Jesuits had received death threats. U.S. Capuchin missionaries working in the country's eastern rain forests were threatened with imprisonment and expulsion, and one of them, Father Evarist Bertrand, was deported. The Capuchin house in Managua was watched by security police; the priests' outgoing mail was frequently censored. American Maryknoll nuns working in the Managua slums were similarly controlled.

The death squad, which went under the name of the Anti-Communist League of Nicaragua, made no secret of its intentions. According to the late Pedro Joaquín Chamorro, editor of *La Prensa*, and himself a victim of assassins, the organization had a list of Nicaraguans and foreigners whom it intended to eliminate. One of them was Central America's famous religious poet, Ernesto Cardenal.[1] His brother, Fernando, a Jesuit philosophy professor, was similarly threatened after he told a U. S. House subcommittee that the Somoza government had been responsible for the deaths of 224 peasants in 1976–77.[2] The Capuchins were on Somoza's blacklist because they provided the proof that peasants in the eastern department of Zelaya had been massacred by Nicaragua's National Guard, which doubled as Army and police. (The government-controlled press called the American missionaries "castrated pigs.")

As in El Salvador, a basic cause of the Church's conflict with the government was land, even though Nicaragua has more than enough to go around. The largest nation in Central America, with only 2.2 million people living in an area about the size of England and Wales combined, Nicaragua does not have the population pressures of El Salvador. But like its neighbor, it harbored a small group of greedy people. Half the arable land was occupied by 1,800 ranches, with 96,000 small farms crowded onto the remainder. Another 200,000 peasants had no land. During Somoza's presidency, the Somoza family alone owned 8,260 square miles, or more than 5 million acres, an area approximately the size of El Salvador. (The Somozas controlled an equally disproportionate share of the country's industry; they owned Nicaragua's twenty-six biggest companies.)

As the country's large cattle ranches spread north along the Pacific, the peasants were progressively pushed off the land until there was nowhere to retreat except to Zelaya, a primitive region of rain forest and jungle that occupies the eastern half of the country along the Atlantic. Each new wave of peasant expulsions was accompanied by a brutal military campaign waged on allegations that the peasants were collaborating with a group of left-wing guerrillas known as the Sandinista Front of National Liberation.

Until recently, Zelaya was little regarded, since the ranchers would not put up with the discomforts of jungle living, and in any case the only outlet to the markets of the industrialized southwest was by river canoe and a single decrepit C-46 that somehow made the rounds of the village dirt runways. Since nobody in Somoza's crowd wanted such land, it was left to the peasants, and in less than a decade Zelaya's population increased by 47 percent. But when roads were constructed to connect the region with western and southern Nicaragua and neighboring Honduras, the pattern of land evictions that had occurred elsewhere was repeated in Zelaya —and with the same excuse: "communist subversion." By mid-1978 some six hundred peasants in Zelaya had been killed by government forces, according to the Capuchin missionaries.

Typical of the ongoing terror was the National Guard's slaughter of ninety-two peasants in 1976 in the Sofana district of northwestern Zelaya. The people there had lived in a state of terror since 1974, when the National Guard brought in twenty peasants from the neighboring department of Matagalpa and shot and buried them in Sofana. In August 1975 guerrillas were seen in the neighborhood, and a delegation from Sofana visited military authorities to ask for protection and thus avoid the appearance of complicity with the guerrillas. A National Guard patrol was stationed in Sofana but left after a month.

Caught between National Guard and guerrillas, Sofana's fifty families met at the district's rustic chapel to decide whether to move to Siuna, a town to the north, or come together in a small village for mutual protection. (There are few proper villages in Zelaya; in most cases, houses are a mile apart.) They never did decide because in February 1976 five National Guard patrols stormed the district. "They had a list of names," said an eyewitness, "and they moved from one isolated hut to the next, taking the men out, beating and torturing them in front of their families, demanding that they divulge the names of guerrilla collaborators in the area. These men were then marched out into the fields and shot." Women and children were also murdered, among them an eight-year-old boy who was hanged and then decapitated.[3]

Among the peasants killed were Fernando García and his family, who had formed the backbone of the community and owned some twelve hundred acres along the Iyás River. The land thereupon became the property of Commander Gonzalo Evertz, National Guard chief of Zelaya until his promotion in 1976 to head the Managua traffic department.* Evertz was remembered in the

_____

* According to one estimate, National Guard officers owned 10 percent of Nicaragua's arable land. This, of course, excluded the holdings of the Somoza family. Other perks of office included a monopoly over prostitution

region not only for his ferocity but also for his unusual suspenders, which were covered with U.S. insignia, souvenirs, no doubt, from one of the nine courses he had taken in counterinsurgency and police training in the Panama Canal Zone and the United States. (Some fifty-six hundred guardsmen were so trained, or three quarters of Nicaragua's Army and police force.)[4]

A similar case of expropriation occurred near the Dudú River, where Evertz's successor, Colonel Gustavo Medina, authorized the take-over of river frontage by a large cattle rancher with adjacent holdings along the Matagalpa-Zelaya frontier. Of the original one hundred peasant families living on these lands, only eighteen remained, the rest having fled or "disappeared."[5]

Many of the massacres were motivated by the National Guard's greed for the spoils of war, including land, cattle, and women, or because of old feuds within the community. Forty-four men, women, and children were shot by the military in the Varilla district of Zelaya in January 1977 after the local sheriff denounced the head of the González family as a guerrilla collaborator. There was no evidence to support this charge—and it was known that the sheriff and González had been at odds ever since the latter accused the sheriff of pocketing a collection taken up in the community to build a fence around the local chapel. Nevertheless, the National Guard slaughtered the entire González family, including their married daughters and their families, including twenty-nine children, burying the bodies in a common pit.[6]

But while "there is no justice in such terror," as one Zelaya farmer said, there were reasons for it beyond greed and revenge. People fearful for their lives would not protest against smaller things like the lack of schools and medical facilities or the slave wages paid by the ranches. "It is enough to stay alive," said an old peasant. And without such basic community services as schools and agricultural clubs and cooperatives, it was unlikely that the Nicaraguan peasant would ever be more than a beast of burden. (Fifty-five percent of the country's population are peasants, with an annual per-capita income of less than $120.)

and gambling, kickbacks from public transport and traffic fines, reduced taxes, and the right to import a duty-free car every two years, usually a Mercedes-Benz. (José Fajardo, *"¿Por qué no ha caido Tachito?,"* El Tiempo [Bogotá, Oct. 9, 1978].)

"Teaching people to think is the worst crime you can commit under the Somoza government," said a rural teacher whose school had been closed by the National Guard. Ex-President Somoza's father, Anastasio, Sr., who founded the family dynasty in 1936, would surely have agreed. While on an official visit to Costa Rica, he listened while his colleague there boasted of the schools the government was building. Finally Somoza could stand it no longer: "I don't want educated people," he snorted. "I want oxen."

"Witness of the Truth"

After four decades of work in Zelaya, the forty Capuchin priests from the United States were beginning to see their labor repaid in rural schools, agricultural clubs, homemakers' associations, and medical units. The Capuchins' message was simple: people who work and pray together can achieve a better life for themselves and their community. Unlike Alliance for Progress programs, which were dependent on the government for personnel and funds, and were frequently a cover for counterinsurgency activities, the Zelaya Christian communities were conceived as local bootstrap operations by encouraging the people to elect representatives to be trained in Capuchin seminars as teachers, midwives, artisan agronomists, and religious leaders. None of these people are experts in their fields; many of the primary school teachers, for example, are themselves barely able to read and write. But because they form part of the community, and therefore have a stake in its progress, they do not quit their jobs, as did all the previous urban-educated teachers, agronomists, and doctors. So eager for knowledge are these people that they will hike for three and four days through the rain forests and mountains to attend a local seminar.

To support these programs, the Capuchins assembled a whole library of pamphlets, posters, and books, all written in the language of the Zelaya peasants and all conveying the same message: Love your neighbor, know your legal rights, and be proud of your Indian peasant heritage. Maps were drawn up to help the peasants establish legal titles to the land; there was even a course for local sheriffs, most of whom had not the faintest grasp of the law.

The Capuchins were able to carry out these programs in 275

different communities primarily because they were priests. Like most Latin-American peasants, the first thing the Zelaya farmers wanted, even before a school, was a chapel where they could marry, baptize their children, and receive communion. Though the peasants may not identify with the official Church, they have a deep sense of piety. (The most precious possession in a peasant hut is the Bible, and these people will save for years to buy one.)

With the Capuchins' support, the people constructed the back-bone of Zelaya's Christian communities, a chain of rustic chapels, each with a communal dining hall. The purpose of these halls is to encourage the people to meet, pray, and eat together once a week. Although the Capuchins rarely visit the remote villages more than twice a year, the lay leaders, or Delegates of the Word, carry on their work with weekly prayer meetings and religious instruction. Unlike the missionaries of old who would appear once a year to baptize, confirm, and marry the village en masse, the Capuchins insist that the people attend religion classes to learn the meaning of the sacraments.

As a result of these regular meetings, Zelaya's Christian communities soon spawned a series of other organizations, including teacher-parent associations and agricultural clubs. In some areas, such as the districts along the Prinzapolca River, the Christian communities saved the people from the National Guard. There were fewer *orejas,* informers, to tell lies, and when a member of the community was falsely accused by the military or a rancher, the people united behind the peasant. Thanks to the Capuchins, these people have some awareness of their legal rights. In other areas, however, many of the community structures built up over the years were destroyed by the National Guard. All but 5 of the 30 agricultural extension clubs in the Siuna area were closed on the ground that they might be "subversive." Zelaya's 186 rural schools were also in trouble. A self-help program begun in 1975 to teach peasants to teach their children, the schools were performing well until 1977, when the government ordered the National Guard to take over their administration as part of its "civic action" programs, a United States–supported operation similar to the strategic-hamlet program in Vietnam.

Zelaya's chapels and community centers also were violated by the military, which used twenty-six chapels as barracks and torture centers and as places to rape the peasant women. Lay leaders were singled out for arrest and torture. One Zelaya Delegate of the Word was left tied up for several days in a chapel, then beaten and tortured for three months. He is no longer a leader but a vegetable.[7]

Despite such setbacks, the Capuchins refused to surrender. Seminars and community meetings continued, and a program was started for the preparation of peasant priests. The Capuchins still rode the backlands of Zelaya, bringing comfort and hope to the farmers, prodding the lay leaders to get on with the formation of a youth club or school, and pestering the local military commanders about the whereabouts of a missing peasant. From all this activity there emerged a single, overriding mission: to be a "witness of the truth," like the Good Samaritan, by defending the poor and the oppressed. As the Apostles Peter and John said, "We cannot possibly give up speaking of the things we have seen and heard." (Acts 4:20)

This was easier said than done, of course. Quite aside from the risks implicit in confronting a dictatorship with its crimes, a missionary's life in Zelaya is no picnic. The house in which the Capuchin Midwesterners live in Siuna is rustically adequate, but there is frequently no electricity in the town, water is scarce, and the sole diversion consists of a hike up a nearby hill to look at the surrounding jungle. The dirt road from the "airport" to town a block away winds around the wooden shacks, then peters out in the jungle. Yet Siuna is a paradise compared to conditions in the bush, where the Capuchins spend half their time. Since there are no roads in these backlands, all travel is by foot, mule, or horse. The average distance between rustic chapels is two hours by horse during the dry season, five to six hours when the rains come. Each community provides a horse or a mule for the next stage of the priest's journey, which averages a month in all. There are snakes in the tall grass, vermin in the swamps, floods in the rainy season, droughts in the dry season, and malaria in the villages. Food consists primarily of rice and beans; sleeping conditions in the chapels are extremely primitive. All this was in addition to the ubiquitous National Guard, which viewed the Capuchins as agitators. After several weeks on the forest trails, the Capuchins' small

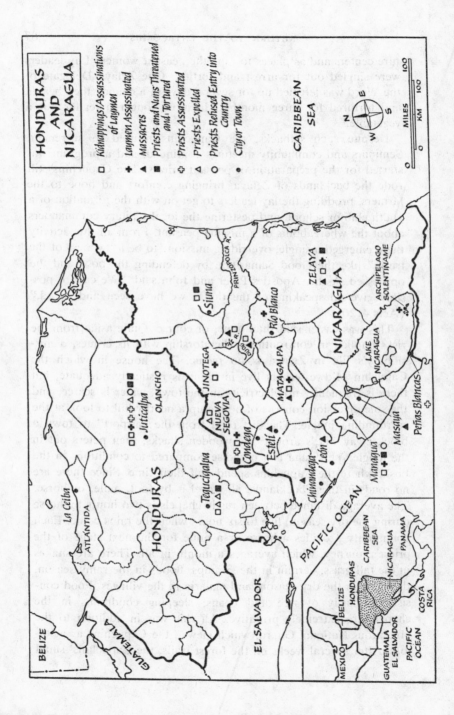

HONDURAS
AND
NICARAGUA

□ Kidnappings/Assassinations of Laymen
✝ Laymen Assassinated
▲ Massacres
■ Priests and Nuns Threatened and Tortured
✚ Priests Assassinated
△ Priests Expelled
○ Priests Refused Entry into Country
● City or Town

CARIBBEAN SEA

N
W   E
S

MILES
KM   100   200

GUATEMALA

BELIZE

HONDURAS

● La Ceiba
ATLÁNTIDA

● Tegucigalpa

OLANCHO

● Juticalpa

□ Siuna

PRINZOPOLCA R.

ZELAYA

● Río Blanco

JINOTEGA

MATAGALPA

NUEVA SEGOVIA

● Comayagua

● Estelí

● Chinandega

● León

EL SALVADOR

PACIFIC OCEAN

LAKE NICARAGUA

ARCHIPELAGO SOLENTINAME

NICARAGUA

● Masaya

● Managua

Peñas Blancas

MEXICO

GUATEMALA
BELIZE
EL SALVADOR
HONDURAS
NICARAGUA

PACIFIC OCEAN

CARIBBEAN SEA

COSTA RICA
PANAMA

house in Siuna seems like a palace, but civilization is still an hour away in Managua, which can be reached only by the decrepit C-46.

"We cannot sit with our arms crossed in our convents."

While conditions had been considerably better in Managua than in Zelaya, the atmosphere there was as oppressive. As in Stroessner's Paraguay, the Somoza regime employed an efficient network of spies, including telephone operators, waiters, taxi drivers, and the corner grocer. Such "troublemakers" as the Capuchins and the Cardenal brothers were listed in a government directory supplied to the police and immigration authorities. Among the prominent Nicaraguans on this backlist was Archbishop Miguel Obando y Bravo, a short, rotund prelate with the half-caste features of his people, whom the government press liked to bait as "that uneducated Indian." Although Obando spoke carefully in public, it was no secret that he opposed the regime. Indeed, his first act as archbishop was to return Somoza's gift of a Mercedes-Benz. (Somoza controlled the Mercedes-Benz agency.) For thus refusing to become indebted to Somoza, the archbishop was threatened with a "car accident" of the sort that killed another progressive Latin-American bishop. His house was ransacked by security agents, and his weekly radio program was censored.[8] Nevertheless, Obando joined the country's other bishops in publicly upholding the Capuchins' denunciations of peasant massacres in Zelaya with a strongly worded statement against "arbitrary detentions, torture, rape, and executions without previous trial."

Jesuit Fernando Cardenal was similarly abused for testifying on Nicaragua's violation of human rights before the U. S. House Subcommittee on International Organizations. The government press described him as a "pervert" and "mental incompetent"; Cornelio Hueck, president of the Somoza-dominated Congress, threatened to try him for treason, and the National University of Nicaragua, where Cardenal taught philosophy, was pressured to dismiss him. Because of media censorship, Cardenal could answer none of the accusations made against him. His telephone was tapped, his letters opened. The Jesuit was not jailed—or murdered—only because Donald Fraser, chairman of the House subcommittee, told the State Department that the U. S. Congress would hold the Somoza government responsible if any harm came to him.

Fernando's brother, the poet Ernesto, was also threatened with charges of treason for denouncing the Somoza government's misuse of AID funds, an accusation backed up by the General Accounting Office in Washington. After Ernesto Cardenal gave a speech in Washington early in 1977, the Somoza newspaper *Novedades* ran a crude cartoon depicting him as a dirty hippie. Cardenal was a dangerous enemy because of his highly respected writings, including *The Gospel in Solentiname,* a series of dialogues with the peasants of the Solentiname Archipelago in Lake Nicaragua, based on Medellín's consciousness-raising techniques in reading the Bible. *Solentiname* is generally agreed to be one of the most damning denunciations of the Somoza dynasty ever printed.†

Though less spectacular, government harassment of other priests and nuns was equally unpleasant. After the 1972 earthquake leveled Managua, a number of religious orders moved to the slums instead of rebuilding their schools for the rich, but even the well-to-do Catholic schools that remained placed increasing emphasis on the sort of "liberating education" that searches out the whys and wherefores of injustice and poverty. Since this went against the Somoza preference for "uneducated oxen," the government, in addition to banning courses in philosophy, logic, psychology, and sociology, burdened these Catholic institutions with endless red tape, arbitrary orders to dismiss teachers, and threats of closure.[9]

Priests and nuns involved in social work in the Managua slums were automatically on the government's blacklist, since attempts to teach the poor their legal rights were judged subversive. Maryknoll nuns in the slum of Open, for example, were persistently badgered because they supported the thirty-five thousand inhabit-

---

† Cardenal's community at Solentiname was destroyed by the National Guard in 1977. All the buildings were razed, including a large library and a museum of pre-Columbian and peasant art.

Cardenal subsequently joined the Sandinista Front of National Liberation in the belief that nonviolent struggle was hopeless in Nicaragua. "Every authentic revolutionary prefers nonviolence to violence," he said, "but he does not always have the freedom to choose."

ants in a protest against the high price for water imposed by Managua's privately owned water company. A parched, dusty shantytown on the capital's outskirts, Open is so poor that its inhabitants lack even a cemetery in which to bury their dead, yet they were paying water rates double those levied on Managua's wealthy suburbs until a peaceful demonstration by one thousand Open inhabitants forced the water company to lower its rates.

Like their Capuchin counterparts in Zelaya, the Maryknoll sisters live with the people, sharing their deprivations, problems, and aspirations. The nuns' tiny house is on the corner of a dusty dirt road in the heart of the slum, their only concession to luxury a battered pickup truck used to transport the people to religious meetings or to a school or hospital in the city. (Open's "health centers" have neither the medicine nor the facilities to treat the people.) Known as the "Peggys" because both are so named, the two resident nuns run a dawn-to-midnight program of community meetings, religious education, civic action projects, and conferences with Maryknoll sisters from outlying regions. Slender, pretty young women dressed in sandals and cotton dresses, they are welcomed everywhere in Open, good examples of the men and women who believe that the religious life in Latin America "has never been richer." There is no whining about poor living conditions or hard work, no nitpicking over theology, sex, or whether the Mass should be said in Latin or Spanish, because the issues these nuns face are so much more immediate—hunger, sickness, misery, and death. "I would have gone home a long time ago," said Sister Peggy Healy, "were it not for the Christian testimony of these poor people. No matter how much they are beaten down every day, they refuse to give up."

Typical of the charity and hope that somehow survive the dirt and the poverty is one young mother who rises every morning at dawn to make tortillas to sell in the distant city market where she works all day. The woman also cares for three nephews and nieces, in addition to her own two children and her husband's parents, all of whom live in a one-room hovel with no electricity. Yet she attends the fourth grade at night school and still finds time to participate in a Christian community. "You have to live with the poor, and be poor yourself, to realize that these people are the real hope and power of the Church," said Sister Peggy.

A trained nurse, Peggy Healy is the educated catalyst so important in motivating a Christian community. Open's inhabitants make their own decisions, as in the case of the water fight, but they need someone like Peggy as advocate. One young Open couple, for example, whose little boy suffered from a partial paralysis of the face, waited months for an appointment at a Managua hospital, only to be sent home by the doctor after a cursory examination. "He didn't tell them anything about rehabilitation or where they could get it," said Peggy, "and they were too afraid to ask him what was wrong or what they should do about it." When Peggy saw the dejected family on their return to Open, she was furious. "I told them to get in the truck, and we drove right back to the hospital. When we arrived, I demanded attention for the child and we got it. But that's because I'm a *madre;* I know the people's rights and am willing to fight for them." For all her slightness, Peggy looks to be a determined young woman, with a set to her jaw and spark in her eye that must have caused consternation in the Managua hospital. The boy is cured of his paralysis.

In the constitution of the Maryknoll nuns' religious order, evangelization "not only is proclaiming the Good News with truth, clarity, and challenge but witnessing it in life and service. We have an urgent call to announce the brotherhood of all men in Christ and to denounce that which deprives man of his legitimate claims for dignity, equality, sharing, and friendship." For that reason, said the Maryknoll sisters in Nicaragua, "we cannot sit with our arms crossed in our convents, as some have said we should. Our role is to be with the people in their struggle to achieve a life of dignity and justice."[10]

Accordingly, the Maryknoll nuns agreed to support a second civic crusade in Open, this time for better public transportation, although they were already under government suspicion for their part in the water fight. The few buses that served the outlying shantytowns of Managua were usually so overcrowded that people literally hung out the door, clawing for a toehold on the crowded steps. After six years of petitioning the government for more buses, the people of Open still wasted two hours to get to Managua by bus, compared to fifteen minutes by car. "If they've waited six years, they can wait a little longer," was the reply of the city transport authorities. A peaceful demonstration was therefore organized at the end of 1977, but was forcibly disbanded by the National Guard. Sister Peggy Dillon, Open's other Peggy, was in the pickup truck, following the parade of demonstrators, when the National Guard stopped the vehicle and took away her driver's license. A freckled redhead, Peggy Dillon, like Peggy Healy, talks back. There were protests against government abuse to the transport authorities and in the press. The same pressures that had earlier forced the water company to lower its rates were now being directed against the transport company.

During the week before Christmas, when the Open transport demonstration took place, seven Managua churches were occupied by students who demanded the release of an estimated 350 political prisoners in Nicaraguan jails.[11] One of the churches was in Open, where the people had put up a sign protesting the lack of buses. Although the Maryknoll sisters and parish priest did not agree with the sit-in, they allowed the students to stay within the church on the condition that they remain peaceful. But they took down the sign on the church in order to dissociate the transport protest from the sit-in. They also agreed to a request by Managua's police chief that they keep order among the students.

On the third night of the vigil the National Guard attacked the students by lobbing tear-gas bombs into the church. When the parish priest tried to intervene, the guardsmen knocked him to the ground, repeatedly kicking him. "You're the cause of all this disorder and subversion, you communist priest," they screamed.[12] The following night one hundred heavily armed guardsmen again descended on Open, attacking a crowd of some three hundred people who had gathered outside the church. A group of nuns and priests were standing in front of the Maryknoll sisters' house when the attack began. Twelve guardsmen fell on Father Benigno Fernández, a Spanish Jesuit who was visiting the nuns at the time. They hit him on the head and slapped him in the face, knocking him to the ground, and breaking his glasses. The nuns kept shouting at the guardsmen to stop hitting the priest, whereupon the guardsmen turned on the sisters, knocking Peggy Dillon to the ground with their rifles and beating her on the head and shoulders with rifle butts. Another Maryknoll sister, Julianne Warnshius, was also felled with rifle butts. Geri Twigg, a lay missioner who works with the Maryknoll priests and nuns in Nicaragua, was beaten.

The following day the group complained to Archbishop Obando and the U.S. Embassy: "We have always been present to try to avoid violence and when necessary to mediate before the authorities to defend our people. This is not communism or subversion. The Church cannot isolate itself inside a temple, as one Guardsman told us, but must be at all times with the people, in their suffering and happiness."[13]

As it turned out, the attack on Open was merely a warm-up for much worse violence. Less than a month later, in January 1978, Pedro Joaquín Chamorro, publisher of the opposition newspaper *La Prensa,* was killed by assassins. A national figure renowned for his unremitting criticism of government corruption and repression, the fifty-three-year-old Chamorro was the leader of a center-left coalition, the Democratic Liberation Union, which included representatives of three political parties and two labor federations. He was a strong contender for the presidency, not only as a well-known newspaper crusader but also as one of the few men of his generation who were never compromised by the Somoza family. As a colleague remarked, in describing the outspoken publisher's frequent stints in jail and exile, Chamorro refused to give up, whereas most Nicaraguans of his age had long since tired of fighting the dictatorship. "Imagine living under the Pinochet junta in Chile for forty-two years, and you have some idea of what it is like in Nicaragua," said a university professor.

According to conservative estimates, some thirty thousand Nicaraguans died in the four decades prior to the 1978–79 civil war for opposing the government of Anastasio Somoza and his sons Luis and Anastasio II. Those who survived, including the sons and daughters of the Nicaraguan aristocracy, were either bought off, forced into exile, or caught up in the economic vise of the Somoza family, which dominated Nicaragua's industry, agriculture, and banks. To silence Chamorro, the president of Somoza's rubber-stamp Congress had threatened him with bankruptcy by demanding damages worth the approximate value of *La Prensa* on a trumped-up libel charge. But Chamorro wasn't frightened. "I will continue to fight no matter what happens," he said.[14]

His last editorial campaign was directed against a Managua

blood-export firm called Plasmaféresis, controlled jointly by Somoza and exiled Cubans, and Somoza tried to pin the assassination on his erstwhile Cuban partner, the director of the company, who was supposed to have masterminded the killing from
Miami. It was a story that only the government accepted.[15]

The ill-advised murder of the popular newspaperman set off a
wave of violent opposition that shook the Somoza dynasty to its
foundations. Family panic had already set in when a sudden upsurge of guerrilla warfare in the fall of 1977 coincided with the
discovery that Anastasio II had a serious heart condition. Nevertheless, the ailing strongman was determined to assure the succession of his son, Anastasio III, who had taken over many of his father's duties. Thus, when the business community protested
Chamorro's murder with a two-week general strike, Somoza responded by ordering the National Guard to bomb, burn, rape, and
pillage cities and villages. At least 350 peasant families were
killed in the department of Chontales in the first two months of
1978, according to the department's Bishop Pablo Vega, who said
the National Guard had used helicopters to massacre the people
and bomb the houses.[16] The Indian quarter of Monimbó, near
Managua, was stormed by eight hundred National Guardsmen in
tanks, armored cars, and helicopter gunships. The toll there will
never be known because the Nahoas Indians buried their dead
and hid the wounded in the hills behind the town, but Red Cross
and Church sources estimated at least thirty dead and hundreds
wounded. Others put the number of dead at over four hundred.[17]
The cities of León, Diriamba, and Matagalpa were also severely
attacked.

As often happens in such repressive situations, increasing numbers of Nicaraguans turned to the Sandinista guerrillas as the only
organization with a hope to overthrow the Somoza dictatorship.
Such was the anger against the regime in the months following
Chamorro's assassination that a number of prominent businessmen publicly sided with the guerrillas. They included landowners, corporate lawyers, bankers, the owner of one of the
largest chains of supermarkets in Managua, and the former treas-
urer of the Managua Chamber of Commerce. Even Alfredo
Pellas, the richest non-Somoza in Nicaragua, urged the strongman
to resign. "Many of my fellow countrymen now believe that the

only way out of this situation is with a gun," said the secretary general of Nicaragua's Conservative Party. "Private enterprise and workers are united in saying, 'No more Somoza!' " Somoza's promises of reform and dialogue fooled no one—the family had broken too many promises in the past. Pedro Chamorro, the only man of sufficient reputation and political support to have conducted a dialogue on equal terms, was dead—killed, most people thought, by Somoza's own men.

One of the few who still believed in the possibility of dialogue, and in Somoza's promise to step down in 1981, was Terence Todman, the State Department's Under Secretary for Inter-American Affairs. Despite the ongoing massacres, he insisted that the human rights situation in Nicaragua had substantially improved. There were good reasons for Todman's inability to recognize facts: while the Carter administration had made known its displeasure at Somoza's heavy-handed way with opponents, it would hardly do for a left-wing guerrilla movement to seize power in Central America. What nobody wanted to admit was that the United States was directly responsible for the popularity of the Sandinista guerrillas. Had it not been for Washington's many years of economic and military support of the Somozas, it is unlikely that conditions in Nicaragua would have reached the point where conservative businessmen were willing to treat with guerrillas. Or as Ernesto Cardenal put it: "Fortunately for us, the United States has never learned the lesson that in supporting cruel and corrupt dictatorships, it only radicalizes the population, causing the very thing it does not want—socialist governments."

The first and fatal mistake was made long ago, in the 1920s, when U. S. Marines attempted to put down a peasant uprising led by Augusto Sandino, a popular leader and the namesake of the current guerrilla front. Anastasio Somoza I was named to head the Army–police force. He used his position to seize the presidency in 1936 and to murder Sandino by first promising amnesty for a conference and then promptly killing everyone who took him at his word. That was a long time ago, but, incredibly, the United States' relationship with the Somozas survived unaltered into modern times. Washington continued to prop up the dictatorship with loans. The Pentagon created, trained, and armed the National Guard, and nearly all Guard officers spent their last year of training in U.S. schools in the Panama Canal Zone.‡ (One of Somoza's chief police advisers, Gunther Wagner, was the former head of AID's police training program in Nicaragua.)[18]

During the 1960s and '70s, the Somoza family regularly cried wolf at congressional aid hearings, falsely claiming that such assistance was needed to fight off a Castro-financed guerrilla invasion. Although there were periodic flare-ups, just as there had been in the thirties, forties, and fifties, guerrilla forces never seriously threatened the government, and even as late as 1976 the Sandinista guerrillas numbered no more than fifty militants.[19] The money, the training, and the arms received from the United States were used for something quite different: to repress the poor people in the slums and rural areas by imprisonment, torture, and death. Very few peasants in the department of Zelaya, for example, wanted any truck with the Sandinista guerrillas,[20] but when thousands of unoffending people are repeatedly hounded from their homes, when their families are tortured and murdered, when their land and goods are seized, they eventually turn to the other side, because, as Ernesto Cardenal said, there is no choice. So one day the wolf did finally appear: the phantom threat of a guerrilla uprising that the Somozas had used to keep Nicaraguans in bondage for so long had become a reality by 1978. But neither communism nor Fidel Castro had anything to do with the guerrillas' success. It was Somoza's own doing—with the loyal help of the United States.

Anyone who studies the history of repression and corruption in Nicaragua will see the obvious parallels with Batista's Cuba prior to Castro's successful revolution. The wonder is that nobody in Washington seems to have bothered with history.

Civil War

By the time of the September 1978 uprising, when several thousand young insurrectionists seized five of the country's largest cities, a majority of Nicaraguans were openly demanding So-

‡ On a per capita basis, the United States trained more Nicaraguan National Guardsmen than any other military or police force in the hemisphere.

moza's resignation. Ten days later, after the insurrection had been (temporarily) put down at the cost of enormous—and unnecessary—suffering, there was "not a decent person left who is not against Somoza," in the words of a Nicaraguan lawyer. "Everyone is cooperating with the guerrillas. He can only stop the killing by resigning—or by killing all Nicaraguans."[21]

Eyewitness accounts of the slaughter by the National Guard suggest that Somoza was prepared to do just that. The Red Cross reported at least five thousand dead, ten thousand missing, over fifteen thousand injured, and twenty-five thousand homeless. The cities of Estelí, Masaya, and León lay in ashes; some sixteen thousand Nicaraguan refugees were in makeshift camps on the Honduran and Costa Rican borders. And long after the guerrillas had been put to flight, the killing continued.

An eighty-one-page report of an on-scene investigation by the Human Rights Commission of the Organization of American States (OAS) described the indiscriminate bombing, strafing, and shelling of Nicaraguan cities and towns by the National Guard: "During the so-called 'mop-up operation,' there was pointed disregard for human life, with the shooting of many people, in some cases children, in their homes or in front of them, in the presence of their parents, brothers, and sisters." The commission also condemned the Somoza government for obstructing Red Cross work;* of killing, arbitrary detention, and other abuses against peasants; and of generalized repression against all young men between the ages of fourteen and twenty-one. One commission member, after a visit to the devastated city of Estelí, called the National Guard an "occupying army."[22]

Typical of the atrocities cited by the commission was the massacre of four innocent people in the city of Matagalpa. The only survivor, a woman, described how her mother, her brother-in-law, a servant, and a guest were fatally shot by guardsmen when they opened the door of their house. Because she was behind the others, the woman managed to escape to the house next door,

---

* *Newsweek* correspondent Ron Moreau reported that "on a road outside the city [of León], Guardsmen for no apparent reason opened fire on a Red Cross truck attempting to carry food into the city. The driver and a passenger were riddled with bullets and died instantly." ("Bloody Nicaragua," *Newsweek*, Sept. 25, 1978.)

where she hid in a garbage dump. During her twenty-four hours in hiding, she could hear the guardsmen looking for her: "'There were five. Where's the other?'

"I could see what they did to my mother after they killed her—they slit her stomach open with a bayonet! They cut off the genitals of my brother-in-law and stuffed them in his mouth. Then they took all my mother's clothing, my brother-in-law's watch, even the keys to his car."[23]

In another incident in Matagalpa, attested to by Amnesty International, the entire family of the owner of the Hotel Soza was machine-gunned by the National Guard, the owner being castrated before he was killed.[24] In their concern for the young, Amnesty International reports coincided with those of the OAS commission. "In some areas," Amnesty International stated, "all males over fourteen years old were reportedly shot dead. In León, eyewitnesses told of the execution on September 15 of twenty-two young men: 'They made the persons kneel in two lines . . . it seemed like thousands of shots . . . we could see a Guard shooting his submachine guns at the people writhing on the ground. They then drove a tractor over the bodies.'"[25] On September 8 most of the young men of the town of Catarina were detained. Seven were later found dead on the outskirts of town.

Ron Moreau of *Newsweek* reported similar scenes: "After retaking León, Guardsmen executed five teenagers—three boys and two girls—in the street. The victims were forced to kneel and were summarily shot."[26]

The Church also had its martyrs, among them Father Chico Luis, founder of an agricultural school for young farmers from the Central American countries. The school, being located on the highway between the badly battered cities of Estelí and Condega, provided refuge for some three hundred people from Estelí. Fearful that the building would be bombed but afraid to venture onto the highway, where they might be machine-gunned, the refugees remained huddled in the school while the priest, his cousin, and a sick woman set off for Condega. They never returned, and though the priest's car was found riddled with bullets, no bodies were recovered. Eyewitness reports stated that the three were machine-gunned by the National Guard when they entered Condega; the bodies were buried in a common grave.[27] "Father Chico Luis gave his life for his brothers," said Sister Joan Uhlen, a Maryknoll nun working in Condega.

On November 2, All Souls' Day, Sister Joan and the people of Condega visited the grave of Father Chico and the others. Said the nun: "The people of the town had adorned his tomb with flowers and beautiful paper decorations with a chalice, a stole with the word 'priest' on it, and many other expressions of the respect and love the people had for Father Chico Luis."

"On the road they were burning stores and hanging people, and even a dog that barked at them, they hung." Thus wrote Ernesto Cardenal of the National Guard—those pupils of the United States. As verified by numerous accounts from foreign journalists who were present during the September slaughter, the National Guard was much better at killing than at fighting. It took, for example, a full battalion, supported by armored cars and planes, to subdue the city of Masaya, which was defended by no more than three hundred youths, armed only with revolvers and sticks! Somoza had survived another round of bloodletting, despite unanimous repudiation by the people, only because of the superiority of his arms—U.S. arms.† After international opinion belatedly

† The National Guard was also aided by an undisclosed number of U.S. mercenaries, including an Oregon-born Vietnam veteran, Mike Echanis, known as "Mike the Merc." Echanis was killed in September 1978 when his plane, piloted by his superior, General José Alegrett, National Guard chief of intelligence and counterinsurgency operations, crashed into Lake Nicaragua in mysterious circumstances. Also killed in the crash were another U.S. citizen, Charles Sanders, and a Vietnamese, Nguyen Van Nguyen. The latter was identified by Fernando Cardenal during his testimony before the House Subcommittee on International Organizations as an adviser to the National Guard. This was denied by the State Department, which said that the man was a "guardsman of Chinese extraction." ("Human Rights in Nicaragua, Guatemala, and El Salvador: Implications for U. S. Policy," Hearings before the Subcommittee on International Organizations of the Committee on International Relations, U. S. House of Representatives, [Washington, D.C., June 8 and 9, 1976], p. 229.)

"Mike the Merc" had been invited to Nicaragua by Somoza's son, Anastasio III, who had been his student at the U. S. Army Special Forces (Green Beret) school at Fort Bragg, North Carolina. It was Anastasio III who led the sacking of such rebellious cities as Estelí and Masaya.

According to Venezuelan Foreign Minister Alberto Consalvi, who interviewed Nicaraguan refugees on the Costa Rican border, a number of the atrocities were committed by U.S. mercenaries. Said Consalvi: "They are

forced the U. S. Government to suspend arms shipments to
Somoza, Israel rushed in to fill the gap with anti-aircraft missiles,
surface-to-surface missiles, and other armaments. Though the
State Department claimed it was none of its business, Israeli manufacturers, most of whom work under U.S. licenses, could not
have supplied the National Guard without Washington's consent.
Only the year before, the U. S. Government had vetoed the sale of
similarly sophisticated Israeli equipment to Ecuador.

Fearful of a Sandinista victory—by November 1978 some six
hundred battle-hardened guerrillas had regrouped in Nicaragua
and on the Costa Rican border—Washington attempted to mediate a peaceful settlement that included Somoza's resignation but
excluded the Sandinistas from government.‡ Predictably, both
sides rejected the proposal, Somoza refusing to step down, the opposition insisting that no government would be viable without
representatives of the guerrillas, by now national heroes to large
segments of the population. The State Department excused its
failure on the ground that "unfortunately another Balaguer could
not be found," a reference to Joaquín Balaguer, who became the
Dominican Republic's perennial President after the 1965 U. S.
Marine invasion. One could only say, thank God, for a U.S. puppet more corrupt and repressive than Balaguer would be hard to
find—except in Nicaragua.

The Nicaraguan Catholic Church, in contrast to the Church's
behavior in Cuba, where most of the clergy and bishops had opposed Castro's guerrillas, not only joined the people's clamor for
Somoza's resignation but also had important and fruitful contacts
with the Sandinista guerrillas. Indeed, it was largely due to Catholic influence that the guerrillas changed from a hard-core Marxist
group to a broader movement that includes numerous Social
Democrats.

---

veterans of the Vietnam war, a war in which genocide was practiced, and
are accustomed to killing." ("Nicaragua: The beginning of the End" and
"Mike the Merc: Soldier of Misfortune," *Latin America Political Report*
[Sept. 22, 1978].)

‡ Washington's policy on guerrillas could hardly be described as consistent. While rejecting the Sandinistas' inclusion in a Nicaraguan coalition,
the United States was attempting to obtain the participation of the Patriotic
Front in a new government in Rhodesia, although the Front was responsible for far worse violence than the Sandinistas.

The Church owed some of its influence to a group called "Los Doce," or "The Twelve," composed of prominent priests, businessmen, and intellectuals, who had relatives in both the guerrillas and the conservative business community and could therefore bridge the gap between them. Thanks largely to The Twelve, opposition to the Somoza government coalesced into a coordinated movement with a specific program for government, including all representatives of the opposition, and a list of reforms, starting with a complete reorganization of the National Guard. (This platform was endorsed by Nicaragua's Catholic bishops.) Among The Twelve were poet Ernesto Cardenal's brother, Fernando, and Nicaraguan Maryknoll missionary Miguel D'Escoto, highly regarded in Nicaragua for his housing projects for the poor.

But if the Church had helped to influence the guerrillas, the justice of the latter's cause also had influenced the clergy. Explained D'Escoto: "In the beginning, the Sandinista Front of National Liberation was Marxist and anticlerical, perhaps because a process of Christianization had not yet begun in the Nicaraguan Catholic Church, and it was identified with the interests of the privileged class. But with our evangelical radicalization, placing ourselves on the side of the poor and oppressed, and not betraying Christ so much, the Front opened itself to Christians because they believed the Church an important factor in the struggle for liberation and because they realized they were wrong in believing that only a Marxist could be a revolutionary. Thus the Front acquired maturity and it became authentically Sandinista."

A young guerrilla on the barricades of Estelí put it another way. "Look at this cross," he shouted at a foreign journalist, waving a revolver in one hand and a cross hanging from his neck in the other. "I am not a communist, as Somoza calls all who fight against his government. I am a Catholic and a Sandinista!"[28]

The Managua Priests' Council hammered on the same theme in a letter sent to President Carter during the September insurrection:

> The Latin American bishops warned us at Medellín that for this type of government "it is very easy to find apparent ideological justifications for these actions" (for example, anticommunism or preservation of "order").

Thus Somoza's tragic rule has evicted many peasants from their land on the grounds that this was necessary to prevent the "communists" from doing the same. Thus the government keeps employment low so that "communists" will not condemn people to forced labor. It disloyally competes with private industry so that "communists" will not be able to obtain financial support. And it sends dissident soldiers to jail so that they will not be tempted by "communism." In Nicaragua it is very difficult to find a social group that the government has not labelled in one way or other as communist or as being an instrument of communism. Even your government, President Carter, has been accused of being "in the hands of leftists."[29]

The Nicaragua Lobby

If the Nicaraguan people ever forgive the United States for foisting the Somoza family on them, it will be because of Americans like the Sisters Peggy and the Capuchins, whose only motivation is a Christian concern for the poor in Open and Zelaya. Unfortunately, the same cannot be said of the U.S. congressmen who, despite ample evidence of corruption and repression, continued to support a dictatorship set up by the State Department more than forty years ago.

Human rights apart, the record shows that the Somoza government had a lot of explaining to do about the misuse of U.S. taxpayers' money, specifically the $76.7 million in AID and other funds designated for the reconstruction of Managua after the 1972 earthquake that killed 10,000 people and left 250,000 homeless. The city's property transfer records tell the story, but even without examining them one can guess who got the aid. Downtown Managua, most of which was destroyed, still looks like a Stanley Kubrick movie set, with block after block of burned-out buildings leaning dangerously over the fields of weeds. This former core of the city has now been replaced by a series of expensive, Los Angeles–like shopping centers distributed around the wealthier residential sectors. The poor, who used to crowd the streets of downtown Managua, got no shopping center, presumably because they could not afford Kentucky Fried Chicken, bowling alleys, or Big Macs. What they received, instead, was a series of slums such as the AID-financed "Las Americas" housing project with its open sewers and matchbox houses.

Typical of the sort of hanky-panky that went on during the reconstruction boom was the purchase of 93.6 acres east of Managua for $71,428 on July 4, 1975, by Rafael Adonis Porras, Somoza's military aide. A little more than two months later, and for $1.7 million, Porras sold the government 56.8 acres of the land for a housing project.[30] Under prodding by the General Accounting Office, AID eventually commissioned a reputable firm of Nicaraguan lawyers to make a study of such land deals. It showed "direct participation of government employees in the land transactions, prior knowledge of land transfer and gain thereof by government officials, inflated land values of up to 1,156 percent over a three-month period, and lack of any ethics in transactions in which the public sector was involved." The Somoza family also reaped millions, not only as owners of the only cement plant in Nicaragua but also as partners in most of the deals. As one Managua businessman pointed out, "In a country as small as Nicaragua where the Somozas dominate the economy, nobody is going to put his hand in the government till without the Somozas' consent."[31]

For a time, in 1977, it seemed that Congress might act to correct such abuses, but then Somoza's powerful Nicaragua lobby stepped in. Following House subcommittee hearings on human rights violations, Representative Edward Koch (D., N.Y.) led a majority vote to cut off $3.1 million in U.S. military aid to Nicaragua for fiscal 1978; this vote was subsequently approved by the full Appropriations Committee. Whereupon, unlike El Salvador and other Latin-American countries that spurned U.S. aid because of such hearings, Nicaragua mounted an expensive campaign to reverse the Koch vote. This was done not so much to get the money, although it would come in handy for arming and training the National Guard, as to maintain Somoza's image in Nicaragua, where Washington's support was psychologically crucial to the government after so many years of U.S. domination.

Apparently on the advice of his childhood friend and fellow West Point graduate, Representative John Murphy (D., N.Y.), Somoza found William Cramer, who was just the sort of influential politician needed to head a lobbying effort. Cramer, a former congressman from Florida, was still accorded many privileges on the Hill but was otherwise a free agent;[32] he had the added advantage of serving as general counsel to the Republican National Committee. Somoza paid him $50,000 as a six-month retainer, in addition to $57,000 earlier paid to his law firm, Cramer, Haber and Becker.[33]

Cramer was supported by the American-Nicaraguan Council, which listed as its members Charles Lipsen, an associate in Cramer's law firm, and Raymond Molina, a Bay of Pigs veteran and businessman who once obtained a $2.5 million contract from the Nicaraguan Government.[34] The council's services cost Somoza $100,000 in 1976, including fees to Joan Worden, a public-relations counselor who had among her clients the Chilean military junta. Also enlisted in the campaign were James Theberge, former U.S. ambassador to Nicaragua and a member of a special Rockefeller commission on Latin America; Fred Korth, an influential Washington lawyer and former Secretary of the Navy; and Korth's good friend Representative Charles Wilson (D., Tex.), a member of Koch's subcommittee. While Korth was convincing Wilson to oppose the aid cutoff, Molina and Lipsen zeroed in on Representative Yvonne Burke (D., Calif.), another Democrat on the subcommittee. At that time neither Molina, Lipsen, nor Cramer was registered as a foreign agent. Cramer claimed he was just a consultant, although he advised Republicans during the subcommittee vote on Nicaragua "with regard to strategy" on how to reinstate aid; Korth was registered with the Justice Department but not with Congress. By U.S. law, all lobbying activities must be registered with both the Congress and the Justice Department *before* they take place. When Cramer finally did register, he cited, among other things, that his services to the Nicaraguan Government would relate to earthquake reconstruction and that he would be lobbying for "economic and military assistance." But as one Justice Department official commented, "It is peculiar they would include military assistance to help in earthquake reconstruction," not to mention that the earthquake occurred in 1972.[35]

As a result of the lobby's campaign, the full House reversed the Appropriations Committee vote and reinstated military aid to Nicaragua, although the very same people had voted the previous day to stop $700,000 in military-training funds for Argentina on the ground of similar human rights violations. But then, Argentina did not have an influential lobby.

Among the members of Congress who switched their vote were nine members of Representative Murphy's Merchant Marine and Fisheries Committee, Wilson's sizable Texas delegation, and all but one of former Representative Cramer's Florida colleagues. Providing the final weight in the balance was a letter from Under Secretary of State Todman supporting military aid to Nicaragua, though Lucy Benson, Assistant Secretary of State for Security Assistance, had earlier stated that she could not think of a single reason why such aid should be continued.[36]

Although the Justice Department later investigated the Nicaragua lobby's activities, Somoza could crow that he and his cronies had put the liberals to flight, not only in the House but in the Senate, where Edward Kennedy abandoned his plan to cut off aid to Nicaragua when a head count showed that he could not muster enough votes to pass the amendment.

In May 1978 the Nicaraguan lobby again used its leverage to unfreeze $12.5 million in U.S. loans for nonmilitary programs and a $32 million soft loan from the Inter-American Development Bank to construct a road between two military garrisons in the northern department of Zelaya. It was in this same area that some six hundred peasants were killed by the National Guard, according to the Capuchin missionaries.

In further support of Somoza, President Carter sent him a letter of congratulations for the improvement in human rights, apparently on the advice of the faction in the State Department that believed the only alternative to Somoza was communism, the very argument of the Nicaraguan dictator. The observation of Nicaragua's former ambassador to the United Nations, Enrique Paguaga Fernández, that "Somoza claims he has more friends in Congress than Carter" may also have prompted the incredible letter.[37]

As if to prove Somoza's claim, seventy-eight members of Congress sent Carter a letter supporting the Somoza regime at the height of the September 1978 slaughter. Initiated by Somoza's good friend Congressman Murphy and by Representative Larry McDonald (D., Ga.), the letter was intended, said McDonald's administrative assistant Fred Smith, "to let the Nicaraguan Government know that not everyone in the United States is against it." Among the signers were Representative Melvin Price (D., Ill.), chairman of the House Armed Services Committee.[38]

The moral of Somoza's lobbying success story is that in Washington money and influence count more than proof of corruption and repression. No one should be surprised to learn, then, that the Nicaraguan word for a Somoza bootlicker is "gringo."

Law of the Gun

While international opinion was shocked by the atrocities committed by the National Guard during the civil war in Nicaragua, the large landowners and military commanders in neighboring Honduras were just as savage. Typical of the barbarities in that country were the torture and massacre of fourteen people, including two priests, in mid-1975, when the military and the landowners arrested and expelled most of the clergy in the eastern province of Olancho.

A rich agricultural area of sugar plantations, cattle ranches, and oak and pine forests, Olancho has traditionally been ruled by the law of the gun, even though the provincial seat at Juticalpa is but 109 miles from the capital, Tegucigalpa. Few of the large landowners who run Olancho have legal title to their plantations or farms, but that hardly matters, since they have the money and the arms. They also control the military government.

As in most of Central America, Honduras is divided between a wealthy few who own the majority of the land and 2 million peasants who own little or no land. Again, it is a question not of too little acreage to go around but of violence and greed: with a population of only 2.9 million in an area nearly the size of Pennsylvania, there is no reason why 23,000 peasant families should starve to death for lack of an acre to plant. But that sort of simple mathematics plays no part in the thinking of the Honduran Government.

The principal difference between Honduras and the other Central American countries is the high degree of political organization of its peasant unions, and for this United Fruit must be thanked. Over the years, conditions on United Fruit's Atlantic Coast banana plantations became so bad that they eventually produced a militant labor movement. The company then employed armed bands to intimidate striking workers, and company planes flew kidnapped union leaders to neighboring El Salvador, where they were dumped. United Fruit thugs took their machetes to the small growers' banana shipments as they lay on railroad platforms. Conditions were not much better on the plantations of United Fruit's principal rival, Standard Fruit. Workers were paid an average seventy-five cents a day and had no right to vacations, medical care, or redress from arbitrary dismissal.[39]

That was until the historic strike of forty thousand workers in 1959, which lasted seventy days despite various deaths and massive arrests of union leaders. All through that terrible period, peasants in the surrounding countryside supported the banana workers, sharing their small portion of beans and bananas with laborers who otherwise would have starved. The banana workers never forgot this solidarity, and it was due to them that the peasants organized their first labor federations.*

The other major impulse toward peasant organization came from the Catholic Church and the young technicians of Venezuela's Social Christian Party (the Venezuelan version of Chile's Christian Democrats), who laid the foundations for a vast network of rural radio schools, peasant training centers, and cooperatives that later came under the umbrella of the Council for Coordinated Development (CONCORDE), financed by various European and U.S. Christian organizations. But while CONCORDE's activities spawned three different peasant federations with a combined membership of 140,000, it could never solve the

---

* Even after the strike, living conditions on the plantations did not noticeably improve. A study of United Fruit's tropical operations by the Rockefeller-financed International Basic Economy Corporation (IBEC), carried out in the mid-sixties at United Fruit's request, showed that the company had created, and was perpetuating, a "culture of poverty." IBEC reported that many of the plantation workers expressed a "desire for freedom." This was not just an abstract longing but a result of the people's total dependence on the "company's mercy" for everything they needed to survive, the report said. Among other recommendations, the IBEC study urged the construction of decent workers' housing. None of the recommendations was ever implemented. (Thomas McCann, *An American Company: The Tragedy of United Fruit* [New York: Crown Publishers, 1976], p. 95.)

basic problem of land distribution. The people knew their legal rights but were repeatedly balked by the country's military regimes which, while they were quick to make promises, and even passed an agrarian reform law in 1974, did nothing to alter the pattern of land tenancy because of the militant opposition of the cattle ranchers and plantation owners. The frustrations caused by this run-around came to a head when twenty thousand peasants marched on Tegucigalpa in 1972, with the usual massacres by the Army and police.

There have been serious clashes between the Army and peasants almost every year since then. Tensions usually begin to build up in April and May, at the beginning of the planting season when the peasants are reduced to eating maize and salt in order to buy seeds. (The annual per capita income of these peasants is thirty dollars!) In mid-1975, at least six people died of hunger every day, according to the Tegucigalpa press, as a result of floods, droughts, and the ravages of Hurricane Fifi, which had worsened the already desperate plight of the peasants during the previous year.[40]

Olancho, one of the areas worst hit, also happened to have, thanks to Nicholas D'Antonio, the province's progressive bishop, one of the country's most advanced programs in peasant leadership training. A good-humored, white-haired New Yorker, the Franciscan had supported CONCORDE's educational programs for the peasants and was therefore thoroughly disliked by the landowners, who called him "the mad communist" and looked upon his priests as "communist agents." The peasants' frustrations and the landowners' hatred produced an explosion on June 25, 1975, when Olancho's military commanders and landowners slaughtered fourteen people, including an American priest. So repulsive were the methods employed in the long torture sessions preceding the massacre that even the national government in Tegucigalpa was shocked.

The excuse for the killings was a "March of Hunger" on the capital organized by the most militant of the country's three peasant federations, the Christian Democrats' National Union of Peasants, as a protest against the government's failure to fulfill any of its promises of agrarian reform. Some twelve thousand peasants were to have participated in the march but only two thousand managed to reach the highway to Tegucigalpa, and they were turned back by Army barricades. In Olancho the march was the signal for the landowners to vent their rage against the Catholic Church. Bishop D'Antonio was in the United States on a fund-raising trip; had he been at home, he also would have died. The landowners had set a price of ten thousand dollars on the bishop's life, his head to be delivered to them on a platter just like that of John the Baptist.[41] Another twenty-five hundred dollars had been paid to the Olancho military commander, Major José Enrique Chinchilla, for the life of Father Iván Betancur, a Colombian priest, by one of the region's richest landowners and lumber exploiters, José Manuel Zelaya.[42]

The terror started in Juticalpa, Olancho's dusty capital of eight thousand, on the morning of June 25 when peasants, teachers, and students occupied the Church's Santa Clara peasant training center in symbolic support of the peasant march on Tegucigalpa. Father Jerome Cypher, a thirty-five-year-old priest from Medford, Wisconsin, was in town that day, seeking medical aid for a peasant. As Cypher was passing the Santa Clara institute, the military and the landowners opened fire on the center, killing five peasants, injuring two, and taking five others prisoner. Cypher, a Franciscan friar who had been in Honduras only eight months and spoke very little Spanish, was standing in front of the center, shocked by the carnage, when someone shouted, "It's one of them. It's a priest." He was immediately set upon, beaten, his clothes ripped off. Bleeding and nude, he was taken to the Juticalpa jail with the five peasants.

At ten-thirty that night, Sergeant David Artica, who was in charge of the jail, had the bound prisoners thrown into the back of a red pickup truck and drove off with them to meet an armed convoy led by Major José Chinchilla. They drove for three hours to the valley of Lepaguare to rendezvous at a lonely bridge with vehicles driven by Carlos Bahr and Zelaya, who escorted them to Zelaya's nearby ranch, Los Horcones. Once at the ranch, the five peasants were given two choices: castration or death in a bread oven. All chose the oven. Cypher was given no choice: he was a priest, not a peasant, and therefore marked to endure far worse.[43]

Meanwhile, in Tegucigalpa, Father Iván Betancur was kissing his elderly mother, Felisa, good-bye, promising to see her next day at the Juticalpa airport. The seven-hour drive to Olancho was too rough for a lady of seventy-two, but Betancur had decided to go by car to show his future sister-in-law, María Elena Bolívar, the countryside. He had invited a young Honduran university student, Ruth García, to accompany them. They drove off, and that was the last time Mrs. Betancur saw them alive.

A frail, white-haired grandmother, Mrs. Betancur had left her family in Colombia to visit Iván, taking with her María Elena, a thirty-one-year-old secretary who was to have married another son, Bernardo, in December. The Betancur family comes from the coffee-growing hills of Antioquia in western Colombia, where the people take pride in their large families (Father Iván was one of eleven children), Catholic faith, and self-reliance. Known as the "Yankees" of Colombia, the industrious Antioqueños are something of a phenomenon in rural Latin America, because, unlike the average peasant, they are proud, independent farmers who own and work their own land, the inheritance of Basque immigrants. Iván Betancur was a typical Antioqueño, hardworking and serious, who could easily have been mistaken for a young bank manager. He was certainly not the sort of priest to endear himself to the landowners of Olancho, since he refused to kowtow to them and saw no reason why the Honduran peasants should be treated like slaves.

Like Bishop D'Antonio a Franciscan, Betancur was a good example of the new breed of young priests in Latin America, men deeply committed to social justice and the cause of the poor. He first came to Honduras in 1968 to work as a layman, and after his ordination in Colombia in 1970 returned to Olancho to serve under Bishop D'Antonio as the parish priest of Catacamas, a village near Juticalpa.

When Betancur set off by Jeep for Olancho with María Elena and Ruth, he was unaware of what was happening in Juticalpa because all radio communications were censored. On the way there he saw that he was low on gasoline and stopped at a ranch near the village of Limones to buy or borrow some. The owner turned him down and, as soon as the priest drove off, alerted the local Army patrol that Betancur was on his way to Juticalpa. Fifteen minutes later, as the car was approaching the valley of Lepaguare, Lieutenant Benjamín Plata and his men intercepted it and took

Betancur and the women to join Father Cypher at Los Horcones. Then the long night of torture began.

Like Cypher, Betancur was stripped, and both men were whipped and beaten. Cypher was castrated and shot, but Betancur endured even worse: his eyes were gouged out, his fingernails, tongue, and teeth pulled out, his hands, feet, and testicles slashed off. The bloody remains of Cypher and Betancur were then dragged out of the ranch house and thrown into a nearby 150-foot well, together with the bodies of the five peasants who had died in the bread oven. The two young women were thrown alive into the well with the corpses, and Lieutenant Plata tossed two sticks of dynamite on top of them to seal the hole, which was later covered with earth. Plata then drove Betancur's Jeep back to the main road, where he doused it with gasoline and set it afire.[44]

Meanwhile, Betancur's mother had arrived at the Juticalpa airport, found no one there to meet her, and made her own way to Betancur's parish house, where a frightened nun told her she did not know what had become of the priest. Soon thereafter, the nun was arrested by the military and the landowners, who systematically pillaged every church, convent, and parish house in Olancho. The parish house at Juticalpa was stormed at midnight, and the four priests sleeping there were taken to jail in their pajamas.[45]

"We were marched into the street and forced to lie face down while armed men sacked the house," said Father Bernardo Arango, another Colombian. "Then they took us to the jail, where they interrogated us till ten in the morning. We were not allowed to eat or drink, even though the people tried to bring us food. A sergeant was stationed in the prision patio to guard and taunt us.

"Later in the day we were herded into an open truck so that the peasants could see us and taken to the airport, where all the landowners in the region had gathered to jeer at us and tell us we would be expelled. There was another long interrogation in Tegucigalpa until nine that night. We were not allowed even a glass of water during all that time. I was thrown naked into a cell and kept incommunicado until the following day, when I was expelled from Honduras."[46]

In all, thirty-two priests and nuns were arrested in Olancho and sent to Tegucigalpa or expelled. The ranchers and the military confiscated church property, including the diocese's cars, and ransacked all the parish houses, among them Bishop D'Antonio's residence. Father Francisco Alonso, the twenty-six-year-old Honduran parish priest of Juticalpa, was taken from jail and marched to the church at gunpoint to say Sunday Mass. He was warned that in the future he would not be allowed near any school or convent, or indeed any place other than the church and the parish house. He was told to state in his sermon that Olancho was calm, that the Army and the Church worked together in harmony, and similar lies. Father Francisco refused to say Mass.

By then, Mrs. Betancur was in touch with Father Bernardo Mesa, one of the few priests who had miraculously escaped arrest. He took her back to Tegucigalpa to see if they could learn anything of her son and the young women, Major Chinchilla having effectively concealed the slaughter at Los Horcones by telling the government in the capital that Fathers Betancur and Cypher had taken to the hills with a pack of six hundred peasant guerrillas. Mrs. Betancur's frantic attempts to locate her son might have come to naught had it not been for the students at the University of Honduras, who organized a march of silence to demand a government investigation of events in Olancho, and the Olancho peasants who had worked with and loved Father Betancur. These latter located the well on Zelaya's ranch and spent eight days digging up the bodies. Faced with embarrassing questions from both the U.S. and Colombian embassies, the military regime finally agreed to investigate. Gonzalo Gálvez, owner of the bread oven in which the peasants had died, described the grisly murders, and Zelaya, Major Chinchilla, and three accomplices were arrested. A few days after giving evidence, Gálvez was found dead under mysterious circumstances.[47]

The military regime's investigation and a private one undertaken by the Betancur family showed that Zelaya and Chinchilla had not acted impetuously or on their own; the campaign against the Olancho Church had been planned two months in advance by all the cattle ranchers in the region and had the financial and political support of both the National Federation of Cattlemen and Farmers, and the business community.[48] Disclaimers to the contrary, the regime itself, headed by General Juan Alberto Melgar, was also involved in the gruesome affair. Church sources asserted that some of the top command must have been accomplices in the plot, because a number of priests, nuns, and lay volunteers who had no connection with Olancho were arrested at the same time in other parts of the country. Those arrested in Olancho were interrogated and expelled by the central government, and the Tegucigalpa authorities forbade any autopsy on the corpses dug up at the ranch. Pedro Martín Bolívar, María Elena's brother, who was sent by the two families to Honduras to bring back Mrs. Betancur and the bodies, said that the Honduras customs authorities told him: "Take the bodies and get out!" (Autopsies were eventually performed in Colombia.) The Betancur family lawyer, who went to Honduras to obtain legal representation for the family, reported that no one in the College of Honduran Lawyers dared touch the case for fear of meeting the same end as the Olancho baker.[49]

Zelaya, who had presided over the torture and slaughter, took up residence in the Central Penitentiary in Tegucigalpa to await trial. He was allowed to build a three-room brick house in the prison courtyard, complete with television, refrigerator, and telephone, where he lived with his wife. He left the prison whenever he pleased, though always with guards to protect him from possible assassins. This special treatment was accorded him as much for his personal connections as for his wealth: his son was married to President Melgar's daughter. When the trial ended in February 1978, Major Chinchilla and Sergeant Plata were found guilty and sentenced to ten years in prison. Zelaya and the others involved in the massacre were exonerated and released.[50]

Zelaya said later that he was reading the Bible and praying that the bishops would lift the excommunication he was under for his role in the murders. "I am a Catholic and the godfather of over six hundred children," he said. "I am completely innocent."[51]

Meanwhile, land invasions, peasant marches, and massacres by the ranchers and the military continued. The government no longer even pretended to be interested in agrarian reform, everyone who had earlier voiced support for the peasants having been fired. Said Lieutenant Colonel Mario Maldonado, former head of the agrarian reform institute, who was exiled to a military assignment in Washington: "Agrarian reform is not communist. It is opposed simply because it affects the traditional privileges of a few wealthy people."[52]

The "Octopus"

Actually, General Melgar would never have countenanced agrarian reform had it not been for the unfortunate scandal that brought down his predecessor, General Oswaldo López Arellano. Unlike the Somozas in Nicaragua, who had decades of experience in the nuances of bribery, López Arellano got caught with his hand in the till when the New York Securities and Exchange Commission revealed that United Brands of Boston—which is the new name for United Fruit, otherwise known as *el pulpo,* the octopus—had paid Honduran Government officials $1.25 million as the first installment of a promised $2.5 million bribe to reduce a banana tax. The tax (50 cents on each forty-pound box of bananas) was established by a fledgling banana cartel of seven Latin-American banana-producing countries to offset spiraling transportation and fertilizer prices. Although the tax was, in effect, the first price rise in twenty years, the companies were outraged. United's competitor, Standard Fruit, threatened to clobber the Central American governments and even went so far as to suspend banana exports from Honduras, but "the octopus" took the more expedient tack of secretly bribing the Honduran Government to halve the tax, thereby saving United Fruit (Brands) $7.5 million annually. The two banana multinationals meanwhile took advantage of the tax to increase their profit from the U.S. consumer by 50 cents a box, all the while crying "extortion" in Central America.[53]

Details of the bribe negotiations came to light in early 1975 after Eli M. Black, the fifty-three-year-old chairman of United Brands, smashed the window in his Manhattan office and jumped to his death on Park Avenue forty-four floors below. When neither Black's relatives nor his business associates could explain the former rabbi's suicide, the Securities and Exchange Commission began to look into the company's affairs. United Brands was in sore financial trouble, thanks to Black's wheeling and dealing; there had been dramatic declines in the price of company stocks, bonds, and warrants and in its share of the banana market. United was also carrying an enormous debt and using questionable accounting practices and was now about to be involved in a scandal of international bribery that would bring down the Honduran Government and give the unpopular *pulpo* yet another black eye in Latin America.[54]

Publicly, at least, Black had always claimed that he wanted to improve the company's image abroad. Immortalized by novelist Gabriel García Márquez's *One Hundred Years of Solitude* for its 1928 slaughter of Colombian banana workers, United Fruit (Brands) is also remembered in Latin America as the cause of the 1954 coup masterminded by Secretary of State John Foster Dulles against the populist government of President Jacobo Arbenz in Guatemala. Arbenz ran afoul of Dulles when the Guatemalan Government expropriated some uncultivated lands belonging to United Fruit, which had at one time employed Dulles and his brother, CIA chief Allen Dulles, as company lawyers. United also employed that illustrious public servant Thomas Cabot, former director of the Office of International Security in the State Department and president of the Gulf Steamship Company. (Despite its name, the company owned no steamships but was a CIA corporate cover to lease land on Swan Island, a base for clandestine radio propaganda in the Caribbean during the Bay of Pigs invasion.)[55] General Walter Bedell Smith, also a former CIA director, had become president of United Fruit in 1955.

Carrying on the company tradition, Black in August 1974 sent United Brands' Vice-President Harvey Johnson to Miami to settle the details of the Honduran bribe with the then Finance Minister Abraham Bennatón.[56] Johnson succeeded in knocking down the Hondurans' original demand from $5 million to $2.5 million, to be paid in two installments into numbered Swiss bank accounts by United Brands' European subsidiaries. The conglomerate's affiliates were already experienced in such dealings, having paid $750,000 in cash to high government officials in Italy to uphold banana import quotas for its Chiquita brand bananas.[57]†

† Despite these revelations, United Brands continued to play according to its own rules. In 1978 the European Court of Justice fined the company $1 million for "abusing" its dominant position in the European banana market. The Court found the company guilty on three counts: discriminatory pricing in the sale of Chiquita bananas, placing undue restraints on distributors, and refusing to sell to a Danish wholesaler who had taken part in an advertising campaign for a rival banana brand. ("United Brands Fined $1 Million," *Newsweek* [Feb. 27, 1978].)

While Johnson and Bennatón were negotiating the details of the bribes, United Brands and Standard Fruit were busy in Honduras laying off workers. Standard did its bit to wreck the Honduran economy, which depends on bananas for its principal source of foreign exchange, by reducing exports from 500,000 to 150,000 crates per week—in an attempt, said the president of the company union, to create economic chaos in the city of La Ceiba, where 55,000 workers depend on the fruit business.

Black's suicide blew the whole rotten banana business wide open, although the scandal caused little surprise in Latin America. Named by *The Wall Street Journal* as the principal beneficiary of the bribes, López Arellano was forced to resign after he refused to allow a government commission to examine his foreign bank accounts. It was not exactly a glorious departure for a man who had led two military coups, but typical of what passes for government in Central America. Once a penniless bus driver's assistant, López Arellano had risen through the ranks of the armed forces to amass a $25 million fortune by the time he was booted from office.[58]

Although President Melgar was certainly no reformer, he could hardly follow López Arellano's act with more of the same. Thus the right-wing general was forced to appear just a bit radical by claiming that his government would be "in favor of the people." There was some talk of nationalizing the plantations of the banana companies, which are the largest landowners in Honduras (United Brands alone has 3.3 million acres), just as there was some talk of agrarian reform. But nothing came of either, and Standard Fruit and United Brands were soon back to business as usual.‡

‡ Melgar in turn was overthrown in a bloodless palace coup in August 1978 by an even more right-wing military regime led by General Policarpo Paz García, head of the armed forces, and Police Chief Amílcar Zelaya. Melgar's fall was due in part to his desire to perpetuate himself in power by becoming president in elections scheduled for 1980, an ambition considered above his station by Paz García and Zelaya, both from relatively elite military backgrounds compared to Melgar, who was press-ganged into the Army as a boy and worked his way up through the ranks. Paz García and Zelaya also reportedly were annoyed with Melgar for failing to squash stories in the local press suggesting that the two were involved in a series of drug and bribery scandals. According to the daily *La Prensa*, Paz García is

One of the companies' first acts was an attempt to destroy the militant banana workers' union, and in this they were aided by the Minister of Labor, a member of the law firm representing the banana companies in Honduras, and by a senior legal adviser to the government, also a member of the law firm.[59] The old union bosses had been voted out of office because of their collaboration with management. (Many of them had been trained by an AFL-CIO branch called the American Institute for Free Labor Development, which had close connections with the CIA.)* The new leadership demanded better living conditions and wages for its members, most of whom earned less than $3.50 a day. To combat this threat, Standard Fruit encouraged thirty-five union members, some of whom had earlier been voted out of office, to agitate against the new union leadership. When this failed to attract any rank-and-file support, the thirty-five occupied union headquarters under the protection of the Honduran Army, which arrested two hundred of the more militant labor leaders. An ensuing wildcat strike of six thousand plantation workers was quickly crushed, and within forty-eight hours Standard Fruit and the Ministry of Labor recognized the thirty-five as the official representatives of the union. To forestall a repetition of this takeover, some one thousand members of United Brand's union occupied their own headquarters.[60]

The Honduran Army also helped Standard Fruit wrest control of a workers' enterprise on banana lands abandoned by Standard Fruit after Hurricane Fifi in 1974. The leaders were arrested on charges of "mismanagement of funds" and "communist control," and new directors, appointed by the military, promptly signed a ten-year agreement to sell all the enterprise's production to Standard Fruit. The workers had earlier considered shifting their busi-

---

co-owner of a large ranch northeast of Tegucigalpa with the recognized chief of the Honduran Mafia, Ramón Matta Ballesteros.

Meanwhile, the chief of the Honduran branch of Interpol, Lieutenant Juan Angel Barahona, was arrested for slander after charging that top-ranking officers were connected with the Mafia and were turning Honduras into a bridge for the United States–bound cocaine traffic. None other than Paz García was appointed to head a commission to investigate Barahona's charges. ("By the way: Honduras," *Latin America Political Report* [June 9, 1978].)

* See Chapter VII, pp. 211–13.

ness from Standard Fruit to COMUNBANA, the marketing arm of the banana-producing countries' association. (Both Standard Fruit and United Brands look upon COMUNBANA as a threat to their marketing monopoly and are determined to starve it of suppliers.) While Standard claimed it had nothing to do with the arrest of the banana enterprise's officials, one of its vice-presidents later admitted that company vehicles had been used in the raid. It also turned out that the district commander responsible for directing and coordinating the attack, Lieutenant Colonel Gustavo Alvarez, was authorized to receive two payments from Standard, totalling $2,850, prior to the raid.[61] Also on the company's payroll, according to a Standard Fruit internal document, was Lieutenant Colonel Juan Angel Arias, the regime's Interior Minister. (United Brands, for its part, said it tended to make its "special" payments directly to the government rather than to officials.)[62]

Following the arrest of the labor leaders, Standard Fruit announced plans to increase banana and pineapple production in Honduras.† The company also began to test vegetable production for the eastern markets of the United States. As the company's diversification manager explained, "Cheap labor and cheap land will enable us to undercut the Florida growers who produce for the winter vegetable market."[63]

Not to be outdone, United Brands began maneuvering to take over a workers' 17,500-acre African palm cooperative as part of its Central American diversification program to produce vegetable oil from the palm's fruit. The secretary general of the 1,339-member cooperative was first approached by United Brands with a proposal to administer and market the plantation's produce, but this was roundly rejected by the members. Shortly afterward, the national police jailed seventeen of the cooperative's leaders on charges of "illegal gambling." Unlike the banana cooperative leaders, who languished in jail for nineteen months, they were freed the following day, but the warning was clear. To make it explicit, the region's military commander told the peasants that if they did not accept United Brands' offer with grace, their cooperative would be smashed, just as the banana enterprise had been. Government funding of the African palm cooperative, essential to its survival, suddenly ceased.[64]

† Standard Fruit is a subsidiary of Castle & Cooke, which markets Dole bananas and pineapples in the United States.

"Uprisings of Despair"

Unlike El Salvador and Nicaragua, where the Church hierarchy repeatedly condemned corruption and repression, most of Honduras' bishops were too frightened to protest, not so much because they were in awe of the military as because they feared the unknown. "They want to maintain good relations with the wealthy classes and the government, and they are afraid of any change in the status quo," explained the director of a European Catholic relief agency working in Honduras.

Actually, the issues were not quite that simple. Like a number of churches in Latin America, the Honduran hierarchy was forced to face the inevitable consequences of consciousness-raising, of Christian communities, and all the other radical reforms that emerged at Medellín. And these consequences are political in nature, because any meaningful reform must eventually topple Latin America's political structures. The Honduran bishops are not alone in preferring the old order, however bad, to the political unknowns of social reform, since no one in the Latin-American Church can predict where such reforms may lead. It always takes a good deal of faith in one's fellow humans to believe that change is for the better.

Few of the country's bishops understood this when they sponsored the formation of radio schools, cooperatives, and peasant-training centers in the 1960s, but by 1974 it was obvious that the National Union of Peasants (UNC), the fastest-growing peasant federation in Honduras, was outdistancing its Christian Democratic mentors to become a powerful political force in itself. Unlike most Latin-American peasants, who can be cowed by a few bloody massacres, the UNC peasantry was well organized, with a tradition of militancy going back to the 1950s. So when faced with death by starvation or a firing squad, these peasants did not hesitate to choose the latter. Not only did they have a cause, they also had the martyrs of Olancho to inspire them. And who was responsible for this situation? All the priests and nuns and lay volunteers working in the CONCORDE radio schools and training programs.

When Honduras' bishops finally saw what was happening, they

retreated, withdrawing their support from CONCORDE and making a sharp distinction between the Church's traditional good works, such as gifts of food and clothing to the poor, and the post-Medellín programs of CONCORDE. Many of the radio schools and training centers were secularized, and Caritas, the international Catholic aid agency, was directed to dissociate itself from CONCORDE.

The bishops explained that they had drawn in their horns to counter criticism from the military and the country's right-wing parties, which claimed that the Church's new programs were advancing the cause of the Christian Democrats. In fact, the Christian Democrats, only slightly less myopic than the political Right, were willing to sacrifice the peasants, and anyone else for that matter, for a promise by the military that they would get their share of the plums of office. Like the Christian Democrats in Chile, who were prepared to take money from the CIA in order to secure a place in government, the Honduran party resorted to such old demagogic tricks as personal attacks, handouts of money, and "communist" smears to bring the unruly UNC peasants under control. But it was too late. Rather than accept political compromise, the peasant federation broke with the Christian Democrats.[65]

"Knowledge is power," and once the peasants understood the country's land laws, they were no longer willing to settle for vague promises of agrarian reform or accept meekly that old maxim "the law is to be observed but not obeyed." "What the large landowners most resent is the peasant leaders' ability to talk and argue about their rights and aspirations in contrast to their previous passiveness," said Bishop D'Antonio. Much of the tension between peasants and landowners in Olancho, for example, stemmed from the peasants' knowledge that the land in dispute did not legally belong to the cattle ranchers. "Legal ownership of land has never been of much importance in Olancho," said New Jersey missioner Vincent Prestera, who worked with Honduras' peasants for seven years. "José Manuel Zelaya, for example, became a millionaire by cutting down timber in the Olancho forests wherever he pleased." Such peasant demonstrations as the March of Hunger on Tegucigalpa were, said the priest, legitimate instruments of pressure on the government to parcel out untilled land that had already been designated for distribution among the peasants.[66]

Appeal to the country's courts is usually hopeless because the large landowners control the judiciary, which invariably rules in their favor. With the government in Tegucigalpa refusing to act, these legal defeats must produce the "uprisings of despair" foreseen by the bishops at Medellín. "All this land," said an Olancho peasant, sweeping the horizon with his hand, "is claimed by one man who doesn't cultivate it but defends it with arms. We have been asking the government to expropriate it, but the government doesn't answer us. Eventually desperation will force us to invade the land, despite the killers who guard it."

That is the sort of talk that frightens the bishops of Honduras, although a minority like Bishop D'Antonio continue to insist that the Church must loudly and actively support social justice in order to stop the unceasing resort to violence. "To remain silent in the face of injustice would make us accomplices of injustice," explained Bishop José Carranza, of Santa Rosa de Copán, in a June 1976 letter to President Melgar that was signed by the Priests Council of Honduras and the Federation of University Students. "What happened in Olancho is only another inducement to continue our Christian work. If the authors of the massacre were trying to intimidate the Church in its evangelical mission, they have not succeeded, for there will always be members of the Church willing to give their lives for their brothers and for the just causes they defend."

Bishop D'Antonio, at least, will be remembered as a man who tried to defend that cause. Sneered at by some of his fellow bishops as "too good' or "too naïve," D'Antonio was prevented from returning to Olancho by Papal Nuncio Gabriel Montalvo, a conservative Colombian prelate. The murder of two priests was bad enough, but the assassination of the popular bishop would have caused irreparable damage to Church-state relations, forcing the reluctant hierarchy to take a strong stand. D'Antonio accepted this prohibition "because I want to live in order to be able to return to work in my diocese."[67]

Having tasted blood, the victorious ranchers were not about to allow the bishop or his clergy to return to work in the province, because "they use the sacred sanctuary to create social agitation and excite the faithful to be disrespectful and disorderly." Since the massacre, vast areas of Olancho have been left without clergy, and any priest or nun sympathetic to the peasants' plight is run out at the point of a gun.

Bishop D'Antonio was eventually relieved of his duties by a Vatican decree, although he retained the title of Bishop of Olancho. In his farewell letter to the peasants, he said that he left his diocese "without resentment of any kind, although my heart is heavy because I cannot personally take care of my flock. Together with my priests, nuns, and laity, I tried to implement the teachings of Vatican II and the Medellín documents. We all know that such work involves risks, and the unprecedented massacre of June 1975 proves this."

Added Archbishop Joseph Bernardin, president of the U. S. Catholic Conference: "The few individuals directly responsible for the Olancho massacre were merely agents and symptoms of a much greater evil—the exploitation and oppression of the vast majority of the Honduran people by a small oligarchy. This situation has been worsened by the monopolistic practices of the multinational corporations in Honduras and their successful efforts to keep the price of bananas low by bribing the Honduran Government in exchange for tax concessions."[68]

A Different Kind of Martyr

"If I disappear, don't look for me. You know where you're going now, and you must carry on." These prophetic words are a fitting epitaph for a shy young priest, Héctor Gallego, whose legend of self-sacrifice lives on in Panama and all of Central America, where the peasants revere him as a saint.

A Colombian like the guerrilla-priest Camilo Torres, Gallego, twenty-eight, was a very different kind of martyr, a humble peasant who preached love, not violence, and who lived with the illiterate poor in one of the most backward regions of Panama. For many people in the Latin-American Church, Gallego was made in the mold of the Twelve Apostles. His work survived his kidnapping and murder in mid-1971 to become an inspiration for priests and nuns throughout the hemisphere.

Only his murderers know what happened to Héctor Gallego

after he was dragged at night from a peasant shack in the province of Veraguas by two men claiming to be Panamanian police agents. It is generally believed, however, that his body was thrown to the sharks of the Pacific from a government helicopter.[69]

Contrary to his exhortation, the Veraguas peasants and the Panamanian Church searched for Gallego for a full year, repeatedly demanding that the government of General Omar Torrijos, Panama's strongman, undertake a thorough investigation. It was all in vain; too many political and economic interests were involved in Gallego's death, including a cousin of Torrijos. And since, unlike Camilo Torres, Gallego had never been involved with guerrillas or a left-wing party, there was no convenient explanation for his murder. He was killed solely because a few selfish and greedy politicians saw their control over the Veraguas peasantry threatened by the Church's agricultural cooperatives and Christian communities. As Panama's Archbishop Marcos McGrath pointed out, Gallego's murder is a sad commentary on a society in which those with a little money and social ascendancy, such as the Veraguas shopkeepers, prefer to hoard their small advantages rather than join the rest of the community for the betterment of all. The attitude is widespread in the Latin-American middle class, which apes the social and political mores of the rich and shows no charity for or understanding of the poor people from whom they themselves have come.

"His way of living could not be understood."

Héctor Gallego's story unfolds against the background of Veraguas Province, a mountainous, isolated land of rain forests and rivers that straddles the Panamanian Isthmus west of the Panama Canal. It has changed very little since the eighteenth century; roads are few and there is no electricity or running water outside the principal towns. In the district where Father Gallego began his work in 1967, ten thousand peasants eke out a miserable living, mainly in hamlets scattered one to four hours apart by foot or mule. The "wealthy" people of the area live in Santa Fe, which has some six hundred inhabitants, a primary school, and an ancient electrical generator. Some work in the town's four stores, others have government jobs—mayor, teacher, policeman—and still others own farms or look after the large ranches of the absentee owners in Panama City. The average townsman can send his children to study in the provincial capital or Panama City, at least through high school; he does not go hungry, and when a member of his family is sick he can afford medicine. The average peasant in the isolated hamlets is illiterate, never sees a doctor, is lucky to eat a plate of beans and rice once a day, and earns less than five dollars a month. Yet extreme as are the differences between hamlet and town, the people in Santa Fe can hardly be described as living in urban splendor, since the town is little more than a cowboy outpost where the principal diversion is a Saturday night beer brawl.

Town and hamlets have stagnated because there are no roads to carry the region's rich produce of coffee, citrus fruits, bananas, potatoes, corn, and sugar cane to city markets. During the six-month rainy season, the only means of transport between Santa Fe and the provincial capital at Santiago are a few four-wheel-drive cars and light airplanes that risk flying into the hill country and landing on the town's dangerous airstrip. Even a mule has trouble getting through the muck and overgrowth between hamlets and town during the torrential downpours, and there are no bridges across the swollen rivers.

Anyone who approached the area's problems logically, as Father Gallego did, would soon conclude that the first priority of townspeople and peasants alike must be an all-weather road, since everyone would gain from the increased trade, services, even tourism it would bring. But, no, the townspeople were happy with conditions as they were. This is not surprising, perhaps, in a people whose feudal mentality locks them into traditional ways impervious to time, excluding any possibility of social change. If the townspeople would not progress, neither would the peasants. They were unable to get the little they grew to the larger towns and were dependent on the Santa Fe storekeepers, who gave them less than the going price during the harvest season, or refused to buy at all, and sold them such essential items as cloth at prices exorbitant by Santiago or Panama City standards. To earn a little cash, fifty dollars or less, the peasants were forced to leave their mountain huts for four months each year to work on the region's large sugar plantations. As a result of these conditions, the peasants were forever in debt to the storekeepers. A peasant who borrowed ten dollars, for example, was expected to repay twenty dollars by the end of the year or go to jail.[70] Totally dependent on the townsmen and their political bosses, or caciques (usually the largest landowners in the region), the peasants were herded to the polls at election time to vote as directed. The townspeople saw nothing wrong in this, since in their opinion the peasants were ignorant and lazy and spent what little they earned on drink, frequently abandoning their women and children to set up new families in another mountain hamlet where they would hack and burn the jungle to plant a little rice or corn for two or three seasons before the unfertilized, eroded land gave out and forced them to move on.

The storekeepers genuinely believed they were being kind to these peasants when they advanced them a little credit, gave them an old dress or worn-out pair of shoes, or employed one of their children as a servant—for food but no pay. Their fathers and grandfathers had behaved that way, and they saw no reason to change. What broke this cycle of poverty and dependence was the introduction of agricultural cooperatives, and for this Héctor Gallego was killed.

Like Father Iván Betancur, who was mutilated and murdered in Honduras, Gallego was born in the Colombian coffee hills of Antioquia. The oldest of eleven children, he was the son of a small farmer who earned just enough to feed his children and send them to high school. Even as a small boy, Héctor wanted to be a priest —a very special kind of priest, one without privileges, a man of the poor. He refused any special celebration of his ordination in 1967, preferring a simple family gathering. "He was forever urging us to give anything extra that we had in the house to needier people," recalled his parents. "Héctor insisted that I pay the people who work with me on the farm a fair wage," said his father, Horacio, a grizzled, broad-shouldered farmer. "The only thing we ever argued about was his decision to leave us for Panama."[71]

A thin, nearsighted young man, Héctor inherited his father's iron will and physical stamina—the priest's hikes through the Panamanian jungles are legendary. Colombia's conservative, inbred Church offered little opportunity for a young man with progressive ideas; whereas Veraguas, which was then under the administration of the forward-looking Archbishop McGrath, was promising ground for new experiments in Church cooperatives and Christian communities. Besides, Héctor told his father, there was greater need of priests in Panama. So Héctor left the safety of a secure but undemanding job as a parish priest in Colombia to work in the rain forests of Veraguas.

From the beginning, he refused any privileges that would distinguish his way of life from that of the peasants. As Yike Fonseca, a Panamanian university student who spent his vacations working with the peasants in Father Gallego's parish, recalled: "He tried hard not to be the sort of priest who is interested only in religious ceremonies. He refused to accept any fees for such rites as baptisms, marriages, and funerals but placed himself totally at the service of the peasants.

"He lived with the bare necessities in the town of Santa Fe, his only income a dollar a day from the church diocese. Normally he ate very little, the same food as the peasants. He never bought extras, not even cigarettes, smoking only if someone offered him one.

"He lived in a tiny shack until the Veraguas shopkeepers burned it down over his head one night when he was sleeping inside: he was lucky to get out alive. That shack had two rooms, made of bamboo, with a small table and a tin locker. Next to it was a larger shack, used for Masses and meetings.

"He dressed simply, like the peasants. He had only one pair of work pants, which he had salvaged from the fire. He went around in hemp sandals, but used rubber shoes if he had to work in the mud. The last time I saw him using them, his toe was sticking out: the rubber shoes had been partly burned in the fire, but he patched them and made them do till one of his peasant friends could get him another pair from Santiago. He wore a mountain hat when he went out. You could pick him out easily at a distance because of his size, his glasses, and that unmistakable hat.

"The last time I saw him he was quite sick. It was his stomach —he frequently suffered from the same trouble.

"When he was at home in Santa Fe, Héctor used to go to bed around midnight. He was always working at something, on parish records for baptisms and marriages or plans for the week's meetings. He would never do this work without the help of some of the peasants. I can still picture him hunched over his table, concentrated on the work he was doing.

"The peasants said that Héctor worked as hard as they did. We university students marveled at him at our volunteer camp at Chilagre, where Héctor worked with a machete and a bush hook for seven days. He was always ready to undertake any job, from cooking to felling enormous trees. When we traveled together to the outlying villages, he used to carry almost twice what we students could. He was thin but tough. His pace was rapid, and I understand he covered great distances.

"Héctor left an unforgettable message for all who are in search of a better world. But his way of living could not be shared or understood by those who are unwilling to give of themselves."[72]

"He showed us the way."

Although the seeds of a cooperative movement had existed before Father Gallego's arrival in Veraguas, his example of self-sacrifice made real what had previously been only good intentions. Contrary to the shopkeepers' assertions that he divided town from hamlet, Gallego began his work of education among the inhabitants of Santa Fe, who promptly rejected his ideas as stupid and improper. They were not interested in joining with the peasants to induce the government to build a road. Agricultural cooperatives would never work, they said, because the peasant was incapable of any real initiative to improve his situation. Besides, it wasn't the parish priest's job to worry about the peasants. He should stick to his clerical duties in the town and not gallivant around the countryside, talking to peasants who were not expected to go to church in any case.[73]

Rejected by the townspeople, Gallego turned to the peasants, who accepted him as one of their own. But it took two years of grueling work, tramping through the jungle and mountains, to form a nucleus of thirty Christian communities with sixty "responsibles," a term Gallego invented to describe the lay leaders. The choice of title is indicative of Gallego's work, which emphasized communal responsibility and encouraged the peasants to think critically about their situation. Meanwhile, McGrath's diocese had set up a peasant training center to give a one-to-three-day course in cooperative management, and young high school graduates trained in cooperative work fanned out into the villages and towns to talk up the advantages of solidarity.

This patient labor eventually paid off with the formation of a federation of cooperatives named after Pope John XXIII that acquired legal title and began to set up stores to buy and sell its own goods, first in the provincial capital at Santiago and then in the principal towns, including Santa Fe. The cooperatives were successful because they worked from reality, not theory, starting with production and consumption instead of the classic cooperative savings and loan institution, for the simple reason that the peasants had nothing to save. In its first year the Santiago store barely broke even; in the second year its sales reached $27,000, and by the fourth year, $500,000. It had become the biggest, best equipped, and most efficient store in town. The lazy, unmotivated peasant was turning out to be quite a businessman.

Production patterns were also changing. Instead of growing a little rice on their tiny plots, the peasants were encouraged to pool their land and to switch from rice to peas, which thrive on the hilly land, particularly with the introduction of fertilizers and irrigation during the dry summer months. Rice, by contrast, is an unprofitable crop and can actually be bought cheaper at the cooperative store.

The financial success of the cooperative movement had an exhilarating effect on the peasants' social attitudes. As Archbishop McGrath described it, "From humble, passive peasants, with heads bowed and straw hats in hand, they had developed into upright persons speaking independently and fairly about religion, their families, and their attempts to improve their situation. They spoke with no bitterness or aggressiveness against others, but rather of their own efforts."[74]

Suddenly, the myths were being destroyed. The so-called laziness of the peasants turned out to be the effect of chronic malnutrition, another result of which was the habit of drinking liquor whenever possible in order to get quick energy for work. The apparent instability of the peasant family was often caused by lack of land on which to build a permanent home. Children were not sent to school because there was no incentive to educate them and they were needed to work the land. With the gradual improvement in their earning capacity, thanks to the cooperative movement, the peasants began to develop greater social stability, participating in Church and community activities and taking over many of the responsibilities of the priest. A number of the couples who had been living together were married, at their own request, and often in the presence of their children. There was a growth of faith, and the basis for a stable society was taking form in the nuclear families. The peasants no longer had to grovel at the feet of the town *patrones* for a ten-dollar loan, since the cooperative lent them money on fair terms. It also provided them with technical assistance and the means to buy seeds, fertilizer, and pesticides.

All this fed the rage of the townspeople and local caciques, who saw their economic and political control eroding. As one of the peasant ballads written about Gallego notes: "Héctor Gallego told us that we must reflect on the steps we take, and that is what the rich resent."[75]

In the beginning, resentment was limited to lies and malicious gossip. The illiterate peasants still under the caciques' control refused to join the Christian communities and their Bible-reading sessions because "the New Testament was a communist book that Padre Gallego had brought from Colombia." (Until Gallego's arrival, many of the peasants had never attended a Mass.) The townspeople also complained that "today's priests are not real priests, because they don't wear cassocks, they smoke, and sometimes they even whistle."[76]

But beneath such patently silly accusations a more vicious hostility was building. Construction materials that belonged to the parish and were to have been used for a new church were seized by the townsmen. On another occasion, when fifty peasants came to Santa Fe for a weekend course in cooperatives, they were insulted by the children of the town who gathered around the hut where the peasants were sleeping, shouting at them to go back to their hamlets and stop bothering the town. The local policeman did nothing, and on the following night, the same children, mostly high school students home on vacation, emphasized their insults by throwing rocks at the shack. The peasants said nothing, but Father Gallego told Archbishop McGrath of the incident.

"I went with the priest to see the mayor," recalled McGrath. "I asked him why neither he nor the policeman had stopped these abuses. He could give me no answer. I told him that unless something were done about it I would bring criminal charges against the parents of these children in the capital city of the province. In view of this he called a meeting of all the townspeople for that very evening.

"At the meeting, one after another expressed their excuses and regret for the incident. I tried to get at the heart of the question. It was true that the cooperative store cut down the sales of other stores in town, but it was quite obvious that the peasants had not only a legal right to the store, but also a moral right to fight for a more decent level of life. This did not impress them. I tried another argument. A more prosperous peasantry would mean economic progress for the whole area. If they all joined in fighting for the year-round road to the town, all would benefit. Instead of fighting over a few pennies, why did they not consider the prospect of a more abundant situation for both the peasants and themselves? Both arguments, the moral and that based on self-interest, were coldly received."[77]

Tempers grew hotter during the 1968 national elections when the peasants refused to vote as the caciques ordered. Alvaro Vernaza, owner of the largest store in the town and a local political power, had thought to buy the district's votes by giving Santa Fe an old electrical generator that he had used on his sugar plantation, but the peasants refused the bribe and burned some of the generator's wires in protest (damage: $7.50). Why, they demanded to be told, was Vernaza giving the town a second-hand generator before elections, when he had done nothing to obtain electricity for the region during his earlier periods in office? Vernaza never forgave the peasants or Gallego for defying him, and two years later Vernaza had the priest arrested on charges of burning the generator.

Gallego's arrest was preceded by another ugly incident when the townspeople, during June celebrations for the district's patron saint, dragged the statue of St. Peter out of Gallego's church-hut and beat the priest, because he and the peasants had wanted a celebration based on prayer and solidarity instead of the drunken brawls that had greeted religious processions in the past. It was the townspeople's saint, and they were not going to share him with any "dirty peasants or that communist priest" Héctor Gallego.[78]

During Gallego's detention at provincial police headquarters in Santiago, hundreds of Veraguas peasants came to his defense. He had not been arrested because of $7.50 in damages to an electrical generator two years earlier, wrote 117 peasants from the hamlet of Vuelto Larga in a letter to the bishop of Veraguas. It was because "he showed us the way to find ourselves. We didn't know what participation was, and now we know. There are strange people in the town who say they don't want to see peasants at the Mass on Sundays, that those of us in Christian communities are communists. We beg of you not to let Padre Héctor leave us in Santa Fe. . . ."[79]

The bishop intervened, and charges against Gallego were dropped, but Bishop Alejandro Vásquez Pinto then insisted on accompanying the priest back to Santa Fe. They were met by the enraged landowner-politician Alvaro Vernaza, who tried to run Bishop Vásquez down with his Jeep. When he failed, Vernaza beat him with an iron cable.[80]

"If the world hates you, bear in mind that it hated me first" (John 15:18), Héctor had frequently quoted Jesus in his talks with the peasants, and now the university students who worked with the priest during their vacation were to learn the same lesson. On their return from their camp at Chilagre, the students were arrested by Panama's National Guard, which claimed that the young people were guerrillas. Two months later, in May 1971, a death warrant was out for Héctor Gallego.

The incidents leading up to Gallego's kidnapping and murder began in the hamlet of Cerro, near Santa Fe, when that community objected to the expulsion of a peasant woman, Juana González, from her tiny, thatch-roofed hut by an influential government official, Saul Ruiz, who wanted to expropriate her property and add it to his own.[81] Although Mrs. González had legal title to her house, the Santa Fe authorities ruled for Ruiz. One morning just before dawn, the entire community of Cerro went to work and fenced the property of Mrs. González, where they left a twenty-four-hour guard. Bishop Vásquez again intervened, and it was quickly established that Juana González had every right to her shack and that Ruiz was in the wrong. The angry townspeople swore revenge, however, and a son of one of the leading families announced that he would "get that bastard Gallego."

Shortly thereafter, on the night of June 9, 1971, two armed men dressed in National Guard uniforms appeared at the hut where Gallego was sleeping and demanded that he come outside for questioning. Gallego was reluctant to do so, but he was also worried about the safety of the hut's two other occupants, and eventually he stepped out to speak to the men. He was instantly knocked to the ground and thrown into a waiting Jeep, in which the two men drove off.

Although the alarm was quickly sounded, the Jeep got a good hour's start on the peasants, who pursued the kidnappers in the cooperative's truck. Within twenty-four hours of Gallego's disappearance every peasant in the district knew what had happened and was combing the mountains and rain forest. Bishop Martín Legarra, who was in charge of the Veraguas diocese, immediately went to National Guard headquarters to protest, and Archbishop McGrath personally took the matter up with General Torrijos in Panama City. To no avail. The government-controlled press threw up the usual smoke screen, reporting all sorts of lies about the investigation. Typical of the allegations was the libel that Gallego's "woman" had been sleeping with him in the hut on the night he was kidnapped. The "woman" in question was one of the two male peasants, whose name happened to be Leonor. It is a common enough name for a man in the Santa Fe district, but that fact the Panama City press conveniently ignored.[82]

General Torrijos, playing Pontius Pilate, stated that he had no knowledge of the kidnapping, a claim hard to credit in view of the political realities of Panama. No military leader who permits himself to be ignorant of anything that happens in that country will last in government more than one week, and Torrijos' survival record is one of the best in Panamanian history. According to him, it was all a plot against the government, although he admitted that he personally had warned Gallego that he was "fomenting violence."[83]

Bishop Vásquez Pinto replied to these disclaimers by charging the National Guard, which doubles as Panama's Army and police, with the kidnapping and with defending the economic interests of the politicians and landowners affected by the Veraguas cooperative movement. By this time Archbishop McGrath and Torrijos were no longer speaking to each other, and for nine months after the priest's abduction the archbishop refused to appear at any government function.[84] Back in Santa Fe, the peasants covered the cross in front of the little church with a picture of Gallego and the huge letters: "Give him back to us alive."‡

"Be careful how you live your life for it is the only Gospel that others will read," Brazil's Archbishop Helder Cámara once said. Gallego left the Veraguas peasantry a message they will remember all their lives. The cooperative movement has continued, as has the work in the Christian communities. "Although Héctor has disappeared physically, he is still with us, because he left us an ideal, an ideal of Christ," said a Santa Fe peasant. "He was a true apostle of God."

‡ Two and a half years after Gallego's death, another foreign missionary who worked in Veraguas was murdered. The body of Gilbert A. Reimer, thirty-five, a Canadian Protestant missionary, was found floating in the Panama Canal. Reimer's corpse bore numerous stab wounds. ("The Way of the Cross in Latin America," *Latinamerica Press* [Lima, April 4, 1974].)

PART TWO

U.S. INTERVENTION

CHAPTER V

MY PAWN TO YOUR BISHOP—
Ecuador Follows Brazil and Chile

Some people believe the "liberation of Christ" is synonymous with guerrilla activity or armed subversion. Such people have never heard the Gospel of Jesus.

The bishops of Santiago,
Talca, and Copiapó, Chile,
August 17, 1976

"Out! Everybody out! *¡Vámonos! ¡Rápido!*"

Forty-eight bishops, priests, and nuns, stunned by the sudden invasion of their peaceful seclusion in the Ecuadorian Andes, couldn't believe what was happening. A platoon of military policemen had burst into the Santa Cruz retreat house, brandishing machine guns, pistols, and tear-gas bombs. No sense could be had from the policemen, who continued to shout and shove, hustling the bishops and priests into a waiting bus. Bishop Leonidas Proaño, who was in charge of the meeting, had a gun stuck in his face when he demanded to see an official order for the raid. What the hell was going on?

An hour earlier, the group had been quietly discussing Proaño's pastoral program for the Ecuadorian Indians. Although the five-day meeting had been formally approved by the Vatican and the Ecuadorian hierarchy months before it took place in August 1976, it was less an official conference than an informal get-together of Latin Americans and Americans, including four U.S. bishops,* who were interested in pastoral work among the poor. Among those present were Archbishop Roberto Sánchez, of Santa Fe, New Mexico; Archbishop Vicente Zaspe, vice-president of the Argentine Bishops' Conference; fifteen bishops; and some of the hemisphere's top theologians. Riobamba, a small provincial city in central Ecuador, had been chosen for the gathering because of Proaño's notable success in educating and organizing the impoverished Indians of the area.

The Santa Cruz house had often been the site of such conferences and retreats, particularly for the region's Indians, many of whom had never slept in a bed or taken a shower until their visit to this peaceful house in the mountain forests. Indeed, everything in the large, rambling building was designed to make the Indians feel welcome, including the conference hall that doubles as a church, with its simple altar made of the trunk of a local cherry tree, an altar cloth woven by Indian hands, and a sanctuary for the Host that is a miniature of the windowless, thatched huts in which Ecuador's Indians have lived for centuries. The group was conferring in this rustic chapel-hall on the afternoon of the fourth day of the meeting when the forty armed policemen burst on the scene.

As Venezuelan Bishop Mariano Parra León tells it, "These barbarians pushed us into a police bus without allowing us to touch any of our personal belongings or even put on a pair of socks. For the first time in my life I knew what it was like to have a rifle shoved in my back.

"We were stuffed into the bus, . . . eighty people in a space meant for fifty, with armed guards pointing their guns at us. We had to take turns standing up during a three-hour trip through the mountains—we didn't know where they were taking us—and even when the bus stopped to allow us to relieve ourselves, there was an armed guard right behind us. Later, when the guards realized who we were—the government hadn't told them—some of them were so ashamed that they wanted to confess their sins there and then."[1]

* Roberto Sánchez, archbishop, Santa Fe; Juan Arzube, auxiliary bishop, Los Angeles; Gilberto Chávez, auxiliary bishop, San Diego; and Patricio Flores, then auxiliary bishop, San Antonio, now bishop of El Paso.

The bus finally came to a halt in its ascent through the darkening Andes at Machachi, a small town below the plateau of Quito, Ecuador's capital. There was more shouting and shoving as Bishop Proaño was dragged from the bus. "We didn't know what they were going to do with him or if they were going to kill him," said Bishop Parra León. "Those gangsters in charge of the military government will murder people without the slightest compunction."

Eventually deposited at the San Gregorio police barracks in Quito at 10:30 P.M., the bishops were forced to walk a gauntlet of eighty armed policemen, whose guard dogs were straining on the leash. The group kept up its courage by singing hymns and praying in unison. Once inside the police barracks, the prisoners were conducted to a large salon with chairs and couches, where the exhausted prelates were told they had been "invited to talk with the Interior Minister." Proaño, meanwhile, was at the Interior Ministry, undergoing a long interrogation about the purpose of the Riobamba meeting. The government officials tried unsuccessfully to force from him an admission that there was subversive literature in the Santa Cruz house, including works by Trotsky and the Colombian guerrilla-priest Camilo Torres. Retorted Proaño: "The only subversive document at the meeting was the Bible."

"This sort of procedure is common practice in Latin America," explained Parra León. "The police try to incriminate peasants, priests, students, and other unfortunate innocents with planted documents to show that the prisoner is guilty of subversion. Fortunately, they stupidly used the same tactic with a group of bishops, which just goes to show the sort of lies and calumny these people are capable of."

Shortly after midnight the group decided to celebrate Mass. The police then offered them coffee, food, and beds, but the prelates refused these amenities out of solidarity with Proaño and "because we felt we were imprisoned in the cause of Christ and the Church, and nobody offered Christ coffee or conveniences on the night of his imprisonment." Parra León, who had just turned sixty-five, said he felt unwell, then collapsed with a heart attack. Meanwhile, Papal Nuncio Luigi Accogli had arrived to inform the bishops that the government had told him "nobody was detained" but that the acting Interior Minister Javier Manrique "wanted a

little talk with them about their subversive meeting in Riobamba."
The outraged bishops told Accogli that nothing subversive had
been discussed at the meeting, unless the minister was referring to
the Vatican's own teachings, and that it "certainly was strange behavior to invite someone for a talk at the point of a gun."† When
the Interior Minister failed to show up—"a coward, that's what he
was," said the indignant Parra León—the imprisoned bishops sent
him a stiff note and a letter of complaint to the Pope as well.

By midmorning the whole government farce was beginning to
unravel, with protests coming from Quito's Cardinal Pablo Muñoz
Vega; the U.S., Venezuelan, and Argentine embassies; CELAM
(the Latin-American bishops' service organization), and a half-
dozen Latin-American hierarchies. Not since President Otto Arosemena had imitated Khrushchev's shoe-banging act in Lyndon
Johnson's presence had Ecuador looked so foolish or received
such bad international publicity. An earlier plan to put all the
prelates on a plane for Panama was dropped when the Interior
Ministry realized that the assault squad had forgotten to bring the
bishops' suitcases with them to Quito—it would hardly do, they
decided, to hustle seventeen bishops off to Panama without their
clothes. Another plan to expel the Colombians, Peruvians, and
Ecuadorians by an overland route to the borders also misfired.
Halfway to the frontier, the police car carrying the Colombians
was ordered to return to Quito by an increasingly worried government. And when Cardinal Muñoz learned that Bishop Victor
Garay Gordobil of Ecuador was to be shipped in a police bus on
a fourteen-hour trip to the Peruvian frontier, he told the Quito
authorities that Church-state relations would never recover from
such a blow. Totally unprepared for the international fracas and
the fury of the Ecuadorian Church's highest officials, the military

† Proaño later accused Accogli of collaborating with the military regime. "The Vatican was never officially informed of the affair by its representative in Quito," said Proaño. "The letters and communications sent by
the imprisoned bishops did not reach the Pope, and this is because there
also exists a Church compromised by members of the Curia that impedes
the Pope from learning of events that injure the sensibility of all Christians.
When the Nuncio visited the bishops in jail, he consoled them by saying,
'You are making a lot of fuss about nothing.'" (José Steinsleger, "Monse-
ñor Proaño: Darle la mano al indio," Cuadernos del Tercer Mundo [Mex-
ico City: Oct. 1978], pp. 48–51.)

regime backed down in a hurry, by 5 P.M. claiming that nobody had been detained; that the bishops were free to go to a hotel or wherever they wished; in short, that it had all been an unfortunate mistake. But Interior Minister Manrique somewhat spoiled this pacific explanation by telling the international press that the bishops and priests had been detained after "friendly governments" had warned the Ecuadorians that the participants at the Riobamba meeting were "subversive communists plotting the government's overthrow."[2]

Although Ecuador has never been admired for either the longevity or the intelligence of its governments, which run the country like a three-ring circus, no one in the Latin-American Church could believe the military regime so stupid as to cause a pointless international scandal without the strong prompting of a more sophisticated and Machiavellian councilor. They looked, therefore, toward Brazil or Chile, and by coincidence many of the bishops and priests present at Riobamba had just come from a pastoral meeting in Vitória, Brazil, that was monitored by Brazilian military intelligence. Also by coincidence, ten Chilean intelligence officers were in Quito at the time, helping the Army's chief, General Guillermo Durán, set up a network of intelligence and security. Chile's military regime gained far more mileage from the affair than did the red-faced Ecuadorian junta; it arranged a rock-throwing reception at Santiago's international airport for the three Chilean bishops who had been at Riobamba.

According to the Chilean Bishops' Conference, Chile's pro-government press knowingly distorted the Ecuadorian story to paint the Chilean bishops as communist subversives. (All three were critical of the government, and Bishop Carlos González of Talca had had several run-ins with Chile's strongman, General Augusto Pinochet.) At a table-pounding press conference chaired by Cardinal Raul Silva, the bishops produced photos and documents to prove that the airport demonstration had been organized by the government's National Department of Intelligence (DINA), Pinochet's secret police. Bishop González reported that a DINA official had threatened to arrest him and his driver. (The official was excommunicated, along with three other DINA agents.) The bishops also said that during their detention in Ecuador the Chilean Embassy "deliberately ignored" them, whereas the U.S. and Venezuelan ambassadors had helped obtain the group's release. "German Catholics knew nothing about the crimes of the Gestapo and the massacre of millions of Jews until after the war, when they were shown the pictures," said Bishop Carlos Camus, permanent secretary of the Bishops' Conference. "I believe something similar is happening in Chile. There are many people who do not know what is going on, but someday they will know the truth, and then they will wonder, how could we have been deceived? But, as Solzhenitsyn says, violence is always disguised by lies and is the justification for those lies."

The situation in Chile was not unique, said the bishops. "The actions that we denounce and condemn are not isolated. They form part of a process or system with well-defined characteristics that threatens to engulf Latin America unresisted. Always on the ground of national security, a justification from which there is no appeal, a model of society is gradually being fashioned that eliminates all basic liberties, tramples on the most elementary rights, and subjects its citizens to a fearful and powerful police state. Were this process to be consummated, we would be mourning the burial of democracy in Latin America."[3]

But Archbishop Alfonso López Trujillo, secretary general of CELAM, put his finger on the real cause of the bishops' mistreatment in Ecuador when he denounced a "concerted campaign against the Church." While there were plenty of skirmishes between national churches and governments in Latin America during the early 1970s, only since 1975 has there been a marked similarity in these anti-Church campaigns, such as planting communist literature on Church premises or arresting foreign priests and bishops on trumped-up charges of "subversion." This was no coincidence: at least eleven countries were following the same geopolitical plan, the Doctrine of National Security, and therefore shared similar strategies in their "war on communism." The military regimes regularly exchanged information about "subversive agents," including churchmen, and regional training programs developed common techniques for dealing with them. The Chileans helped the Ecuadorians set up their national security system; three years earlier the Brazilians had done the same for the Chileans.

A typical contribution to this common strategy was the "Banzer

Plan," hatched in the Bolivian Interior Ministry in early 1975 and named for Hugo Banzer, Bolivia's right-wing military dictator. Although the original plan was not committed to paper, it was discussed at length in the Interior Ministry, a publicly acknowledged subsidiary of the CIA, after the Bolivian Church began to make trouble for the government by denouncing the massacre of tin miners.[4] The plan was leaked to Bolivia's Jesuits by an Interior Ministry official, who was horrified by the government's intention to smear, arrest, expel, or murder any dissident priest or bishop in the Bolivian Church. The authenticity of the Banzer Plan, which boasted many of the classic "dirty tricks" employed by the CIA in Latin America during the 1960s, was subsequently confirmed by the government itself when it followed, word for word, all the original tactics. The plan was later repeated verbatim by the Bolivian delegation to the Third Congress of the Latin-American Anti-Communist Confederation (CAL) during its March 1977 meeting in Asunción, Paraguay.[5]

The three main thrusts of the campaign were to sharpen internal divisions within the Church, to smear and harass progressive Bolivian Church leaders, and to arrest or expel foreign priests and nuns, who make up 85 percent of the Bolivian clergy. According to the plan, "The Church as an institution should not be attacked, much less the bishops as a body, but only a part of the Church, the vanguard, such as [La Paz's] Archbishop [Jorge] Manrique."[6] The idea is to "separate him from the hierarchy and create problems for him with the national [Bolivian-born] clergy." Nationalism should be encouraged among Bolivian priests, nuns, and laymen to "isolate foreign missionaries and damage their prestige, particularly such religious orders as the Catalan Jesuits and the Canadian Oblates." To this end, continued the plan, propaganda should emphasize "the idea that they have been sent to Bolivia for the exclusive purpose of directing the Church toward communism." All progressive Catholic media, such as radio stations and newspapers, should be censored or closed. Among the methods recommended to discredit Catholic progressives was the planting of subversive documents on Church premises. Arrests and expulsions of foreign priests were to be "quietly" carried out so as to "present the bishops with a *fait accompli.*" "Priests who are found to be dangerous must be arrested away from their parish houses and, if possible, outside the city."[7]

The backbone of this strategy was a central depository of intelligence containing dossiers on all progressive laity, clergy, and bishops, with which to "monitor and denounce Marxist infiltration in the Church." The CIA was particularly valuable in "providing full information on certain priests—personal data, studies, friends, addresses, writings, contacts abroad, etc. The CIA also has information on other priests and religious who are not North Americans." John LaMazza, the U.S. labor attaché, was mentioned as "very helpful in this work," along with two Bolivian Interior Ministry officials, Freddy Vargas and Alfredo Arce. Although LaMazza denied the charges, fifty U.S. Maryknoll missionaries refused to meet with U. S. Ambassador William Stedman, Jr., during the priests' annual conference when Stedman showed up at the meeting with LaMazza. As one Maryknoll priest explained: "Whether he is a CIA agent or not, we weren't taking any chances after he was mentioned in that plan." Vargas, the Interior Ministry's Under-Secretary, also denied the charges, claiming that relations between government and Church were "perfect."‡[8]

In fact, those relations steadily deteriorated as the Banzer Plan's recommendations were put into effect. Between 1975 and 1978 twelve foreign missionaries were arrested, half of whom were deported. In October 1976 Father Raymond Herman, a diocesan missionary from Dubuque, Iowa, who worked with the Indians in Cochabamba in central Bolivia, was found strangled in the parish rectory with two bullet wounds in his head. Cochabamba's Archbishop Armando Gutiérrez wrote to the Bolivian Interior Ministry indignantly demanding a thorough investigation of the murder after the accused assassin, Omar Baeza, escaped from a Cochabamba prison under suspicious circumstances. Herman's murder was never solved.

‡ Former Maryknoll priest Jim O'Brien, now with the Inter-American Foundation sponsored by the U. S. Congress, states that he saw a confidential State Department report, written prior to the exposure of the Banzer Plan, that described State Department officials' visits to progressive priests in Bolivia. The report, he said, described the priests' work and outlined their movements. (Interview with author, Jan. 1978, Colombia.)

The smear campaign proposed in the Banzer Plan was carried out with a series of letters and denunciations in the local press from previously unknown organizations, such as the "Anti-Communist Catholic Traditionalists," the tactics and even the names of which were the same as those listed by former CIA agent Philip Agee in his description of CIA activities in Ecuador during the 1960s.[9] Archbishop Manrique and Bishop Jesús López de Lama, both mentioned in the Bolivian documents presented at the CAL meeting in Paraguay, were harassed, and López de Lama's residence was searched by the police. An organization calling itself the "Bolivian National Social Legion" of Cochabamba implied in a letter to the city's newspaper, El Diario, that Bishop López de Lama, a Spanish Passionist, was the leader of a communist conspiracy "that has infiltrated the Church by way of the false post-Conciliar Church." The "Anti-Communist Catholic Traditionalists" demanded that López de Lama be "indicted and imprisoned." El Diario also published a communiqué in which the "National Meeting of Catholic Laymen" asked for the "expulsion of every foreign person, no matter what his mission or situation in the country, who is the intellectual or material author of books or pamphlets that tend to distort the Bolivian mentality or incite subversion in any way."[10]

The Banzer Plan was later adopted by ten governments belonging to the Latin-American Anti-Communist Confederation, including Chile, Brazil, and Honduras. At CAL's 1977 meeting the Bolivians proposed that these governments take the plan a step further by creating a hemispheric organization to help keep watch on progressive Church leaders and to distribute propaganda against that sector of the Church. Also proposed were a special "economic fund" for "anti-Marxist" priests and bishops, support for "anti-communist governments in their fight against infiltration of religious schools," public denunciation of such "communist bishops" as Chile's Cardinal Raul Silva, and support for ecclesiastical right-wingers like Colombia's Cardinal Aníbal Muñoz Duque, a brigadier general in the Colombian Army.[11]

The Brazilian delegation to the meeting enlarged on the Bolivians' denunciations by claiming that the Pope was a puppet of Marxist cardinals and accusing President Carter of having violated "the human rights of Latin-American nations" when he opposed Brazil's bid to become a nuclear power. But perhaps the most curious suggestion came from the Mexican Anti-Communist Federation (FEMACO), whose proposed solution to the "Red Menace" was to recite the Apostles' Creed. "Communism," said FEMACO, "is caused by religious ignorance."[12]

Silly or not, CAL's anti-communist fulminations could not be dismissed as the ravings of a lunatic fringe, since the confederation was supported by half a dozen Latin-American dictators, including Chile's Pinochet, Paraguay's Stroessner, and Nicaragua's Somoza. Just how far CAL was prepared to go in its anti-communist crusade may be judged by its financing of a Croatian separatist movement that was responsible for the murder of the Yugoslav ambassador to Sweden, for attacks on diplomatic missions in West Germany, and for the assassination of the Uruguayan ambassador to Paraguay, whom a Croatian dissident killed by mistake in 1976. The man's boss, Dinko Zakio, was later arrested in Paraguay on charges of stealing $3.5 million from CAL.[13]

CAL's attack on the Church was one of the cornerstones of the Doctrine of National Security, which defines any challenge to the status quo as "communist subversion." Clownish though it was, the Ecuadorian junta's imprisonment of Bishop Proaño and his foreign guests was intended to disgrace Proaño because he had questioned the established order. (Several of the prelates present at Riobamba were also on the Bolivian delegation's black list.)

A square-faced, graying man in his late sixties, Proaño is a good example of the sort of "communist bishop" under attack from the Latin-American dictatorships. Soft-spoken, gentle, and clothed in a threadbare Indian poncho, the shy bishop abhors violence. (Like Mahatma Gandhi, his model, Proaño believes that nonviolence is the only road to change.) When the Ecuadorian Indians are in his presence, an almost physical change comes over them, transforming them from sullen, bent beasts of burden into laughing, happy human beings. Said a wizened Indian woman, "Only since Taita Amitu Obispu [an affectionate Quechua title for Proaño] has come has the eye begun to see and the mouth to speak."[14]

The son of an impoverished provincial hatmaker, Proaño is neither a mystic nor an intellectual but a man of the people (he dislikes being addressed as "Your Excellency," insisting that everyone call him Leonidas). As such, he has taken a down-to-earth approach to the Indians' problems, including such unglamorous but practical projects as a Riobamba hostelry, hospital, and bathhouse for the Indians, who would otherwise on their visits to town sleep and eat in the city's mud ditches. It is by this sort of concern for the Indians, by this belief that they, too, are human beings, that Proaño has antagonized the region's large landowners.

Ever since his arrival in Riobamba in 1954, when he broke with tradition by traveling to the smallest villages in his diocese in the province of Chimborazo, Proaño has embarrassed and annoyed the area's few wealthy, white families. Proaño grew up in the northern valleys of Ecuador, near the Colombian frontier, where live the pigtailed Otavalo Indians, a poor but proud people quite unlike the Chimborazo Indians, who have been dehumanized by generations of feudalism. Proaño never adjusted to the latter situation. It was bad enough, complained the Chimborazo landowners, that the bishop demeaned himself by shaking hands with the Indians, but he wanted as well to "open the eyes of the Indians" by organizing schools and cooperatives. Although the ranchers offered financial aid to build a new cathedral in Riobamba, they would have nothing to do with the bishop's educational programs, and with good reason: an illiterate Indian is unlikely to protest against the land-tenure system or demand the payment of the legal minimum wage if he does not know that he has any rights.

"Why is there hunger, if the oil is ours?"

Even today, when the discovery of petroleum has made Ecuador South America's second-largest oil exporter, the nation remains one of the poorest, least developed in the hemisphere. Visitors who look behind the plush villas that are rising in Quito will see miserable Indians bent double under loads of wood as they trot up and down the capital's back streets. Ecuador's rags-to-riches petroleum story involves only a privileged few, the 7 percent who receive 50 percent of the country's income. The Indians, who comprise 36 percent of the 6.8 million inhabitants, have never seen a penny of the millions of oil dollars that have been pouring in since mid-1972. In fact, few of them are aware that the oil exists. They know tragically little—according to a survey by the University of Ecuador, 70 percent of the highland Indians cannot name their country or its President, or the colors of its flag.[15]

The Indians continue to scratch a subsistence living in the Andean sierras, or they form part of the burgeoning marginal populations of Quito and the banana port at Guayaquil, which has the worst slums in South America (not even the shantytowns ringing La Paz, Bolivia, can compare). Although change is coming to some areas such as Riobamba, thanks to people like Bishop Proaño, most of the Indian provinces have not altered since the Spanish Conquest.

As in Venezuela, which is Ecuador's oil tutor, "sowing the profits from petroleum" in the countryside is an empty phrase, although the military government and everyone else seemed to agree that the agrarian sector, with 70 percent of the country's marginal population, was Ecuador's foremost problem. But while the military regime had more money to spend than any previous government, its agricultural policy was no more successful than that of its predecessors because of the large landowners' grip on national politics. The military only appeared to rule Ecuador; the ranchers controlled most of the political parties and were allied with the large Quito and Guayaquil import houses that dominate Ecuadorian industry. Any government that tries to restrict the privileges of this group soon finds itself out of a job. That happened to a previous military junta (1963–66), which was overthrown when it attempted a mild agrarian reform.

A backward banana republic until the 1972 oil boom, Ecuador is still the politically most retarded country of South America, with no more than 100,000 of its people able to distinguish between a conservative and a communist. Thus it is relatively easy for the educated elite to make and break governments, often with the United States' support.[16] Any move to alter the inefficient pattern of land tenure is quickly squelched, because the government of the moment will immediately back down when threatened with a coup (which eventually happens anyway; the coup average in Ecuador is one every three years). Thus, four decades after the first attempt at agrarian reform, 0.1 percent of Ecuador's farms, all larger than 2,500 acres, still occupy 14.4 percent of the arable land, while 74 percent of the farms, each less than 12.5 acres, cover only 10 percent.

"Why is there hunger, if the oil is ours?" demand the wall graffiti in Quito. "Because the rich get richer and the poor, poorer," wrote Clotario, columnist for the conservative Quito daily *El Tiempo*. The statistics of poverty are such that the National Medical Congress urged the government to declare a "national emergency." Sixty percent of the children are malnourished; 33 percent of the people are illiterate, and 70 percent are without running water, sewage systems, medical attention, or decent housing. These are the marginal Ecuadorians, the 52 percent of the labor force that is unemployed or underemployed. Nevertheless, the Ministry of Health stated that "the situation is not so bad compared with India, where people are starving to death."

Maybe not, but it is hard to imagine worse conditions than those in Chimborazo Province, which has the highest concentration of landholdings, the largest Indian population, and the worst standard of living in Ecuador. Although the land is majestic, with towering, snowcapped volcanoes and deep, green valleys, the people are dirty and sad. At the Saturday market in Riobamba, Chimborazo's capital, the plazas overflow with this mass of Indian poverty that has trotted long miles across the Andes to sell a few vegetables or eggs to the white and mestizo townspeople. (Although the peasant may keep chickens or a cow, eggs and milk are too precious for his consumption. Only by selling them can he buy such necessities as salt and kerosene.)

Many of the Indians earn a few cents as pack animals for Riobamba housewives, staggering barefoot through the muddy markets with loads of food or firewood on their backs. The fair is also the one day in the week allowed for such luxuries as a piece of fruit and for getting drunk on a cheap corn brew fermented with human bones, among other substances. The Indians drink to forget the hovel that awaits them at night—a windowless hole in the ground topped by a thatched roof, where up to fifteen people sleep in the dirt with the family's pigs and guinea pigs, the Indians' only source of occasional protein.

Although Chimborazo is but sixty miles from Quito, 83 percent of the population never see a doctor. Malnutrition and lack of hygiene among the province's 220,000 Indians are so severe that six out of ten children die in their first year. About the only thing the Chimborazo Indian does not die of is old age.

Barely touched by agrarian reform, Chimborazo is Ecuador's worst example of *latifundio-minifundio,* or large landholdings and tiny plots, with farms of more than 1,250 acres hogging 68 percent of the land, while farms under 12 acres, 83 percent of the total number of parcels, are squeezed onto 8.6 percent of what remains.

When Chimborazo's well-to-do would give no money for the Indians' education, Bishop Proaño went to Europe to obtain financial and technical help to start a series of cooperatives and radio schools. Today there are 120 cooperatives and an Indian adult-education school in Riobamba, the Santa Cruz retreat house on the outskirts of the city, and a radio station transmitting fifteen hours of educational programs a day to Indian schools. All these programs are aimed at "liberating" the Indians, opening their eyes to their condition as human beings.

Of all the programs begun by Proaño, none was so controversial as the gift to the Indians in 1964 of 27,300 acres of Church lands. Since that historic event, the struggle for land in Chimborazo has intensified as the Indians have become more aware of their legal rights and the means to enforce them. In a desperate rearguard action, the angry landowners have employed armed bands to beat the Indians—and Proaño's priests—back into their traditional submission. But although the Riobamba clergy has been threatened and imprisoned, Proaño's followers believe that violent retaliation would weaken the Indians' moral cause and give the landowners a pretext to call in the Army or the police. Father Delfín Tenesaca, for example, turned the other cheek innumerable times after beatings and threats by the landowners, who put a price on his head. Yet this Indian priest and the thirty-two communities with which he works continued to press the Ecuadorian Institute of Agrarian Reform and Colonization (IERAC) for land they were entitled to under the law. In Father Tenesaca's area alone, seven cases were under study by IERAC. The 2,000 acres the Indians were claiming were few compared to the 25,000 acres of the landowners' local "cooperative," but they symbolized the long-feared awakening of the Indians: any Indian willing to go to law to demand that his land title be respected is unlikely to work on the haciendas for daily wages of twenty-eight cents or less. And without cheap labor, the undercapitalized, poorly administered ranches of the absentee landlords cannot produce their large profits.

Through the radio schools and the Riobamba diocesan newspaper, *Jatari Campesino* (*Peasant, Rise Up*), the Indians have learned what a minimum wage is and what facts can be raised to achieve agrarian reform, such as underproductivity or the monopoly of natural resources by one family in an area that is under heavy population pressure. This may not seem like much of an advance in the face of the poverty and land structures in Chimborazo, but it is an enormous improvement over conditions of a few years ago, when the Indians dared not even speak in the presence of a white man. That, at least, is the view of Father Valentín de Lucas, a member of a group of Spanish clergy and laymen who work with Proaño.

"When I first came here in 1968, I was very angry at the way the Indians were treated, but I soon realized that violence was not the answer," de Lucas said. "Without education, self-realization, and a sound community organization, the peasants are incapable of improving their standard of living. There have been cases, for example, where land distributed under the agrarian reform was allowed to lie fallow because the Indians did not know how to farm it. Our approach is to educate the people so that they can develop their own solutions. It is important that the Indians make their own decisions with a sense of communal responsibility, as in a community action program to install running water with everyone contributing according to his income and ability. We always give the Indians moral support in disputes with the estate owners or government officials, but we insist that the Indians speak out for their rights. They must learn to be their own spokesmen."

Although the diocese's educational programs are beginning to have some effect, progress must often be paid for in blood. In one case, Proaño sent a priest to work at Iltuz, with an Indian community that had received legal recognition from IERAC for a claim to communal lands earlier annexed by the neighboring hacienda. Through the priest's mediation the rancher agreed verbally

CHAPTER VI

THE DOCTRINE OF NATIONAL SECURITY—TERROR—
The United States Teaches Latin America How

> You have a gun
> And I am hungry
>
> You have a gun
> because
> I am hungry
>
> You have a gun
> therefore
> I am hungry
>
> You can have a gun
> you can have a thousand bullets and even another thousand
> you can waste them all on my poor body,
> you can kill me one, two, three, two thousand, seven thou-
> sand times
> but in the long run
> I will always be better armed than you
> if you have a gun
> And I
> only hunger.

Arms
by M. J. Arce[1]

The stories of the Chimborazo Indians in Ecuador and of Héctor Gallego and Iván Betancur in Central America are not bizarre instances of cruelty but common occurrences in Latin America, endured by thousands of innocent people. The more industrially advanced the country, the more sophisticated the form of torture and death: in Ecuador, a horse bridle; in Honduras, a bread oven; in Brazil, computerized terror, truth serum, and electric shock. So systematized is torture that it has become a way of life in many Latin-American countries. Yet these countries claim to share the cultural values of the Western world, to show the same respect for liberty and human rights.

There have been many explanations for this situation. Some said it was a collective sickness in the land; others, a return to the bloodthirsty lawlessness of the early conquistadors. Still others claimed that, just beneath the cultured surface, Latin America has always been a brutal continent. There may be some truth in all these explanations, but the key to the current terror and repression lies elsewhere—in the values of the Western world itself.

When Eli Black jumped to his death from the forty-fourth floor of his Park Avenue office, there was considerable speculation that he had killed himself because he knew he would be exposed in a case of international bribery—almost no one suggested that the United Brands chairman might have felt any moral scruples about his role in the Honduras banana scandal. Quite apart from the ethics of using stockholders' money to enhance the personal fortune of a greedy Latin-American dictator, United Brands has a long history in Honduras—and elsewhere in Central America—of financial and political support for repressive military regimes that allowed or encouraged such atrocities as castrating priests and roasting peasants in bread ovens. United Brands also used the AFL-CIO's Free Labor Institute to undermine and destroy such legitimate unions as the banana workers' federation on its Honduras plantations.[2] Even so, such tactics might not have achieved the desired degree of corruption and repression had millions of U.S. taxpayers' dollars not been spent to train and arm the Honduran military and police, and always with the same objective: to crush any expression of popular aspiration that might endanger the "stable" business climate in which United Brands and its Honduran partners could exploit the people. Yet United Brands is not an exception; its outrages are no more unusual than were the murders of Gallego and Betancur. The sickness that has engulfed Latin America, that endorses torture and assassination as routine in most of these countries, was to a significant extent bred in the boardrooms and military institutes of the United States.

Americans who once shook their heads in disbelief at the idea of CIA agents overthrowing a democratically elected government were shocked into some awareness of the truth when the CIA's role in the downfall of Salvador Allende was thoroughly documented by the United States Congress. And Chile was but part of the story. However the Department of Defense may try to duck its responsibility, the Pentagon's courses for Latin-American military officers were instrumental in formulating the Doctrine of National Security, and it was this doctrine that gave rise to totalitarianism in eleven Latin-American countries. Even the RAND Corporation, the State Department's think tank for Latin America, worried about what the Pentagon had done.*

While Defense Department officials could not be accused of deliberately encouraging the emergence of Latin-American Hitlers, and while no one was suggesting an international conspiracy, cause and effect worked as they had during United Brands' long history of corruption of Central American governments: United Brands did not itself put the peasants in the Honduran bread oven, but it helped create the political conditions necessary for such atrocities.†

At the Nuremberg trials in postwar Germany, a number of individuals and companies were found guilty of crimes against humanity. It was no defense to say, "I was only following orders, I

---

* Reported RAND: "United States preconceptions about the seriousness of the Communist threat and about the subsequent need for counterinsurgency and civic action for the Latin-American military are producing undesired results. Paradoxically, U.S. policies appear simultaneously to encourage authoritarian regimes and to antagonize the military who lead them." (Luigi R. Einaudi, Richard L. Maullin, and Alfred C. Stephan III, "Latin-American Security Issues" [Santa Monica, Calif.: RAND Corporation, Apr. 1969], p. v.)

† "We must produce a disembowelment of the incipient economy of the country in order to increase and help our aims," a United Fruit (Brands) manager wrote a company lawyer about Honduras. "We have to prolong its tragic, tormented, and revolutionary life; the wind must blow only on our sails and the water must only wet our keel." (Richard J. Barnet and Ronald E. Muller, *Global Reach* [New York: Simon and Schuster, 1974], p. 87.)

didn't know what was going on," or "I was just doing what everyone else did"; that was judged morally indefensible. Three decades after World War II, it must again be asked if the support by bribery of right-wing totalitarian governments that have killed thousands of innocent people is morally defensible because "if I don't do it, my competitor will." Or whether it is acceptable to teach Latin-American paramilitary organizations how to make bombs or to instruct governments in press censorship and the persecution of the Catholic Church. That is the United States' record in Latin America since World War II, and there is not even the weak excuse that the Americans responsible for this immorality were acting in the greater cause of their country. Unlike the Germans, these people cannot possibly claim that the American people have gained anything from the repression and poverty of their Latin-American neighbors—only a few companies have done so.

Certain ideals, such as freedom and respect for the individual's rights, form part of the United States' heritage, but how is anyone to respect that heritage when Americans say one thing at home and do another in the poorer countries? "In the face of the facts, it must be said that our recent performance has been high on rhetoric but poor in real terms," said Archbishop Peter L. Gerety, of Newark, New Jersey. "Whether the case cited is the Soviet Union, Korea, Chile, South Africa or Rhodesia, the actual influence of human-rights considerations in U.S. policy-making does not appear to be substantial or sustained."[3]

The Catholic Church has been severely persecuted in Latin America for denouncing the Defense Department and the immoral business practices of a host of U.S. corporations, yet it is merely asking the American people to respect their own ideals. "We only want for ourselves what you want for yourselves," Nicaraguan Jesuit Fernando Cardenal told the U. S. Congress. "If you don't want dictators in this country, do not support them in other countries. What is good for you is also good for us."[4]

Creole Fascism

Ever since 1823, when the Monroe Doctrine became the cornerstone of U.S. policy for Latin America, Washington has befriended dictators. Before World War II these were usually yes-

men who identified with U.S. interests, an example being Anastasio Somoza, who held Nicaragua in reserve for the United States
in case Washington should ever want to build a second transisth-
mian canal in Central America. (One of Somoza's predecessors
was booted out of office for opening canal negotiations with the
Japanese.) After World War II U.S. interests were broadened to
include cold-war priorities. Even when no specific economic or
political advantage was to be gained, Washington supported
Latin-American dictators who claimed to be anti-communist,
as in the case of General Stroessner in Paraguay. But the result of
this preoccupation with communism was the revival of another
monster: a creole version of European fascism.

A latent force in several of the most important South-American
countries, fascism—particularly Mussolini's corporate state—had
long attracted certain military and civilian sectors. During the
1930s it was also popular within an influential wing of the Catholic Church because of its virulent anti-communism and emphasis
on "God, Fatherland, and Family." Called "integralism" in South
America, this creole brand of European fascism made its greatest
impact on Argentina, although the Brazilian populist dictator
Getúlio Vargas (president 1930–45, 1951–54) also flirted with
integralism, especially after 1937, when he seized total power and
established his *Estado Novo*. Chile and Paraguay were also
influenced by fascism.

Based on a rigid hierarchical society in which people are de-
partmentalized according to social class and productive function,
the integralist corporate state was well suited to Latin America's
older feudal order and also accommodated economic and political
changes brought about by industrialization. While all sectors of
society theoretically have equal political representation in a corporate state, integralism as it evolved in Latin America essentially
meant that the military, large landowners, and industrialists tightened their control over the government and the economy. Unlike
Vargas, who eventually outlawed the fascist Brazilian Integralist
Action Party in favor of his own personalist brand of dictatorship,
Argentina's Juan Domingo Perón remained an outspoken admirer
of Benito Mussolini to the very end of World War II, breaking
relations with the Axis powers only under severe pressure from

the United States in the final months of conflict, when the outcome was no longer in doubt. Nor did Brazilian integralism ever develop the anti-Semitic overtones of Argentine fascism, possibly because the Brazilians themselves are such a heterogeneous mix of races, religions, and cultures, or because the Jewish community in Argentina, the largest in Latin America with 400,000 people, offers a more visible target than does the smaller group in Brazil. In any case, a strain of anti-Semitism that has persisted in the Argentine armed forces ever since Perón's first period in government emerges again whenever the country comes under military rule.

In contrast to Brazil's armed forces, which took a technological approach to totalitarianism, the Argentine military reverted to the mysticism and fervor of the medieval Christian knights to justify fascism. Though both see Catholicism as a necessary component of military dictatorship, Argentina's generals, with their Augustinian vision of a world of order and discipline ruled by God's chosen few in the Argentine military, are more sincere and therefore more dangerous Catholics than their Brazilian counterparts. General Juan Carlos Onganía's 1966–70 dictatorship, the forerunner of Argentina's virulently right-wing regimes in the late seventies, was a clear example of this mystical, barracks-born corporate state, with its emphasis on the "Christian and military virtues" of Spanish knighthood. Onganía felt himself "personally called" to shape the country's destiny during a religious retreat he made shortly before his mid-1966 coup, and many of the generals and industrialists appointed to his Cabinet shared his belief that these "virtues" would restore mental, cultural, social, and political discipline to Argentina.[5] The feudal aspects of integralism particularly appealed to these men, who were convinced that God had ordained an obedient, hierarchical society in which everyone knew his place. It was natural that they should think so, for many of these values, particularly obedience and loyalty to the chain of command, formed part of the military mentality. Onganía's notion of an elite corps of rulers called by God to serve and save the nation was totally out of step with a modern Argentine society searching for more democratic forms of government, and popular discontent eventually forced the military to replace him with a less dogmatic ruler. Nevertheless, many of his ideas survived and thrived in the right wing of the Argentine armed forces, particularly among the hard-liners in the Army and the Navy because these men had been influenced by U.S. counterinsurgency courses that polarized the world forever between Western capitalism and Eastern communism. Onganía converted this into a medieval-like crusade against communism, which he called the "West Point Doctrine" in honor of the academy where his ideas were first formulated.

Although Onganía and his military successors harped constantly on the Christian nature of their dictatorships, only far-right wings of the Argentine Church took their claims to God-given superiority seriously, in part because the Church itself was undergoing a social revolution, and in part because the "saviors of the nation" frequently turned out to be bloodthirsty crooks whose real ambitions were power and money. The military's principal support within the Church came from another throwback to the Middle Ages known as "Tradition, Family, and Property" (TFP), whose knights errant go forth in flowing red capes to do battle with the communist dragon.

There was no such confusion of medieval mysticism with twentieth-century totalitarianism in Brazil, although the results were similar. Brazil's military also views itself as the "chosen few," but less on religious than on technological grounds, the Brazilians believing themselves "nation builders"; the Argentines, "nation saviors." Like Hitler, Brazil's generals view Catholicism as a useful weapon to control the masses, but they neither expect nor accept active participation by the Church in the field of social action or human rights. As in Argentina, however, the Brazilian branch of TFP was a useful ally of the military, particularly during the period leading up to the coup against President João Goulart.

Whereas Argentina's generals want to drag the bishops physically into the crusade against communism, the Brazilian military considers the critical, post-Conciliar Church a political nuisance because it won't restrict itself to its nineteenth-century role as caretaker of souls or fit in with the military's new scheme to replace God with a bank of computers. General Golbery do Couto e Silva, the principal ideologist of Brazil's Doctrine of National Security, believes that Catholicism, though outdated as a faith, still has its social uses—in teaching children, for example, to respect their parents, or discouraging them from killing one another. This essentially materialistic view of religion is to a degree an extension of the military's consuming faith in technology as the solution to all mankind's problems and its commitment to the welfare of the amoral multinationals. But there is also a strong streak of the superiority complex so obvious in Argentina's armed forces: Brazil's generals are devout in one respect—they sincerely believe that they know better than anyone else, bishops included, what is good for Brazil.

A basic difference between the two armed forces is that the Argentines needed very little outside help to convince themselves of their natural superiority, since they had run the country for most of this century, whereas it is unlikely, in view of Brazil's democratic traditions, that its military would ever have viewed itself with such satisfaction had it not been for the influence of the U. S. Department of Defense. The American brass not only taught their Brazilian counterparts to see themselves as the chosen few, but also encouraged them to resurrect and update integralism as part of the great cold-war anti-communist crusade. Because of Perón's lasting influence, fascism never died in Argentina and could be revived with little or no outside prompting; in Brazil it was reborn thanks largely to Brazil's "greatest friend," the United States. And today Brazil, not Argentina, calls the shots in Latin America.

Grad School for Juntas

Ironically, Brazil's modern military state had its origins in the Allied invasion of fascist Italy in 1945, when a number of Brazilian officers participating in the campaign were exposed to American military ideas and tactics. General Humberto de A. Castelo Branco, who was to lead the 1964 coup against João Goulart, returned to Brazil with a lasting admiration for U.S. military methods, as did General Golbery do Couto e Silva, the Brazilian military's grey eminence. Castelo Branco's roommate in Italy, General Vernon Walters, later deputy director of the CIA, was also to play an important role in the 1964 putsch.

Couto e Silva, who served two Brazilian military rulers and at one time was head of Dow Chemical's Brazilian division, was particularly influential in the formation of Brazil's Advanced War

College, popularly known as the "Brazilian Sorbonne," which is responsible for national security studies, the development of military strategy, and a variety of specialized courses for officers and businessmen. Founded in 1949 during the height of the cold war, the War College incorporated many of the Pentagon's ideas on national security and nation building, the latter an outgrowth of the U. S. Army's experience in reconstructing postwar Japan.

The cornerstone of United States–Latin American military cooperation had already been laid in 1947 at Rio de Janeiro with the Inter-American Treaty of Reciprocal Assistance, itself the culmination of a series of bilateral military pacts that were signed during World War II to combat the Axis powers. It was under the Rio treaty's umbrella that the Defense Department in 1951 set up its Military Assistance Program (MAP) to arm and train Latin America's armies. Although MAP, like the treaty, was conceived as a defense against external military threat, it soon became a mechanism to promote U.S. military strategy and the "American way of life," one of the principal goals being to keep the hemisphere safe from internal subversion of the sort that occurred in Guatemala, where in 1954 the Arbenz government was overthrown for its temerity in trying to expropriate some United Fruit lands. By 1959, when President Eisenhower convened the Draper Committee to evaluate MAP's effectiveness, the pretense of external threat had been dropped: the principal objective of U.S. military assistance was to influence the region's future military leaders. "There is no single aspect of the military assistance program that produced more useful returns for the dollars expended than these training programs," the committee found, adding that the relations developed with Latin-American military officers would help instill in them a sense of U.S. priorities and policies.[6]

MAP became yet more important after Castro's successful 1959 revolution, not only in developing counterinsurgency programs but also in encouraging Latin-American military officers to look upon themselves as an elite. As Defense Secretary Robert McNamara explained to a House Appropriations Committee:

> Probably the greatest return on our military-assistance investment comes from the training of selected officers and key spe-

cialists at our military schools and training centers in the
United States and overseas. These students are hand-picked
by their countries to become instructors when they return
home. *They are the coming leaders,* the men who will have
the know-how and impart it to their forces. I need not dwell
upon the value of having in positions of leadership men who
have firsthand knowledge of how Americans do things and
how they think. *It is beyond price to us to make friends of
such men.* [Emphasis added.][7]

Professor Lucian Pye, one of MIT's cold-war social scientists,
was even more specific about U.S. military goals, arguing that the
armed forces "have been consistently among the most modernized
institutions in their society" and that therefore the United States
should support military governments. Poorer countries, he said,
should not "be deprived of the developmental value of the military organizations simply because the ideological basis of the military in advanced societies rejects the appropriateness of the military openly touching upon essentially civilian functions," adding
that this was particularly true "in countries faced with serious insurgency or subversion."[8] Pye's ideas, published in 1961, were
echoed almost word for word by Nelson Rockefeller eight years
later, when, after his historic tour of Latin America, he announced that the military was "the essential force of constructive
social change."[9]

The United States fostered the idea of armies as nation builders
in several ways, including civic action programs in which the
Latin-American military took over a number of civilian functions,
such as building roads. The purpose was to improve relations with
the local populace, but such projects were never popular with the
military, which felt it had been reduced to the status of a local
Peace Corps, or with the civilians, who, quite properly, suspected
the military's motives. More to the point, courses designed to give
the Latin-American military officers a broader background in government were introduced at U.S. military schools and academies.
Explained the Department of Defense:

Normally the subjects available in United States institutions
denote a degree of academic sophistication far beyond that

achieved in the schools of the less developed countries. Yet in these countries . . . the need for training in management, economics, public administration, the social sciences, and related fields is most critical. In many of these countries where the military plays a predominant role in national development, the collateral benefits accruing from the training of senior officers are obvious.[10]

At the Inter-American Defense College (IADC) at Washington's Fort McNair, for example, Latin-American officers study industrial and financial management, transportation, trade, agriculture, energy, communications, and international finance. "The college is training people to more efficiently manage a government," said Admiral Gene LaRocque, IADC director from 1969 to 1972. Although he admitted that "it's unhealthy to build up a cadre of military governors all over the world and this is what we do to some extent," he immediately added that in Latin America "the more efficient the military are, the more powerful the military are, and the more powerful *our* military are. These days when you need a problem solved, you go to the Pentagon. The admiral there knows the admiral in Latin America."[11] (Someone, perhaps, like Admiral Emilio Massera, an IADC graduate and ultra-rightist, who used his position as head of the Argentine Navy to set up a network of torture and terror in Buenos Aires.[12]) ‡

But undoubtedly the Pentagon's strongest motive for pushing its idea of nation building was its reliance on the military as the "guardian of national security" in the ongoing crusade against communism. Almost all the courses, whether in ballistics or communications, were, and still are, heavily laden with pro–United States, anti-communist propaganda that encourages the Latin

‡ LaRocque's successor, Air Force General Kermit C. Kaericher, took a more optimistic view of dictatorship in Latin America, stating that "if problems were left to the military, we would have a lot less war and problems." Asked what sort of model government he had in mind, General Kaericher said he certainly had been impressed by Paraguay. Recalling a visit to that impoverished South American country, Kaericher said he had told President Stroessner that he had "never been to a place where the people were so poor and looked so happy." (Jeffrey Stein, "Grad School for Juntas," *The Nation* [May 21, 1977], pp. 621–24.)

Americans to abhor as subversive anything that seems to run counter to U.S. interests. Moreover, as builders—and saviors—of the nation, only the armed forces can judge what is and is not subversive. As evolved in Latin America, these ideas led the military to believe that their job was to defend traditions and the status quo; any suggestion of change, whether agrarian reform or a return to democratic government, was per se subversive of the established order. It was but a short step from this definition to the use of terror and torture in defense of the "need for order," and here again the United States provided the necessary training and arms. Among the subjects taught Brazilian officers in U.S. military courses, according to information supplied to a U. S. Senate Committee, were the following:

> . . . censorship, checkpoint systems, chemical and biological operations, briefings on the CIA, civic action and civil affairs, clandestine operations, counterguerrilla operations, cryptography, defoliation, dissent in the United States, electronic intelligence, electronic warfare and countermeasures, the use of informants, insurgency, intelligence, counterintelligence, subversion, countersubversion, espionage, counterespionage, interrogation of prisoners and suspects, handling mass rallies and meetings, nuclear weapons effects, intelligence photography, polygraphs, populace and resources control, psychological operations, raids and searches, riots, special warfare, surveillance, terror, and undercover operations.[13]

According to U.S. government officials, these courses, and $4 billion in aid,* served the national interests of the United States in Brazil. But when questioned more closely about exactly what those interests were, the AID director, William A. Ellis, admitted to the U. S. Congress that they were "the protection and expansion, if possible, of our economic interests, trade, and investment."[14] Yet a multitude of independent surveys, including those made by the State Department's think tank at the RAND Corporation, have shown that the only economic interests at stake were, and are, those of a few large U.S. corporations.

* Foreign aid for 1964–72. Source: AID.

A Regional Policeman

An unabashed apologist for U.S. military and economic expansion, Couto e Silva, Brazilian general and erstwhile Dow Chemical director, shaped his ideas on national security around the central premise that, as "keeper of the beacon for Western civilization," the United States could do no wrong in Latin America. Accordingly, it was Brazil's duty as a "privileged satellite" to protect U.S. interests in Brazil and the rest of South America; for, in the war to save the Western world from communism, were not Brazil's interests the same as those of the United States? (Put another way, in the terminology of the Nixon administration, Brazil was to serve as the United States' regional policeman.) Explained Couto e Silva: "What imperils us today as yesterday, is a threat that is leveled, not really against us, but through us against the United States."[15]

Couto e Silva dressed up his model of a Brazilian Praetorian Guard with such geopolitical propositions as "dominant antagonisms" and "living frontiers," the former to explain a permanent world war of opposing ideologies,† the latter to justify Brazil's acquisition of large tracts of frontier land belonging to Paraguay, Bolivia, and Uruguay, which were to serve as Brazilian subsatellites in the hemisphere defense system. "[Our goal is] to launch a manifest destiny, as long as it does not clash with that of our brothers to the north," he explained. This satellite relationship reflected Couto e Silva's belief in a world dominated by technology where the strong nations become stronger and the weak, weaker. A country's survival depended, therefore, on its rela-

† Though his admiring biographers give Couto e Silva a place in history with some of Europe's leading military theoreticians, much of his writing reads as though copied from the Defense Department's course manuals for the Latin-American military. For example, Course 0-47 at the School of the Americas in the Panama Canal Zone (Doc. 5489, p. 5): "Democracy and communism clash with the firm determination of the Western countries to conserve their own traditional way of life." Couto e Silva's translation: "Let the West not indulge in dreaming. Its profoundest self, its most precious traditions are threatened by a bloc of communist countries firmly set on dominating and conquering it, on imposing on it their alien ideology." ("*Escuela de las Américas: Entrenamiento y Control,*" *Diálogo Social* [Panama City: Feb 3, 1977].)

tionship with and submission to the dominant power—in Latin America's case, the United States. Domestic policy could not be separated from foreign policy; thus it was in Brazil's interest, as a satellite, to protect United States foreign investments.

How a Latin-American general, and a self-avowed nationalist at that, could support such an apology for economic colonialism in the latter half of the twentieth century seems beyond comprehension, unless one accepts Belgian theologian José Comblin's explanation that, unlike the elites of Asia or Africa, who have deep roots in the cultural history of their people, the Latin Americans are totally alienated from the Indians, half-castes, and blacks who make up the majority of their society. The Brazilian military, Comblin argues, identifies with U.S. interests because it would like to be American. "Not merely do [the Latin-American elites] reject the genuine origins of their nations—African, Indian, and Iberian—but they regret that they themselves are not French, English or North American: this is alienation of a kind to be found nowhere else."[16]

Thus men like Couto e Silva were predisposed to U.S. military and political policies even before the Pentagon began its postwar training; any lingering doubts were swept away by the United States' massive indoctrination of Brazilian officers and the overwhelming U.S. presence in Brazil itself. (At one point, the U.S. mission in Brazil had so many employees, 588 Americans and 811 Brazilians, that Senator Frank Church was moved to wonder: "Relative to population, we have twice as many people in Brazil as the British had in India when they were providing the government for the entire country."[17] The U.S. air attaché's office alone employed seven professionals to maintain a special Military Airlift Command for weekly military flights to Rio de Janeiro.)

To encourage their identification with the "typical American way of life," the Pentagon regularly sponsored expensive tours of the United States for Brazilian officers. Among the highlights of such junkets, which averaged one hundred thousand dollars each, were floor shows at the Flamingo and Stardust hotels in Las Vegas, visits to the Astrodome, Disneyland, Universal Studios, Fisherman's Wharf, Radio City, Connecticut beach parties, and extended stays at the Plaza Hotel in New York.[18] Such, according to Major General George S. Beatty of the Joint Brazil–United

States Military Commission, was the "scholastic atmosphere under which this training is conducted and these visits are made."[19] Beatty failed to mention that representatives of a number of U.S. corporations—including Exxon, Humble Oil, and Coca-Cola—with heavy investments in Brazil also participated in these "scholastic" sessions,[20] or that such "typical American" life-styles are possible in Latin America only if you belong to the wealthy elite, say as a representative of Dow Chemical. Nevertheless, Defense Secretary McNamara continued to insist that such exposure paid off, and the results supported him: 80 percent of the officers who carried out the 1964 coup against President Goulart had been trained by the United States.[21]

Shortly before the putsch, U. S. Ambassador Lincoln Gordon told Washington, "To maintain the pro-American tendency within the Brazilian military, it is necessary to supply equipment in accordance with the internal-security role, the efficient establishment, and sense of dignity of the armed forces of a great nation."[22] Washington responded by sending to the South Atlantic to support the coup a naval task force that included an aircraft carrier, six destroyers, a helicopter carrier, four oil tankers, and one hundred tons of arms and ammunition. Dubbed "Operation Brother Sam," this flotilla is described in documents in the Lyndon B. Johnson Library; they establish that, long before Allende in Chile, the United States was actively involved in the overthrow of constitutionally elected governments. (A year before the coup, Goulart had been confirmed in office by a four-to-one vote.) As it turned out, Ambassador Gordon was able to call off the fleet within hours of Castelo Branco's putsch, but, public denials to the contrary, both Gordon and the U.S. military attaché, General Vernon Walters, participated in the plotting.[23]

Why was this thought necessary? Comblin points out that the United States felt threatened, or, more specifically, certain U.S. companies felt threatened. The threat in Goulart's Brazil included controls on foreign drug companies, among other multinationals, and these were removed by the military government. The Johnson Library documents also show that Ambassador Gordon was later to have doubts about the monster Washington had helped unleash, but no one else in the Johnson, Nixon, or Ford administrations had such second thoughts. To cement Washington's special relationship with the generals, Secretary of State Kissinger visited Brazil in February 1976 and there signed a "consultative agreement" with the regime for semiannual talks on trade, world problems, and the transfer of technology, bringing Brazil into the United States' exclusive club of allies with Japan, India, Canada, and Iran. Kissinger said that he was particularly happy to be back in Brazil because "there are no two peoples whose concern for human dignity and for the basic values of man is more pronounced in the day-to-day lives of their people than Brazil and the United States."

Obviously Kissinger had not read Amnesty International's documented reports of the repression suffered by "one out of three Brazilians," or the lists of thousands of Brazilians arrested, tortured, exiled, murdered, or deprived of their civil rights.‡ On the contrary, Washington consistently refused to admit that anything was amiss. The AID public safety program, which drilled some one hundred thousand Brazilian policemen in the latest skills in repression, had, according to Theodore Brown, chief AID public safety adviser, helped develop the police's "democratic conscience, their respect for human rights, and dedication to their country . . . the love of liberty and active participation in the nation's development." When asked by Senator Frank Church during a subcommittee hearing whether he really believed this in light of all the reports of torture coming out of Brazil, Brown replied that, yes, he really thought the training program had been a success. As to such crudities as torture and assassination, well, he re-

‡ Although there are no exact statistics on repression because so many Brazilians have been arrested by paramilitary or para-police squads, or have just "disappeared," some indication of the terror is given by Amnesty International's conservative estimate of 1,801 cases of torture as of August 1976 and the arrest of 28,304 people "on suspicion" by the police and military in the city of São Paulo during the first two months of 1977 alone.

Brazil's Church-supported National Amnesty Congress estimated that, as of November 1978, two to three hundred political prisoners had died under torture, while another fifty to sixty had "disappeared." In addition to some two hundred political prisoners, approximately ten thousand Brazilians were in exile, many of whom faced imprisonment if they returned to Brazil. The Congress also stated that 4,877 Brazilians, including congressmen, professionals, and government employees, had been stripped of their political rights or dismissed from government service for political reasons.

ally couldn't explain how such things happened in Brazil: "Why do some people beat their wives, these things why do they occur, it is difficult for me to answer." There had been a few slipups, to be sure, Brown admitted, such as the Brazilian police's failure to paint out U. S. Army Chemical Corps markings on anti-riot gas equipment, or the loquacity of a member of the U.S. naval mission, who complained to an Associated Press reporter in Rio, "I have been hearing screams and groans for about two years" from rooms next to mission headquarters in the Brazilian Navy Ministry, where political prisoners claimed they had been tortured. Other U.S. personnel were reported to have seen Brazilian Naval agents dragging people to and from the interrogation rooms. Nevertheless, Admiral Clarence Hill, commander of the U.S. mission, said he knew nothing "about that kind of thing." Nor did State Department officials, who claimed that "though naturally concerned about allegations of torture in Brazil, we've been assured in conversations with high Brazilian officials that the Brazilian Government does not condone torture."[24]

The U.S. ambassador to Brazil, William M. Roundtree, was similarly sanguine about the country's future under the military: "The dedication of the Brazilian leaders, with the support of the Brazilian people, to this program of progress, is really very impressive. Their progress is being made under a free enterprise system that I think serves as a very good example to others who might be considering other forms of economic systems for the achievement of their objectives."[25]

Contrary to Roundtree's assertions, however, the Brazilian people were less than enthusiastic about the "progress." Despite the billions of dollars in foreign aid and investment, and the brief mirage of the "Brazilian miracle," the country's military regime was unable to demonstrate, either with statistics or elections, that the majority of the people supported its model of free enterprise or had gained anything by it. Every time the government risked even limited electoral forays it was rebuffed; it could not command the sympathies of even the small middle class that had obtained some benefits. Thus the military could remain in power only by repression and by continuing to assert that the people did not understand what was good for them or for the country. All criticism of repression was answered with statistics, and when the statistics did not produce the answers the government wanted, they were manipulated, as in the case of the 1973 increase in the cost of living. The regime originally claimed it to be only 14 percent; four years later Finance Minister Mario Henrique Simonsen admitted that it had been 26.6 percent. Since wages are keyed to the cost-of-living index, this statistical sleight of hand further eroded the workers' purchasing power. But despite the outcry from labor, the government announced that it had "no intention whatsoever" of making good the workers' loss.[26] The idea of submitting such policy to popular debate was anathema to both the regime and the large foreign corporations, whose profits in the developing countries depend in large part on low wages and strict controls over the local labor movement—not to mention the need for security and established order.

Although Brazil's apparatus of repression resembled that of European fascism, its lack of popular support distinguished it from its German and Italian counterparts and made it intrinsically Latin-American. Brazilian economist Helio Jaguaribe described it as "colonial fascism"—fascism because it was "a model for promoting economic development without changing the existing social conditions"; colonial, because it depended on "the West in general, and the United States in particular, due to its need for foreign assistance and foreign markets."[27] Far from encouraging social mobility, capitalism's marriage to "colonial fascism" only intensified class differences as the rich grew richer and the poor, poorer. The development promoted by such foreign aid programs as the Alliance for Progress was as much a farce as the periodic elections staged by the Brazilian military. The rich local elites refused to accept change, and Washington was unwilling to do anything that might adversely affect U.S. corporate interests. As U.S. political scientist James Petras pointed out, "By building up and indoctrinating the Latin-American armed forces to the point where they influence policy and exercise a personal veto and then using them to protect U.S. economic interests, Washington's military has gone straight to the heart of the hemisphere political system." Because the rulers of Brazil, the "privileged satellite," were economically and militarily dependent on the United States,

Washington was able to do away with the outdated military intervention implicit in the Monroe Doctrine.*

Underpinning Brazil's repressive apparatus was a series of "institutional acts" decreed between 1964 and 1971 that allowed the regime, when it saw fit, to suspend Congress, habeas corpus, civil rights, unions, student federations, and freedom of the press—all in the name of national security. The death sentence, abolished in 1922, was reintroduced for political crimes, and a number of common crimes, such as armed robbery, became political ones. Heads of university faculties were given police powers to bar professors from teaching for five years and students from studying for three years, and to order their arrest and trial by military tribunal. Any Brazilian whom the armed forces considered undesirable could be banished from the country, which amounted to "civil death." And the President of Brazil was authorized to draw up a series of secret decrees in the area of national security.

Under the Code of Military Penal Procedure, Brazilians and foreigners could be arrested by the military police of the Army, Navy, Air Force, or one of the many special paramilitary groups that "assisted" in security operations, such as "Operação Bandeirantes," a right-wing vigilante force created by the Second Army Command in São Paulo and responsible for the deaths of five hundred to one thousand people between 1964 and 1970. Prisoners could be held incommunicado indefinitely until they confessed under torture. According to Amnesty International, prisoners "who attempt to rescind testimony given under torture, and refuse to sign the statements given to them during the police inquiry phase of the proceedings against them, are tortured again until they agree to do so."[28] All political crimes are judged by military tribunals, and, reported Amnesty International, "numerous cases are known of last-minute shifts of both military and civilian personnel, when the authorities feared that the verdict would not go as the government wished. Although the trial, including the hearing before the military tribunal, should be completed within a maximum time limit of seventy days, hundreds of cases are known where prisoners have awaited trial for more than three years."[29]

---

* There have been sixty-nine cases of U.S. military intervention in Latin America since 1850.

Under Brazil's Doctrine of National Security, all power rests in the executive branch, which is composed of the military community, represented by the general staff of the armed forces; the organs of intelligence and repression such as the National Information Service; and an alliance of the military with the business community in the National Security Council. The executive branch is not only responsible for enforcing the institutional acts; it also has the power to ensure that the Brazilian people "think correctly" in Orwellian fashion. Under the Moral and Civic Education Program created in 1969, for example, all schoolchildren spend two hours a week studying courses designed to "promote a regard for obedience to law, fealty to work, adjustment to the community, and the responsibility of every Brazilian for national security."[30] Children are encouraged to "denounce enemies of the fatherland," with specific instruction on how to identify and report such traitors, including their parents. Religion's importance is instilled, in a step-by-step progression, from a correct "scale of values" to the legitimization of the military government and its "present development effort" and "Brazil's membership in the Western bloc." Any teacher who refuses to sign a written agreement to support the goals of this indoctrination program can be barred from teaching.

Cultural repression ranges from censorship and blacklisting (the works of two Latin-American Nobel Prize winners are banned) to imprisonment of writers, actors, and journalists. A partial count by the influential, pro-business daily *O Estado do São Paulo* showed the banning in 1976 of seventy-four books, seven theater scripts, thirteen films, five TV series, and various TV documentaries. In addition, a "freeze" was placed on one hundred films and plays, meaning they were neither banned nor approved. Eight newspapers were subject to prior censorship.

In that repressive a society, atrocities proliferate. The "dragon chair," for example, is a device invented in the Rio military police barracks whereby the prisoner receives electric shocks while a dentist's drill shatters his or her teeth; after which, if the prisoner is a man, he is held upside down while his testicles are crushed. Parents are tortured in front of their children, or vice versa, as in the case of a three-month-old baby who was tortured to death by

police in São Paulo's notorious Tiradentes Prison.[31] After a while, reported U.S. Methodist missionary Fred Morris, who himself was tortured for seventeen days at Recife in northeastern Brazil, such horrors become routine. "These people had a nine-to-five job, except that their job was to torture for a living." (Chilean prisoners described a similar attitude, their inquisitors calling for a prisoner with the phrase "It's time to go to work.") According to one European psychiatrist, Brazil's hierarchical, authoritarian order is eminently suited to attract the type of mentality that can be developed into an efficient torturer, one who seeks and accepts authority and obeys orders without question, who is fanatically patriotic and self-righteous but unbalanced and vindictive toward anyone who does not share such views.[32]

It was people of this sort whom the United States trained in its ten-year public safety program in Brazil, the largest in Latin America and the most costly, with over one hundred thousand federal and state police and six hundred high-ranking officers. The United States can also take credit for the construction, equipment, and development of curriculum, faculty, and staff for Brazil's National Police Academy, National Telecommunications Center, and National Institute of Criminology and Identification, as well as for the expansion of training programs for other Latin-American policemen, as in Chile, where the Brazilian prototype of national security was copied to the last detail, including a Superior Academy of National Security, patterned after General Couto e Silva's "Sorbonne," and a new periodical with the original title *National Security*. Paraguay, Bolivia, and Uruguay also sent police agents and military officers to be trained in Brazil's schools of counterinsurgency, and Ecuador developed a national security philosophy: it was under the country's April 1976 National Security Act that the forty-eight bishops and priests were arrested in Riobamba. According to Bishop Proaño, the Riobamba affair was a direct outgrowth of the Banzer Plan against the Catholic Church that was drawn up in Bolivia, an economic and political satellite of Brazil.†

† The Brazilian Government played a crucial role in Bolivian President Hugo Banzer's successful 1971 coup by supplying arms to his supporters in the eastern city of Santa Cruz. (J. Nash, "Cultural Imperialism," *Russell Tribunal*, Third Session, Rome.)

"A great blind spot"

After reading case after nauseating case of the atrocities committed in the name of national security, and after recognizing the United States' involvement in the creation of military, police, and paramilitary agencies responsible for these horrors in El Salvador, Honduras, Guatemala, Brazil, Chile, Bolivia—seventeen Latin-American countries in all—one comes to the conclusion either that the Americans who helped to establish and run these military and police training programs were deranged or that they never considered the predictable results of their work—possibly didn't want to consider them. For any normal person, the idea of torturing a three-month-old baby to death or putting a human being through the torments of the "dragon chair" is so appalling that it does not bear thinking about. In the words of AID Administrator David Bell, trying to justify the police assistance programs to the U. S. Congress: "It is obviously not our purpose or intent to assist a head of state who is repressive. On the other hand, we are working in a lot of countries where the governments are controlled by people who have shortcomings."[33] In other words, better stick to the nine-to-five job and not ask too many questions. This was relatively easy to do, since very few U.S. personnel ever bothered to study the real causes of popular discontent or repression in Latin America. Few could speak Spanish or Portuguese with any fluency, and for most of them Latin America was merely a two- or three-year tour en route to some other part of the globe. The majority lived and worked exclusively with Latin America's social and military elites, feeding each other's fears and rationalizations, unable or unwilling to penetrate the slums or rural villages where most Latin Americans live, because they could not communicate with the people or because it was just too uncomfortable. The rich Latin Americans, in contrast, were well educated, well mannered, eager to please their friends the Americans, and of course spoke English. Four decades after Secretary of State Henry Stimson appointed Anastasio Somoza to head the National Guard in Nicaragua on the sole qualification that he spoke English, many Americans still judge this to be the primary qualification for a leader, or a business partner. But however much U.S. historians try to explain the United States' behavior in Latin America as "inadvertently misguided" or "unthinking"—Arthur Schlesinger, Jr., called it "a great blind spot"—there is no way they can avoid their country's responsibility for the results of that behavior.

When did it all begin? Although the groundwork was laid in the 1940s and 1950s under the Truman and Eisenhower administrations, it was during the years of John F. Kennedy's Camelot that the terms of traditional U.S. military and political strategy were redefined. After France's defeat at Dien Bien Phu and the Bay of Pigs disaster in Cuba, classic military strategy was replaced by counterinsurgency methods to contain and destroy guerrilla or popular insurrections and provide the necessary "security for development." As Secretary of Defense McNamara explained, "The goals of the Alliance [for Progress] can only be achieved within a framework of law and order."

The factor missing in this dual strategy—and the cause of so much subsequent suffering and bloodshed in Latin America—was any appreciation of the political and social conditions responsible for popular discontent, or indeed any reference to the U.S. military's own definition of insurrection as a revolution or uprising against a *constituted* government. All the Latin-American Presidents overthrown with U.S. help in recent years represented *constituted* governments: Arbenz in Guatemala (1954), Goulart in Brazil (1964), Allende in Chile (1973). It mattered not whether the perceived threat was a democratically elected government or a guerrilla group; it was a dangerous precedent to be eliminated by military force. As General Maxwell Taylor told Third World police graduates of AID's International Police Academy in Washington:

The outstanding lesson [of the Indochina conflict] is that we should never let another Vietnam-type situation arise again. We were too late in recognizing the extent of the subversive threat. We appreciate now that every young, emerging country must be constantly on the alert, watching for those symptoms which, if allowed to develop unrestrained, may eventually grow into a disastrous situation such as that in South Vietnam. We have learned the need for a strong police force and a strong police intelligence organization to assist in identifying early the symptoms of an incipient subversive situation.[34]

The cost-conscious Secretary of Defense put it another way: It was cheaper politically and economically to let the Latin Americans put out local fires. The United States could not be everywhere at once, said McNamara, and, besides, it cost a lot less to keep a Latin-American soldier than an American—$540 per year against $4,400. Neither Taylor, McNamara, nor anyone else in the Kennedy administration ever stopped to think that there might be good reasons for the local fires, such as decades of dictatorship. It was much easier to explain the appearance of Marxist guerrillas in Latin-American countries as part of an international communist conspiracy, although most guerrilla uprisings in Latin America have occurred in response to internal influences, Castro's insurrection against the corrupt, repressive Batista dictatorship being the obvious example. It is quite possible that had Cuba enjoyed more social mobility, a better distribution of wealth, and less repression, Castro would never have carried off his revolution. Costa Rica, the only stable democracy in Central America, has no recent experience of insurrection. In contrast, its neighbors, governed by military or quasi-military regimes, have long histories of guerrilla movements, some of them, as in Nicaragua, dating back to the 1920s.

Because it was beyond the capacity of the Pentagon's counterinsurgency strategists to grasp the real causes of popular discontent in Latin America—and because Washington would not have sanctioned meaningful social change if they had—every potential disturbance had to be met with military and police tactics. Moreover, to recognize that there were legitimate causes for revolution would have cost the counterinsurgents their reason for being. Long hours were spent in study of the writings of Mao Tse-tung, General Vo Nguyen Giap, Ernesto "Che" Guevara, and other Marxist revolutionaries, the idea being to beat the revolutionaries at their own game by adopting guerrilla tactics, though these writings had no meaning to the average Latin American or practical application to his problems. Liberated zones became strategic hamlets; a political organization, psychological warfare; and guerrilla units, Special Forces. Frequently unable to communicate with or understand the people, U.S. military advisers assumed that the guerrillas could win over the people only by terror; therefore they responded in kind. But for every peasant shot by guerrillas, at least fifteen were killed by U.S.-supported government forces.[35] The tragedy is that in most instances of rural guerrilla warfare, as in Bolivia and Venezuela, the peasants caught in the crossfire were entirely neutral and wanted only to be left alone. In the rare cases when they eventually did identify with a guerrilla movement, as in Nicaragua, it was not because of guerrilla terrorism but because they were being repeatedly massacred by government troops. Yet the Americans never learned that repression is the surest way to transform apathetic peasants into political militants. Thus, when questioned about the legitimacy of terror tactics in Guatemala, Colonel John Webber, the U.S. attaché, responded, "That's the way the country is. The communists are using everything they have, including terror. And it must be met."[36] When the 1966–68 counterinsurgency campaign finally ended in northeastern Guatemala, six thousand to eight thousand people were dead. That was how the "spiral of violence" began, of which Brazil's Archbishop Helder Cámara so frequently speaks; eventually, everyone is touched by terror. In the lexicon of the counterinsurgent these are "limited wars." But they are so only in their consequences for the intervening power; for the people and the countries under assault they are total.

Thus the counterinsurgents' preoccupation with military and police techniques, with repression and terror, became an end in itself. As I. F. Stone put it:

> In reading the military literature on guerrilla warfare now so fashionable at the Pentagon, one feels that these writers are like men watching a dance from outside through heavy plate glass windows. They see the motions but they can't hear the music. They put the mechanical gestures down on paper with pendantic fidelity. But what rarely comes through to them are the injured racial feelings, the misery, the rankling slights. So they do not really understand what leads men to abandon wife, children, home, career, friends, to take to the bush and live gun in hand like a hunted animal; to challenge overwhelming military odds rather than acquiesce any longer in humiliation, injustice, or poverty. . . .[37]

In reading the courses that the United States devised for them, one can also understand how the Latin-American military came to see communists at every turn. Course O-47 on urban counterinsurgency operations, taught at the U. S. Army School of the Americas in the Panama Canal Zone, is illuminating on this point. It suggests ways whereby the presence of communist guerrillas may be detected:

   a. The disappearance or movement of youths possibly indicates the recruitment to form guerrilla bands in the area. You should report the reluctance of families of said missing youths to speak about them.
   b. The refusal of peasants to pay rents, taxes, or agricultural loans or any difficulty in collecting these will indicate the existence of an active insurrection that has succeeded in convincing the peasants of the injustices of the present system, and is directing or instigating them to disobey its precepts.
   c. Hostility on the part of the local population to the government forces, in contrast to their amiable or neutral attitude in the past. This can indicate a change of loyalty or of behavior inspired by fear, often manifested by children refusing to fraternize with members of the internal-security forces.
   d. Short, unjustified, and unusual absences from work on the part of government employees.
   e. Networks of police and informants don't provide the kind of reports they should. This could indicate that the sources of information have become allied with the insurgent movement, or that they fear the retaliation of the insurgents or their sympathizers.
   f. A growing hostility against governmental agencies and agencies of public order. . . .[38]

Subversion, according to Course O-47, is not limited to armed insurrection; it can also take the form of nonviolent action, such as consciousness-raising work (as promoted by the Catholic Church), demonstrations, strikes, "compromised social sciences," and so on, that "attract the discontented among the populace, although those who protest are not the people themselves but an atomized group of malcontents and adventurers." Anyone who differs with the established order must be obeying foreign, communist influences. Such is the case of intellectuals or students who are "manipulated by insurgent theses" that "deform" history and speak of imperialism. Any attempt to get at the real historical, sociological, or economic causes of poverty and injustice in Latin America is judged "subversive."[39] A number of methods are suggested to deal with such "subversion," as in the Pentagon's course on "Utilization and Containment of Rumors," which teaches the student how to use white or black propaganda. (See appendix.)

More than 64,000 Latin-American soldiers and officers, including 170 heads of state, ministers, commanding officers, and directors of intelligence, were exposed to such methods and ideas between 1950 and 1973 in the School of the Americas, better known as the "School of Coups." Similar ideas were drummed into the heads of Latin-American police agents during psychological operations courses (PSYOPS) at the U. S. Army Institute for Military Assistance at Fort Bragg, North Carolina. In one symposium euphemistically described as "Population Protection and Resources Management," the Latin Americans were taught such techniques as a national identity card system, search operations, checkpoints, curfews, and block controls to monitor the movement of people and goods. The semester concluded with a discussion of the role of the mass media and propaganda in building support for the government, "since by their nature most [of these] measures are rather harsh . . . [and] they should be coordinated with an intense PSYOPS campaign to convince the population that these harsh methods are for their own good."[40]

Some of the material used in the courses was purposely simplistic; for instance, the U. S. Information Agency issued comic books in which American Supermen battled the communist monster. This "literature" occasionally backfired; in Colombia, university students rioted when the comic books were distributed during a U.S.-sponsored concert. But for the average Latin-American soldier, with at best a primary education, there was nothing exaggerated or false about the communist threat. Stationed in a village or city far from his hometown, he had no point of contact with the people except through the medium of fear and authority, which only increased the local hostility. So communication was reduced to a war between "them" and "us." If the peasants did not provide the sort of information the military wanted, it was automatically assumed that they were guerrilla collaborators, yet in ninety-nine cases out of a hundred they had no dealings with the guerrillas. A Bolivian Indian in an Andean village, for example, is not apt to tell a stranger his life story, or divulge the recent movements of his family. It would be as plausible to expect that an Appalachian coal miner would air his grievances to a New York cop who just happened into town. But this, according to U. S. Army Course 0-47, was sufficient grounds for suspecting the peasant of being a collaborator. "Look at all those communists out there," said a Nicaraguan National Guard commander in the northern rain forests of Zelaya, pointing to the peasants at work on the slopes below him. "They're all guerrilla collaborators, every one of them." The man's attitude was typical of that held by many Latin-American military officers trained, like himself, in the School of the Americas.

U.S. military and police advisers rarely questioned the effect of such training, because the programs became an end in themselves. Thus, asked what he conceived his job to be, a member of the U. S. Military Group (MILGP) in Guatemala replied instantly that it was to make the Guatemalan Armed Forces as efficient as possible. The next question, as to why this was in the interests of the United States, was followed by a long silence while he reflected on a point that had apparently never occurred to him.[41] Nor could the MILGP itself think of a sufficient reason for the U. S. Government to have given the Guatemalans $1.7 million (plus $5 million in Guatemalan cash) to purchase eight A-37 aircraft, particularly after the Guatemalans destroyed two of the planes in a midair collision within two weeks of delivery. According to Pat Holt, a staff member of the U. S. Senate's Subcommittee on Western Hemisphere Affairs, it was first said that "the planes were for anti-guerrilla operations, though it was emphasized that the United States refused, as a matter of policy, to sell napalm or even to sell the empty containers for napalm. When asked what good was a plane with the A-37's performance characteristics in anti-guerrilla operations, the answer was that the planes were useful in patrolling the Guatemalan territorial sea to prevent poaching by Salvadorans. When pressed as to the threat that Salvador presented to Guatemala, it was said that the planes were sold for a political reason—namely, to keep the Air Force happy so that it would not overthrow [President Carlos] Arana. But not thirty minutes before, the same people had emphasized Arana's support among the military.

"One is left with the strong impression that the MILGP views its job as an end in itself. When pressed, MILGP officers list U.S. national interests in Guatemala as (1) to keep them 'on our side' so that they vote with us in the UN and OAS, and (2) to help them develop socially and economically so that they can be a leader in Central America and so that they can avoid a communist takeover. Guatemala has so far voted 'on our side' in the UN and the OAS. It has so far avoided a communist takeover. Its economic and social development is severely retarded, and it doesn't look like much of a leader in Central America. As in the case with AID public safety (police training), the military assistance program carries a political price. It may be questioned whether we're getting our money's worth."[42]

It may also be questioned whether the bloodletting caused by the counterinsurgency programs had any real military significance. The RAND Corporation, which advises both the State Department and the Defense Department, holds that U.S. military assistance programs in Latin America were successful only because the conditions necessary for rural and urban insurgency never obtained. Had they done so, U.S. arms and training would have been insufficient to put down an uprising, as they were in Vietnam. In other words, most of the killing has been for nothing. As RAND points out, "Violent revolution in rural insurgency did not have the conditions to succeed and . . . these conditions cannot be readily created even by determined bands of rural guerrillas."[43] This was in part because many of the self-styled revolutionaries were romanticizing students with "capabilities for little more than dramatic acts of terrorism that made good international press copy without being of direct political consequence" (such as the small guerrilla groups in Colombia that have been active since the 1950s without ever threatening the central government). What the military assistance programs did do, reported RAND, was to "facilitate preoccupation with military response to national security" and encourage the United States in the belief that all rebellion in Latin America, even if necessary for social change, was bad by definition, with the result that Washington automatically defended reactionary or status quo governments from such violence.[44] Or as Senator William Fulbright once put it, Latin-American dictators "need us much more than we need them." U.S. support of these governments can be explained, he said, only by "the anti-communist crusade that for years impregnated U.S. foreign policy. The attraction of right-wing dictators has consisted in their decided anti-communism, and this appears to have been enough to compensate for their despotism and corruption."

To be fair to them, not all Latin-American soldiers were convinced that the United States' preoccupation with counterinsurgency and anti-communism was a good thing; there have been occasional demurrals, as at the Tenth Conference of Latin American and U. S. Armies in 1973, when the Argentine and Peruvian generals complained that they were tired of talking about communism, and shouldn't the conference consider other threats to the Latin-American countries, such as the multinationals and economic imperialism? According to Juan Domingo Perón, who was President of Argentina at the time, the United States was "maneuvering to have the armed forces, rather than the political forces, direct international policy." His words proved prophetic: less than two years after his death in 1974, Argentina's armed forces once again seized power.

General Carlos Prats, who was commander-in-chief of the Chilean Army under the Allende government, had similar doubts before he and his wife were assassinated in Buenos Aires in 1974, just a year after the Chilean coup. According to his private diary, published in Mexico City under the title *A Life Within the Law*,[45] neither Allende nor the government parties knew "how profound the North American influence is on our armed forces and especially on the mentality of the Chilean military man." Prats wanted to limit or at least balance what he called this "influence without counterweight." Convinced that politicization of Chile's military was inevitable, he said the country's officers should understand Chile's social reality and participate in the task of development, but that it was urgent to send Chilean officers to Europe, Africa, and Asia—"not to copy them, but to understand that the world does not begin and end with the schools of the Pentagon." In the School of the Americas and other U. S. Army training centers, he wrote, Chilean officers have learned to respond "to the stereotypes and reflexes of those courses." "While thinking they were liberating the nation from 'the enemy within,'" Prats added, "they have committed a crime that can be explained only in terms of their ingenuousness, ignorance, and political shortsightedness." Proof of the "simplicity" of Chile's military mentality, he said, was its exclusive concern with "activities and terrorism of the left, while the right was just as dangerous and stockpiling more arms."

The warnings of Perón and Prats have long been forgotten, and at the most recent Conference of Armies, the subject was, as usual, communist subversion. The only thing lacking in the otherwise united march of the hemisphere's armies is an Inter-American Defense Force under U.S. command, a Pentagon dream that dates from the Truman administration but has not materialized because of regional differences among the Latin Americans. In Central America, however, the Defense Department brought the armies of El Salvador, Guatemala, Honduras, Nicaragua, and Panama and the Costa Rican police force together under the umbrella of the Defense Council of Central America (CONDECA). It had fourteen thousand soldiers, trained in the Panama Canal Zone, and served as a mutual-aid society for the region's dictators. Thus when presidential contender José Napoleón Duarte of El Salvador threatened to lead a popular uprising in 1972, after being deprived of victory by a fraudulent vote count, Nicaragua and Guatemala sent combat planes to help General Arturo Armando Molina put down the insurrection. There were also twenty-two U.S. military advisers on hand to counsel Molina, at an annual cost to U.S. taxpayers of $25,000 to $50,000 each.[46]

"A real good, close relationship"

While Nicaragua's Somoza was the most infamous case of a Central American dictator set up and financed by the U. S. Government, plenty of lesser-known strongmen came to power because of U.S. support. Such a one was Colonel Carlos Arana of Guatemala, who was tapped by the U. S. Military Mission to head the country's counterinsurgency program. A former military attaché in Washington, Arana had "a real good, close relationship" with U.S. military personnel, according to a Special Forces adviser.[47] He soon revealed his abilities by organizing the slaughter of eight thousand Guatemalans between 1966 and 1968.[48] Some one thousand Green Berets were on hand to help him, accompanying Guatemalan patrols on counterinsurgency raids. Official denials notwithstanding, U.S. pilots flew U.S. planes to drop napalm on the peasants, and under the leadership of the U.S. military attaché, Colonel John Webber, paramilitary groups composed of large landowners were encouraged to collaborate with the Army in hunting down "subversive" peasants.[49] These groups were the forerunner of the White Hand, a right-wing vigilante group responsible for thousands of deaths. According to Amnesty International, most of the bodies were so severely mutilated that identification was impossible.

When Arana became President in 1970, a second reign of terror was unleashed, this time with the help of thirty-two thousand Guatemalan policemen trained by AID's public safety program. Some seven thousand people were murdered or "disappeared" between 1970 and 1971, most of them killed by the White Hand. In all, fifteen thousand people died during the first three years of the Arana government. For every Guatemalan murdered by the extreme left, fifteen were killed by the extreme right.[50]

Arana turned over the presidency to the head of the Army, General Kjell Laugerud García, in 1974, but continued to be a power in the land. Through blatant bribery in the Guatemalan Congress ($5,000 per vote), he succeeded in having a loyal follower elected president of that body in mid-1976.[51] He was also linked to a private terrorist squad run by his "old friend" Elías Zimeri, a White Hand militant allegedly involved in the kidnapping of María Olga Novella, the daughter of an important local industrialist; in the shooting of a prominent Guatemala City official; and in the wounding of Manuel Colom Argueta, head of the opposition coalition. In addition, the Zimeri-Arana gang was thought responsible for a series of death threats to members of the Committee of National Reconstruction, an agency charged with administering foreign aid for the reconstruction of Guatemala after the February 1976 earthquake. Arana was particularly piqued when he failed to gain control of the committee and its

bank accounts. Terrorism, thus, was not always political; sometimes it was a matter of money, as with the kidnapping of Ms.
Novella, whose family paid $1.3 million in ransom.[52] When the
police finally raided a number of private and business properties
belonging to the Zimeri family, they found machine guns, rockets,
grenades, army uniforms, and the remains of a young Army
officer who had been kidnapped in 1975.[53] Arana's son Roberto,
a notorious drug trafficker, maintains the family tradition.[54]

Guatemala is but one example of U.S. involvement with repressive police and military agencies. In the Dominican Republic,
Kennedy's ambassador, John Bartlow Martin, strongly encouraged the police and military to adopt terror tactics. "I found
myself urging . . . methods once used by the police in Chicago,"
he said. "There, if a policeman saw an ex-convict or a known
hoodlum on the street, he picked him up 'on suspicion,' took him
to the station, held him the legal limit, then released him only to
raid his flat that night, rout him out of bed, and start all over;
time after time harassing him, hoping finally to drive him out of
town. It was illegal detention, and often worse—prisoners were
sometimes beaten."[55] After the 1965 Marine invasion of the
Dominican Republic, Martin's suggestions were enthusiastically
adopted by the local police, who had the benefit of an eighteen-
man public safety program, one third of whom were CIA agents,
according to David Fairchild, an AID official who worked in the
Dominican Republic in 1966 and 1967.[56] The police organized
the Dominican Republic's equivalent of the White Hand, called
"La Banda," whose victims were averaging fifteen to twenty a
month by 1971, most of them inconspicuous, apolitical people,
including five young men who were brutally murdered although
they had no known political connections. When six members of
La Banda sought asylum in the Mexican Embassy, they claimed
to have worked with the police and been threatened with death by
high-ranking police officers when they refused to carry out orders.
They named Lieutenant Oscar Nuñez, chief bodyguard of Police
Chief Enrique Pérez y Pérez, as the leader of the gang.[57]

Police officers also used terror to ensure the reelection of the
country's perennial President, Joaquín Balaguer, who had run the
Dominican Republic with U.S. support ever since the 1965 invasion. As Balaguer assured the American Chamber of Commerce

in Santo Domingo, "We cannot allow ourselves the luxury taken by other countries in Latin America, of shaking off the so-called yoke of North American imperialism to accept others that are, indeed, ignominious."[58] Activities by opposition parties, such as street meetings, were violently suppressed by the police; opposition leaders were beaten up, arrested, and, in a number of documented cases, killed or kidnapped and never seen again. Particularly vulnerable were members of the Dominican Revolutionary Party of Juan Bosch, who was overthrown in 1963 for attempting a few mild reforms. According to a *Wall Street Journal* report, "The U.S. embassy has done nothing publicly to dissociate itself from the terror. The United States continues to provide substantial aid, including training, equipment, and arms, to the Dominican police and Army."[59]

U.S. public safety advisers and CIA agents were also instrumental in the formation of Uruguay's para-police and military organizations. Contrary to popular opinion in the United States, most of Costa-Gavras' controversial film *State of Siege* was based on fact. At one point in the movie, for example, a Uruguayan police officer is shown receiving training in the manufacture and use of explosive devices at a secret school in the southwestern United States. The officer is later linked to a right-wing death squad responsible for numerous murders, some performed with explosives, of prominent Uruguayan radicals. U.S. audiences could hardly be blamed for assuming that this episode was a figment of Costa-Gavras' imagination—so much that goes on in Latin America is too terrible to be believed. But State Department documents unearthed by Senator James Abourezk proved that the U. S. Government was indeed involved in training foreign policemen in bomb design at a remote camp in Texas and that sixteen of these policemen were Uruguayans. In a memorandum to Senator Abourezk, AID's Matthew Harvey acknowledged that the public safety program had provided instruction in the design, manufacture, and use of homemade bombs and incendiary devices to at least 165 foreign policemen, most of them from Latin America, Africa, and Asia, at the U. S. Border Patrol Academy in Los Fresnos, Texas. U.S. taxpayers paid the entire cost of this training, $1,750 per student.[60]

According to the AID documents, students in this "Technical Investigations Course" first attended a four-week session at the

International Police Academy in Washington, D.C., for lectures on: basic electricity ("problems involving electricity as applied to explosives are given"), introduction to bombs and explosives ("a lecture/demonstration of incendiary devices"), and assassination weapons ("a discussion of various weapons that may be used by the assassin"). The trainees were then flown to Los Fresnos for a four-week field course at an outdoor "laboratory" run by the CIA. (Harvey stated that the subject matter of these courses was so sensitive that the Defense Department refused to provide instructors, forcing AID to rely on the CIA.)‡ The field sessions included "practical exercises" with "different types of explosive devices and booby traps" of the sort shown in *State of Siege,* including bombs exploded in buildings, automobiles, and a public plaza full of dummies.

Almost every country in Latin America sent students to the Los Fresnos academy, among them Brazil, Guatemala, and the Dominican Republic, all three of which were infamous for their death squads. (These countries were condemned for human-rights violations by the Organization of American States, Amnesty In-

‡ The CIA also used a secret installation in the Panama Canal Zone to train Americans and Cuban exiles in paramilitary warfare. One former officer of the CIA's Clandestine Service described how students were familiarized with an "army of outlawed weaponry . . . which included bullets that explode on impact, silencer-equipped machine guns, homemade explosives, and self-made napalm. We were taught demolition techniques, practicing on late model cars, railroad trucks, and gas-storage tanks. And we were shown a quick method of saturating a confined area with flour or fertilizer, causing an explosion.

"And there was a diabolical invention that might be called a minicannon. It was constructed of a concave piece of steel fitted into the top of a No. 10 can filled with a plastic explosive. When the device was detonated, the tremendous heat of friction of the steel turning inside out made the steel piece a white-hot projectile. There were a number of uses for the minicannon, one of which was demonstrated to us using an old Army school bus. It was fastened to the gasoline tank in such a fashion that the incendiary projectile would rupture the tank and fling flaming gasoline the length of the bus interior, incinerating anyone inside. It was my lot to show the rest of the class how easily it could be done. It worked, my God, how it worked. I stood there watching the flames consume the bus. It was, I guess, the moment of truth. What did a busload of burning people have to do with freedom? What right did I have, in the name of democracy and the CIA, to decide that random victims should die?" (As quoted in Victor Marchetti and John D. Marks, *The CIA and the Cult of Intelligence* [New York: Dell Publishing Co., 1974], p. 125.)

ternational, and the International Commission of Jurists.) As in the case of the Dominican Republic's La Banda, no serious attempt was made to disguise police links with these gangs of assassins. "The members of [Brazil's] death squad are policemen, and everyone knows it," said Nelson Fonseca, São Paulo's top criminal judge.[61]

The involvement of U.S. police and CIA agents in the training and arming of Uruguay's parapolice organizations, which Costa-Gavras treated at length, was confirmed by Nelson Bardesio, a police photographer and death squad member who was kidnapped and interrogated by Uruguay's Tupamaro guerrillas in 1972. His testimony was recorded in the presence of the politically moderate president of Uruguay's Chamber of Deputies, Senator Héctor Gutiérrez Ruiz, who allowed himself to be "kidnapped" by the Tupamaros in order to talk with Bardesio.* According to the police photographer, the Department of Information and Intelligence (DII), which was an official cover for the death squad, was set up with the advice and financial assistance of U.S. public safety adviser William Cantrell. Bardesio, who had occasionally served as his chauffeur, said that Cantrell made daily trips among the DII, Montevideo police headquarters, and the U. S. Embassy to ensure the steady transfer of intelligence data and the effective coordination of extra-legal operations. As part of this process, he said, U. S. Embassy personnel periodically requested specific information from the DII for their own intelligence work. Bardesio speculated that Cantrell worked for the CIA, a guess confirmed by ex–CIA agent Philip Agee, who had been assigned to Uruguay and who later fingered Cantrell as CIA operations officer in Montevideo.[62]† Bardesio also named a number of Uruguayan police

* Gutiérrez Ruiz was later kidnapped and murdered by Uruguayan agents working with the Argentine police in Buenos Aires, where he had taken refuge after the 1973 military coup in Uruguay.

† Agee also reported that the CIA Montevideo station supplied the Uruguayan police with a long list of left-wing Argentines, Paraguayans, Brazilians, and other Latin Americans not resident in Uruguay as part of security measures during President Johnson's visit to Punta del Este for the 1967 hemispheric summit conference. (Philip Agee, *Inside the Company: CIA Diary* [England. Penguin Books, 1975], p. 537.) These lists were subsequently added to the military regimes' central pool of information on political dissidents.

and military officers who had participated in assassinations and bombings with the approval of the Ministry of the Interior. He said that this death squad had ample supplies of explosive materials used in the manufacture of homemade bombs and booby traps.[63]

The Brazilian Arsenal

As a result of mounting evidence linking the public safety program to such terror squads, the U. S. Congress voted to phase out the program in 1974. Military grants to purchase arms met a similar fate, but the training programs were continued. By this time, however, there was less need for such assistance, because Brazil had taken over many of the United States' functions as regional policeman in training and arming its neighbors. With a $2 billion–plus annual budget, Brazil's defense establishment has amassed an impressive arsenal of weapons, including Australian anti-submarine rockets, British frigates, and the Seacat and Sea Dart naval missiles, 48 Northrop F-5E Fighters, and 331 French Mirage jets. Though still one of the United States' biggest arms customers ($400 million in aerospace equipment in 1974 alone), Brazil has begun to establish itself as a major weapons manufacturer in the Third World through licensing agreements with U.S. and European firms. Among the matériel it now produces are West German anti-tank "Cobra" missiles, the Belgian 7.62 NATO Round FN rifle, the French Roland surface-to-surface missile, the Italian 9 mm Beretta submachine gun, the British Argus 700 minicomputer system for naval weapons systems, and armored personnel carriers. The chemical weapon Mace is purchased from the United States' Smith & Wesson, part owner of the Brazilian arms firm Forjas Taurus. Brazil is also producing a subsonic military jet trainer called the "Xavante" under a licensing agreement with Italy's Aermacchi, helicopters under agreement with France's Aerospatiale and Britain's Westland, structural parts for Northrop's F-5E Fighters, and a twin-engine turboprop called the "Bandeirante."

But undoubtedly the most frightening addition to the Brazilian arsenal is West German know-how and material for the entire nuclear cycle, thereby enabling Brazil to produce atomic weapons.

While insisting that its intentions were entirely pacific, Brazil steadfastly refused to sign the Nuclear Non-Proliferation Treaty. In the meantime, while developing Brazil's nuclear capacity, the government has devised another plan to form a 7,000-man parachute brigade with 48 Lockheed C-130 Hercules transport planes to operate anywhere in Latin America within forty-eight hours.[64]

The regime has already given more than a little help to its friends in Bolivia and Uruguay, where it supported the coups of 1971 and 1973 respectively. Two Brazilian Air Force planes loaded with arms were flown to Santa Cruz in eastern Bolivia, which has sizable Brazilian interests, to aid General Hugo Banzer in his successful putsch. And just in case Banzer needed more help, the Airborne Joint Brigade of Corumbá, Army II Corps, under General Ramiro Gonçalves Lima, was lined up along the Brazilian-Bolivian frontier and at some points even inside Bolivian territory. (The importance of Washington's Operation Brother Sam as a standby support for Brazil's 1964 coup was not lost on the generals.) A week after Banzer took power, Brazil repaid the allegiance of the Santa Cruz ranchers by granting them a $5 million loan. The Bank of Brazil advanced a similar amount to the Banzer government, at the same time launching an expensive publicity campaign throughout the country with the slogan: "Bolivia, you can count on me!—Bank of Brazil, S.A." Banzer counted not only on the bank but also on the Brazilian military, which sold him tanks, arms and ammunition, and eighteen "Xavante" jet fighters.[65]

Uruguay was saved from outright Brazilian occupation in 1971 only because a left-wing coalition known as the Broad Front failed to win Uruguay's presidential elections, thereby eliminating the need for Brazil's "Thirty-Hour Operation." But according to Wilson Ferreira Aldunate, head of the centrist Uruguayan National Party and the real winner of the elections, the result was much the same, since Uruguay's armed forces had Brazilian support in both preparing and carrying out their putsch two years later, including Brazilian fuel and transportation supplies during a general strike called to protest the military take-over. Uruguayan police agents belonging to the country's death squad also received training and arms from Brazil.[66]

Chile's generals were the recipients of similar Brazilian know-how, particularly in the weeks after the 1973 coup, when Brazilian agents taught their Chilean counterparts new techniques of torture and surveillance.[67] Both Chile and Uruguay purchased Brazilian aircraft, and Chile bought $2 million worth of army supplies from the Brazilian firm of Diana Paolucci. Brazil is also marketing armored carriers to Bolivia, Paraguay, Chile, and Peru.

One result of this mutual aid has been the regionalization of terror, from Washington to Buenos Aires, with no guarantee of safety in political asylum. Several dozen political refugees were assassinated in exile, including General Prats; former Bolivian President Juan José Torres, overthrown by Banzer and, like Prats, killed in Argentina; and two prominent Uruguayan senators, Zelmar Michelini and Héctor Gutiérrez Ruiz, kidnapped and murdered in Buenos Aires. Bernardo Leighton, a founder of Chile's Christian Democratic Party and one of the most distinguished Chileans of his generation, narrowly survived an assassination attempt in Rome. Orlando Letelier, Allende's Foreign Minister and a former Chilean ambassador to the United States, was less fortunate. He was killed in September 1976 when a remote-control bomb exploded beneath his car as he drove along Washington's Embassy Row. Ronni K. Moffitt, a staff member and colleague of Letelier at the Institute for Policy Studies, also died in the explosion.

A subsequent FBI probe showed that Letelier was killed by right-wing Cuban exiles working for DINA, the Chilean secret police. The Cubans belonged to Brigade 2506 of the abortive Bay of Pigs invasion. Brigade 2506 had eight to nine hundred members, most of them in Miami, and was believed to be linked to a right-wing, anti-Castro umbrella organization known as the Co-ordination of United Revolutionary Organizations (CORU). CORU's leader, Orlando Bosch, was arrested in Venezuela in connection with the explosion of a Cuban airliner in October 1976 in which seventy-three people died.[68] Brigade 2506 veteran Rolando Otero was convicted in a Florida circuit court in 1977 for a bombing at Miami International Airport that caused considerable damage but no injuries.[69]

Both Bosch and Otero had close Chilean connections. The former lived in Chile from the end of 1974 to late 1975, after fleeing the United States following the assassination of Cuban leader José

Elías de Torriente. At the time of his flight, Bosch was on probation after having served four years of a ten-year sentence for attacking a Polish ship with a bazooka gun in the port of Miami.

George Crile III, an expert on the Cuban community in the United States, stated in a Washington *Post* article that Bosch—after a stay of almost a year in Chile—"was interviewed in Curaçao by a journalist in exile who reported that Bosch had an escort of armed Chileans and access to all the money he needed."

Crile said, "State Department files indicate that the Chileans were offering safe haven, passports, and even the use of diplomatic pouches to some Cuban terrorists. One government investigator says that a remote-control detonating device, used in the assassination of the exile leader Rolando Masfere in 1975, had been brought into the United States in a Chilean diplomatic pouch."[70]

Bosch later met with José Dionisio Suárez, who was cited as responsible for detonating the bomb that killed Letelier, at a CORU meeting in the Dominican Republic in mid-1976.[71]

Otero, alias "the Condor," visited Chile as DINA's guest in early 1976, but DINA turned him over to the FBI, which took him back to the United States. Otero told the FBI that General Manuel Contreras, a Pinochet protégé who headed DINA at the time of Letelier's murder, had asked him to go to Costa Rica to expedite a plot to assassinate Andrés Pascal Allende, head of the Chilean Movement of the Revolutionary Left (MIR) and Anne Marie Beausire, who, as asylees in the Costa Rican Embassy, had recently fled from Chile. Otero told the FBI that DINA asked this "favor" of both Otero and Bosch, offering to provide arms and funds to support Cuban exile action against Castro in return. Otero accepted, but the killing never took place because Allende and Beausire left Costa Rica for Cuba.[72]

The Chilean Government's involvement in Letelier's murder was originally dismissed as "too stupid to be believed"—anyone who did not know Pinochet's Chile would snort at the idea of a government deliberately courting an international scandal by murdering such a well-known diplomat. This assumption was strengthened by a cover-up operation in which FBI investigators —or persons with access to the investigation—leaked to the press the contents of Letelier's briefcase, recovered from the bombed car. The resulting stories by U.S. columnists created the impression that Letelier was a Cuban or Soviet agent, because letters in the briefcase mentioned funds paid to him from Cuba. Since many of the key figures in the worldwide Chilean exile organization have their headquarters in Cuba and enjoy the public support of Castro, it was hardly surprising that Letelier was receiving funds from his countrymen there. But the story served to distract attention from the Chilean connection and create a plausible motive for anti-Castro Cubans to ambush Letelier.[73] Although FBI agents knew of Chile's involvement in early 1977, they did not disclose this information until February 1978.

The Chilean connection started with Michael Vernon Townley, an American who had lived in Chile for fifteen years and had been a CIA armaments trainer,[74] and Captain Armando Fernández, a member of DINA. A month before Letelier's assassination, Townley and Fernández went to the United States under assumed names on official government passports, where they made contact with the Cubans. The Chilean Foreign Ministry had sent the U. S. Embassy a letter requesting A-2 visas (official travel on government business) for Townley and Fernández under the names Juan Williams Rose and Alejandro Romeral Jara. Guillermo Osorio, the Foreign Ministry's director of consular affairs and the man who requested the visas, later died of gunshot wounds in mysterious circumstances, an alleged suicide.

A successful diplomat who had been appointed to an ambassador's post shortly before his death, Osorio had no motive for killing himself and, according to his relatives, was not noticeably depressed in the days before his death.[75] He was last seen alive at a diplomatic function at government headquarters in Santiago and was driven home from the reception by three generals, including General Contreras, the DINA chief who was named by U.S. columnist Jack Anderson as the mastermind of the Letelier killing.[76] After Osorio's death, General Carlos Forestier, second-in-command of the Army, arrived at the house to supervise the handling of the body, claiming that an autopsy—an automatic requirement under Chilean law for all violent deaths—was unnecessary. When an autopsy was finally performed, at the insistence of Osorio's family, he was reported to have died of a heart attack, despite a bullet wound in his head. Because of the angle of the bullet and the absence of scorch marks, the suicide theory was physically improbable.

Michael Townley, a key figure in the Letelier investigation, had earlier been involved in clandestine operations with an extreme right-wing guerrilla squad called Fatherland and Liberty, and funded, according to the U. S. Congress, by the CIA.‡ Fatherland and Liberty was responsible for a series of terrorist acts during the Allende administration, including an unsuccessful CIA-sponsored military coup. A radio and electronics expert, Townley was in charge of training Fatherland and Liberty commandos. One of their operations, of which Townley later boasted, was a raid on a government radio installation; the group stole the equipment and murdered the caretaker. A Chilean member of the commando was later arrested, and through his confession the CIA's connections with the incident became known.[77] After the coup, Townley went to work for DINA.

Under strong pressure from the Carter administration, Townley was eventually expelled from Chile and taken to the United States for questioning, where he confessed his part in the Letelier assassination as the leader of the Cubans.[78] According to a 700-page dossier assembled by the FBI, Townley's wife admitted that the couple had been in Buenos Aires at the time of General Prats's murder and in Rome during the attempt on Leighton's life.[79] Townley subsequently told an Italian television program that he had been involved in the Leighton affair.[80] The dossier also revealed that DINA had used Cuban exiles in two unsuccessful attempts on the life of the former Chilean Foreign Minister and Christian Democrat leader Gabriel Valdés, in 1975 and 1976 in New York. A Cuban exile mission sent to Mexico to kill Carlos Altamirano, secretary general of the Chilean Socialist Party, also failed, according to the dossier.[81]

"Would you sell a computer to Hitler?"

In addition to regional assassinations and kidnappings, there were regular exchanges of political prisoners among Latin-American governments, such as the thirty-two Bolivian tin miners who were exiled to a police camp in southern Chile, and the body brigade

‡ For more details, see Chapter VIII, pp. 292–93.

that shuffled corpses across the River Plate between Uruguay and Argentina. When ten manacled, mutilated corpses showed up on the riverbanks of Uruguay, the government at first claimed they were Orientals, a play on the country's official name, the Oriental Republic of Uruguay, but later admitted that the dead were Uruguayans, probably some of those who disappeared weekly from their homes or jobs in Argentina.

Computers are important for collecting and exchanging information on these political refugees. According to *Computer Decisions,* a reputable trade journal, U.S. firms were selling sophisticated systems to Chile, Uruguay, Argentina, and Brazil to spot political suspects for interrogation, torture, and elimination. The magazine reported that the Argentine Federal Police "are using electronics so advanced that the most modern American police forces have no comparable gear," including the Digicom system, which connects patrol cars to police dispatch systems. Although the Digicom procedure of submitting the name of a person picked up in the streets to police headquarters and to a data-base system is common in the United States, the Argentine equipment had the added capability of projecting any area reporting a disturbance on a circuit screen map. The Argentine police also used a special radio transmitter, called the Wheelbarrow system, which detonates explosive devices.[82] It was sold to the Argentine military by E-Systems, a Garland, Texas, "supplier of military and police electronics with gross revenue of nearly $250 million."[83] Among the members of its board of directors, according to *Computer Decisions,* was Admiral William Rayburn, "a high Central Intelligence Agency official during the Johnson administration." E-Systems was the owner of Air Asia, which it purchased in 1975 from the Air America Company, owned and operated by the CIA.[84]

Computer Decisions also reported receiving a document, dated in 1973, that disclosed "IBM plans to sell a 370/145 and forty 3270 terminals to the security department of the State of Guanabara [Rio de Janeiro], Brazil." The document showed that IBM was aware of the Brazilian authorities' purpose for buying such complex and sophisticated equipment: among the normal police projects listed was one labeled "J41, Political Activists." Later investigations by *Computer Decisions* showed that the document did indeed belong to IBM but that the deal did not go through at the time.[85] However, IBM did sell 370/145 computers to Chile. They were sent to Chilean universities, which are controlled by the military, and formed part of the military's communications system. IBM's rationalization, according to the company's director of information, was that "we are in a position similar to a car manufacturer. If General Motors sells you a car, and you use it to kill someone, that doesn't make General Motors responsible."[86]

The National Council of Churches disagreed. Using proxies totaling two hundred thousand shares of IBM stock, the Council unsuccessfully tried to dissuade IBM from selling computers to the Pinochet regime. Said William Wipfler, Latin-American director of the Council: "When you know who Hitler is, you can't pretend you don't know what he's doing with your equipment."[87]

Attempts by members of Congress and journalists to ferret out more information on computer exports were stonewalled by the U. S. Government, although it is required by law to monitor such sales. Senator Edward Kennedy complained that the Ford administration had denied him access to information on whether "American computer firms have been selling computers to foreign police agencies," unless he would promise "to keep the information confidential."[88] Michael Klare, a visiting fellow of Princeton's Center of International Studies, got a similar response from President Carter's Secretary of Commerce, Juanita Kreps, who informed him that it would be contrary to the "national welfare" to release data on the export of U.S. computers to foreign police and intelligence agencies.[89] But Kreps's reasoning was contradictory: after first claiming that the Commerce Department had taken precautions to prevent the delivery of computers to repressive regimes, so that no public disclosure was necessary, she went on to say that the nation's trade position would suffer if the government provided damaging information on the behavior of U.S. corporations overseas.

The computer case was yet another indication that, no matter who is President, there is more rhetoric than substance in U.S. concern for human rights. Shortly after taking office, Secretary of State Cyrus Vance reaffirmed Kissinger's "memorandum of understanding" with Brazil and that country's special relationship with the United States in a letter to the Brazilian Foreign Minister. And when Hodding Carter was asked if it was true that various

U.S. ambassadors in Latin America were privately assuring local officials not to worry about all the human rights talk in Washington, that it was really just for internal political consumption, the State Department spokesman said that it was a problem and "we are trying to deal with it."[90] Certainly a good many people in government have not changed their stripes. Typical of their attitude was an exchange on the advisability of U.S. military intervention in Latin America between Representative Edward Koch and Stephen Winship, director of the State Department's Office of Security Assistance, during military appropriations hearings in 1976:

> *Koch:* Your position is that if there is an internal threat . . . or force in Brazil, we will provide aid to the government of Brazil to put down an internal insurgency.
> *Winship:* . . . that is considered by the foreign governments a very essential element in their relationship with us.
> *Koch:* I will bet, for them, but how about for us?[91]

In fact, much of the *mea culpa* criticism of the United States' counterinsurgency programs veiled an obvious relief over the disappearance of such distractions as guerrilla uprisings and populist governments, the idea being that now the United States could get on with initiatives in Latin America, though what those initiatives were supposed to be no one seemed to know—the Alliance for Progress was certainly too shopworn to be resurrected. Sol Linowitz, a former U.S. ambassador to the OAS and negotiator for a new Panama Canal treaty, came up with a series of high-sounding generalities in 1975 as chairman of a gilt-edged study group known as the Commission on United States–Latin American Relations. Although the commission's conclusions, popularly known as the Linowitz Report,[92] were adopted in broad outline by the Carter administration, no attempt was made to get at the real causes of repression and underdevelopment in Latin America. Washington had found a convenient scapegoat in international communism a decade earlier, and it was now judged convenient to sweep all the mistakes of that period under the rug. But without recognizing why Latin America's death squads came into being or how fascism could rise again, Washington was simply compounding its errors.

One of the basic issues so conveniently ignored is that military governments are a destabilizing force, despite the oft-repeated preference of large business corporations for a "law and order" regime. The constant intervention of the armed forces in politics and government, both overtly and covertly, has made civilian political development virtually impossible in most Latin-American countries. The military has staged innumerable coups, ousted elected Presidents, dismissed Congresses, changed and discarded Constitutions, imposed states of siege, closed universities, expelled and imprisoned political opponents, and established censorship—all this in addition to its own internal feuding.* "Law and order" is a myth in many of the regimes, where narcotics traffickers, blackmailers, and thieves operate with impunity under the protection of parapolice organizations, and anyone can hire an assassin to knock off a business rival. In Brazil, where the law of the strongest was institutionalized under the Doctrine of National Security, street crime rose in all the major cities, and entire areas, such as Rio's Nova Iguaçu suburb, have been taken over by the local Mafia.

The promise of elections by some of the region's regimes has done little to change the picture, because the military continues to exercise a veto on civilian policies. Or the local dictator, as so often happens in Bolivia, simply trades his military uniform for a three-piece suit when he stands for office. Change, to be meaningful, has to start from another premise—that it is not to the advantage of the peoples of either North or South America to encourage the military to assume civilian functions, no matter what the Rockefeller—or any other—report claims. Far from being "the essential force of constructive social change," the Latin-American military in the overwhelming majority of cases is an agent of reaction.

* Although Argentina, Ecuador, and Honduras are the most obvious cases of such internecine warfare, with frequent changes in the dictator of the moment, even the most stable regimes suffer from the same tensions. Brazil's President Ernesto Geisel, for example, narrowly escaped a coup by his Defense Minister, General Silvio Frota, in late 1977.

The Church Responds

Unlike Washington's, the Catholic Church's response to Latin-American militarism has at least begun to achieve some coherence, and many of the region's priests and bishops now recognize that threat for what it is. Brazilian Archbishop Helder Cámara's observation that "I don't understand why it is necessary to combat communism with facism" has become a generalized complaint. The fact that so many priests and bishops have personally been persecuted by the military regimes has also enriched the Church's understanding of itself as a religious and political force. When local hierarchies cite papal encyclicals against human rights violations, for example, it is not just an obligatory exercise or empty exhortation, but the result of personal experience. The papal encyclicals *Mater et Magistra, Populorum Progressio, Gaudium et Spes,* and *Pacem in Terris* form the basis of the Church's answer to the Doctrine of National Security, together with the Medellín documents and the personal witness of the Latin-American Church's martyrs. And the message is entirely clear: that the state exists to serve the people, not the other way around; that the individual's dignity and rights must be respected; and that totalitarianism, in whatever form, is inhuman. By upholding this doctrine, priests and bishops are saying, for the first time in history, that the Latin-American Church cannot coexist with military regimes—and, more, that it must actively oppose dictatorship. But they are also saying something of profound religious significance: that the Gospel is a mandate to join in the struggle for human rights, the first imperative of which is to speak out.

Today a constant flow of denunciations against military repression emanates from the Latin-American Church. Men like Chile's Cardinal Silva and São Paulo's Cardinal Arns are not afraid to tell the truth, in their own countries, in Europe, and in the United States. Nor are they in the least persuaded that, by speaking out, they hurt their country's image. The same argument was used four centuries ago by the Spanish colonists in Latin America against Bartolomé de las Casas, one of the Church's great humanitarians. They claimed that he was giving the Protestants in England and

Holland more fuel for the "Black Legend" against Catholic Spain by denouncing abuses the Indians suffered at the hands of Spanish settlers. The colonists did not want to admit—nor do their descendants today—that the root of the evil lay, not in the denunciation, but in the deeds themselves.

Because the abuse is not limited to Latin America, neither is the denunciation. Many bishops in the Latin-American Church blame the U. S. Government for the upsurge in militarism under the Doctrine of National Security, rightly pointing out that U.S.-trained and -armed police and military have been responsible for the destruction of Christian communities and for the persecution and even murder of Catholic clergy. Unlike the United States, where the human rights question has been confused by political expediency, the issue is clear in Latin America. Said a Brazilian bishop: "Were it not for the guns, for the torture, and the terror, Brazil's military regime could not survive. And were it not for this regime, foreign corporations could not continue to make enormous profits at the expense of the people. The government has all the legal instruments necessary to control these companies, and so has the United States, but the military ignores them."[93]

CHAPTER VII

U.S. CAPITALISM AND
THE MULTINATIONALS

*Money isn't everything. Love is the other 2 per cent. I think
this characterizes the United States' relationship with Latin
America.*

> Nathaniel Davis,
> U.S. ambassador to
> Guatemala, addressing the
> U. S. Chamber of Commerce
> meeting in Guatemala,
> April 20, 1971.[1]

When Nelson Rockefeller made his "goodwill" trip to Latin
America in 1969, a collective groan went up from the U.S. business community there. "Who the hell in Washington thought that
one up?" could be heard in offices and embassies from Buenos
Aires to Quito. True, Mr. Rockefeller had diplomatic and business relations with the Latin Americans dating back to the
Roosevelt years, but didn't Washington realize whom he represented? Standard Oil, that's who, and you know how the Latins
feel about U.S. oil companies!

Sure enough, there were riots in La Paz, bombings in Montevideo, and an impressive display of Argentine terrorist technology, which demolished a string of Rockefeller-owned supermarkets within seconds of one another. "I don't see why we
should have to pay the penalty for the oil industry's un-

popularity," a U.S. bank manager beefed as he gazed at a sidewalk of shattered glass, all that remained of the bank's windows. Everyone was relieved when Mr. Rockefeller returned home to write for President Nixon a series of recommendations on hemispheric policy, the most important of which urged more military and police aid for the Latin Americans.

There is something quite comforting about an industry that everybody can stick pins into, and foreign oil serves that purpose in Latin America. The belief is that if an oil representative shows up anywhere south of the border to negotiate U.S. policy, all the good guys with refrigerators and drugs to sell will suffer from the backlash. What most U.S. businessmen fail to grasp is that, as far as the Latin Americans are concerned, a delegate from, say, Sears, Roebuck or Citibank is as unwelcome as someone smelling of U.S. oil. The Rockefeller mission was just an unusually tactless demonstration of what most Latin Americans take for granted: that U.S. foreign policy is run by corporate business.

Thanks largely to United States congressional investigations of the past eight years, that assumption has been amply justified; it can now be seen that many of the men who approved counterinsurgency training for the Latin-American military, assassination courses for the police, and CIA activities against democratically elected governments were also pillars of the U.S. business community. For example, the majority of those responsible for the decisions that helped scuttle Allende's government in Chile, including Treasury Secretary John Connally, CIA Director William Colby, Kissinger, and Nixon himself, were closely tied to corporate industry.* With few exceptions, the military coups of the past fifteen

---

* John McCone, a former CIA director, was a member of ITT's board of directors and a CIA consultant when ITT offered the CIA $1 million to fund the political campaigns of friendly candidates in the 1970 Chilean presidential elections. Though the CIA did not take the money, ITT channeled at least $350,000 into the elections; other U.S. companies contributed a similar amount. McCone knew that CIA funds had been used in 1964 to support the successful presidental campaign of the Christian Democrats' Eduardo Frei. CIA documents indicate that McCone informed Harold Geneen, ITT's board chairman, of these facts. ("Covert Action in Chile, 1963–73," staff report of the Select Committee to Study Governmental Operations with Respect to Intelligence Activities, U. S. Senate [Dec. 18, 1975], p. 12.)

years in Latin America have been related in some way to U.S. business, the payoff after the coup—as in Brazil, Bolivia, and Chile—being special concessions to U.S. companies.

Although the United States never hesitated to use a big stick to protect its interests in Latin America, it was only after World War II that government and business became so interdependent as to be indistinguishable. The Dulles brothers' connection with United Fruit, though a particularly blatant example of the use of government power to benefit business interests, typifies an era in which corporate presidents and lawyers use their position in government to promote company goals. This is not to suggest that all such people were, or are, guided solely by selfish motives —a good many executives-cum-bureaucrats genuinely believe that what is good for business is good for the United States, and therefore for Latin America. The trouble with this logic is that, just as the Defense Department's counterinsurgency courses became ends in themselves, corporate growth is used to justify every kind of villainy, including military dictatorship.

With such businessmen as the Dulles brothers in charge of foreign policy, it is easy to understand why Washington was persuaded that the only solution to Latin America's social and economic problems was the infusion of foreign capital and a sustained growth of the gross national products, and why these imperatives shaped the Alliance for Progress and other attempts at "development" that became so popular in the 1960s. As things turned out, foreign investment and aid only compounded the region's problems. GNP statistics may have looked good on paper, but in most cases economic growth was achieved at the expense of the people. Between 1958 and 1970, for example, the real wages

---

During the trial of ITT executive Robert Berrellez, who was accused of perjuring his 1973 testimony on Chile during hearings before the U. S. Senate, evidence came to light that the CIA had helped Berrellez and another ITT executive, Edward J. Gerrity, Jr., prepare the testimony in which they denied any knowledge of ITT payments to Allende opponents or association with the CIA. The trial also produced evidence, as revealed by the Los Angeles *Times,* that the Pinochet government's Foreign Minister, Hernán Cubillos, had been an "important" CIA agent. (*"Falsos testimonios," United Press International* [Washington, D.C., Oct. 8, 1978] and *"Canciller chileno habría trabajado para la CIA," Associated Press* [Washington, D.C., Nov. 14, 1978].)

of Brazilian workers declined by 64.5 percent.[2] Whatever U.S. taxpayers may have believed, the Alliance for Progress was an excuse for business to gouge Uncle Sam as well as the Latin-American treasuries. Or as Senator Frank Church put it: "The present foreign aid program has been turned into a grotesque money tree, sheltering the foreign investments of our biggest corporations and furnishing aid and comfort to repressive governments all over the world."

President Kennedy chose Peter Grace, the archconservative chairman of W. R. Grace, to head a group of businessmen from twenty-five major corporations who were to evaluate the Alliance and recommend useful projects. They did their job so well that by 1964 David Rockefeller detected a "marked change in the attitude of those responsible for the Alliance" and could praise the State Department for recognizing that the Alliance "had had too much emphasis on social reform."[3] AID orders accounted for one third of all U.S. steel exports by 1969; the following year, AID-financed fertilizer exports ran to just under $100 million. According to AID officials, some $2 billion per year in U.S. exports were financed by the foreign aid program.[4]

U.S. aid buttressed corporate interests in America in a host of ways. It was a marvelous stick to hold over recalcitrant governments. Bolivia, for instance, was gradually forced to abandon the reforms begun by its 1952 revolution as the country fell increasingly into debt to the United States. By 1967 AID could boast that "the adoption of reforms . . . in the nationalized tin mines, a revised mining code favorable to private investments . . . and a new investment code and a revised and more equitable royalties schedule designed to encourage private investment is largely attributable to AID assistance."[5] AID could also take credit for undermining Bolivia's attempts to become self-sufficient in wheat and quinoa, a hardy grain grown since pre-Columbian times in the high Andes. Under the P.L. 480 (Food for Peace) program, which was a convenient way to dump surplus U.S. commodities on the world market, Bolivian wheat and quinoa were gradually replaced by cheaper U.S. flour. Of course, when the market for U.S. wheat improved, there were no more handouts, and wheat and flour now represent 43 percent of Bolivia's agricultural imports. That is exactly what the proponents of P.L. 480 had in mind. Said Senator Hubert Humphrey, one of its most enthusiastic supporters:

> I have heard . . . that people may become dependent on us for food. I know that was not supposed to be good news. To me that was good news, because before people can do anything they have got to eat. And if you are looking for a way to get people to lean on you and to be dependent on you, in terms of their co-operation with you, it seems to me that food dependence would be terrific.[6]

Local currency funds acquired from the sale of P.L. 480 commodities were earmarked for low-interest loans to U.S. firms or their subsidiaries, or for the purchase of arms by local governments ($693 million on military equipment between 1966 and 1971). These funds also proved a handy way to circumvent the limitations imposed by Congress. Because of human rights violations, Congress placed a $26 million ceiling on economic aid to Chile for fiscal year 1975 and cut off all military funding; yet the Chilean junta received the largest P.L. 480 allotment in Latin America, $65.2 million out of $80.2 million.† When Allende was

† While Congress insists on a State Department human rights report for each country requesting aid, fully 69 percent of the foreign aid the United States sends the Third World, either bilaterally or through multilateral institutions, is not reviewed by Congress. Thus in 1976 Chile received $357 million in credits, guarantees, and insurance, of which only 21 percent was debated and authorized by Congress. Between 1973 and 1978 the Pinochet junta received nearly $1.1 billion in bilateral and multilateral assistance from the United States.

As reported by Michael Moffitt and Isabel Letelier, whose spouses were killed in the DINA-sponsored Washington, D.C., bombing (See pp. 193–96), this was no accident:

> According to a U. S. Senate Report, the CIA helped Chilean economists and businessmen who were plotting to overthrow Allende to prepare a "blueprint" for the Chilean economy based upon the conservative "monetarist" theories developed by Milton Friedman and others at the University of Chicago. Following the coup, Pinochet selected the "Chicago Boys" as his top economic policy-makers. These economists, most of whom were trained at the University of Chicago, began almost immediately to dismantle the public sector of the economy in order to reverse decades of social change. To implement the Chicago "shock treatment," as *Business Week* put it, the junta had to eliminate politics

in office, P.L. 480 shipments to Chile were suspended, adding to the country's severe food shortages. The White House even turned down a government request to buy U.S. wheat for cash shortly before the 1973 coup, but within weeks of Allende's overthrow the Agriculture Department's Commodity Credit Corporation extended the junta credits of $54 million to buy wheat and corn.[7]

In addition to low-interest loans to U.S. companies, AID funds paid for 50 percent of their pre-investment surveys, which often, and particularly in mining, saved these companies large sums. Senator Jacob Javits, one of the promoters of ADELA, a giant multinational Latin-American investment company, tried to defend such subsidies on the ground that "it enables AID to get smaller enterprises which are not in the field into this area of private investment." Among the "smaller enterprises" cited by Javits as beneficiaries of the program were United Fruit, Kaiser, Allied Chemical, American Metals Climax, and Standard Fruit.[8] Once

---

from Chilean society. After four years of starving social services, holding down wages, and increasing unemployment, Central Bank President Alvaro Bardon declared that: "The success of the economic program has been fantastic. Who would have thought that you could do such a thing in Chile? We were always too political. We never wanted to make sacrifices." (Michael Moffitt and Isabel Letelier, "Private International Banks Support Chilean Junta," *Multinational Monitor* [Washington, D.C.: Winter 1978–79], p. 4.)

The junta also received $1.3 billion in loans from foreign banks between 1975 and 1978, the majority American, led by Morgan Guarantee Trust, Bankers Trust, Wells Fargo, Chemical Bank, Citibank, and Chase Manhattan. The latter is tied into Exxon—both are dominated by the Rockefeller interests—which became the first major foreign investor in Pinochet's Chile by purchasing the $130 million La Disputada copper mine nationalized under the Allende government.

Although Senator Edward Kennedy and Congressman Tom Harkin questioned private banks' support of the Pinochet government that circumvented congressional sanctions, President Carter stated: ". . . it would be inconceivable to me that any act of Congress would try to restrict the lending of money by American private banks . . . under any circumstances." Added Carter: "The American business community . . . support[s] completely a commitment of our nation to human rights." (Ibid.; "Exxon in Chile," *Noticias,* National Foreign Trade Council, Inc. [New York, Jan. 9, 1978]; "Chilean Copper Sale Disputed," *Newsweek* [June 19, 1978]; Ernesto Tironi and Jorge Barria, "La Disputada: De la ENAMI a la EXXON," *Mensaje* [Santiago, Aug. 1978]; "Chile: Exxon et al.," NACLA *Report on the Americas* [May/June 1978].)

the investment was approved, the U. S. Government provided money for the country involved to build the necessary infrastructure, such as the highway and port facilities that serve International Nickel's giant concession in Guatemala. However, no local firm or government agency could obtain a loan that might enable it to compete with a U.S. subsidiary. Thus, while Washington had no qualms about advancing the Guatemalans $13.5 million for the nickel project, for years it refused to lend them money for a road to the Atlantic Coast that would have put United Fruit's inefficient International Railways out of business. Moreover, AID construction loans could be used only to employ U.S. companies, often at a cost higher than the Latin-American governments would have paid if there had been competitive bidding. Such was the case in Costa Rica, where AID refused to honor a loan for a water supply system after a local firm underbid its U.S. competitor, and in Colombia, where the World Bank insisted that the government specify that railroad rails, which it proposed to buy through international bidding, be of a size manufactured only by U.S. companies.

All AID loans were tied to U.S. products and, by 1969, 99 percent of AID-financed goods and services were being bought in the United States, often at prices 30 to 40 percent higher than the international rate.[9] What this cost the U.S. and Latin-American taxpayers may be judged by the inflated prices U.S. drug companies charged AID under a program called Commercial Import Loans, or dollar loans made by AID to foreign governments, which in turn allocated them among U.S. subsidiaries to import products and equipment from the parent company. According to 1970 hearings by the Senate Subcommittee on Small Business, the drug subsidiaries took advantage of AID loopholes to inflate prices at the expense of U.S. tax money, the foreign consumer, and the foreign country's balance of payments. Comparing the prices AID was paying with those quoted on the European market, the subcommittee found that AID payments ranged from 3 to 113 times the European prices for equivalent products. AID's explanation was that "American suppliers are insulated from foreign competition," but as Senator Gaylord Nelson pointed out, that was no consolation to the poor Latin-American consumer, who "must pay 20 to 30 times as much as he would have to pay if [the drug] was coming from another country."[10] AID later collected $1 million in refunds for overpricing and still had claims outstanding for some $2 million. The largest claims were against Wyeth ($218,573), Eli Lilly ($238,281), Abbott Laboratories ($371,903), Merck, Sharp & Dohme ($394,067), Roussel Corporation ($699,860), and Gedion-Richter Pharmaceuticals ($802,617).[11]

AID also forced Latin-American governments to sign investment-guarantee agreements that protected U.S. companies against losses from inconvertibility (inability to convert local currency into dollars for remittance), expropriation, war, revolution, and insurrection, thereby involving the U. S. Government in what initially were disputes between U.S. companies and Latin-American governments. Why the U. S. Government, or taxpayer, should be asked to bail out companies whose sharp practices were an open invitation to nationalization apparently never entered the discussion, nor did U.S. support of these companies' inflated claims for compensation. On the contrary, AID and the State Department threatened reprisals if the Latin-American governments did not sign the investment guarantees. Legislation was enacted requiring a cutoff date for aid if guarantees were not accepted, and when that did not work, the State Department began issuing guarantees without the Latin-American governments' consent. When Mexico steadfastly refused to sign, a group of seventeen companies led by Ford Motors told the State Department to step up the pressure, but Mexico, having wisely phased itself out of the Alliance for Progress, was not in the position of Bolivia or Brazil and could resist such pressure.[12]

None of the high-sounding goals of the Alliance for Progress were achieved, including income redistribution or tax reform—and not just because the local elites opposed such reforms. Had the tax loopholes been closed and the labor force been given a greater share of national wealth, foreign companies could not possibly have developed lucrative new markets in Latin America. During the Alliance years, according to U. S. Department of Commerce statistics, three dollars went back to the United States for every dollar invested. Foreign subsidiaries compensated for the smallness of the consumer market—in Brazil, for example, it was only a fourth of the 110 million population—with enormous markups that gave these companies twice the margin of profit they earned in the United States.[13] When the Alliance was finally buried at the end of the 1960s, about the only thing the Latin-American countries had to show for it was an enormous foreign debt—$19.3 billion, compared to $8.8 billion in 1961, when the program was launched.

Not only did the Latin-American people fail to benefit from the generosity of the U.S. taxpayer; AID—and CIA—money was also used to help destroy one of the few established outlets of popular opinion, the free trade unions. Not content with funneling Alliance funds into corporate industry, Peter Grace promoted the American Institute for Free Labor Development (AIFLD), a Trojan horse for the multinationals sponsored by the AFL-CIO. Created in 1962 with the financial support of AID, the State Department, W. R. Grace, ITT, Exxon, Shell, Kennecott, Anaconda, American Smelting and Refining, IBM, Koppers, Gillette, and 85 other large corporations with interests in Latin America, the AIFLD was organized, ostensibly, to combat the threat of Castroite influence in Latin-American labor unions; in reality it was a way for U.S. companies, working in cahoots with repressive governments, to replace independent unions with company ones. Explained Peter Grace, AIFLD's board chairman, the Institute "teaches workers to increase their company's business."

The AIFLD drew 92 percent of its annual $6 million budget from AID and the State Department and was also reported to have received sizable sums from the CIA.‡ This money was used to train 300,000 union members at the AIFLD's Front Royal school in Virginia, where courses were, and are, heavily spiked with pro–United States, anti-communist propaganda. AIFLD money was also used to support the military coups in Guatemala, Brazil, and Chile, and the terrorism and racial violence directed against the leftist government of Cheddi Jagan in Guyana.[14] AIFLD Executive Director William C. Doherty, Jr., who has been

‡ Drew Pearson in his February 24, 1967, column in the Washington *Post* claimed that the CIA was pumping $100 million a year into U.S. labor organizations, including the AIFLD. And Senator J. William Fulbright told labor columnist Victor Riesel in August 1966, "I have had suggestions that they [the CIA] had taken a very strong part in labor union organization in the Dominican Republic."

identified as a "CIA career agent,"[15] publicly boasted that AIFLD graduates "were so active [in the Brazilian coup] that they became intimately involved in some of the clandestine operations of the revolution before it took place."[16] When U. S. Marines invaded the Dominican Republic, the AIFLD union was the only one to welcome them. Although the governments of Brazil, Chile, and the Dominican Republic arrested and murdered workers, and destroyed their unions and bargaining power, the AIFLD could not praise them enough, even going so far as to become their apologists at international labor gatherings. The AIFLD's National Workers' Confederation was the chief labor spokesman for Chile's junta.

Working through tame unions, the AIFLD collected detailed information about Latin-American labor leaders, the pretext being that such surveys were necessary for AID-financed workers' housing projects. Though precious few houses were built, and most that were proved too expensive for the average worker, the AIFLD was able to obtain a personal and political history of every union member, with addresses and photographs. Given the AIFLD's close CIA connection and the CIA's documented role in the Chilean, Uruguayan, and Brazilian coups, among others, it is all too probable that this information was passed on to the military regimes and their secret police.

The AIFLD also proved adept at smearing as communist such democratic labor movements as the Christian Democrats' Latin American Federation, in splitting the Dominican Republic's labor movement, and in providing such backers as United Brands and Standard Fruit with docile unions for their Honduran banana plantations. As AIFLD Director Doherty explained, "We welcome [the] co-operation [of management] not only financially but in terms of establishing our policies. . . . The co-operation between ourselves and the business community is getting warmer day by day."[17] Thanks to such "good" business-labor relations, nineteenth-century sweatshops, complete with child labor, were reintroduced in the textile mills of Brazil,[18] and hundreds of workers languished in the prisons of Chile. Still, it was in character—the AFL's foreign department got its start by supporting Nazi collaborators in the postwar unions of France.[19] It was as a result of that work that the CIA agreed to finance its activities, according to Thomas Braden, director of the CIA's European operations from 1950 to 1954.[20]

Trickle-up

As the AIFLD's career in Latin America shows, the political costs of foreign aid and investment may be higher than the economic benefits they bring. Indeed, many of the arguments for corporate investment, while reasonable enough in theory, do not apply in a region like Latin America, where governments have neither the will nor the means to control or guide a transnational empire of companies that comprises the world's third-largest economy after the United States and the Soviet Union. If the U. S. Internal Revenue Service, which employs some of the world's best technicians, is hard put to control these companies, what can be expected of poorly educated, grossly underpaid Latin-American bureaucrats without access to typewriters, much less computers? Thus some Latin Americans who a few years ago were enthusiastic promoters of capitalist development now question the arguments of big business. Said Argentine economist Raul Prebish, one of the fathers of the Alliance for Progress: "What is good for the consumer society is not necessarily good for development."

A key argument of these critics is that, whereas unemployment is among the most serious problems facing Latin America, foreign investment creates very few jobs. A company can hardly be blamed for wanting to reduce labor costs by increasing automation, yet automation is the last thing needed by a continent with 50 percent unemployment and underemployment.[21] Petrochemical plants may reduce a country's imports and add a few points to the GNP, but they do not promote human development. On the contrary, capital-intensive investments have checked the post–World War II expansion of the labor base in Latin America. While industry's share of Latin America's GNP has grown from 11 to 23 percent during the past five decades, it employs exactly the same percentage of workers today that it did in 1925, a mere 14 percent of the labor force. In several countries, among them Chile and Peru, the percentage has actually declined. Some of this can be attributed to the population explosion, but the essential issue is the model of development: Do you make refrigerators and air conditioners or shirts and shoes? Do you build sophisticated hospitals or rural clinics, universities or primary schools? By choosing to encourage foreign investment in such technologically sophisticated industries as television sets or computers, a Latin-American country may actually be postponing any hope of real development.

Because they identify with the Americans and Europeans, Latin America's elites have chosen the industrialized world's model of development—for example, it is a matter of intense national pride with these people that their country has a steel industry, though there may be no economic or social justification for the expensive toy. The argument for promoting this model of development is the trickle-down theory—that as countries become richer, trade union organizations, rising food prices, and shortages of certain types of labor begin to improve the conditions of some of the poorest classes—small farmers, unskilled and semiskilled industrial workers, and so on. Such was the case in nineteenth-century England and in Japan. Of course, wealth takes a long time to trickle down—even in Japan it took at least a century—and it is doubtful that the Latin-American masses will wait that long. Indeed, it may never happen at all if, as in the Latin-American military regimes, trade unions are banned or severely limited, food prices and agricultural production are controlled by the rich themselves, and there is no possibility of political opposition or civic development. Certainly there has been very little trickle-down since World War I, when Latin America began to industrialize. The richest man in Latin America earns over $550,000 a week; the poorest, $90 a year; and the gap is still widening. Latin America's "burgeoning" middle class still accounts for only 20 percent of the population[22] and, given the present growth of poverty, there is little likelihood that it will go higher in this century. Moreover, the price of foreign investment, quite apart from the issue of jobs, is now so high in political and economic terms that it can be seriously challenged on that ground alone.

The licking AID took from U.S. drug companies is a minor bit of chicanery compared to what goes on in Latin America itself. Although investigations thus far have barely stirred the ant hill, they suggest that, contrary to the multinationals' claims, foreign investors have bilked the Latin Americans of hundreds of millions of dollars. In 1968 the Colombian Government asked the Greek economist Constantine Vaitsos to make a study of its situation. The Colombians could not understand why foreign companies were so eager to invest, since their declared profits were a mere 6.7 percent, local firms were showing higher returns, and the interest rate in financial markets was running between 16 and 20 percent. It looked fishy, the Colombian Government decided, and so it put Vaitsos and a team of researchers to work in the Customs Office.

One of the first things Vaitsos discovered was the extraordinary number of restrictive clauses, in contracts between the foreign companies and the government, that obliged local subsidiaries to buy all their raw materials and intermediary products from the parent company. Other similar clauses prevented a subsidiary from exporting to or purchasing machinery from anyone but its parent. There lay the key to the mystery: a practice known as "transfer pricing." To avoid showing profits in a country where taxes or inflation are high, or to shift money for other reasons from one affiliate to another, a company can manipulate the costs of machinery, technology, or raw materials it sells to itself or among its various subsidiaries. A Latin-American company that assembles washing machines may buy electric motors from its parent company at an inflated price, thus for tax reasons increasing the profits of the parent and reducing those of the subsidiary. Or, if the tax situation is reversed, the subsidiary can overcharge the parent for raw materials or the goods it produces.

Vaitsos studied the transfer prices of four major industries: electronics, pharmaceuticals, chemicals, and rubber. To find out what the goods were, where they came from, where they were going, what the price was, and whether there was any price variation because of quality or specification, his team spent eleven months in the Customs Office tabulating invoices on more than fifteen hundred products. What they were interested in was the "FOB price," which is unaffected by the product's destination. To determine what the FOB price should have been, Vaitsos set up dummy companies and solicited quotations from all over the world. Colombian commercial attachés also interviewed suppliers in the exporting countries.[23] When Vaitsos compared world prices with those the Colombian subsidiaries were paying, the differences were astounding. In electronics the transfer price was 16 to 60 percent above the FOB price; in chemicals, 25 percent; in rubber, 40 percent; in pharmaceuticals, 155 percent. For some individual products the price difference was even greater: a record-changer spindle worth $.30 was being sold by a Dutch electronics subsidiary in Colombia for $2.10. One paper manufacturer wanted to import a used machine for $1.2 million when the price for a new one was $800,000. The drug metronidazole was overpriced by 3,390 percent. Gouging in the pharmaceutical industry alone was costing Colombia $20 million in lost foreign exchange and $10 million in tax revenues.

As a result of Vaitsos' revelations, the Colombian Government established a royalties committee to review contracts between subsidiaries and parent companies. It negotiated royalty payments that were 40 percent less than the original demands, saving Colombia $8 million, and reduced by 90 percent the tie-in clauses that required subsidiaries to buy only from parent companies. Although hundreds of contracts were reviewed, not a single company withdrew from Colombia.

A similar study carried out by economists at the University of Lund, Sweden, showed that 64 U.S. mining companies working in Peru had understated their profits between 1967 and 1969. While these companies reported profits of $60 million to the Peruvian Government, the same operations declared profits of $102 million to the U. S. Government. A Peruvian congressional investigation of the United States–controlled Southern Peru Copper Corporation found that during 1960 and 1965 the company had reported net profits of $69 million to the Peruvian Government but $135 million to the U. S. Securities and Exchange Commission.[24]

Another lucrative trick of overpricing is to introduce a third country like the Bahamas, Curaçao, or Panama that maintains a tax-free port. This is known as the "triangular trade," named after the eighteenth-century trade in cotton, rum, and slaves among Africa, the Caribbean, and New England. As Vaitsos described the trade in pharmaceuticals:

. . . 17 foreign-owned firms (which constitute 40 to 50 per cent of the national pharmaceutical industry in Colombia) receive intermediate goods from abroad at FOB prices 155 per cent higher than standard market prices in Europe or the United States. This is done by shipping the goods to Panama, a virtual tax haven, then raising the price substantially before sending the products on to Colombia. Thus the United States or European supplier shows low profits and pays low taxes, while the high profits are realized in lenient Panama. The Colombian purchaser uses the high cost of inputs to keep profits and taxes low.[25]

Drugs

Even when a government is aware of such trickery, it may be hard put to force foreign companies to obey the law. That was Mexico's experience with the foreign companies that control 85 percent of the country's drug industry. According to a United Nations survey, markups through transfer pricing averaged 200 to 1,300 percent, costing Mexico an estimated $41 million a year.[26] Hoffman LaRoche, the world's largest drug company, was selling its tranquilizers, Librium and Valium, in Mexico and other countries at price inflations of 425 to 1,000 percent.[27] Despite fines, official threats, and considerable bad publicity, the industry stubbornly refused to observe government price controls. After the 1976 peso devaluation, drug prices jumped 32 percent, although the government had authorized only a 10 percent increase. Some drugs soared by as much as 200 percent. The government fined twenty laboratories for these unauthorized rises, including Eli Lilly, Pfizer, Roussel, Gedion-Richter, Syntex, Upjohn, Ayerst ICI, and Richardson-Merrell. To no avail: two months later, prices were again climbing, some by as much as 1,000 percent. Many of the drugs, such as Sidney Ross's aspirin, which is sold as Mejoral, were simply repackaged with a higher price tag. The government again fined twenty-one laboratories, including Pfizer, Gedion-Richter, and other repeaters, along with the newcomers Abbott, Armstrong, and Parke-Davis.* But prices continued to climb. Another thirty-five companies were fined, without the slightest effect on the price spiral.[28] Since developing countries

* Three of the offenders—Eli Lilly, Abbott, and Gedion-Richter—were also involved in the AID scandal.

spend 50 to 60 percent of their health budgets on drugs (compared to 15 to 20 percent in the industrialized nations), this sort of exploitation is devastating.

Pharmaceuticals are big business in Latin America, with sales of about $1.5 billion per year and growing fast, thanks in part to the unscrupulousness of companies that overcharge, oversell, and, worst of all, dump unsafe drugs on unsuspecting publics. Because of the enormous variety of drugs on the market (fifteen thousand brand names in Colombia with a population of 25 million compared to nine thousand brand names in Britain with 56 million people), the Latin-American consumer is totally at the mercy of the companies. Unable to afford a doctor and frequently unable to read or write, he depends on the local druggist to recommend medicine, although the druggist himself may be semiliterate and is in any case dependent on the drug companies' literature—when the companies bother to supply it.† (Few Latin-American countries require a prescription for the purchase of any drugs except narcotics, so most Latin Americans doctor themselves.) One result of drug proliferation is that Latin Americans spend more for medicine than their ailments require. A poor patient suffering from tuberculosis, for instance, can be treated cheaply with isoniazid or thiacetazone, but if the druggist or the doctor recommends streptomycin, he will pay seventeen times as much. He may buy as much as he can afford, only to be forced to interrupt the treatment before it is completed.

But undoubtedly the worst aspect of this free-for-all is the sale of drugs banned or severely controlled in the United States and Europe. (The parents of 146 Brazilian infants born with defects, whose mothers had taken thalidomide, initiated judicial action against three pharmaceutical companies in October 1976.[29]) Altogether, four hundred drugs on sale in Brazil have been condemned as dangerous by the Medical Association of Rio de Janeiro, and a good many of them are sold by the foreign com-

† In one study of medicines marketed in Central America and the Dominican Republic, it was found that a number of drugs, including the highly dangerous dipyrone, were sold without any instructions. (Octavio Paredes López, "Consideraciones sobre la actividad de las empresas farmacéuticas en México," Revista del Banco Nacional de Comercio Exterior, Vol. 27, No. 8 [Mexico: August 1977], p. 940.)

panies that control 80 percent of the country's pharmaceutical business. They range from long-acting sulfonamides to synthetic male sex hormones and birth-control pills, and they are sold throughout Latin America, not just in Brazil. Among them is an antique drug called cinchophen, introduced in 1902 as a treatment for gout, but long since abandoned in the United States and Europe because it can cause fatal hepatitis. It is still marketed by Abbott under the brand name Cincofeno to "stimulate the elimination of uric acid."[30] A similarly dangerous drug, chloramphenicol, known for more than twenty years to cause the fatal blood disease aplastic anemia, is marketed by Dow Chemical, USV-Grossman, and Parke-Davis. According to studies by a group of Colombian doctors in Bogotá and Cali, the introduction of chloramphenicol led to "aplastic anemia becoming a dreadfully common disease" in Colombia.[31] Although Parke-Davis has paid over $1 million in damages in the United States for failing to warn users that the antibiotic Chloromycetin can produce undesirable side effects, it continues to promote this drug in several developing countries with no warning whatsoever of the six circumstances under which the drug should not be used. According to a United Nations study, "the company could hardly claim to be unaware of the possible adverse reactions, yet it took advantage of the developing countries' lack of controls to sell its product (for which no prescription is required in many countries) as if it were wholly safe."[32]

One of the most popular drugs sold in Latin America is dipyrone, a pain-killer that can also kill the user. Both the U. S. Government and the American Medical Association restrict its use "as the last resort to reduce fever when safer measures have failed" because it can cause fatal blood diseases, including a severe depression of the bone marrow called agranulocytosis. Sterling insists that it markets the drug under the same conditions as in the United States, by prescription only.[33] Yet this drug is sold everywhere in Latin America as a harmless pain-killer and its advertising leads the customer to believe that it is safe for small children. In Colombia, where it is called Conmel, it ranks twentieth on a list of best-selling drugs. It is used for everything from headaches and toothaches to the common cold and can be purchased in any Colombian drugstore without a prescription.[34]

The foreign drug industry's performance in Latin America also destroys the claim made by multinationals that foreign investment funnels technology to the less-developed countries. In fact, these companies keep a stranglehold on patents, often using them to prevent the development of local technology that would compete with products they might decide to sell in Latin America at a future date. Forty-five percent of the patents registered in Argentina between 1957 and 1967 were for products neither manufactured in nor imported to Argentina, and of these, 315 were held by chemical and drug companies.[35] In Colombia the Royalties Committee canceled a number of contracts on the ground that the technology was out of date or "absolutely unnecessary," since it was freely available in the country.[36] Raul Prebish, former head of the United Nations' Economic Commission of Latin America, charged that the foreign companies are selling as patented knowledge in Latin America information that is in the public domain at home.‡[37]

When a company cannot control a market through patents, there is always the possibility of gaining a monopoly over raw materials, as Brazilian diabetics learned to their cost in 1975, when there was a sudden shortage of insulin. The only company making insulin in Brazil was Eli Lilly, which imported insulin crystals from its Argentine plant, where the crystals were manufactured from the pancreas of cattle and hogs. The crisis moved Brazilians to ask why their country, with one of the world's largest cattle herds, was not making its own crystals, particularly since Brazil had had the know-how since 1945. Eli Lilly claimed it was uneconomical to manufacture the product in Brazil until it was revealed that Farbwerke Hoechst, the German pharmaceutical and chemical firm, was profitably buying 400 tons of pancreas a year from Brazil.[38]

The insulin scandal also pointed up the drug industry's heavy dependence on imports—75 percent of the raw materials used in the Brazilian pharmaceutical industry are imported, and 90 percent in Central America's foreign-controlled drug industry. Con-

‡ According to a Cornell University study, 79 percent of U.S. subsidiaries in Mexico and 59 percent in Puerto Rico use secondhand machinery. Another study showed that the average age of equipment imported by the foreign companies in Latin America ranged from two to fifteen years.

trary to the companies' claims that they encourage exports, the drug industry, at least, imports more than it exports. In Mexico, drug imports between 1970 and 1975 were three times exports. Yet according to the Mexican Secretariat of Industry and Commerce and the Mexican Institute of Foreign Trade, over one hundred chemical imports could be produced locally. Other, more conservative studies estimated that at least twenty-nine raw materials could be manufactured in Mexico.[39] As to the argument that the drug industry creates jobs, the technology transferred is so labor-saving that labor accounts for less than 4 percent of total costs.[40]

As with other manufacturing in Latin America, foreign companies have come to dominate the drug and chemical industries in large part by acquiring local firms. Of 294 foreign subsidiaries in Mexico's chemical, food, textile, and glass industries, for example, nearly half were obtained by buying out local capital, and the practice is becoming ever more common—in 1949, 10 percent of "new investments" in Mexico were acquisitions; in 1972, 75 percent![41] The overall picture is much the same. Of the 717 manufacturing subsidiaries established in Latin America by the United States' top corporate industries between 1958 and 1967, 45 percent were set up by buying local firms; 85 percent of the money to buy these operations, or to establish new ones, came from the Latin Americans themselves. Ironically, the poorer the region, the more foreign companies draw on its resources. Thus fewer dollars are exported by U.S. companies to Latin America than to Europe or Canada.[42] Moreover, there is strong statistical evidence to suggest that corporate industry is financing expansion in the United States from profits in the poorer countries. Between 1965 and 1968, U.S. manufacturing subsidiaries in Latin America sent 52 percent of their net profits back to the United States; mining and petroleum subsidiaries sent 79 percent. And in both cases most of the original investment came from Latin-American sources. So much for the argument that foreign investment injects new capital into the Latin-American economies. Forty percent of the continent's manufactured exports are now controlled by U.S. companies, and half of Latin America's exports and one third of its imports are traded between U.S. subsidiaries and parent companies.[43]

Bribes

For some of these companies no deceit is too mean to increase profits, whether it be deliberately shortening the life of light bulbs, as a cartel of General Electric, Osram, Tokyo Electric, and Philips was alleged to have done,[44] or bribes to local officials. Among the long list of prominent U.S. corporations that have resorted to bribery or "questionable payments" in Latin America are Exxon, Philip Morris, Lockheed, Boeing, Gulf Oil, General Telephone & Electronics, and, of course, United Brands.[45] U.S. corporations are not the only offenders: Atomic Energy of Canada was called on the carpet by the country's auditor general for $2.4 million in "questionable payments" to Argentine Air Force officials,[46] France's Renault has been fined by the Colombian Government for tax evasion, and Colombian customs authorities have accused West Germany's Siemens of trafficking in contraband.[47] The competition's resort to bribery is a highly dubious justification for such practice, particularly when there is evidence that honesty can be its own reward. Northrop discovered that to be so in Colombia when it steadfastly refused to match the bribes offered by the French and British competition for a multimillion-dollar government contract for airport navigational aids. The story of the promised bribes leaked out, causing a major scandal in the Colombian Congress and forcing the government to drop its negotiations with the Europeans.

Contrary to its pose as a benevolent big brother, the government in Washington has abetted U.S. companies in cheating the Latin Americans whenever that suited its interests. A case in point is the Allende Government's nationalization of the U.S. copper companies, one of the factors behind the Nixon administration's decision to bankrupt Chile. The principal issue in the 1971 nationalization, which was approved unanimously by all the political parties in the Chilean Congress, was compensation, the Allende Government claiming that Anaconda and Kennecott, the biggest companies, had made $744 million in excess profits. According to independent surveys, between 1915 and 1968 the two giants earned in Chile $2 billion in net profits and depreciation on an initial investment of $3.5 million. Anaconda averaged 21.5 percent

contain debris and the leavings of freely running animals. The stench of Cartavio's public toilets (the only ones for many residents) is quite unbelievable."[54] Nor was there any evidence on the plantations of Grace's oft-repeated belief in "consensus" between labor and management. When three thousand Peruvian workers struck in 1960, the company called in the police, who killed three workers and injured sixteen.[55]

Of course, there is more than one way to bring a Latin-American country to heel. In contrast to its open hostility to the Allende government in Chile, the Nixon administration used a more sophisticated carrot-and-stick approach to force Peru's nationalistic generals to agree to compensation and to roll back some of their earlier social and economic reforms. This was accomplished, not through the application of sugar quota penalties or the equally onerous Hickenlooper Amendment, which cuts off aid to any country that nationalizes U.S. property, but through the good offices of the foreign banks and the International Monetary Fund (IMF), which these days increasingly call the shots in Latin America.

Like many Latin-American countries, including Mexico and Brazil, the Peruvian regime borrowed heavily abroad to finance internal development. Foreign commercial banks were happy to accommodate the Peruvians because such loans are extremely profitable. Citibank's Citicorp, for example, earned 20 percent of its worldwide profits in 1976 in South America, compared to 28 percent in the United States and 22 percent in Europe, though only 6 percent of the company's assets were invested in Latin America. Led by Citibank, Chase Manhattan, and the Bank of America, U.S. banks have dramatically increased their Latin-American operations in the past decade, establishing 460 branches and a portfolio of investments that range from sugar to giant mining ventures. In contrast to the Alliance for Progress era, when they held less than a third of U.S. loans to Latin America and the bulk of the money came from government agencies, the private banks now provide approximately 55 percent. However, the banks' willingness to lend the money has proved a double-edged sword. Not only has Latin America run up an appalling $90 billion foreign debt, the highest in the developing world, but U.S. banks, which account for half this debt, are also in a tricky position—there is always the possibility that some of these countries may default or simply declare a moratorium on their debts. To protect themselves, therefore, the banks and their chief watchdog, the IMF, are playing an increasingly important role in local political and economic decisions. As matters now stand, the banks can often exert more influence than the U. S. Government on the lives of the Latin-American people.

In Peru's case, the government had no choice but to accept the banks' ultimatum in order to obtain refinancing of $400 million in loans in 1976. With a $5 billion foreign debt, the country is barely able to keep afloat and must spend nearly half its revenue from exports to service the debt. Among the conditions set down by the banks, most of which are American, were compensation to the U.S.-owned Marcona Mining Company, nationalized in 1975; periodic reviews of Peru's economic performance, with a threat to cut off money if the banks were not satisfied; and strict adherence to an austerity program specified by the IMF. While the IMF has never been noted for its understanding of political problems in Latin America, the demands it made on the Peruvians were so stringent that, to meet them, the relatively moderate regime would have had to establish a dictatorship at least as harsh as the Pinochet government in Chile. They included a 13 percent devaluation, a wage freeze, whopping rises in public utility rates, and a 60 percent increase in the price of gasoline. Caught between the IMF's intransigence and bankruptcy, the government tried to put through the price hikes in mid-1977, only to set off the worst national strike in sixty years. The military reacted by massacring students in the southern sierra region of Huancayo and arresting seven hundred labor leaders in Lima alone.[56] Industries were authorized to dismiss three thousand striking workers. Not all the generals approved of these tactics, however, and, after some cosmetic changes in price and wage policy, calm was temporarily restored. The government is still trying to live up to the IMF's demands without provoking a civil war, but the generals are now thoroughly fed up with an impossible balancing act. One unforeseen result of the economic squeeze exerted on the country was the military's announcement that it would turn the government and the financial mess over to the civilians by 1980—that is, if a Peruvian Pinochet did not emerge before then to ram through the IMF's demands.

There is no doubt that the bankers feel their money is safer with tough military governments that have no qualms about public opinion or human rights. "As long as Mario Simonsen is Finance Minister, Brazil will pay its foreign creditors before everything else, including social welfare," said an executive of a large U.S. investment banking firm.[57] "We're not interested in the politics of military governments but in how they run the economy," said a Citibank manager, who, like most of his fellows, listed the dictatorships in Brazil, Chile, Argentina, and Bolivia as examples of good government.[58]

Of course, Peru's dilemma was not entirely of the banks' making—nobody forced the generals to borrow so heavily. Like their counterparts in Brazil and Argentina, the Peruvian military has expensive tastes, and one of the reasons for the enormous debt was uncontrolled military spending (some $700 million in arms purchases were contracted in 1976, or approximately one third of all Peruvian imports that year). So while the banks could be said to have grown fat on the government's spendthrift ways, the Peruvians themselves were responsible for the economic mess. The same could be said of the sins of foreign investors. Were it not for the venality, selfishness, and short-sightedness of the Latin Americans who rule these countries, it would be more difficult, though probably not impossible, for foreign firms to get away with so much chicanery. But when a company can buy both dictator and democrat, as United Brands bought Honduras' General Oswaldo López Arellano and Costa Rica's President José Figueres,† Latin America's elites are in no position to cast the first stone.

"Consumer Democracy"

The Council of the Americas, spokesman for U.S. corporate interests in Latin America, claims that "consumer democracy" can and

---

† Shortly before assuming the presidency in 1970, Figueres received several lucrative contracts to produce banana sacks for United Brands in his Costa Rican factories. Once President, Figueres returned the favor by authorizing a number of generous concessions and benefits to United Brands. ("United Fruit Is Not Chiquita," *North American Congress on Latin America* [New York: October 1971], p. 10.)

should replace political democracy. In sharp opposition, the Catholic Church rejects that model of development as a mask for privilege: so few Latin Americans can afford more than one pair of shoes a year—much less refrigerators, cars, television sets, and the other enticements of an affluent society—that talk of consumer democracy is no more than mockery. It could hardly be otherwise when the formula for Latin America's development is based on a wage freeze and an unbridled price policy that often distorts the cost of even locally produced goods, as in the case of Brazilian-made shoes, which sell for four times as much at home as they do in England. By itself, the free play of prices should not be an obstacle to the development of a large consumers' market, but when other mechanisms of a free market, such as competition, are eliminated and high tariffs are imposed to protect monopolies, when fiscal and tax policy favors the concentration of wealth in the hands of the few, there is little possibility of a substantial or sustained growth of consumption. Indeed, recent Department of Commerce statistics indicate that U.S. investment in the traditional manufacturing sectors is approaching saturation in Latin America, a finding confirmed by statistics on the underutilization of plant capacity, which ranges as high as 60 percent in some countries. The Latin-American market for nonessential products like TV sets is shallow, and once the initial demand is satisfied the assembly plant faces limited growth. It can attempt to export its televisions sets, but that is not easy when the market for such products is in the industrialized countries, where the competition in technology-intensive goods is toughest. So in the end U.S. manufacturing subsidiaries must depend primarily on the local market and, to compensate for small volume, must charge higher prices.‡

This vicious circle started with the wage freeze of the early

‡ A number of foreign subsidiaries in Latin America produce components for sophisticated equipment marketed in the industrialized world, such as computer memory spools that are manually wound. But the profits from the sale of the finished product remain in the country of the parent company through "transfer pricing" (see pp. 215–16). Once the components are assembled by the parent company, the product is re-exported to Latin America at a markup, even though many of the parts may have been made there. The classic example of this triangular trade is the Brazil nut, which is sent in its natural state to England to be processed and re-exported to Brazil in cans.

1960s. The argument that wages must be temporarily sacrificed to a country's greater need to replace imports with locally manufactured products, or to expand exports in order to earn more foreign exchange, makes no sense in terms of either consumer growth or social development when, as in Latin America, the income from these industries merely increases the power and wealth of the privileged few who never lacked money for television sets and automobiles. Whatever the technocrats' strategy, it is difficult to justify in human terms the progressive conversion of Brazilian farmland formerly planted in black beans, the staple of the Brazilian diet, into cattle ranches for meat exports, when a significant portion of the foreign exchange earned from this new trade goes to finance Brazil's annual $2 billion defense budget. It must be acknowledged, however, that the guns and tanks bought with the hunger of the Brazilian people serve effectively to silence any protest against their deepening impoverishment. That is what Brazil's bishops had in mind when they said they were no longer willing to accept a situation "in which the people receive only the crumbs from the table of the rich." As theologian José Comblin points out, "There can be a great increase in production at all levels and that production can improve the State's economic potential and enable it to compete with the other power centers of the world. It can build a complex of awesome weaponry and an economic power capable of penetrating the international markets. But it will never better the lives of the workers."

The only people who benefit, Comblin says, are the "engineers, technicians, economists, and producers of strategic products or competitive goods for the international market," a charge supported by income statistics: executives earn more in Brazil than in any other country, including the United States. (The difference in Brazil between minimum wages and top executive salaries is five hundred to one; in the United States it is sixty to one.) Comblin charges that "the economy is not supposed to produce for the people, but for foreign markets, for the military, and for a few privileged technocrats. This marginalization means that the masses do not work for themselves, or have any hope of advancing themselves by their work. The elites are absorbed in quantitative goals, and they have no time to worry about the masses, who exist merely to serve the state. Thus there are two categories of citizens: those who share in the state's power, and to them goes every reward; and those who do not, and they do not exist. They never appear in society. In the statistics, they are negative numbers.

"Matching this economic and social marginalization is a political marginalization. Political direction is in the hands of the military, which subordinates every facet of the nation's life to military discipline, depoliticizing the country, and destroying all associations through which its citizens could strengthen their demands and rights. Economic direction is in the hands of pseudoscientific economists, usually bright young men recently graduated with the highest honors from U.S. universities. Most have no experience of getting along with people—they are interested only in statistics and graphs."[59]

They are the people, says Comblin, who have sold out to the multinationals. Or, as Father Virgilio Rosa Netto, director of the Brazilian Church's National Pastoral Institute, put it, "The amazing thing is that so many of these technocrats have turned their backs on their own earlier education as Christians to adopt the religion of the global corporations." Norman Saramelli, a member of the U. S. National Catholic Coalition for Responsible Investment, which counsels U.S. religious orders on their investments, says that the multinationals "are functioning today in the same way the missionaries functioned in the nineteenth century. Just as the Christian missionaries went out bringing the gospel of salvation to the heathen, our corporate missionaries are going out preaching the gospel of secular salvation, the gospel of consumer lifestyle, and they're doing it to a far more effective degree than the missionaries of the nineteenth century." The trouble with this new gospel, said Saramelli, is that social responsibility is a "secondary priority" with the corporations, which by their nature are "a conservative force" in developing countries because of their desire for stability. "But you have to worry about stability because somebody's stability is somebody else's repression. It always works out like that.

"Not that we can expect the corporation not to act like a corporation, any more than we can ask a camel to fly across the Atlantic. We should not expect these companies to be philanthropic institutions. That's not their purpose." On the other hand, religious institutions have a right and a duty to "insist on corporate responsibility and even to go beyond that to see the real contradictions in the industrial, capitalistic system."[60]

Although the Medellín documents touched on this subject, most Latin-American churchmen would probably agree with Saramelli that the Church has seldom dealt with the hard facts of economics. "Even our theologians talk about a political theology," he said, "but I have yet to hear anybody talk about an economic theology. I think we're going to have to develop one." While few Latin-American bishops would go that far, the mainstream in the Church has begun to identify economic and political priorities. During a series of meetings of theologians and bishops in Colombia in 1977, held to prepare for a follow-up of the Medellín conference, one of the issues that emerged was the need to clarify responsibility for the region's economic problems and to make concrete recommendations for their solution—as, for example, demanding tough new tax laws to encourage a redistribution of income. Both CELAM and CLAR, the service organizations of the Latin-American bishops and religious, agree that Latin America should stop passing the buck: if foreign investors are able to get away with overpricing, bribery, and other abuses, it is because they are abetted by Latin Americans.

This is not to suggest that foreign investors are to be let off the hook, since a good many churchmen agree with Brazil's Archbishop Helder Cámara that "often the big companies have sucked from the poor more than they have given, and introduced automation into our unemployed areas, and stunted our local industries." But more and more, the Church avoids the sweeping denunciations of the past to attack specific abuses, as in the Dominican Republic, where the Church has taken on Gulf+Western and Rosario Resources.*

The latter exploits the largest gold mine in the Western Hemisphere at Pueblo Viejo, a Dominican mine controlled jointly by Rosario, Simplot Industries, and the Dominican Government. Since the concession was approved in 1972, Rosario has invested approximately $40 million in the mine, although 70 percent of the capital was raised through Dominican private and state banks.

* Headquartered in New York City, Rosario Resources has mining interests in several countries, including Nicaragua.

Among the benefits granted Rosario were exclusive access to Pueblo Viejo for seventy-five years and the right to market gold, previously the sole prerogative of the country's Central Bank.[61]

Before Rosario came on the scene, the area around Pueblo Viejo was primarily agricultural, with small farms producing fruit, cocoa, and coffee. Most of the farmers were poor, and they welcomed Rosario for the employment it promised. However, few of the six hundred jobs created by the mining operation went to local people, since they lacked the requisite skills. Meanwhile, some seventy peasant families were forced off their land as the mine expanded its operations, and the region's principal rivers were diverted for the mine's use and severely polluted. According to Church studies, Rosario decided what, if anything, it would pay for the land it wished to expropriate, then confronted the peasants with the choice of quitting the land with little or no compensation or having it bulldozed by tractors. Parish priest Carlos Guerra charged that one third of the peasants received no compensation at all, and those who did were represented by the company's own lawyer![62] Evicted peasants were moved to El Callejón de las Lagunas and Los Cacaos, where as many as five families were crowded onto one small plot. Houses built by the company were defective; two latrines were constructed for fifty-four people. And the Mejita, Arroyo Hondo, and Margajita rivers that water the region were so polluted with cyanide and mercury gases from the mine that they can no longer be used for agriculture or drinking.[63] Pollution has killed thousands of fish and many farm animals, particularly poultry. According to local press reports, four children died after drinking the brackish water,[64] and now the peasants fear even to wash in it because of skin diseases, or worse.

The peasants' attempts to seek redress for pollution and eviction were ignored by the company, and when they staged a peaceful demonstration against Rosario in July 1975 the police and armed forces arrested two hundred of them. President Joaquín Balaguer refused to consider a petition by the peasants, who then beseeched Bishop Juan Antonio Flores, of La Vega, to intercede. Flores and other Church representatives visited the area and were so shocked by what they saw that they started a nationwide publicity campaign on behalf of the peasants. When Rosario announced plans to expand into another 10.4 square miles in the mining region, the peasants produced a series of documents demonstrating the inevitable destruction of agriculture and further pollution. Under pressure from the Church, Balaguer admitted in August 1976 that the peasants' complaints were justified; the expansion program was suspended, pending further government study. Miffed by the government's action, which Rosario claimed was counter to its agreement under the country's mining code, the company announced that it was no longer interested in the project. But Rosario later changed its tune when Homestake Mining expressed interest in the area.[65]

Bishop Flores, in the meantime, continued to press for indemnification of the peasants. The problem, he said, was not a lack of legal mechanisms, since the country's mining code provides for adequate compensation, but "the lamentable failure to apply this code when the people affected are poor, uneducated peasants. Over two years have passed since these people were evicted, and while their cases are still under discussion, they are starving to death. This is not the first time that the peasant has been legally stripped of his land, even though his ancestors cultivated it for decades." According to Flores, the peasants' squatters rights were not respected,† whereas the large landowners, who could afford a notary and a lawyer, received handsome compensation. "Here is a case where what is legal is unjust," said the bishop, adding that "these [foreign] companies make a lot of propaganda out of the benefits and progress they bring to countries like ours, when in reality the only people who benefit are a small group of rich Dominicans living in Santo Domingo."

Flores also scored the government for failing to control pollution. The state Commission against Environment Contamination had never produced a scientific report on the effects of pollution at Pueblo Viejo, he said, and "it certainly is not to the country's advantage to leave environmental control in the hands of private companies." Furthermore, the harm "caused in these peasant communities by this sort of exploitation cannot be offset by a few alms from the company. Vital problems like the source of employment—and land is the peasants' only livelihood—cannot be solved by the construction of a primary school or the weekly

† As elsewhere in Latin America, few of the illiterate peasants possess a written title to the land.

visit of a doctor. These are palliative aspirin, which can answer some of the necessities of a small group but do not alter the basic problems of the peasant."[66]

Flores was not the only Dominican bishop to support the peasants in their struggle against the multinationals. Indeed, it was largely pressure from the Church hierarchy that caused the Balaguer government even to consider agrarian reform in the rich, sugar-producing eastern part of the country, headquarters of the U.S. giant Gulf+Western. Although the government did its best to delay land redistribution, the Church kept up the pressure. According to Bishop Roque Adames, of Santiago, the vast majority of the Dominican Republic's arable land was in the hands of 1.2 percent of the 4.5 million population. At the rate the Balaguer administration was carrying out agrarian reform, said the bishop, it would be two decades before the country's 100,000 landless peasants could till their own soil. Government statistics support Roque Adames' charges: only 9 percent of the acreage distributed under the 1964 land reform law has been titled to peasants; the rest is listed under companies or individuals closely associated with the government or the top echelons of the Army.[67] The Balaguer administration's manipulation of the agrarian reform law was yet another symptom of the "unspeakable levels" of corruption in government, said the archbishop of Santo Domingo and the country's six bishops. (Balaguer, once a crony of the late dictator Rafael Trujillo, tried to shrug off this criticism with the comment that corruption "is not a phenomenon of Dominican society but a plague of our times.")

The "Sugarization" of the Dominican Republic

A mountainous, semitropical land that covers the eastern two thirds of the Caribbean island of Hispaniola (Haiti occupies the rest), the Dominican Republic is crisscrossed by four almost parallel mountain ranges that confine the arable land to one third of the country's surface. The most fertile area is in the southeast, where Gulf+Western Industries (G+W) has its plantations. As the largest landowner, private sugar grower, and foreign investor in the Dominican Republic, G+W is at the heart of the struggle for agrarian reform and therefore the target of Church criticism.

One of the largest corporations in the United States, G+W came to the Dominican Republic two years after the 1965 invasion by U. S. Marines during a period when Washington was heavily involved in Dominican politics and for this reason upheld artificially high U.S. prices for Dominican sugar. Expanding its sugar and coffee interests, G+W purchased the South Puerto Rico Sugar Company (SPRS) owned by investors close to the Rockefeller interests. SPRS had developed large sugar holdings in Puerto Rico under the protection of the U. S. Government after the Spanish-American War, and in 1917, a year after the U. S. Army occupied the Dominican Republic, it expanded its operations to that country, acquiring large tracts of land in the eastern part of the country through the eviction of peasants by U.S. soldiers.[68] When G+W bought the company, SPRS owned 9 percent of the Dominican Republic's arable land and one of the world's largest sugar mills.

G+W was aided in its expansion program by Chase Manhattan, which made funds available and provided advice and services,[69] and by the Wall Street law firm of Simpson, Thacher & Bartlett, of which G+W is a client. It was by working in this law firm that Secretary of State Cyrus Vance got his start in government—his boss then, Edwin Weisl, was a confidant of Lyndon Johnson, and Weisl introduced Vance to important government and financial circles, including the Department of Defense, where he was appointed Assistant Secretary in 1964—just in time to help plan the Dominican Republic's invasion. Johnson later sent Vance to arrange a provisional government in the Dominican Republic, and about then G+W began acquiring SPRS shares. By 1976 G+W was paying Simpson, Thacher fees of over a million dollars a year; Simpson's senior partner, Donald Oresman, was a member of G+W's board of directors.[70] (The law firm had its ups and downs, however, and was involved in a number of scandals, including a 1974 suit by investors in Homestake Productions' oil tax-shelter scheme on charges of a $100 million fraud.[71])

One of G+W's first acts on buying SPRS was to break the union on its Dominican plantations. Cuban exile Teobaldo Rosell, a self-styled "specialist in busting unions,"[72] was appointed vice-president and general administrator of G+W's La Romana plantations. Police Colonel Simón Tadeo Guerrero González, an official in the Trujillo regime who had been transferred from La Romana because of brutality to workers, was reassigned to the plantations. On his arrival, Rosell denounced the workers' union, Sindicato Unido (SU), as communist-controlled, and shortly thereafter the union's lawyer, Guido Gil, was arrested. On releasing Gil, Colonel Guerrero warned him, "We don't guarantee your life here." The next day Gil was kidnapped by plainclothes police while on his way to Santo Domingo and never seen again.[73] Union leaders claimed that Gil and another popular leader, Miguel Fortuna, had been murdered. When the union protested the replacement of a weekly pay system with a biweekly one, the company annulled SU's contract, with the government's blessing, and fired eighty-three union members, virtually the entire SU leadership, while police occupied the company plant. Some $86,000 in SU funds was frozen, and union documents were requisitioned by the police. G+W then called in the AIFLD to form a new union, Sindicato Libre, which government officials immediately recognized. One result of this labor-management "consensus" was that cane cutters earned less in 1975 than in 1964.[74]

By destroying the SU, G+W effectively eliminated any threat of labor militancy. Seventy percent of the cane cutters employed during the harvest season are starving, illiterate Haitians, people so desperate for work that they defy organization. Most of them earn less than two hundred dollars during the seven-month harvest, for which they are trucked across the border to the eastern sugar plantations, but that is a small fortune by the standards of the average Haitian, whose annual income is one hundred dollars. The Haitian Government is perfectly willing to go along with the arrangement, since the Dominican Republic agreed that the dictatorship of Jean-Claude ("Baby Doc") Duvalier be paid ten dollars for every Haitian wetback. Five percent of the workers' wages also goes to the Haitian Government, and middlemen take another slice of their paltry pay.‡ Because of the poor

‡ Dominican officials also exploit Haitian laborers by threatening to deport those who stay on illegally unless they agree to work without pay on the large sugar plantations. The going price for a Haitian worker, according to Ramón Antonio Veras, a well-known columnist for the Dominican Republic's *El Nacional de Ahora,* is fifty to seventy-five dollars, and for this "the person has the right to take the Haitian to his farm and put him to

wages and living conditions—the cane cutters are housed in unhygienic, openair camps—many Dominicans refuse to work on the plantations. "The last time I worked in the harvest, I spent six months cutting and I couldn't even buy a pair of pants," said one Dominican, who claimed he earned more in one day as a wood-cutter (ten dollars) than he could make all week in the cane fields (cane cutters average seven to eight dollars per week).

G+W, producer of one third of the country's sugar, was favored with a number of handsome concessions by the Balaguer administration, including a twenty-year extension of a tax exemption Trujillo had granted to La Romana. G+W also received a twenty-year tax exemption on its Romana free port, the only industrial free zone in the country under private control. The free zone attracted eighteen U.S. companies, many of which had left the United States for the lower wages of Puerto Rico, only to "run away" again to the Dominican Republic because of still cheaper labor—thirty cents an hour. According to an investment analyst's report on Caribbean Leisurewear, a G+W tenant, the Dominican Republic offers, in addition to low wages, a huge labor pool, and "with four to five applicants for every company job in the Dominican [Republic], the company has the opportunity to expand rapidly within a framework of labor peace and dedication to work."[75] The report does not mention that such runaway shops reduce the number of jobs available in the United States or that they exploit cheap labor in the developing countries.

G+W also acquired substantial holdings in the Dominican tourist industry and a huge cement factory that supplies some 50

---

work without pay; he need only furnish this slave with basic needs, that is, take care of him so that he can cut sugar cane. [The master] has the right to kick him and even kill him if the subject refuses to cut cane." (Raymond Alcide Joseph, "Border Strife in Hispaniola," *The Nation* [Nov. 27, 1976], pp. 558–62.)

Veras' charges are borne out by *Caribbean Contact,* an ecumenical, Barbados-based newspaper supported by the Caribbean Conference of Churches, which described how a truckload of Haitians returning to the border from a sugar factory in the eastern Dominican Republic was stopped by a large landowner who said he needed some laborers to work in his house. When the men refused, the landowner fired on the Haitians, wounding several. ("Exploitation of Haitian Sugar Workers in Dominican Republic," *Caribbean Contact* [Nov. 1972].)

percent of the construction industry, in addition to a controlling interest in the Pablo Duarte Olympic Center, a new sports complex built for the Pan American Games. The latter is tied into the Madison Square Garden Corporation, also controlled by G+W, which in turn has reportedly attracted the interest of persons in the gambling underworld.*

* G+W's connection with organized crime has already been the subject of U. S. Government investigations. During a 1970 hearing by the Illinois Racing Board, for example, it was shown that G+W was a partner with Philip Levin, a G+W director, in the Acapulco Towers Hotel in the Mexican resort and that the hotel was run by "Moe" Morton, not as a hotel, but as a private club for himself and his friends. Among Morton's friends who stayed at the hotel during a two-week period in early 1969 were: Meyer Lansky, reputed financial chief of organized crime in the United States; Las Vegas gambling figures Dean Shendel, Moe Dalitz, and Hyman Segal; Tony Roma, connected with organized crime in Montreal; Sidney Korshak of Chicago and Los Angeles, a labor relations consultant reportedly connected with underworld crime; and Delbert Coleman, a businessman who was accused of stock manipulation with Korshak and others by the Securities and Exchange Commission. The hearings also established that Lansky had used the hotel to evade police surveillance during a conference of organized-crime figures in Acapulco in early 1970, and described a series of meetings among Lansky, Levin, Korshak, and Newton Mandell, general counsel of the G+W subsidiary that owned the hotel. ("Smoldering Conflict: Dominican Republic, 1965–1975," NACLA's *Latin America & Empire Report* [April 1975], pp. 79–80.)

Levin, who bought into G+W in 1968, was not the only dubious character associated with G+W. Another partner, Sicilian banker Michele Sindona, was the principal shareholder in the $5 billion Franklin National Bank, whose failure in the United States led to a high-level investigation in Italy into Sindona's business interests and underworld connections and his subsequent sentencing *in absentia* to three and a half years in prison. (Ibid.; also *"Escándalo financiero,"* Associated Press [Rome, Aug. 31, 1978].)

Sindona, in turn, was in partnership with the Vatican. One of his first actions following his appointment as financial steward by Paul VI in 1969 was to transfer $40 million in Vatican funds to the Luxembourg bank Paribas Transcontinental, $15 million of which was acquired by G+W. Charles Bluhdorn, G+W president, subsequently joined the board of the Vatican-controlled Società Generale Immobiliare (SGI), a multinational real estate firm with property on both sides of the Atlantic, including the Watergate complex in Washington, D.C. The collapse of Sindona's empire cost the Vatican some $240 million, according to Swiss banking sources. (Malachi Martin, *The Final Conclave* [Briarcliff Manor, N.Y.: Stein & Day, 1978], pp. 29–31.)

G+W's tourist, sports, and gambling interests in the Dominican Republic, its connection with organized crime in the United States, and its cozy relationship with the admittedly corrupt Balaguer government made the conglomerate the object of various charges and rumors in the Dominican Republic. It was not merely a question of bigness (with some $200 million at stake in the Dominican Republic, G+W was the largest foreign investor in the country). As London's *Financial Times* pointed out, the Balaguer administration had "apparently done everything possible to help G+W despite local objections,"[76] including the manipulation of Dominican laws to further the corporation's interests, such as an amendment of the industrial incentives law to exempt G+W's free-zone operations from any exchange restrictions. But undoubtedly the most serious accusations centered on G+W's sugar-growing operations.

The owner of 109,642 acres of prime Dominican land, G+W also had contracts on nearly 50,000 acres under what is known as the *colonia* system. This arrangement has become increasingly popular with U.S. food conglomerates in Latin America because it guarantees a regular supply through contract growers without burdening the company with such potential political-economic liabilities as land ownership or labor unions. At the same time, since the company dominates processing and marketing, it retains control of local production. In the Dominican Republic the contract system became particularly attractive because the law prohibits foreigners from buying more land to plant cane.

The only drawback of the *colonia* system from the company's viewpoint is that the land must be relatively near its sugar mill and loading stations, and not all farmers on the perimeter of G+W's holdings want to plant sugar. That is especially true of the smaller farmers, who prefer a modest income from yucca, beans, fruit, and rice to the wild fluctuations of the international sugar market. Moreover, a number of farmers are reluctant to sign contracts that they say make them economic vassals of G+W. According to Alberto Giraldo, who was president of an association of four hundred *colonos* who sell their sugar cane to La Romana, the company is "a state within a state stronger than the government itself."[77] The owner of a 1,500-acre farm in the town of Pintado, near the Romana mill, Giraldo claimed that two attempts had been made on his life because of his opposition to G+W.[78] (While president of the *colonos,* Giraldo tried unsuccessfully to improve the contractors' bargaining power and persuade the government to establish tighter controls over G+W.) Small farmers in the town of La Otra Banda in the sugar cane belt also complained of "heavy aerial spraying of herbicides that damage plants and trees on land adjacent to cane fields, fences being mysteriously broken at night, access being denied to certain roads, and the company police force making sure that animals that stray into the cane fields are either destroyed or taken to a distant police station where the owner must pay a stiff fine to retrieve them."[79]

The principal victim of "sugarization" is not the small or medium-sized farmer like Giraldo but the landless peasant, who has been sacrificed to the greed for land. Once a landowner signs a contract with G+W, a whole way of life is destroyed. Under the terms of the agreement all the acreage must be planted in sugar, and the peasants who have worked on the estate in return for the use of a small parcel of land lose not only their source of food, but also the basis of their social relationship to the landlord and society. Father Juan Miguel Pérez, coordinator of peasant affairs for the diocese of Higüey in the heart of the sugar-growing region, describes this process as one of progressive dehumanization:

> Before he was consumed by the lust for land, the landowner had a deep sense of dignity and honor in dealing with the peasant. He was feared for his power, yes, but at the same time he was respected for his honor and humanity. The *señor* was a patriarch. You could turn to him, as the peasants did, in any crisis. He was the cement that held that semifeudal world of the countryside together. Now, because he is so often absent, but particularly because he is so land-hungry, the *señor* no longer serves that integrating social function. In fact, he has become the single most powerful force for social disintegration.
>
> But it is not only because of his absenteeism and his obsession with acquiring more land that the landowner lost that social role. It is also because of his new concept of private property, which today is exclusive, total, and unconditional.
>
> Before, the peasants could get a good number of the simple

things they needed from the *señor*'s largesse: hand-me-downs, the odd jobs he would provide, etc. Today, all that has changed: the fences are higher, and if a peasant's animal strays onto the landowner's property, it will probably never get home again. Before, peasants were free to help themselves to wild mangos or oranges, to firewood, etc., on his property. But now the peasants can be jailed for taking such things.

This heightening of the privateness and exclusivity of the *señor*'s notion of ownership has stifled his humanity and paternal generosity. He would also flatly deny any suggestion that private property has a social function.

Consequently, the peasant has lost his regard for the *señor*, and any sense of dependence on him. Before, social relations were vertical, from the person above to the one below, from superior to inferior, and that was perhaps not ideal. But now there are no interpersonal relations at all. The landowner's craving for self-sufficiency has grown so that he neither needs nor wants the peasant's work or thanks. With his sense of autrachy, he has lost all identification with the peasant.[80]

A green plague that has multiplied twenty times since the turn of the century until it occupies one quarter of the cultivated land in the Dominican Republic, sugar cane has aggravated both social and economic divisions in the countryside. Thus agriculture's per capita production of food for local consumption has declined by 60 percent since 1961 because of the emphasis on export crops, the growing concentration of land in a few estates, and the population explosion; 64 percent of the island's food production is exported, and of this three quarters goes to the United States, mostly in the form of sugar. Because of malnutrition, infant mortality is 10 percent of live births. Of those who survive, half are anemic and suffer chronic malnutrition, according to a survey by New York's Columbia University.[81] The average monthly income of a Dominican family of five is less than fifty dollars in rural areas, and two thirds of the population remains outside the mainstream of the country's economic, cultural, and political life.[82] Because of the desperate situation in the countryside, 6 percent of the rural population migrates to city slums each year, swelling the already high 22 percent unemployment rate, while another four hundred thousand Dominicans have fled to New York and New Jersey. One Dominican out of four depends on U.S. food supplies distributed by CARE and other private agencies. Bishop Roque Adames, whose diocese spans the country's central mountain range, reported that were it not for the monthly remittances of Dominicans in the United States, half the people in his diocese would be starving to death. "For these poor farmers, the country up north—which to them means New York—promises a job and money for their families," he said. "As one peasant told me, 'It may be hard there, but it can't be worse than this.'" The irony is that, while the United States consumes the Dominican Republic's food, it also imports its poverty, and all because of corporate profits and the greed of a few wealthy Dominicans. It is pointless for U.S. officials to lament the failure of such poor countries as the Dominican Republic to feed themselves when most of the food grown goes, not to the people who live there, but to the United States.

Like United Brands and Standard Fruit in Honduras, where anti-labor policies eventually led to the formation of militant unions, G+W's "sugarization" of the Dominican Republic has mobilized the peasantry and the Catholic Church. Typical of the clashes that have become regular occurrences in the eastern part of the country was the seizure in 1974 of a thousand acres of land that were about to be planted in sugar cane, under contract to G+W, by fifteen hundred people from La Otra Banda, Higüey, and neighboring towns who demanded that the Balaguer Government fulfill its promise of agrarian reform. Merchants from Higüey provided tractors and seeds, and the people planted yucca, beans, and plantains. Although the Army disbanded the people and plowed the crops under, the peasants made their point, as did the Catholic Church. Bishop Juan F. Pepen of Higüey not only scored the government for political repression but also publicly supported Father Juan Torres, an outspoken priest who called President Balaguer a "paper kite" for bowing to sugar interests. Like the Jesuits, who run a radio school for eight thousand peasants, Torres angered the landowners by promoting social awareness among the peasants. And as Father Pérez noted, the Dominican peasants "have learned to use their most effective weapon—their numbers—and this factor is going to be decisive.

Yet, though he has changed from passivity to direct action, the peasant does not use violence. He simply pays no attention to the social and legal framework of the established order."

In one community in the diocese of Higüey, cited by Pérez to illustrate the causes of this new solidarity, a large landowner seized a portion of a peasant's property by stretching a barbed wire fence across it and sending in his dairy cattle to destroy the peasant's crops. When the peasant took the large landowner to court, the police arrested not the landowner but the peasant The man's appeals to higher courts were repeatedly delayed, and two years later, having run out of money and patience, the peasant sold his plot to the large landowner for $125 in a "friendly compromise." That was at the end of 1972. A few weeks later, the large landowner used the same trick to get possession of a farm belonging to the peasant's neighbor. The man called in the local sheriff to witness the destruction caused by the landowner's cows, then sued the landowner in the district court. When the judge, who was a friend of the landowner, threw out the case, the stubborn peasant appealed to a higher court in Santo Domingo. Six months passed, during which the peasant made innumerable trips to the capital, often with witnesses and at considerable expense, and still no date was set for the hearing. "Come back tomorrow," he was repeatedly told. Meanwhile the landowner's cattle had wiped out his crops, forcing the peasant to look for odd jobs to support his family.

Encouraged by these easy expropriation methods, the landowner next proceeded to run barbed wire across a number of peasant properties, again sending in his cattle to destroy the crops. But there comes a time when even the most fatalistic peasant will stand for no more abuse, and so it was that fifty peasants agreed to act together to defend their interests. With their wives and children, they cut down the barbed wire and began preparing their fields for the September planting, whereupon the large landowner called in the police, as the peasants had expected. Instead of jailing all the peasants, which would have caused an uproar, the police arrested only three of the organizers, believing that this would end the protest. But these peasants were replaced by others from neighboring communities. The next day there were more arrests. By the end of the week fifty peasants were in jail, and, sure enough, there was a scandal in the press and the government was forced to name a commission of inquiry, which promptly released all the peasants. "Events like this," said Father Pérez, "convince the peasant that he won't get justice under the present legal system." Explained the priest:

When he is hauled into court and sent to jail for doing what he knows is right, he isn't looking for a fight. He has simply decided to disregard the procedures and provisions of court action because the established order has ceased to be a real order in his eyes. Jail is no longer an ignominy for him but an honor, a sign of his total and definitive break with the old ways of life and their workings. He has made up his mind to break out of the closed circle in which he was living.

Some say that this is active nonviolence. Well, certain of the peasants may have heard about this method and its tactics in a lecture. But they did not need outside ideas; they found this posture of unity and solidarity all by themselves.

The peasants have outgrown their old individualistic view of life. They have learned a new social sense, a new social cohesion. As a member of a peasant class that is marginalized, each one feels solidarity with all the other members of that class. When one of them goes to jail without resisting, he knows that his fellow peasants will see his disobedience to the law—and his scorn for its penalties—as an act of solidarity with them. And in his eyes it is much more important what his peers think than what the establishment thinks.

The peasant never could trust the courts to be fair. Today he goes farther: he is convinced that courts are instruments of oppression, legal devices that society uses to keep him down, in permanent inferiority. He doesn't understand how the great landowners can have deeds to lands that he and his neighbors have been living and working on for so long. But he also knows that the landowners covet those lands. And that his and his neighbors' cases are as good as lost—legally, that is—before they walk into a courtroom.[83]

Support of such civil disobedience has not improved the Catholic Church's relations with the government. Several priests were arrested or refused reentry into the country because of their work with the peasants. Lay leaders were also arrested; Florindo Muñoz Soriano, a regional director of the Union of Christian Farmers, was shot to death by the foreman of a large landowner.[84] Church sources further claim that the government insisted, at G+W's behest, that Bishop Pepen, an eloquent critic of the corporate giant, be transferred from his diocese in the sugar-growing region of Higüey to Santo Domingo. But Pepen's politically conservative replacement, Bishop Hugo Polanco Brito, proved equally recalcitrant, supporting both the peasants and the priests who work with them. When three of his clerics were accused by a Dominican senator representing the sugar interests of "subverting" the agrarian reform, Polanco defended the priests for their evangelization, education, and radio programs, and for their aid to the peasants. "The agrarian-reform program is opposed by large landowners who see their holdings threatened," said the bishop. "They are the real opponents of reform, not the priests." To prove the bishop's point, several thousand people demonstrated in support of the priests, and even the national police chief was forced to admit that they had "done nothing subversive."[85]

"In the past, religion was an escape, a kind of magic dream, a flight from reality," explained Father Pérez. "But that God who arbitrarily distributed fortune, health, and social position is dead. For the Dominican peasants, God is no longer the capricious Being who makes and unmakes the course of history. A new God is calling, one who stimulates man and encourages him."[86]

A Model of Development

The Dominican Church's campaign on behalf of the peasants is a small-scale model of what is happening in northern Brazil and the Amazon, where bishops, priests, and nuns are in open, often violent conflict with the multinationals, local ranchers, the military, and the police. As in the Dominican Republic, land is at the root of most of Brazil's social problems. Within the last two decades, all the unoccupied territory that once relieved the pressure of the land-starved peasants has been taken up, and they are moving by the millions into the already swollen slums of the industrial South. Brazil's last reserve, the Amazon jungle, has been appropriated by the multinationals, and there is no place left for either the peasants or the rapidly dwindling Indian population. The *posseiro,* or squatter without land title, has become the *posseiro urbano,* or slum dweller without wages. Some 30 million of these dispossessed are on the move, according to government statistics, in an avalanche of human misery that is both the backbone of Brazil's new industrial wealth and the source of its social problems, including a rising crime rate and frequent epidemics in the big cities.

While the skewed division of land has always been a barrier to social development in Brazil, the problem was magnified by the military regime's model of development, with its heavy emphasis on exports and foreign investment. The latter was a built-in feature of the 1964 coup that overthrew the elected government of João Goulart and the principal condition of U.S. support. Goulart's left-wing, populist government had established a series of controls on foreign investment, including tough restrictions on profit remittances. It had nationalized the telephone company of the Canadian conglomerate BRASCAN and was about to obtain the Supreme Court's sanction to expropriate Hanna Mining Company's high-grade iron ore concession in the state of Minas Gerais. As *Fortune* magazine pointed out in 1965, "For Hanna, the revolt that overthrew Goulart . . . arrived like a last minute rescue by the 1st Cavalry."[87] Much the same could be said of BRASCAN, whose stock rose fivefold within a year of the coup.[88]

When a CIA outlay of $20 million to opposition candidates in the 1962 state and congressional elections failed to achieve the desired results,[89] the U. S. Embassy began to conspire directly with military leaders to overthrow Goulart. After the coup, the properly grateful Brazilian generals repaid U.S. support by accepting an entire package of U.S. demands, including a generous new profit remittance law, an investment guarantee treaty covering U.S. subsidiaries, and the return of the Hanna concession.[90] So eager was the military to show its appreciation for foreign intervention and investment that, within two years of Goulart's overthrow, foreign companies had gained control of 50 percent of Brazilian industry[91]—often through the expediency of what the Brazilian Finance Ministry called "constructive bankruptcy," a combination of fiscal and monetary measures that forced local firms to sell to foreign interests or go broke.[92] By 1971, fourteen of the country's twenty-seven largest companies were in foreign hands; of the remainder, eight were state-owned and only five were private Brazilian firms.

The military justified this heavy reliance on foreign investment by claiming that Brazil could become an industrial power only through exports and that the only companies with the technology, money, and marketing skills to develop exports on a large scale were the multinationals. But as the country's balance of payments showed, there were major flaws in this thinking: imports by these companies were higher than exports, and profit remittances abroad were more than twice the original investment.[93] Moreover, in order to pay for the technology, services, and industrial development—as usual, most of the money for the multinationals' expansion came from local sources—Brazil ran up the highest debt in the developing world, some $50 billion (compared to $3 billion under Goulart). Two fifths of Brazil's export earnings go to service this debt. Yet the government wanted to borrow another $50 billion over the next decade to finance its development programs.

Perhaps the biggest flaw in the military's scheme was social, though the generals would hardly entertain that sort of objection. Other countries could offer foreign companies political stability and attractive investment terms. And the Brazilian market, while large by Latin-American standards, could not compare with the riches available in Europe, the United States, or Japan. But the military regime could and did offer foreign capital one undeniably competitive commodity: a huge pool of cheap labor, 30 million *posseiros*. Wages were frozen or progressively reduced in terms of real purchasing power, with the result that half the country's 38 million workers earn less than the government's own minimum monthly wage of $70. Strikes were outlawed and job security legislation abolished, thereby encouraging many companies to adopt a job rotation policy, laying off workers in the first three to four months of the year when corporations are obliged to increase wages, albeit at a rate that lags behind inflation, and hiring new ones to replace them at lower wages. General Motors, for example, fired 1,792 workers in the first quarter of 1974 while hiring 1,970 new ones. Many of these workers came from GM's competitors at Volkswagen, Toyota, or Ford; they, too, had been laid off in the rotation game.[94] In a 1974 study of labor rotation, São Paulo's Department of Statistics and Social Economic Studies reported that "the Brazilian subsidiaries of the multinational corporations mainly owe their expansion to a more intense exploitation of labor, employing workers at wages lower than the level required by the government's present wage policy."[95] Thanks to such low labor costs, Volkswagen President Rudolf Leiding could report in 1974: "The situation of our corporation had worsened because of a reduction of almost 30 percent in exports to the U.S.A. and of 17 percent in sales in the German market, [but] in 1973 profits coming from our Brazilian subsidiary were so high that [they] covered losses from our other productive units."[96]

One result of this wage policy is that Brazilian laborers now work twice as many hours as they did a decade ago to buy the same minimum necessities. They do so by working overtime—110 hours per month on top of 240 normal working hours in the construction industry[97]—or by finding jobs for other members of the family. Fourteen textile factories in the state of Minas Gerais, for example, decided that the best way to "reinforce the family income" and increase production was to employ the wives and children of factory workers.[98] Weavers go to work at 6 P.M. and do not leave the plant until 1:30 P.M. the following day. Working conditions are such that Brazil has one of the highest job accident records in the world, according to the government's own figures. In 1975, 1.9 million work accidents affected one third of the industrial labor force. Many employers view such accidents as inevitable. Explained the spokesman for one large construction company: "Four deaths per kilometer is the ideal for tunnels. Six deaths means the existence of medium risks; eight, high risks; and ten, impossible conditions." He then proudly disclosed that in its current construction program the company "hadn't even filled its quota."[99] Instead of attempting to control such exploitation, the government encourages it. The governor of the state of Pernambuco in northeastern Brazil, for example, based his sales pitch to foreign companies on the state's extraordinarily cheap labor. The average monthly salary in Pernambuco, boasted the governor, was among the lowest in the country, a mere $43.83.[100]

Whether the issue is labor rotation or frozen wages, the search

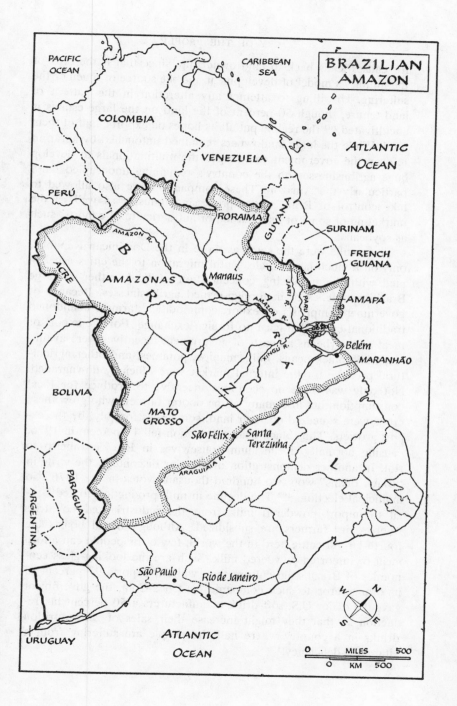

BRAZILIAN
AMAZON

PACIFIC
OCEAN

CARIBBEAN
SEA

COLOMBIA

VENEZUELA

ATLANTIC
OCEAN

PERÚ

RORAIMA

GUYANA

AMAZON R.

SURINAM

FRENCH
GUIANA

ACRE

AMAZONAS

Manaus

B
R
A
Z
I
L

P
A
R
Á

JARI R.

PARU R.

AMAZON R.

AMAPÁ

Belém

MARANHÃO

XINGU R.

BOLIVIA

MATO
GROSSO

São Félix

Santa
Terezinha

ARAGUAIA R.

PARAGUAY

ARGENTINA

São Paulo

Rio de Janeiro

URUGUAY

ATLANTIC
OCEAN

MILES   500
0

0   KM   500

N
W   E
S

for causes leads back to land ownership, since that is the crux of the military's model of development and the source of much of the suffering. Unwilling to attempt any alteration in the pattern of land tenure, though 50 percent of the land on the large estates is uncultivated,[101] the regime put all its hopes on exports, half of them food. While the large landowners remained untouched by agrarian reform, the government encouraged the multinationals to develop huge agribusinesses on the country's remaining unoccupied land, particularly the Amazon. These companies were also allowed to take control of Brazil's food-processing industry as well as the marketing of some of its most important agricultural exports, such as soybeans.

The results were the same as those in the Dominican Republic, only on a much larger scale. Rural migration to the cities accelerated with the increasing concentration of land, either in large Brazilian ranches or in foreign-owned agribusinesses. Because of government emphasis on export commodities, farmers abandoned traditional crops that earn no foreign exchange. For the export of meat and soybeans all sorts of government incentives were available, while black beans, milk, manioc, potatoes, and other agricultural produce for the internal market were officially downgraded. Not only was there no economic incentive to produce for local consumption, but also many of the poorer farmers who grew these crops were squeezed off their land, sometimes forcibly, by the export growers. Thus black-bean production fell 17 percent in 1976, causing normally docile slum housewives in Rio de Janeiro to riot. In another demonstration of popular discontent, the write-in "Black Beans" won two hundred thousand votes in the 1976 Rio municipal elections.[102] The decline in milk production forced Brazil to import powdered milk from the industrialized countries where dairy farmers are subsidized. Although Brazil boasts the fourth-largest cattle herd in the world, few of its people can afford meat or imported powdered milk. Such are the looking-glass economics of Brazil's agriculture that, while it exports 97 percent of its orange crop to such companies as Coca-Cola, the government gave the major U.S. soft-drink manufacturers a 50 percent tax reduction so that they might increase their sales of zero-nutrition drinks in a country where half the people are suffering from a vitamin C deficiency![103]

Although Brazil's annual agricultural growth rates of 5 percent and more outstripped those of other Latin-American countries, the government could hardly claim that the people had benefited when 75 percent of the population was suffering from malnutrition.† On the contrary, at a meeting of international nutritionists sponsored by the New York Academy of Sciences, Brazil was singled out as an example of how a people fail to benefit from agricultural progress.[104] The argument of a pro-military foreign agronomist that "the rest of the world is better off because Brazil can export more than 10 million tons of soybeans a year" was not convincing when the Brazilians themselves were left with nothing to eat. But then neither was the government's pride in the cattle ranches, since these had ousted thousands of peasant families in the Northeast and the Amazon in order to put steaks on the tables of the rich, industrialized nations. With an average daily wage of seventy-three cents—when there is work on the cattle ranches—the Brazilian peon is lucky to eat plantains and manioc. At a dollar a pound, black beans are his filet mignon. Yet this, to the minds of Brazil's military, is progress.

Nor is it at all clear that the native gains anything by emphasizing export crops at the cost of internal consumption. In the case of soybeans, for example, market manipulations by the international commodity traders cost Brazilian farmers $100 million in 1974, according to the president of the Brazilian Rural Society.[105] This loss was due in part to a 40 percent price drop between 1973 and the first half of 1974—after Brazilian farmers had planted soybeans on a large scale at the urging of such conglomerates as the United States' Anderson, Clayton and Argentina's Bunge & Born. When prices seemed likely to rise, the Brazilian Government announced a temporary ban on exports, ostensibly to protect the internal market, thereby forcing soybean prices down again. Informed in advance of the pending ban, the conglomerates registered a series of export contracts with the government but did not purchase the soybeans until the prices had fallen. At the time of the scandal, July 1974, these exports were running at 300,000 to 400,000 tons a day.[106]

Brazilian Agriculture Minister Cirne Lima was so disgusted that

† Ministry of Health statistics.

he quit in protest. In a letter to the President of the country, Lima said that the regime had lost a splendid opportunity to increase internal food consumption, preferring to subsidize the foreign companies:

> For the first time in twenty years, agricultural prices were rising on the international market, and in view of your earlier wise and sound decision to increase agricultural production for the sake of the domestic Brazilian consumer, our country seemed likely to have enough foodstuffs and fibers for export, too. It was an opportunity that, with skillful handling, could have given the farmer in the backlands his first chance at prosperity in many years.
>
> But the steps your government took to expand agriculture to meet domestic needs never really helped the urban consumer. Instead, the industrial and commercial export firms, which are increasingly foreign-owned, were favored, so that the country's prosperity now redounds less and less to the advantage of Brazil.
>
> The government's insistence on efficiency and productivity has sacrificed not only the small- and medium-sized farmer, but the small- and medium-sized businessman and industrialist—all of whom are Brazilians—to the advantage of multinational corporations, which undoubtedly have a valid role to play provided they are obliged, here in Brazil and everywhere else, to serve the common good of the host country. Capital has been given special breaks that have nullified the nation's over-all planning for needs and priorities. The profits siphoned off by this capital (which each year becomes less and less Brazilian-owned) are increasing our external indebtedness, our balance-of-payments deficit, and the cost of borrowing in Brazil. And the war on inflation is practically a lost cause, almost the entire cost of which is dumped on other sectors of the economy, particularly agriculture.‡[107]

‡ Cirne Lima was allowed to get away with such criticism because of his position as a minister. Other, less influential critics of the government's economic policy were not so treated. Kurt Rudolf Mirow, the president of a small Brazilian firm that makes electrical generators and motors, was harassed and threatened by Rio de Janeiro police after he wrote a book

Brazil's bishops agreed. Indeed, by 1973 the bishops of northern and central Brazil, where land tenancy is the most stubborn social and economic problem, were already in conflict with the government over peasant rights, having denounced the military for its inhuman agrarian policy in a series of scathing documents. By the mid-seventies the entire Church hierarchy had taken up the cry, the bishops of the industrial South rightly blaming the growth of urban slums on rural migration from the North.

The first of these philippics, called "I Have Heard the Cry of My People," was signed by three archbishops, ten bishops, and the heads of five important religious orders in the Northeast, and was so explosive that it was immediately banned. No sooner had the government recovered from this affront than it was confronted by two equally critical documents: "Marginalization of a People," a documented survey of injustice in central and western Brazil, including the Amazon, which was signed by six bishops; and "Y-Juca-Pirama" (in the Tupi Indian language, "The One Who Must Die"), a description by the bishops and missionaries working in the Amazon of the plight of the dwindling aboriginal population. By 1974, when the Brazilian Church published "Church and Politics," a broadly based document that criticized the government for its authoritarian policies, the hierarchy was at open war with the government.

These denunciations were especially embarrassing to the authorities because they were scrupulously based on fact—on examples and statistics gathered over the years by Church economists,

---

about the attempts of multinational cartels, particularly in the electrical industry, to squeeze out small, nationally owned businesses such as his own. Mirow said the police first attempted to seize the unpublished manuscript of the book at the publishing house. When that failed, a bomb was planted on the premises of the publishing company. Mirow also reported that he and other members of the firm had "repeatedly been threatened with physical violence in order to stop our research on the activities of an international electrical cartel." Most of the copies of the book were seized by the police when it was published.

Mirow filed suit in Brazilian courts against the alleged cartel, citing such firms as Siemens and Telefunken of West Germany, Westinghouse and General Electric of the United States, Toshiba and Hitachi of Japan, and the Swiss firm Brown, Boveri. ("Brazil Police Seize Books Attacking Cartels," Miami *Herald* [Mar. 2, 1977].)

sociologists, anthropologists, and the priests and nuns who live with the people—and were not the usual vague appeals to Christian conscience that can be easily shrugged off. "Marginalization of a People," for example, listed case after case of injustice in the countryside, including sixteen pages of graphs and statistics. Some were similar to Father Pérez's account of the large landowner and the barbed wire in the Dominican Republic. Others described how government agencies that had been set up to benefit the people of the region were used to promote the interests of foreigners and wealthy Brazilians from other parts of the country. Industrialists from São Paulo and Rio de Janeiro, for example, were given 50 percent tax write-offs to invest in the Northeast and the Amazon, in addition to government credit and technical aid. As the bishops pointed out, this meant that the government was subsidizing the wealthy to increase their holdings at the expense of the region's small and medium-sized farmers who could not compete with the large companies for bank loans or other benefits offered by the regional development corporations. Forty percent of the projects receiving tax incentives from SUDENE (Regional Development Superintendency for Northeast Brazil) belonged to foreign corporations.[108] "The only thing we can conclude is that this policy has been undertaken to favor those who least need it, wealthy people who already own property," said the bishops, citing a series of statistics to support their charges, including the upward redistribution of wealth between 1960 and 1970.* "It is time we stopped confusing the 'development of Brazil' with economic growth," said the bishops. "Brazil is, first of all, its people. Thus development without the people or their participation or, worse, a development that sacrifices the people cannot be described as the 'development of Brazil' but merely the growth of a few through the exploitation of the majority or the sale of our riches to increase the wealth of rich foreigners. This is the accusation of our people, the cry suffocated by suffering: 'You are inhuman, you are criminals, you don't want us to be people.' "[109]

One has only to look at the government's own statistics to un-

---

* In 1960 the richest 1 percent of the population received 11.7 percent of the country's total wealth. Ten years later, that 1 percent received 17.8 percent of the wealth. In the same period, the income of the poorest 50 percent of the population fell from 17.7 to 13.7 percent.

derstand what the bishops meant. In the Northeast alone, there are 28 million undernourished people whose annual per capita income is less than one hundred dollars. Infant mortality is eight times that of the United States, and 20 percent of the children suffer from such severe malnutrition that it has permanently damaged their brains. Yet the government talks of nothing but efficiency and productivity. Brazilian agriculture must be "modernized," insists the government, and those who cannot meet this challenge "must stop being small farmers and become workers for the large rural enterprises," even if the National Institute of Colonization and Agrarian Reform (INCRA) has to tax them out of existence.[110] Brazil does not want *posseiros,* or marginal farmers, said the Interior Minister, explaining the government's preference for large agribusinesses. Thus 3.1 percent of the landowners control 80 percent of the arable land,[111] and the multinational corporations are establishing ranches of 500,000 acres and more in the Amazon.

But are these rural enterprises really any better than the feudal *latifundio?* Brazil's bishops think not. "Some people say the rural enterprises are not *latifundio* because *latifundio* are large areas of uncultivated land, while the rural enterprise exploits the land," wrote the bishops in "Marginalization of a People." "This may be true for students of economics who see things from the viewpoint of production and profit. But for us, the people, *latifundio* means only one thing—a large piece of land. It can be cultivated or uncultivated, productive or unproductive, but it's all the same because it does not produce for us. So rural enterprise is the same old *latifundio* with another name.

"The difference lies in the rural enterprise's commitment to a project, a plan of production or cultivation. But a commitment to whom? To the government that finances these programs. But if that is so, it must be asked whether these rural enterprises are going to resolve the problems of the peasant, or really help [the government] to achieve peace in the countryside, or 'regional security.'

"A study carried out in the Amazon shows that none of these three objectives is achieved by rural enterprises. On the contrary, they lessen employment opportunities, agricultural production is reduced to a few large cattle ranches, and this in turn engenders discontent and tensions between a people without jobs or land and the large landowners, not to mention the fact that many of these new *latifundio* are foreign-owned."

The government was in such a hurry for quick results, said the bishops, that it never considered alternatives to agribusiness. "If the same amount of government money were used to finance the *posseiros*, improve their education, standard of living, and technical know-how, if these people were organized in production cooperatives, wouldn't this also lead to increased productivity? And this would have the advantage of collaborating in the human and social development of the people of these regions. But, no, it wouldn't do, because obviously it would take longer and the rich would not get richer!"[112]

The bishops' argument was sound, if one may judge by the reaction of such organizations as AID, the Ford and Rockefeller Foundations, and the United Nations' Food and Agriculture Organization (FAO). Contrary to expectations, the much publicized "green revolution," which so dramatically increased crop yields through new hybrids, fertilizers, and tractors, has not resolved the problems of malnutrition and rural poverty, but has actually contributed to them. As both Brazil and the Dominican Republic demonstrate, the marginal farmers are being forced off their land by more efficient export growers. It is cruelly pointless to tell a peasant he should use fertilizer or eat a balanced diet when he can afford neither. According to an AID evaluation of agriculture extension programs between 1942 and 1967, the "green revolution" was so successfully applied by large and medium-sized farmers to develop export crops that in a number of cases food shortages occurred in areas that had been self-sufficient. Many of the small farmers who formerly supplied vegetables and fruit to the local market were forced out of business by the export estates, obliging the government to import these products or let the people go hungry—usually the latter. If Latin America were to convert the coffee, cotton, sugar, and banana plantations to food for local consumption, says FAO, it could double its wheat production or increase the rice crop by 250 percent. Yet many Latin-American nations are now importing such basic foodstuffs as wheat, corn, and beans.

José Pires, the archbishop of João Pessoa in the northeastern

Brazilian state of Paraíba, relates a typical case of this progress in reverse that occurred in the municipality of Serra da Raiz on an estate called Lameiro, where the crops of the *posseiros* were destroyed by the neighboring rancher's cattle. "It makes you sad and indignant to see what happened," said the archbishop. "Thousands of banana plants were destroyed by the cattle, which eat everything." Pires said that the peasants made innumerable trips to the appropriate government agencies to obtain legal redress, to the local labor union, the federation of farm workers, the police station, county judge, Secretaries of Security, Interior and Justice, even the federal police:

> There was no door on which the representatives of Lameiro had not knocked in trying to get legal protection for their rights. But the result of the long, difficult pilgrimage is, so far, nothing. In fact, their situation is worse because they have nothing left with which to support their families, and several have eight and nine young children.
>
> It is painful and revolting to see in Lameiro the way food is taken from the mouths of so many children. Peaceful men, good Christians, these brothers of ours had no wish to harm anyone; they wanted only to live in peace and do their work. But they have begun to have no faith in justice or the government. This is because a farmer has no security. But who should have the greater right to the use of the land, the men who were born there and cultivated it for so many years, or those who acquired it with money, sometimes borrowed from government agencies like SUDENE, but have never shed one drop of sweat on it?
>
> The policy of SUDENE is harmful to farming in Paraíba, and the people have a very bad image of the agency. Many tears have been shed because of SUDENE and many families ruined by it. For most people SUDENE is the owner of all land that bears its sign. Bordering the Lameiro land is a hacienda that everyone says belongs to SUDENE. We know it is not theirs even though a big sign has only one word you can read from a distance—SUDENE. Everyone knows there are property owners who justify themselves before the people by saying, "This land belongs to SUDENE now." "You have to

leave because SUDENE ordered us to plant grass here."
SUDENE is not the owner; it was the agency that financed
the owner to pay insignificant indemnifications, make deals—
often iniquitous—knock down fruit groves, run a tractor over
and raze crops, destroy houses, plant grass, expel men, and
introduce a bull. SUDENE encourages this exploitation.

The places we mention are located in regions suitable for
farming. Now they are becoming increasingly less productive.
Beans, cassava, vegetables, and fruit are disappearing from
the markets or have to be imported. One Lameiro peasant
alone was taking eight thousand to ten thousand bananas a
month to the market.

But the time is coming when the wrath of God will be
kindled against some landholders of Paraíba, as it was
against King Ahab and his wife Jezebel, who were responsible for the death of Naboth. In the Book of I Kings, Chapter 21, you can read the story and check the similarities with
what is going on in Lameiro and many other places.

Ahab, King of Israel, had palaces, haciendas, and other
properties at his disposal. Near the King's residence there
lived a man of modest means called Naboth. He had a small
plot of land where he kept a vineyard. The King wanted to
beautify his palace and decided to change Naboth's vineyard
into a garden. But Naboth did not agree to his proposal; he
wanted to stay on his land, the inheritance of his fathers, and
cultivate his vineyard. The King was greatly vexed by his refusal.

His wife Jezebel then took recourse to justice and arranged
for witnesses to make false charges against Naboth. He was
condemned, stoned, and killed, and Ahab took possession of
his vineyard. But God was angry and sent Elijah, the
prophet, to tell the King that in the place where the dogs
licked up the blood of Naboth, they would also lick up the
blood of Ahab and his wife. And so it came to pass.[113]

The Brazilian Amazon

The archbishop's biblical tale of greed and bloodshed could also
be applied to the Amazon jungle, a land of natural beauty that is

the object of a mineral and land rush matched only by the most turbulent period of the Wild West. The world's last surviving huge natural park, the Amazon extends over 3 million square miles, an area equal to 83 percent of the United States, and covering half of Brazil as well as smaller portions of Colombia, Ecuador, Peru, Bolivia, Venezuela, Guyana, Surinam, and French Guiana. When foreigners speak of the Amazon, they always resort to superlatives —the largest tropical forest and river system in the world, the hemisphere's longest river, the world's largest iron and tin reserves. Yet most of the people who live in the Amazon know nothing but misery, eking out an existence in a thatch-roofed lean-to on the muddy banks of some river, a prey to every imaginable plague, from malaria to piranhas. Still, for all the hardships of life in the Amazon, it has had one overriding attraction—hope —for if the peasant could not find land anywhere else, he could always migrate to the vast, untouched reserves of the Amazon, hoping that one day he might own his own farm.

For a good many years this illusion was shared by Brazilian governments, which saw the Amazon territory, with its minuscule 5 million population, as a natural overflow basin for the country's peasant population, particularly from the Northeast. Thus it was that President Emílio Garrastazú Médici embarked on a crash program to populate the Amazon in the early 1970s by constructing roads, the most ambitious of which was the 3,400-mile Transamazonian Highway stretching from the Atlantic Coast to Brazil's frontier with Peru. An additional 6,000 miles of roads were to crisscross the Amazon basin, many passing through Indian lands. To support this scheme, the government created the Superintendency of Amazon Development (SUDAM), which was supposed to plan, execute, and coordinate the development of the Amazon, and the Bank of the Amazon, to finance this development. Never given to thinking small, the Brazilian Government envisioned the resettlement of 30 million peasants in the Amazon, mostly in the regions where roads were under construction. Some eight thousand colonists were actually moved into the region, given seeds, six months' minimum wages, a rough wooden house and—what most of them had never had—a 250-acre plot to call their own. There were several drawbacks to the grandiose scheme, however, including lack of sufficient money and the danger to the environment. As one prominent Brazilian agronomist pointed out, "To put primitive labor into the Amazon is to create a desert. The government does not allow anyone to say the soil is no good for farming, but it is no good. [The Transamazonian Highway] is the most stupid project in Brazil—up to now."[114]

Latin-American governments have always preferred colonization schemes to agrarian reform, since the former raises no political problems with the landowners. But while these colonization projects may look good on paper, they invariably prove impractical, particularly in jungle regions, where most of them are located. The isolated peasant usually has no access to government funds or technical aid and is unable to get his crops to market because the government never has enough money to build the necessary infrastructure, such as roads and bridges. Moreover, jungle farming is a complex ecological challenge quite beyond the technical or financial capabilities of the illiterate peasant, who employs the traditional slash-and-burn method to clear the land. Slash-and-burn has already caused serious erosion in many parts of Latin America; in areas like the Amazon jungle, where the entire ecological balance depends on the topsoil, it brings certain disaster.

Unlike Médici, his successor, General Ernesto Geisel (1974–79), took the view that marginal farming was uneconomical in the Amazon, a position that ecologists and agronomists would support. But Geisel's policy for the Amazon's development was far more destructive than anything envisioned by Médici, for instead of encouraging peasants to burn a few thousand acres, the Geisel government gave rich Brazilian industrialists and foreign companies official subsidies to destroy millions of acres of jungle to make room for cattle ranching, the worst possible solution for the Amazon. In the state of Pará, for example, pasture that flourished in the first year after planting died off after three years. Said Wilhelm Brinkmann, a German ecologist working at the Amazon Research Institute near Manaus, the Brazilian Amazon's capital: "I am against the great cattle ranches in the Amazon not because the forests are more beautiful. The severe cutting should be avoided for economic reasons. In a short time it will be necessary to fertilize the pasture to produce meat, and this is uneconomical."[115] (Fertilizer prices in the Amazon are four times those in southern Brazil, where sugar and coffee are grown.)

According to SUDAM studies, cattle ranching in the Amazon yields an 18 percent profit on investment, but agricultural projects would yield 28 percent and forestry, 55.4 percent. Professor Rodrigues Lima of the Amazon School of Agronomy takes a similar line, urging the cultivation of rubber, cacao, babaçu, coconut, and palm-oil plants, fruits, black pepper, guaraná, and cashews, all of which are native to the environment. "Nature itself is giving us a lesson in how to use these soils, and that is with forests," he said. "If the soil was covered with trees of a certain type of vegetation, why should we row against the current?"

While a few multinationals operating in the Amazon have followed this advice, among them Belgium's corporate giant Socfin, which is planting 82,500 acres of jungle with palm-oil plants, most have confined their interests to cattle or mining. The size of some of the ranches boggles the imagination: the Italian conglomerate Liquigas has carved out a 1.4-million-acre spread in the Mato Grosso between two tributaries of the Amazon, yet that is nothing compared to the holdings of the U.S. multimillionaire Daniel Keith Ludwig, who owns 3.7 million acres of Amazon land along the Jarí and Parú rivers, an area equivalent to half of Belgium. Altogether, foreign firms own some 50 million acres in the Amazon territory, according to a survey by the Brazilian Congress. Nearly 250 million acres of jungle forest have been cut down for cattle pasture.†

The Amazon has always excited foreign interest, particularly during the rubber boom in the early part of the century, but only since the 1964 military coup have foreign companies moved into the region in a big way, thanks to changes in the mining code and

† Brazilian newspaper reports in late 1978 suggested an even larger scale of destruction. Citing sources in the government forestry institute, the Brazilian press described a project to cut down an additional 140 million acres of trees under lumber "risk contracts" with foreign corporations similar to those with the oil companies. Sale of the trees would be used to pay part of Brazil's foreign debt, the newspapers reported. The Brazilian Environment Association sent President Geisel a cable imploring him "not to put your name on this black page of our history." (Guillermo Real, *"Destrucción de selva amazónica provocará un desastre mundial,"* EFE [Rio de Janeiro, Dec. 16, 1978].)

land legislation that encourage foreign ownership, and tax exemptions for up to fifteen years. Some of the world's biggest mining and metals conglomerates have obtained concessions in the Amazon, including Kaiser Industries, Royal Dutch Shell, National Bulk Carriers, Rio Tinto Zinc, Hanna Mining, Nippon Steel, the Aluminum Company of Canada, Reynolds Metals, Alcoa Aluminum, Falconbridge Nickel Mines, Canada's BRASCAN, U. S. Steel, Bethlehem Steel, and Gulf+Western. An equally impressive roster of twenty-nine multinationals is involved in cattle ranching, the United States leading with fifteen companies.

Normally such land is acquired through local intermediaries who frequently use questionable tactics, such as forgery of real estate documents and the forced eviction of squatters by armed bands in the pay of the company. Americans have also been active in land speculation. Robert MacGohn was embroiled in a dispute over a matter of 250,000 acres with Georgia-Pacific Corporation, the Oregon plywood giant that owns a million acres in the Amazon. Although MacGohn was the protagonist in a land-selling conspiracy uncovered by a Brazilian congressional inquiry, he was never brought to court.[116] U.S. entrepreneur John Weaver Davis, who owned a 250,000-acre cattle ranch in the Amazon, was killed, along with two of his sons, by a group of sixty *posseiros* (homesteaders) in July 1976, following a three-year land dispute. While Davis' family described the *posseiros* as invaders who moved in on the land and stole logs and machinery, other sources asserted that the *posseiros* were settled on the land before Davis bought it. (Under Brazilian law, a *posseiro* is entitled to the land after ten years' occupancy, but both SUDAM and the agrarian reform institute have ignored these rights when selling titles in the Amazon.) In 1973 the *posseiros* on the Davis estate went to the state authorities when Davis fenced 70,000 acres with barbed wire, cutting off ninety families from their only source of water. Shortly thereafter, a police patrol caught Davis carrying illegal weapons and driving with three peasants roped in the back of his truck.[117] Still no action was taken by the government, and, as so often happens in the Amazon, the issue was eventually settled with guns.

Unlike the *posseiro,* the Amazon Indian has no defense whatsoever against the land greed of foreigners, since the government's Indian institute, FUNAI, which is supposed to protect the aboriginal population, has repeatedly stated, "The Indian cannot stand in the way of progress." Or as the governor of the Amazon territory of Roraima put it, "I am of the opinion that an area as rich as this—with gold, diamonds, and uranium—is not able to afford the luxury of conserving a half-dozen Indian tribes who are holding back development."[118] Accordingly, Brazil's Indian population declined from 2 million Indians at the beginning of the century to 200,000 in 1963 and to a mere 100,000 by 1978.[119] At the current rate of attrition, predict Brazilian anthropologists, the Indians will be extinct within a decade. That bleak forecast is shared by the military governor of the Amazon center at Boa Vista, who said that the Indians would never survive the Amazon road construction program.

A number of multinationals, European, Canadian, and U.S., have been accused of contributing to the Indians' plight. Dr. Jean Chiappino, a French doctor, charged that seven large companies which had been given permission to prospect on an Indian sanctuary in the territory of Rondônia were responsible for a 1972 epidemic that decimated the Cintas Largas Indians. Three of the companies named were owned by the Bolivian tin magnate Antenor Patiño, known in Bolivia as the "Metal Devil" for his company's exploitation of workers in the Patiño tin mines, which were nationalized by the Bolivian Government in the early fifties.[120] According to a study by the World Council of Churches, the meat packing company Swift Armour, which is now a subsidiary of the Canadian conglomerate BRASCAN, and its partner, King Ranch of Texas, carved out a 180,000-acre ranch in the state of Maranhão that had been set aside as a reservation for the Urubú-Kaapor and Tembe tribes. Thanks to the intervention of the Brazilian Interior Minister, FUNAI's objections to the purchase were overruled and jurisdiction transferred to state officials, who approved the deal with Swift and King.[121] King Ranch Brazil's director, Guilherme Cardoso, defended the ranching project on the ground that "there are no Indians in the region,"[122] but a 1973 study by the Aborigines Protection Society of London confirmed the World Council of Churches' report that the land had indeed belonged to the Indians.[123]

Part of Daniel Keith Ludwig's vast Amazon empire occupies land that once belonged to the Apalaí tribe, and Volkswagen's 287,000-acre cattle ranch in the Araguaia region includes the territory of the Northern Cayapo tribes. According to Camilo Martin Vianna, president of the Brazilian Society for the Preservation of Natural Resources, Ludwig's employees are clearing large areas of Amazon forest with chemicals identical to those used by U.S. troops to destroy jungle areas in Vietnam. (Known as "agent orange," these toxic 2, 4-D and 2, 4, 5-T herbicides are considered by U.S. scientists to be 700 times more dangerous to human beings than thalidomide.[124]) Both the Brazilian forestry institute and Brazil's leading landscape designer, Robert Burle Marx, denounced Volkswagen for burning 7.5 million trees in a 23,500-acre area, a charge substantiated by the Skylab satellite. Company officials claimed that the trees' destruction was part of the contract they had signed with SUDAM and added that they intended to clear another 172,500 acres of trees in 1976.‡[125]

‡ Ecologists have frequently voiced the fear that destruction of the Amazon jungle, popularly known as the "lungs of the world," will reduce the amount of oxygen in the earth's atmosphere by as much as 50 percent. Preliminary investigations by Brazil's Center for Nuclear Energy in Agriculture refute this theory. However, the investigation says nothing about the adverse effects of large increases in carbon dioxide. According to Dr. Harold Sioli of the Max Planck Research Institute in West Germany, burning extensive areas of forest in the Amazon generates dangerously high levels of carbon dioxide in the atmosphere. (Each acre burned gives off 120 tons of carbon dioxide.) Sioli calculates that if the unthinkable happened and most of the Amazon jungle were burned to make way for cattle ranches, there would be a 10 percent increase in carbon dioxide in the earth's atmosphere, thereby raising the earth's temperature about seven degrees Fahrenheit. Among other effects, the polar ice caps could melt and the sea level rise by more than one hundred feet. ("What Shall We Do to Save Amazonia?," *Oiga* [Lima, May 18, 1973], reproduced in *Latin America Documentation*, [Washington, D.C.: U. S. Catholic Conference, Jan. 1974], p. 8.) (Sioli, who lived seventeen years in the Amazon and has dedicated his life to its study, is highly respected in Brazil for his work on the Amazon.)

Brazilian ecologist Vianna believes that the unthinkable could very well happen. If the current process of destruction continues, said Vianna, the Amazon jungle will be a desert within forty years. Vianna's fears are shared by scientists at the Amazon Research Institute at Manaus, who describe the jungle's rapid destruction as a "catastrophe caused by ignorant technicians." According to the institute's botanists, some eighty thousand Amazon species of plants have yet to be classified, at least one hundred of which are believed medicinal, yet many of these plants are bound to disappear in the ongoing onslaught. Also endangered are some two thousand species of fish, which are already suffering the effects of river pollution from industrial waste and open-pit mining.

But perhaps the worst example of the multinationals' slash-and-burn methods in the Amazon is provided by the Italian conglomerate Liquigas, which purchased 1.4 million acres in the heart of the Xavante Indians' territory. Sixty Indians died when the military forced them to move from their land,[126] and now only a few charred stumps remain of the forests where the Xavantes once hunted, the land having been seeded in grass. Like most Amazon cattle ranches, the Liquigas project produces only for the export market, using an airstrip big enough to accommodate chartered 707s that fly direct to Italy with the meat packaged in supermarket cuts and the price stamped in lire.*[127]

However much U.S. and European consumers may benefit from such exports, there can be little doubt that the cattle and lumber enterprises in the Amazon are producing the same mass poverty already evident in the Northeast. Even some government officials, such as the head of the National Housing Bank, are predicting disaster, for most of the 120,000 laborers who now work on the multinationals' estates have no assured jobs, no land, and almost no purchasing power. It is unlikely that the highly mechanized rural enterprises will employ more than 20,000 of these workers permanently, and the remainder can end up only in new slums on the edges of the estates or in the Amazon's towns. And 10 million landless peasant families in other parts of the country are already considered "surplus population."

"We want land on earth . . ."

The Catholic Church has not only suffered vicious persecution because it defends Brazil's Indians (see Chapter IX); its priests, nuns, and bishops have also been jailed and tortured for supporting the *posseiros* in the Amazon's ongoing struggle for land. At

* Liquigas' Brazilian associates have also been credited with some ingenious innovations. Henning Albert Boilensen, director of Liquigas' Brazilian partner, Associgas, was killed by urban guerrillas after insistent reports that he was one of the financial pillars of the notorious Operação Bandeirantes (OBAN), a joint Army–political police torture network responsible for the deaths of some one thousand Brazilians. Some of the people detained by OBAN reported that Boilensen personally assisted in torture sessions. He is also remembered in connection with a device called the "Boilensen pianola," which delivers electric shocks to political prisoners. ("By the Way: Brazil," *Latin America* [London: Aug. 6, 1976].)

the center of this conflict is the prelature (a type of pre-diocese) of São Félix do Araguaia, a 58,000-square-mile area with only 100,000 people in the state of Mato Grosso bounded by the Araguaia and Xingu rivers. The prelature includes two Indian reservations and a large number of *posseiro* homesteads, as well as Brazilian- and foreign-owned cattle ranches such as the Liquigas spread: in short, all the elements for conflict in the Amazon. The villages are without electricity; there are no paved roads, no telephones, newspapers, or television; and the only communication is by river or potholed dirt road. One doctor serves the entire region.

At the head of this far-flung prelature is a diminutive bishop of Spanish origin, Pedro Casaldáliga, who fears nothing and no one. Born in Catalonia in 1928, Dom Pedro learned early what persecution and courage mean. During the Spanish Civil War he made his confession in stables and received communion at secretly held Masses. His uncle, a priest, was killed by the communists in a concentration camp. Casaldáliga soon distinguished himself as a priest by his writings, particularly his sensitive poetry with its concern for the suffering of others. A writer for Catholic radio programs and magazines, in 1967 he left the comfort of a Claretian seminary in Spain for the jungles of Brazil. Four years later he was named the first bishop of São Félix.

Recalled Dom Pedro:

> When I arrived in São Félix with one other companion, we were the only priests in the entire region, and naturally we had no idea of what sort of pastoral program should be developed. So we began to walk, to see, to feel, to make contact with reality. We soon realized that, with the exception of the Indians, most of the people came from other parts of Brazil, particularly the Northeast, a land scourged by drought, *latifundio*, and the most cruel colonization. We also felt that these people were facing the same problem here in the "promised land" that they had suffered in the Northeast, or the gradual loss of their farms to *latifundio*. We began to understand that these people who had been unable to obtain land where they were born were not going to obtain it here either. So we decided that if we really wanted to establish a Church of the People based on the local communities we

would first have to confront the principal social problems. How can you bring together in a permanent church community people who are constantly migrating?

We also began to perceive the exploitation of the peons, an exploitation so scandalous that you could call it a new form of slavery. The large ranches employ these peons, sometimes in the thousands, with no regard for the labor laws or minimum health standards, with no schools for their children or even the possibility of leaving the ranches, which are patrolled by gunmen paid by the owners; in sum, a "Wild West" that isn't in the least picturesque but a genuine social tragedy. And then there is the problem of the Indians, who also are being forced off their land through brutal contact with civilization, its diseases and vices, which have contributed to the increasing disintegration of the tribes.

The regime's official policy for the Amazon is based on enormous fiscal incentives that benefit only the large ranches owned by wealthy national and international interests, opening up huge highways to serve these same interests. Cattle are supposed to replace men, and if things continue as they are, I may end up as a bishop of cows and oxen because there won't be any people left.

For all these reasons the prelature chose to work with the poor, and automatically, without wanting to, it came into conflict with the powerful and the rich. It was also necessary to develop a pastoral program with less emphasis on traditional sacramental methods of evangelization and more social content—the defense of land rights, education, and medical assistance.[128]

Alone in the Amazon forest one day, Dom Pedro brought these ideas together in a single stanza of poetry that he scratched on the back of a wild banana leaf with the point of a pocket knife. The poem has since become the rallying cry of 10 million landless peasant families:

> We are the people of a nation
> We are the people of God
> We want land on earth
> We already have it in heaven.

As poor as the people he serves, with nothing to set him apart as a bishop, Dom Pedro lives in a humble house in São Félix, where he washes his own clothes, cooks meals, cleans dishes, and shares other chores with the priests who live and work with him. This "unseemly" behavior and his constant struggle on behalf of the Indians and *posseiros* have earned him the enmity of the region's landowners, who were at odds with Casaldáliga even before his appointment as bishop because of a document he had sent government authorities on white slavery on the ranches. But despite strong pressure on the papal nuncio, Casaldáliga was named bishop of São Félix. He used the occasion to launch a pastoral letter, "The Church of the Amazon in Conflict with the *Latifundio*," that caused him to be briefly jailed; he was one of the first of numerous bishops to be so treated in recent years. The letter achieved its desired effect, setting off a series of documented denunciations by the Brazilian hierarchy, the first of which was "I Have Heard the Cry of My People." It was also largely because of Casaldáliga's letter that the federal government issued a decree in April 1972 stating that all agricultural enterprises financed by fiscal incentives had to respect the rights of *posseiros* already living on the land, and that these *posseiros* were entitled to form villages. In theory there was no reason why such rights should not have been respected, since there was more than enough land to go around. But as the governor of the state of Mato Grosso himself admitted, the same land was frequently sold or claimed by several different owners.[129] Although Mato Grosso has an area of 463,200 square miles, 656,200 square miles were actually sold, and these fictitious 193,000 square miles are the source of most of the land disputes in such areas as the prelature of São Félix.

Among the chief disputants was CODEARA (Company for the Development of the Araguaia), a land development company backed by São Paulo banking interests and one of several Brazilian intermediaries that clear Amazon land for sale to foreign companies. Like many of these firms, CODEARA acquired the land by signing a deed in a distant city office without ever inquiring into the legal rights of the hundreds of *posseiros* who already occupied it. Nor did CODEARA scruple to use questionable methods in its employment of local labor or the eviction of *posseiros* when it began clearing the land.

One of the areas claimed by CODEARA was the town of Santa Terezinha, with a population of some one thousand people, and the surrounding Araguaia River valley in northeastern Mato Grosso. It was here that the company first clashed with Father François Jentel, a gaunt, forty-eight-year-old French priest who had worked among the region's Indians and poor settlers for two decades. Jentel was appalled by CODEARA's labor practices and initiated legal proceedings that eventually led to a federal police investigation. According to Leonard Greenwood of the *Los Angeles Times:*

> Their report caused an international scandal when they told how twelve hundred men were being held at gunpoint in slave conditions in the jungle camps of CODEARA. Men were ill and dying with malaria. Others died in the jungle trying to escape. Some were beaten and there were reports that others had been shot while trying to escape. In a report that could hardly have been clearer or more specific, the police team named eight men as being responsible for the conditions. But now, almost three years later, the men immediately responsible for the conditions and the powerful company owners that employed them are still at large. There has been no trial.[180]

CODEARA never forgave Father Jentel for his meddling, and by 1971 government authorities were warning the Church and the French embassy of his pending expulsion. CODEARA took matters into its own hands by constructing a building in the middle of Santa Terezinha's main street and bulldozing a partially completed health clinic that Jentel and the peasants were building on Church property. A member of the prelature was beaten up when he attempted to photograph the destruction. The local police corporal, who had attended parish religion courses and therefore had some idea of what Father Jentel was trying to achieve, defended the people's right to build a clinic, and for this he was later brutally beaten in a local bar by CODEARA's henchmen. Although the Church lodged an official protest, no action was taken.[131]

After consulting with the *posseiros* and Bishop Casaldáliga, Jentel authorized the reconstruction of the clinic. CODEARA representatives meanwhile had unsuccessfully tried to persuade the government that the company was the victim of the prelature's aggression. When this failed, the company threatened to send in a band of armed men to destroy the new clinic "with many bullets and machine guns."[132] Jentel told the people there would be no bullets or guns because anyone who questioned the clinic's reconstruction, whether the police or the company, would have to deal with the rightful owner of the property, the Church. But he was wrong. A month after the first attack in February 1972, CODEARA vehicles arrived in Santa Terezinha carrying thirty armed men, including several policemen from other parts of the state. They converged on the clinic, where they first threatened the workers with machine guns, then announced that all were under arrest. But the *posseiros,* who were armed with shotguns, were not prepared to submit without a fight, and shooting erupted between the two groups in which eight people were wounded.[133] Jentel, who was half a mile away in the parish house at the time, arrived after the CODEARA men had fled, leaving behind in their haste two incriminating cables from regional police headquarters ordering the arrest of all the town's civic leaders.

Although Jentel had repeatedly informed state and federal authorities of the trouble in Santa Terezinha and for five years had prevented the *posseiros* from taking the law into their own hands by attacking CODEARA, the French priest was accused by Brazil's military regime of leading an armed assault on state police and therefore endangering national security. Five *posseiros* were arrested, and forty others were forced to go into hiding for three and a half months while CODEARA's henchmen and thirty soldiers ranged the forests in search of them. Jentel was put on trial, along with José Norberto Silveira, director of CODEARA; but while Silveira was exonerated, Jentel was sentenced to ten years' imprisonment. According to Church documents, there was never any doubt of the outcome. Two officers of the Justice Department sent instructions to the four military judges, and an attempt was made to replace the lone civil judge in the case. Jentel's lawyer was threatened, two peasant witnesses for the prosecution were jailed and forced to sign statements that they later said they did not even understand, and the third witness, Colonel Euro Barbosa, was the same military officer who had led the attack on the Santa Terezinha clinic.[134]

The lone dissenting voice, Civil Judge Plinio Barbosa Martins, said he was in "total disagreement" with the military court's ruling and that there was "absolutely no basis for finding Father Jentel guilty of criminal conduct." Said the judge:

> On the contrary, I admire him for his courage to leave a developed nation like France to spend twenty years of his life here in the Amazon of Mato Grosso to bring a little civilization and Christian goodwill to the Indians and Brazilians who live in these inhospitable lands. He has exposed himself to countless dangers, known serious illnesses, and all this for love and human solidarity, the very same qualities that have been recommended and encouraged by numerous Popes in their well-known encyclicals. There are some who call the Church communist because of its concern for human rights. But no authentic Christian can willingly accept the sufferings of others.
>
> In all conscience, I profoundly believe that the condemnation of Jentel is neither just nor humane. All the facts and everything that he has done demonstrate that Jentel is far from being a Marxist. If he were, why would he bury himself in the forests of the Amazon when he could live in a city and indoctrinate the young in class warfare? I find in Father Jentel's conduct a Christian example to follow. He deserves a prize, not prison![135]

But despite protests from the Brazilian Bishops' Conference, the papal nuncio and the French Embassy, and an international outcry against the injustice of Jentel's imprisonment, government authorities continued to insist that the priest was a communist agitator, and a foreign one to boot. If that were the case, said Bishop Casaldáliga, "I, too, can be detained and expelled because I am just as foreign as Jentel and, as bishop, have more responsibility than he does for what happens in the prelature. Furthermore, I personally gave the order for the reconstruction of the clinic, and I have approved and do approve of his solidarity with the *posseiros* whom he defended. I assume all responsibility for what he did, and if there are any 'consequences' to be suffered, I state publicly that I will not seek any intervention on my behalf by the Brazilian Conference of Bishops or the papal nuncio. When I was consecrated a bishop, I was not invested with any superior order of privilege. I gave myself, through the merciful choice of our Lord Jesus, to a life of total sacrifice."[136]

Casaldáliga was to suffer the "consequences" sooner than he expected. Within days of Jentel's sentencing, one hundred military police from the Army and the Air Force invaded the town of São Félix under the command of the same Colonel Euro Barbosa who had led the attack on the Santa Terezinha clinic. The entire staff of the prelature's high school was rounded up for questioning and identification, as were Casaldáliga's assistant Father Pedro María Sola Barbarín, another priest, and a nun. The bishop's house was searched, church files were carried off by the police, and when Casaldáliga protested, Air Force Captain Monteiro, shouting insults and threatening reprisals, slapped him in the face. Meanwhile, another contingent of sixty military police descended on the village of Serra Nova, where they searched all the houses, including the prelature mission, and arrested the local priest and several laymen. The mission house in the village of Pontinópolis also was raided, and police invaded the Tapirapé Indian mission of the Sisters of Jesus, the first such incident since the nuns founded the mission in 1952. Said one of the *posseiros* whose house was repeatedly searched: "I've never seen such badly educated people. . . . If they were local police, one could understand it, but these were lieutenants, captains, colonels!"[137]

Casaldáliga and the four priests who work with him were taken to a nearby ranch, and there the priests were tortured. Father Leopoldo Belmonte, a thirty-two-year-old Spanish missionary, said, "They tied my hands tightly behind my back and then made me run, sit, and stand up for a very long time." Belmonte also reported that "they kicked us and beat us on all parts of our bodies. . . . Father Eugenio Consoli vomited blood from the terrible blows he received."[138] Casaldáliga said later: "No matter how much we are lied about or condemned, we will continue our work of consciousness-raising and evangelization, which for the Church of Christ means a total concern for man and not just for spiritual matters, contrary to the opinion of that presumed theologian Colonel Euro Barbosa."[139]

The attack on the São Félix prelature immediately brought down the censure of the entire Brazilian Church. Dom Fernando Gómez dos Santos, archbishop of the city of Goiânia, protested to the Ministries of Justice and the Army, and eighteen bishops sent a letter of solidarity to Casaldáliga. In August, on the feast of the Assumption of Our Lady, the bishops and their representatives gathered in São Félix for a co-celebration with Dom Pedro, his parents, all the priests, nuns, and brothers working in the prelature, and hundreds of peons and *posseiros* who had come to town from deep in the jungle to express their support for "such a beautiful testimony of evangelical courage and love." Government authorities were not impressed, however, and after seizing the prelature high school, which was taken over by the State Office of Education, they closed the Church's health clinic in São Félix, saying it was superfluous because the Department of Health intended to open its own clinic. (The clinic was duly inaugurated, but it is open only once every two weeks, when medical students from Campo Grande, the nearest city and 666 miles away, are flown in for the day.[140])

But these incidents were petty when compared to the smear campaign against Casaldáliga by the prelature's large foreign and Brazilian cattle interests and subsequent attempts by the military regime to expel the bishop from Brazil. The landowners bought advertisements in the local press to denounce Casaldáliga as a communist agitator; flyers criticizing the prelature's work were sent to churches throughout Brazil; and the powerful Rede Globo radio and television chain reported that Casaldáliga had printed in the prelature newspaper a communist manifesto that urged the peasants to rebel in the name of religion. According to Casaldáliga, the majority of Rede Globo's attacks were "ordered by the administrators and technocrats of the multinational *latifundio*," including the Brazilian representatives of the 287,000-acre Volkswagen cattle ranch, who are among Rede Globo's most important clients.[141] Relations with the Brazilian cattle ranchers were no better, said Dom Pedro, adding that "there is no longer any sense in saying Mass on the same estates where peons, Indians, and *posseiros* are mistreated." Tensions were running so high at one point, reported a fellow bishop, Tomás Balduino, that professional killers were hired to eliminate Casaldáliga.[142]

Balduino's accusations formed part of a dossier taken to the Pope by Cardinal Paulo Evaristo Arns of São Paulo, when the Church discovered that the Ministry of Justice had initiated proceedings to expel Casaldáliga. The day after Arns's interview with the Pope, the government denied that it had ever intended to expel the bishop, no doubt because of the Pope's pointed warning: "Whatever is done to the bishop of São Félix is done to the Pope."

The Church was less successful in defending Father Jentel, who was released after a year in prison when Brazil's Supreme Military Court reversed the lower tribunal's decision. Following a study and home leave in France for a year and a half, Jentel returned to work in Brazil, only to be kidnapped by security police as he was leaving the residence of Cardinal Aloisio Lorscheider, president of the Brazilian Bishops' Conference. Jentel was shipped out the next day on a plane bound for France. In a gesture of solidarity and friendship, Rio de Janeiro's conservative, pro-military Cardinal Eugenio de Aráujo Sales accompanied him to the plane. "This event," said the country's bishops, "was a step backward for justice, and we protest it as a Church and in the name of the people."

Despite such setbacks, the Church of the Amazon continued to grow: Starting with the original two priests who came to São Félix in 1967, Casaldáliga's team increased to seven priests, eight brothers, four nuns, and eighteen laymen. Among the prelature's many projects were adult literacy classes; youth and housewives' clubs; the only newspaper in the region, *Alvorada;* a producers' and consumers' cooperative, founded by Father Jentel, that now has eighty enthusiastic members; and in Santa Terezinha a health cooperative with three hundred members that sells medicine at reasonable prices. None of these self-help projects received any support from the prelature's bourgeoisie. On the contrary, Manoel Aírton Alves e Limoeiro, the subprefect of São Félix and owner of its only drugstore, spoke for the majority of the landowners when he said, "We don't want to see priests around here."[143] But Casaldáliga's team is undeterred, believing that the only way to end the exploitation of the peasants is through more education, better health facilities, and a government administration that is not in the pocket of the *latifundio*. "Around here," explained Father Pedro María Sola Barbarín, vicar of São Félix, "people quickly learn the meaning of Darwin's selection of the species."

"We came to the region a bit late because there was no existing church," added Bishop Casaldáliga, "but we had the luck to arrive after Vatican II and Medellín, so we don't have the right to commit the errors that others naturally made."

Casaldáliga and the Brazilian Church are not alone in their concern for these landless people—Indians, *posseiros,* or peons. Ralph Nader spoke as follows at a conference on Brazil's Indian policy at Washington's Brookings Institute:

> The word genocide is often used a little too liberally in other areas of the world, but if anybody wants to know what the definition of it is in a contemporary way, then you need to look at the documented trends of destruction over the last few decades in the Amazon basin. While almost every day, students in the United States recoil with horror when they read about the destruction of the Carib Indians in the Caribbean centuries ago . . . exactly the same thing is going on in the Amazon areas with very, very little attention being paid thereof.
>
> Now, what American companies do in other countries is clearly of interest to U.S. citizens, and there's been an amazing neglect of multinational corporate activity in South America generally in the last decade. I think that this area has got to be probed by one or more of the following agencies: the U. S. Senate Foreign Relations Committee, the House Foreign Relations Subcommittee, and the Subcommittee on Multinational Corporations, looking directly for activities pursuant to multinational effects in foreign lands and how they affect U.S. policy.
>
> Second, there needs to be an inquiry into the funding role by U.S. agencies. The taxpayer, unwittingly, is supporting a great deal of what is being done in the Amazon area through government lending agencies, through the AID program, and through other protective U.S. agencies, such as the government insurance program.
>
> When U.S. corporations interfere in the internal affairs of

Brazil, that is a U. S. Government concern. And when taxpayers are funding activities, lending activities, surveillance
activities of the Amazon basin, that is a U. S. Government
concern.[144]

Nader is correct when he says that very little is known about
the activities of U.S. corporate giants in Latin America. The little
that is known is due almost entirely to probings by the U. S.
Congress, whose various committees and subcommittees have investigated some of the multinationals' more notorious ventures
south of the border, such as ITT's attempt to prevent Salvador
Allende from assuming the presidency in Chile.[145] And some information has filtered out because of investigations by the Securities and Exchange Commission, which exposed many recent cases
of bribery by U.S. corporations, and because of lobbying by
religious pressure groups. The latter include a number of Catholic
and Protestant organizations, such as the National Council of
Churches, which have used their stock in the large corporations to
initiate proxy battles, either to prevent a company from investing
in a country with a repressive government, such as Chile, or to extract information on, say, working conditions on Gulf+West-
ern's Dominican Republic sugar plantations.

In themselves, these actions have little effect on corporate decisions. It is typical, for example, that attempts by an ecumenical
group of U.S. and Canadian Church officials to dissuade General
Motors from investing in the Chilean automobile industry were
unsuccessful. The group's argument that it would be both "immoral and economically unwise" to lend support to Chile's military regime because of its "numerous violations of human rights
and documented cases of torture" could hardly impress General
Motors—or any other company whose sole concern is making
money. According to a General Motors spokesman, the corporation's management does not believe that its activities will either
strengthen the government or imply approval of it.[146]

On the other hand, such protests do help publicize the issues
and increase the amount of information available to the public,
and it is only with such knowledge that U.S. taxpayers/share-
holders and their representatives in Congress can determine
whether corporate industry should be held to an ethical account-

ing. Following testimony in Congress describing bribes by 306 U.S. corporations, for example, Congress passed a tough law, with fines of up to $1 million and five years in prison, for any U.S. executive caught suborning foreign officials. "I share the opinion of Congress that bribery is ethically repugnant and competitively unnecessary," said President Carter when signing the bill into law. "The corrupt practices among corporations and foreign public officials undermine the integrity and stability of governments and harm our relations with other countries. The recent revelations about frequent bribes abroad have weakened public confidence in our fundamental institutions."

Without such revelations, bribery—and much worse—will continue unchecked. Not that anyone should expect the multinationals to take ethical stands; by their own definition, they are amoral institutions.[147] But that does not excuse the failure of others, usually out of indifference, to question these companies' behavior or to demand some ethical restraints on the race for profit. Quite apart from the moral issues of whether one wants to buy a car or a steak from a company that is responsible for the suffering and death of defenseless Indians and peasants in the Amazon basin, there is the practical question of law. When an American buys shares in a U.S. company, he does not expect that company to be involved, even indirectly, in the murder of innocent people or the overthrow of a legitimately constituted government, since that is against the law. Or are there two sets of laws, one for the foreign subsidiaries and another for the parent companies in the United States? It is a question that must concern the shareholder when many of these companies are earning half their profits abroad. Whatever the multinationals may believe, there must come a day of reckoning, as it came for W. R. Grace in Peru. Nationalization with compensation is the mildest form of retribution. And then who will explain to the stockholders why a company had to write off its investment in Latin America?

For religious institutions such as the Catholic Church, the issue goes much deeper, for if a Christian acknowledges a code of moral behavior, it cannot condone, even by default, the unethical practices of U.S. executives or government officials in the poorer countries that are most in need of justice and real charity—not handouts, but an attempt at understanding. The business of making money should not be an end in itself, wrote the Vatican's Secretary of State Cardinal Jean Villot, in a letter of support to the Chilean Church for its opposition to the military regime's ruthless free-market economic policies. What is needed, said the cardinal, is an economy with a human objective that satisfies the real needs of the community, and not an unbridled capitalism that creates artificial desires and mere consumerism in a small, privileged minority. "We are not denying the legitimate right to property," said the cardinal. "But it must be clearly understood that property rights are subject to the needs of the community and that it is not possible to accept a society divided between a selfish, privileged minority and a mass of people deprived of life's essentials."

CHAPTER VIII

VILLAINS AFOOT—The CIA Linked to the Tradition, Family, and Property Movement— German Finance Replaces CIA Funding in Support of Military Dictatorships and Multinationals

The CIA goes to church but not to pray.

Popular saying

Adolfo Centeno Alancastro was suitably sympathetic. It really was a shame, he told the Uruguayan Jesuit, how brutish Uruguayan police agents were, but what could you do with people who thought that Medellín* was the name of a person and confused pictures of Christ with Che Guevara.

The police had just ransacked the priest's house in Montevideo, carrying off his entire library to burn, including a rare collection of theological treatises, and here was their boss commiserating with him over the loss of his life's work! According to Centeno, such incidents would never happen if Church officials would only cooperate with educated policemen like himself.

Whatever his claims, Centeno had bona fide credentials, for

* The historic conference of Latin-American bishops held in the Colombian city of Medellín in 1968 that set the hemisphere's Church on a new course for social justice (see Chapter II).

like his counterparts in Brazil and Chile he could demonstrate an intimate knowledge of theology and Church politics, as well as an expertise in intelligence and "dirty tricks," courtesy of the CIA. After years of using and abusing local and foreign religious groups in Latin America, the CIA now appears to be seeking a lower profile in this area, partly because of the ruckus caused by indignant Catholic and Protestant organizations in the United States following revelations in 1975 of CIA penetration of missionary groups. More to the point, the Latin-American security agencies can now do the job themselves. Centeno, for example, was trained in the Panama Canal Zone;[1] his boss at the Uruguayan Interior Ministry, Luis Vargas Garmendia, was an old CIA hand who worked with former CIA agent Philip Agee in the 1960s. The pair spent their time making life difficult for diplomats from the socialist countries accredited to Uruguay back in the days when Uruguay was still a democracy.[2] Vargas Garmendia was generally thought to have planned the murders of two former Uruguayan senators in Buenos Aires in 1976.[3] He was later made secretary to President Aparicio Méndez, front man for Uruguay's repressive military regime.

Because of his background in Church affairs, acquired during a stint in Central America, Centeno was chosen to monitor and persecute Uruguay's critical Catholic Church. Also useful were his credentials as a militant in Catholic Action, a laymen's movement that was influential in Latin America during the 1960s. Centeno professed not to understand why Uruguayan priests were so "strangely" reluctant to answer questions, whereas his experience with Catholics in Central America had been "just the opposite."[4] But in view of the regime's arrest and/or expulsion of fifteen religious between 1972 and 1976, the closure of five Church publications, and a smear campaign against Montevideo's Archbishop Carlos Parteli, labeled a communist because he defended human rights, such reticence was well founded. Though an "educated" policeman, Centeno specialized in the "black propaganda"† of half-truths or outright lies practiced by the CIA in its work with Church groups in Ecuador, Brazil, and Chile during the sixties and early seventies. When such important Montevideo bookstores

† For more details on how U.S. agencies encouraged the use of black propaganda by the Latin-American police and military, see appendix.

as Ramos y Mosca refused to stock *The Church of Silence,* a slanderous attack on Chile's bishops by a right-wing Catholic group known as Tradition, Family, and Property (TFP), Centeno threatened the owners.[5] The Uruguayan branch of TFP later came out with its version of the Chilean smear in a dreary tract titled *Leftism in the Church: Communist Fellow Travelers in the Long Adventure of Failures and Changes,* a 384-page denunciation of Uruguay's clergy for "completely abandoning their duty and aiding the enemy of religion and country." (The enemy included such strange bedfellows as the U.S. Democratic Party and the Soviet Union.) Heavily advertised in the government press, *Leftism in the Church* was eulogized as "among the best-selling books in Montevideo," another undocumented exaggeration, according to the bookstore owners.[6]

Men like Centeno owe their skills in part to AID's police training programs (see Chapter VI), but they also adhere to a long tradition of Church spying that dates to the CIA's forerunner, the Office of Strategic Services (OSS), formed during World War II. Later, during the cold war, U.S. missionaries routinely collaborated with the CIA and, on their return to the United States, visited the State Department to be debriefed. In those days there was nothing conspiratorial about this relationship, nor any suggestion of moral conflict: most missionaries shared the concerns of their government, particularly about the spread of communism. A number of Foreign Service personnel came from missionary backgrounds, and it was not uncommon for missionaries to take sides in military/ideological confrontations, the classic example being John Birch. A Baptist missionary who worked with the OSS in World War II and was later killed by a Chinese communist while leading a patrol of Chinese nationalists, Birch was canonized by Robert Welch and the radical Right as the "first martyr" of the cold war.

Because of their personal relationships with the people they serve and the status of their profession, the forty-five thousand U.S. Catholic and Protestant missionaries stationed abroad were and are an obvious source of intelligence, in some areas perhaps the only source. This was particularly true in Latin America, where twelve thousand U.S. missionaries work and where most of the cases of CIA collaboration have been documented. During the

1960s when the Alliance for Progress was in vogue, nobody questioned this relationship, since Church groups and the U. S. Government were agreed on the twin priorities of economic development and anti-communism. "Part of the problem stems from the fact that the great Latin crusade by the churches in the 1950s and 1960s merged, at times almost totally, with the thrust of the Alliance for Progress and its Truman-Eisenhower predecessors," said Thomas Quigley, assistant director of the Division for Latin America of the U. S. Catholic Conference. "The stated goals were to promote development and contain communism, and few then realized the ambiguities contained in that statement. Only later was it learned that development, as practiced, benefited the rich at the expense of the poor, and that containment of communism was often simplistically equated with protecting an unjust and un-Christian status quo. Now we see those aspects. But at that time, the average missionary—perhaps especially the socially progressive ones—sensed a greater affinity with certain people from the local United States embassy or consulate than with fellow missionaries from another country or even congregation. The prime targets for CIA contact were precisely such pragmatic liberals sent in large numbers during the period to Latin America from the United States churches—the 'concerned' missionaries from the mainline Protestant Churches and from Catholic societies like Maryknoll and the Jesuits."[7]

Typical of this sort of collaboration was the Protestant missionary in Bolivia who regularly met with a CIA agent to pass on "all sorts of information about unions and farmers' cooperatives," according to a highly placed minister in the same denomination. "Now," said the minister, "if a missionary had a similar connection, I would call him in and fire him."[8] U.S. missionaries today wonder how they could have been so easily deceived. Looking back, one priest who had worked in Bolivia at the time when United States Special Forces were combing the jungles for Che Guevara and his guerrillas, explained: "The maneuver was to butter one up as to one's knowledge of the terrain and the people, a kind of anthropological recognition of one's merits as a person who knew the area. At that time, most missionaries were very naïve and it usually worked. I don't know what good I was but I talked a lot over beers, feeling flattered by the attention. Later I realized who my drinking companions were."[9]

Darryl Hunt, a Maryknoll missionary who headed the Lima-based *Latinamerica Press* news service covering hemispheric Church affairs, recalled that CIA visits to Maryknoll headquarters in New York were routine up to a decade ago, when the order's superiors were alerted to the agency's intentions. "They tried to get information from the missionaries in the field by developing friendships with them and appearing to ask disinterested questions without identifying themselves as CIA," he added. "U. S. Embassy officials in Lima asked me questions about progressive priests' movements in Peru that later seemed highly suspect."

Jim O'Brien, a former priest who worked in Guatemala in the late 1960s, described how CIA agent Sean Holly used his background as a Maryknoll seminarian to develop contacts with U.S. missionaries. Officially listed as the labor attaché, Holly was later kidnapped by a Guatemalan guerrilla group and freed in exchange for four political prisoners held by the Guatemalan Government. Holly's job, said O'Brien, was to keep tabs on U.S. missionaries, particularly Maryknoll priests and nuns.[10]

According to John D. Marks, a former State Department intelligence analyst and co-author of the controversial *The CIA and the Cult of Intelligence,* 30 to 40 percent of the churchmen he interviewed, during an investigation of the subject, knew of a CIA-Church connection.[11] Marks also reported a retired CIA agent as stating: "Hell, I'd use anybody if it was to the furtherance of an objective. I've used Buddhist monks, Catholic priests, and even a Catholic bishop."[12]

It is precisely this amoral—some would say immoral—attitude that altered the thinking of many missionaries: that and political conditions in the countries where they worked. In the days before Vietnam and Watergate, few missionaries questioned U.S. support of right-wing dictatorships, because those governments claimed to be anti-communist. But as the United States expanded its role as world policeman, its police methods becoming ever more dubious, the missionary was forced to face the conflict posed by his dual role as American citizen and bearer of Christ's universal Good News. Indigenous Christians were suffering imprisonment, torture, and death, as well as hunger and social discrimination, at the hands of repressive governments; and yet these governments were receiving U.S. economic and military aid, and in some instances had been brought to power by the United States. For the missionaries working and living with these people, this was not a remote issue of foreign relations but a question of neighbors and friends. As one Protestant writer put it, "Most missionaries loved the countries and the people where they worked far too much to knowingly damage them."[13] Thus, when these missionaries realized that they had been used as tools by their own government to harm the interests of the people they had thought to serve, they were shocked and angry. The crux of the matter was the blatant violation of freedom of worship, one of the fundamental guarantees in the United States Constitution, by an agency funded by American taxpayers, and all on behalf of right-wing political interests. According to U. S. Senate investigations, the CIA attempted to play God in Latin America, deciding who should be President, who should be eliminated, how the people should live, and whom they should have as allies and enemies. Foreign missionaries and local religious groups were among the many means used to achieve these ends, but because of what they believed and taught, their manipulation must be viewed as an act of calculated cynicism.

CIA Director William Colby's assertion that CIA use of clergy and churches was "no reflection upon their integrity or mission" was absurd: there is conclusive proof that the CIA used religious groups in Latin America for its own secret ends. At the same time it contributed to the persecution and division of Latin America's Catholic Church by supporting right-wing Catholic groups and financed and trained police agencies responsible for the imprisonment, torture, and murder of priests, nuns, and bishops, some of them U.S. citizens. That is why missionary groups in the United States have changed from complacent collaborators to harsh critics of the CIA—they have seen the results of the agency's intervention with their own eyes.

After President Ford announced his approval of illegal U.S. intervention in the internal affairs of the Latin-American countries, sixteen officials of Catholic and Protestant mission agencies wrote him: "Contrary to what you would have us believe, CIA covert actions in the Third World frequently support undemocratic governments that trample on the rights of their own people. We missionaries have felt first-hand the effects of such interventions, which are certainly not in 'the best interests' of the majority of the citizens of those countries. . . . Nor do such actions, which are prohibited by international law and by Article 6 of our own Constitution, serve 'our best interests,' as you stated. Gangster methods undermine world order and promote widespread hatred of the United States."

Warned *New World Outlook,* published by agencies of the United Methodist and United Presbyterian churches: one cannot "defend democracy by destroying it." As long as U.S. citizens shrug their shoulders, romanticize "spy thrillers," and pass the buck to politicians, it added, there will be blood on our hands, "for it is our money and our government that pay for the regimes that do the killing."[14]

To avoid a repetition of the CIA connection of the fifties and sixties, a number of Church groups set up watchdog committees. The Church of the Brethren's General Board, for example, instructed its missionary personnel to "avoid any relationship with the CIA," and a Washington-based ecumenical organization representing Catholic and Protestant missionary groups went so far as to prepare a primer on "how to identify spooks."

Judging by the statements of CIA officials, there were good reasons for such caution. In response to a letter from Senator Mark Hatfield, who had expressed concern over the CIA's continued use of religious organizations, CIA Director Colby said he believed "it would be neither necessary nor appropriate to bar any connection between the CIA and the clergy and the churches." It "would be a mistake and impose a handicap on this agency that would reduce its future effectiveness to a degree not warranted by the real facts of the situation."

David A. Phillips, the CIA's former chief of Latin-American operations and a self-appointed public relations spokesman for the agency, said that "any information-gathering organization would be derelict if it did not take advantage of the in-depth experience of American clerics working in the area." He added that CIA contacts with U.S. missionaries were "to mutual advantage,"[15] though he failed to specify what advantage a missionary might gain from collaborating with an agency involved in the arrest and abuse of priests. Phillips is himself a good example of the mentality that has alienated and shocked so many religious groups. His book *The Night Watch,* a CIA whitewash that does not even try to refute ex–CIA agent Agee's *CIA Diary,* makes it evident that in the CIA no means, however illegal or unpleasant, is ever questioned if it achieves the desired goal. While admitting reservations about the CIA's operations in Chile, for example, Phillips justified the agency's intervention by arguing that orders were orders—after all, who was going to deny President Nixon if he wanted Allende's head? There is no room for moral distinctions in that line of reasoning, and collaboration with the CIA is indeed a reflection on the integrity and mission of U.S. churchmen, whatever Colby may say. Phillips' assertion that CIA contacts with missionary groups have declined in recent years is undoubtedly true, but that is more because missionaries have learned to be suspicious than because the CIA has resolved to be scrupulous.

Whereas it sought out U.S. missionaries primarily for information, the CIA funded and directed local religious groups in Latin America for all manner of covert activities, from bombing church buildings to overthrowing constitutionally elected governments. It ranged the political spectrum from extreme right to center-left, but usually preferred the former, particularly for dirty tricks. The choice was often dictated by the politics of local bishops. In Ecuador, for example, where the majority of the Catholic hierarchy is conservative, the CIA used right-wing Catholic groups. In Chile, the CIA played both sides of the street, conservative and liberal, because most of the bishops favored reform.

In *CIA Diary,* Agee documented a typical campaign that had enlisted local Church support to force the Ecuador Government to break relations with Cuba in the years 1960 to 1962. According to the book, Cardinal Carlos María de la Torre wrote several pastoral letters denouncing communism and Cuban subversion at the behest of Aurelio Dávila Cajas, a leader of Ecuador's Conservative Party, president of the Chamber of Deputies, and a CIA political action and intelligence agent. When Ecuadorian leftists criticized the cardinal, Dávila got CIA money to organize a campaign in support of de la Torre, which included letters and lists of signatures that were published by local Church groups in the Ecuadorian press. Agee reported that Dávila also used the Catholic University youth organization to protest the 1961 visit of a Soviet delegation that had come to discuss possible banana purchases with the Ecuador Government.

Relations between President José María Velasco Ibarra and the Church hierarchy declined rapidly in April 1961, after a religious procession in Quito turned into an anti-communist, anti-Velasco rally because he had refused to break relations with Cuba. To whip up more support for the anti-Cuban cause, wrote Agee, goons from the CIA-financed Social Christian Party stoned a Jesuit church and bombed the cardinal's residence and the offices of the Anti-Communist Front. They had hoped to pin the violence on Cuban sympathizers, but the police caught them red-handed.[16] (Velasco was overthrown in 1961; his successor, Carlos Julio Arosemena, was ousted in 1963. The principal cause of both coups was the Cuba issue.)

In neighboring Colombia, where the hierarchy is unanimously conservative, the CIA financed anti-communist propaganda in the countryside under the guise of a Church radio literacy program, Radio Sutatenza, for some one million peasant listeners. The project also supports peasant leadership courses and a weekly newspaper for rural readers, El Campesino, with a 60,000 circulation. The CIA money was provided through a resident U.S. businessman who was supervised by Raymond Warren, the CIA station chief who later directed the agency's operations against the Allende government in Chile.[17] AID also contributed generously to the project—$4.4 million between 1973 and 1978. Sutatenza, a mixture of propaganda and intelligence disguised by the literacy campaign, was relatively innocuous as CIA operations go. Monsignor José Joaquín Salcedo, the high-living prelate who founded and directed Sutatenza, later broke with Colombia's bishops because the radio station supported birth control programs, a prerequisite for AID funding. Since 1973 Sutatenza has faithfully followed the AID line that Latin America's problems are caused not by unjust social and economic structures but entirely by the population explosion.

Like Sutatenza, Belgian Jesuit Roger Vekemans' Centro Bellarmino, with its myriad peasant and union programs in Chile, was funded and used by the CIA as sops to genuine reform in order to

prevent the masses from becoming too restless.‡ But while Sutatenza was a relatively successful safety valve, according to a study
by the West German Government's Institute of Development,[18]
Vekemans' programs boomeranged when Allende took office.
Moreover, the financial management of the fast-talking Jesuit left
a good deal to be desired, judging by the hanky-panky uncovered
in an AID audit. The free-spending Vekemans was saved from an
AID criminal investigation only because the U. S. Embassy in
Chile insisted that to "mark him as a criminal" would damage the
Christian Democrats, whom the CIA had financed through vari-
ous Vekemans projects.

Unlike the CIA, AID must account for the money it spends.
After its population expert, George M. Coleman, visited Vekemans' headquarters in Santiago to see how the center was
progressing on a population study for which it had received a
$1.34 million AID grant, the agency began to worry. Coleman
said he became suspicious when he observed "the lifestyle there,
the dinners, the lunches, and the building." Believing it improper
for U.S. taxpayers to support such luxurious living, he requested
an audit. When the interim investigation was completed in August
1970, the U. S. Ambassador to Chile, Edward M. Korry, cabled
the State Department that it "implicitly suggests the possibility of
fraud and explicitly states that four contract claims presented and
certified may be in violation of the Foreign Assistance Act."
When the audit was finished the following year, it found the following items:

• $92,840 for unsubstantiated travel and transportation ex-
penses.

• $67,907 for thirteen research and eight seminar contracts that
the terms of the AID grant did not authorize.

• $61,615 in bonuses from surplus funds to Vekemans' staff
that were neither required by labor-management contracts nor by
Chilean law and were, in fact, violations of the AID grant.

• $44,413 for Vekemans' salary and $10,641 for a librarian's
salary, although Vekemans and the librarian worked primarily for
the Jesuits' Center for Research and Social Action (DESAL) and
not for the population study.

‡ See Chapter II, pp. 26–27.

• $16,420 for a study to be conducted by Sergio Silva, brother of the assistant director of the AID-funded projects. Pinedo Hermanos y Cía., the accounting firm Vekemans hired to audit his books, certified the $16,420 expense as accurate, but AID auditors learned the study had not been started. They labeled this expense a "false claim."

• $7,000 for printing two books, although there were no records that the money had ever been spent.

• $3,500 for a course on "Population and Family" in Colombia that was never given.

• $2,000 as part of a contract agreement with the Mexican Social Secretariat to study abortion in Mexico. Auditors learned that the contract was never formalized and the money not spent.

• $7,800 for a contract with the archdiocese of Santo Domingo to study immigration from Haiti to the Dominican Republic. Although the expense was verified by Pinedo Hermanos, AID auditors found that Vekemans had drafted two contracts on the same day—one for $7,800 and one for $6,450. He signed the smaller contract but billed AID for the larger one.

• $1,189 for liquor and entertainment, although AID grants never cover such expenses.

The auditors also reported that Vekemans began destroying financial records before the investigation was completed.[19]

AID never made good its threat to prosecute Vekemans. (The matter now lies in an inactive government file: Case No. 4872, "Fraud Against the Government," April 26, 1971.[20]) Nor did it force him to reimburse the agency. As Ambassador Korry put it, such actions "would specifically contradict our objectives in Chile"—meaning there were too many skeletons in the closet. But the audit did scotch any hope Vekemans may have had for further funding in Colombia, where he and his staff moved after Allende's election. Colombia's AID director, Marvin Weissman, said he had "no intention of funding anything of Father Vekemans'," and that "he was happy to see that Inspections and Investigations Staff had an interest in his activity."[21]

Although Vekemans has collected some powerful friends during his career, including Colombia's Cardinal Aníbal Muñoz Duque and West Germany's bishops, the principal reason for the U. S. Government's reluctance to move against him was his close involvement with Washington's attempts to stop Allende from becoming President. In addition to fellow Jesuit James Vizzard's assertion that Vekemans received $5 million in CIA money after a meeting with John and Robert Kennedy in the White House,* there is conclusive proof of CIA funding through a front organization called the International Development Foundation (IDF), whose cover was blown in 1967. IDF backed such Vekemans projects as the National Association of Farm Workers, the Union of Christian Peasants, and the Institute for Union and Christian Training, as well as a slum dwellers' organization. Moreover, IDF's vice president, Edward Cohen, admitted that "we used Roger Vekemans" and that "Vekemans and the Centro Bellarmino were close to the kinds of groups and forces—in an informal and sometimes formal way—that we were working with."[22] Among other CIA sources, reported Jesuit Vizzard, was a prominent Philadelphia businessman who contributed $25,000 for a Latin-American conference on agrarian reform through the auspices of the Washington office of the National Catholic Rural Life Conference, for which Vizzard worked at the time. When Vizzard commented on the businessman's generosity, his boss, Monsignor Luigi Ligutti, told him, "Oh, it's not his money; it's the CIA's money." Vizzard understood at the time that other conferences had been similarly funded. Vekemans, he said, was secretary of a number of these conferences.[23]

Actually, Vekemans' projects were tame (although somewhat costly for the U.S. taxpayer), compared to the activities of other Chilean Catholic groups funded by the CIA, particularly the notorious Fatherland and Liberty goon squads that formed the guerrilla arm of the extreme Right before and after Allende's election.† A modern version of the Spanish Inquisition—the Pinochet junta later employed a number of the organization's members as police interrogators—Fatherland and Liberty received CIA funds for a variety of purposes, ranging from an attempted military coup to violent demonstrations at political rallies, which its militants at-

* See Chapter II, p. 26.
† Chase Manhattan Bank was also involved in its support through the Yarur textile and financial group in Chile, in which it owned substantial stock—Yarur employed one of Fatherland and Liberty's principal propagandists. (Robinson Rojas Sandford, *The Murder of Allende* [New York: Harper & Row, 1975], p. 112.)

tended in full riot gear. Its CIA contact was Keith Wheelock, then secretary of the U. S. Embassy in Santiago.[24] According to a U. S. Senate investigation that revealed CIA funding of Fatherland and Liberty,[25] the organization's tactics came to parallel those of the Movement of the Revolutionary Left (MIR), but whereas the armed forces treated MIR's guerrillas as outlaws, they allowed Fatherland and Liberty to act with impunity. In the waning months of the Allende government in 1973, Fatherland and Liberty spokesmen boasted to a U.S. correspondent about their arsenal of weapons, classes in target practice, and attacks on Allende's followers.‡[26] Some of the most bloodthirsty militants were women, many of whom had participated in the much-publicized "Empty Pots March," a supposedly middle-class women's demonstration against the Allende government that was composed principally of the wives of high-salaried employees, managers, senior executives, and industrialists.[27] During the march the women attacked several boys who shouted "Viva Allende," all but castrating them.

Fatherland and Liberty organized an abortive CIA-sponsored military coup in June 1973, for which it took public responsibility in the Santiago press. It also took credit for 70 attacks (of an estimated 290) on government offices, public works, and Allende newspapers; assassinated Allende's naval aide, Commodore Arturo Araya; and abetted a truck owners' strike by strewing *miguelitos,* three-pronged steel spikes, on the highways. Two months before Allende's overthrow, Fatherland and Liberty's second-in-command, industrialist Roberto Thieme, announced that the organization would unleash a total armed offensive to destroy the government.[28] After Allende's death, Thieme's followers joined the junta's security police, DINA, which was responsible for the torture and death of hundreds of Chileans.

Vigilante Squads

Though dangerous, the Fatherland and Liberty fanatics were less influential than their counterparts in the Chilean branch of a

‡ Most of the arms were smuggled from Argentina, Brazil, and Bolivia with the cooperation of the commanding officer of Atacama Province in northern Chile.

right-wing Catholic movement known as Tradition, Family, and Property (TFP), principally because TFP's militants had an intellectual base that appealed to a large number of officers in the armed forces. Founded in the early 1960s by the Brazilian philosopher Plinio Correa de Oliveira, TFP has followers in most Latin-American countries, including Argentina, Chile, Uruguay, and Brazil. While akin in some respects to twentieth-century fascism, particularly to Mussolini's corporate state, TFP is really a throwback to eighteenth-century Europe, as yet untouched by the French Revolution, when the Catholic Church defended aristocratic privilege as a divine right. Indeed, TFP's insignia is a medieval lion. Most of its members are from the wealthy, propertied classes and yearn for an earlier time when the Latin-American Church upheld the right of a few *patrones* to rule a mass of peons.

TFP's first commandment is the utter sanctity of private property, and in countries with progressive bishops, such as Chile and Brazil, this has forced it into repeated clashes with the hierarchy on the issue of agrarian reform. The movement's members tend to be narrow-minded nationalists with a xenophobic reaction to any suggestion by foreigners that there might be something wrong with their country, particularly if the government is running the country for the benefit of the wealthy, as in Pinochet's Chile. They are also blindly anti-communist, seeing subversion in anything remotely resembling reform, and are convinced that reds lurk everywhere in Latin America's new, socially conscious Church. Thus TFP divides the Catholic Church into "our" Church, which is a class Church, rooted in another century, and "their" Church, which is a classless Church and therefore subversive.*

While the organization exists primarily to maintain the privileges of the rich, that goal has been disguised by jargon about "degenerate political systems," which TFP claims have caused the Western countries to succumb to Marxist penetration. Society is to be purified, along the lines of Mussolini's corporate state, by

* According to TFP founder Plinio Correa, "It is an injustice and a utopian view of things to suppress the inequality of classes. What is important is to strengthen the cooperation between them in a harmonious inequality."

Typical of TFP attitudes toward class divisions is the symbolic front-row pew reserved for the *patrones* still to be seen in Latin-American village churches—the peons stand at the back.

replacing traditional political parties with special-interest groups, to which people are assigned according to job and social class. This is supposed to produce a society in which everyone knows his place and is happy to keep it. What TFP doesn't say is that its model of government effectively nullifies any social or economic gains made by Latin America's middle and lower classes.

TFP's activities in Chile, Brazil, and elsewhere are an important part of the CIA story in Latin America, because its members were the intellectual and financial backers of military coups supported by the agency. After the military took over, TFP members and fellow travelers were active in these regimes' persecution of the Catholic Church, as in the case of police agent Adolfo Centeno and the smear campaign against priests and bishops in Uruguay. In some countries—Brazil, for example, where TFP established a series of training camps near Rio de Janeiro—members were instructed by the Army and the police, who, in turn, received military training and political orientation from the CIA, the Pentagon, and AID.† But there were still closer ties: in Chile and Brazil the evidence points to both financial and political links between TFP and the CIA in plotting the overthrow of the Allende and Goulart governments.

When it supported right-wing Catholic groups, the CIA had principally in mind the political objective of removing left-wing governments by military intervention, but one result of the collaboration was to strengthen such organizations as TFP, which emerged as religious vigilante squads for the military regimes. Thus the CIA could be accused—and was accused by a number of prominent Catholic leaders, including Brazil's Archbishop Helder Cámara—of inciting one sector of the Church to attack another. Moreover, in some countries, Bolivia being one, this collaboration extended to persecution of U.S. citizens when the CIA provided military governments and right-wing Catholic organizations with confidential dossiers on American priests and nuns.‡

A good example of TFP's connections with both the CIA and the military is the branch in Chile, which supplied the Chilean armed forces with a social philosophy—the generals had none—

† See Chapter VI.
‡ For more details, see description of the CIA Banzer Plan, Chapter V, pp. 142–46.

and a religious basis for the regime's political witch-hunts. Chile's TFP first attracted attention in the mid-1960s, when Jaime Guzmán, later the junta's chief ideologist, led a movement called the *gremialistas,* meaning special-interest groups, to victory in student elections at the Catholic University in Santiago. Guzmán's ideas soon gained a significant following among Chile's business and landowning interests, which provided the backing for a TFP journal, *Fiducia.* A publication highly slanted to appeal to Chile's right-wing Catholics, *Fiducia* described the country's bishops as "soft on communism" because they supported agrarian reform, and urged adoption of a Mussolini-style dictatorship that would eliminate the country's traditional political parties. After the coup in 1973, the military, which had no clear idea of political or economic objectives beyond the elimination of Allende, adopted TFP's theories in their entirety. Guzmán's ideas formed the basis of the Declaration of Principles published by the junta in March 1974, which announced a "new institutionality . . . cleansing our democratic system of the vices that facilitated its destruction,"[29] these "vices" including political parties, unions, freedom of the press, and the progressive wing of the Catholic Church. Guzmán also helped to stage a 1978 election farce that was supposed to confirm popular support for the Pinochet regime.*

After the coup, TFP gained control of a tripartite organization, composed of the National Secretariat of Women, the National Secretariat of Youth, and the *gremios,* or business and professional organizations. These last had been effective in setting the conditions for military intervention (for example, the truck owners' strike, which was also supported by Fatherland and Liberty).

In the last months of the Allende government, TFP, the *gremios,* Fatherland and Liberty, and other right-wing opposition groups merged in a common front. The National Agriculture Society, for example, was controlled by Fatherland and Liberty and

---

* The plebiscite was a one-sided affair that left nothing to chance: the political opposition was barred from using the government-controlled media, political meetings and demonstrations were banned, and the ballots were transparent, thereby ensuring identification of any Chilean who voted against the government. Such were the defects of the hastily called election that two members of the junta were moved to deplore publicly Pinochet's insistence on carrying out the farce.

received CIA funds through an organization called the Congress for Cultural Liberty.[30] The society, in turn, worked with the Association of Manufacturers, whose president, Orlando Saenz, was one of the directors of the TFP-backed *gremios* as well as a secret leader of Fatherland and Liberty.[31] A month before the coup Saenz publicly thanked the president of the Agriculture Society for "the services lent earlier by you to our cause."[32] Both groups had close ties with *El Mercurio,* Santiago's largest newspaper, which was financed by the CIA and used as an outlet for anti-Allende propaganda, according to U. S. Senate investigations.[33] They also shared important Brazilian connections. Fatherland and Liberty obtained arms from Brazil through a Chilean coffee-importing firm which brought in, via the port of Valparaiso, crates of guns disguised as raw material for the manufacture of instant coffee. Saenz was in close touch with the financial and ideological backers of Brazil's TFP, which had been in at the kill of Goulart's regime. (Several of the tactics used in Chile were tested by TFP in Brazil. With CIA help, TFP sponsored in São Paulo a march of several thousand middle- and upper-class women that was psychologically crucial to the coup ten days later. Similarly, women's groups sponsored by TFP and Fatherland and Liberty held their largest demonstration five days before Allende's overthrow.) †

U.S. congressional investigations have established that the CIA spent $13 million to thwart Allende, but with some exceptions, such as *El Mercurio* and Fatherland and Liberty, details of how the money was allocated have not been revealed. How much the CIA gave the TFP may never be known, but there are numerous links between the two organizations, particularly through Fatherland and Liberty, in addition to an established connection in the campaign to discredit the country's Catholic Church.

Even before the coup, TFP had been at odds with the hierarchy because the bishops refused to side with the right-wing Catholics

---

† The TFP *gremios* also copied a Brazilian think tank called the Institute of Research and Social Studies, which served as a bridge between the armed forces and private enterprise before the 1964 coup. The Chilean version, called the Center for Public Opinion Studies, prepared strategies for anti-government strikes, press campaigns, the spreading of rumors, and the use of shock troops during street demonstrations. (Marlise Simons, "Whose Coup?," *Brazilian Information Bulletin,* No. 12 [Berkeley: American Friends of Brazil, Winter, 1974], pp. 7–9.)

in TFP and Fatherland and Liberty (the bishops also condemned the left-wing priests in the pro-Allende Christians for Socialism movement). After the coup, the breach was formalized over the Church's defense of human rights. As in Uruguay, where police agent Centeno and TFP attempted to discredit the hierarchy, the Chilean Government used the movement and its CIA connections to undermine the Church. The tactics were the same: smear campaigns in the government-controlled media; harassment, imprisonment, and/or expulsion of bishops and clergy; and attempts to divide the Church between those who supported the military regime and those who opposed it and therefore had to be communists.

Typical of the smear campaign was Bishop Carlos Camus's experience during an off-the-record discussion with members of the Foreign Press Association at a dinner in Santiago. At that time the secretary general of the Chilean Bishops' Conference, Camus spoke frankly in criticism of the military government and its supporters, believing that his remarks would not be attributed. However, a member of the association taped the conversation, copies of which later turned up in military and pro-government newspaper offices. Although Camus's statements concentrated on the country's social and economic situation, certain remarks were taken out of context by the afternoon daily *La Segunda,* part of the *Mercurio* chain, to suggest that the Church was controlled by Marxists.

Alvaro Pineda Castro, the Colombian journalist responsible for the leak, had gained access to the dinner as the correspondent for a small Bolivian newspaper. Between 1960 and 1968 Pineda worked in Chile as general manager of a news agency, Orbe Latinoamericano, and Philip Agee's *CIA Diary* describes Orbe as "financed and controlled by the CIA through the Santiago, Chile, station." Pineda's office was in the building that also housed the headquarters of the Chilean junta. When, after the Camus incident, the Foreign Press Association expelled Pineda for "a grave breach of ethics," the government retaliated by canceling the credentials of the foreign correspondents.

Although the junta gained effective propaganda from the affair, it failed to divide the Church; the hierarchy closed ranks behind Camus, reelecting him secretary general of the Bishops' Conference. However, the same tactic worked with Chile's Lutheran

Church which split on the expulsion of Bishop Helmut Frenz, half the congregation supporting government claims that he had engaged in "activities that defame the national image." Frenz's principal sin, in the eyes of the junta, was his position as co-chairman of the ecumenical Committee of Cooperation for Peace in Chile, which was established by the Catholic, Protestant, and Jewish faiths for the defense of political prisoners and human rights in the months following the coup. (For his work with Chilean refugees, Frenz was awarded the United Nations' Fridtjof Nansen medal in 1974.)

Unable to split the hierarchy, TFP continued to put out scurrilous propaganda aimed at driving a wedge between laity and clergy. It included *The Church of Silence,* a long, slanted book, widely publicized in the government press, that followed upon another TFP hatchet job, by a Brazilian lawyer, called *Frei: The Chilean Kerensky,* (blaming former Christian Democrat President Eduardo Frei for Allende's election), and called on the Chilean laity to "show their love for the Church by refusing obedience to their pastors."[34] Backed by the papal nuncio, Chile's hierarchy retaliated by announcing that it would excommunicate all spokesmen for the book. "They divide the world into extremes of either 'good' or 'bad,' and they deny all rights for the 'bad,' especially the vanquished," the bishops asserted. *"Church of Silence* is a title, a name, that commands respect. We can only deplore the fact that those attempting to exploit it neither know silence nor are the Church."[35] Cardinal Silva, whom the book singled out for criticism, added that he was pleased to be called a heretic. "It's another feather in my cap. I consider it a sign that I am in line with the Gospel that they attack me."[36]

Despite the Vatican's public disapproval of *The Church of Silence,* TFP brought out three different editions, the last of which was published by the government-controlled University of Chile. Advertising for the book included billboards previously used for government propaganda.

Meanwhile, TFP ideologist Guzmán went on national television to accuse Cardinal Silva of protecting extreme leftists, and a series of stories describing the bishops as anti-Chilean appeared in the government press. When the bishops defended lawyer Hernán Montealegre, arrested for his work with the Church on behalf of political prisoners, *La Segunda* claimed the Church was supporting Marxist subversion.[37] It came as no surprise, then, that when France's schismatic Bishop Marcel Lefebvre came to town in 1977, on a tour to drum up support for his medieval ideas, his hosts were members of TFP. Lefebvre returned the favor by calling Cardinal Silva a subversive.

A Disgraceful Affair

Not to be outdone by its Chilean coreligionists, Brazil's TFP published its version of *The Church of Silence,* which focused on the Amazon's Bishop Pedro Casaldáliga, and particularly on his "subversive" poetry.‡ As in Chile, the organization's militants did much to establish the philosophical underpinnings for Brazil's military regime. Many of the first teachers at Brazil's Superior War College, birthplace of the Doctrine of National Security, belonged to TFP, and it was they who introduced the compulsory teaching of "moral and civic education" in Brazilian schools and universities.* According to María Nilde Marcellani, a Brazilian academician who was commissioned by the World Council of Churches to make a study of the subject, "moral and civic education" had its intellectual origins in the Nazi philosophy of education.†

But whereas in Chile the hierarchy presented a united front, TFP was able in Brazil to establish a small beachhead in the Church, thanks to Archbishop Dom Geraldo Proença Sigaud of Diamantina, a wealthy landowner, staunch opponent of agrarian reform, and TFP founder. Sigaud belongs to the old school of Latin-American bishops who still live in palaces and own huge tracts of land. He was tolerated by his fellow bishops, most of whom are political moderates, in the belief that Brazil's Church was sufficiently flexible to accommodate both the Right and the

‡ See Chapter VII, p. 269.

* See Chapter VI.

† Shortly before her book was due to go to press, Ms. Marcellani was arrested by the regime's security police and tortured for seventy days on charges of spreading subversive propaganda and attempting to "turn the people against the constitutional authorities." A military court later acquitted her on a technicality. ("By the Way: Brazil," *Latin America* [London, June 24, 1977].)

Left. But when Sigaud agreed to front for the military regime by claiming he had positive proof that two Brazilian bishops were communists and that another seventy-eight subversives were probably lurking in the hierarchy, he was unanimously disowned by the other bishops, including such staunch conservatives as Rio's Cardinal Eugenio de Aráujo Sales and Porto Alegre's Cardinal Vicente Scherer, who called the charges "disgraceful."

Sigaud said he had documents showing that Bishop Casaldáliga and Bishop Tomás Balduino, president of the Church's Indian Mission Council, were "encouraging communist infiltration," but he failed to deliver any such proof to either the Brazilian Bishops' National Conference or Papal Nuncio Carmine Rocco, saying only that he would get around to it "when my catechism activities allow me the time."[38] Sigaud also repeatedly contradicted himself in declarations to the press. Said Dom Adriano Hipólito, bishop of the Rio suburb of Nova Iguaçu: "These statements are not proofs of anything. They are nothing more than libelous accusations." According to Dom Avelar Brandao Vilela, the politically moderate cardinal of Salvador: "The word 'communist' is abusively bandied about today. Any disagreement of an ideological order, of a political nature, of interpretation in the field of economics, is immediately identified as a communist doctrine or a communist attitude. Such a procedure, instead of creating opposition to communism, is lamentably favoring its cause."

The hierarchy believed that Sigaud's accusations were timed to coincide with the release of a highly critical document, "Christian Requirements of a Political Order," published by the Brazilian Bishops' Conference in 1977. Approved by a vote of 210 to 3 at the bishops' biennial assembly, it attacked the government for violation of human rights and failure to allow the majority of Brazilians any political voice. Its force was blunted by the outcries in the pro-government press following Sigaud's denunciations, and, as if to confirm the bishops' suspicions, government leaders in the rubber-stamp Congress immediately took up Sigaud's cause. After a meeting with Brazil's Minister of Justice, Deputy José Bonifacio labeled Casaldáliga "an instrument of subversion in Brazil"; Senator Eurico Rezende called him "a communist dressed as a bishop."

Bishop Balduino said that at first he was perplexed by the slander: "It seemed like a case of mental imbalance, but now we are absolutely certain that Dom Sigaud was used by the government. Both the timing and the sensationalism indicate that it was a well-planned maneuver expertly carried out, using Dom Sigaud to distract the public's attention just when 'Christian Requirements' was about to be published. At the beginning, it seemed to be an attack against two bishops, but we now believe the real objective of the battle is the entire Church, specifically the Church that manifested itself through a document that threatened the government. We two bishops suffered a repetition of previous confrontations. For example, when in 1976 the commission representing the Bishops' Conference released an entirely realistic document called 'Pastoral Communication to the People of God,' which described the assassination of two priests, the kidnapping of a bishop, and similar occurrences, there were immediate repercussions: interrogations of bishops, the detention and torture of a priest, and the deportation of another."

Casaldáliga agreed: "Past experience shows that the government tactic is to give blow for blow. In response to a document by the bishops, there is an attack against the Church, with accusations, prison, etc. We know that the landowners, the government, national security, and military personnel have tried unsuccessfully at various times to expel me. Then they concocted a plan at the Superior War College, the 'Gregorianum' of the armed forces, since there was no basis for expulsion through the regular channels. I was a bishop and therefore possessed some power and I belonged to the Vatican. They also had to deal with national and international public opinion. Therefore, they concluded the only way to get rid of me was to get help from the Church. We know this from someone at the War College. Dom Sigaud was used as their spokesman. Now that the government has destroyed all the political parties that could signify real opposition, silenced the students and the free press, it is natural that they should become frightened when a new popular force emerges, even though this force stems from the Gospel and the Church."[39]

While Sigaud's accusations may have overshadowed the bishops' denunciations in "Christian Requirements," they failed in the end to divide the Church. Hundreds of letters poured into Casaldáliga's Amazon diocese expressing support for the bishop's stand on social justice. The affair "reaffirmed the people's commitment . . . and bestowed on them a sense of collective martyrdom in belonging to a persecuted Church," said Casaldáliga. "It also seems positive to me that the hierarchy itself has been touched in its honor. Some good always derives from every evil, and the Church has reacted very well. Of course, Sigaud or his masters used the wrong tactic when they claimed that there were not merely two communist bishops but fifty-one and maybe even eighty. Imagine, almost a third of the angels have fallen—one third of the Brazilian bishops are communists. It is so ridiculous that no one believes it."[40]

Bishop Ivo Lorscheiter, secretary general of the Brazilian Bishops' Conference, left no doubt about the government's participation in the TFP defamation campaign. "The police are investigating bishops and priests in Brazil in an attempt to prove communist infiltration in the Church," he said, describing how police agents were required to fill out a two-page questionnaire on local bishops and priests, even though the questions did not cover police matters or crimes in the penal code.[41] "Imagine an ordinary policeman trying to answer the first question, on whether the bishop or priest is disfiguring the person of Christ!" exclaimed Lorscheiter. "Or whether he tries to disfigure the person of God!" Any talk of Christian communities is also noted in these confidential police dossiers, such communities presumably being proof of communist subversion.‡ As Brazilian writer Roberto Barbosa pointed out, "The presence of bishops in areas of great social tension, living and identifying with the suffering people, is an embarrassment to the government and a barrier to be eliminated if land-development companies are to have their way [see previous chapter]. It is evident that the government prefers to have bishops living, like Sigaud, in splendorous traditional residences, rather than in humble quarters, like Casaldáliga."[42]

While there is no proof of CIA support of the Brazilian Gov-

‡ Typical of the Brazilian Government's vigilance was a police check of Latin-American bishops, theologians, and grass-roots leaders who attended a meeting on Christian communities in Vitória, Brazil, in 1976. By an interesting coincidence, most of the bishops and priests arrested in Riobamba, Ecuador, at the conference sponsored by Bishop Proaño, had just come from the meeting in Vitória. (See Chapter V.)

ernment's campaign against the Church, a number of bishops blame the agency for having contributed to the problem by its earlier intervention in Brazil. "We are not suggesting that the Brazilian police could not have done this on their own," said a bishop, "but the training they received from AID and the CIA certainly made them more efficient at their job." Mexican Bishop Samuel Ruiz put it another way: "Roger Vekemans may not have actively sought CIA money, but it came down to the same thing. A similar observation could be made about the CIA and the military regimes' persecution of the Church."

The German Alliance

Despite the heightened awareness of CIA activities in Latin America, a drama similar to that of the 1960s, when AID and the CIA funded religious groups, was staged in the late 1970s with different actors, although the ubiquitous Roger Vekemans was once again in a central role. If not as well informed about events in Latin America as Washington, the West Germans run it a close second, and they early came to the same conclusion as did the Rockefeller mission*—that the rebel Church in Latin America was a fast-growing threat to their interests. But whereas the United States relied on government agencies for its principal contact with Latin-American religious groups, in West Germany the Catholic hierarchy set itself up as the watchdog, albeit with financial support from Bonn. As in the 1960s, when U.S. missionaries shared the CIA's fear that communism might be spreading, German Church groups worked with the continent's Christian and Social Democrats to encourage the growth of Christian trade unions and political parties, including the Christian Democrats in Chile and the Social Christians in Venezuela, as an alternative to Marxism. With the U.S. hierarchy's interest in Latin America gradually waning, the German Church's concern and influence grew, until it became the principal foreign source of funding for the Latin-American Church. Nowadays, when a Latin-American bishop or priest wants money, he goes to Germany.

The two principal sources of funding are Misereor, which supports social projects such as schools and hospitals, and Adveniat,

* See Chapter VI.

which is concerned with traditional Church work such as the training of priests. Both are supported by obligatory contributions from German taxpayers, who pay the church of their choice a sort of tithe, and by additional voluntary offerings from Germany's 28 million Catholics. Misereor is essentially concerned with good works, but Adveniat is involved in politics—the politics of the Right. With this orientation and plenty of money, Adveniat gradually replaced the CIA in the 1970s as helpmate of the military regimes and the chief foreign source of division in the Latin-American Church.

Though founded specifically to meet the needs of Latin America, Adveniat derives its political ideas more from Western Europe than from the New World. Few German bishops have more than a superficial knowledge of Latin America, according to their own advisers, but their experience of a divided Germany has made them militant anti-communists, and the growing threat of Eurocommunism, particularly in Italy and France, has added to their fervor. Moreover, a number of the men who are bishops today belonged to conservative Christian groups in their youth when fascism was on the rise. Their outlook is similar to that of Opus Dei, the Spanish right-wing Catholic organization that flourished under Franco, with strong ties to the Catholic Right in Latin America. (Opus Dei and Fatherland and Liberty worked together in Chile during the Allende years, and General Juan Carlos Onganía, dictator of Argentina from 1966 to 1970, seized power after making a religious retreat sponsored by Opus Dei.) While none of Germany's bishops could be described as Opus Dei militants, a number are "sympathetic to its aims," in the words of an adviser to the German hierarchy. It was natural, then, that the German bishops should seek allies in the right wing of the Latin-American Church. What made this alliance so baleful was the economic muscle achieved by the Germans, in Rome as well as Latin America, just at the time when right-wing military dictatorships were seizing power in the Western Hemisphere.

The point of contact was Roger Vekemans, who was energetically attacking the theology of liberation.† The Medellín Conclusions had seemed innocuous enough, and caused little excitement in Europe, until Vekemans began to point out, in a series of

† See Chapter II.

persuasive articles and books, that the theology of liberation was subverting the Latin-American Church by using a radical political and economic analysis to study the historical causes of the continent's underdevelopment. He identified the new theology with such left-wing religious groups as the pro-Allende Christians for Socialism in Chile, whom he said were "like a contagion" being multiplied around the world by the "carriers of the bacillus." His arguments found fertile ground in Germany, particularly after the Christians for Socialism movement spread from Chile to Italy and elsewhere in Europe, and by the mid-1970s the German hierarchy had convinced itself that, if something were not done to stop the growth of this rebel Church, an Iron Curtain would descend in Latin America. It was an opinion wholeheartedly shared by the hemisphere's military governments.

The German bishops were, however, immune to the arguments of their brothers in Latin America that the theology of liberation could not be equated with the Christians for Socialism movement. (Contrary to Vekemans' assertions, the movement had ceased to be important in Latin America by 1975, both because of military repression and because the Church was moving toward a consensus that, to be effective, an option for the poor had to exclude partisan politics.) Nor did the West German Church take into account the different historical experiences of Europe and Latin America, with the result that socialism was confused with communism and anti-imperialism with Marxism. When Peru's bishops issued a strong denunciation of foreign capitalism, the West German hierarchy was horrified, because it did not understand that capitalism has produced one standard of living in Germany and quite another in Latin America.

Vekemans, who in Chile had been getting up to $25 million a year from the German Church, continued to receive large contributions from Adveniat when he moved to Bogotá, only now the money was directed at fighting the theology of liberation and the progressive wing of the Latin-American Church instead of Salvador Allende. According to the Belgian Jesuit, the charge that he took CIA money in Chile was due entirely to the fact that "I was the first in Latin America to attack the theology of liberation," an explanation not entirely supported by the record. But Vekemans was probably correct when he claimed that "I never enjoyed such prestige with the hidalgos of the Church, nor received so many offers of money from the foundations, until I was accused of working for the CIA."[43] (Vekemans' life-style in Bogotá, where he lives in an elegantly furnished mansion, is no less sumptuous than what AID auditors observed in Chile.) The hidalgos of the Church included the unanimously conservative Colombian hierarchy, which joined with the West German bishops to combat the spread of the theology of liberation with books and magazines, religious courses, and conferences, and by exerting unremitting pressure on the Vatican through the good offices of Cardinal Sebastiano Baggio, an Opus Dei sympathizer and president of the Pontifical Commission for Latin America, the Vatican's principal authority on Latin-American affairs.

The campaign had a number of serious weaknesses, however, including its reliance on a rehash of the Church's social doctrine that dated from the nineteenth century and had gone out of fashion with Vatican II. ("Vekemans sounds like a broken record," was the comment of Jesuit Bartolome Sorge, the Vatican's most knowledgeable critic of the Christians for Socialism movement.) And while attacking the theology of liberation and Church progressives, Vekemans and company offered no solution of their own for the continent's growing social problems. But undoubtedly the worst failing of the Adveniat campaign was that it played into the hands of the military regimes by giving them more ammunition to attack large sectors of the Church as communist simply because they worked with and defended the poor and the oppressed. "These attacks are actually helping the military dictatorships," said Brazilian Bishop Cándido Padín. During an emotional confrontation between the Church's progressive and conservative wings at a meeting in Peru, Archbishop Helder Cámara, with tears on his cheeks, begged his conservative colleagues to consider the harm they were doing by harping on Marxist infiltration in the Church. Like other progressives, Cámara wanted the conservatives to broaden their horizons. The military regimes and the multinationals were as great a threat in Latin America as communism, said Cámara, and the Church ill-served the mass of the people when it swept such issues under the rug in the name of anticommunism. Cámara's remarks were directed specifically at

Vekemans, from whom he demanded an answer to charges of CIA collaboration.

The Brazilian archbishop was not the only churchman to criticize Vekemans. Back in Germany, over one hundred influential Catholic and Protestant theologians, including Karl Rahner, Herbert Vorgrimler, Johannes B. Metz, Martin Niemöller, and Ernst Kasemann, publicly upbraided Adveniat for creating divisions in the Latin-American Church by backing Vekemans' campaign against the theology of liberation. They also criticized Adveniat's director, Essen's Bishop Franz Hengsbach, military bishop for the Armed Forces, for his cozy relationship with Bolivia's military dictatorship, which had given Hengsbach the country's highest honor, El Condor de los Andes. The decoration was "grotesque," they said, when one considered that the very same government that had honored the bishop was collaborating with the CIA in the persecution of progressive elements in the Bolivian Church.†[44] There was reason to believe, added the theologians, that German Church funds had been "abusively used for imperialist ends" and "for oppression." "How are German Catholics to interpret the contradictions they find here? For example, while collaborators of Misereor [the other German Church aid agency] are being interrogated by the Brazilian police, the directors of Adveniat state publicly that repression in Brazil is not a real threat. Are those in the German Church who approve of the campaign against liberation theology aware of whose interests they serve and how much damage they cause the Latin-American Church? Do they realize how much fresh suffering their behavior will inflict on many Christians and priests who have already suffered enough under the yoke of military dictatorships? We cannot accept," concluded the theologians in an allusion to the Church's record under Hitler, "that once again the German Church is under suspicion of making agreements with the powerful and of not seeing—whether in good or bad faith—the inhuman behavior of dictatorships that call themselves Christian."[45]

The German document echoed earlier statements by some of Latin America's leading theologians, who had asked the Latin-American bishops' hemispheric organization, CELAM, to investi-

‡ See Chapter V.

gate funding of Church groups by foreign agencies, particularly the CIA. While one sector of the Church was receiving funds from such agencies, said the theologians, another sector identified with the common people was persecuted by "intelligence services, state police, and ultra-right movements" also financed by such funds. The work of the Church was therefore distorted and, when the facts became known, its credibility questioned.

Just how tangled a web these agencies weave may be judged by the experience of the labor unions in Ecuador, where there was a direct link among the CIA, the German Church, and the German Government. Once again, the man who forged the chain was Roger Vekemans.

As Agee documented in *CIA Diary,* the agency penetrated most of Ecuador's important Catholic organizations. Among them was a Catholic labor federation called CEDOC, which had an elaborate structure of agencies for education, rural and urban services, and social research. The latter was conducted by a Church institute known as INEDES and headed by Isabel Robalino, a lawyer who was a CIA agent.[46] Ms. Robalino was also the Ecuadorian representative of Misereor, and of a hemispheric Christian Democrat labor organization, the Central Latinoamericana de Trabajadores (CLAT). CEDOC is an affiliate of CLAT and depends on it for the bulk of its money. CLAT, in turn, gets approximately 6 million Deutschmarks a year from the Konrad-Adenauer-Stiftung, an agency of Germany's Christian Democratic Party.

When Vekemans was receiving CIA money in Santiago, his Chilean organization maintained close contacts with Robalino's INEDES institute in Ecuador. Despite Agee's revelations of her CIA contacts and testimony by prominent Ecuadorians supporting his assertions,[47] Ms. Robalino continued to work for both CLAT and Misereor in Ecuador.* But her influence in CEDOC came to an abrupt end in 1976 when the increasingly rebellious membership threw out the CLAT-sponsored leadership and replaced it with its own, more militant executive. The rebellion

* Misereor was similarly uninterested in revelations of Vekemans' CIA funding. "Whether he worked for the CIA or not is of no interest to us," said a Misereor representative. Asked about Vekemans' misuse of AID funds, he said, "Why should we be concerned if the Americans didn't want to do anything about him?" (Author's interviews [Bogotá, 1978].)

caused quite a flap in Germany because the new CEDOC leadership took a strong line on workers' rights and agrarian reform, whereas the whole point of CLAT had been to dissipate such militancy by pacifying the workers with pseudo-reforms. That, too, is more or less the line taken by the United States' Latin-American labor organization, the AIFLD, which is supported by the CIA and the multinationals,† although CLAT takes an anti-American position that suits the economic interests of the West Germans, who are challenging U.S. hegemony in Latin America.

When all the bits and pieces of this maze of interests come together, they form two parallel lines, one running from West Germany, the other from the United States. Their mutual goal is to hold down the lid on Latin America, on the rebel Church, and on the increasingly militant unions. This common design is not always apparent because of the anti-Americanism of the German Church agencies and trade unions, which depict Uncle Sam as a grasping capitalist. In fact, the Germans are every bit as capitalistic as their Yankee counterparts. Thus what appears to be an ideological conflict between "liberal" Germans and "conservative" Americans is in fact a contest between U.S. and West German business interests for the pickings in Latin America. When CEDOC's membership threw out the CLAT leadership, CLAT immediately labeled the rebellion a CIA conspiracy, although CLAT delegate Robalino was a CIA agent of long standing. Having lost CEDOC, the Germans then tried to woo Ecuador's other labor federation, CEOSL, away from the Americans' AIFLD. Meanwhile, the Germans set up a foundation in Quito to publish material and organize seminars on the role of the modern businessman in Latin America, the meetings usually being scheduled to coincide with West German businessmen's missions to the city. Though the infighting between West German and U.S. business interests is keen, it does not prevent them from sharing a wider objective, which is to maintain a favorable business climate in Latin America. And that, translated into political terms, means military regimes.

† See Chapter VII, pp. 211–13.

PART THREE

THE AWAKENING

CHAPTER IX

CLOCKWORK ORANGE—Torture, Murder, Repression, and Anti-Semitism in Brazil, Argentina, and Mexico

If you want peace, respect life.

Pope Paul VI

The atmosphere in the church was tense. Crowded inside were several hundred young Brazilians, there to attend an afternoon Mass for a fellow student killed by the military police. Outside the church, stationed in the plaza and all along the thoroughfares that crisscross this part of downtown Rio de Janeiro, were soldiers from the 1st Division of the Brazilian Army.

Earlier in the week, after the first funeral Mass for the student, mounted police had attacked all those leaving the church. On the morning of this, the second Mass, the city had been readied as though for war, with machine-gun nests at the crossroads, armored cars, barbed-wire entanglements, and aerial patrols. When the Mass ended, the unarmed people inside the church would have to confront the military. Set in the middle of a large plaza/parking lot that straddles Avenida Presidente Vargas, the Candelaria church is an unprotected island, with no narrow side streets or alleys for refuge. Surely more people would die this afternoon.

One of the priests forbade any in the congregation to leave the church ahead of the clergy. Dressed in alb and stole, the fifteen priests then followed Bishop José Castro Pinto out into the plaza, where, holding one another by the hand, they formed a line to confront the drawn sabers of a row of mounted military police. Slowly, slowly, this strange procession forced the horses to fall back. The priests then moved down Avenida Presidente Vargas to Avenida Río Branco, the crossroads of downtown Rio, forming a protective arc around Candelaria until the last person had left. It was only then, in the crossroads, that the cavalry and soldiers lashed into the crowd with their batons, hurling tear-gas grenades, but at least there was somewhere to flee, someplace to hide.

"That afternoon," recalled one Brazilian journalist, "veterans and hardened campaigners of the press came back to their editorial offices, their voices full of emotion as they told of the miracle —of the massacre that had not taken place because a dozen priests offered themselves as the first victims. That afternoon the Church discovered a new dimension of grandeur that prompted a former priest, who is today a professional journalist, to say: 'That's how the Church should be! If I were not married with three children, I'd go straight back to my monastery.'"[1]

The Candelaria incident occurred in Rio de Janeiro in 1968. Since then there have been countless instances of similar courage by priests, nuns, and bishops, not only in Brazil but throughout Latin America. Though the setting and circumstances vary, such sacrifice has invariably been inspired by the motive that led Bishop Castro Pinto and his priests to confront the mounted police: to protect the people, to "give voice to the voiceless."

"Martyrdom is part of our march."

"Don't hit me again! Please don't hit me again!" The middle-aged peasant woman was sobbing, half slumped on the floor of the primitive jungle jail. For days now, she had been forced to kneel on jagged bottle caps while the police beat her with clubs and stuck needles and pins into her breasts and under her fingernails. Her niece, just recovering from childbirth, had been similarly tortured after the police, having gang-raped her, burned down her small shack and the family's rice patch. Everyone in the small village of Ribeirão Bonito could hear the women screaming, but they were too frightened to intervene. Here, as elsewhere in the Brazilian Amazon, the military police did as they pleased.[2]

While many of the village's one thousand inhabitants had been similarly abused, only one man, Jovino Barbosa, had dared to strike back, and now his sister and daughter-in-law were paying. Barbosa had killed a police corporal, a man notorious in the region for his torture and murder of peasants, after he had jailed and brutalized Barbosa's two sons. A detachment of military police had been sent to the village to capture Barbosa; when they could not find him, they arrested and tortured the two women.

By coincidence—the villagers say it was the hand of God—the Amazon's Bishop Pedro Casaldáliga and Jesuit missionary João Bosco Penido Burnier stopped at Ribeirão Bonito to bless some baptismal water from the village river while en route from a regional meeting on Indian affairs in another town. As they walked back from the river, a boy approached the bishop and told him of the women who were being tortured. Casaldáliga immediately set off for the jail. As soon as he and Father João entered the police station, said Casaldáliga, two corporals and two soldiers began to harangue and insult them, threatening to kill the bishop. "We tried to talk calmly, but when Father João said he would inform the policemen's superiors of their undisciplined action, police officer Ezy Romalho Feitosa hit him and then shot João in the head."

The desperate bishop dragged Burnier out of the police station to give him first aid, then drove to the nearest ranch that had a small airplane, a distance of four hours on the jungle roads. The bishop and the missionary were flown to the city of Goiânia the next morning, but it was too late—Father João died the same day. During the long ride through the Amazon jungle, the priest was conscious for much of the time. "His was a profoundly Christian agony," said the sorrowing bishop. "He repeatedly offered his life for the Indians, for the people. He invoked Jesus. Repeating the last rites of our Lord, he told me: 'Dom Pedro, carry on our work.'"[3]

Father João was the second Brazilian missionary to be murdered in the space of a few weeks in the fall of 1976. Had it not been for the social prominence of his family, which included two generals in the Brazilian military, and his standing in the Jesuit community, the government would probably have dismissed his death as another case of Church subversives obstructing justice in the Amazon. A former secretary of the Jesuits' superior general in Rome, the fifty-nine-year-old Jesuit was highly respected for his tireless work on behalf of the Bacairi Indians in the Brazilian Amazon. Unlike Casaldáliga, who had had frequent run-ins with the military, Burnier had not been tagged by the government for repression or harassment. Thus the regime could hardly write him off as a subversive, particularly when the entire Brazilian hierarchy was up in arms over his murder. To pacify the bishops, the government ordered the temporary arrest of the Ribeirão Bonito policemen. President Geisel also met with Burnier's cousin, Archbishop Geraldo Penido, to tell the hierarchy that he did not himself condone torture, but that there was no way he could prevent his underlings from resorting to it.

While Geisel was officially washing his hands of the matter, spontaneous retribution was suddenly and violently exacted in Ribeirão Bonito. All the villagers were present for Burnier's funeral Mass, and many had come from nearby towns to witness what Bishop Casaldáliga called "a silent protest against the oppressors and the exploiters represented by the police who are responsible for so many injustices and so much of the people's suffering. Let this celebration make us more conscious . . . that it is ourselves, and only ourselves, who are going to attain our liberation."[4]

When the Mass was over, the two women who had been tortured by the police led a procession to the now-empty jail, where the people put up a cross with the inscription: "Here is where the police killed Father João Bosco, who was defending freedom."

But would the police not pull down the cross as soon as they returned? asked a peasant. Would they not desecrate Father João's memory, too? Carmosina Pereira, a middle-aged woman who had been imprisoned in the jail, began to shout: "Many innocent people have already been imprisoned here. Many people have suffered. The jail must be destroyed."[5] Someone kicked at its walls; another slammed the door. Then, in a single movement, the villagers fell on the jail, literally tearing it apart with their hands.

One of the first acts of the police on their return was to take down the inscription on Father João's cross. The people put another in its place, but it, too, was destroyed. A third plaque was then made in bronze and soldered to the cross, whereupon the police dug up the cross and placed it "under arrest." But the police could do nothing about Ribeirão Bonito's new church, which was built in Father João's honor by the grateful villagers. It has become a shrine for settlers from other parts of the Amazon, who already revere Father João as a saint, and sing songs in his memory.

On the first anniversary of João's murder, Casaldáliga, six fellow bishops, thirty priests, several dozen nuns, Protestant pastors, and representatives of the Bororo and Bacairi Indian tribes gathered in Ribeirão Bonito to pay him tribute by inaugurating the village church. But the occasion was marred by the presence of a detachment of military police, who arrested a layman working with Casaldáliga as soon as the dignitaries had left the village. Unable to imprison Casaldáliga or his colleagues, the police derived some satisfaction from abusing an innocent man whose sole crime was his connection with the Amazon's bishop.

As Bishop Tomás Balduino had said in his sermon at the dedication of the Ribeirão Bonito Church, "What we are celebrating here is the suffering we bear. Martyrdom is part of our march, the march of the People of God. In the celebration of the Eucharist, the Church remembers those who gave their lives for their brethren.

"The work of the Church in evangelization is also a political work, a work for transformation and change. And it was for this that Christ came to the world—to bring change."

A Lesson for a Bishop

"Communist traitor! We're going to kill you, and the other bishops, too!"

Bishop Adriano Hipólito was lying doubled up on the back seat of a moving car, his hands tied, a hood over his head. Shouting threats and insults, his tormentors first ripped the buttons from his cassock, then tore off his clothes, throwing them out the window. When Hipólito refused to drink the cheap cane alcohol they were trying to force down his throat, he was punched and beaten. "We're from the Brazilian Anti-Communist Alliance," they told him.

An hour earlier, Dom Adriano had left the diocesan chancery of Nova Iguaçu, a huge slum on the outskirts of Rio de Janeiro, accompanied by his nephew and his nephew's fiancée. Within blocks of the chancery, the bishop's Volkswagen was intercepted by two cars. Six men with pistols dragged the bishop and his nephew from the Volkswagen—in the confusion the girl managed to escape—and sped off to an isolated place where they beat up Hipólito's nephew and splashed Hipólito with red paint. The bishop was then taken to another Rio suburb far from Iguaçu, where he was dumped on the sidewalk, bound hand and foot. He was found by a group of men who gave him clothing and took him to a nearby parish house. Meanwhile, the kidnappers blew up his Volkswagen in front of the headquarters of the National Conference of Brazilian Bishops in downtown Rio.[6]

Like Father João in the Brazilian Amazon, Bishop Hipólito was mistreated because he had dared to protest, but Hipólito's complaint had been directed against not the rural military police but the gangs of common criminals who terrorize the people of Nova Iguaçu under the protection of such military and police death squads as the Brazilian Anti-Communist Alliance (AAB). A fearless journalist who used the diocese's weekly newspaper to condemn police connivance with bands of drug traffickers and extortionists, Hipólito was "punished" as a warning to the Church to stay out of police affairs, announced his AAB kidnappers. But the kidnapping had the reverse effect: after his humiliating experience, many of the priests and laymen who had earlier doubted the wisdom of his newspaper crusade closed ranks with the bishop. The kidnapping also pushed such Church conservatives as Cardinal Vicente Scherer into the political mainstream: Father João's murder had been bad enough, but the degradation of a bishop was too much even for those in the hierarchy who had previously advocated a dialogue with the military.

As with Burnier's murder, the government promised a full investigation of Hipólito's kidnapping with no intention of conducting it—too many people in the AAB had important police connections. Seven months after the incident, Hipólito learned from reports in the press that the military had closed the case without even making a preliminary investigation[7]—and the threats continued. In 1978 the AAB warned Hipólito that "next time you're going to spend several months in hospital because you won't shut up." It was futile to complain to the police or the military, said Hipólito, since they had refused to investigate the kidnapping: "I have no contact with the people in power. I don't know a general or even a police corporal whom I could call if something happened to me. I have the protection of the law, as do all citizens. But since the laws don't function, I am without protection, just like other citizens."

As Hipólito noted, survival is a daily challenge in Nova Iguaçu, where 1.2 million slum dwellers subsist without running water, schools, or a single hospital. Those with jobs in the city must rise at 3:30 A.M. to wait for a series of buses that will eventually deposit them in Rio by 7:00 A.M. Few return to their homes in Nova Iguaçu before 10:30 P.M., with the result that the people are "too tired even to think of protesting," as one priest said. The average monthly income of a family of eight is fifty dollars, yet even from these starvation wages the people are forced to pay protection money to the racketeers who terrorize the slum. Life is cheap in Nova Iguaçu—murders average seventeen a week —and it is a courageous priest or layperson who ventures forth at night to attend a Church meeting. "The police play an important role in this situation," said Bishop Hipólito, "for the simple reason that they are never present."

Like Ribeirão Bonito in the Amazon, Nova Iguaçu reflects a basic contradiction in Latin America's military regimes—a lawless society ruled by a government whose stated reason for being is law and order. In practice, the law is designed and applied to serve the interests of the few, while order is an excuse for corruption and repression.* The regimes pay lip service to such Western

---

* By the fall of 1978, even members of the Brazilian military were describing the presidential palace as a "sea of mud." General Hugo Abreu, who was head of the military household under President Geisel, was arrested after he published an open letter describing "the lawlessness of the palace group, which has been preparing for a permanent stay in power. We must do away with a regime based on denunciations and espionage," he said. "In contravention of the Constitution, the government opens our letters, hears our phone calls, and even penetrates the intimacy of our homes, using what it hears for blackmail. This is pure nazism. . . . We must pre-

They wanted to keep me suspended the whole night on the *pau de arara* [literally, the "parrot's perch": the prisoner is bound in a crouching position and suspended from a rod thrust under his knees]. But Captain Albernaz said: "No, that won't be necessary. He will stay with us a few days. If he doesn't speak, his insides will be destroyed, and we know how to do these things without leaving visible marks. If he survives, he will never forget the price of his insolence."

I couldn't sleep in my cell. The pain kept getting worse. My head seemed three times larger than the rest of my body. I was haunted by the thought that my brothers would have to go through the same sufferings. It was absolutely necessary to end it all. I was in such a state that I didn't feel capable of suffering more. There was only one way out—to kill myself!

In my cell, littered with trash, I found an empty sardine tin. I started to sharpen it on the floor. The prisoner next door, hearing the noise and guessing my intention, tried to calm me. He had suffered more than I, having his testicles crushed, but had not yet despaired. But what I meant to do was to prevent others from being tortured, and to denounce before public opinion and the Church what happened inside Brazilian prisons. I was sure that this could only be done through the sacrifice of my own life. I had a New Testament in my cell and read the Passion according to St. Matthew. The Father called for the sacrifice of the Son as a proof of love for mankind. I fainted full of pain and faith.

Friday morning a policeman woke me. A new prisoner was next to me. He was a young Portuguese and was crying from the tortures he had suffered at daybreak. The jailer told me, "You have only today and tomorrow to make up your mind to talk; if you don't the 'tough ones' will get you through the same treatment. They have already lost patience and are ready to kill you slowly."

The same thoughts I had the previous day kept coming back. I had already marked on my wrists where I should cut. I went on sharpening my tin. At mid-day I was taken out of my cell to shave. I was told that I would be sent back to the Tiradentes Prison [the notorious prison for political prisoners in São Paulo]. I shaved myself badly and went back to my cell. A policeman walked by. I asked him for a razor blade to finish my shave. The Portuguese was sleeping.

I took the blade and thrust it firmly into the inner part of my left wrist. The gash was deep. It had slashed both the vein and the artery. The blood started to fall on the cell floor. I stuck my arm into the latrine hole, thinking it would flow faster. I regained consciousness on a bed in the first aid sector of the prison hospital. The same day I was transferred to the military hospital.

Fearing a scandal, the Army kept secret what had happened. At the military hospital, Captain Mauricio was desperately telling a doctor: "Doctor, this one cannot die. We must do everything possible to keep him alive; otherwise we are lost." The Operaçao Bandeirantes [one of the military's death squads in São Paulo] put six soldiers in my room to guard me.

The next day psychological torture began. They would tell me: "Now your case is going to get worse because you are a suicidal and terrorist priest. The Church has expelled you," and so on. They would not let me sleep. All the time they spoke in loud voices, joking, and telling strange little stories about flying saucers. I realized that they were trying to absolve themselves of responsibility for what I had done by driving me crazy.

On Monday night a judge visited me. He came with one of the priests of my convent and the auxiliary bishop of São Paulo. They had learned what had happened through the prisoners at the Tiradentes Prison. One of the hospital doctors examined me in their presence, showing the scars on my body, the place where I had been stitched at the prison hospital, and the torture marks. The judge said that this was pure folly and that he would find the people responsible for it. I begged him not to be returned to the Operaçao Bandeirantes, and he promised to intercede for me.

I was well treated by the military at the military hospital, except for those from Operaçao Bandeirantes, who kept guard on me. The nuns of St. Vincent gave me all necessary assistance. But the judge's promise was not kept. Early on Friday morning, I was again transferred to the Operaçao

Bandeirantes prison. I was kept in a cell till late at night with nothing to eat. I felt giddy and weak from loss of blood, but my wounds were beginning to heal. During the night I was taken to the Tiradentes Prison, where I had been for several months.

It must be said that what happened to me was not an exception, but the rule. There are very few Brazilian political prisoners who have not suffered indescribable tortures. Many, like Chael Schreider and Virgilio Gomes da Silva, died during torture. Others were left dumb or sterile or were otherwise maimed.

These political prisoners place their hope in the Church, the only institution in Brazil that is not controlled by the military state. Her mission is to preserve and promote human dignity. When a man suffers it is the Master who suffers. It is time for our bishops to say "enough" to the tortures and injustices of the regime, before it is too late. The Church must not protect itself. We carry on our bodies the evidence of torture. If the Church does not speak up in a case like this, who will? Or is it necessary that I die for something to be done?

At times like these, silence is omission. If a word is a risk, it is also a testimony. The Church exists as a sign and a sacrament of God's justice in this world.

I make this appeal and this denunciation to prevent another death under torture in the future.‡[10]

Father Tito did not cry out in vain. Fittingly, the man who took up his appeal was the cardinal archbishop of São Paulo, Brazil's largest metropolis and most important industrial hub, the city where the young priest was imprisoned, and the center for some of the most sophisticated torture methods used in Latin America. The crimes committed in Ribeirão Bonito and Nova Iguaçu were minor compared to what went on in São Paulo, where Sergio Fleury, police commissioner and narcotics kingpin, ran a chain of horror houses, including the rat-infested Tiradentes Prison.*

‡ Following his release from prison, Father Tito hanged himself.

* Fleury was one of four torturers identified by Father Tito. ("Report on Allegations of Torture in Brazil," [London: Amnesty International, 1976], pp. 58–60.)

Among his subordinates was a proven psycopath and drug trafficker, José Alves da Silva, who was assistant director of the Tiradentes Prison despite his indictment for homicide in fourteen cases.[11] Fleury himself was accused of murder by Brazilian civilians in eleven different cases, but was repeatedly exonerated by military judges because of his "good record." The judge in Fleury's eleventh trial based his decision on the opinion of "eminent figures from Brazilian judicial, political, and social circles" who claimed that Fleury was an "individual of irreproachable conduct, both in his professional and private life."[12] Among Fleury's "irreproachable" activities were a São Paulo narcotics ring[13] and the local death squad—he was known to have played an active part in the deaths of over two hundred Brazilians.[14] Yet this record weighed not at all with his many character witnesses, including the commander in chief of the Second Army of Brazil in São Paulo, the former state prosecutor, the director of the State Department for Investigating Crimes, the secretaries of labor and tourism, and the chief of the Air Force's Investigative Committee in São Paulo. Such was Fleury's prominence that, after he was arrested in connection with the death of a narcotics dealer, the military regime changed the law to exempt murder suspects of "good record" from preventive detention. The amendment was immediately dubbed the "Fleury Law."[15] As a further sign of the government's regard, the regime increased Fleury's area of jurisdiction to include Europe, where he was sent to investigate the activities of Brazilian exiles.[16]

Not all Brazilians were convinced of Fleury's innocence. It was strange, said the prosecutor in his last trial, that the military government should claim that Fleury was "an exceptional element in the maintenance of the military regime, since this implies that the survival of the regime depends on one police official, because he killed a few subversives. Yet the truth is that, while the police wallow in the mud of corruption, they mask their criminal and immoral conduct by claiming to combat subversion."[17] The real reason that Fleury was "being touted as an anti-terrorist hero," added the Brazilian bishops, "was that he belonged to the notorious Death Squadron," a charge supported by a São Paulo security agent who turned state's evidence.[18] "To whitewash and exonerate the members of this squadron," said the bishops, "prestigious persons in high social and political positions have been asked to write endorsements for them. Moreover, the witnesses against them have been discredited, and the Church is being accused of involvement, to prove once again that it is 'mixed up in subversion.' And why have these charges been made against the Church? Because two of the incriminating accusations against the Death Squadron come from priests."[19]

A Cardinal at War

It was to combat such men as Fleury that São Paulo's archbishop, Cardinal Paulo Evaristo Arns, took up the banner of human rights shortly after his appointment in 1970. The first shot in what was to become an open war between the archdiocese and the military came in January 1971, when the military's secret police arrested an Italian priest and his assistant. The pair had been involved in programs for the city's workers, and when the police raided the priest's house, they found a stencil demanding better wages for workers. This was immediately seized upon as proof of subversion, and the two Italians were taken to police headquarters, where they were brutally tortured, although no charge was made against them. As soon as Arns learned of their arrest and mistreatment, he went to see the governor of the state of São Paulo, who told him that he must obtain proof of torture. When Arns went to the prison with two doctors to verify the charges, the police refused to admit him. Normally an even-tempered diplomat, Arns was outraged by this treatment and immediately denounced the incident in the archdiocese's newspaper and radio programs. A description of the Italians' arrest and torture was nailed to the door of every church in the city. Arns then summoned all the priests in his archdiocese to discuss the issue of torture, and from this meeting came a strongly worded document clearly defining the difference between social work and subversion.

The angry cardinal again brought up the question of torture during the annual conference of the country's bishops. "His declaration was the strongest, most courageous affirmation ever made by a Brazilian prelate against the torture of prisoners," in the words of the New York Times.[20] A pragmatic leader in the mainstream of the Brazilian Church, Arns received a respectful hearing from his fellow bishops. As a result of his intervention, the hierarchy made its first strong statement on behalf of human rights, and the torture of the Italians was publicized throughout the country. In response to these denunciations, the commanding general of São Paulo charged that several priests and two archbishops were agitating against national security.[21]

Because of his earlier defense of human rights, Arns was asked in 1972 to mediate on behalf of thirty-six political prisoners in the Tiradentes Prison. They had gone on a hunger strike to call attention to the terrible conditions in the nineteenth-century prison. Arns's plea that "we must all act . . . we must all intervene to save the lives of the thirty-six prisoners" called worldwide attention to their plight and may have saved their lives. The strike ended when the prisoners were moved to another São Paulo jail, but because of his intervention Arns was banned from the prisons.

The cardinal struck back with a series of editorials in his newspaper, *O São Paulo,* the largest Catholic publication in the country. The government's reaction was to censor *O São Paulo* and shut down Arns's Nove de Julho radio station. Torture continued as usual, but was expanded to include children. Hilda Gomes da Silva, the mother of three children, was tortured, along with her four-month-old son. Teresa Cristina, the daughter of lawyer Antonio Expedito, also underwent military interrogation—she was ten years old. Mrs. Fanny Akselrud was tortured because she would not reveal the whereabouts of her "dangerous" son—the ten-year-old Irineu. A year-old boy was given electric shocks in front of his father.[22] And Manoel Santiago da Silva, sixteen, was arrested, beaten by five men, and gang-raped.[23] Meanwhile, the Army, Navy, and Air Force expanded their joint courses in "interrogation" for junior officers. In one such class, an Army lieutenant showed slides of torture sessions while lecturing the assembly about each type of torture, its characteristics and effects. Ten male political prisoners were then brought into the classroom and forced to strip. One by one, they were tortured by corporals and privates in a "live" demonstration before the one hundred officer students.[24]

Typical of the regime's heavy-handed methods was the death of a young university student under torture in the spring of 1972. A top student at the geology faculty of the University of São Paulo, Alexandre Vanucchi Leme died after his arrest by the São Paulo military police. The government tried to pass his death off as the result of a car accident, but the cover-up was so ill-conceived that no one believed it. Among other things, the military said that it had had to bury Leme's body within twenty-four hours "since no one claimed it," although the young man was well known at the university faculty and came from a socially prominent family. In fact, his parents first learned of his death in a press report—they had not been informed, it was explained, because the police "were busy with various other investigations." Moreover, the police refused to allow the parents to exhume the body for a postmortem.

Leme's death might have passed without notice—so many prisoners die in Brazil†—had it not been for the shattering effect of the memorial Mass held for him in the cathedral of São Paulo by Cardinal Arns; Dom José Melhado Campos, the bishop of Sorocaba; and twenty-four priests. The Mass was scheduled for 6:30 P.M. but by midafternoon downtown São Paulo was occupied by armed police and shock troops, while the university was surrounded by military police. Nevertheless, three thousand students managed to enter the cathedral. The first song on the service sheet, specially prepared by an archdiocesan commission, was no hymn but a work written by a Brazilian exile and prohibited by

---

† A famous opinion poll taken in São Paulo in 1975 showed that seven out of ten people were afraid of being arrested by the police, while only six were worried about being attacked and robbed. There was good reason for this fear, according to a 1977 document, "Violence against the Meek," prepared by the Human Rights Commission of the archdiocese of São Paulo. The study showed that police violence was often gratuitous, as in the case of Djalma Arruda da Silva, a São Paulo shoemaker who was arrested at home while drunk, beaten by the police before they put him into the patrol car, and beaten again on arrival at the police station. As a result, he became comatose and died. A police inquiry concluded that "excessive violence was not used." ("Brazil: The Practice of Violence," *Latin America Political Report* [London, Apr. 7, 1978].)

The same study showed that rich people were treated quite differently. In a raid on an illegal casino in a private Rio mansion, police arrested thirty-one gamblers, but as the newspaper *Folha de São Paulo* pointed out, "Perhaps due to the social position of many of them—members of the armed forces, lawyers, industrialists, and traders, not to mention three policemen —none was charged."

the Brazilian censors. The liturgy was similarly "subversive," the sermons almost revolutionary. The bishop of Sorocaba openly accused the government: "God knows the truth of the accusations against this young student, and he will be the judge. But I believe that he was barbarically liquidated." Cardinal Arns, in the first words of his sermon, pointed out, "Even Christ after his death was returned to his family and friends; the representative of Roman power was able to do that much justice."[25]

The Leme affair was the prelude to a much more serious break with the Church when the National Conference of Brazilian Bishops published the United Nations' Declaration of Human Rights, with a stern warning to the regime to end the use of torture. The bishops said that the jails could not hold the "avalanche of citizens of every social class who had been detained, making it necessary to turn Army barracks into dungeons in which the military operated free from any observation so that no one could denounce what was happening there." To put teeth into their criticism, they announced the organization of diocesan departments as tribunals for the promotion of human rights, and urged priests to use their pulpits "to denounce discrimination against workers, small farmers, marginal sectors of society, women, blacks, and Indians." As Cardinal Arns explained, "It is impossible to pray in peace when dignity is being trampled on and ignored. The lack of respect for legal guarantees means social insecurity: for the people who have been imprisoned and subjected to harsh treatment on the basis of mere suspicion or even by mistake; for families in which one of the members has suddenly disappeared; and for a society that ends up losing faith in those responsible for its protection. How many people have spent months and even years in prison, who one day will be released without even being tried?"[26]

In an attempt to appease the Church and an increasingly critical world opinion, the regime temporarily eased press restrictions, but this taste of freedom was brief. Alarmed by published criticisms of its political and economic policies, the government once again resorted to repression by arresting twelve journalists in São Paulo. Among those seized was a distinguished Jewish journalist, Vladimir Herzog, who died under torture. Once again, Cardinal Arns summoned the people to protest at a cathedral funeral Mass, this time an ecumenical service with Jewish rabbis and a Presbyterian minister. Over eight thousand people defied a military siege of the city to attend the ceremony, and thirty-two thousand students at the University of São Paulo demonstrated their solidarity by refusing to attend classes.

Following the Mass, Arns and the bishops of São Paulo issued another stern pastoral letter, entitled "Do Not Oppress Your Brother":

> We would fail the command of our conscience if we did not take up again the phrase of John the Baptist, and say with the prophet, "It is not lawful for you." (Mark 6:18)
>
> It is not lawful to make arrests as they frequently are carried out, without identification of the authority or of the agents who make the arrest, without a trial from a competent judge within the legal period of time.
>
> It is not lawful to use physical, psychological, or moral means of torture in the interrogation of suspected persons, especially when they are carried to the degree of mutilation, destruction of health, and even death, as has happened.
>
> It is not lawful to deprive the accused of his right to full defense or to threaten or prejudge him as a criminal before trial or to postpone for an indefinite time the due process of law when our Constitution expressly provides that "the law will assure the accused of full defense with the recourses inherent in it."
>
> We also deplore the suspension of the full guarantee of habeas corpus. We stand behind those who plead for the total return of this guarantee. It is precisely its absence that contributes to the creation and maintenance of a climate of social insecurity.
>
> The warnings we voice emerge from the depths of human conscience, expressed in the Universal Declaration of Human Rights, a direct echo of the word of God: "You shall not kill." (Ex. 20:13)

To emphasize the seriousness of the Church's charges, Cardinal Arns and two million Catholics in São Paulo went on a twenty-four-hour hunger strike—which immediately brought a reaction from the government. Censorship of Arns's newspaper was tightened, the cardinal's life was threatened, and he was subjected to a defamation campaign similar to those against the outspoken Archbishop Helder Cámara and the Amazon's Pedro Casaldáliga. Anonymous letters accused Arns of sexual misconduct, grossly fabricated photomontages being offered as evidence. At the same time, the hitherto unknown "Confederation of Catholic Organizations in Brazil" circulated a statement condemning "red fascists" in the hierarchy, "red fascists" being a favorite phrase of General Eduardo D'Avila, the military commander of São Paulo. But these attacks only strengthened the Church's solidarity, and in December 1975 three thousand priests and six bishops gathered in São Paulo to attend a Mass in support of Cardinal Arns.

In the end, General D'Avila, not the cardinal, was forced to leave his post, when still another political prisoner, this time a worker, died under torture in the São Paulo prisons. Reaction to the man's death was spectacular, with yet another Mass in the São Paulo cathedral and long reports in the country's principal newspapers detailing how he had been arrested and commenting on government attempts to suppress the news of his death. In panic, President Geisel fired General D'Avila, without even bothering to give him advance notice.

D'Avila's dismissal may have been a victory for the Church, but it was greeted with dismay by the city's business community. According to the chairman of the Federation of Industries of the State of São Paulo, altogether too much attention was being paid to human rights, and this could backfire on the business community. General D'Avila was considered a staunch friend by São Paulo firms, which showered him with gifts and honors. Their gratitude was not misplaced: an important function of the military police was to pick off militant labor leaders and thus prevent effective union activity.[27] In fact, D'Avila's removal placed little curb on São Paulo's repressive apparatus; by 1976 it had become so sophisticated that it could even boast a public relations office. Nor did the attacks on Arns cease. By the end of 1977 the government had declared the cardinal to be the principal leader of the opposition.

But Cardinal Arns was not intimidated. "The Church," he said, "is a community of people, and if there is social injustice in that community, the Church must be concerned. In the Old Testament, God's prophets were always against the oppression of the weak. And Christ very clearly identified himself with the humble people."

Sheer, Open Terror

The "institutionalization" of violence in Brazil was rationalized by both Washington and corporate industry as an unpleasant but necessary corollary of development, the theory being that only a strong government could drag Brazil into the twentieth century. As long as Brazil's gross national product could show a reasonable growth, and as long as the regime's representatives spoke piously about human rights and democracy in international forums, the rest of the world would look the other way.

Not so with Argentina. Unlike Brazil, whose dictatorship was dressed up with military doctrines and economic miracles, Argentina in the late 1970s was a land of sheer, open terror. Nothing in Latin America, not even Pinochet's Chile, could equal the levels of violence that followed the military coup of March 1976. Indeed, the only regime to create a state of fear approximating that in Argentina was Hitler's Germany. (There were other parallels to nazism, including a government-sponsored hate campaign against the country's four hundred thousand Jews.) Nor was there any economic excuse for this reign of violence, with the economy in a shambles and the inflation rate the highest in Latin America. Yet Argentina had been the most literate, best-fed nation on the continent, a country whose cultural accomplishments could rival those of Europe and the United States, one that produced the best scientists in Latin America, not excepting Brazil. That such a people could be reduced to a state of terror, in which no one was immune from the midnight knock on the door, must be seen as one of the great tragedies of Latin America in this century.

Some idea of the scope of the terror may be gained from the statistics compiled by Amnesty International, the United Nations, the Catholic Church, and the World Council of Churches: approximately twenty thousand people had been detained or had disappeared by July 1978; at least twelve thousand political prisoners were in prison or in concentration camps in September 1977. (The State Department had a list of seventy-five hundred

Argentines who had been jailed or had disappeared.) Political killings were averaging seven a day in 1977. Nor were Argentines the only victims. An estimated fourteen thousand refugees from other South American military regimes were told to leave the country or face the possibility of arrest. Torture was automatic for anyone arrested, according to a spokesman for the World Council of Churches.

Although the causes of the violence in Argentina were complex, they could be traced to the tensions between, on the one hand, the military institution and its allies in the wealthy upper classes and, on the other, the labor movement and its allies in the middle class. The fundamental issue was popular rule. Unlike other Latin-American countries where labor is largely ineffectual, Argentina had developed during the 1940s a cohesive, literate trade-union movement. This was due in part to the makeup of the workers—first- and second-generation immigrants from Italy and Spain—and in part to the country's rapid industrialization. The third and crucial factor in this process was Juan Domingo Perón, who organized the labor movement as his principal power base during his first period in government (1943–55). Though Perón was overthrown in 1955, successive military and civilian governments were unable to lay his ghost, and in 1973 he was allowed to return to Argentina to win the presidency in popular elections. His death the following year set off the spiral of violence that culminated in a reign of terror in the late seventies.

During Perón's years in exile, the man became so indistinguishable from his myth that few Argentines were able coldly to assess the failings and successes of his first period in government: if you were a Peronist, the man was a god; if you were an anti-Peronist, he was the devil. Thus Perón had enemies and allies on both the Right and the Left—everyone thought to exploit the legend; few looked at the record. The fact is that Perón was a poor economic administrator and a corrupt dictator with strong fascist leanings (Mussolini was his model). But he was also a consummate politician and a nationalist who tried to steer a course independent of the United States. By building a base in the labor movement, thus outside the traditional alliance between the military and the wealthy, he changed the balance of power in Argentina. It was a brilliant stroke, transforming Perón from just another run-of-the-mill dictator into a populist leader with a mass following.

During the sixties, when civilian governments were regularly overthrown by the military because of the threat of a Peronist coalition or election victory, the image of Perón, the monster dictator, was repeatedly invoked. But the real danger, never stated, was that posed by the working and middle classes to the alliance of military, industrialists, and large landowners. Politician that he was, Perón from his exile in Spain encouraged young Argentine leftists to mount armed attacks on the military regime, and the growth of guerrilla violence finally convinced the military, or at least those in charge at the time, to allow Perón to return and run for President, the belief being that only he could unite all Argentines. (There was no one else, in any case.) This was part of the myth, of course—the fascist dictator of the forties and fifties had not changed, but it was politically expedient for him to make the young people on the Left think so. And while some union leaders privately questioned Perón's real commitment to the poorer classes, few dared say so publicly, lest they lose the workers' support.

Once Perón was back in power, it became apparent that he could not be all things to all men, even with his considerable gift for dividing and ruling his heterogeneous following. While protecting his power base in the labor movement by encouraging the enactment of advanced labor legislation and upholding the workers' share of the national income, Perón also repressed strikes and dissident union leaders and generally supported the suppression of the center-Left by paramilitary groups. There was nothing new in this policy—much the same had happened during his previous period in government. But most of the students and union militants were too young to remember those years—their only reference was the myth. When that collapsed, the disillusioned young turned to the guerrilla movements that Perón himself had earlier encouraged. Their opposite numbers in the paramilitary and police squads on the extreme Right had deeper roots, dating to the first Perón government, and their orientation was decidedly fascist. Their authority had been expanded under the 1966–70 dictatorship of General Juan Carlos Onganía, who also shared fascist leanings, at the same time that young leftists were forming guerrilla groups with Perón's support.

Thus the stage was set for a national bloodbath when the old man died. María Estela (Isabel) Perón succeeded her husband in the presidency, but having neither the intelligence nor the political skill to control the antagonists, she surrendered her power to the Peronist movement's right wing, and it fed the violence by sponsoring a proliferation of such paramilitary death squadrons as the Argentine Anti-Communist Alliance (AAA). By the time the military intervened in 1976, a vast repressive apparatus had been established.

The original objective of the coup—to destroy the left-wing guerrilla movement—was largely accomplished by the end of 1977. But at the same time repression became so pervasive that anyone who criticized the government was liable to be kidnapped and murdered, even if he was equally critical of leftist politicians and guerrillas. By the end of 1976 three quarters of the political deaths could be attributed to the extreme right,[28] yet not a single Argentine from that side of the political spectrum was arrested or tried. On the contrary, the government gave dozens of paramilitary and para-police organizations a free hand to torture, murder, and blackmail their victims: thuggery was thus institutionalized on a national scale.

President Jorge Videla and his junta tried to pass the buck by claiming they could not control their subordinates. In fact, there were strong historical reasons for the repression. Argentina's military has always mistrusted civilian rule (there have been only four freely elected, relatively democratic governments since the country achieved independence), and it became particularly wary after the rise of the labor movement under Perón in the forties. The generals' refusal to countenance popular rule was largely responsible for Perón's enduring influence in absentia—civilian leaders could never hold office long enough to carry out their programs or attract a mass following—and for the rise of violence on the Left. Yet very few in the military establishment understood that their constant interference in the country's political life was itself the basic cause of instability.

The military's principal dread—a mass mobilization of workers, students, and the middle class—was also of its own making. Everyone could remember the "Cordobazo," a spontaneous uprising in the industrial city of Córdoba that toppled General Onganía in 1970, but the generals refused to see that military repression had sparked the revolt. Instead of allowing the people an outlet for their hopes and frustrations through elected government, they chose to beat the Argentines into submission. Repression against left-wing guerrillas and students was expanded to include union leaders, moderate politicians, lawyers, journalists, scientists, priests, even right-wing businessmen. It was enough to deplore the carnage to become a victim. As one Argentine general succinctly put it: "No one can be neutral or ambivalent. Some will succumb for being indifferent. Others will be shot as collaborators."[29] Or in the memorable words of General Benjamín Menéndez, commander of the Army III Corps in Córdoba and its notorious concentration camps: "While [President] Videla governs, I kill!"[30]

Underlying this bloodthirsty boast was the military's belief that it was engaged in total war. As the Jesuit magazine *Mensaje* pointed out, "Anyone who was not a trusted ally, anyone who did not have a 'good-conduct pass,' was suspect as an undercover agent who somehow was or might be in league with the enemy, and who therefore had to be destroyed or neutralized."[31] But since the enemy was not a foreign army but the Argentines themselves, the "war" became generalized violence.

To justify the need for such a "dirty war," Argentine officers frequently cited French doctrines of counterinsurgency, particularly as applied to Algeria's struggle for independence in the 1950s. But as three French generals wrote President Videla, such methods could lead to kidnapping, torture, and long periods of imprisonment without trial—a form of war inconsistent with military methods and traditions. We know from our own experience, they said, that military men sometimes described as "subversion" the disagreements normal to a democracy.[32]

Typical of the "inconsistent" methods used by the military on thousands of Argentines was the torment suffered by Dr. Laura Bonaparte, an Argentine psychology professor, and her daughter Aida. A teacher in a slum school near Buenos Aires, Aida was kidnapped by the military in December 1975, apparently because she had organized a committee of neighbors to help the families of those who had been wounded during an Army bombardment of the slum. Dr. Bonaparte appealed for help to the Church, police, and military headquarters, and to former Argentine senators and representatives. She also filed dozens of petitions of habeas corpus, to no avail. In desperation she joined other relatives of political prisoners in a demonstration at the 601st Army Battalion Headquarters. "Through the gates, we yelled the names of our sons and daughters, hoping that the guards would tell us if they were being held in that prison," she said. An officer told them to go to the Avellaneda Cemetery in Buenos Aires and request a list of the dead. "The odor was unbearable," she recalled, "and I did not have the strength to continue. Five blocks from the cemetery I turned and left."

On January 8, 1976, Dr. Bonaparte received official notification that Aida had "died in a confrontation." "They also provided me with the number of a jar, No. 24, which I was supposed to request at La Plata police headquarters. My daughter's hands were in that jar, and they wanted me to identify her from them." Two Army officers later told Dr. Bonaparte that her daughter had been raped and then shot, along with other prisoners. "The executions were performed under orders from the Minister of the Interior, General Albano Harguindeguy," she said. "The prisoners' corpses were piled up and later dismembered."[33]

Aida's husband was killed by the military in March 1976; Dr. Bonaparte's husband was abducted that June. In September a sister-in-law and her husband disappeared, and in May 1977 Dr. Bonaparte's other daughter, Irene, and her husband were kidnapped from their home in Buenos Aires, leaving behind two baby sons. Dr. Bonaparte was able to give testimony of these events in a letter to U. S. Congressman Donald Fraser only because she had fled to Mexico and most of her family was presumed dead. Countless other Argentines who suffered similar barbarities were afraid to tell their stories because they or their relations would be marked for revenge.

Such was the case of two elderly spinster sisters whose twenty-one-year-old niece was dragged from the family apartment in Buenos Aires by military agents. Her father, who was recovering from a prostate operation, suffered a heart attack as a result. The niece had already been through more than a lifetime of suffering. Her husband had been shot by a right-wing para-police squad and permanently paralyzed. Depressed and worried about the physical strain on his pregnant wife of dressing and moving him, he committed suicide. She lost the baby anyway. The family went to the Buenos Aires morgue to examine thirty corpses after someone called to say that the young woman was among them. She was not, and from a contact in the military the family later learned the bare fact that she was still alive. "We are afraid to go to the government office for missing persons to report the case because this may be a ploy to implicate the rest of the family," explained the aunts. "She was such a sweet girl and pretty, too," sobbed one of the old ladies. "She had freckles and blue eyes and long blond hair. You wouldn't have thought she was more than seventeen. And we'll never see her again!"[34] The niece's crime? She had been a social worker in a Buenos Aires slum.

From an American's point of view the Argentine situation was all the more tragic because of the U. S. Government's part in the carnage. CIA agents stationed in Buenos Aires during the Onganía dictatorship in the late sixties knew about the formation of right-wing paramilitary and police squads and the growing use of torture. "If you think the Brazilian police's torture methods are bad, you should see what goes on in Argentine prisons," was the comment of one CIA agent.[35] But apparently torture was accepted as routine—in any case, the CIA Buenos Aires station had other matters to think about, including the overthrow of Allende in neighboring Chile and the elimination of the Tupamaro guerrillas in Uruguay.‡ According to Agee's *CIA Diary,* the Argentine federal police were the CIA's principal liaison in Buenos Aires, assisting the agency in telephone tapping and other operations under the code name "Biogénesis." There is ample evidence that the AAA death squad and similar organizations were creatures of this same police force. For example, many political prisoners kidnapped by the AAA were jailed and tortured in federal police headquarters.* The head of the police, Héctor García Rey, had been trained in the Panama Canal Zone, with eighty Argentine policemen. Additional training and funds for the police were supplied through the International Narcotics Control Program of the State Department and the Drug Enforcement Administration,

‡ See Chapter VI, pp. 188–91.
* See Father Rice's testimony, Chapter I.

which became the chief source of U.S. aid for Latin-American police agencies after Congress abolished the AID training program in 1974.†

In May 1974, after the U. S. Government agreed to give the Argentine police increased training and funds for narcotics enforcement, José López Rega, the Minister of Social Welfare and principal power in Isabel Perón's government, held a nationally televised press conference with U.S. Ambassador Robert Hill to announce the new U.S.-Argentine program. Said López Rega: "We hope to wipe out the drug traffic in Argentina. We have caught guerrillas after attacks who were high on drugs. Guerrillas are the main users of drugs in Argentina. *Therefore, the anti-drug campaign will automatically be an anti-guerrilla campaign as well.*"[36] (Emphasis added.)

From 1974 to 1976, 260 Argentine police officers attended seminars in Argentina, the United States, and the Panama Canal Zone under the narcotics program. The U. S. Government also supplied money for vehicles and communications and laboratory equipment. But one may ask how much of this equipment and training was used to combat the drug traffic, given the activities of the Argentines in charge of the program, including Social Welfare Minister López Rega, who controlled the country's police appara-

† A study by the General Accounting Office (GAO) published in 1976 indicated that U.S. narcotics assistance could well be serving the same objectives as those of the earlier AID public safety program, which was shown to have encouraged the use of torture and assassination by Latin-American police and para-police organizations. (See Chapter VI, pp. 186–91.) According to the GAO, U.S. aid to Latin-American police agencies through the narcotics program increased by nearly 600 percent between 1973 and 1974, compensating almost exactly for the money cut off from the public safety program. The types of armament and equipment previously furnished the Latin-American police through AID were now being supplied by the narcotics program, and the police merely added narcotics control to their other activities, thus complying, at least superficially, with U.S. regulations. But even in countries with special anti-narcotics police squads, there was no guarantee that the equipment and training supplied by the U. S. Government would not be used by other police agencies for different purposes, the GAO said.

The Drug Enforcement Administration has also replaced the public safety program as a cover for CIA agents. According to columnist Jack Anderson, sixty-four former CIA employees now work for the DEA and thirteen narcotics agents were trained at a CIA counterespionage school.

tus, and Federal Police Chief García Rey. According to an investigation by the Argentine Congress, López Rega was the founder of the right-wing terrorist AAA, a charge supported by numerous other sources.[37] There was also considerable evidence linking him to Argentina's cocaine traffic, particularly in the northern province of Salta near the frontier with Bolivia, South America's major coca leaf producer. Military intelligence reports‡ showed that López Rega and his son-in-law Raul Lastri, who had served briefly as President of the country before Perón's election, were in partnership with a Peronist senator from Salta, owner of the province's only newspaper and television station, in a three-way cocaine operation involving Bolivia and Paraguay.[38] Among the drug ring's operations were an 87,500-acre coca leaf plantation near the Bolivian frontier and a cocaine processing laboratory. When the provincial legislature began an investigation of cocaine smuggling, the provincial government was placed under the control of federal authorities. In 1975 alone, the police were reported to have marketed 2 tons of marijuana and 186 pounds of cocaine. Yet these were the people who received training and equipment from the U. S. Government. As in São Paulo, Brazil, where Police Chief Sergio Fleury combined a drug ring with a death squadron, so in Buenos Aires the federal police were responsible for both the AAA and the narcotics traffic.

In addition to the police, 3,676 Argentines from the armed forces, including the head of the dread secret service, were trained in the United States and in the Panama Canal Zone. And Argentina received $352.4 million in U.S. military credits between 1950 and 1976. As with the police, there is overwhelming evidence that the military sponsored such death squads as the AAA, which eventually became a catchall for right-wing terrorist groups. Senator Hipólito Solari Yrigoyen, known for his firm defense of human rights during the Peronist years, reported that he was kidnapped and tortured by Army officers in the city of Bahía Blanca, at a time when the Argentine Government was denying all knowledge of his whereabouts. The target of an earlier bomb attack, Solari Yrigoyen said that his Army captors were quite open about their membership in terrorist organizations. "You want to know

‡ This was during the interval between Perón's death and his wife's overthrow by the military in March 1976.

all about the Triple-A," they told him. "Well, we're the Triple-A. We put the bomb in your car." They went on to list the assassinations for which they claimed responsibility.[39]

According to a U.S. missionary in Argentina, military and police often worked independently, and the frequent instances when people were kidnapped and tortured because of mistaken identity occurred, he said, from the profusion of security agencies, usually working at cross-purposes. The missionary's testimony was borne out by a U.S. businessman, who described how Buenos Aires was divided into small fiefdoms with a local colonel in charge of each area and "safe houses" in which political prisoners were tortured and murdered. Both businessman and priest considered the police force a disaster. "They have almost no training . . . and are notorious for graft and crime," said the missionary.[40]

The profusion and irresponsibility of para-police and paramilitary gangs were frequently cited by the Videla government to excuse the government's failure to control right-wing violence. But every time sufficient international pressure was brought to bear, as when there was an upsurge of anti-Semitism, lo and behold, the regime found it could contain the violence. When American Jewish leaders complained to the U. S. Congress about an outbreak of unprecedented attacks on the Argentine Jewish community, Videla's government attempted to placate the Americans by closing Editorial Milicia, an Argentine publishing house responsible for a flood of Nazi literature, and by ordering the terrorist squads to reduce the number of bombings of Jewish establishments.[41]

"Be a patriot [in Argentina]! Kill a Jew!"

The hate campaign against Argentina's four hundred thousand Jews was particularly revealing of the military mentality. While Jews have always been ostracized by the wealthy, landowning aristocracy and by the military (no Jew can aspire to the highest ranks), anti-Semitism did not become an issue until Perón's first period in government, when the regime was pro-Axis. After World War II, Perón gave hundreds of fleeing Nazis a safe refuge. As in Germany, Argentine Jewry was singled out as a scapegoat for the country's economic and social ills whenever there was a serious political crisis. Thus there was a rash of anti-Semitic incidents in the first months after General Juan Carlos Onganía seized power in 1966. German and Argentine Nazis played on the military's gut feeling that the Jews were Marxist traitors to the Fatherland, and grasping capitalists to boot. Their principal instrument in this hate campaign was Nazi literature. In 1969 a Nazi publishing house was founded in Bariloche, an Andean lake resort in southern Argentina where many Nazis had taken refuge. It published neo-Nazi books in German and Spanish. A ten-page anonymous pamphlet was also circulated that purported to describe a secret Jewish plot to form a breakaway state, "Andinia," in the southern part of the country. Such books and pamphlets were regularly mailed to military officers and university students. Julio Weinvielle, an anti-Semitic priest and author of *The Jew in the Mystery of History,* encouraged the campaign as spiritual adviser to several high-ranking officers. One of the most avid readers of anti-Semitic tracts was General Menéndez, the self-styled butcher of Córdoba.[42]

But it was on Perón's return to Argentina in 1973 that anti-Semitism really surged. Editorial Milicia came out with a series of anti-Semitic classics, including works by Mussolini and *The Protocols of the Elders of Zion,* as well as books by Argentines, among them two famous Jew-baiting novels, *El Kahal* and *Oro.* It also published a series of tracts blaming the Jews for the world's problems, including capitalism, communism, and both world wars. Milicia was one of several anti-Semitic publishing houses and magazines, among them *El Caudillo* and *Puntal.* The latter received government advertising from the Ministry of Social Welfare, the original architect of the AAA, and *El Caudillo* is particularly remembered for printing a poem calling for a pogrom: "Nine at night is a good hour for this. . . . The place you already know: the Quarter of Usury. Wave a thousand truncheons; bloody a thousand heads . . . that all will be devastated."[43]

Within months of Perón's recapture of power, Argentina had become a world center for the publication and distribution of Nazi literature, according to the Anti-Defamation League of B'nai B'rith.[44] The liberal Buenos Aires daily *La Opinión* also warned that Argentine Nazis with direct contacts in Germany were publishing Spanish translations of their colleagues' work in Germany.

After Perón's death and the military coup, attacks on the Jewish community escalated. Bookstores and kiosks were flooded with cheap editions of works by Hitler and Goebbels; Jewish schools, synagogues, newspapers, and businesses were bombed; prominent Jewish citizens were kidnapped, blackmailed, and generally intimidated. In August 1976 unidentified thugs drove through Buenos Aires' Jewish quarter, Barrio Once, strafing shops and synagogues with machine guns. A group calling itself the Argentine National Socialist Front, one of several Nazi organizations in Argentina, including the Tacuara and the National Restoration Guard, took credit for the attack. The story of the "Andinia plot" to create a Jewish state was again circulated, this time by the government news agency, and a series of crude anti-Semitic programs appeared on television. The walls of the city of Mendoza in northwestern Argentina were painted with swastikas and such slogans as "Be a patriot! Kill a Jew!"* In April 1976 the public was invited by two groups calling themselves the Aryan Integral Nationalist Fatherland and the Pious Christian Crusade to attend Masses in the Buenos Aires cathedral "for the eternal rest of our blood brother in Christ, Adolf Hitler." (The Church refused to sanction the ceremonies.)

Jewish leaders also reported that political prisoners were treated more harshly if Jewish. According to a woman who was detained and tortured by the military, most of the officers had Nazi ideas. "The head torturer told me that he had previously worked in Algiers and that he had a Nazi ideology," she said. A partly Jewish couple from Uruguay, arrested at the same time, were subjected, she said, to particularly barbarous treatment. "They insulted the Uruguayan man because his mother was Jewish. 'How could you marry such a filthy pig?' they asked his wife."[45] The police showed similar Nazi sympathies, according to the Irish priest Patrick Rice (see Chapter I), who mentioned swastikas painted on the walls of the federal police headquarters in Buenos Aires. Jews were also singled out for extortion and blackmail. To secure the release of Dr. Alfredo Stein, a prominent Argentine physician, from the Campo de Mayo military barracks

* A variation of the slogan used by the White Warriors Union against Catholic priests in El Salvador. See Chapter III.

on the outskirts of Buenos Aires, his family was forced to pay $23,000 ransom.[46]

President Videla's gesture in closing Editorial Milicia turned out to be empty: the publishing house continued under a new name, ODAL, and a second Nazi publishing house, Editorial Occidente, began publishing anti-Semitic books. On the other hand, the Videla government banned a Jewish magazine and closed the offices of the American Jewish Committee, harassment and threats against his life forcing the committee's representative, Jacobo Kovadloff, to leave the country. Meanwhile, government television seized upon a local financial scandal involving a prominent Jewish family to whip up more anti-Semitic feeling. Emphasizing the Jewish surnames in the case, Channel 11 commented: "Very Argentine these names, aren't they? Not all the country is like this. The rest is honest."[47] The son of the president of the Delegation of Argentine Israeli Associations, spokesman for the Argentine Jewish community, was kidnapped in July 1977 and held in military premises where the walls were decorated with swastikas and pictures of Hitler, Mussolini, and Franco. Thanks to his father's prominence, he was later released, but bombings of Jewish schools and homes continued.

In this period, Nazi criminals were given official protection. Edward Roschmann, better known as the "Butcher of Riga" for his part in the slaughter of forty thousand Jews in that city, was allowed to leave Argentina in July 1977, after West Germany requested his extradition. Believed to have been the head of the ODESSA network responsible for smuggling Nazis to Latin America, Roschmann died of a heart attack shortly after arriving in his new haven, Paraguay. Heinrich Muerk, another well-known figure in Nazi circles in Argentina and once a close associate of Adolf Eichmann, was released by the government after being arrested in connection with the rape-murder of a five-year-old boy in a Buenos Aires suburb. Witnesses claimed to have seen Muerk in the boy's company the day of his death, and police sources admitted he had a long record of sexual obscenity in the neighborhood. Local newspapers speculated that ODESSA had secured his release.[48]

The anti-Semitic campaign was coupled with an equally ugly attack on the progressive sector of the Argentine Catholic Church.

Military repression of priests and nuns coincided with a barrage of anticlerical propaganda by Editorial Milicia and other Nazi publishing houses, which charged that the Church was in league with world Judaism and Marxism. This line was used by the military and paramilitary organizations to persecute religious working in slums and rural areas, and by the end of 1977 seventeen priests and nuns had been murdered, thirty were in prison, and the country's most outspoken bishop was dead, killed by security forces in a fake automobile accident. Some, such as Fathers José Tedeschi and Francisco Soares, were murdered because they had protested against violence. Soares was killed by a para-police squad in the San Isidro diocese of Buenos Aires after he denounced the murder of a woman catechist found bleeding to death with one of her breasts ripped away. Soares' invalid brother died with him. Four months later, in June 1976, three Irish priests and two seminarians working in the Irish suburb of Belgrano were shot to death by the Buenos Aires police in revenge for a guerrilla attack on police headquarters. The priests had nothing to do with guerrillas or left-wing politics, but one of them had earlier preached a sermon against the death penalty, and this was seized upon as an excuse to massacre the five in the Belgrano parish house. Violence had reached such a point that any victims would do, even innocent bystanders.

Government denials to the contrary, the Belgrano murders were clearly the work of the federal police. On the night of the massacre, the son of a senior military officer who lived in the area noticed a Peugeot, with four occupants and flashing lights, parked near the parish house. He reported this suspicious circumstance to Station No. 37 of the federal police, but the information was ignored until the young man identified himself. The police then offered him a ride home in a police car. He refused and on his way home saw a police car approach the parked Peugeot, stop for a brief exchange of words, and then drive off. The young man described the incident to the police guard at his door, who told him that the occupants of the Peugeot had identified themselves as members of the secret police who had said "they had come to do away with lefties." From his house the young man saw armed figures entering and leaving the parish house. He thought they had asked the priests' permission to go through their house for greater convenience. At 2:55 A.M. the Peugeot drove off.

The next day one of the boys from the parish knocked at the door of the priests' house. When there was no response, he entered through a window, and found the three priests and two seminarians dead in their rooms. The priests bore signs of beatings on the mouth with rifle butts. On one of the carpets in the house had been spray-painted: "For corrupting the virgin minds of the young," and with chalk on one of the doors: "For our dead comrades in federal security." The words in chalk were erased by the police immediately on their arrival.[49] According to the judge's report on the murders, which was suppressed by the government, the killers were members of the federal police.[50]

While the massacre of the Irish priests was an act of mindless vengeance, there was reason enough to kill Bishop Enrique Angelelli and two of his priests the following month. An outspoken man with a strong social conscience, Angelelli worked in the "other Argentina," the backward, impoverished Northwest with its huge haciendas and hungry Indians, a world away from the sophisticated capital of Buenos Aires and the rich industrial and agricultural cities of the pampas. The son of Italian immigrants who had made their fortune in Argentina, Angelelli spent most of his working life in the industrial city of Córdoba. Leaving Córdoba for La Rioja in 1968, when he was named bishop of the diocese, was, said Angelelli, like going to another country.

Isolated by a sea of scrubland and the blue foothills of the Andes, La Rioja has changed very little since the Spanish colonists enslaved the Indian tribes four centuries ago, huge ranches of twenty-five thousand acres contrasting with squalid adobe Indian settlements. The Indians are used on the ranches as peons, to tend the vineyards and the walnut and olive groves. Although their ancestors built splendid cities, bridges, and highways and developed the art of ceramics and weaving to a level rivaling that of the Inca civilization, the Rioja Indians are literally treated as work animals by the white landowners.

One way whereby the ranchers maintained this cultural and economic repression was the Catholic religion, which had always identified the region's patron saints with the white man's dominance over the Indians. This conveniently racist cult dates to the second half of the sixteenth century, when a Franciscan friar, St. Francis Solano, persuaded the Indians to lay down their arms in submission to the Child Jesus, supposedly after a series of miracles and because the friar had some skill on the violin. In the best cross-and-sword tradition, Solano talked the Indians into accepting a statue of the Child Jesus as the mayor of the town of La Rioja, in place of the Spanish official, whom they hated and feared. Duly named to office, this statue of a white child in warrior's robes has ever since been the center of an annual ritual reaffirming the Indians' submission.

The symbol of this submission is the figure of a black St. Nicholas, which is taken from the cathedral in a procession to pay homage to the Child Jesus. An arrogant, frightening statue, St. Nicholas is venerated by the people of La Rioja as a malevolent spirit who must be placated. During the annual procession, the descendants of the Indian slaves take the part of St. Nicholas; the wealthy white landowners, that of the Child Jesus. The local bishop presides over the procession, kneeling three times with the statue of St. Nicholas in front of the "Mayor of the City" in an act of submission. Thus the superior power of good over evil, white over Indian, is symbolically reaffirmed—year after year.

During Angelelli's first year as bishop, the procession was held as usual, with Angelelli kneeling in submission to the Child Jesus. But unlike his predecessors, he wanted to rid the cult of its racist symbolism. As the bishop explained to the crowd of worshippers, submission to the "Mayor of the City" did not mean submission to any other authority. "No man," he said, "has the right to put his foot on the neck of another."

Angelelli's teaching was rightly interpreted as a challenge to the white landowners, who promptly dubbed him "Satanelli." But this was a minor insult compared to a hate campaign initiated by Tradition, Family, and Property, the right-wing Catholic movement. It published a series of advertisements in local newspapers denouncing the bishop and his clergy as Marxist, even taping sermons by the priests in the town of Chamical. Angelelli had regular run-ins with the large landowners and the local government, which the bishop chastised for failing to provide the people with even the minimum in public services. "Must the people wait forever for the government to keep its promises?" he demanded. In

1972, when two of his priests were arrested on vague charges of subversion, Angelelli attempted to hold a religious ceremony in front of the local government building. This being banned, he organized a protest Mass in the cathedral. The following year he imposed ecclesiastical sanctions on thirteen wealthy ranchers who had attacked him for defending workers' rights. The landowners then denounced him to the Vatican, but this backfired when the Vatican delegate sent to investigate the situation concluded that Angelelli's work was in complete accord with papal teachings and that he "deserved praise and support."

The bishop made more enemies among the military when he refused to attend a presidential reception in La Rioja, saying, "A bishop cannot shake the hand of a man who represses his people."[51] He had words with Córdoba's General Menéndez over the Church's failure to support military repression, and he was disliked by the Air Force, which has an air base at Chamical. When the bishop preached against a coup during a Mass celebrated at the base a few days before the military takeover of 1976, the commanding officer stalked out of the church, complaining that he did not go to Mass to hear about politics. But what probably assured Angelelli's death was his promotion of an ecumenical group to aid political prisoners and their families after ten of his collaborators were jailed. Later released, the ten took refuge in Angelelli's home.

During all these crises, the corpulent bishop managed to keep his sense of humor and a zest for life. "A little is a lot for someone who has nothing," he would say, appearing at the hut of an Indian peasant with a bottle of cheap local wine, a can of sardines, and a loaf of bread for the family's supper. "He was constantly on the firing line," said an admiring friend, "but this never affected his joy in being alive, the happiness of someone who knew he was loved by all those poor people."[52]

One of those poor, a community leader called Wenceslao, was shot at point-blank range at the door of his house in July 1976. Before his assailants killed him, said his wife, they asked, "Where are the priests?" The priests were Father Gabriel Longueville, a Frenchman who had worked in La Rioja for five years, and Carlos Díaz Murias, an Argentine born in Córdoba who had been in La Rioja for a little over a year. Before studying for the priesthood, Murias had been a pupil at the Military College in Córdoba; many of his classmates were now officers in the Argentine Army.

Longueville and Murias were having supper in the home of the nuns next to the rectory in Chamical when two men with federal police credentials appeared at the door, asking the priests to accompany them to La Rioja to identify some political prisoners. The priests went with the police. Later that night the nuns drove to La Rioja to report the incident to Angelelli. The following day railroad workers found the priests' bodies on the railroad tracks in Chanar, a few miles south of Chamical. The bodies were covered with Army blankets. Murias' body showed signs of torture, and a list of priests' names had been left with the corpses. The Army blankets were burned as soon as the bodies arrived in the local mortuary. Meanwhile, Angelelli had arrived in Chamical in search of the priests. During their funeral the following day he spoke of the two men's spirit of self-sacrifice and the reasons for their murder: they were killed, he said, "to silence the voice of the Church, the voice of the voiceless."

The night before Angelelli was due to return to La Rioja with his vicar general, Father Arturo Pinto, the two men noticed strange movements in the empty lot behind the parish house, where they had left their Fiat van. A vehicle without lights was seen to leave by a side street. The next day, when Angelelli drove out of Chamical with Father Pinto, a Peugeot followed at some distance. When the Fiat was on a particularly empty stretch of road, said Pinto, the Peugeot overtook them and forced the van off the road onto the hard shoulder. Pinto said that when the bishop tried to apply the brakes, they stuck, as if the van had lost a wheel. The Fiat crashed, ricocheted sixteen yards, landed upside down, and bounced another thirteen yards, rolling over several times. Angelelli was thrown through the windshield and died instantly of a broken neck. Pinto, who was still alive, was picked up by a private car, which took him to Chamical. Angelelli's body remained on the road till late that night, but the military promptly removed the van to the air base, where its tires were stripped. Church sources unanimously agreed that, contrary to the official report, there was no puncture in the back left tire.[53] The bishop's attaché case, containing reports on the deaths of the priests in Chamical, disappeared, and a police squad was sent to the diocesan offices to search the bishop's private room. Angelelli's vicar general refused them entry, citing canon law.

When Angelelli's body was already dressed for the funeral, the local judge ordered an autopsy, and not until the next day was the bishop delivered to his friends for burial. Ten bishops, eighty priests, and a huge congregation—all the Indian peasants whom Angelelli had loved—attended the ceremony. Said Archbishop Vicente Zaspe: "Now, for the first time in my life, I know what being a bishop means."

The "Glorious Revolution"

"What forces are so powerful that they can operate with impunity and anonymity in our midst?" the Argentine bishops had asked. "What guarantees, what rights remain the ordinary citizen?" In Argentina such questions had become rhetorical, but how can one explain similar questions in Mexico, a country so different from Argentina in history and cultural makeup, one of the few enduring democracies in Latin America? Or was it? The statistics certainly did not suggest a happy society: an average of fifty-two thousand arrests and seven thousand murders a year, thirteen murders a day in Mexico City alone.[54] According to the popular weekly magazine *Impacto,* the police had become Public Enemy No. 1.[55] Out in the countryside, peasants and landowners were forever clashing, often in showdowns involving thousands of people. Infant mortality was on the rise (a 10 percent increase between 1966 and 1973), the illiteracy rate was soaring, unemployment was estimated at 40 percent, and the gap between rich and poor was growing.†

As in Argentina, where the Peronist myth failed to answer the country's political and social problems, Mexico's myth of the 1910 revolution gradually lost its promise. While that "glorious revolution" still figures prominently in the obligatory rhetoric of Mexican politics, it is no longer seen as a genuine social revolu-

† Figures for income distribution show that the poorest 40 percent of the population receive only 11 percent of the national income, one of the lowest figures in Latin America for this class. The richest 5 percent, on the other hand, take 29 percent of the country's wealth.

tion—had it been such, Mexico today would be unlike any other Latin-American country. In fact, the vast majority of the people live in the abject conditions that are all too familiar elsewhere in Latin America.

Fought and won by armies of hungry peasants who had rebelled against Mexico's feudal landowners, the revolution gradually came under the control of a rising industrial class. Although many of the feudal estates were broken up and distributed to the peasants, the system of land tenancy gradually returned to the old pattern of *latifundio,* only now the large estates were called agribusinesses and were controlled by local political bosses, urban industrial interests, or foreign companies. By 1976 three quarters of the land belonged to such estates.[56] This skewed pattern of land ownership was responsible for the annual migration of some 2 million Mexican farm workers to the United States, as well as for the explosive growth of the cities and the urban and rural violence.

Nearly seven decades after the revolution, Mexico was politically bankrupt, its ruling Partido Revolucionario Institucional (PRI) a wasteful and corrupt octopus unable to cope with the spreading social malaise or to manage a modern economy. In hock for the staggering sum of $32 billion, the country was sliding backward in many of the areas considered yardsticks for development, including literacy, nutrition, and health. Though still predominantly a rural country, Mexico was forced to import huge quantities of grain to feed its people.

As in Brazil, the source of the problem could be traced to the model of economic development. Since World War II, Mexico has concentrated its resources on industrialization, at great cost to the working class and the peasants, whose earlier gains in land reform and labor legislation were gradually effaced. The argument for industrialization was that commonly offered by developing countries: the need to substitute domestic production for imports, to increase exports and create more jobs for the growing labor force. To achieve this, Mexico welcomed foreign investment, primarily from the United States, and borrowed heavily in the international market to subsidize cheap oil, electricity, railroads, and the like for private business. But as so many developing nations have learned to their sorrow, industrialization did not reduce Mexico's unemployment, nor did it significantly alter the country's dependence on imported capital equipment. Most of the import substitute industries are concentrated in such consumer areas as packaged foods and drugs. Moreover, a high percentage are foreign-owned, and profits go not to Mexico but to the company's home country.‡ By 1974, 40 percent of the manufacturing sector was controlled by multinationals. Three quarters of the investment, or about $3 billion in twelve hundred firms, came from U.S. interests. Altogether, four thousand companies in Mexico are foreign-controlled.

Because of its heavy dependence on the United States, the Mexican economy nosedives every time the United States suffers a slight recession. Thus Mexico suffered a trade deficit of $3 billion in 1976, largely because of economic conditions in the United States. (Or as the Mexican dictator Porfirio Díaz once put it, "Poor Mexico. So far from God and so near to the United States.")

To prop up sagging industries, the Mexican Government was spending $1.3 billion a year in subsidies—and borrowing more and more abroad to keep its place on the treadmill. Yet Mexican taxes remained among the lowest in the world, because the government feared an outflow of foreign capital and an outcry from native businessmen if they were raised. Consequently Mexico's spending on social services has lagged far behind that of other large Latin-American countries. Mexico City, the country's capital and largest city, was bankrupt, according to Governor Carlos Hank González.[57]

Unlike Brazil or Argentina, however, the Mexican Government did not have to institute a reign of terror to support its development model. The people's apathy and fatalism, the lack of national leaders, and the enduring magic of the Mexican Revolution combined to give the country a veneer of social stability and democracy. But down on the state and municipal levels, there was an enormous amount of violence, particularly in rural areas where landless peasants were many. With some 175,000 land petitions backlogged in the government's Agrarian Reform Ministry, it is

‡ According to the Bank of Mexico, these companies repatriated profits over two and a half times the amount of their investment during 1975 and 1976. (*Noticias*, National Foreign Trade Council, Inc. [New York, June 20, 1977].)

no wonder, as the Mexican Bishops' Conference put it, that "farm workers are tired of listening to promises, speeches, and demagoguery."[58] After the Army twice massacred peasants during land disputes in Sonora and Sinaloa, some 35,000 of them stormed the northwestern states in 1976, seizing several hundred thousand acres of land belonging to agribusinesses, many of them jointly owned by U.S. interests.

The causes of the violence were apparent. In Sinaloa, 85 families controlled one quarter of the irrigated land, while 126,000 peasants had no land at all. Migrant workers on Sinaloa's vegetable and cotton farms, these peasants live in temporary cardboard, tin, and tar-paper camps, or sleep outside in their cotton bags or tomato bins. Outhouses straddle the canals that supply the workers' drinking and bathing water; intestinal disease is common, as is sunstroke. In 1975 nearly eight hundred people, mostly children, died in Sinaloa of diarrhea or dehydration. Hundreds of families, unable to find work on the farms, follow the cotton shipments down the highway, gathering the fiber that blows off the trucks and selling it to middlemen.[59]

This human misery is the backbone of Mexico's $100 million-a-year vegetable business with the United States and the cause of the land invasions. As Mexican President José López Portillo himself admitted, "How would we like it if our children had to live as the peasants do, without a single piece of meat to eat all year? Well, the golden rule of life is to treat others as we would like to be treated and not demand of others what we ourselves are not prepared to give. It wasn't Marx who said that; it was Christ. Either our children will live together in harmony with the children of the common people, of the peasants, or they will confront each other in violence."

In Oaxaca in southern Mexico, where conditions are even worse than anything seen in Sinaloa, violence was so prevalent as to rival Argentina. Populated by 500,000 hungry Indians and another 1 million landless peasants, Oaxaca is a good example of the lopsided division of land in Mexico. All the best land, with adequate irrigation, belongs to the large estates, which cover over 125,000 acres. Most of the rest of the population eke out a subsistence on tiny plots or work as peons on the cattle ranches. In recent years the problem has been aggravated by speculation in timber and oil, with the landowners expanding their holdings at the expense of Indians and peasants. In 1976, for example, eight Indian villages were razed by soldiers in the pay of the ranchers.[60] The villages had existed for nearly a decade and the Indians' land titles were being processed by the government's Agrarian Reform Ministry. Nevertheless, the ranchers denied that the Indians had any right to the land; five Indians were killed in the confrontation. Later in the year, seventy soldiers threatened the community of Lázaro Cárdenas, where the peasants have struggled for over forty years to obtain legal title to the village's 1,135 acres of communal land.* Although a presidential decree deeding the villagers this land dates to 1964, a decade later they had received no titles, despite innumerable, costly trips to Mexico City to unravel the red tape in the Agrarian Reform Ministry.

Increasing repression caused the Indians and peasants to seek common cause with Oaxaca's workers and university and high school students, one result of which was a strike by urban transport workers in solidarity with the peasants. The region's landowners and businessmen responded with an armed attack on the university. By January 1977 repression had become generalized, with the arrest of hundreds of people belonging to the peasant-student-union front. When high school students demonstrated in front of the local jail for the release of thirty-eight of their fellows, the police opened fire, injuring fifty and killing two boys, aged thirteen and eleven. The bodies of three young men who had been arrested were later found on a highway, so mutilated as to be unrecognizable. Fourteen others "disappeared": that is, they also were killed. In February, twenty-nine Mixtec Indians were massacred by the local police. They had been pressuring the Agrarian Reform Ministry to process deeds for community lands that had been held up by red tape for thirteen years, according to Church sources.[61] The head of the Oaxaca Peasant and Workers Union was also murdered.

The federal government's response to the violence was to name a general as governor and send in soldiers trained for anti-guerrilla warfare. Said one Oaxaca peasant woman, "The same thing

* The structure of villages with communal lands, known as *ejidos,* dates to pre-Columbian times. It was to reassert their rights to these lands that Mexico's peasant armies rose up in 1910.

always happens: anyone who complains that we peasants are the victims is immediately accused of being a communist, an enemy of God, and a subversive. He is tracked down, tortured, and murdered, and afterward his corpse, totally mutilated, is dumped on some road."[62]

Arturo Lona Reyes, the bishop of Tehuantepec, issued a strong protest against the killings of students, peasants, and workers. "We cannot remain silent," he said, "in the face of these murderous deeds and we denounce the lack of respect for human life. We repeat the motto of the Pope: 'If you want peace, respect life.'" Echoing his colleagues in Argentina, Lona Reyes asked what forces were responsible for so many deaths. "There is no doubt," he added, "that the poorest people are once again the victims. We will neither accept the excuse of incompetence [by the authorities] nor are we satisfied with vague promises that these gory deeds will be investigated and justice done. The people have a right to be served with loyalty and efficiency and without more sacrifice of innocent victims."[63]

Because of this denunciation, assassins attempted to murder Bishop Lona Reyes in April 1977. He escaped only because he had left his car minutes before it was strafed by gunmen who suddenly appeared on the highway in another vehicle. The priest driving the bishop's automobile was severely wounded.

Lona Reyes was not the only bishop to be attacked. In Guerrero State in southern Mexico, where two hundred thousand Indians were literally starving to death,[64] Bishop Fidel Cortés Pérez was repeatedly threatened with death by telephone and letter. The chancery was robbed, gunshots were fired into the church patio, and the bishop's chauffeur was set upon by three men and a woman who tried to strangle him.[65]

As in other Latin-American countries, violence against the Mexican Church was directly related to the increasing identification of bishops and priests with the poor and oppressed. This commitment became evident in Mexico in the early 1970s when a handful of bishops and priests began to speak out against political and economic structures responsible for "institutionalized violence." They were joined by Mexico's Jesuits and Marist Fathers, seminarians, and lay leaders. Though still a minority, these Mexicans represented the same prophetic voices that a decade earlier had sounded the alert in the Brazilian Church.

Mexico's extreme Right was not slow to recognize the threat. Its first attack came in 1972, when a paramilitary group calling itself the Anti-Guerrilla Squadron kidnapped two Marist priests, one of whom was severely tortured. Father Oscar Núñez was repeatedly submerged in icy water until he nearly drowned, while his kidnappers punched him in the stomach and reviled him. He was then given electric shocks on various parts of his body. During the priests' thirty-six hours in detention, eleven other people were brought in and tortured. Their kidnappers followed military discipline, addressing each other as "Commander" and "Captain," and appeared by their conversation to have plenty of money, the priests said.[66] After their release, Núñez was forced for safety to leave the country. He had previously worked in an education program in a Mexico City slum.

The Marists' superior, Father Carlos de Anda, said he was "shocked to think that such a torture organization could exist in Mexico," adding that "these paramilitary groups are clearly against the Constitution. They subvert lawful order and public peace, creating the kind of climate that spawns guerrilla uprisings and terrorism. The torture of a priest and the illegal detention of a second priest and eleven other people sadden us because these events show that our country is faltering in its progress toward democracy."

Persecution of the Church did not become widespread until 1977, however, when Bishop Lona Reyes barely escaped assassination, two priests were murdered and two kidnapped, and several Church organizations were raided. In every case the persecution could be traced to the victim's work with Mexico's slum and rural poor. Father Rodolfo Aguilar, for example, was murdered in March 1977 in the city of Chihuahua in northern Mexico "only because he dared to cry out for justice on behalf of poor people," said Chihuahua's Archbishop Adalberto Almeida Merino.

Like most Mexican cities, Chihuahua has grown explosively in recent years because of migration from the countryside (three quarters of the people in the state of Chihuahua now live in cities; a high percentage of the remaining peasant population earns their living as migrant laborers in the United States). As wave after wave of peasant migrants arrived, a belt of misery gradually surrounded the city, and by 1977 there were fifty-two shantytowns with an estimated population of 150,000 people. One of the oldest of these was Nombre de Dios, and it was here that Father Aguilar came to work shortly after his ordination in 1974.

Aguilar was typical of the new breed of priests graduating from the Latin-American seminaries. In his letter to Archbishop Almeida Merino asking for ordination, Aguilar said that he wanted "to make my life a prophetic and priestly response to the call of God, my Father, and of man, my brother. I admire and accept the evangelical life that Jesus led. I have an obligation to my brothers who are oppressed, and I want to give my life for their liberation and for my own."

When Aguilar arrived in Nombre de Dios, a community of some twenty thousand inhabitants, there were no running water or electricity, no sewage system, no telephones, mail service, parks, or high schools. Yet next door to this shantytown were the industrial park of Chihuahua, site of the city's most important industries, and a residential sector containing huge mansions and splendid gardens.

Aguilar early impressed the slum dwellers as a "new kind of priest" by celebrating Mass each day in a different neighborhood, whereas his predecessors had refused to hold Mass outside the parish church. Working with Nombre de Dios' catechists and pastoral agents, the young priest gradually began to awaken the collective conscience of the slum. When the Villar family was threatened with eviction from its one-room hovel, a community movement was formed to protect the family's rights (the Villars had acquired the house a decade earlier and had been paying for it ever since). Out of this incident grew a more organized movement called the Committee for Social Rights, and in mid-1975 two hundred members of this group went to see the state governor to ask for mail service, a sewage system, and land for housing. When the governor saw Aguilar among the crowd, he became furious and violently threatened the priest. Shortly thereafter, police agents entered Nombre de Dios, beating up and abusing the people. Nevertheless, the movement grew, and when the authorities demanded Aguilar's removal from Nombre de Dios five thousand slum dwellers demonstrated in his support. By this time, some five hundred people were meeting in Sunday assemblies to organize civic action programs. As a result of the movement's pressure on the local government, Nombre de Dios got mail service, a high school, sufficient land for the construction of four hundred houses, running water, and the start of a drainage system that would eventually benefit one hundred thousand people in Chihuahua's slums. But the struggle was not without violence. Aguilar's parish house was set afire, an act the people attributed to the police when they refused to investigate the crime. And the priest was constantly threatened by the police, the governor, and spokesmen for the city's financial interests.

But it was the Nombre de Dios sewage system that caused Aguilar's death. Already alarmed by the growing militancy of the inhabitants, local authorities were outraged when the Nombre de Dios civic movement announced that the people would build their own sewage system because the government was asking an exorbitant price for the work. The owners of neighboring factories and wealthy residences were equally opposed to the project because it would connect with a nearby river. Though the river was already polluted by industrial waste, it was one thing for the factories to dump refuse in the river and quite another for a slum to use it for drainage. But since the government had no alternative to suggest, slum sewage being low on the city's list of priorities, the people of Nombre de Dios went ahead with the project. During this fight over the sewage system two men appeared at the parish house one morning and asked Aguilar to accompany them to give last rites to a dying person. They took the priest to the house of Aguilar's co-worker, Sergio Durán, and there killed him. Durán, who was away on his honeymoon, found the priest's body on his return. He and his wife were immediately arrested, as was another co-worker. But because their innocence was patent, the police jailed yet another member of the movement and extracted from him a confession under torture, which he later denied. Although the man continued to protest his innocence, the state authorities announced that the case was closed.[67]

Contrary to expectations, the Nombre de Dios civic movement did not collapse with the priest's death. Other priests and nuns appeared to take his place. Work on the sewage system went forward; a cooperative, a health center, and a parent-teachers association were founded; and the government was coerced into providing parks and running water in the shantytowns. "The organizations most directly hurt by Father Aguilar's murder have not disbanded or given up their legitimate fight for liberation," announced a communiqué from the Church's social and pastoral departments in the northern states of Mexico. "On the contrary, his death has encouraged the people to close ranks. It is clear [Aguilar] would not have been killed if he had not worked with and for these people and had his work not conflicted with powerful political and economic interests.

"We invite those who are glad of his death to open the pages of the New Testament and to ask themselves if they truly believe in Christ, for two thousand years ago another Man was similarly criticized by those with economic and political power. His intentions were also misunderstood: he, too, was accused of popular agitation and of blasphemy for predicating a God who wanted equality and fraternity among men, and, because of this, he was condemned as a political leader opposed to the Roman Empire."

Within weeks of Aguilar's murder, another priest was shot to death in Mexico City in almost the same circumstances. Father Rodolfo Escamilla had worked for eight years with the slum poor in one of the hundreds of "lost cities" on the outskirts of Mexico's capital, helping the people to obtain land titles and organize cooperatives. As in the Aguilar case, the police tried unsuccessfully to pin his murder on his co-workers.

The people of La Troja, the shantytown of eight thousand inhabitants where Escamilla had worked, were stunned by the death of their beloved "professor," as they called him. "He was a good person," said a shopkeeper. "He never did anything bad here. He came only to help us organize the cooperative and to defend us against the people who wanted to take our land away from us. He taught us what it means for people to work together."

In a moving tribute to Escamilla, Bishop Sergio Méndez Arceo and seventy priests led five thousand Catholics in a procession to Mexico's famous Guadalupe Basilica in May 1977. Though the event was covered by a great many police, the participants were not intimidated. In a joint statement read by the bishop, the seventy priests declared that they were not asking for any special immunity for the clergy but were protesting the suffering of the Mexican people and the murder of a man who had dedicated his life to alleviating that misery.

Despite—or because of—these protests, police repression continued, and in July nearly one hundred police sacked the Mexico City offices of the Center for Social Communications (CENCOS), one of the country's principal ecumenical organizations. Eleven people were arrested. According to Police Commander Arturo Cisneros, the CENCOS offices contained "a great deal of subversive material."[68] Among the "subversive material" were files on Latin-American political refugees, collected in collaboration with the United Nations' high commissioner for refugees. Also sacked during the raid were the offices of the World Council of Churches and the Latin-American Evangelical Commission for Christian Education. While the CENCOS files were eventually returned by the police, "all this leaves a bad taste in the mouth because these acts are part of a pattern," said a CENCOS spokesman. As if to confirm his charge, the Mexico City police next raided the Jesuits' house in the parish of Los Angeles, carrying off files and equipment. Several Jesuits were arrested.

Here, again, there was a clear connection between police harassment and the Jesuits' work with the poor. In line with the religious order's new, worldwide commitment to peasants and workers, the Mexican Jesuits had closed their upper-class schools, including Mexico City's prestigious Instituto Patria, to devote themselves to educational programs in the slums. The need for such schools is desperate: approximately a fifth of the country's 63 million people are functional illiterates; 50 percent of the adults in city slums cannot read or write. In the capital alone, fifty thousand young people are without schools, and the statistics will get worse, according to all projections, with four hundred thousand new illiterates in Mexico City by 1990. Thus, if the Jesuits had limited themselves to teaching the poor how to write their names and add two and two, there would have been no objection. But because their programs encourage social awareness and the need for a more equitable society, they have come under increasing attack.

What particularly annoyed upper-class Mexicans was the Jesuits' "betrayal" of class interests, for it was the Jesuits, more than any other religious order in Latin America, who traditionally educated the sons and daughters of the rich. And it was by such education that the continent's social and economic structures had been built. So why were the Jesuits suddenly denying their own heritage? Because, said the order's superior general, Pedro Arrupe, the Jesuits "have a moral obligation to make up for their sin of omission in failing to seek social justice through the education of the poor." The idea that the Jesuits could influence social change by educating a wealthy minority was wishful thinking, added the Mexican Jesuits. "These people have never been the agents of social progress and never will be. The only force for change is the people who are most affected by poverty and political disenfranchisement: the poor, the workers, the peasants, this mass of humanity forcibly marginalized by society. We want to make it very clear," the Jesuits concluded, "that we are not going to be intimidated by criticism or by police repression."

The Jesuits' challenge was a courageous gesture, given the increasing persecution of socially conscious Christians. As the churches of northern Mexico had noted in their tribute to Father Aguilar, "His death occurred at a time when there is an upsurge of violence everywhere in Latin America against those sectors of the Church dedicated to making this world a more just and Christian society. Chile, Brazil, Uruguay, Argentina, Ecuador, Nicaragua, Guatemala, and El Salvador have been the scenes of violence and death for many Christians in a campaign to silence the Church. And now the same is happening in Mexico. But Jesus foretold this:

"I will send them prophets and messengers; and some of these they will persecute and kill; so that this generation will have to answer for the blood of all the prophets shed since the foundation of the world. I tell you, this generation will have to answer for it all."

Luke 11:49–51

CHAPTER X

THE CHURCH'S ROLE

Today everyone recognizes that in certain circumstances religion can be an opium but that under others it can foment development: Everything depends on how the message is delivered.

Brazilian theologian
Eduardo Hoornaert

A man sits in a mansion in the northern suburbs of Bogotá, watching the evening news. By most standards, he is to be envied: he has a lovely wife and two children, a six-bedroom house, two expensive cars, and six servants, including a butler. But the television news disturbs him: three more kidnappings today; one victim, the head of an insurance company, was an acquaintance.

There is a price to be paid for this life, he thinks, looking at the steel bars on the windows. The doors have triple locks, and an alarm system protects the windows and doors. The garage doors open automatically as the car enters the gates—the time lost if the chauffeur had to jump out and open them could cost the man his life. An armed guard watches the gate; a civil defense patrol prowls the neighborhood. The chauffeur carries a gun, as does the man. When the children walk down the street to visit friends, another armed guard must accompany them. The man has received three threats by telephone and letter: if he does not pay up, he or his family may be kidnapped and murdered.

It is useless to appeal to the police; they cannot protect him. Indeed, every day the newspapers carry new reports of police involvement in the kidnappings—fifty a month in Bogotá alone* His wife cannot wear a watch, rings, or earrings in the street for fear of being robbed—if the mugger cannot pull off the jewelry, he will slash her fingers and ears.

What sort of life is this, the man wonders, a prisoner in an armed fortress—afraid to go anywhere lest he be robbed, kidnapped, or murdered? If he moved to Miami, as have many of his friends, he would not have six bedrooms or six servants, but he would have something he cannot buy in Colombia: security. He seriously considers the move.

The man lives in the most dangerous city in the Western Hemisphere, some say in the world, where thousands of street urchins begin their apprenticeship in crime at the age of four or five.† If it is dangerous now, when there are 5 million people in Bogotá, most of them poor, what will it be like in twenty years, when the population has doubled? The man has seen the future, not just of Bogotá but of all Latin America, and he wants no part of it.

Yet, consciously or not, this man has helped to create the future. Because he and others like him have consistently opposed any redistribution of the national wealth,‡ because they ignored the laws they themselves had made, a lawless society has arisen perforce to impose its own redistribution of wealth through kidnappings, bank robberies, murder, smuggling, and the narcotics trade.*

* Colombian police officials estimated that as many as ten thousand kidnappings took place in 1975, ransoms ranging from over $1 million, to less than $100, depending on the victim's ability to pay. The overall increase in crime in Colombia between 1974 and 1975 was 46 percent.

† Bogotá police statistics show that of 17,000 street crimes committed in the first half of 1975, 14,000 were the work of Colombians younger than fourteen.

‡ Eighty-four percent of the Colombian labor force earns sixty dollars or less a month.

* As elsewhere in Latin America, Colombian laws are so designed and applied that only the rich and powerful benefit. One result of this "legal morass," as Colombian lawyers describe it, is widespread government corruption, particularly in the judiciary. Corruption is further fueled by Colombia's United States–bound cocaine and marijuana traffic, which earned local smugglers some $3 billion in 1978, or more than the value of all other Colombian exports, coffee included.

Colombia is not the only Latin-American country where crime is epidemic. The number of homicides in Mexico is nearly twice that of Colombia, and Colombia itself records six times as many murders as England, with half of England's population. Yet Colombia and Mexico are among the few surviving formal democracies in Latin America. The military regimes have legalized crime in the name of national security; in Brazil, for example, by small-time racketeers in the Rio slums and big-time drug operators like Sergio Fleury, Police Commissioner of São Paulo. Thus "institutionalized violence" affects and infects rich and poor alike. Contrary to the old fear that the Latin-American slums would explode in political revolution, they are spawning a different kind of violence—one that seeks material gain or vengeance, but not justice.

As everywhere in Latin America, the violence in Colombia can be traced to the land. Because of the physical and economic insecurity in rural areas, millions of peasants and small farmers migrated to the cities during the 1950s. Today, with 93 percent of the arable land occupied by 25 percent of the farms, the rural exodus continues. By the end of the century the majority of Colombians will live in cities. The same trend can be observed on the entire continent: by the year 2000 two thirds of the projected Latin-American population of 630 million people will be crowded into megalopolises, nearly half their areas given over to slums. Or 210 million people living in tin and cardboard shacks with no running water, no electricity, no schools, no jobs—with nothing to hope for and nothing to lose. The statistics are overwhelming and terrifying: Mexico City, already circled by shantytowns, will be the largest city in the world, with 32 million people; São Paulo, where everyone, rich and poor, now spends on average three hours a day getting to and from work, will explode to 26 million people.

Urbanization is a world phenomenon, but what makes it so dramatic in Latin America is that, whereas in Europe industrialization preceded the vast growth of cities, here big-city life is what lures the peasant. The urban industries, which have copied the developed nations' labor-saving technology, cannot supply jobs for these new millions. But once in the city, the peasant cannot go home again. Agribusiness has mechanized the countryside and agrarian reform has nowhere changed the pattern of land tenancy, not even in Mexico for all its myths of the "glorious revolution." Mortgaged to the international banks and corporate industry, faced with an ever-mounting oil import bill, these city-nations have set up their own nemeses of social alienation and economic privation: just beyond the glass skyscrapers distrustful, frustrated people subsist in miles and miles of slums. However mean their rural past, these people had at least a set of values that held agrarian society together; in the cities most of those values are denied or forgotten, and nothing replaces them.

Fifty Million Slobs

One institution, at least, has begun to appreciate the scope of the problem—the Latin-American Church. While there are different interpretations of the problem, and as many solutions are proposed, the most dynamic sector of the Church is coming to believe that the only answer is to make over society from the bottom up. The idea is not as farfetched or as paternalistic as it may sound. In these churchmen's opinion, Latin America is governed by an elite of wealth, totally alienated from its own people and its own culture. Hence the attempt to ape the industrial programs of Europe and the United States; hence the unquestioning adoption of the Pentagon's national security theories, and an almost slavish imitation of American culture, to the denigration of indigenous customs and beliefs. Whether the country be El Salvador or Brazil, the rich inevitably view the common people with contempt. As one Brazilian government official put it: "There are one hundred million of us Brazilians. Fifty million are no more than poor, ignorant slobs whom the other fifty million must civilize. And even of those others, forty million are incapable of civilizing anyone. That leaves an elite of ten million whose job—and right—is to rule the other ninety million."[1]

An inheritance of the Spanish and Portuguese colonizers, this superiority/inferiority complex admirably suits the multinationals' desire to homogenize the world's wants and tastes (Coca-Cola must be better than the native fruit juice because it is American), though it is precisely this ambiguous attitude that has brought Latin America's city-nations to their desperate plight. Foreign aid and local development programs have failed repeatedly because they imposed foreign, elitist solutions on the people, with no thought to their real needs or wants. During the 1960s, when literacy programs were in vogue, university students went into the slums and villages to teach adults how to read and write. The early enthusiasm waned, however, when it was found that the adults were "inattentive," "lazy," and "uninterested." Yet there were good reasons for the apathy. These conventional literacy programs gave no heed to the world in which the illiterates lived, to their environment and subculture. Adults were treated as children, and the primers, in both words and pictures, were totally alien to them. How could they become interested in stories about foreign white children, wearing nice clothes, living in charming homes, and eating three good meals a day? Most of the ragged, hungry adults in these programs quickly lapsed back into functional illiteracy.

The same happened with community action programs, when higher authority decided who should be the leader of a village or a slum project, what the project should be, and how it should be paid for (usually by voting for the party in power). A similar parallel between inferiors and superiors marked the relations of the local elites with foreign powers, particularly the United States. Unable, unwilling, to listen to the people, those in government assumed that foreign solutions for underdevelopment must as surely be superior to local ones as Coca-Cola was better than native fruit juice. The result was the same as with the literacy programs, but on a far larger scale. The idea that development could be achieved by following the processes of the developed societies was historical folly, for the conditions that gave rise to industrialism in Europe and the United States in the nineteenth century had ceased to exist by the middle of the twentieth century. Trade patterns, science, economics, and the balance of power had changed so radically that no developing nation could hope to repeat the same process successfully.

Yet very few wealthy Latin Americans perceived that they were mere satraps in the industrialized world's empire. Like the man who beats his wife after his boss has bawled him out at the office, these "decision makers" could always compensate for their dependence on foreign ideas, companies, and gadgets by demonstrating their superiority to the "slobs." To see such men fawning on the foreign executive who has dropped by to check on how they are running the corporation's subsidiary is to wonder if anything has changed since colonial times: the Spanish viceroy has simply been replaced by the vice-president in charge of Latin-American operations.

The Catholic Church, a mainstay of this master and slave system ever since the New World was discovered, now believes that it is not only morally wrong but also the principal cause of Latin America's underdevelopment. As in the case of the primers for illiterates, Latin-American history and mores as taught in the educational system do not reflect reality but reinforce the social complexes and political myths of the wealthy minority.† National heroes are usually white descendants of the Spanish and Portuguese settlers; important historical events are almost always described in terms of the white minorities. Latin Americans religiously honor such independence leaders as Simón Bolívar, but never say anything of the peasant soldiers who made it possible for these men to win their wars of independence. Little attention is paid to the culture and history of the native peoples. True, they comprise the majority of the population, but they are looked down on as the colonized, the uneducated, the fifty million Brazilians who need to be civilized. "History has been written by a 'white hand,' " says Gustavo Gutiérrez, one of Latin America's foremost theologians. "I believe that our job today is to rewrite history in terms of the poor, the humiliated, and the rejected of society, to rewrite the struggles and the fights that have taken place in the last century. We all know the efforts that have been made to have those who have been beaten, the losers, forget their past." The new approach to history is not to be seen as an intellectual exercise, says Gutiérrez, but as a spiritual and cultural identification with the peasants and slum dwellers who have their own vision of the world.

From the perspective of the poor, Latin-American history is a

† President Carter encountered a similar problem when trying to get the new Panama Canal treaties through Congress: many Americans opposed the treaties as an "unconstitutional giveaway" of U.S. property. Contrary to popular belief, and unlike the Louisiana and Alaska purchases, the United States paid Panama $10 million in 1903 for treaty rights, not for property. But few U.S. schoolbooks made this important distinction.

story of religious, political, and economic repression. Although they are unable to express the causes of their situation in scientific language, their popular legends and beliefs repeatedly reveal this sense of oppression. When history is looked back upon from where the losers stand today, it turns out that neither European colonialism nor U.S. capitalism has been a good thing for Latin America, not, at least, for the majority of the people (native fruit juice is cheaper and more nutritious than Coca-Cola, propaganda notwithstanding).

For Latin-American Christians who view the world through the eyes of the poor, who see the slums beyond the glass skyscrapers, the next logical step is to reexamine their faith in the light of reality, and this leads them to reread the Bible. Gradually the biblical story is perceived to be more than a history lesson; it also describes the contemporary scene. As U.S. religious writer Robert McAfee Brown points out, these Latin Americans "see the Bible as a very revolutionary book, which is from first to last the account of Jahweh's liberation of his people. The exodus story is the paradigm event: Jahweh frees his people from oppression. The oppression is not just the oppression of sin, but also the oppression of unjust social structures, enforced by a political tyrant and a repressive economic order. So the story is about political and economic liberation as well. The Old Testament prophets pound home the same theme, inveighing against corrupt judges, against the rich exploiting the poor, against religious leaders siding with the rich, against the few living in outrageous comfort while the many starve. Jesus stands in this same prophetic tradition: He, too, denounces exploitation, and proclaims a gospel of 'freedom to captives' and 'liberation to the oppressed.' His story of the Last Judgment indicates that nations (and not just individuals) are held accountable to God for whether or not they have fed the hungry, clothed the naked, taken sides with the oppressed.

"The biblical account of the liberation of oppressed Israel is likewise a description of the possibility of the liberation of oppressed peoples today. If the God of the Bible took sides back then, it is clear that He continues to take sides today, identifying with the oppressed and challenging their oppressors. And this means that all who claim to believe in Him and are trying to carry on His work *must take sides, too.* Those who reject that conclusion usually argue that the Church should not take sides. They ignore the fact, however, that the Church has always taken sides in the past, but that it has almost invariably been on the side of the rich oppressors. The plea now is not that the Church should take sides for the first time but simply that it should *change* sides. Having sided with the wealthy, it must now side with the poor; having been the support of those with power, it must now cast its lot with those deprived of power; having enjoyed privilege in the past, it must undergo risk in the future."[2]

From reflections like these evolved the theology of liberation, the Third World's controversial, politically explosive contribution to theology that marks religion's coming of age in Latin America. It is an outburst similar to the flowering of fiction and art on the continent.‡ For Gustavo Gutiérrez, leading proponent of the new orientation, theology is not only a body of spiritual and rational knowledge but also a critical reflection on the Church's pastoral work. The challenge now facing the Church in the midst of growing violence, poverty, and repression, says Gutiérrez, is "how to say to the poor, to the exploited classes, to the marginalized races, to the despised cultures, to all the minorities and nonpersons, that God is love and that all of us are, and ought to be in history, sisters and brothers. This is our great question. If theology has any meaning, it is an attempt to respond to this question and to discover ways in this social struggle to form a new society of sisters and brothers."

Gutiérrez believes "liberation" is a more appropriate word than "development" in the context of poverty and repression, because it suggests that "man can begin to change himself as a creative being, directing his own destiny toward a society in which he will be free of every kind of slavery. When history is seen as the process of man's emancipation, the question of development is placed in a larger context, a deeper, more radical one. Man is not seen as a passive element but as an agent of history."

This is a political theology, as Gutiérrez readily admits, but by political he does not mean party politics, or even an ideology, but a focus on the social dimensions of the biblical message. "The Bible tells us not only of a *vocation* to communion with God but

‡ See Chapter II for a historical description of the theology of liberation.

also of a *convocation,* and this must have an effect on the political behavior of Christians." The Church thus becomes an "institution of social criticism" and a stimulus for liberation. The key difference of this approach to previous attempts at reform in Latin America is that the Church does not lead or organize the struggle for liberation; it is done by the people themselves, through their own institutions in their villages and slums. The Church is the prod from within, not a superstructure imposing its ideas from without, and it is the prod at the bottom, where the mass of the people are. "Christ was a religious, not a political leader," explained Segundo Galilea, a popular Chilean religious writer. "But through his religious message, he generated a dynamism for political and social change."

"The sad fact is that for recent centuries the Christian Churches seem often to have forgotten or conveniently overlooked the revolutionary nature of the Way they were both to preach and practice," says Philip Scharper, director of the Orbis religious publishing house. "As a result, many of the things that were God's were placed on Caesar's desk almost with a sigh of relief. Christians were encouraged to wash their hands in innocence over the injustice of 'the world,' and 'Thou shalt not rock the Ark' became the Eleventh Commandment. Against this background, a theology based not on the 'social teachings of the Church' but on 'the social teachings of Christ' becomes less than banal and will seem, to some at least, a suspicious novelty." But, cautions Scharper, this is not just another theological fad, such as urban theology, the theology of secularization, or "the death of God."

"Liberation theology is new in our time because its object is the transformation of society rather than purifying and forming the faith for the Church," explained C. Ellis Nelson of the Union Theological Seminary. "This stance makes a radical difference in how the Church is understood. The Church is not a colony of heaven; it is not a neutral institution in society. The Church is part of society, and if it does not speak against social injustice, it silently supports the oppressors. The task of liberation theology is to analyze and criticize the role of the Church in order to help the Church use its institutional power to change society.

"Because liberation theology has society as the object, everything in theology is turned upside down. One does not start with

God, one starts with man. One does not seek truth and apply it to man's condition. One does not take the past and find a lesson for the present, one takes the future. One does not ask: 'What must I do to get to heaven?' but 'How can I find fulfillment of my life here on earth?' Humanity, according to liberation theology, is the temple of God."[3]

But it is most concerned with a particular type of temple—"the wretched of the earth." In Scharper's words, "the Scriptures have been used too long to comfort the afflicted; the Scriptures are also meant to afflict the comfortable."[4]

This is all very well, skeptics might say, but how do you go about it? For such a gigantic endeavor, there must obviously be faith. Or as Brazil's Dom Helder Cámara says, "It is high time that Don Quixote rode forth again." No one in this endeavor pretends that conditions in Latin America can be changed quickly— even the most optimistic speak of two generations. Nor is there any illusion of a mass conversion. On the contrary, the emphasis is on small, committed groups in order to avoid the supermarket atmosphere of Latin America's huge parishes, where the priest is reduced to "a vending machine of the sacraments." Dom Helder calls these groups "Abrahamic minorities," people who, like the Hebrews' great patriarch, are not afraid to risk security and comfort in order to seek the "promised land." "We must have no illusions," cautions Dom Helder. "We shall not walk on roses, people will not throng to hear us and applaud, and we shall not always be aware of divine protection. If we are to be pilgrims for justice and peace, we must expect the desert."[5]

The fundamental task of these Abrahamic minorities, in Cámara's opinion is education, but education of a particular kind. In line with the theology of liberation, it must be a two-way process whereby the poor instruct the teacher, who is known as a coordinator, while learning more about themselves and their reality, thus acquiring a desire to change that reality. This is the consciousness-raising technique of Brazilian educator Paulo Freire. In this *Pedagogy of the Oppressed,* the title of his most famous work, dialogue entered into with humility is essential. "How can I converse if I always see ignorance in others and never perceive my own?" Freire asks. "Dialogue implies trust in, and love for, men."

Using this approach, Freire has demonstrated in numerous experiments in Brazil and Chile that adults can be taught to read and write in six weeks. Equally important, the adult does not lapse into functional illiteracy once the program is over, but moves to a new stage of awareness through some need felt in common with the group. This usually produces a simple form of people's council, a parent-teacher association, say, or a cooperative to buy cheap medicine. The pace varies, depending on the illiterates' political awareness and the degree of repression: it is faster in Chile, slower in northeastern Brazil.

At first, reports Freire, the poor tend to associate their values with those of the rich. "If they long for agrarian reform, for instance, it is not in order to become free men, but to get their hands on land, to be owners themselves; or more exactly, to be the bosses of other workers. It is the rare peasant who, promoted to foreman, is not harsher on his former associates than the boss himself. This is so because the peasant's situation of oppression remains unchanged; the new foreman feels he must be as harsh as the owner, maybe more so, to protect his job. That is why we say that, during the initial phase of the struggle, the oppressed find in the oppressor their ideal man."

These poor also scorn themselves. "They hear it said so often that they are lazy, weak, and unproductive that they end up believing in their own inability," Freire says. "The peasant feels inferior to his boss, because the boss seems to be the only one who knows, the only one able to make things work. As long as this illusion continues, the people are completely without self-confidence, totally unable to protest. In some vague way, they believe in the boss's invulnerability and omnipotence. . . . A sociologist friend of mine tells the story of a group of armed peasants who took over a *latifundio*. For some reason, they decided to hold the owner as hostage. But no one had the courage to stay and guard him. His very presence cowed them, and maybe they had some sort of guilt feelings. In any event, there was certainly a bit of the boss in each of them."[6]

Self-awareness and self-esteem rise together when people learn to read and write by the Freire method. Most of the classes are small (no larger than twenty-five) and freewheeling, with the coordinator helping the discussion along but not dominating. The texts that are used stress "generative" words that are phonetically rich and have a social, political, or economic meaning in the illiterates' world. Such a word is *favela,* the Brazilian word for slum. The phonetic families are developed from the syllabic divisions— fa-fe-fi-fo-fu, va-ve-vi-vo-vu, and la-le-li-lo-lu. Finally, the students are encouraged to form other words built on each of these phonetic families. In northeastern Brazil, where Freire developed the technique, every "literacy circle" opened with a discussion of culture as opposed to nature, in order to help the people discover, before being exposed to any utilitarian learning, that they are already creators of culture, and not absolutely at the mercy of nature. In the second stage of this program students concentrate on themes instead of words, such as the meaning of democracy and of nationalism. This is not any "ba-be-bi-bo-bu" exercise, as Dom Helder points out, but a means of encouraging the poor to find "their own name for the world."

Freire's methods are not new; in the late 1950s he was experimenting with the idea in Brazil, and after the military took over there, he continued his work in Chile. But the combination of right-wing military coups and the lack of any hemisphere-wide structure to support these educational efforts limited their effectiveness. While a few local churches had used Freire's methods, notably in Brazil, it was not until Medellín that the Church adapted and expanded consciousness-raising techniques to include religious as well as secular education.

The Church had a ready-made text in the Bible, which is the one book universally read or quoted in Latin America. The story of Palm Sunday, for example, can be developed into a discussion among villagers about what happened when an important government official visited their community. What were his motives for coming? Did he change anything? How did the people react? Well, he made a lot of promises and everybody got drunk at a big fiesta, but the ground he inaugurated for a new health center is still an empty field, and a year and a half have gone by. Demagoguery, that's what it was. What's demagoguery? It's when somebody important comes from the capital in a big car and makes a lot of promises so you'll vote for his party.

By the end of a four-hour discussion along such lines, even the most obtuse peasant begins to have an inkling of why the important official came to his village. When this sort of discussion is repeated weekly for several years, using the limitless themes of the Bible, the impression made on the people is both profound and revolutionary. It matters not that they are illiterate or that they use their own simple language to describe politics, economics, or social relationships. The important thing is that they understand their reality and, in so doing, attempt to change it. "We must discourage the idea that economic and political problems can be solved only by those in power," explained Chilean theologian Ronaldo Muñoz.

Because of the emergence of three other factors affecting pastoral work, consciousness-raising programs have spread like wildfire across the continent. The first factor was the rise of right-wing regimes with an ideology of power—the Doctrine of National Security—and a determination to remain in power for several decades. The unprecedented repression unleashed by these governments forced many churchmen to take their stand with the oppressed and the poor. The second and third factors were the rediscovery of folk Catholicism, or "popular religiosity," and the small Christian communities that were the foundations of the primitive Church. At the same time, the theology of liberation was emerging to provide an intellectual framework for the Church's commitment to the poor and its role as social critic.

Popular Religiosity

Freire's emphasis on the need for dialogue in education of the poor was echoed in the Latin-American Church, which had become acutely aware of the lack of sufficient religious vocations to serve the exploding population and of the increasing gulf between the people and the institutional Church. Though 90 percent of Latin Americans are baptized Catholics, no more than 20 percent regularly attend Mass or identify with official Church teachings. Gradually, therefore, churchmen began to listen to what the people were saying about Catholicism. It was a sobering experience, for the people's ideas of God, Christ, the Virgin Mary, and the saints were quite unlike those of the Church. Their religion was fatalistic, syncretic, and paternalistic: God was like the large landowner, to be appeased and bribed; his Son, Christ, who appears everywhere in Latin America as a crucified man, epitomized the suffering and death of the poor. Few understood the Resurrection and its message of hope. For them, Christ had been beaten down, tortured, and killed by a higher authority, just as they had been and their fathers before them.

All this had been obvious to anthropologists for years, but it came as a shock to bishops and priests, who suddenly realized that the people did not understand what they were saying. On the other hand, it was also obvious that, however superficial the evangelization had been, Catholicism, or rather popular Catholicism, had sunk deep roots in the Latin-American cultures. Unlike the industrialized world, where religion has succumbed to materialism and a flexible social structure, Latin America is still profoundly influenced by the Church. Farming traditions, health, education, social mores, politics are all imbued with religious folklore. This popular religiosity is a genuine form of cultural expression and creativity—indeed, the only one for most Latin Americans. Whatever the rigor of his political, social, or economic deprivations, the Latin American can always turn to the spirits or saints for comfort and help. These are very real, personal friends to whom he speaks in his own language. Thus, while Catholicism had played a fundamental role in creating the fatalism inherent in Latin-American poverty, it also had the means, through its enormous influence over the people, to liberate them from that fatalism.

One of the principal reasons that the clergy did not share the religious vision of the people, many priests now contend, is that they did not share the life experience out of which it grew. Father Felipe Berryman, a U.S. priest living in a Panama City slum, cited the question of birth control. "The furor in the Church has been basically a middle-class phenomenon, for it is the middle class that feels compelled to practice it, and it is a religious problem only for bourgeois Catholics who feel the need for confession. A poor woman in a favela or barrio quite likely does not yet feel impelled to use contraceptives. Should she decide to do so, she most probably does not go to confession and is not married by the Church. For her, the Pope's position is probably unintelligible and in any case would cause her no real anguish. On the other hand, the suppression of many saints from the liturgical calendar and the elimination of saints of doubtful authenticity caused a commotion in popular Catholicism. One man told me it was as though the Pope had lined up people's favorite saints in front of a firing squad."[7]

The importance of the saints in the lives of the Latin-American poor is in direct proportion to the diminished importance of Christ. The Christ they know is a poor guy without influence, like themselves, not the teacher or the leader who defeated death and who inspired his people with a new vision of heaven and earth. In Brazil, for example, there are any number of legends about how Christ had to call for help from more powerful spirits, and in some areas "to put up with Christ" means "to deal with an idiot." For all practical purposes, heaven is ruled by St. Peter, and hell by the devil. Mary is universally recognized as a type of earth mother.

Once the Church began to pay attention to the anthropologists, however, it soon began to purify and redirect popular religiosity. Midway through a Sunday afternoon Mass in Vitória, Brazil, for example, nine peasants gathered before the altar to present a playlet about the problems of the land-starved people in northeastern Brazil. "My family is hungry and we have no land," said the first peasant to the second, who wore the large white sombrero of Brazil's wealthy ranchers.

"I don't want to hear your troubles," replied the rancher/peasant. "Get off my land."

Another peasant with a priest's collar then approached the rancher to tell him how Christian he was for donating money to build a cathedral (much laughter).

"What shall we do?" asked the first peasant of the rest of the troupe. "The rancher tells us we must leave this land."

"Let's go to the cities to find work," suggested one.

"No," said another. "We will only end up in the slums. We must stay and fight for our rights."

"That's right," said a third peasant, who began to chant a Brazilian version of "We Shall Overcome."

"Yes, we shall overcome, we shall overcome with Jesus Christ," sang all the peasants as they were joined by the ten bishops behind the altar and the three thousand people in the Church.

While such goings-on undoubtedly shock more conservative churches, the people of Vitória obviously enjoyed the play and approved its message of solidarity. And the formula certainly works from the Church's point of view, to judge by the religious response (all three thousand people received communion), or by the aggressive spirit of the new Christian peasant communities in Brazil.

Farther south, in the working-class outskirts of Buenos Aires, 25,000 people a week visit the shrine of San Cayetano, carrying noodles, cans of meat, and powdered milk, flour, soup, and clothing to the Italian immigrants' saint. These offerings, which total 15,000 tons of food and 250 bags of clothing a month, are later distributed to Argentina's slum and rural poor. Until 1970, when a team of priests led by Father Angel Sallaberremborde took over the shrine's administration, the statue of San Cayetano was so smothered in peso notes, flowers, and candles that no one ever saw it. Through an education program that includes a monthly magazine, *Bread and Work,* Father Angel's team convinced the people that "they should thank San Cayetano by helping their brothers." Previously, he said, "it was a closed relationship between the saint and the worshiper."

Since democracy is basic to the Church's new programs in popular religiosity, any innovation at the shrine is discussed in advance with the congregation. The idea for the change in offerings, for example, came from the worshipers themselves. "I heard one man tell a woman that she should bring food instead of candles, because 'San Cayetano helps you and you should help other Argentines to have bread,'" recalled Father Angel. But when the shrine's priests replaced the altar's crucifix with a more modern one, the people complained. "They feel the shrine belongs to them, that it is like the house of their father, and we respect their feelings," the Argentine priest said. The old crucifix has been put back.

Though irregular churchgoers, Latin-American Catholics never fail to visit their local shrines. Consequently, with the resurgence of devotion, sanctuaries that were thought obsolete only a decade ago have suddenly taken on new importance in the Church's eyes. Moreover, these shrines can become national symbols for a people with no means of political expression. More than one hundred thousand Argentines participated in the 1976 procession to the sanctuary at Luján, there to pray for peace in strife-torn Argentina. It was the largest religious gathering in the country's history.

A shrine can also provide the people with an outlet for their worries and sufferings. At San Cayetano a confessor is on duty twenty-four hours a day, not so much to listen to sins as to provide some comfort in an atmosphere of repression and fear. A typical case was the mother of a two-year-old child who was dissuaded from the suicide she contemplated because her husband had "disappeared," almost certainly the victim of a right-wing paramilitary kidnapping.

In neighboring Paraguay, where General Alfredo Stroessner was busy selling off large chunks of the country to the Brazilians, the shrine to the Virgin Mary at Caacupé became a symbol of national identity. Long at odds with the Stroessner dictatorship, the Paraguayan Bishops' Conference believes the Church's first priority is to give the average citizen a sense of personal worth and pride in the nation. Because of Church propaganda, Caacupé is now seen as the essence of all that is Paraguayan. It was from there that the Church also launched a massive evangelization program to encourage solidarity and faith. Representatives of peasant groups and urban workers were invited to the shrine for a candle-lighting ceremony in honor of the Virgin that emphasized all the positive aspects of popular religiosity; each returned to his village or slum with a candle and a statue of the Virgin to repeat the ceremony. The program was enormously successful because the bishops chose the Virgin of Caacupé to convey their message.

Like most Latin Americans, the Paraguayans feel a special closeness to the Virgin Mary, but they have also a particular historical reason for this attachment. After a series of ruinous wars with its neighbors in the nineteenth and twentieth centuries, Paraguay had lost the bulk of its male population, leaving the women to care for families and farms. Motherhood, as symbolized by the Virgin of Caacupé, is therefore deeply revered.

By recognizing the need for religious symbols, Paraguay's Church took an enormous step forward in communicating with the largely Indian population. "We are not the people," said Paraguayan theologian José Blanch. "We think of them as 'them,' and this is a true reflection of the difference in our social status. It is necessary to live and be with the people, to be poor as they are, in order to interpret what they think." That is precisely what worried the Stroessner government—all those religious living with the people; and bishops as well! Were it not for the critical Church and its civic education programs, Paraguay would be a nice, quiet dictatorship with no social unrest.

One of the first hierarchies to see the connection between political awareness, poverty, and popular religiosity, the Paraguayan Church also took the lead in applying the basic principle of Freire's popular pedagogy—listening to and learning from the people, instead of trying to impose alien ideas upon them. The flood of literature that has since poured forth on the subject strikes a persistent note of humility and regret; for by studying popular religiosity the clergy has discovered how blind it was to the depth of the people's simple faith. "If only 20 percent of Latin America's baptized Catholics regularly attend Mass, this does not mean that the remaining are not Christians," said a Colombian priest. "It means that we priests have not bothered, or known how, to bring these people into the community of the Church."

A Paraguayan *pai,* or priest of the Guaraní Indians, put it another way: "The white men who call us pagans are themselves un-Christian. For them, I am not a Christian because I have my ritual dances and long orations and live in a community without social classes or private property, believing that we are all sons of God, baptized or not, gringos, Brazilians, or Paraguayans. But the white men are without prayer, egotistical, violent, and deceitful, using force and disdain to make us afraid and to diminish us. In the name of their religion they treat us like animals. Yet we are the true inhabitants of this land, the favorite sons of the Great Grandfather, and we know there is a place for all of us in the heavens that he created."

Joaquín Alliende, a Chilean priest and one of the hemisphere's most eloquent spokesmen for popular religiosity, feels that the Latin-American Church's slavish imitation of the Europeans, and particularly intellectual snobbery, has done much to alienate such people as that Paraguayan *pai.* "If we don't watch out, we may find we are strangers in our own land," says Alliende. "If we are discovering what is Christian in the Marxists, why can't we discover the same in our brother who has a statue of the Virgin in his hut or goes to the shrines to fulfill a promise?"

Many Latin-American religious agree with Alliende that the continent's Church has been too long under the influence of French and Belgian theologians and that it is time to "deintellectualize the Church." The colleges of such institutions as Rome's Pio Latino Americano and Pio Brasileiro are held responsible for the Church's alienation in Latin America, and nowadays few seminarians go to Europe to complete their studies. Father José Ayesterán, Pio Latino's rector, foresees a time when the college will have no Latin-American applicants (the Latin-American enrollment dropped from one hundred to thirteen in only six years). "The young Latin Americans say they want to stay home and study their own people."

Though paternalistic, the earliest missionaries were anything but intellectual snobs; from the beginning of the conquest they tried to build on existing Indian structures. Most of the first churches were adaptions of Indian temples, and pre-Columbian rites were often included in the ceremonies. In 1558 Pope Paul IV ordered "that the days dedicated [by the Indians] to the sun and their idols should be selected for special celebrations to Christ, the Blessed Mother, and the saints." The first Masses were recited, sung, and, especially, danced. One of the early bishops of Guatemala told all new missionaries that the first thing they had to do was to teach the Indians to dance the Gospel.

Despite its superficiality and cruelty, this forceful evangelization of Indians and African slaves produced a syncretic religion, one of Latin America's few genuinely indigenous creations. Latin-American colonial art is rich in examples of the fusion, such as the use of moon and sun in religious paintings to represent the creator and his wife/mother, or the Bolivian Indians' golden-haired Virgins with one breast longer than the other, symbolizing the Aymaras' earth mother.

Like many Latin American tribes, Mexico's Otomí Indians adapted pre-Columbian rites to Catholic ones, for example the *njadana* ritual of praying to the dead on All Souls' Day—only the Otomís do not pray to comfort the dead but to propitiate them, for if not given such attention they will inflict disease upon the living. Mexico's Zenacantecos Indians have similarly altered the message of the crucifixion to fit their own pre-Columbian religion. The thousands of crosses scattered across southern Mexico are places where the Zenacantecos' ancestral gods meet to discuss the affairs of their living descendants—from whom they expect offerings of black chickens, white candles, and *aguardiente,* the local firewater.

Even baptism, the most universally accepted sacrament in Latin America, has extra-Christian meanings. Among the Indian tribes of the Andes it is an insurance against thunderbolts. For the Zenacantecos its purpose is to attach a soul to its body. In Paraguay, baptism prevents the child's head from growing too large, and in Central America it guarantees that "the child will not remain a Moor," a hazard that popular belief retains from the Spanish Middle Ages.

As Brazilian theologian Eduardo Hoornaert pointed out, the Indians and the Africans soon concluded that Christianity and their religions "were not so different after all, because of the readiness with which the white men's priests baptized their children." Thus Catholicism gradually came to be regarded as a "magnificent expansion of their own fetishisms." The plasticity and superficiality of the early missionaries' Catholicism actually made it more acceptable than Islam had been to the blacks brought from Africa to Brazil. As in Haitian voodoo, Brazilian Macumba attached the characteristics of Christian saints to the African *orixas,* or minor deities. Hence Xango became St. Jerome, and Abaluae, St. Lazarus. Oxala, Macumba's most powerful spirit, is Christ.

Macumba is so popular that it has thirty-two thousand centers, or *terreiros,* in Rio de Janeiro alone. Catholic sources estimate that 30 percent of the Brazilian population practices Macumba; the other great African cult in Brazil is Candomblé, the religion of Bahia. In Rio the Macumbistas are grouped into four federations, which regularly elect middle-class deputies to the local assembly, although Macumba, like the samba, belongs to the counterculture of the Rio slums. Government officials are delighted by Macumba's growth because, unlike Catholicism, it preaches an authoritarian government and insists on a rigid hierarchy. "You never hear any talk about politics or 'liberation' in a *terreiro,"* said a Macumba priest.

Macumba and Candomblé are not the only challengers to Catholic hegemony in Brazil: the Protestants are making sizable inroads. But these are not the mainline, middle-class denominations; the Pentecostal sects account for 75 percent of Brazil's 8 million Protestants. Like Macumba, the Pentecostals abjure political involvement, taking an otherworldly approach.* Its particular attractions for Latin Americans are its emphasis on the laity instead of a priestly hierarchy, and the opportunity for self-expression.

As a result of its new interest in popular religiosity, the Catholic Church is paying closer attention both to the African cults and to the Pentecostals, learning from their success. One result has been more lay participation in the Church, including a Mass largely conducted by the communicants. Catholic religious are also trying to reach an ecumenical understanding with Macumba and Candomblé priests. Jesuit Francisco Barturen, who counsels a fishing cooperative in Bahia, claimed that the basis of its success was his participation in annual Candomblé fishing rites. "The fishermen told me that if I, a Catholic priest, could join in their rites, then I must really understand them."

To develop a coherent and dynamic pastoral program for popular religiosity, the Church had recourse to both psychology and anthropology. Anthropological studies prompted the Church to discard its former disdainful attitude toward legends; these are now understood to be a form of historical communication among the people. Anyone who has tried to interview Latin-American peasants will acknowledge that they often seem to talk in riddles, saying one thing and looking another, smiling when they tell you about the death of an infant brother, for instance. "That is because they cannot, or are afraid to, express their true feelings," said a Brazilian social worker. Religious legends, symbols, and gestures are means of self-expression; the challenge is to unlock the riddle. "Unlike Europe or the United States, where secularization has sidelined religion, here it has a strong influence on social, economic, and political conditions," said Chilean sociologist Renato Poblete. "In discovering what is really important to the people in a religious sense, we will also discover new political solutions."

---

* There are exceptions, however, such as the Brazil for Christ Evangelical Pentecostal Church, whose leader, Manoel de Mello, is active in social causes. Mello is also president of Brazil's Ecumenical Service Commission.

In Andean rural societies, religion, politics, and economics merge in the tradition of *cargos,* or obligations, incurred during annual religious celebrations that honor the local patron saint. But a *cargo* is not only an obligation; it also designates the highest office, because the men selected to pay for the festival's food, drink, music, and decorations gain enormous social prestige. In Ecuador they can be more important than local government officials. A way to redistribute wealth and eliminate class differences, the *cargos* are changed annually so that each villager has an opportunity to pay. Anthropologists say these festivals are also a collective unburdening, a brief time of mythological magic and color when the Indians can return to a past when there was no white *patron* or cultural oppression.

"In a culture impregnated with religion, as Latin America's popular culture is, the religious message penetrates where the school can never reach, and by very subtle means," said Father Hoornaert. "Thus religion can really determine a society's evolution."

The problem has been that, until recently, the message encouraged fatalism. Because God is viewed as remote and powerful, like the local dictator, most Latin Americans ask the saints or souls of the dead to intervene for them. There is a saint for almost every activity, from lottery-ticket selling to bread making, and for every conceivable problem. St. Patrick cures snake bites; St. Anthony is invoked to attract boyfriends. Each country also has its own unofficial saint, among them Venezuela's María Leonza, an Indian princess who doubles as earth mother and goddess of the Caracas freeways; José Gregorio Hernández, a Venezuelan doctor much revered by the Colombians and Venezuelans; and Argentina's "Dead Correa," a young mother who died of thirst in the deserts of western Argentina around the year 1835.

The saints and souls of the dead are as real to these people as their neighbors. At an Aymara religious festival for St. James in Bolivia, a mourning Indian woman harangued the effigy and even struck it to elicit a response. Malnutrition and lack of medicine were not responsible for her baby's death; it was the saint's fault. Similarly, any sudden improvement in the family's fortunes is attributed to offerings or promises made to a particular saint or soul. The highways abound with crosses and miniature chapels to the souls (*animitas*) of the dead, some of which, such as the *animita* housed in the central rail station in Santiago, are believed to have miraculous powers.

The principal fault of this narrow you-me relationship with the saint or *animita* is that it induces an acceptance of all things and events as inevitable. Church studies conducted in 1972 in the Santiago slum of La Victoria showed that the people believed that it is their destiny to be poor. Nor did they expect any happiness in the afterlife, since dead souls spend their time haunting the living, a concept similar to that of Mexico's Otomís. "Religiosity/animism is basically something that helps the person to get through this life," said Chilean theologian Antonio Bentue, the author of the survey. "The person at least has the possibility of offering the saints or souls a gift to intercede." In this very narrow relationship, he said, change is impossible "because authority and tradition are accepted without criticism. Nor is there any social conscience within the community. If there were, the people would join together to protest the economic and social realities responsible for their poverty, instead of trying to bribe God through the saints or the souls of the dead."

But popular religiosity need not be narrow and fatalistic— much depends on where the emphasis is placed. Any number of historical experiences have shown that when the Church emphasizes the positive aspects of folk religion, such as willingness to share in happiness and suffering, the people respond with a heightened sense of solidarity. Brazilian theologian Hoornaert cites the example of Father José Antonio María Ibiapina, a remarkable lawyer-priest who worked in northeastern Brazil in the second half of the last century. Ibiapina encouraged the discipline of work by giving the people a sense of dignity and by emphasing the value of their manual labor. To do so, he used such peasant traditions as the *mutirão,* a Brazilian form of community barn-raising, and the *compadre* system, which is based on the godfather and godmother relationship but is much deeper than those ties in Europe or the United States. Because Ibiapina was everybody's *compadre,* he could get the people to accomplish an incredible number of public works, from dams to homes for orphan girls who later formed the backbone of the Northeast's elementary school faculties. Unlike his European predecessors, Ibiapina did not patronize the people or their beliefs but helped them break the culture of oppression. His legacy is Juàzeiro do Norte, a progressive town in the otherwise backward fiefdom of northeastern Brazil.

When popular Catholicism's positive values are linked to a new understanding of Christ through Freire's consciousness-raising techniques—particularly with reference to the Resurrection's message of hope—magic and spiritual bribery can be replaced by the conviction that the people are "co-creators with God." "This brings forth protest, not against destiny, but against injustice that is not consecrated by destiny and is therefore vincible," explained Chilean theologian Bentue. "Protest leads to the conviction that the future can be better, and thus places more emphasis on the future and change than on the traditional past." What Church groups are basically saying, explained José Miguez Bonino, South America's foremost Protestant theologian, is that many of the gestures, devotions, and symbols of popular religiosity have been substitutes, through magic or providence, for human initiative and action. "When the structural relation between capitalism and unemployment or the social causes of infant mortality are discovered, the relation changes between the believer and the saint whom he was beseeching for work or health. Basically it is a question of a new kind of faith, not mere growth. Whatever the form in which the change takes place, popular piety that alienates must die in order to give birth to an adult and responsible faith. The qualitative change involved in this shift to a faith that mobilizes people implies a different concept of the role of the Church and pastoral and theological interpretations. This cannot occur as a mass phenomenon but means the formation of informed and committed Christian minorities, which really are the only kind of community corresponding to the resolute character of the Gospel."[8]

When at last the Church saw the connections among poverty, popular religion, and education, it could open a new, more authentic dialogue with the people. Local churches began to rewrite the liturgy in the language and symbols of the natives, new forms of instruction were developed to reflect Indian traditions, and old taboos, such as dancing in church, were swept aside. But perhaps the most important revelation to come out of this dialogue was the realization that the religious leader in Latin America must be a man of his people. While priests and nuns could live with the poor and identify with them, they would always carry with them their own cultural inheritance. Thus their interpretation of what the people were saying would inevitably be tinged by their different cultural experiences. Once the local churches recognized this gulf, many came to the conclusion that the only long-term answer for Catholicism in Latin America was lay ministers and married priests.

This conviction is based on necessity as much as a desire to rebuild the Church from its foundations. While religious vocations began to pick up in some countries in the late 1970s as a result of the Church's commitment to social justice, it has proved impossible to close the gap between the exploding population and the number of religious available to serve the population. In most countries at least half the clergy is foreign, and in Venezuela, Bolivia, Panama, and Honduras the percentage of foreigners is over 80 percent. Because of the downturn in vocations in Europe and the United States, fewer foreign priests and nuns are available for Latin America.

A great deal of money and time went into the development of indigenous vocations, but with negligible results. In Bolivia and Peru, for example, a twenty-four-year program run by U.S. Maryknoll missionaries for eight hundred Aymara Indian seminarians produced only fourteen priests. A similar program sponsored by U.S. Capuchin priests in Nicaragua graduated one native priest. Both the Maryknollers and the Capuchins now recognize that one of the problems has been the culturally alienating character of seminary courses. "In the traditional seminaries, our surrounding, our education, and the examples held up for us as models all pressure us to renounce our culture and make us ashamed of being Indian," said a Yaqui priest from Mexico. "I left my people and went off to study many miles away in a city. It was as if I had gone to study in Japan or China, in a different world, completely alien to our own; we Indians felt cramped, diminished.

"We don't need the sort of intellectual training given in most seminaries, where they try to pour us all into an identical mold. Our Lord didn't demand five years of Latin from his apostles, or make them pass philosophy exams before they could begin theology. He trusted the Holy Spirit and sent country people, ignorant fishermen, out into the world to preach the gospel."

Added Father Isidoro Tehuintla, a Nahuatl Indian: "They uprooted me from my own folkways and trained me in Western culture. When I returned home as a priest, I was a total failure. I couldn't understand my own people, and they began to nickname me *pinotl* [Spaniard]."[9]

Even when the courses are geared to Indian culture, there remains the problem of chastity, for in a number of native cultures, such as the millennial Aymara nation, a man cannot be a religious leader unless he has a family. The standards demanded of the Aymara holy men, or *yatiri,* were and are high: they are expected to be faithful to one wife, honest, and generous. On the other hand, it mattered little if a Western-educated priest was *convivente* (living with a woman) or greedy for money, since he was not one of them but a representative of the *misti,* mixed-blood class that dominated the Indians. The priest was primarily needed for ritualistic purposes but never expected to give spiritual guidance, which remained the function of the *yatiris.* Aymara boys who entered the seminaries were viewed as strangers who had left for another culture. In contrast, the *yatiris* lived with their families in the community and therefore "would not go away and abandon us." Because of these cultural differences, there were almost no native vocations. In a typical area, the prelature of Juli in the Peruvian highlands, there were twenty-four priests for four hundred thousand Aymara Indians dispersed in over a thousand communities. All but three of the twenty-four were North Americans.

Situations like that led the Peruvian and Brazilian bishops to urge Rome to change educational requirements for the priesthood and to authorize married priests. "I believe in celibacy as a charismatic gift and consider it indispensable for the Church, but it should be accepted in a realistic way," explained Bishop José Dammert Bellido, of Cajamarca, Peru. We are not advocating the abolition of the traditional celibate priesthood but are seeking additional options with different people exercising different powers of the priesthood, explained Cardinal Aloisio Lorscheider, president of the Brazilian Bishops' Conference. This has already occurred in all but name in dozens of Latin-American dioceses where lay "Catholic pastors" celebrate paraliturgical services, baptize, distribute communion, witness marriages, and perform other functions of the priest. Few have more than a minimum education but all are respected members of the community with high moral standards. They are elected by their own people and almost always turn out to have the qualities that bishops normally look for in a priest.

Grass-roots Communities

While the Vatican steadfastly refused to countenance married priests on the grounds that "they have no European training" and that such approval would open the floodgates elsewhere in the world,[10] celibacy became increasingly a moot point with Latin-American bishops, who were placing so much emphasis on lay leaders. In its search for popular roots, first in consciousness-raising and later in folk piety, the Latin-American Church was reaching back to the historical origins of the universal Church in the primitive Christian communities. As more and more poor Latin Americans began to take responsibility for Church affairs, a model emerged for small groups of committed Christians. Some call them "Abrahamic minorities"; others, the "People of God"; but everywhere they are known as *comunidades de base* (Christian grass-roots communities). The Christian communities are the building blocks of a new society—religious groups that are also people's councils, linking Catholicism with civic action, education with freedom, and solidarity with Christ. That association of piety, learning, and civic action is revolutionary on a continent where the only solidarity hitherto known has been one of oppression. Needless to say, most of the military regimes think the whole idea subversive.

The communities vary according to country and region but all exhibit certain basic traits. They are definitely communities for adults, a shift from the Church's earlier practice of concentrating its educational efforts on children and youths. (Experiments in Chile showed that attempts to duplicate such communities among young people were premature, because the young were not yet ready to set up stable, closely knit societies.)

The communities also discourage individualism. There is no "your" God and "my" God, "your" saint and "my" saint. People are urged to pool their experiences and feelings, thus liberating themselves from the sense of isolation and insecurity caused by political and economic repression. The sharing is extended to other Christian communities, so that there is mutual support, each encouraging the others and exchanging experiences. The communities are also strong antidotes to defeatism, since every member must commit her- or himself in one way or another. Nor does any member stand above or below another.

The most successful communities are in rural areas or poor neighborhoods on the outskirts of the cities where social values have survived. They are almost always composed of poor people because, despite repeated efforts to interest the upper and middle classes in such organizations, very few churches have succeeded.

Some communities place more stress on religion; others on civic action. Some are just beginning; others are advanced. All have the structural support and protection of the diocesan priests and bishops, who act as advisers and coaches. Unlike the rigid parish structure, however, the communities are encouraged to develop on their own and not depend on the Church to solve their problems. Here again, the cardinal rule is to listen and learn, to talk together with humility. Thus, when fifteen Brazilian bishops met at Vitória in 1976 with representatives from the country's eighty thousand Christian communities, it was the peasants and the slum dwellers, not the bishops, who did the talking, who drew up the list of priorities for the grass-roots communities, at the top of which was land.

During the week-long meeting it was agreed that if the peasants were threatened or driven from their land, they should lodge a protest with the authorities, hire a lawyer, and themselves study the law to see that it was enforced, and join with other people having the same problems (small landowners and landless peasants often find themselves in conflict with one another when in fact they are all victims of the large landowner). If all else failed, the peasants and bishops decided, the people should attempt to stay on the land for as long as possible. Observed a worker from São Paulo at the end of the meeting: "Up till now I thought we were struggling alone in our own corner. Now I know that all

over Brazil we have brothers and sisters involved in the same struggle and living the same faith." In this new Church the bishop's role is changing. A brother amongst brothers, he regards his authority as a service. At Vitória only the ring distinguished the bishops from the others.

"There is an amazing process of evangelization astir," reported Canada's Bishop Remi de Roo after a trip through Latin America. "Christians by the thousands are experiencing the redemption of Christ in the flesh, in their own persons, in the midst of poverty and persecution. Deprived of their human rights, cheated out of their natural resources, frequently enduring torture for the cause of truth and freedom, they are coming together in small but increasingly dynamic Christian communities to proclaim their allegiance to the Gospel."[11]

In Honduras six thousand Christian communities sprang up in ten years. With only 204 priests for a population of 2.6 million, the situation had become desperate. Then one day a missionary in the prelature of Choluteca gathered together a number of young people to help him prepare the Holy Week procession. Their response was so enthusiastic that he invited them again, this time to read a Sunday liturgy. He organized for them a course in liturgical training: some to read the Epistle and Gospel, others to lead the hymns, still others to be acolytes. The new ministry appealed to a great many youths and men, so he picked out ten of them for an intensive course in private liturgical services. Thus was born the Association of Delegates of the Word, the Central American term for "Catholic pastors."

"At first, the delegates were not too warmly received," recalled Bishop Bernardino Mazzarella. "Some people looked on them as Protestants, until finally the bishop came in person to introduce them as his representatives to preach the Gospel when priests were unavailable. He even gave them a document with his signature."

The delegates divide up responsibilities; some distribute communion and baptize; others lead catechism classes. All are trained in simple, short courses that do not take them away from their communities for years or alienate them from their people. "Deacons [a position between layman and priest] must be trained for years in theology," said Bishop Mazzarella, explaining why the

Honduran Church preferred lay ministers. "They usually do not come from the neighborhood where they serve, nor are they expected to live there. But delegates, as natives of the place, can guide their brothers and sisters better, see more effectively to the Christian formation of families, understand better the problems of the People of God there, and in general work more successfully at that grass-roots level. Moreover, they need no salary from the Church. And this is of great importance in areas where cash is not readily available."[12] Today no town or hamlet in Honduras is deprived of Sunday services.

Roque Adames, the bishop of the city of Santiago in the Dominican Republic, tells of a similar experience with "presidents of the assembly," as "Catholic pastors" are called there. Starting in 1968 with 3 men, whom he appointed in a special ritual, Adames by 1975 had trained 350 "presidents." All were elected by their communities; none could be a political leader or hold civil office—a ban imposed to avoid the temptation, almost routine in Latin America, of becoming a source of patronage. Each "president" receives a series of books containing outlines of the rites of the Church, as well as suggestions of topics for Sunday discussions. "The people of these communities say they have never lived so close to the liturgy," said Bishop Adames.[13]

To help the lay leaders gain confidence, the bishop or priest attends the Sunday celebration as though a member of the community. He sits with the people while the lay leader gives the readings, and receives communion from the minister in charge of that sacrament. As the lay leaders grow more assured, the communities develop a dynamism of their own. Dom Tiago Cloin, the bishop of Barra, Brazil, said that only after the ecclesiastical ministries had been divided up among the laity in the Christian communities did it dawn on them that "this was starting us toward a new pluralistic system of parish life in which the community had a new sense of collective responsibility." Not only did the sharing of responsibilities reduce the work of the local priests, whose parishes were scattered over huge areas, but also the sacraments took on a deeper meaning. In one parish, said Dom Tiago, the priest "used to have to perform fifty baptisms and five or six marriages in each chapel he visited, and on occasion between one hundred and one hundred and fifty baptisms and as many as twenty weddings! We were convinced that when a lay minister, however uneducated, baptizes only two or three, the sacramental rite means more pastorally than when the priest baptizes twenty-five or more children, amid a commotion so great that he can hardly make his voice heard over the babies' wailing."

But a Church that "limited itself to strictly religious ministries could hardly increase its strength," Cloin felt. "The people had a greater sense of corporate responsibility now, but was their religion sufficiently incarnated in daily life? And was an excessive emphasis on the sacraments alienating them? After a while we saw that as the sense of community increased, certain communities built a school. Others focused on public health questions (practically none of these rural communities has a doctor or a nurse). They picked out a young woman who, after a basic first-aid course organized by the diocese, could at least give injections and bandage wounds. Twenty-five communities now have such 'mininurses.'

"We see that out of these developments a new sort of priest will emerge. The day will come when certain communities insistently ask the bishop to have the full Eucharist more than once or twice a year, as at present. Since there will just not be enough of the present sort of priests for that, the bishops will have to consider the possibility of a solution in these lay ministers in their chapel communities. And we are convinced that these communities, despite their rudimentary nature, have a right to this new kind of priest—at least if, as we believe, divine law offers no absolute barrier to their hopes. Church law, in principle, cannot be an absolute impediment, since its function is to serve evangelization and edification of the Church. The contrary makes no sense.

"In the diocese of Barra, we foresee a general outline of this new sort of priest: he will normally come from the class of small businessmen, dirt farmers, and low-level civil servants; he will continue to work at his job and thus support himself without being a burden on his community. That means he will not exercise his priestly work full-time. His community will choose him because it sees in him a notable perseverance and maturity in the Christian life. Consequently, he will usually be a married man, and in all likelihood at least thirty-five years old. He need not be a university or even a high-school graduate, since he normally lives where such education is impossible. Nor will he have to be the traditional ecclesiastical factotum of the past: the system of differentiated 'ministers,' each with his or her special respon- sibilities, should continue to operate as an expression of the com- munity's corporate responsibility. He will not receive any exten- sive specialized training. It will be enough if he has a clear and vivid vision of the meaning of Christ in the life of both the indi- vidual Christian and the Christian community and if he has a solid sense of what Christian morality demands, particularly in the question of love of neighbor and of justice.

"To avoid the dangers of concentrating too much power in this one man, particularly since his capacities are limited, he will exer- cise a sort of collegial government with those responsible for the other 'ministries.' His particular task will be to help administer the sacraments and to encourage the community's unity, espe- cially that of the team leaders; he must be the expression, the 'sac- rament,' of that unity.

"He would be ordained exclusively for the service of the com- munity that asked for him as minister; hence he would have only diocesan faculties. And his mandate would come to an end when the community decided that, from repeated and clear evidence, he no longer had the necessary physical, intellectual, or moral quali- ties.

"This new sort of priest will not make the traditional priest superfluous; even in places like Barra the latter will always be needed. They will be needed for full-time work in the cities, in particular, and to train mobile teams of specially prepared, full- time lay experts to supervise the ongoing education of the com- munities and, above all, their new type of priests."[14]

What distinguishes Latin America's new grass-roots communi- ties from earlier unsuccessful experiments in people's councils is precisely the Christian framework in which they are developing. Dom Helder Cámara, Latin America's leading proponent of a nonviolent struggle for liberation, firmly believes that the Chris- tian communities are more likely to bring about change than a group of people committed to nonviolent action.[15] However ideal- istic the latter, they are not founded on religion—the one element common to all Latin-American cultures, and still the strongest so- cial influence. Moreover, they usually start from a political premise, whereas the Christian communities start from the essential message of the Gospel: love of God and of man. Only when the community understands and lives this concept can it begin to participate responsibly in politics (in Christian communities it is more important to be a brother than a boss).

For all the successes of the Christian communities, they have created enough problems to convince churchmen that the process is a long, hard pull, particularly when the community attempts to live up to the Gospel's stricture, "Love thy neighbor." Father Alfredo Schnuettgen, a Franciscan priest, describes the frustrations he has met in the communities of Brazilian fishermen with whom he works in Rio Doce, northern Brazil. Adapting the Church's new guidelines to listen and learn, Schnuettgen spent five months on the beaches of Rio Doce just talking to the fishermen, and by the end of that time had not made a single friend. Called *jangadeiros,* the fishermen put out to sea in fragile canoes or rafts at 3 A.M., and came back between 3 and 5 P.M., having eaten some dry bread or a banana. All they wanted then was to sell their fish, get drunk, and play dominoes, said Schnuettgen, and because they had eaten almost nothing they were stone drunk on one or two glasses. There were frequent fights in which the *jangadeiros* used their long fish knives. They ignored Schnuettgen as another city slicker out to fleece them.

In the summer, with a bit of luck and plenty of work, the fishermen earn fifty dollars a month, but if they have to rent their canoe or raft, the owner takes half their catch. In the rainy season their income drops to just over a dollar a month. Intermediaries buy the fish from the *jangadeiros* and sell it for two and three times as much, often in the presence of the fishermen. "I'd see them walk away with their heads down," said Schnuettgen. "'God wants it this way,' they'd say. 'Some are born rich, some poor. And there's nothing we can do about it.' They were completely fatalistic and frustrated."

Over half the fishermen are illiterate. Few of their children go to school because the family cannot afford the books, writing paper, and uniforms. Most of the fishermen's families live in adobe shacks or thatched huts, without toilets, running water, or electricity. Their relationship to God is the usual narrow, superstitious one. "When I'm fishing and I feel I have a big fish biting, I make the sign of the cross so God will give me the fish," explained a *jangadeiro*. "But when I feel it's a small fish, I don't make the sign of the cross." St. Lucy and St. Peter are the patron saints, and anyone who works on St. Lucy's feast day will be punished with fish that are blind to the bait.

One member of the fishermen's colony had fought with the local wholesaler when the latter cheated him. The fisherman decided henceforth to sell his fish direct to the consumers; some of his fellows agreed that he should market their catch as well. It was at about this time that Schnuettgen met the man on the beach. The priest had been urging the *jangadeiros* to share their catch with the colony's elderly and sick, and they had been giving more to the needy. But when the rainy season came, they sought out the priest and asked, "Now, Father, what about them—and what about us, too?" Remembering his conversation with the dissident fisherman, Schnuettgen proposed that the *jangadeiros* get together and talk over their problems. To solve the problem of the sick, they set up a common fund, but it went broke in a month. They then decided to establish a mutual aid society, which was the forerunner of a cooperative.

The men got together enough money to make a down payment on wood for seven rafts. After visiting several merchants who refused to give them credit, they finally found one who would let them have the wood on terms, principally because the priest had accompanied the group. "It was a great sacrifice for them, but they managed to pay off the debt without coming to me for further help," Schnuettgen said. "During the rainy season the president of the colony, as head of the association and manager of the fish stall they now had, underwent great hardships. Some days, the fish they sold barely produced enough cash to meet the payments, and there was nothing left to pay him his fee for buying and selling his colleagues' fish. But so firm was his determination that he and his family went almost unnourished without complaining."

Seeing what sacrifices the fishermen would make to keep the aid society alive, Schnuettgen obtained a loan from a European Church agency to build an ice locker for fish storage. The fishermen built a hut to house the locker, but the day after they put up the roof, a torrential storm swept hut and locker away. That same morning the men were at the site, trying to patch things together.

When Dom Helder Cámara heard of their plight, he got enough money for them to repair the locker and make a down payment on a twenty-four-foot motorboat. By this time the association was doing fairly well, selling its own fish direct to the consumer at a price lower than the wholesaler would offer, with the result that more and more customers were patronizing the stall.

But there were constant fights in the association, said the priest. "At the meetings, for instance, the men sometimes quarreled so violently over trivial matters that I was sure the association would break up. And yet on other occasions they would surprise me by their spirit of cooperation. The day after some of the bitterest quarrels, for example, I would find the men at their headquarters, seated around a basket, shucking shrimp together.

"Even the purchase of the motorboat brought out petty jealousies. Some of the men invited me to go along with them to inspect boats at several shipyards. The day before we were to go, some suspected others of trying to double-cross them; violent words ensued. I hoped that during the night tempers would cool, but at 7 A.M. I found the group waiting in front of the fish hall, silent. One of them said: 'If so-and-so goes, I don't,' and they all felt more or less the same way. I tried to get them to forget their differences and work together for the good of the society. We argued till eight forty-five and finally set out. For some miles, we rode in silence. Gradually, one or another said a few words, until we got to the first beach and they saw the boats, when all rivalry and suspicions disappeared. From that day on, that group was the solid nucleus of the association.

"Petty squabbles like that were happening all the time. Some of the fishermen, when any little difference of opinion arose, would simply walk out of the association, even though they owed it money. There would be arguments when the men came to the fish hall drunk, looking for loans. And one time, one of the members beat me up. The officers of the society wanted to expel him, but I persuaded them that everyone should have a second chance."

Helping the men organize the association was all very well, since, in a way, this "consciousness-raising was a sort of evangelization," said Schnuettgen. "But someone had to announce the word of God to them, too." The priest got in touch with a nun who was working with a similar group of fishermen on another beach, and after a number of meetings, they brought together representatives from seven beaches. Out of these meetings grew a series of Christian communities, known as the Leme Movement and comprising 350 fishermen's families. The movement organized pastoral work and drew up a program to pressure the government to provide social security for fishermen. It also agreed that the various communities should share their experiences, in religious matters as well as such practical ones as the marketing of fish. But while the Leme Movement has made an important start, it still has a long way to go in overcoming the fishermen's fatalism and individualism, in their relationship with God as well as with men.

Even in the associations, said Schnuettgen, "there are fishermen who, on principle, perform no service, acknowledge no duty toward the rest. On shipboard, they have to obey the captain, because a common peril forces them to work together. But ashore, they feel completely free, with no obligations toward their mates. A fisherman will ask his captain for a loan, and then refuse to pay him back; he feels he has done enough by taking the captain's orders. He has the same attitude in his mutual-aid society, where he does nothing—but demands his annual premium. When the colony organizes a block party, he will come, insisting on his right to participate, though he has done nothing at all to prepare the party or to play his part in the neighborhood: 'I have a right to come, because I'm a fisherman.' "[16]

Such attitudes can be overcome, but only with years of patient labor. Schnuettgen spent five years with the fishermen before the Leme Movement crystallized. And even when the patient work begins to pay off, there is always the threat that the government will arrest the leaders of the community and disband its members. That happened in Paraguay, where the bishops had helped the peasants organize a network of agrarian Christian communities, many of which were wiped out in 1975–76 by the Stroessner government, which feared the seeds of democracy in these people's councils. Yet the seeds somehow survive, and the Church begins the work all over again. Said Bishop Aníbal Maricevich, who was busy rebuilding the communities in his diocese of Concepción: "We refuse to be domesticated."

An Institutional Umbrella

Because of the obvious dangers, Christian communities avoid publicity. There are no press releases or manifestos, and many of the bishops and priests take a protective attitude toward them when strangers are about: one can never be sure who the stranger represents. Indeed, without the shield of the established Church, these people's organizations probably could not survive, particularly in the military regimes. Even in Paraguay the Stroessner government was unwilling to risk a formal break with the Church hierarchy, and after the bishops issued a stinging rebuke the regime released several hundred political prisoners arrested during the 1975–76 purge.

Chile provides a vivid example of how Church institutions can protect and comfort the people. There the Catholic Church, alone of all the institutions in the country, has been able to talk back to the Pinochet regime. Thousands of Chileans, whatever their political persuasion, will forever remember the Church as the single organization that stood up for the rights of political prisoners, the homeless, and the unemployed in the desperate years following Allende's overthrow. Church representatives never questioned the Chileans they helped about their political beliefs, or whether they had supported or opposed Allende. It was enough that these people needed help.

In contrast to Honduras, where Christian communities grew out of a commonly felt religious need, in Chile the impetus was hunger. Under the Christian Democratic government of President Eduardo Frei (1964–70), peasants and slum dwellers had made some small progress; after Allende's election more jobs were created for the poorer classes and food supplies were redistributed to ensure that the poor got enough to eat. Every slum child, for example, received a free ration of milk. When the Allende government was overthrown, several thousand people were jailed, most of them from the lower classes. Moreover, the regime's economic policy created unprecedented unemployment—20 percent by 1978. Thousands of Chileans who had worked all their lives were suddenly jobless, and beggars, heretofore unknown, became a common sight on the streets of Santiago.

Shortly after the September 1973 coup the Church helped organize an ecumenical group, the Committee of Cooperation for Peace, to defend the thousands of political prisoners. When the government forcibly disbanded the committee, Cardinal Raul Silva founded a similar organization, the Vicariate of Solidarity, under the direct protection of the Church. But it soon became obvious that the Vicariate would have to do more than supply legal aid to prisoners. Because of the sudden upturn in unemployment, many families were nearing starvation. Studies by the Vicariate's medical team showed that 60 percent of the children in Santiago were suffering from severe malnutrition. The Church founded a free school lunch program, ensuring that each child got at least one meal a day. Dioceses were divided into zones to centralize the collection and distribution of food, with a board composed of laypersons and priests to organize communications.

In response to this program, countless poor Chileans came forward to share the little they had with their neighbors. Housewives pooled their small resources—a cup of rice, an ounce of oil, a couple of onions—and this was supplemented from the local church's food stores. Dining rooms were set up in chapels and schools, but more often in the people's own homes. One of them was Señora Rosa's house in a poor sector of Santiago. Every morning several women gathered there to cook the children's lunch in huge caldrons in the tiny backyard. At noon all the furniture was carried out of the living room and replaced by tables and benches where several dozen children took turns eating. After lunch all the furniture was put back. The chairs and tables took quite a beating from this constant moving, but whenever anything was broken, the neighborhood carpenters repaired it without charge: their children also ate at "Aunt" Rosa's. And what was her payment for this bother? "What do you mean, 'payment'?" she demanded. "To see children eat! Isn't that enough?"

All the neighborhood mothers took turns preparing the lunch, a piece of bread and a soup of seaweed and onions. Often the children took the bread home to save till night, there being nothing else to eat until the next day's lunch. So many parents arrived fainting from hunger at these school restaurants that Church dioceses began a program to feed adults and teenagers as well. By 1977 nearly twenty-four thousand children were being fed lunch.

Because the school lunch centers were an obvious comment on the regime's economic record, the government did its best to destroy them, intimidating storekeepers who contributed food and sending police inspectors into the slums to harass the women in charge of the program. "After our restaurant had functioned for a few months, a municipal sanitary inspector arrived," said a Chilean housewife. "He said the place wasn't adequate for so many children and that conditions weren't sufficiently sanitary. But the place where we feed the children is the best house in the neighborhood. As to sanitary conditions, the government never bothered before about the conditions in our homes. But as soon as we started the lunch program it was different."[17] Other housewives complained that the police had threatened to close the dining halls if the women did not answer questions in a survey they were taking. "We told the police we didn't have to answer them," said a housewife. "These halls belong to the Church, and they can't take from us the only means we have of feeding our children."

Supported by donations from Catholic and Protestant groups in Europe and the United States, the lunchrooms also depended on the solidarity of the people. "Whenever possible we try to connect one group with another so that we can confront the problem together," explained a spokesman for the Vicariate. Thus a peasant cooperative that had received a loan from a Protestant organization to buy seeds repaid the loan in vegetables for the Vicariate to use in the school lunch program. The poor also organized brigades to solicit free food, although this was a humiliating experience for many Chileans, who are not accustomed to begging. An electrical technician, who had worked in the construction industry and never been without a job, reflected the feelings of many Chileans when he said, "As a man I am accustomed to supporting my wife and children without begging. One must put on a very hard face to go out and ask for food." Even with a letter from the archdiocese, members of these food brigades were frequently turned away as "lazy, good-for-nothing beggars." "Why don't you get a job?" one storekeeper asked a woman member. "I didn't dare say anything because the man in the store next door had just given me some food and I didn't want to get into an argument," she said. "But his insults hurt. I'd be glad to have a job, but where, what? Everybody on our block is unemployed."

A number of Chilean Catholics also censured the Church for failing to use the school lunch program to teach the children their catechism. But evangelization takes many forms, explained a Chilean priest. "In Chile today it begins with a long tunnel a little over 2.4 feet in length that is called the digestive tract."[18]

By not preaching religion in exchange for food, the Church was rewarded with the spontaneous growth of Christian communities. A typical experience was that of a nun who helped organize a school lunch program in a neighborhood where there was no community. "We were always very respectful and never insinuated anything about religion. But with time a desire for such a community grew out of the people themselves, and today they are organizing their own."[19]

The absence of paternalism from the lunch program, and from the 127 community industries sponsored by the Vicariate, contributed to the growth of solidarity among the poor that had just begun to take shape during the Allende years. Only now there was less political partisanship and more charity. "We have gone through a difficult period, but we are learning that hunger and all the other daily problems can be solved only in solidarity," said a member of a Christian community who had charge of a lunch program. "We are all stuck with the same dance, so we'd better learn to dance together."

The Chilean Church hammered at this theme in its religious propaganda: everyone must help his neighbor, and no crying to the saints or souls of the dead about the injustices of destiny, the bishops said. One of the principal conveyors of this message was the Virgin Mary, who "went out" to the slums to bring the people together in Christian communities. Letters from the Virgin were sent to everyone in a neighborhood, inviting the people to join these groups; married couples, carrying statues of the Virgin, went into the homes of their neighbors to talk up the need for solidarity. Because the Virgin is the country's patroness, and deeply revered, these efforts were enormously successful. Moreover, the Virgin who carried the message was not the "Generalíssima" of the military regime but the Virgin of popular song: "She sews, irons, cleans, sweats. She is a *chinita* [country girl] just like you."[20] The depth of love for this *chinita* may be judged by the unusual experience of a Santiago housewife who came back from shopping to find her husband cleaning the house in preparation for the Virgin's visit.

The Chilean Church believed that there were valid historical reasons for the communities, which they called "a people's synod." Suffering in solidarity would purify the Church, said Santiago's Bishop Enrique Alvear, but only if the people participated in the change. Since the coup the Church had been working as a "fire-fighting ministry," rushing here and there to extinguish flare-ups, but with no long perspective. "What must we do so that the Church of the Poor may emerge from the poor themselves?" the bishop asked. "How do we evaluate our present experiences? Are they important only because they reflect the social and political organization of Chile? Or should we discover through them a new image of the Church, more gospel-oriented, in greater solidarity with people, more independent from state and economic powers, more committed to an integral liberation for all persons, and more open to everything and everyone?"[21]

Out of the experience of the communities in the synod came the answers to these questions, a popular theology that was later published in comic book form under the title *What Kind of Church Does Christ Want?* Just asking such questions as "Are we truly Christians?" and "Do we know and care about each other?" produced a remarkable reexamination of faith in the eighty-five communities that participated in the program. They, in turn, formed missions to go into other slums. Many people were stunned to discover that anyone was interested in them. "What does the Church care about me, about what I think or would like, I who am so poor, a nothing?" remarked one woman. Those who went to church, either out of curiosity or because they had promised a member of the mission to do so, were surprised by the new atmosphere, with its emphasis on laity, Christian solidarity, and such religious gestures as raising arms to heaven and embracing everyone in the Church. For the first time in memory, people were making a genuine effort to know one another. There were many signs of this new kinship, such as a meeting attended by thirty-five hundred people at a Chilean shrine, where they reflected on what it meant to be witnesses of the Church, commissioned by their bishop to make and receive testimonies. The women brought flowers from their gardens, filling the grotto with color and fragrance. At the offertory there were gifts of flour. As Christ had invited all to partake of his bread, so the poor offered gifts to be shared later with Chileans more destitute than themselves. The flour filled several wheelbarrows.

The success of such evangelization programs was related to the emphasis on popular religiosity. Like the Brazilian peasants who presented the playlet in the church at Vitória, Chilean slum families found occasions for collective expression in the Church. That involved such innovations as dancing in front of the altar during Mass. At the religious dance festival at La Tirana in northern Chile, the people are encouraged to join their dances to the Mass, instead of performing them, as in the past, apart from the Church. Dating from the sixteenth century, these dances are a deep expression of reverence for La Tirana's Virgin of Carmen. In northern Chile, where there are more religious dance groups than sports clubs, some forty-five thousand participants practice two hours daily, five days a week, for four months—all in honor of the Virgin.

Once disdained as "illiterate cowboys," Chile's colorful *huasos* were urged to attend the annual festival of Cuasimodo at the national shrine at Maipú, where Cardinal Silva, dressed in a cowboy poncho, welcomed two thousand *huasos* who had come on horseback and bicycles to reenact the ancient tradition of accompanying the priest on his round to distribute communion to the sick. Mass was later celebrated with dancing and folk singing. This was not a once-a-year event, for the *huasos* and their families continued to meet with Maipú's pastoral group throughout the year.

Farther west, on the Chilean possession of Easter Island, the natives carved a superb statue of the Virgin that looks very like the island's ancient Maori carvings, which have bewildered archaeologists and anthropologists for decades. The occasion for the carving was a nationwide crusade to encourage and purify devotions to Chile's patroness, the Virgin of Carmen. "The islanders were disappointed when we arrived without the statue of the Virgin of Carmen," recalled Father Joaquín Alliende, who was in charge of the program. "But we explained to them that she was Western and white and that they should make their own Polynesian Virgin, because Christ and the Virgin were not Italian or European. All people had made images of them according to their own cultural characteristics."

While the islanders have a tradition of counterpoint singing in Church, they had never attempted a religious carving or painting. After holding an election to choose the island's ten best artisans, the people picked out one of the rare trees that grow in the sacred grounds of the Maoris to be carved into the Virgin and Child. Standing on a map of the island, the Virgin now looks to sea from the fishermen's harbor, her black stone eyes dominating a long, Romanish face, with a crown of seashells on her head.

During the religious ceremonies that took place before, during and after the carving, people buried old feuds over stolen boats or fishing nets. To climax the ceremony on the day of the Virgin's arrival at the harbor, an out-of-season swallow appeared in the sky, a symbol of happiness and the Holy Spirit.

In the Chilean Church's opinion, the Tirana dance clubs, Maipú *huasos,* and Easter Island carving rites are the best possible stimuli for Christian communities. But it is also true that none of these groups could have existed without the institutional Church's commitment to the poor. And no one could doubt where the Chilean Church stood. Although the hierarchy was careful to avoid the appearance of favoring any political group, and took special precautions to ensure that Church institutions were not used for political proselytism by Allende's followers, the bishops repeatedly denounced the lack of respect for human rights and the suffering caused by the Pinochet government's economic policies. As in Paraguay, the Church paid dearly for its criticism—165 priests and nuns were expelled, 3 were murdered, and prelates as high-ranking as Cardinal Silva were subjected to smear campaigns in the government press. Nevertheless, both the Paraguayan and Chilean hierarchies were able to sustain their critical postures because they had connections and power. Communication lines were never completely cut by the governments, which were willing to make private concessions to the bishops and thus avoid an open break with the institutional Church. Again and again, for example, political prisoners were quietly released when the local bishop made his personal interest clear to the President or an influential general. As the advocate of the poor and the oppressed, the

Church provided the Christian communities with a vital lifeline, particularly in the military regimes, where normal communication channels through political parties no longer existed.

The importance of such institutional support in changing the attitudes of Latin America's poor has been demonstrated in a series of studies of the Santiago shantytowns. They refute the conventional wisdom that Latin America's slum dwellers tend to be either tinder for revolutionaries or conservative drones. On the contrary, the studies support the thesis of the theology of liberation that when small groups of poor people achieve a reasonable level of solidarity *with* the support of an institutional power such as the Church, they can effect radical change from within the community. That is quite different from the procedures in socialist countries where change was imposed from the top, and it may be that this combination of popular solidarity with institutional power is the key to solving the problems of alienation in Latin America's burgeoning cities.

Conducted by Santiago's Center for Urban and Regional Development during the last years of the Allende government, the study of twenty-five shantytowns discovered many things about the attitudes and structures that lead to political mobilization among the slum poor. It showed, for example, that when the poor were given a chance to develop their own institutions, they were highly creative in solving such community problems as local administration, housing, criminal justice, and the maintenance of law and order. The Santiago shantytowns instituted a court system, based on the community's moral force, that was quite unlike traditional systems. There were no imprisonments, and fines and physical punishment were rare. Rehabilitation rather than punishment was stressed, to raise the level of social awareness. People could be brought to trial for not participating in community meetings or for drunkenness (several communities banned liquor because of widespread alcoholism). Some communities even had appellate courts. These were genuine "people's courts," outgrowths of the communities themselves, and thus were unlike those in Yugoslavia or China, where the state developed such courts and retained ultimate authority for their administration. The shantytowns also created work brigades to provide jobs for the unemployed and special committees to pressure the government for schools and hospitals. The more homogeneous the social and economic background of the slum inhabitants and the smaller the group, the higher the level of social cohesion.

Breaking away from the client-patron relationship between Latin America's poor and those with political power and money, the Santiago slum dwellers proved quite independent, and many learned to distinguish between what was owed them as citizens and what was given them as a political favor. Thus they absorbed a fundamental element of democracy, learning to use the political parties instead of being used by them. Although these communities tended to confine their political aspirations to concrete demands, such as a school, the survey indicated that the shantytowns would in time become political forces to be reckoned with by the national government. Nor was there any doubt that, given a free choice in elections, increasing numbers would vote for some form of socialism.[22]

While the Santiago slums obviously could not be used as a prototype for the estimated twenty thousand shantytowns throughout Latin America, they disproved the theory that slum dwellers were socially irresponsible, politically conservative, and prone to crime. Only in Chile, of all the Latin-American nations, were the slum poor given an opportunity to develop their own institutions and to express their political preference in free elections where all ideologies were represented. Even in countries that permitted populist or left-wing candidates to run for office, the poor soon learned that they were wasting their votes on such people, because they would either be illegally deprived of victory, as occurred in the 1970 presidential elections in Colombia, when a populist ex-dictator won the count but lost the elections, or eliminated by a military coup. Indeed, it was the fear of a people's socialism that ended the experiment in Chile.

However, the solidarity and hope experienced by the slum poor under the Allende government did not entirely die. It was the backbone of the school lunch program and the new Christian communities. While the people running these programs were afraid and economically insecure, theirs was not the fatalistic fear sociologists ascribe to the culture of poverty, but the result of the military's ongoing political and economic repression. None would dream of shouting "Down with Pinochet" in a public plaza, yet these slum dwellers were neither cowed nor resigned. "We have not forgotten the social gains we made in the past," said a slum mother. "We cannot say anything now, but there will come a time when 'those people' must go, and then we will build a better society in which there is equality and justice for all of us."

CHAPTER XI

THE CHURCH DIVIDED

The voice of the Church, echoing the voice of human con-science, . . . deserves and needs to be heard in our time when the growing wealth of a few parallels the growing poverty of the masses.

Pope John Paul II

Very few of those now planting the seeds of a better society in the political desert of Latin America will live to see the fruit ripen. Political liberty, for example, remains a remote prospect in most Latin-American countries, given the military's determination to stay in power through the end of the century. Such is the future of Chileans, Paraguayans, and Argentines. Even in countries like Uruguay and Peru the armed forces, having reluctantly agreed to allow elections, announced their intention to supervise the civilians' running of things. "I see no possibility of liberation for Latin America in this century," was the grim summation of theologian José Comblin, a specialist in military affairs. "We have to look forward to twenty years of slavery."

The Catholic Church therefore faces some hard decisions. In the political and economic context of Latin America, any option for change implies the use, and risk, of the Church's institutional power. Support of the status quo, on the other hand, demands accommodation, albeit critical, with the military regimes and rich minorities that govern the majority of the Latin-American countries. Either way it is a gamble.

Recent experience has shown that when the Church is sharply critical of existing powers, it attracts persecution of its representatives and the loss of institutional structures such as schools and radio stations, sources of much of its influence on and communication with the people. But if it fails to be sufficiently critical, the Church risks losing the mass of the people. For the first time in years, the Church is experiencing a renaissance in vocations and lay participation in many Latin-American countries, a revival closely related to its commitment to social justice.

The choice between a prophetic and a traditional Church also calls into question the cherished ideal of a Church so united that it can speak to and for all people. This ideal denies the existence of class conflict, a reality in Latin America, and neutrality is thus an illusion: either the Church takes a critical position in favor of the poor, or it silently supports existing structures.

Progressive churchmen readily admit this reality, charging that existing power structures are the primary source of the conflict. Hence it is not enough, say the bishops, to oppose violent revolution; the Church must also condemn the violence of the military and the wealthy minority. Or as one theologian put it: "As a Christian, I am opposed to violence. But if I support those who oppose guerrilla violence, I cannot do so without opposing other kinds of violence as well—the violence that keeps people oppressed and feeds the soil out of which guerrilla movements grow."

There is also the question of prevailing economic and political systems. Capitalism is on the block—even conservatives in the Latin-American Church question the behavior of the multinationals and the terms of trade imposed by the industrialized nations, particularly the United States. But if capitalism is the wrong formula for Latin America, what are the alternatives? The record in Chile shows that the poor, if given the opportunity for self-development and expression, will choose socialism. Although the Christian communities started from a different premise than that of the shantytowns in Chile, they are tending toward the same conclusions. Indeed, some churchmen working with these communities, among them the bishops of northeastern Brazil, openly support a grass-roots Christian socialism. São Paulo's Cardinal Arns describes it as a Christian system of socialism based on solidarity and charity, nonviolent and genuinely Latin-American; a creation of the poor, not the pseudo-copy of U.S. and European economic systems imported by the rich. According to the cardinal, this tendency is "emerging spontaneously" from the people.[1] "We have no objection to private property," adds Dom Helder Cámara, "provided that each person can own it."

Though the forms of socialism are many, as the Vatican itself admits, the word smacks of communism to Latin-American Church conservatives. "Too frequently," says Guadalajara's Cardinal José Salazar López, "Christians attracted by socialism tend to idealize it in very generous terms: good intentions of justice, solidarity, and equality. They deny the historical basis of socialistic movements, which were and are conditioned by the ideology of Marxism."[2]

Helder Cámara disagrees. "There is no such thing as a universal model of socialism. Socialism is not necessarily linked with materialism, nor need it designate a system that destroys the individual or the community. I do not accept the Russian 'model.' It appears to me primitive, elementary. Russia continues to interpret Marxism as a dogma: what was true in Marx's time is still professed in Moscow as THE TRUTH. Since Marx denounced a religion that was, in his time, the opium of the people, communists continue to see and to persecute religion as an alienated and alienating force; whereas we have, right here, the living proof of a Christianity that is no longer either alienated or alienating, but the contrary. Soviet Russia cannot concede that a certain pluralism exists within socialism.

"What we need to find for Latin America is a line of socialization adapted to Latin-American needs. I am thinking of a conscious participation by more classes of the population in the control of power and the sharing of wealth and culture. The world trend is toward socialism. At this time, Christians offer to it the mystique of universal brotherhood and hope."[3]

For men like Cardinal Salazar López, however, such views are ingenuous. Only when it is too late, he warns, will it be perceived that socialism is a façade for totalitarianism.[4]

The difference in viewpoints goes deeper than rhetoric; it has divided bishops and priests, fellow prelates, and even entire hierarchies of one country and another. Much depends on whether the country is controlled by a repressive military government, as in Brazil, or by a formal democracy, as in Mexico. In military regimes, where the principal threat is fascism, the bishops are more disposed to discuss the merits of socialism; many also understand the distinctions made by Cámara. Conversely, the majority of bishops in Latin America's remaining democracies still believe that the foremost danger is communism. (Their colleagues living under military regimes point out that they have had no experience of military repression.) While the Brazilian Church harbors a dissident minority of conservative bishops and a progressive minority persists in the Mexican hierarchy, for all practical purposes the Brazilian Church seeks basic structural changes and the Mexican Church supports the status quo. The split also affects priests and nuns, although statistical evidence shows clear support for change. The laity tends to divide between the rich, who identify with the conservative sector of the Church, and the poor, who find hope in the progressive wing.

The increasingly open divisions in Latin-American Catholicism refute the conservatives' claim of a united Church, and in fact the Latin-American Church has never been homogeneous. A tradition of division and dissent dates back to the sixteenth century, when Fray Bartolomé de las Casas criticized the Spanish Empire's mistreatment of the native population. But only progressive churchmen admit such differences and see merit in a pluralistic church.

If a head count were taken, it is unlikely that many Latin-American bishops would align themselves with either Mexican Bishop Sergio Méndez Arceo's open support of Marxism, or Brazilian Archbishop Geraldo Proença Sigaud's public alliance with the military against the Brazilian bishops.* Those are the extremes. But a substantial group of bishops believe the Church should be concerned with social issues, and these men comprise the innovating minority who are shaping the consensus of the Church of tomorrow. A floating middle vacillates between the innovators and a minority of well-financed conservative bishops allied to the Roman Curia.

The ideological issues that divide the Latin-American Church

* See Chapter VIII, pp. 300–3.

reflect the lack of consensus on how the Church should see itself. If it is a servant of the people—and the majority of the people in Latin America are poor—it must take the side of the poor and be poor itself. But if it is a representative of power, concerned primarily with institutional survival, it must help preserve what prevails: any talk of a people's socialism or an alternate economic system threatens existing structures.

Further complicating the controversy is a dispute over ideology and reality, conservatives insisting that the former is the principal issue, progressives holding to the latter. Thus, while only a minority of Latin-American bishops could be said to advocate the theology of liberation, many agree, if not with the use of Marxist analysis, at least with the reality which that theology describes. These men say they are interested not in ideologies but in realities. Yet the issue has become so confused that to speak against injustice, poverty, and capitalism, as the Brazilian and Peruvian bishops have done, is immediately to raise suspicions in Europe and the United States that Marxism has penetrated the Latin-American Church.

These conflicts became apparent in 1977 as the Church prepared for a follow-up to the historic Medellín meeting, a third extraordinary conference of the hemisphere's bishops, to be convened in the colonial city of Puebla, Mexico. Conservative churchmen had long urged such a meeting, hoping there to put an end to the ferment begun by Medellín, but had been balked by more moderate Church leaders who judged such a convocation "inopportune." Once the Vatican had approved the Puebla gathering, however, it was no longer possible to ignore the divisions.

Unlike Medellín, where the progressives held sway, preparations for the 1979 Puebla conference were largely controlled by a conservative faction led by a triumvirate composed of Colombian Archbishop Alfonso López Trujillo, secretary general of the Latin-American Episcopal Conference (CELAM); Belgian Jesuit Roger Vekemans; and the Roman Curia's Cardinal Sebastiano Baggio, president of the Pontifical Commission for Latin America and López Trujillo's power broker at the Vatican. Vekemans and López Trujillo were singularly well equipped to achieve their ends, the one a European intellectual, the other a shrewd Latin American versed in church intrigue. (Both men are superb organizers with excellent contacts. Vekeman's specialty is Church and government foundations in Europe and the United States; López Trujillo's, the Roman Curia and the conservative members of the Latin-American hierarchy.) Of the two, Vekemans is the more polished, but they have both been notoriously outspoken in their disdain for "those bastards" in the progressive wing of the Church. López Trujillo, in particular, is disliked and feared for his rough-shod tactics; he will accuse anyone who disagrees with him of communist leanings, sometimes in angry public scenes.[5] Yet these very qualities were what earned him the respect of the conservative bishops who stood firm against any further liberalization of the Catholic Church: there was to be no turning of the other cheek, no dialogue, no compromise.

Like Vekemans, López Trujillo gained power by his early attacks on the theology of liberation. He leaped from a minor position in the Colombian hierarchy to the powerful post of secretary general of CELAM in 1972, when the Latin-American bishops began to worry about the radical forces unleashed at Medellín. It was a period of clerical rebellion against bishops; of emerging religious movements committed to left-wing parties, such as Christians for Socialism in Chile; and of an unprecedented number of desertions by priests and nuns, either from political motives or to marry. At about this time, too, the radically new theology of liberation began to emerge. "The ordinary bishop didn't know what was going on," recalled Vekemans. "But he knew he didn't like this sex business."[6] Sex, clerical and political rebellion, and the theology of liberation, then, were subtly connected in the minds of many bishops, thanks to publications by Vekemans and López Trujillo. In a widely publicized document written for the West German Church, Vekemans also claimed that liberation theology was an excuse for violent revolution, although the theology's proponents oppose violence in any form.

Allende's overthrow and the growth of military repression in Latin America helped to define the issues. Faced with a common enemy in the military regimes, priests and bishops found new reasons for dialogue; the vocational crisis subsided as nuns and priests discovered opportunities for expression and service in a socially committed church. The fear of communism was becoming

less immediate than that of fascism: Cuba was the hemisphere's single communist country, and it had not managed to export its revolution to the other Latin-American nations. On the other hand, eleven Latin-American countries had by 1978 succumbed to right-wing totalitarian regimes.

Meanwhile, conditions had also changed in Europe, but in the reverse direction: Eurocommunists were participating in national governments, inching ever closer to an election victory. Pope Paul, who had helped unlock the doors at Medellín, was aging and sick, his encyclicals no longer gifted with the vision and openness of such earlier work as *Populorum Progressio*. Orthodox prelates in the Vatican worried that Latin America was going off on its own, promoting socialist Christian communities, married peasant priests, and other disquieting novelties.

The Brazilian Church was particularly alarming. When Roman wags say that the Vatican will move to Brazil by the year 2000, they are only half joking: by the end of the century more than half the world's Catholics will live in Latin America, and by far the largest number will be in Brazil, which also has the continent's most progressive Church. Pre-conclave maneuvering in 1978 indicates that the Curia feared competition from the Brazilian Church, which the Romans claim is "too horizontal," meaning too democratic. (Helder Cámara's retort: "The cross to us is not only vertical. It is also horizontal."[7]) Brazil's progressive Cardinal Aloisio Lorscheider was a papal contender in the 1978 conclaves, when he was president of both CELAM and the Brazilian Bishops' Conference. His success at enlisting groups from eighty countries to participate in a Brazilian Church project, "The International Study for a Society Overcoming Domination," did not find favor in Rome, where the project was interpreted as a possible platform to launch Lorscheider's candidacy. The Brazilian bishops received an unsigned letter on Curia stationary urging them to withdraw from the project. Similar pressure was applied to the U.S. bishops through Apostolic Delegate Jean Jadot.[8]

Such Curialists as Cardinal Baggio saw López Trujillo as the ideal man to stop the "nonsense" in Latin America. "The responsibility of the Puebla [conference] is to put the Church in Latin America back on the right track," said Cardinal Agnelo Rossi,

ranking Latin American in the Vatican Curia. Thanks to Vekemans' groundwork, the Colombian prelate also had the uncondi-
tional support of the West German bishops, the richest and most
conservative hierarchy in Europe and the largest contributor to
the Church in Latin America.†

This not so subtle support enabled López Trujillo to maintain
his position in CELAM even after the issues in Latin America
had been clarified—few bishops wanted an open break with the
Vatican. López Trujillo not only ran the CELAM machinery as
secretary general; such was his influence in Rome that he frequently overruled Cardinal Lorscheider and the gentle Argentine
Cardinal Eduardo Pironio, who was Lorscheider's predecessor in
the CELAM presidency. Under López Trujillo's management,
CELAM was gradually stripped of the departments and personnel
that had made Medellín possible; it became just another organization, with little political or moral weight. The national conferences of bishops did as they pleased: whether they followed
Medellín's guidelines, as in Paraguay, or opposed them, as in
Colombia, depended on local circumstances, not the CELAM
leadership.‡

A Chorus of Dissent

Nearly two decades had passed since the early 1960s, when Roger
Vekemans first approached the U. S. Government for money to
launch projects in Chile. During that time much had happened to
change the Latin-American Church's understanding of itself and
of the society it was supposed to serve. The Alliance for Progress
was dead; so were Camilo Torres, Che Guevara, and Salvador
Allende. Almost every statistic of social development showed a
decline in the living standards of the average Latin American. The
region's foreign debt was staggering, the highest in the developing

† See Chapter VIII, pp. 304–10.
‡ A service organization for regional communications, CELAM was used
as a political platform by the progressives and, later, by the conservatives,
but it has no juridical authority. The landmark decisions taken by the
Latin-American Church, such as the Medellín and Puebla documents, were
approved by the representatives of the local hierarchies meeting in a hemisphere conference.

world, with some nations spending up to 40 percent of export earnings just to pay the interest. Meanwhile, South America had been engulfed by military dictatorships.

Yet the first working document for Puebla barely touched on these questions. Written by López Trujillo's conservative CELAM team, with the intellectual support of Vekemans, the 214-page document rejected Medellín's strong call for social justice. Known as the "green book," the document avoided the central issue of poverty by resurrecting the colonial church's fatalistic message of resignation: the poor were once again to accept misery in the hope of a better hereafter, because "even when they are deprived of everything, they possess the richness of having a God and faith that will enable them to live with fortitude and the joy of the Kingdom which no human pain can take away."[9] The "development" models of the 1960s that had been rejected by Medellín were once again presented as the only solution to Latin America's economic and social problems, although it had been proved, in country after country, that such models served only to increase the gap between rich and poor. Similarly, the wealthy elites trained at the continent's universities would continue to be the leaders of Latin America and the Church's "chosen few."

So narrow was the vision of the document that within weeks of its release in December 1977 a chorus of indignation and dissent rose throughout the region. While no bishops' conference publicly rejected the document, such being contrary to Church diplomacy, a majority criticized it for failing to deal with the principal challenges to the Church. ("An encyclopedia of everything and nothing," as Dom Pedro Casaldáliga put it.) The Brazilian Bishops' Conference even went so far as to draft an alternate document containing 128 "Contributions," or specific recommendations, for Puebla.

The public release of the "green book" was the first of López Trujillo's several tactical errors. Contrary to expectations, the obscurantist document became an instant best seller, reprinted by the thousands in Latin-American countries. As the liberation theologians have frequently noted, no amount of chicanery can change reality; and at the time when the "green book" came out, the reality of Latin-American Catholicism was an increasingly "horizontal" Church in which bishops consulted with laity in the thousands of Christian grass-roots communities that had sprung up since Medellín.

Thus, on a continent dominated by dictators, the release of the document proved an extraordinary event, sparking a democratic debate on political, economic, and social issues for the first time in more than a decade. University groups, labor unions, peasant federations, women's movements, and ecumenical organizations were all involved in its discussion; enough publications were written on the subject to fill a library. Nowhere was the debate more fruitful than in the Christian communities, typical of which was the Chilean experience. Thousands of copies of a document summary were printed for distribution among the local communities, plus a companion booklet with forty-nine questions for debate. The grass-roots results were then sent to six committees appointed by the Chilean bishops to summarize recommendations for the Puebla conference. Such consultation would have been unthinkable a decade earlier, not only because few prelates would have been prepared to submit a private bishops' document to public scrutiny, but also because the infrastructure for such consultation did not exist.

Thousands of poor Latin Americans in the communities were given an opportunity, most of them for the first time in their lives, to express their opinions about the causes of poverty, military repression, and political and economic discrimination. For example, members of one community in a working-class section of Santiago, Chile, described how unemployment and declining wages had contributed to an increase in suicide, prostitution, alcoholism, crime, and destruction of family life. "The Church is the only place where it is possible to speak of such things," they said. In a number of nations—Brazil, Peru, Chile, and even conservative Colombia among them—such denunciations formed the substance of exceptionally critical reports that the bishops' conferences made on their countries in a 1,258-page auxiliary document for Puebla.

Discussion of the "green book" proved an enriching experience in evangelization, the very subject of the Puebla conference, and a bench mark of how far the Church had come since Medellín. Even so severe a critic of the document as Peruvian theologian Gustavo Gutiérrez admitted that the method used to achieve a critical consensus had been an important step forward in "conscientization." Chilean theologian Segundo Galilea attributed the depth of debate to the amazing number of study courses, workshops, encounters, and publications for clergy and religious in recent years, all of which, he said, had served to stimulate creative thought and prophetic commitment. "More has been done for the renewal of evangelizers in the past fifteen years than in the last hundred." Protestant theologian John C. Bennet, former president of the Union Theological Seminary, New York, agreed with him: "The most provocative theological questions, as well as a courageous defense of human rights of both Christians and non-Christians, are currently coming from the Latin-American Church, which only a generation ago was commonly considered theologically obscurantist, socially reactionary, and religiously intolerant."

In response to widespread criticism of the "green book," a small group of bishops representing South and Central America met at CELAM headquarters in Bogotá in mid-1978 to rewrite the working document for Puebla under the guidance of Cardinal Lorscheider, the organization's president. Based on the reports submitted by the individual bishops' conferences, the second document was shorter and more concise, its main purpose being to reaffirm the Church's commitment to social justice in the strong language used at Medellín. For Lorscheider, who wears a pacemaker, the price of this achievement was high: such were the tensions between the cardinal and López Trujillo that Lorscheider was twice confined to his bed with a serious heart condition.[10]

A humble man who has never publicly criticized López Trujillo, even when the latter went over his head to enlist the aid of Baggio at the Vatican, the normally jovial Brazilian eventually lost patience with the pugnacious Colombian, according to members of the rewrite team, who reported that Lorscheider told López Trujillo to leave the bishops alone and attend to his duties in the city of Medellín, where he had recently been appointed archbishop coadjutor with right of succession.[11] But López Trujillo had the last word. After the cardinal's group left Bogotá, the rewrite completed, López Trujillo's CELAM team appended to the document fifteen jarring "Notes" which were a throwback to the "green book." Several were frankly offensive, such as the treatment of Protestants in the "Note" on Christology.

"Badly educated, little smart alecs"

The dispute over the working document was part of a larger struggle that included the Latin-American Confederation of Religious (CLAR), representing the region's religious orders; the region's leading theologians; the Vatican; the West German bishops; and a right-wing U.S. religious organization called the DeRance Foundation, with headquarters in Milwaukee.

López Trujillo had long been at odds with CLAR, which carried the banner for the theology of liberation and had employed theologians and social scientists dismissed from CELAM for their association with Medellín. Father Luis Patiño, a Colombian Franciscan who was secretary general of CLAR, had several times been the victim of López Trujillo's wrath, on one occasion receiving a tongue-lashing in the presence of a gathering of bishops. With control over the CELAM machinery, and Baggio as power broker in Rome, López Trujillo was able to exclude CLAR from the Puebla conference, whereas at Medellín its directors had had both voice and vote.

Meanwhile, a book by Alberto Methol Ferré, a Uruguayan lawyer belonging to CELAM's Lay Department, was distributed throughout Latin America for the bishops' edification. A collaborator with López Trujillo and principal advocate of the "green book's" argument for an accommodation with the military, Methol Ferré singled out such critics as CLAR and the liberation theologians for vitriolic attack. CLAR was "like a bunch of students . . . badly educated, little smart alecs" who "talked nothing but drivel." Such respected liberation theologians as Brazil's Clodovis Boff, Chile's José Comblin, Argentina's Enrique Dussel, and Peru's Gustavo Gutiérrez were "irreverent," "negative," and "irresponsible."[12]

Though not in a class with Vekemans' more polished denunciations of liberation theology, which were also sent to the bishops, Methol Ferré's book caused quite a stir—the knives were out for all to see. The book also evoked old memories of Vekemans' CIA connections, since its publication was financed by the DeRance Foundation,* which had contributed $200,000 to Vekemans' campaign against the theology of liberation through its affiliate, the Institute of the Sacred Heart of Jesus, of which Vekemans is Latin-American director.[13] (This was in addition to the money Vekemans received for the same purpose from the West German bishops' agency, Adveniat.) † ‡

As in the case of the working document, Lorscheider went at once to the aid of CLAR, threatening to resign his CELAM post unless the religious were invited to Puebla. A Franciscan who is held in great respect by CLAR, Lorscheider served as the principal bridge between CLAR and CELAM during the height of the in-fighting, not only because he is a religious but because he has always advocated communion and dialogue, a stand that helped propel him into the two most important positions in the Latin-American Church, the presidency of CELAM and that of the Brazilian Bishops' Conference. Thanks to Lorscheider and similar pressure from Cardinal Pironio, former CELAM president and now prefect of the Sacred Congregation for Religious, Cardinal Baggio was forced to extend a belated invitation to the CLAR directorship and sixteen additional religious.

As Father Patiño later observed: "Tensions are always present when the Church wants to grow—tensions between the prophetic, the charismatic, the inspirational, the disciplinarian, the traditional . . . which are values and currents complementing one another. But sometimes the actors in this historical process do not have the right temperament to understand it. Thus CLAR, which is viewed as dangerous by a few bishops, including the secretary general of CELAM, was deliberately excluded from Puebla. The conference was organized from the viewpoint of a vertical church, directed from above, and not as a church of a people of God, in which we all have obligations, as in a community."[14]

While López Trujillo was unable to bar CLAR from Puebla,

---

* Headed by Harry John, the foundation is identified with such traditionalist Catholic movements as the Family Rosary Crusade.

† See Chapter VIII, pp. 306–7.

‡ The DeRance Foundation also contributed $140,000 to the Puebla conference; Adveniat, $100,000; and the U. S. Bishops' Conference, $70,000. (Gary MacEoin and Nivita Riley, "Velvet Curtain Shields Bishops at Puebla," *Latinamerica Press* [Lima, Feb. 15, 1979].)

the defeat was more than offset by his success in obtaining papal approval for an additional 181 delegates to be selected by himself in consultation with Baggio, and thereby assuring conservative control at Puebla. Of the 356 delegates, only 175 were elected by the national bishops' conferences. The majority of the other 181, including bishops, clergy, and laymen, were chosen by López Trujillo; most were conservative, including twelve additional right-wing bishops, and several of them military chaplains, such as Cardinal Aníbal Muñoz Duque, a brigadier general in the Colombian Army. All but one of the theologians and sociologists were hostile to the theology of liberation. Obscure men, for the most part, their chief characteristic was loyalty to López Trujillo. The choice of lay delegates was equally surprising; it included a Helena Rubinstein executive from Guatemala who is spokesman for that country's military regime. Representatives of the DeRance Foundation, Adveniat, and similarly oriented foundations were invited, while members of progressive aid institutions were not. Pope John Paul I approved the list in the last days of his brief papacy—under pressure from Baggio, according to Vatican sources.[15] John Paul II reconfirmed the list as a formality, but neither Pope knew the delegates or understood the parts assigned to them in the scheme to end the movement begun at Medellín by a specific condemnation of the theology of liberation.

Again, the principal flaw in that scheme was its failure to acknowledge reality. While conservative and moderate bishops in the Latin-American Church might criticize CLAR and the theology of liberation, few were of such little good will, or intelligence, that they wished the Church further polarized by excluding its most renowned thinkers from so important a conference. On the contrary, the deliberate exclusion of men as eminent as Gustavo Gutiérrez merely helped to substantiate the progressives' claim that López Trujillo was manipulating the conference.

Although it is undoubtedly true that the progressives had prevailed at Medellín, they did not do so by excluding opposition groups. Colombia's conservative Cardinal Muñoz Duque, for example, led a delegation that presented an alternate document. Nor was the atmosphere preceding the meeting nearly so venomous, if only because Medellín was a "sleeper," as Panama's Archbishop Marcos McGrath observed. In the last tense months before the

January 1979 meeting in Puebla, accusations of conspiracy were made by both right and left, López Trujillo claiming a conspiracy of defamation, the liberation theologians alleging a conspiracy of "mystification," one that implied they were attempting to establish a parallel church. The Vatican newspaper *L'Osservatore Romano* and Jesuit publications in Latin America joined the fray, the former siding with López Trujillo and the five most influential Jesuit magazines in Latin America unanimously rejecting the Colombian's claims.

As fears and distrust mounted, Sergio Torres, a Chilean priest and secretary of the New York–based "Theology in the Americas" project, set off on a ten-nation tour of Latin America to consult with the progressive bishops. Torres believed that the liberation theologians could contribute to Puebla, even though they had been officially excluded, by becoming personal advisers to bishops who would be attending the conference, much as similar experts had given semiofficial support to delegates to the Roman synods. The plan found favor with a number of bishops in Brazil, Uruguay, Chile, Peru, Ecuador, Venezuela, Panama, and Guatemala, and twenty-two theologians and eight social scientists, comprising the continent's leading spokesmen for liberation theology, were unofficially invited to Puebla. Gustavo Gutiérrez, for example, was personal adviser to eight bishops, including Brazil's Dom Helder Cámara and Ecuador's Bishop Leonidas Proaño; José Comblin, the adviser of Cardinal Arns; Segundo Galilea, of Chile's Bishops Enrique Alvear and Fernando Ariztía. Each had the personal protection of a bishop, as well as direct lines of communication into the conference through the progressive bishops and CLAR, which included three leading liberation theologians in its official delegation.

These links to the conference were tenuous, however, and no one could predict reaction to the group's arrival in Puebla. "We were very worried," Torres admitted. But the "signs of the times," so clearly identified at Medellín, favored the liberation theologians at Puebla. In two years of preparation for the conference, many of the uncommitted bishops had been forced to study their own reality, in itself a process of "conscientization." For example, the conservative Colombian bishops, who for years had supported the country's two traditional, center-right parties, found the political system corrupt, incompetent, and unjust, a "formal democracy" in which the vast majority of the people had no part. Peru's bishops charged the country's military regime with "encouraging an abysmal difference" between social classes and participating in a "run-away arms race at the cost of the hunger of the people." The normally conservative Ecuadorian bishops were equally scathing in their denunciations of that country's military government and "prostituted politics." In Venezuela, the bishops condemned "demagoguery and empty promises."

São Paulo's Cardinal Arns summed up the general feeling of malaise: "The Church has become convinced and has begun to preach that three elements are responsible for the marginalization of the people: land and industry concentrated in the hands of less than 5 percent of the population; political power concentrated in 1 percent of the population; and the almost total dependence of Latin America on the First World. In my city alone, three million people are without housing, food, schools; without participation in the city's life, or the possibility of practicing their religion in a free and integral manner." "If the church were to summarize the past decade of 'development' in Latin America, it would have to state that the result is more hunger," agreed the Theological Commission of the bishops of northeastern Brazil. "The situation of the vast majority of Latin Americans totally contradicts the teachings of Jesus Christ," concluded Brazil's Bishop Cándido Padín.

Nor was poverty the only issue. As Amnesty International noted, in a plea to the Puebla delegates to continue the Church's work on behalf of human rights: "At a time when conservative figures indicate that there are 17,000 political prisoners in Latin America, with over 30,000 disappearances, thousands of victims of torture, and innumerable families separated and without protection on the continent, the call for radical action for the defense of the fundamental rights of the Latin-American peoples is increasingly urgent."[16]

Thus when the bishops traveled to Mexico for the Puebla conference, they carried with them a new understanding of reality as well as "a sense of shame that after five centuries of colonization, there is still such a gap between rich and poor in a Catholic continent," said Panama's McGrath.[17] Even Cardinal Baggio described Latin America as "the Galilee of our time," just as the Galilee of

Christ was "the scene of poverty, ignorance, sickness, and malnutrition, with the presence of an invading foreign force rejected by the Galilean people."[18]

Something Untainted

It was to Galilee, then, that a complex, seemingly enigmatic Pole addressed his first concern as Pope. A religious scholar with an independent mind, and a man of courage and charm, John Paul II was yet a mystery to the First and Third Worlds. His record in Poland was clear, but how would he respond to vastly different circumstances in Latin America? That question was on everyone's mind when, four months after his election, John Paul made his first trip abroad, to the "continent of hope," to inaugurate the Puebla conference.

What none foresaw, least of all the officially anticlerical Mexican government, was the delirious reception accorded him. Contrary to police predictions of a maximum crowd attendance of 8 million, over 18 million Mexicans thronged streets and plazas to pay homage to the Pope. The entire country was paralyzed as Mexicans left home and office to wait hours for the thin, sunburned "Papa," if only to glimpse him for an instant as he passed in a car. No man in Mexican history had drawn such crowds; by contrast, President Carter's Mexico City reception a few weeks later seemed almost ludicrous.

While John Paul's warm personality obviously delighted the Mexicans, the size of the crowds, and their spontaneous sense of respect and discipline, were due less to the man himself than to the symbol of his office. The phenomenon could not be explained solely by popular piety, but reflected the people's identification—repeatedly stressed by John Paul in Mexico and, later, in his first encyclical, *Redemptor Hominis*—with a higher moral force, something untainted by the corruption, cynicism, and falsehoods of an alienating political system, something almost divine. In an extraordinary gesture, as the Pope was leaving, hundreds of thousands of people climbed onto rooftops in Mexico City and waited for his plane to appear. When it did so, they took out mirrors, pieces of broken glass, and shiny metal and flashed the sunlight toward the plane. A Catholic radio announcer explained that in this way the Pope would have one final look at each and every individual soul.[19]

The Puebla delegates were also awed by John Paul's tremendous reception, and this—in addition to his authority as new Pope —gave extraordinary weight to his thirty-seven speeches in Latin America. Had he chosen to do so, he could at that moment in history have set a specific direction for the Latin-American Church, and no bishop, however outspoken, would have gainsaid him. But John Paul wisely chose otherwise, providing guidelines sufficiently broad to let the Latin Americans make their own decisions.

A dialectical thinker whose logic can be appreciated only in its totality, John Paul seemed to say one thing in the Dominican Republic, en route to Mexico; another in Mexico City; and still another in Puebla and the other cities he visited during his week-long tour. Thus his early speeches in Mexico City appeared to emphasize popular devotion and religious discipline at the expense of social commitment; yet only the day before, in the Dominican Republic, he had spoken of the rights of the workers and the poor. In the aftermath of his journey, when all the speeches could be absorbed and put into the clear focus of *Redemptor Hominis,* John Paul's guidelines were obvious, but at the time of his visit both the press, which numbered over one thousand journalists, and a sizable group of bishops interpreted the speeches according to their own lights, seizing on one point or another to support personal preferences. There were a few voices of caution, of course, including that of the ever prophetic Helder Cámara, who warned against taking the Pope's statements out of context.

The broad outline of John Paul's analysis covered several crucial points, including the relationship between God and man, religion and ideology, and human dignity and evangelization. For John Paul, love of God and love of man are the same: If "God 'gave his only Son in order that man should not perish but have eternal life,'" how can man love his brother less? That is the meaning of redemption. "God wants us to be responsible for each other," the Pope told the crowds at the Zapopan Sanctuary in Guadalajara. He wants "an authentic commitment to our brothers, especially the poorest and most needy, and to a transformation of society."[20]

The Church has a specific role in this transformation, the Pope told the bishops at Puebla, and that is to be a "teacher of the truth" about Jesus Christ, the Church's mission, and man. "Not a human and rational truth, but the truth that comes from God, the truth that brings with it the principle of the authentic liberation of man: 'You will know the truth, and the truth will make you free.'" (John 8:32).

The truth about Christ, said John Paul, is that he was not a "political figure, a revolutionary," a mere "prophet" whose "divinity is passed over." "By confusing the insidious pretexts of Jesus' accusers with the—very different—attitude of Jesus himself, some people attribute his death to a political conflict, and say nothing of the Lord's will to deliver himself and of this consciousness of his redemptive mission. The Gospels clearly show that for Jesus anything that would alter his mission as the servant of Yahweh was a temptation. (Luke 4:5) He unequivocally rejects recourse to violence. He opens his message of conversion to everybody without excluding the very publicans. The perspective of his mission is much deeper. It consists in complete salvation through a transforming, peacemaking, pardoning, and reconciling love."

Thus to "reread" the Gospel from an ideological viewpoint is to miss the essence of the message and to destroy the originality of the Church's fundamental mission, exposing religion to "monopolization and manipulation by ideological systems and political parties." On the contrary, ideologies should be interpreted from the viewpoint of the Gospel, and thus Christianity can help mold political beliefs, although its message is more profound than any ideology.

The Church "does not need to have recourse to ideological systems in order to love, defend, and collaborate in the liberation of man," insisted the Pope. "At the center of the message of which it is the depository and herald it finds inspiration for acting in favor of brotherhood, justice, and peace, against all forms of domination, slavery, discrimination, violence, attacks on religious liberty, and aggression against man, and whatever attacks life.

"It is therefore not through opportunism or thirst for novelty that the Church, 'the expert in humanity,'" sees the defense of human rights and the promotion of the dignity of man as its foremost mission. "It is through a true evangelical commitment, which as Christ showed, is a commitment to the most needy. In fidelity to this commitment, the Church wishes to remain unencumbered by competing [political and economic] systems in order to work solely for man.

"The voice of the Church, echoing the voice of human conscience and never ceasing to make itself heard down the centuries in the midst of the most varied social and cultural systems and conditions, deserves and needs to be heard in our time, too, when the growing wealth of a few parallels the growing poverty of the masses.

"There is no economic rule capable of changing [unjust economic] mechanisms by itself. It is necessary, in international life, to call upon ethical principles, the demands of justice, the primary commandment of which is love. Primacy must be given to what is moral.

"The Church sees with deep sorrow the sometimes massive increase of human rights violations in all parts of society and of the world. . . . Who can deny that today individual personal and civil powers violate with impunity the basic rights of human beings—rights such as the right to be born, the right to life, the right to responsible procreation, to work, to peace, to freedom and social justice, the right to participate in the decisions that affect people and nations? And what can be said of the use by various groups and individuals of physical and psychological torture against prisoners or political dissenters? The list grows when we turn to the instances of abductions for political reasons or material gain which attack so dramatically family life and the social fabric. We cry out once more: Respect man! He is the image of God!"[21]

How can man achieve a more just world? "By making every effort to ensure that children are no longer undernourished, without schooling and instruction, or that youths do not lack essential vocational preparation; that peasants are not left without land and the means to develop themselves with dignity; and that workers are not mistreated or deprived of their rights. Systems that allow the exploitation of man by man should not be permitted, nor should corruption or situations in which some have too much while others, through no fault of their own, lack everything. Let there be no families that are destroyed, separated, and without sufficient help; let there be no one without the protection of the law, which is to protect all without distinction. Force should never prevail over truth and law, nor economic and political systems over the dignity of man."22

The Pope's speeches to the Indians in Oaxaca and the workers at Jalisco were even stronger. Nobody knows why—whether it was the spectacle of some two million impoverished Mexican peasants lining the road from Mexico City to Puebla, or the confusion caused by his earlier, more conservative speeches in Mexico City—but John Paul rewrote the Oaxaca speech on his return from Puebla at eleven at night. "The Pope wishes to be the voice of the voiceless," John Paul told some forty thousand Indians the next day. "You have a right to be respected and not deprived of the little you have, often by methods that amount to plunder. You have a right to throw down the barriers of exploitation.

"For your part," John Paul told Mexico's wealthy landowners, "you have at times left the land fallow, taking bread from so many families who need it. Human conscience, the conscience of the people, the cry of the destitute, and, above all, the voice of God and the Church repeat with me: it is not right, it is not human, it is not Christian to maintain such clearly unjust situations. . . . If the Church defends the legitimate right of private property, it teaches with equal clarity that there is always a *social mortgage* on such property, that the goods of the world were destined by God for the good of all. And if the common good so demands, there is no doubt that expropriation is the best measure.

"Individualism is a widespread evil among rural workers," John Paul told the peasants, "whereas better coordinated action in greater solidarity might be very helpful. Think about this, my dear sons."23

"For the Christian it is not enough to denounce injustices," the Pope later told Mexican workers in Jalisco. "He must be a witness and agent of justice, working for rights that must be defended legally, but also fulfilling duties with generosity.

"I want to tell you with all my soul and strength that I am deeply pained by the injustices against workers, by the conflicts, the ideologies of hate and violence that are not evangelical and cause so many wounds in contemporary humanity."[24]

"This is the strongest language we have heard from any Pope," said Archbishop McGrath after reading the Oaxaca and Jalisco speeches. Agreed Brazil's Bishop Cándido Padín, one of the architects of Medellín: "John Paul's statements were much stronger than those of Pope Paul when he opened the Medellín conference."

Had John Paul used such language on his arrival in Mexico, there would have been less confusion at the start of the Puebla conference. True, he had talked about human rights in his speeches in the Dominican Republic and at Puebla, but world attention was focused on his references to clerical involvement in politics and, by implication, to the theology of liberation, although John Paul never once mentioned the latter in his speeches. "You are not social directors, political leaders, or functionaries of a temporal power," the Pope told priests and male religious in a Mexico City address. "Much less would it be admissible for priests and religious to set up an authority parallel to that of the bishops—the authentic and only teachers of the faith—or the conference of bishops."[25]

These statements—as well as his caution against "rereading" the Gospel in ideological terms, and an inaccurate wire service report that John Paul had condemned liberation theology—produced the erroneous impression that the Pope had admonished priests and nuns to return to their sanctuaries, and to eschew social causes having political overtones. Chile's strongman, General Augusto Pinochet, gleefully pounced on such reports as proof that the Church "has a specific mission in this world that has nothing to do with politics," adding that "the Church appears to have stopped in order to reexamine its situation and once again follow the course it is meant to take."[26]

John Paul's later speeches, statements on his return to Rome, and the encyclical *Redemptor Hominis* showed that that was not at all what he had in mind. As Cardinal Lorscheider pointed out, the Pope's directive to the bishops to be "teachers of the truth," with a priority option for the poor and for human rights, clearly means that the Church must question all structures that deny the dignity of man. "That specifically means totalitarian military regimes," Lorscheider warned. "But we are questioning these governments from faith, not from a political party or ideology," cautioned Chilean Bishop Enrique Alvear. "As the Pope said, this gives us more freedom and moral authority to continue our mission."

In that context, said Panama's McGrath, "the Church has been talking politics ever since Moses talked back to Pharaoh. When the Pope tells the peasants they have a perfect right to organize, as he did in Oaxaca, that has a tremendous political impact. But this is quite different from saying that a priest should get involved with a political party or pressure groups that are politically aligned." In any case, said Lorscheider, "the trend in Latin America has been away from participation in political movements. I don't know of a single priest active in partisan politics in Brazil." We should look at the issue from another angle, urged Ecuador's Bishop Proaño: "Christ, without being a political person, without having founded political parties, overturned the political and religious structures of his time by his denunciations and his preaching."

The Puebla delegates also insisted that John Paul had not condemned liberation theology. "He never even used the term," said Brazil's Padín. "When interpreting the Pope's speech, people would be better advised to consider his references to capitalism, which is what he was talking about in his description of unjust economic systems," added Jesuit Pierre Bigo, the conservative director of the Social Action Division of CELAM's Theological-Pastoral Institute and a close associate of López Trujillo.

John Paul himself later clarified the issue by telling an audience in Rome that "the theology of liberation is often connected, sometimes too exclusively, with Latin America," when in fact there is "reason for a theology of liberation on a universal scale." Emphasizing the close links between Christ's message of liberation and "knowledge of the truth," the Pope said that "it is necessary to call by name every social injustice, discrimination, and violence inflicted on man against his body, his spirit, his conscience, and his convictions"—which is just what the theology of liberation does. He also praised a basic tenet of liberation theology, or "conscientization," that awakens the poor to their dignity and rights as human beings; and he deplored the ways whereby social, political, and economic injustices suppress that dignity.[27]

But the Pope also made clear, both in Mexico and in Rome, that he opposes any Marxist theories of revolution and class warfare that claim the injustices in Latin America cannot be ended by peaceful means. Progressive bishops and liberation theologians at Puebla were in complete accord, not only because violence is un-Christian, said Helder Cámara, but because it does not work. "Those who attribute violence to the theology of liberation do not know what they are talking about," added Gustavo Gutiérrez. "The theology's position on violence is the same as the Church's traditional teaching on 'just wars' that dates to St. Thomas Aquinas: that violence is possible as a lesser evil and last resort against a greater violence, such as tyranny, but that no Christian willingly accepts such a choice. One of the crucial decisions in that choice is whether counterviolence is effective. If it is not, it should not be chosen.

"I think the source of confusion lies elsewhere. If I say my priority is to evangelize the poor, the rich in Latin America immediately say that this is communism, because questioning structures that keep people poor is considered subversive. If a Latin-American priest had spoken out against injustice as the Pope did in Mexico, he would have been accused of subversive political activity."[28]

"Teachers of the Truth"

Overwhelmed by the Pope's presence and not entirely certain of his message, the bishops began their historic third conference in an atmosphere of distrust and doubt. Unlike Medellín, when the first week was spent in open debate, the Puebla delegates were immediately put to work writing draft documents. But what were they to write? After the Pope's speeches, the working document prepared by Lorscheider's group no longer seemed adequate, yet many bishops were reluctant to take the initiative, less they misinterpret John Paul and come down on the wrong side in a divided Church. The Pope had told the bishops to continue Medellín, but there was no consensus on the direction.

It fell to Cardinal Lorscheider to break the ice. In a simple but moving speech, the CELAM president outlined the essential points in John Paul's message: to be "teachers of the truth" and to adopt human rights as their foremost mission, with a priority for the poor:

> The theme of this conference is *Evangelization in the Present and Future of Latin America*. To proclaim today and tomorrow the evangelization of our peoples—who are inspired with hope but at the same time tortured in their deepest beings by the assault on their dignity—is not only a fraternal, noble, and enriching work; it is our mission, our duty, our life. The cry of hope and anguish of our peoples that reaches us in this conference and that seeks a *prophetic response* demands a commitment to the word of God in our lives and our preaching. We are here as shepherds leading their flocks. (John 10:4)[29]

In the climate generated by Lorscheider's speech, the delegates selected twenty-one themes for study. At the same time, the bishops rejected López Trujillo's plan to have the CELAM staff appoint a steering committee to oversee the work of the twenty-one corresponding commissions. Instead, they elected the committee. This group of five bishops, headed by Panama's Archbishop McGrath and all of them progressives or moderates, played an important part in shaping the final document. The liberation theologians also influenced the conference in the first days of uncertainty and suspicion, though making contact with the bishops was akin to storming a fortress.

Puebla was not chosen by chance as the site of the conference. Ringed by churches—one for almost every day of the year—the colonial city is controlled by a local party machine in alliance with right-wing business interests and an ultraconservative Church. The poverty of the city's Indians, encamped on the back streets of the native markets, contrasts with Puebla's palatial colonial houses and magnificent churches: here is an Indian selling cucumbers for a few cents, with a dying child beside him in a box of leaves; and behind him rises a church covered in gold leaf. The Indian has never heard of Medellín; he thinks it may be a person or place—not a hope, a dream.

The city's wealthy families, on the other hand, know all about Medellín. Thus, when such progressive lobbies as the liberation group arrived in Puebla, they encountered harassment, even threats. The group's first meeting place, a parish house, was abandoned when the local priests received stern warnings from police and church authorities. Representatives of a women's lobby reported anonymous telephone threats of excommunication and physical violence; the women were forced to leave their meeting place at a local museum after the woman director was threatened with dismissal.[30]

At the high-walled Palafoxiano Seminary, where the Puebla delegates were housed, guards patrolled the entrance gate around the clock. No one could enter the grounds without authorization from the CELAM secretary general, and López Trujillo's staff told the bishops that they should avoid contact with outsiders. That was the atmosphere when the liberation theologians tried to approach the progressive bishops behind the "wall of freedom," as López Trujillo cynically described the seminary enclosure.

Brazilian Bishop Alano Pena was the first to defy the wall. On the morning of the second day of the conference, he came out from the seminary to meet with the liberation theologians and carry their analysis of the Pope's Puebla speech back to the sequestered bishops. At the same time, Gustavo Gutiérrez sent a note to Archbishop McGrath, stating that the group had come to Puebla only to be of service to the bishops and that it was in no way attempting to set itself up as a parallel church.

Within a week of the opening, the liberation group's papers were freely circulating throughout the conference, and were even officially recognized by the CELAM staff. After Cardinal Arns's personal secretary had a shouting match with the guards at the seminary entrance, when they refused to let him in, the "wall of freedom" came tumbling down and delegates were soon mingling with the eight lobbies gathered outside. The collapse of the elaborate security measures proved two important points: that the bishops were not to be manipulated and that it was impossible to exclude the Latin-American Church's best brains from the meeting, if only because the mediocrity of the work produced by the official theologians within the conference encouraged the bishops to read the one-hundred-plus papers prepared by the liberation theologians. Or as one bishop graphically put it, midway through the meeting: "We have a sick man inside and everyone wants to cure him, but the doctor is outside."

Meanwhile, the Mexican daily *Uno más Uno* published the tape of a dictated letter that López Trujillo had addressed to Archbishop Luciano Cabral Duarte, president of CELAM's Social Action Department and leader of the conservative minority in the Brazilian hierarchy. López Trujillo described his maneuvers to gain control of the Puebla conference, and to link it to the March 1979 CELAM elections, which are "always dangerous." The Colombian characterized his former boss at CELAM, Argentine Cardinal Eduardo Pironio, as a weak director of the Confederation of Religious who had allowed CLAR too much influence. He mentioned as "upsetting" a proposal made by CLAR theologian Leonardo Boff of Brazil for a wider selection of lay ministers. He also criticized as detrimental to the conservative cause an invitation to Jesuit Superior General Pedro Arrupe to attend Puebla. "I am convinced," he said, "that these persons [or such progressives as Arrupe and Pironio] . . . must be told to their faces that they must change their attitude." López Trujillo urged Cabral Duarte to "prepare your airplane bombers for Puebla" and to "get into training just like boxers before entering the ring for a world match."[31]

Although López Trujillo claimed he had not actually sent the letter, he did not deny the tape's existence. Informed news sources reported that it was obtained, quite unintentionally, by a Mexican journalist who interviewed López Trujillo at his Bogotá headquarters: the CELAM secretary general had given the reporter what he thought was an empty tape in order to complete the recording of the interview. Three other letters were said to have been on the tape, but *Uno más Uno* published only one of these, from López Trujillo to Colombian Bishop Darío Castrillón, president of CELAM's Department of Social Communications, in which he complained that "a large number" of the journalists covering the conference were "opponents of the Church."[32]

The letter to Cabral Duarte was read by all within the conference, but elicited no public comment. A number of bishops privately deplored its publication, but they also agreed that it put López Trujillo's credibility in doubt. However, a widespread impression that "López is fried," as one of his associates put it, proved premature, particularly when he continued to enjoy the solid backing of Cardinal Baggio, co-president of the Puebla conference, who praised the Colombian for his high moral qualities. Indicative of the conservatives' continuing influence was the narrow defeat of Archbishop Cabral Duarte by Cardinal Arns for election to a key editorial committee, despite the bad publicity caused by the letter addressed to him.

As the meeting progressed, it became obvious that neither the conservatives nor the progressives had sufficient votes to swing the conference; as at Medellín, the floating middle would decide. Although the personal testimony of such men as Cardinal Arns and Bishop Proaño obviously helped the progressives' cause, as did the papers prepared by the liberation group, the conservatives had the advantage of the physical presence of like-minded theologians and sociologists within the conference. They "imposed their view," said a Dutch delegate, "by telling the bishops that the documents had to be written in proper theological language," a language that also happened to be conservative. Thus each side was defeated on some issues and victorious on others. Arns, for example, could not get approval for a document on torture; nor could the progressives persuade the other delegates to denounce specific cases of repression, despite the presence in Puebla of several human rights lobbies, including the relatives of people who had "disappeared" in Argentina and El Salvador. El Salvador's Archbishop Oscar Romero and Nicaragua's Archbishop Miguel Obando y Bravo, both of whom had received death threats because of their opposition to the military regimes in their countries, pleaded in vain with the bishops to denounce the Salvadoran and Nicaraguan governments. (Near tears, Romero said that if the bishops did not give him some sign of support, the military would "kill my church.") Over forty cardinals and bishops, representing eleven Latin-American countries, subsequently signed two letters, to Romero and to the Nicaraguan bishops, strongly denouncing tyranny, the abuse of human rights, and the persecution of the Church in those countries. But a majority of the delegates refused to incorporate such denunciations in the final document, on the ground that it should be sufficiently general to enable local bishops' conferences to make their own condemnations.

The conservatives, on the other hand, were forced to accept in the document a subtle approval of the theology of liberation. Similarly, attempts by the conservative Argentine delegation to ban the word "liberation" were rejected, as was the suggestion that the document take a softer line on military dictatorship. Bishop Proaño described these differences as an "obvious division between the church that relishes the soup of the people and another that looks at it from afar."*

After eighteen days of private debate and plenary sessions, often lasting until three and five in the morning, the exhausted delegates produced a fourth and final draft of the Puebla document, which was approved by all but one vote. A compromise that reflects the conflicts and ambiguities in the Church, it is nevertheless a confirmation of the commitment made at Medellín, with the same clear language of social criticism and an even stronger option for the poor. Although none of the Puebla delegates was entirely satisfied with the results, the two years that had gone into the document's preparation, and the conference itself, forced the bishops to clarify their position. Less prophetic than Medellín, and therefore more realistic, Puebla cannot be rejected, as Medellín was, with the allegation that the bishops did not know what they were signing: every line in the document was closely scrutinized. Then too, the Medellín delegates had been given a clearly prophetic document to work from in the conclusions of Vatican II, whereas at Puebla John Paul's as yet unassimilated speeches served as the principal framework. Thus no clear line connects the twenty-one themes in the document, and in some sections there is considerable repetition, even contradiction. Yet both the document and the tensions that produced it are signs of a vigorous Church. As CLAR Secretary General Patiño commented, "No one could say that there has been the peace of the cemetery here."

On the contrary, the great themes of Puebla—a commitment to the poor and to human rights—represent a major advance over Medellín. For whereas the Medellín document dedicated only

* This was literally true of the Roman Curia, which stayed at the luxurious Mesón del Angel, the most expensive hotel in Puebla; the Latin-American bishops were billeted in the seminary's small dormitory rooms.

three sections to these issues, the sequel written at Puebla is imbued throughout with an overwhelming concern for the poor and oppressed. Its opening statement sets the tone:

When we look at Latin America, what spectacle confronts us? It is not necessary to probe deeply. It is evident that the gap is constantly increasing between the many who have little and the few who have much. The values of our culture are threatened. The fundamental rights of man are violated. The devastation of wars continues. The great plans for man's betterment have not adequately solved the problems that challenge us. . . .

What have we to offer you, in the midst of the grave and complex problems of our time? In what way can we collaborate in the betterment of our Latin-American peoples, when some persist in maintaining their privileges at any cost, while others feel downtrodden and must struggle for their survival and a clear affirmation of their rights? . . .

Like Peter, when he was appealed to at the temple gates, we declare to you, as we consider the great structural challenges of our time, "we do not have gold or silver to offer you, but what we have, we give to you: In the name of Jesus of Nazareth, arise and walk." And the sufferer rose up and proclaimed the great works of the Lord. Here the poverty of Peter becomes the riches of Peter. . . .

Because we believe that a reexamination of the religious and moral behavior of men and women ought to be reflected in the political and economic processes of our countries, we invite all, without distinction of class, to accept and take up the cause of the poor, as if they were accepting and taking up their own cause, the very cause of Jesus Christ. . . .

The civilization of love rejects subservience and dependence which undermine the dignity of Latin America. We do not accept the condition of satellite of any country in the world, nor of their ideologies. We want to live fraternally with all because we repudiate all narrow nationalisms. But it is time that we as Latin Americans tell the developed countries not to immobilize us, not to put obstacles in the way of our progress, but rather to help us with greater encouragement to overcome the barriers of our underdevelopment by respecting our culture, our principles, our sovereignty, our identity, and our natural resources.

The Church's option for the poor is repeated throughout the document, an option for the peasants, workers, slum dwellers, Indians, Afro-Americans, and all those "who have no voice":

> From the heart of Latin America, a cry rises to the heavens ever louder and more imperative. It is the cry of a people who suffer and who demand justice, freedom, and respect for the fundamental rights of man. The Medellín conference reflected that cry. If it seemed deafening then, it now is clear, growing, impetuous, and, on occasion, threatening.
>
> In [the people's] pain and anxiety, the Church discerns a situation of social sin, of a magnitude all the greater because it occurs in countries which call themselves Catholic and have the capacity to change. . . .
>
> We identify, as the most devastating and humiliating scourge, the situation of inhuman poverty in which millions of Latin Americans live, with starvation wages, unemployment and underemployment, malnutrition, infant mortality, lack of adequate housing, health problems, and labor unrest.

These unjust economic, social, and political structures are the result of the "materialism" of Latin America's wealthy elites:

> To this situation of misery must be added the anxieties arising from the abuses of power, typical of military regimes. Anxiety because of systematic or selective repression, accompanied by informers, violations of privacy, undue pressures, torture, and exile . . . guerrilla violence, terrorism, and abductions by extremists of different ideologies. The lack of respect for human dignity is reflected by the lack of social participation on different levels . . . in the repression of unions and political movements.

Today the Church's mission is to help create "a more fraternal society which respects and defends human rights, in which goals are decided by consensus and not by force or violence, in which no one feels threatened by repression, terrorism, kidnappings, or torture, and structural changes are possible which assure just living conditions for the masses."

In this search for liberation, "the Church is overcoming a fear of freedom through its greater confidence in the force of truth, and in an education that teaches freedom and responsibility, instead of creating protective walls, prohibitions, and distrust."

Thus the poor are seen no longer as objects for paternalistic charity. As the principal victims of the ongoing repression in Latin America, says the document, the poor must also be the primary agents of change. The Church's role in this change is to be the companion—and servant—of the poor, of the majority, in their struggle to construct a more just and Christian society. To achieve this, bishops, priests, and nuns must divest themselves of their riches in order to live by the Gospel's strictures and become independent of all governments and political movements. "The Church has begun to fight on the side of the dispossessed sectors of society, who claim their rightful and integral development," says the document. "If in the past it gave special attention to certain social classes, the Church now has greater awareness of the evangelizing value of poverty that makes us available to build a more just and fraternal world." The Church wants no privileges in Latin America, says the document, save the right to express its prophetic voice. It "desires to become increasingly independent of the powers of the world, thus to enjoy a greater liberty to accomplish this evangelizing mission." "But the Church cannot be effective unless we pastors ourselves are challenged by the reality in our personal and institutional behavior. Consistency, creativity, courage, and total self-giving are demanded of us" because "our social conduct is an integral part of our following of Christ." In serving the poor and oppressed, the Church is "constantly challenged . . . and invited to conversion, . . . a conversion that carries with it the *need for an austere life-style.*"

In Puebla's rejection of privilege and worldly goods, the Latin-American Church has taken the lead in world Catholicism: it is the first church formally to renounce a tradition dating to Constantine when power became the principal basis for evangelization of the masses.

The document makes similarly important breakthroughs when it directs that all evangelizing efforts incorporate the culturally unique, and diverse, forms of Latin-American religious and social life, and when it places strong emphasis on the Church's duty to promote intermediate organizations, or the new "constructors" of Latin America, such as labor unions and peasant federations, thus to encourage greater participation by the people. The Christian grass-roots communities are mentioned as offering "hope and joy" of a new, more just society, but the document carefully avoids any ideological claim for such activism, basing its defense of the right of the poor to organize solely on the Gospel imperative for social justice.

Though criticized by the progressives for failing to go to the roots of Latin America's political and economic problems, the document unequivocally denounces capitalism, the multinationals, Latin America's wealthy classes, and the military regimes as atheistic, idolatrous, selfish, and inhuman:

> No one can deny the concentration of corporate, rural, and urban property in the hands of the few, thus making agrarian and urban reforms a pressing necessity. There also is a concentration of power in civil or military technocracies, which frustrates the people's desire to participate in government and denies the guarantees of a democratic state.

"We acknowledge, sadly, the presence of many oppressive regimes in our continent," continues the document, which are "subject to more powerful centers, operating at the international level [meaning the multinationals]." It is therefore imperative to establish a new international order that will respect the rights of nations to "*defend and promote* their interests in relationship to the multinationals" which "often look to their own interests at the expense of the nations in which they are located." Otherwise, warns the document, existing "international economic and political systems" may condemn the hemisphere to "permanent underdevelopment."

Communism is also criticized, but, in a surprising break with traditional Church policy, the document acknowledges that "the fear of Marxism impedes many from facing the oppressive reality of capitalism."

Not all of the text is that strongly worded; the sections on Christology, the laity, grass-roots communities, and popular piety are ambiguous and weak. Doctrinal aspects are confusing, with one section of the document, obviously prompted by the progressives, praising liberation theology for its encouragement to "live liberating evangelization in its fullness," while another section, written in conservative lingo, cautions against "ideologization of theological reflection when it uses as a point of reference a praxis with recourse to Marxist analysis."[33]

Aimed primarily at an audience of pastoral agents, including priests, nuns, and lay leaders, the Puebla document early underwent the same selective excerpting as did the Medellín Conclusions, only three sections of which—"Justice," "Peace," and "Poverty"—caught the world's attention. The doctrinal portions of the Puebla document, which the conservatives most influenced, will be of continuing interest to theologians, but as one bishop remarked, "Most people will say, well, that's theology, and won't read it." For the vast majority of laity and clergy, the most important sections deal with social, political, and economic issues, where the progressives prevailed. In that sense, the document is a "platform for a new social order in Latin America," as Brazil's Bishop Luciano Mendes contends.

Even before the Puebla meeting, those seeking change were committed to continue the struggle, whatever the document said, but as it turned out, far from hindering, many of its sections support the progressives. This was largely due to the leadership of such men as Arns, Proaño, and McGrath; to the work of the liberation theologians at Puebla; and to the recognition of the overwhelming reality of poverty and oppression in Latin America. Perhaps not unwittingly, Pope John Paul II played an unforeseen role in this drama, setting aside the speeches that had been prepared for him by Baggio's group in Rome to pronounce his own judgments on social injustice. *Get organized,* he had told the Indian peasants in Oaxaca. Private property has a "social mortgage," and expropriation, he warned the landowners, may be "the best measure." Such language had never been heard from an

Italian pontiff—it took a Pole, and a victim of communism, to call the capitalists to order.

In retrospect, it can be questioned whether the bishops would have made such a strong commitment to the poor and to human rights had it not been for John Paul's statements. Certainly his refusal to condemn liberation theology—or even to mention it— was a key factor in López Trujillo's failure to insert a denunciation in the document. And that had been the conservatives' primary purpose in convoking the Puebla meeting.

Neither Pope Paul nor John Paul I had intended to be present at the Puebla Conference, which was postponed by three months because of the latter's sudden death. In his letter to Archbishop Cabral Duarte, López Trujillo had said he supposed him to be "radiant with joy with the election" of John Paul II, since "he already has begun to speak very clearly" (meaning that López Trujillo expected the Pope to condemn liberation theology). He also told Cabral Duarte that it was imperative to hold the Puebla conference in order to clear up "confusions and ambiguities." Otherwise, CELAM elections would be held (in March 1979) "without an ideological platform."[34] The Pope's visit to Mexico, and its "conscientizing" effect on him when he was repeatedly confronted with the poverty of the masses in the overflowing streets and plazas, had effects that López Trujillo had in no way anticipated. Thus the conservatives' certain success at Puebla, carefully plotted for more than two years, turned into a victory for the progressives. Contrary to all predictions, the document produced by the conference is a worthy successor to Medellín.

On the other hand, the conservatives' well-oiled machinery worked perfectly in March, when López Trujillo was elected president of CELAM. Archbishop Cabral Duarte, the addressee of the famous letter, was elected first vice-president; Argentina's Antonio Quarracino, the conservative bishop of Avellaneda and former head of the CELAM Lay Department, its secretary general. Planned by Cardinal Baggio during the Puebla meeting, the elections were dominated by the almost unanimously conservative CELAM department heads and a largely right-wing delegation of bishops. For the Roman Curia, the outcome was crucial, since the church that produced the Puebla document is challenging the Vatican to renounce its power and wealth, including stocks in the multinationals,† in order to make a truly Gospel commitment to the poor.

The "business" of running the Church in Latin America therefore remains in the hands of such conservatives as López Trujillo and Vekemans, who enjoy wielding power. The elections must also have eased the fears of the West German bishops, who have close ties to Baggio, and of such right-wing groups in the United States as the DeRance Foundation, which had financed the attack on the "Church of the People." A "hard-nosed businessman," as Father Guillermo Saelman, the Dutch bishops' representative at Puebla, described him, López Trujillo now presides over the conservative redoubt he constructed with such care at CELAM, but that it is any stronger than the "wall of freedom" at Puebla is open to question. On the one hand, John Paul, a strong, relatively young Pope, is determined to put Christianity's stamp on an unjust world; on the other, a "horizontal" church based on the Christian communities, though still a minority, is the most dynamic, fastest-growing sector in the Latin-American Church. In the ongoing struggle between traditional and prophetic churches, López Trujillo's fortress could well become a tower of isolation, since CELAM has no executive authority to enforce its will and the Pope has committed himself to the cause of the people.

The struggle will doubtless be bitter, yet if only a fraction of the Puebla document's multiple objectives are achieved, such as a priority on education for the poor, the results will be far-reaching. As the Pope's amazing reception in Mexico showed, the power of the Church to sway Latin America is far greater than that of any government or political system.

"Another Iran"

It was precisely the fear of an unassessed religious power that led President Carter to order the CIA to intensify its watch on the Latin-American Church, according to a report on closed hearings of the Senate Foreign Relations Committee. Disclosed by Mexico City's influential center-right newspaper *Excelsior,* the report brought a letter of protest from Harvard theologian Harvey Cox

† See Chapters VII and XII, pp. 240 and 455.

and other representatives of the one hundred and fifty or so Americans gathered at Puebla, who described the order as "an insult to our neighbors, friends, and brother Christians in Latin America. What would President Carter think if a Latin-American government announced a plan to examine and study the churches of the United States, including his own church, the Baptist church? How would Carter like to have a spy in his Bible class? It is a very grave violation of the most basic human rights and of the heart of the Gospel."

Fausto Fernández Ponte, the newspaper's Washington correspondent, reported that Carter had ordered the agency to study and examine the movements of religious and lay dissidents in Latin America after committee members, noting U.S. "unpreparedness" regarding religious currents in Iran, expressed concern that a Latin-American country might become "another Iran." ("Study and examination" is a euphemism for infiltration and surveillance.) No intelligence representative on the National Security Council, it was said, could identify leaders or describe religious influences in Latin America. According to the report, one member of the committee inquired whether some groups that had been receiving aid from Moscow were now receiving aid from Rome!

Another reaction, similarly based on ignorance of the Latin-American Church, was sparked by an article, circulated in parts of the United States, by Malachi Martin, a conservative writer and author of *The Final Conclave,* who claimed that the Latin-American bishops were "seething with the will and the power to destabilize" the U. S. Government. Subsequently, a caller who identified himself as a Latin-American expert at the Pentagon telephoned the U. S. Catholic Conference to inquire about obtaining the Medellín Conclusions. He, too, mentioned "destabilization plans."[35]

Business groups were also concerned, among them spokesmen for the right-wing Puebla Chamber of Commerce, said to have ties to Mexican subsidiaries of the multinationals.[36] The businessmen's group charged that "Marxists in priests' dress" were to blame for "independent unions, economic instability, crazy strikes, and inflationary salaries." Among several "Marxist" bishops named was Peru's moderate Cardinal Juan Landázuri, the then vice-president of CELAM.[37]

The multinationals themselves remained discreetly silent, possibly because past experience had shown there were other means of influence. A decade earlier, for instance, a blue-ribbon committee that included the chairman of Citibank, the president of Ford Motor Company, and other business luminaries had by quiet maneuvering persuaded Pope Paul to deny that he had meant to debunk capitalism in his encyclical *Populorum Progressio,* one of the inspirations for Medellín. The "clarification" was necessary, said Citibank's then Chairman George C. Moore, because "it is nonsense for us to try to achieve economic development in Latin America if we haven't got the Church with us. If the priests are telling people to throw out businessmen, we [shall] have a rather hard time. . . . Everybody thinks we have self-interests, which we do. Now we want to convince the priests that economic democracy—I think that's probably a better expression than 'capitalism'—is in their interest. They are looking for social progress. This is how to get there. We're glad they're listening to us. Latin America is the key. If they can make economic democracy work there, then it can be applied elsewhere."[38]

As of 1979, when the bishops met at Puebla, "economic democracy" had produced a neocolonial system in which the multinational banks and corporations controlled the region's finances, the majority of its industrial exports and capital imports, and its natural resources. As to "social progress," both the Pope's speeches and the Puebla document clearly stated that there had been none.

"The dominant groups in the United States and their partners in Latin America want to maintain a social and political system that enables them to continue exploiting the people," said Gustavo Gutiérrez. "Because the Church is a strong institution in Latin America and a legitimate part of the social and political fabric, its commitment to the struggle of the people is a source of concern. They cannot attack religion frontally; they cannot say that the struggle to eat is atheistic, communist. But the multinationals are obviously worried."

And with good reason. By all accounts at Puebla, the 1980s will be a decade of nonviolent struggle, just as the 1960s were a period of change for blacks in the United States. "The blacks were talking about the same things a decade ago—the right to exist, to speak, to eat, and to think," said Gutiérrez. Such diverse spokesmen as CELAM's conservative theologian Pierre Bigo, Nicaragua's moderate Bishop Salvador Schlaefer, and Brazil's progressive Cardinal Arns agreed that the future struggle in Latin America will depend on such nonviolent measures as strikes, hunger strikes, and sit-ins, and solidarity marches and demonstrations, or all the techniques used by Martin Luther King and Mahatma Gandhi, the two leaders in contemporary history most respected by Latin-American churchmen. Even before Puebla, these techniques had been tried, with varying success, in Chile, Bolivia, and El Salvador, where local churches supported hunger strikes and sit-ins, and in Brazil and Peru, where the bishops defended the workers' right to strike.

There will also be more martyrs, the Puebla delegates predicted, men such as Rutilio Grande in El Salvador and Héctor Gallego in Panama, who were not politicians, said Bigo, but "who gave their lives defending their brothers." "Let's face it," said Archbishop McGrath, "anyone who preaches the Gospel in Latin America is going to be condemned." "Nowadays, we have to worry about a Church that is not persecuted," commented Plácido Erdozaín, a Spanish priest expelled from El Salvador by the country's military government.

The Puebla document also reflects the growing realization that the people of God and their pastors, like Christ himself, will have to pass through pain, suffering, and conflict to achieve redemption. "Jesus well knows what today is so often silenced in Latin America: that pain must be liberated through pain," says the document. "This means taking up the cross and converting it to the source of a paschal life."[39]

That the time has come seems in little doubt. The peasants cannot wait longer for justice, said Dom Ivo Lorscheiter, secretary general of the Brazilian Bishops' Conference. Even "if it costs them imprisonment or their lives, they must demonstrate their opposition to the exploitation they suffer, with audacious solutions that do not lead them to violence, nor yet force them to die in silence." Added Helder Cámara: "Those who think that we are acting too precipitously in [seeking] a change in structures in Latin America should remember that the continent has been waiting for nearly five centuries."

The principal base for this new thrust toward active nonviolence, the bishops said, will be the Christian grass-roots communities, which are growing by the thousands every year.‡ So, while the techniques will be those employed by King and Gandhi, they will capitalize on specific Latin-American traits, such as popular religiosity. The step-by-step progression from truth to justice is already outlined in the Puebla document. As Cardinal Arns explained, "The Church's foremost mission in this option for change is to establish the truth and to seek justice. Then it must help train the Christian communities to seek their own solutions. At the same time, the Church must encourage the universities, research institutions, and others to seek alternatives that are neither capitalist nor communist. And, finally, it must attempt to demonstrate to the privileged classes and those in power that Christian equality, based on the principle that we are all sons of God, produces a broader development in both the individual and society."

There will be no turning back in this march. "Puebla is not the end," announces the introduction to the document. "The process begun cannot be concluded with the publication of a document. Rather, it is the beginning of a new era in the development of our ecclesiastical life in Latin America.

"These pages have the force of a new directive, that which Christ gives to us: 'Go and preach the Gospel to all peoples.' "[40]

‡ As of 1979, there were over 100,000 such communities in Latin America, according to the Mexico-based Federation of Christian Communities.

CHAPTER XII

THE U.S. CONNECTION

Come, Lord, do not smile and say you are already with us. Millions do not know You and to us who do, what is the difference? What is the point of Your presence if our lives do not alter?

Dom Helder Cámara,
Archbishop of Recife,
Brazil[1]

Can Americans understand what is happening to their neighbors, the Latin Americans wonder. The two societies are so different. True, there are poor people in the United States, and economic and social prejudice, but not on the scale of Latin America, with its sharp class divisions. Minority groups in the United States have protested, though usually on racial or sexual grounds. In Latin America, in contrast, race and sex are less important than a person's social condition, his or her place in a wealthy minority or among the abundant poor. Black theology and women's liberation seem esoteric to the Latin Americans, who are looking at the bigger picture of poverty and repression. Conversely the Latin Americans' theology of liberation can be understood only in the context of a region where two thirds of the people live in desperate poverty.

Nevertheless, there have been attempts at comprehension, the principal bridge being the United States' 16 million Hispanos, who can speak to both worlds. Most of these people either fled poverty in their own countries or grew up with economic and racial prejudice in the United States. Unlike the average white, middle-class American, they have had a first-hand experience of poverty.

Already a growing cultural influence in the United States, the Hispano population will double by the end of the century, thereby replacing blacks as the largest minority in the country. Unlike other minorities that have been absorbed into the American melting pot, the Spanish-speaking people have preserved much of their cultural heritage, less because they wanted to than because they were rejected on racial grounds by the white American. Typical of this prejudice was the experience of El Paso's Bishop Patricio Flores. A former migrant worker, Flores was repeatedly rejected by his local seminary because he was a Mexican-American.[2] As one Chicano journalist put it, "When I was growing up Catholic, I thought religion was white-faced."[3]

Like the poor in Latin America, the Hispanos, and the Mexican-Americans in particular, began to reflect on the cause and effect of social and economic oppression. They saw that they were racial and cultural hybrids, neither Latin Americans nor Anglos, but "at the intersection of two histories, two nations, two cultures, two languages converging, colliding, blending, embracing. . . ."[4] Such reflection was the beginning of cultural pride and of a more militant attitude toward Anglo institutions, including the Catholic Church. Hispanos comprise a quarter of the Catholics in the United States, but they are woefully shortchanged in the hierarchy and at the clerical level. Only after two hundred Hispano priests founded the PADRES movement in 1969 did the U.S. Church begin to pay attention to its Spanish-speaking minority. One of the first demands of the PADRES was for Hispano bishops, and by 1977 five had been appointed, mostly in the Southwest. The number is still small, considering the size of the Spanish-speaking congregation,* but at least a start has been made. The presence of Hispano bishops helped to revive the Hispanos' interest in their Church. More than thirteen thousand attended the consecration of Santa Fe's Archbishop Roberto Sánchez, a turnout unmatched at

* In contrast, Irish-Americans, who represent 17 percent of U.S. Catholics, have sixty-seven bishops.

any other episcopal consecration. Hispano vocations are also on the rise; in Los Angeles, 40 percent of those studying for the priesthood in 1978 were Spanish-speaking.[5]

Catholic support of Cesar Chávez's struggle on behalf of farm workers also brought Hispanos back to the Church, particularly the young, who had been alienated by its refusal to concern itself with social causes. Chávez said he "would have been surprised if I had not gotten their support all these years" because such support was a Christian duty. "We don't ask for more cathedrals," he said. "We don't ask for bigger churches or fine gifts. We ask for its presence with us, beside us, as Christ among us. We ask the Church to sacrifice with the people for social change, for justice, and for love of brother. We don't ask for words. We ask for deeds. We don't ask for paternalism. We ask for service."[6]

Chávez's words were echoed in many Hispano communities, where the Catholic Church was asked to use its prestige and influence to help an impoverished minority. The terms of the plea were those heard in Latin America. The Church will be the deciding factor in social change, predicted Gil Cano, a founder of the National Chicano Moratorium Committee.[7]

The use of identical language is not accidental. One of the most influential organizations in the Hispano Church, the Mexican American Cultural Center, has a direct link with the progressive members of the Latin-American Church. Founded in 1971 in San Antonio, Texas, the center has filled a need neglected by Catholic universities and other centers of learning that had provided no theological or pastoral guidelines for the Hispanos' Church. Because of the Latin Americans' rich experience in this area, they were invited to give courses to Anglo and Hispano religious and laity at the center. Thus the theology of liberation passed to the United States, just as *cursillos* (marriage encounters aimed at giving a deeper spiritual meaning to married life) had infiltrated the U.S. Church via Latin America and Spain.

The center is a particularly fertile field for cultural exchange, and not just because of its Hispano origins. Father Virgilio Elizondo, the center's director, went to Latin America to learn what the Latins were doing in theology and pastoral work. Soon a procession of Anglo and Hispano priests and nuns was heading south to study. Because of this experience, they have contributed substantially to the dialogue between the religious of North and South America. The Hispano bishops are a similar link between hierarchies. Four of the men arrested by the military during the bishops' 1976 meeting in Riobamba, Ecuador, were Hispano bishops, and thus could give firsthand testimony of repression in Latin America.†

Thanks to the influence of the Hispanos and to U.S. missionaries who had worked in Latin America, the U.S. hierarchy has begun to shed its cautious approach to Latin-American affairs, even in such controversial matters as a new Panama Canal treaty, which the bishops supported. But the U.S. Church, in the opinion of many Latin Americans, has a long way to go before it reaches its potential. With eleven cardinals (only Italy has more), it has a decisive weight in the councils of the Vatican. Moreover, it belongs to the richest, most powerful country in the world. Yet the U.S. Church seems more interested in finance and efficient management than in taking a prophetic stand for justice, said Father Jesús García, a former member of the Vatican Justice and Peace Commission and director of the Mexican Catholic Social Secretariat:

The first thing that strikes an outsider looking at the U.S. Church is the lavishness and comfort of its chancery buildings, rectories, schools, and convents. Those located in posh neighborhoods look like well-adjusted components (and hence props) of the surrounding affluent society. As for Church institutions in poor neighborhoods, especially in the big cities, where minority groups of Mexicans, Puerto Ricans, and blacks abound, the ecclesiastical and religious lifestyle led in them contrasts sharply with the prevailing poverty. One gets the impression that the chief emphasis in these parishes is on punctuality and dispatch in dealing with persons, sacraments, and records. The neatness and completeness of files for parish and family records, the smart decorum of Masses and sacramental celebrations, and an impeccable financial management seem to exhaust many parishes' pastoral zeal and initiative.

† See Chapter V, pp. 137–38.

The sermons given in them, their liturgical celebrations, and financial efficiency seem to have precious little effect on the social, racial, political, or civic problems of the neighborhood, the nation, or internationally. And if they do have some effect, does it reflect the spirit of the Gospel? Or are these human and social problems treated as technical matters, things quite apart from the Church's faith and preaching, its liturgy and pastoral care? Are they handled with a merely humanitarian Rotary Club approach, rather than because of their vital connection with God's saving plan?

The Church in the United States does not seem to notice the connection between its Christian faith and that plan, on the one hand, and its chance (and obligation) to help us out of our grinding distress, on the other. We would like to see the U.S. Church's energies and creativity used prophetically, to criticize the type of society and the kind of development its countrymen are spreading around the globe. U.S. Catholics have certainly been most generous in supplying both funds and personnel to the whole world, but most of them seem quite unaware of the unique responsibility they bear because of their country's expansionism, its economic, political, and military imperialism and hegemony. Thus their aid, important and beyond a doubt earnestly intended, seems an insignificant repayment for the immense profits and resources that the United States takes from the Third World, a conscience tranquilizer against remorse over basic structural wrongs.

It isn't cash that the Third World wants from the United States and its Church, but a questioning of—and a change in—the worldwide economic and political setup that the United States maintains. For the present international system is why we are dependent, it is how we are exploited.[8]

Harsh words, yet some Christians in the United States are saying the same, and not just about Catholicism—Protestantism is also on the carpet. Perhaps one reason why so many Americans are disaffected by organized religion, say these critics, is that the churches have lost sight of Christianity's original message. According to the U. S. Conference of Catholic Religious Superiors, substance has been sacrificed to formality. "U.S. Catholics, though they were and still are a minority group, looked upon with some suspicion in a society where the Protestant ethic is dominant, nevertheless wanted very much to succeed and be accepted," said the men superiors. "Such was the case, too, for U.S. religious men. They prized as highly as the majority of U.S. citizens material success, building programs, efficient techniques. Thus they came to enjoy the 'good life' in the United States, had confidence in the national goals and aspirations, and did not see fully the need to challenge and confront the prevailing norms as thoughtful witnesses to the Gospel's imperatives. Rarely did they challenge the false gods and false values of Western civilization. In specific religious matters, there was a tendency to be legalistic and to moralize, with little concern for deeper questions of substance and spirit, so long as certain forms were observed.

"But now [U.S. religious] are beginning to awaken under the influence of Watergate, the Vietnam War . . . and an awareness that the American people consume 40 per cent of the world's resources though they represent only 6 per cent of its population. They are beginning to discover that vows lose their meaning unless the community in which they live tries to challenge society's dehumanizing elements."[9]

In the opinion of Catholic and Protestant critics, the consumer society has reduced biblical faith to a private relationship similar to that of the Latin American and his favorite saint—only in the American's case the saint is material success. John Dewey made the same point nearly half a century earlier: "Nowhere in the world at any time has religion been so throughly respectable as with us and so nearly totally disconnected from life. . . . The glorification of religion as setting the final seal of approval on pecuniary success, and the adoption by churches of the latest devices of the movies and the advertiser, approach too close to the obscene." So ingrained has this habit become, reported Protestant critic Frederick Herzog, that there are ministers who actually believe that God is a capitalist.[10] And with good reason: the U.S. churches have obtained staggering material wealth from capitalism. The Catholic Church alone owns some $25 billion in real estate, stocks, and bonds, not including the assets of individual religious communities, such as the Society of Jesus, with estimated assets of $250 million.[11] The concern for material security and growth clearly limits the churches' capacity to assume a critical role in U.S. society. As one fund raiser for a U.S. Catholic mission society bluntly put it, too much emphasis on social causes, particularly when they question the structures of capitalism, antagonizes potential contributors.

That is also true for the Protestant churches, most of which have corporate executives on their boards and rely on members of the country's largest firms to guide them in their investments. Eight main-line Protestant denominations were investors in Gulf Oil, which was prosecuted for paying bribes in Bolivia. Six were also stockholders in Merck, which was involved in the AID rip-off of the U.S. taxpayer.‡ The Episcopalian and Presbyterian churches held stock in Kennecott Copper, one of the principal beneficiaries of the military coup in Chile.[12] The United Church of Christ's Board for World Ministries bought 1,000 shares of the Rockefeller-owned International Basic Economy Corporation (IBEC), which owns supermarkets, poultry, chemicals, and mutual funds in the developing countries. Incredibly, the board also loaned the multimillion-dollar enterprise $250,000. Still more incredibly, it claimed that this transaction was done out of a "Christian obligation" to the developing nations, such obligations being, of course, subject to "provision of maximum return consistent with due prudence with reference to safeguarding of principal," said the board.*[13]

But increasing numbers of Protestants and Catholics are questioning religion's marriage to corporate mammon. Religious groups have begun to use their stockholdings to demand some moral accounting from the companies, particularly those operating in the poorer countries. Ten major Catholic organizations have formed a traveling symposium on "responsible investment" to urge bishops, major superiors, chancellors, and the like to use their financial leverage for effective change in corporate decisions, policies, and practices. The National Council of Churches is moving in a similar direction.

‡ See Chapter VII, pp. 209–10.
* The Vatican also holds sizable stock in such multinationals as General Motors, General Electric, Shell, Gulf Oil, Bethlehem Steel, IBM, TWA, and Pan American. (Malachi Martin, *The Final Conclave* [Briarcliff Manor, N.Y.: Stein & Day, 1978], p. 29; *"Escándalo Financiero"* [Rome: Associated Press, Aug. 31, 1978].)

Though admittedly only a beginning, such action is viewed as a panacea for a more complex problem by some Catholics and Protestants, who believe a whole reeducation is needed, to encourage Americans to face up to their responsibilities, in their own country as well as abroad. Frederick Herzog called the process "consciousness-altering," instead of consciousness-raising.[14]

It isn't pleasant to be called an oppressor, yet that is how many people in Latin America see the United States. And there is considerable documented evidence to support the Latin Americans' point of view—in the Pentagon's encouragement of military regimes, in the CIA's interference in Latin-American political affairs, and in corporate industry's business practices. Critical Christians are asking Americans to look at the record and reflect on it. "Whether we like it or not, to be white Americans in the latter part of the twentieth century is to be part of that group in the world that has the most power, influence, and affluence," wrote Robert McAfee Brown, one of the most eloquent spokesmen for a new moral order. "The record is pretty clear that all these things are used for self-aggrandizement rather than for the welfare of others. Of those who have much, the Scriptures inform us, much shall be required. There are still ways within a democratic society that individuals, by banding together, can have an effect on policy, and no argument that totally disengages us from the actions of our nation is finally defensible."[15]

Part of the problem, from the religious point of view, is that Americans have lost touch, in their language and concepts, with the biblical Christ. Put more harshly, in Philip Wylie's assessment of the pulpiteers in *Generation of Vipers:* "These simpering or clamorous windbags preach Christ the Redeemer, Christ the meek and mild, Christ who died for your sins, Christ who suffered agonies unparalleled, Christ the mystical, Christ the worker of miracles . . . Christ the simple man, Christ the great academic philosopher, Christ the Torquemada of Jehovah, Christ the prince of peace, Christ the tolerator of adultery, Christ the bigot, the spigot, the wellspring of joy and man of sorrows, Christ the scourge of the temple, Christ the physician, Christ the know-it-all, Christ the Miss fix-it, Christ the mineral spring, Christ the autocrat of the breakfast table, and bingo on Friday night. They never preach, teach, screech, or beseech the truth, come hell or holy water."

Americans also have lost touch with their past, in this view. They have forgotten that the United States was conceived as a refuge for the rejected of the world—the persecuted, the condemned, the poor. However romantic it may sound today, the Statue of Liberty still recalls those origins: "Give me your tired, your poor . . . the wretched refuse of your teeming shore."[16] In the process Americans have somehow lost the will to change, not only in their relations with other people in distant lands but also in their own country. "Knowledge of our socioeconomic dilemmas is widely disseminated, certainly among the intelligentsia," said Herzog. "The horror is, we do not have the will to get well. Because of our blind spot to exploitation, we are blind all around to the causes of rising crime, the drug problem, etc."

El Paso's Bishop Flores agreed: "We may shed tears at the murders at Southern University in Louisiana, at the sight of a child screaming from napalm burns, at the eighty-dollar annual income of a family in one of the nations of Latin America," he told the ninth General Assembly of the U.S. National Council of Churches. "Often we give thanks for our blessings and say: 'All the rest is just too complex to deal with.' We permit the injustice that imprisons both the affluent and the poor to go on and on.

"The use of capital and the development of a corporate economy have without doubt procured great benefits for mankind. But it has become increasingly evident that large corporations reaching across national boundaries drain natural resources and labor from poor countries primarily for the benefit of a small proportion of affluent people in the world. Such an ordering of a world economy is immoral and must be rejected and fought by the Church. It is not sufficient to weep for the priest who is martyred by the regime in Brazil, without acting to prevent the complicity of the United States of America in that act of murder. The system as we know it holds in bondage, not only those who are exploited to maintain the flow of wealth largely in one direction, but it also holds in the bondage of unslaked thirst for goods and power and sense of superiority those who reap the benefits.

"Typically, when we speak of modern corporate life, we are speaking of companies where ownership is so diversified that corporate managers are really responsible to no one. Our government has proved unable to regulate corporate life to produce for the benefit of all; indeed, if one looks at the large corporation and its alliance with the military, or its behavior overseas, it is apparent that government and corporate managers are hand in glove. Even at home it is representatives of capital management who most often sit on and control the very regulatory agencies that were once designed to see that the corporation served society.

"Some say the system is not perfect, but that it is the best ever devised by man. Well, it is not perfect. Man must do better, or the large corporation, managed by men shielded from public control, will otherwise be the imperialism of the twenty-first century."[17]

And how escape this vision? Critical Christians argue with Flores that it must begin with the system of education. The bishop gives the example of the educational problems in Texas, citing the state government's own report:

> Most Texans recognize the role of the public schools in building socially acceptable behavior. . . . But it is clear that traditional forms and methods have failed to equip the disadvantaged for constructive citizenship in modern complex society. That failure has contributed heavily to such crucial problems as delinquency, unemployment, and soaring welfare costs.

"Examples like this abound throughout the United States," said Bishop Flores. "Education in the West has become a handmaiden of corporate production, of a bourgeois society, of a society bent on acquisition. Western education imprisons the affluent in a psychology of acquisitiveness and exclusivity of moral vision, and at the same time perpetuates the dominance of the affluent over the poor."[18]

Yet to acknowledge that "our entire social structure is sick at the core is not only a message we may not like, but a message with which we may not, in fact, be able to come to terms," warned Robert McAfee Brown. "It may challenge the social legitimacy of the kind of work we do to earn our incomes, it may leave us with the nagging question of why we are entitled to such splendid homes when most of the human family lives in substandard dwellings, and it may leave us unsure that the creation of a few splendid human relationships is really a sufficient answer to the not-so-splendid squalor that continues unchallenged in the midst of those relationships."

Still, such unease is a step toward rethinking faith and of challenging institutions and goals previously taken for granted. And it is this, more than aid or personnel, that the Latin American Church is seeking from the United States. Giving up a hamburger will not provide grain for people who need it unless there is a real change in the distribution system. Likewise, well-intentioned Peace Corps members are neither needed nor wanted in a Latin-American slum, any more than they are in a black ghetto in the United States. The challenge is elsewhere, in white America, where power and affluence are concentrated.

Commitment to change is not easy, as the Church of Martyrs has learned in Latin America. But it was always thus. As Gabriel told Joseph, in Auden's *For the Time Being:*

> To choose what is difficult
> all one's days
> as if it were easy,
> that is faith.

APPENDIX

MARTYR SURVEY

The following survey is of necessity a partial list of ecclesiastical and lay martyrs in Latin America during the period between 1964 and 1978. Because of censorship and poor communications, particularly in rural areas, detailed information is not available on the thousands of people threatened, arrested, tortured, kidnapped, exiled, or murdered during a time of rising repression. This is particularly true of the laity, many of whom do not even figure in official statistics, nameless Latin Americans whose disappearance or death is denied by the military regimes. Thus the survey includes only well-known Christian lay leaders, such as the heads of *comunidades de base*, although, again, it is impossible to verify the number who have died or suffered in countries where the *comunidades* are under military attack, as in El Salvador, Honduras, and Guatemala.

It is likewise impossible to cite exact statistics on the number of people forced to flee their countries, as for example the exodus from Argentina and Chile.

Most of the martyrs listed are Catholics, although Protestants have also suffered repression in some countries, including Uruguay and Chile. Only the dead have been named, to protect the living.

While the majority of the statistics cover the decade between Medellín and Puebla, or 1968 to 1978, the survey dates to 1964 to include the repression in Brazil arising from the military coup that year. An accompanying graph shows the periods of particularly harsh repression against the Catholic Church, starting in 1969–70 and peaking in 1975–77.

Sources for the survey include Church and human rights groups, local and foreign publications, particularly the Paris-based Bureau of Information on Latin America (DIAL), a church-related agency directed by Charles Antoine, a well-known writer on Latin-American religious affairs. DIAL also prepared the graph on repression.

Symbols: Mgr. . . . . Bishop
Name without symbol . . . . Priest (or Pastor)
o . . . . Religious
oo . . . . Seminarian
+ . . . . Layman (+o: woman)
++ . . . . Ex-priest

TABLE ONE

List of Murdered Bishops, Priests, Religious, and Laity

ARGENTINA	1974	C. Mujica
	1975	C. Dorñak
		++H. Ferreiros
	1976	F. Soares
		J. Tedeschi
		A. Kelly
		P. Duffau
		A. Leacen
		ooJ. Barletti
		ooS. Barbeito
		G. Longueville
		C. Díaz Murias
		Mgr. E. Angelelli
	1977	+E. Kasseman
		+R. Walsh
	1978	Mgr. H. Ponce de León
		oA. Domon
		oR. Duquet
BOLIVIA	1970	+N. Paz Zamora (joined guerrilla band)
	1971	M. Lefebvre
	1977	R. Herman
BRAZIL	1969	A. Henrique Pereira Neto
	1972	ooW. Bolzan
	1976	J. B. Penido Burnier
		R. Lukembein
		A. Pierobon
CHILE	1973	J. Alsina
		M. Woodward
		G. Poblete
		+oE. Reyes V.
COLOMBIA	1966	C. Torres (joined guerrilla band)
	1974	M. Pérez (joined guerrilla band)
	1976	L. Rueda (joined guerrilla band)
		F. Agudelo (joined guerrilla band)

DOMINICAN REPUBLIC	1965	A. MacKinnon
	1977	$+_0$F. Muñoz
ECUADOR	1974	$+$L. Condo
EL SALVADOR	1972	N. Rodríguez
	1977	R. Grande
		$+$M. Solórzano
		$+$N. R. Lemus
		A. Navarro Oviedo
		$+$L. Torres
		$+$M. Baranhona (tortured)
		$+$F. Chacón
		$+$S. Vásquez
		$+_0$F. Puerta
		$+_0$F. Delgado (tortured)
	1978	$+$O. Guardado
		$+$M. Guardado
		$+$T. Vásquez
		E. Barrera (tortured)
GUATEMALA	1978	H. López
HONDURAS	1975	I. Betancur (tortured)
		J. Cypher (tortured)
		$+_0$M. E. Bolívar
		$+_0$R. García
		$+$O. Ortiz
		$+$B. Rivera
		$+$J. B. Montoya
		$+$L. Coleman
		$+$R. Andrade
		$+$A. Figuero
		$+$F. Cruz
		$+$A. Gómez
		$+$M. Aguilera
		$+$F. Colindres
MEXICO	1977	R. Aguilar
		R. Escamilla
NICARAGUA	1977	$+$R. Videa
		G. García (joined guerrilla band)
	1978	C. Luis
PANAMA	1971	H. Gallego (kidnapped)
	1974	G. Reimer (Protestant missionary)
PARAGUAY	1976	$+$M. Arzamendi (tortured)
URUGUAY	1969	I. Rosa (joined guerrilla band)
		$+$J. Sposito
		H. Jurado (Methodist) (tortured)
VENEZUELA	1975	M. Soto

TABLE TWO

Quantitative Survey of Repression against the Catholic Church, 1964–1978

		Threats/ Defamation	Arrested	Tortured	Killed	Kidnapped/ Disappeared	Exiled/ Expelled
Total *	:	314	935	73	79	37	288
Bishops	:	60	35	2	2	2	3
Priests	:	118	485	46	41 †	11	253‡
Religious	:	18	44	7	3	3	26
Laity	:	12	371	18	33	21	6
Groups/Organ.	:	64	–	–	–	–	–

* In some cases the total is higher than the sum of individuals because over the years the same person suffered the same type of repression.

† Six were killed while fighting with guerrilla groups.

‡ Over 100 priests were forced to leave Chile; 7 priests were refused reentry into Venezuela because of the local hierarchy's decision.

TABLE THREE

Quantitative Survey by Country

ARGENTINA		Threats/ Defamation	Arrested	Tortured	Killed	Kidnapped/ Disappeared	Exiled/ Expelled
Total	:	19*	93	11	18	9	2†
Bishops	:	4	–	–	2	–	–
Priests	:	12	89	7	11	2	1
Religious	:	1	1	3	2	2	–
Laity	:	–	3	1	3 ‡	5	1

BOLIVIA							
Total	:	16	38	2	3	–	12
Bishops	:	2	–	–	–	–	–
Priests	:	6	28	1	2	–	11
Religious	:	–	9	1	–	–	1
Laity	:	–	–	–	1	–	–
Groups/Organ.	:	6	–	–	–	–	–

BRAZIL							
Total	:	107	488	31	5	11	28
Bishops	:	28	11	2	–	1	–
Priests	:	27	185	23	4	1	25
Religious	:	12	19	1	1	1	2
Laity	:	12	273	5	–	8	1
Groups/Organ.	:	14	–	–	–	–	–

See Note* in Table Two.

† Precise statistics on priests and religious forced to leave the country because of threats to their lives are not available.

‡ Including one ex-priest.

CHILE

Total	:	10	77	1	4	2	117
Bishops	:	4	1	–	–	–	1
Priests	:	–	63	–	3	2	108*
Religious	:	–	1	–	–	–	6
Laity	:	–	12	1	1	–	2
Groups/Organ.:		2	–	–	–	–	–

COLOMBIA

Total	:	14	22	–	4	–	25
Bishops	:	3	–	–	–	–	–
Priests	:	3	21	–	4†	–	23
Religious	:	1	1	–	–	–	2
Groups/Organ.:		5	–	–	–	–	–

CUBA

Total	:	–	–	–	–	–	1
Bishops	:	–	–	–	–	–	1

DOMINICAN REPUBLIC

Total	:	10	2	–	2	–	4
Bishops	:	1	–	–	–	–	–
Priests	:	9	2	–	1	–	2
Religious	:	–	–	–	–	–	2
Laity	:	–	–	–	1	–	–

ECUADOR

Total	:	9	66	–	1	1	3
Bishops	:	1	17	–	–	–	–
Priests	:	5	30	–	–	1	3
Religious	:	–	5	–	–	–	–
Laity	:	–	14	–	1	–	–
Groups/Organ.:		1	–	–	–	–	–

EL SALVADOR

Total	:	30	13	9	15	8	21
Bishops	:	4	–	–	–	–	–
Priests	:	19	5	4	4	–	19
Religious	:	–	–	–	–	–	2
Laity	:	–	8	5	11	8	–
Groups/Organ.:		7	–	–	–	–	–

* The majority were forced to leave because of threats to their lives.
† Joined the guerrillas.

	Threats/ Defamation	Arrested	Tortured	Killed	Kidnapped/ Disappeared	Exiled/ Expelled
GUATEMALA						
Total :	5	2	–	1	1	8
Bishops :	–	–	–	–	1	–
Priests :	3	1	–	1	–	7
Religious :	–	1	–	–	–	1
Groups/Organ.:	1	–	–	–	–	–
GUYANA						
Total :	–	–	–	–	–	1
Priests :	–	–	–	–	–	1
HAITI						
Total :	–	–	–	–	–	11
Priests :	–	–	–	–	–	10
Laity :	–	–	–	–	–	1
HONDURAS						
Total :	8	29	3	14	3	6
Bishops :	1	–	–	–	–	–
Priests :	3	17	3	2	3	6
Religious :	–	4	–	–	–	–
Laity :	–	8	–	12	–	–
Groups/Organ.:	3	–	–	–	–	–
MEXICO						
Total :	15	26	3	2	–	1
Bishops :	6	5	–	–	–	–
Priests :	4	4	3	2	–	1
Laity :	–	17	–	–	–	–
Groups/Organ.:	1	–	–	–	–	–
NICARAGUA						
Total :	14	12	–	3	–	7
Bishops :	1	–	–	–	–	–
Priests :	6	1	–	2*	–	7
Religious :	3	–	–	–	–	–
Laity :	–	11	–	1	–	–
Groups/Organ.:	5	–	–	–	–	–

* One belonged to a guerrilla group.

PANAMA

	1	2	3	4	5	6
Total :	3	–	–	2	1	–
Bishops :	1	–	–	–	–	–
Priests :	1	–	–	2	1	–
Groups/Organ.:	1	–	–	–	–	–

PARAGUAY

	1	2	3	4	5	6
Total :	29	33	7	1	–	17
Bishops :	3	–	–	–	–	–
Priests :	13	16	1	–	–	14
Religious :	1	1	–	–	–	3
Laity :	–	16	6	1	–	–
Groups/Organ.:	7	–	–	–	–	–

PERU

	1	2	3	4	5	6
Total :	3	5	–	–	–	3
Bishops :	–	1	–	–	–	–
Priests :	3	2	–	–	–	3
Laity :	–	2	–	–	–	–

URUGUAY

	1	2	3	4	5	6
Total :	18	29	6	3	1	8
Bishops :	2	–	–	–	–	1
Priests :	3	20	4	2*	1	2
Religious :	–	2	2	–	–	4
Laity :	–	7	–	1	–	1
Groups/Organ.:	10	–	–	–	–	–

VENEZUELA

	1	2	3	4	5	6
Total :	2	1	–	1	–	13
Priests :	1	1	–	1	–	10†
Religious :	–	–	–	–	–	3
Groups/Organ.:	1	–	–	–	–	–

* One joined a guerrilla group.
† Seven were expelled on the decision of the local hierarchy.

TABLE FOUR

Periods of Intense Repression Against the Church

SAMPLE U.S. COURSE

The following is an outline of a Pentagon course for Latin-American military officers on "Utilization and Containment of Rumors." It covers white, gray, and black propaganda but emphasizes black propaganda. The supposed aim of the course is to combat "subversion"; in fact, the techniques described have been used to censor the press, create fear and mistrust among the civilian population, and whitewash the crimes of the military. The Somoza government in Nicaragua and the Uruguayan and Argentine regimes in South America proved particularly adept at "Utilization and Containment of Rumors."

A copy of the course was published by the North American Congress on Latin America in "The Pentagon's Protégés" (Jan. 1, 1976), an in-depth study of U.S. military penetration of Latin America. Copies of this and other courses taught at the School of the Americas in the Panama Canal Zone have also appeared in the Jesuit magazine *Diálogo Social,* published in Panama City.

A. Introduction

   1. *Objective:* To teach the dynamic of the procedure for disseminating rumors.

   2. *Reasons:* Through this knowledge, to be able to employ or control rumors as the circumstance or situation demands.

B. Explanation

   1. *Generalities*
     • Recall the concept of Psychological Operations: "Utilization of Propaganda" and other means of influencing ideas, attitudes, and behavior of hostile elements, neutrals, and friends in such a way as to gain their support in carrying out their objectives.
     • *Classes of propaganda:* gray, white, and black propaganda: radio transmission, cartoons (comics), leaflets, posters, and . . .

• *The rumor* (*definition*)

"Specific or generalized proposition, to make someone believe in a thing without there being any concrete proof. Its diffusion is generally verbal, by word of mouth."

2. *Characteristics*

• Its source is not obvious, thus avoiding the resistance encountered by white propaganda efforts.

• It doesn't require a normal system of communication, thus its importance increases with the scarcity of such means.

• This technique is more important the lower the literacy rate.

• By divulging it in a situation of friendly confidence it tends to seem more trustworthy.

• Objective verification is generally difficult, since its content is open to varying interpretation depending on the knowledge, values, and attitudes of the individual.

3. *Basic Law of the Rumor*

PR=I×A.

PR=Power of the rumor.

I=Importance of the theme it refers to.

A=Ambiguity present, lack of concrete facts that would allow its negation or verification.

4. *Motivations for the Rumor*

• Three basic emotional impulses constitute it.

• *Fear.*

• The rumor tends to impart reality to the fearful anticipation of people who are "ready for the worst."

• *Objective:* To cause fear and terror; to demoralize.

• *Hope*

For people with a sense of frustration motivated by unfulfilled desire, the rumor relieves the tension of wishing.

• *Objective:* Complacency, to later deal a blow to the morale by catching them off guard.

• *Hatred*

For disillusioned persons or those with frustrated desires it tends to provide an escape by giving them someone to blame, subject to suspicions, hatreds, or prejudices.

• *Objective:* To create internal disunity in order to debilitate the activity.

5. *Reasons for Dissemination of Rumors*

• In an atmosphere of crisis or tension caused by an emergency

situation, the individual is predisposed to listen to and repeat whatever he hears, whether it be a rumor or true information.
• Some specific reasons:
• *Provide a response to important questions*
The insurrection sharpens the interest of the public, and the rumor gives an answer to problems about which you can't give complete information for the moment. When the situation is so complex that information about it is difficult to understand, the rumor distorts it and presents it in a simple form.
• *Provides an excuse for behavior*
PROJECTION IS ONE OF THE MOST POWERFUL DEFENSE MECHANISMS FOR AVOIDING THE PANGS OF CONSCIENCE: FOR THIS REASON YOU CIRCU-LATE A RUMOR THAT PRESENTS ANOTHER PERSON DOING SOMETHING MORE OR LESS CENSURABLE. [Emphasis added.]
• *Provides a means of escaping one's own responsibilities*
IT IS USED TO EXPRESS HATRED OR HOSTILITY OPENLY, WITHOUT HAVING TO ASSUME THE IN-HERENT RESPONSIBILITIES. [Emphasis added.]
• *Give the teller a sense of importance*
The prestige of a person increases when in a time of doubt or confusion he can provide "information." When the information isn't important enough the agent dramatizes or exaggerates it. The latter is characteristic of the rumor.

6. *Methods of Dissemination*
   • *Use of agents*
   Friends in the affected region originate the rumor within the group.
   • *Use of means of communication*
   Generally by means of questions that insinuate their responses. They can be easily distorted.
   • *Use of sympathizers*
   Encourage sympathizers to disseminate stories. Also subject to distortions.

7. *Opportunity*
   • *Little information about important events.* [READ PRESS CENSORSHIP.]
   • *Breakdown of formal means of communication.* [READ CENSORSHIP.]
   • *Inactivity or monotony.*
   • *Periods of extreme tension.*

NOTES

Latin America is as much an emerging part of the world as Africa and, to the industrialized world, just as much of a mystery. Its publications, both those that originate in Latin America and those that are published outside it, are becoming known to North American and European readers, but it is my feeling that the readers of CRY OF THE PEOPLE should know a little of the background of those publications.

A. *Latin America* and its successor, *Latin America Political Report.* This is a weekly newsletter published by the London-based Latin American Newsletters, Inc., which also puts out a weekly newsletter called the *Latin America Economic Report,* a weekly report on Latin American commodities, material on Latin America for high schools and universities, and listings of publications on Latin America in Spanish, Portuguese, and English. Latin America Newsletters is widely regarded as the best source in English on the area for breaking news. No other publication covers the region in such depth. It is frequently cited as a source by other publications on Latin America, in Spanish, Portuguese, and English.

B. Amnesty International's credentials are such that it received the Nobel Peace Prize.

C. *Latinamerica Press.* Headquartered in Lima, it publishes a weekly newsletter on church affairs in Latin America. It is run by an ecumenical staff and financed by the Maryknoll Missionary Society.

D. The North American Congress on Latin America (NACLA) is a research organization with offices in New York and California. It is politically left-wing, but this does not affect its careful research work. It is one of the few U.S. organizations doing serious investigative reporting in Latin America. Like the *Latin America Political Report,* it is cited by publications specializing in Latin America.

E. A number of the sources cited are sponsored by or affiliated with the Catholic Church, such as *Latin America Documentation,* published by the U. S. Catholic Conference; the Catholic Institute for International Relations, and the Latin American Bureau in London; the Latin American Working Group (LAWG) and *Latin America & Caribbean Inside Report* of Canada; and the ecumenical publications *Caribbean*

Contact, put out by the Caribbean churches, and *CENCOS* magazine, published in Mexico. Also cited are *Sendero,* the Paraguayan bishops' newspaper, and *Noticias* and *Editora Vozes,* sponsored by the Brazilian bishops.

In response to the Jesuits' worldwide mandate to investigate and publicize socially significant issues, the order is publishing monthly magazines in several Latin-American countries, also used as sources. Among them: *CEAS* of Brazil; *SIC* magazine, Venezuela; *Centro de Investigación y Acción Social,* Argentina; *Diálogo Social,* Panama; and *Mensaje,* Chile.

F. Other sources cited are human rights lobbies, such as the respected Washington Office on Latin America, which works closely with the human rights group in the State Department, and EPICA, also based in Washington, D.C. Publications of country lobbies include *Paraguay Watch, Brazilian Information Bulletin* of the American Friends of Brazil, and *Outreach,* published by the Argentine Information Office.

G. The Latin-American newspapers cited are the most prestigious in their countries. They include *El Tiempo,* dean of the Colombian press; *El Espectador,* largest-circulation daily in Colombia; *La Prensa,* of Managua, whose editor Pedro Joaquín Chamorro was murdered by paid assassins; and *El Caribe* of the Dominican Republic. Among the nonreligious magazines cited are *Visión,* published in Bogotá; *Veja,* the leading news magazine of Brazil; and the *Latin American Research Review,* published by the Latin American Studies Association representing U.S. university faculties with Latin-American studies.

Financial sources cited include the magazine of Mexico's National Bank of Foreign Trade and the bulletins of the National Foreign Trade Council, headquartered in New York.

H. The international news agencies used as sources are: Associated Press (AP) and United Press International (UPI) of the United States; France Press (AFP) of France; Latin (the Latin-American wire service of the British news agency Reuters); and EFE of Spain.

Notes—Chapter I

1. *Amnesty International Newsletter* (London, July 1976).

2. *Report of an Amnesty International Mission to Argentina,* Amnesty International (London, June 15, 1976), pp. 30–31; also author's correspondence with Father Patrick Rice, 1977.

3. Number of refugees registered with the Buenos Aires regional office of the United Nations High Commissioner for Refugees. Source: letter to author from George Koulischer, Chief for Americas, Iberia, and Oceania Sec-

tion (Jan. 5, 1978). The total estimate of all refugees in Argentina goes much higher, between eighteen thousand and twenty thousand.

4. "Human Rights in Uruguay and Paraguay," Hearings before the Subcommittee on International Organizations of the Committee on International Relations, U. S. House of Representatives (Washington, D.C.: June 17, July 27 and 28, and Aug. 4, 1976), pp. 10–16, 20–21, 38.

5. *Report of an Amnesty International Mission to Argentina,* op. cit., p. 38.

6. Ibid.

7. World Council of Churches report by Professor Georges Casalis as described in "Torture 'to perfection' on Enemies of Fascism," Geneva dateline (London: *The Times,* Nov. 30, 1972).

8. See Chapter VI, p. 174.

Notes—Chapter II

1. Luigi Einaudi, Richard Maullin, Alfred Stepan, and Michael Fleet, *Latin American Institutional Development: The Changing Catholic Church* (Santa Monica, Calif.: RAND Corporation, 1969), p. 51.

2. Father Eduardo Hoornaert, "The Church in Brazil and the Ethic of Development," *Latin America Documentation* (Washington, D.C.: U. S. Catholic Conference, May 1974), pp. 18–35.

3. Penny Lernoux, *"1984* Revisited: Welcome to Paraguay," *Alicia Patterson Foundation Newsletter* (New York, Oct. 11, 1976).

4. Gustavo Ibáñez, "Church and Political Parties Suffer Under Stroessner Regime," *Latinamerica Press* (Lima, Aug. 19, 1976); Iván Vallejo, "New Arrests Silence Opposition in Paraguay," *Latinamerica Press* (Aug. 25, 1977); author's interviews, Asunción and eastern Paraguay (1976); *Paraguay Watch* (Washington, D.C., Sept. 6, 1978), p. 2.

5. Arsenio Rodríguez, "The Silent Penetration," IDOC Bulletin No. 10 (Rome: International Documentation and Communications Center, Oct. 1978), pp. 10–12; "Paraguay: Crucial Dialogue," *Latin America* (London, Nov. 15, 1974); J. Tirado Montero, *"El río que se va," Acción* (Asunción, June 1975), p. 23.

6. "Paraguay: Stroessner Never Sleeps," *Newsweek* (Feb. 21, 1977); "Paraguay: Mopping Up," *Latin America Political Report* (London, May 13, 1977); author's interviews, Paraguay (1976).

7. Penny Lernoux, "Our 'Cost-Effective' Diplomacy," *The Nation* (Nov. 13, 1976), pp. 487–93; "U.S. Leads Global War on Drug Abuse," *Current Foreign Policy,* Department of State (Washington, D.C.: U. S. Government Printing Office, 1972), p. 4.

8. "Paraguay: Church Militant," *Latin America* (London, July 2, 1976); *Muertes en la tortura y desapariciones de presos políticos en Paraguay*, Amnesty International (Oct. 1977), p. 2; Paul L. Montgomery, "Heroin Is Shown at Ricord Trial," New York *Times* (Dec. 8, 1972); "The World Narcotics Problem: The Latin American Perspective," *Report of Special Study Mission to Latin America and the Federal Republic of Germany* composed of Morgan F. Murphy, Ill., and Robert H. Steele, Conn. Pursuant to H. Res. 267 authorizing the Committee on Foreign Affairs to conduct thorough studies and investigations of all matters coming within the jurisdiction of the Committee (Washington, D.C.: U. S. Government Printing Office, Mar. 21, 1973), p. 12; "The Global Connection," *Time* (Aug. 28, 1972); "Paraguay: Too Many Crooks Spoil the Broth," *Latin America* (Nov. 30, 1973); "Human Rights in Uruguay and Paraguay," Hearings before the Subcommittee on International Organizations of the Committee of International Relations, U. S. House of Representatives (Washington, D.C.: U. S. Government Printing Office, June 17, July 27 and 28, and Aug. 4, 1976), pp. 100, 169–70.

9. *Report on Allegations of Torture in Brazil*, Amnesty International, 3rd ed. (England, Mar. 1976), pp. 58–60.

10. "Colombia: "The Coke Trade," *Newsweek* (Dec. 20, 1976). Also author's interviews, Colombia (1974–78).

11. Orlando Fals Borda, Germán Guzmán Campos, and Bishop Eduardo Umaña, *La violencia en Colombia* (Bogotá: Editorial Punta de Lanza, 1962), pp. 1–430.

12. Richard Rashke, "Chile Connection: White House, Church, CIA," *National Catholic Reporter* (July 29, 1977).

13. Ibid.

14. Interview with author, Bogotá (Mar. 1976).

15. Rashke, *National Catholic Reporter*, op. cit.

16. Penny Lernoux, "Latin America's Insurgent Church," *The Nation* (May 22, 1976), pp. 618–25.

17. José Comblin, "The Church's Ministry of Promoting Human Rights," *Maryknoll* (Sept. 1976), pp. 3–8.

18. *Inflación, deuda y desempleo, flagelos de América Latina en 1976* (Rio de Janeiro: Associated Press, Dec. 23, 1976); also *Deuda latinoamericana* (Washington, D.C.: Associated Press, Sept. 9, 1970).

19. "Yanqui Dollar" (North American Congress on Latin America, 1971), p. 51.

20. Archbishop Marcos McGrath, "Ariel or Calibán?," *Foreign Affairs* (Oct. 1973), pp. 16–36.

21. Lernoux, "Latin America's Insurgent Church," op. cit.

22. *Medellín Conclusions* (Bogotá: CELAM, 1973), pp. 28–110.

23. Ibid., p. 36.

24. Penny Lernoux, "Prophets of Change in Latin America," *Alicia Patterson Foundation Newsletter* (New York, Apr. 27, 1976).

25. "Human Rights in Uruguay and Paraguay," op. cit., pp. 10–21, 31–74.

26. Segundo Galilea, *"El Pueblo y el estado: cruz pastoral,"* *Mensaje* (Santiago, Apr. 1977), pp. 131–35.

27. *"Estudio sociográfico de los religiosos y las religiosas en América Latina,"* *Colección Perspectiva,* No. 2 (Bogotá: Secretariado General de CLAR, 1974), pp. 78–82.

28. Alain Gheerbrant, *The Rebel Church* (London: Penguin Books, 1974), p. 233.

29. *Congressional Record* (U. S. Senate, June 15, 1977), p. S9891.

30. Luigi R. Einaudi and Alfred Stepan, *Latin American Institutional Development: Changing Military Perspectives in Peru and Brazil* (Santa Monica, Calif.: RAND Corporation, 1971), pp. 108–9.

31. As quoted in "The Pentagon's Protégés" citing Miles Wolpin, *Military Aid and Counterrevolution in the Third World* (Lexington, Mass.: D. C. Heath & Co., 1972), North American Congress on Latin America (Jan. 1976), p. 11.

32. André Gunder Frank, *Lumpenburguesia Lumpendesarrollo* (Medellín: Editorial Oveja Negra, 1970), p. 107.

33. "Quality of Life in the Americas—Report of a Presidential Mission for the Western Hemisphere," Department of State Bulletin (Dec. 8, 1969), p. 18.

Notes—Chapter III

1. *Diálogo Social* (Panama City, June 1972), pp. 24–29; "El Salvador: Missing a Murderous Deadline," *Latin America Political Report* (London, July 29, 1977); Margaret Goff and correspondents, "Business Groups and Government Combating the Church," *Latinamerica Press* (Lima, June 16, 1977).

2. "Human Rights in Nicaragua, Guatemala, and El Salvador: Implications for U.S. Policy," Hearings before the Subcommittee on International Organizations of the Committee on International Relations, U. S. House of Representatives (Washington, D.C., June 8 and 9, 1976), pp. 47–48.

3. Ibid., p. 44.

4. Ibid., p. 39.

5. "El Salvador Bishops Protest Murder of Six Farm Workers," *Latinamerica Press* (Lima, Jan. 9, 1975); also "Bishop Protests to Government Against Killing of Farmers by Troops" (San Vicente, El Salvador: National Catholic News Service, Dec. 26, 1974).

6. "The Recent Presidential Elections in El Salvador: Implications for U.S. Foreign Policy," Hearings before the Subcommittee on International Organizations and on Inter-American Affairs of the Committee on International Relations, U. S. House of Representatives (Washington, D.C., March 8 and 17, 1977), p. 50.

7. "Policemen Excommunicated for Mistreating a Priest," *Latinamerica Press* (Lima, June 19, 1975); "El Salvador Bishops Protest to the Government over Police Conduct," *Latinamerica Press* (June 26, 1975).

8. "Human Rights in Nicaragua, Guatemala, and El Salvador," op. cit., p. 84.

9. *"General Romero asume gobierno de El Salvador"* (San Salvador: Associated Press, June 30, 1977); *Mensaje* (Santiago: Aug. 1977), pp. 439–40.

10. Jeremiah O'Leary, "Latin Official Arrested in N.Y. Gun Plot," Washington *Star* (May 17, 1976), and "El Salvador-Honduras Talks in Doubt After Gun Arrest," Washington *Star* (May 18, 1976).

11. "Violence and Fraud in El Salvador" (London: Latin American Bureau, July 1977), p. 21; also *"General Romero asume . . ."* (Associated Press), op. cit.

12. "Man in the News: General Carlos Humberto Romero," *Latin America Political Report* (London, July 1, 1977); "Violence and Fraud in El Salvador," op. cit., p. 33.

13. "Salvadoran Church Leaders Decry Repression and Injustice," *Latinamerica Press* (Lima, Apr. 14, 1977); also "Human Rights in Nicaragua, Guatemala, and El Salvador," op. cit., p. 83.

14. "Violence and Fraud in El Salvador," op. cit., p. 12.

15. "The Recent Presidential Elections in El Salvador," op. cit., pp. 22–24, 51–53.

16. Ibid., pp. 55–57. Also *"Más de un centenar de muertos en El Salvador"* (San Salvador: Agencia France Presse, Mar. 1, 1977).

17. "El Salvador," *La Prensa* (Managua, Feb. 21, 1977).

18. *SIC* (Caracas, Apr. 1977), pp. 170–74, 185–87.

19. Karen De Young, "Catholic Church, Military Draw Battle Lines in El Salvador," Washington *Post* (May 22, 1977); also letter from Washington *Post* correspondent Karen De Young (Guatemala City, May 16, 1977).

20. "Violence and Fraud in El Salvador," op. cit., pp. 26–27.

21. *Diálogo*, No. 23 (Guatemala City, July 1977), pp. 20–25, 27–32.

22. Ibid., p. 29.

23. "The Situation in the Country at the Present Time," statement by the Permanent Committee of the Catholic Bishops' Conference of El Salvador (San Salvador, Mar. 5, 1977), reproduced in "The Recent Presidential Elections in El Salvador," op. cit., pp. 82–85.

Notes—Chapter IV

1. Author's interviews (Managua, Mar. 1977).

2. "Human Rights in Nicaragua, Guatemala, and El Salvador: Implications for U.S. Policy," Hearings before the Subcommittee on International Organizations of the Committee on International Relations, U. S. House of Representatives (Washington, D.C., June 8 and 9, 1976), pp. 249–53; author's interviews in Managua (Mar. 1977).

3. *The Republic of Nicaragua: An Amnesty International Report Including the Findings of a Mission to Nicaragua, May 10–15, 1976* (London), p. 27; also author's interviews in Zelaya (Mar. 1977), and letters to author from U.S. Capuchins in Nicaragua (May 20, June 13, and Oct. 16, 1977).

4. "Human Rights in Nicaragua, Guatemala, and El Salvador," op. cit., pp. 12 and 231; *The Republic of Nicaragua*, op. cit., pp. 51–52; author's interviews, op. cit.; and Alan Riding, "Bishops in Nicaragua Say Troops Kill Civilians in Fighting Leftists," New York *Times* (Mar. 2, 1977).

5. *The Republic of Nicaragua*, op. cit., pp. 52–56, 58–59; also author's interviews, op. cit., and "The Idi Amin of Central America," *To The Point International* news magazine (Antwerp, May 16, 1977).

6. *The Republic of Nicaragua*, op. cit., p. 57; author's interviews, op. cit.; New York *Times*, op. cit.; also "Nicaragua: Somoza's Reign of Terror," *Time* (Mar. 14, 1977).

7. "Human Rights in Nicaragua, Guatemala, and El Salvador," op. cit., p. 243.

8. (No title) National Catholic News Service (July 1, 1975), and "Burglary of Archbishop's Office Censored from Newspapers," National Catholic News Service (Nov. 3, 1975); also author's interview in Managua with Pedro Joaquín Chamorro, publisher of *La Prensa* (Mar. 1977).

9. Author's interviews in Managua (Mar. 1977).

10. Letter published by the Maryknoll nuns in Pueblo Nuevo, Tola, León, and OPEN 3, Nicaragua (Dec. 28, 1977); mimeograph copy.

11. "News in Brief: Nicaragua," *Latin America Political Report* (London, Dec. 23, 1977).

12. *"Exposición de Padres del OPEN,"* *La Prensa* (Managua, Dec. 23, 1977).

13. Ibid.; also letter published by Maryknoll nuns, op. cit.

14. Author's interview with Chamorro, op. cit.

15. "Nicaragua: Shotguns Silence a Critic," *Time* (Jan. 23, 1978).

16. "Church Sustaining Protest in Nicaragua," *Latinamerica Press* (Lima, Feb. 16, 1978).

17. "Nicaragua: Nail in the Coffin," *Latin America Political Report* (London, Mar. 10, 1978).

18. *The Republic of Nicaragua,* op. cit., p. 26.

19. Author's interviews in Managua and Zelaya (Mar. 1977).

20. Ibid.

21. "Bloody Nicaragua," *Newsweek* (Sept. 25, 1978).

22. "Nicaragua: Sifting Through the Rubble," *Latin America Political Report* (London, Oct. 13, 1978). And *"Por qué condenó la CIDH al gobierno de Somoza"* (Washington, D.C.: Associated Press, Nov. 18, 1978).

23. Associated Press, op. cit.

24. "Nicaragua: Executions and Disappearances," *Amnesty International Newsletter* (Nov. 1978).

25. Ibid.

26. *Newsweek,* op. cit.

27. Mimeographed letter, Sister Joan Uhlen (Condega, Nicaragua, Sept. 1978).

28. José Fajardo, *"¿Por qué no ha caido Tachito?,"* *El Tiempo* (Bogotá, Oct. 9, 1978).

29. "Nicaraguan Priests to President Carter: Stop All Aid to Somoza," *Latinamerica Press* (Lima, Oct. 12, 1978).

30. Managua Public Registry Deed No. 045970. Also Alan Riding, "Nicaraguans Accused of Profiteering in Help the U.S. Sent After Quake," New York *Times* (Mar. 23, 1977).

31. "Nicaraguans accused . . . ," New York *Times,* op. cit.; also author's interviews, op. cit.

32. Max Holland and Cressida McKean, "Out of the Public Eye, Nicaragua's Washington Lobby Wins Again," "Opinion," Los Angeles *Times,* Part IV (Aug. 21, 1977).

33. "For the Record: Somoza's United States Lobby," *Latin America Political Report* (London, Aug. 26, 1977).

34. Holland and McKean, op. cit.

35. Ibid.; also "For the Record," *Latin America Political Report,* op. cit., and "State Department: Mixed Signals Secure Somoza Aid," *Update Latin America* (Washington, D.C.: Washington Office on Latin America, May–June, 1977).

36. Holland and McKean, op. cit.; also "Nicaragua: Guns for Somoza," *Latin America Political Report* (Aug. 19, 1977).

37. *"Renunció Embajador de Nicaragua"* (United Nations: Latin-Reuters, Sept. 28, 1978).

38. "Nicaragua: Managing the Crisis," *Latin America Political Report* (Oct. 6, 1978); Catherine Myers, "Congressmen Ask Support for Somoza," *National Catholic Reporter* (Oct. 6, 1978).

39. Richard J. Barnet and Ronald E. Muller, *Global Reach* (New York: Simon and Schuster, 1974), p. 87; also *"Campesinos Hondureños," Diálogo Social* (Panama, June 1976), p. 14.

40. "Honduras: Shooting Season," *Latin America* (London, May 7, 1976); *"La Tragedia por la tierra," Visión* (Aug. 1975).

41. *"Diez Mil dólares por la cabeza de obispo hondureño"* (Tegucigalpa: Associated Press, Aug. 1, 1975); "Blood and Land," *Time* (Aug. 18, 1975); and James Goff, "Burgeoning Peasant Movement a Potent Force in Honduras," *Latinamerica Press* (Lima, Feb. 26, 1976).

42. "Honduras Landholders 'Put Price on My Head,' U.S.-Born Bishop Says" (National Catholic News Service, Aug. 6, 1975). Also *"Sepultados el sacerdote y la joven," El Tiempo* (Bogotá, July 21, 1975).

43. *Visión,* op. cit., and *Latin America,* op. cit.

44. *"Colombia en Busca de Justicia," El Espectador* (Bogotá, Oct. 19, 1975); and official military report of government of Honduras on events in Olancho as reported by Spanish news agency EFE: *"Revelan Informe oficial sobre crímenes de Olancho, Honduras"* (Tegucigalpa, July 23, 1975).

45. *"Regresó ayer sacerdote expulsado de Honduras," El Tiempo* (Bogotá, July 4, 1975).

46. Ibid.

47. *"Sepultados el sacerdote y la joven,"* *El Tiempo* (Bogotá, July 21, 1975). Also *El Espectador,* op. cit.

48. EFE report, op. cit. Also *"Dirigente agrario hondureño niega culpa en el genocidio"* (Tegucigalpa: Associated Press, July 26, 1975).

49. *El Espectador,* op. cit., and *El Tiempo,* op. cit.

50. "Honduras Church Reacts to Court's Judgment," *Latinamerica Press* (April 27, 1978); also "Honduran Court Absolves Landholders Who Killed Campesinos," *Latinamerica Press* (June 15, 1978).

51. "Honduras Church . . ." and "Honduran Court . . . ," *Latinamerica Press,* op. cit.

52. *Visión,* op. cit.

53. Penny Lernoux, "The Great Banana War," *The Nation* (June 29, 1974), pp. 813–17.

54. Thomas McCann, *An American Company: The Tragedy of United Fruit* (New York: Crown Publishers, 1976), p. 220.

55. Ibid., p. 29; also David Atlee Phillips, *The Night Watch* (New York: Atheneum, 1977), p. 90.

56. McCann, op. cit., pp. 214–16; *"Exministro de economía de Honduras propuso soborno"* (New York: EFE, May 7, 1975).

57. McCann, op. cit., p. 233; also *"Los Tentáculos del pulpo,"* *Visión* (May 15, 1975).

58. Ibid., *Visión.*

59. *"Asesor presidencial acusado de trabajar para empresa bananera"* (Tegucigalpa: EFE, June 11, 1978).

60. "Honduras, Good-bye to Reformism," *Latin America Political Report* (London, May 6, 1977); also "Union Busting: Castle & Cooke in Honduras," North American Congress on Latin America, Vol. XI, No. 8 (Nov. 12, 1977), pp. 40–41.

61. "Honduras: Challenging Castle & Cooke," North American Congress on Latin America, *NACLA Report* (Mar./Apr. 1978), pp. 43–44; "By the way: Honduras," *Latin America Political Report* (June 9, 1978); "Honduras: Political Medicine," *Latin America Political Report* (Apr. 28, 1978).

62. "By the way: Honduras," op. cit.

63. North American Congress, op. cit. Also *NACLA Report,* op. cit.

64. "Honduras: TNC Land Grab, *NACLA Report* (May/June 1978), pp.

45–46; "Peasant Leaders Freed in Honduras," *Amnesty International Newsletter* (Nov. 1978).

65. *Latin America Political Report* (May 6, 1977), op. cit.

66. Moises Sandoval, "Tragedy in Honduras," *Maryknoll* (Dec. 1975), pp. 17–19.

67. *"La iglesia y el Estado en negociaciones"* (Tegucigalpa: EFE, July 2, 1975); "Honduras Church . . . ," op. cit.; "Honduran Court . . . ," op. cit.

68. *"Iglesia de E. U. denuncia violación de derechos del hombre en Honduras"* (Washington, D.C.: United Press International, Sept. 17, 1975).

69. *"Si desaparezco no me busquen, sigan el trabajo,"* *Diálogo Social* (Panama, June 1976), p. 5.

70. "Interview with Father Gallego on His Parish Organization," *Latin America Documentation* (Washington, D.C.: U. S. Catholic Conference, Feb. 1972), pp. ii, 19d.

71. *"Entrevista con los padres y familiares de Héctor,"* *Diálogo Social,* Special Edition, Nos. 34–35 (Panama City, May–June 9, 1972), p. 10.

72. Yike Fonseca, "Father Gallego: A Typical 'New Priest,'" *Latin America Documentation,* op. cit., pp. ii, 19a.

73. "Archbishop Marcos C. McGrath and the Panamanian Situation," *Latinamerica Press* (Aug. 23, 1973).

74. Archbishop Marcos McGrath, "Ariel or Calibán?," *Foreign Affairs* (Oct. 1973), pp. 16–36.

75. *"Héctor a través de la poesía popular,"* *Diálogo Social,* Special Edition, op. cit., p. 35.

76. *"Por los campos de Santa Fé,"* ibid., p. 76.

77. McGrath, op. cit., p. 20.

78. *"Sus años en Panamá,"* *Diálogo Social,* Special Edition, op. cit., p. 16.

79. *"Héctor para los Santafereños,"* ibid., p. 32.

80. Ibid., p. 17.

81. Ibid., pp. 17 and 88–89.

82. *"Domingo 27,"* ibid., p. 103.

83. Germán Castro, *"Habla el general Torrijos: 'El Caso del cura Gallego formó parte de una conjura,'"* *El Tiempo* (Bogotá, Feb. 14, 1975).

84. Penny Lernoux, "Pan American Report: Missing Priest Causes Political Concern" (Bogotá: Copley News Service, Aug. 3, 1971).

Notes—Chapter V

1. "El Caso Riobamba," *SIC* (Caracas, Sept. 10, 1976), pp. 377–84.

2. Ibid.; also "Ecuador Expels Bishops," *Latin America Documentation* (Washington, D.C.: U. S. Catholic Conference, July–Aug. 1976), pp. 32–46; "Riobamba, *Editora Vozes,* Serviço de Documentaçao, Vol. 9 (Petrópolis, Rio de Janeiro: Jan.–Feb. 1977), pp. 813–18.

3. Press conference, Bishops' Conference of Chile (Santiago, Aug. 17, 1976).

4. Victor Marchetti and John D. Marks, *The CIA and the Cult of Intelligence* (New York: Dell Publishing Co., 1974), pp. 143–44. "Bolivia: The War Goes On," NACLA's *Latin America & Empire Report,* Vol. VIII, No. 2 (Feb. 1974), p. 7. Author's interviews with heads of Bolivian religious orders, 1976–77.

5. *"Acuerdo Presentado por la Comisión de Lucha contra la infiltración comunista en los medios religiosos,"* Bolivian Delegation, Third Congress of the Latin-American Anti-Communist Confederation, Asunción, Mar. 28–30, 1977, Documentation RRC-AMM, signed by Rvdo. Wilfredo López S., secretary, and Dr. Salvador Rubén Paredes, president (photocopy). Also *"Ponencia—Delegación Boliviana,"* signed by Lic. Wilfredo López Suárez, Third Congress (photocopy). And *"Principios tácticos de enfrentamiento a la infiltración marxista en la Iglesia Católica,"* Bolivian Delegation, signed by Dr. Julio Vera and Ms. Margarita González, Third Congress (photocopy).

6. See No. 5; *"Acuerdo . . . ," "Ponencia . . . ,"* and *"Principios . . . ,"* ibid.; also Gonzalo Arroyo, "Repression of the Latin American Church: Armed Purges and the CIA," *Latinamerica Press* (Lima, Nov. 27, 1975); "The Bolivian Government Plan Against the Church," *Latin America Documentation* (Washington, D.C.: U. S. Catholic Conference, June 1975), pp. 1–4; *"Los Cristianos en la Balanza,"* *Diálogo,* Vol. 33 (Guatemala City, July 1977), pp. 8–14.

7. See Nos. 5 & 6, *"Acuerdo . . . ," "Ponencia . . . ," "Principios . . . ,"* Arroyo, "The Bolivian Government Plan . . . ," and *Diálogo,* op. cit.

8. Luis del Río, "Escalating Campaign Against Progressive Foreign Clergy in Bolivia," *Latinamerica Press* (Lima, June 19, 1975); also "CIA's Involvement Suspected in Repression of Mission Work in Bolivia" (Cochabamba, Bolivia: National Catholic News Service, June 6, 1975).

9. Philip Agee, *Inside the Company: CIA Diary* (London: Penguin Books, 1975), pp. 144–316.

10. del Río, op. cit.

11. See No. 5.

12. *"Persecución Contra La Iglesia Popular en A.L.,"* *Diálogo Social* (Panama City, Sept. 1977), pp. 32–33.

13. "The Great Latin-American Anti-Communist Jamboree," *Latin America Political Report* (London, Apr. 29, 1977).

14. Penny Lernoux, "Ecuador: Rags and Riches," *The Nation* (Dec. 27, 1975), pp. 682–86.

15. Ibid.

16. Author's interviews with U. S. Special Forces (1964).

17. *"Chimborazo: Solo Promesas. La Explotación Continua,"* *Nueva* (Quito, 1975), p. 23.

Notes—Chapter VI

1. "Guatemala" (North American Congress on Latin America, 1974), p. 208.

2. "Honduras: Good-bye Reformism," *Latin America Political Report* (London, May 6, 1977).

3. Most Rev. Peter L. Gerety, Archbishop of Newark, N.J., "Human Rights and Foreign Policy," *Maryknoll* (Nov. 1977), pp. 3–7.

4. "Human Rights in Nicaragua, Guatemala, and El Salvador," Hearings before the Subcommittee on International Organizations of the Committee on International Relations, U. S. House of Representatives (Washington, D.C., June 8 and 9, 1976), p. 73.

5. Ignacio Barker, *"Las fuerzas armadas y el Cristianismo en algunos países de América,"* *Mensaje* (Santiago, June 1977), pp. 267ff.

6. "The Pentagon's Protégés" (North American Congress on Latin America, Vol. X, No. 1, Jan. 1, 1976), p. 3, quoting the Institute of International Education, Military Assistance Training Programs of the U. S. Government, Committee on Educational Interchange Policy, Statement No. 18 (July 1964).

7. Ibid., p. 11, quoting U. S. House of Representatives, Committee on Appropriations, Foreign Operations Appropriations for 1963, Hearings, 87th Cong., 2nd sess., Part I, p. 359.

8. Michael Klare, *War Without End* (New York: Vintage Books, 1972), pp. 273–75.

9. "Quality of Life in the Americas—Report of a Presidential Mission for the Western Hemisphere" (Department of State Bulletin, Dec. 8, 1969), pp. 502–15.

10. Klare, op. cit., pp. 273–75, and "The Pentagon's Protégés," op. cit., p. 13.

11. Jeffrey Stein, "Grad School for Juntas," *The Nation* (May 21, 1977), pp. 621–24.

12. Ibid., p. 621. And *Report of an Amnesty International Mission to Argentina, Nov. 6–15, 1976* (Amnesty International), p. 32; also "Argentina: The Navy Way," *Latin America Political Report* (July 29, 1977); Howard Lambert, "Argentina Junta Avoiding Reply to U.S. Charges of Human Rights Violations," *Latinamerica Press* (April 7, 1977).

13. Taylor Branch, "Aid to Brazil: From Dungeons to Disneyland," *Washington Monthly* (Washington, D.C., Sept. 1971) as reproduced in *Latin America Documentation* (Washington, D.C.: U. S. Catholic Conference, Nov. 1971), pp. 1–3.

14. Ibid.

15. Michel Schooyans, *Le Destin du Brésil* (Belgium: Duclot, 1973), pp. 1–222.

16. Alain Gheerbrant, *The Rebel Church in Latin America* (London: Penguin Books, 1974), p. 225.

17. Branch, op. cit.

18. San Francisco Sunday *Examiner & Chronicle* (July 25, 1977).

19. Branch, op. cit.

20. Ibid.

21. "The Pentagon's Protégés," op. cit., p. 12.

22. "Castelo Branco and the CIA's War Games," *Latin America Political Report* (Jan. 21, 1977).

23. Gayle Hudgens Watson, "It All Began with 'Brother Sam,' " *The Nation* (Jan. 15, 1977), pp. 51–54; also Lincoln Gordon, "The 1964 Revolution Made in Brazil," Washington *Post* (Mar. 8, 1977); Klare, op. cit., p. 309.

24. Branch, op. cit.

25. Ibid.

26. "Brazil: Remember Us?," *Latin America Political Report* (Aug. 26, 1977).

27. As quoted in Stein, op. cit., p. 623.

28. *Report on Allegations of Torture in Brazil* (London: Amnesty International, 1976), p. 17.

29. Ibid., p. 20.

30. Hugo Assmann, *Perspectivas de Diálogo* (Montevideo, Aug. 1970); also "By the way: Brazil," *Latin America Political Report* (June 24, 1977).

31. "Report on Allegations . . . ," op. cit., p. 47.

32. "Torture as Policy: The Network of Evil," *Time* (Aug. 16, 1976).

33. As quoted in "The Iron Fist and the Velvet Glove: An Analysis of the U.S. Police," *Center for Research on Criminal Justice* (Berkeley, Calif., 1975), p. 94, quoting *Foreign Assistance 1965* (a U. S. Government publication), p. 82.

34. Ibid., p. 90, quoting Maxwell D. Taylor, Address at Graduation Exercises, International Police Academy, Washington, D.C. (U. S. Department of State press release, Dec. 17, 1965).

35. *Le Monde,* English edition (Feb. 17, 1971).

36. "Guatemala," op. cit., p. 202.

37. I. F. Stone, *In Time of Torment* (New York: Random House, 1968), pp. 173–74.

38. Quoted in "The Pentagon's Protégés," op. cit., p. 22.

39. Raul Leis and Herasto Reyes, *"Escuela de las Américas: Entrenamiento y Control," Diálogo Social,* (Panama City, Feb. 3, 1977), p. 54.

40. "The Iron Fist . . . ," op. cit., p. 91.

41. "Guatemala and the Dominican Republic," A Staff Memorandum Prepared for the Use of the Subcommittee on Western Hemisphere Affairs of the Committee on Foreign Relations, U. S. Senate (Washington, D.C., Dec. 30, 1971), pp. 1–6.

42. Ibid.

43. Luigi R. Einaudi and David F. Ronfeldt, *Internal Security and Military Assistance to Latin America in the 1970s: A First Statement* (Santa Monica, Calif.: RAND Corporation, Dec. 1971), pp. 7–32.

44. Ibid., pp. 7–15.

45. Marlise Simons, "Diary of Murdered Chilean General Surfaces in Mexico," Washington *Post* (Mar. 8, 1977).

46. "Human Rights in Nicaragua, Guatemala, and El Salvador," op. cit., p. 124.

47. As quoted in "Guatemala," op. cit., p. 197.

48. "Guatemala" (London: Amnesty International, June 1977), p. 4.

49. "Guatemala" (North American Congress), op. cit., pp. 198, 202–3.

50. *Le Monde,* op. cit.; "Guatemala" (Amnesty International), op. cit., p. 5; James Goff, "Guatemala's Earthquake Vies with Decade of Violence in Death Toll," *Latinamerica Press* (Lima, Feb. 19, 1976).

51. "Guatemala: 6,000 Pieces of Silver," *Latin America Political Report* (London: June 25, 1976).

52. "Guatemala: Stern Warning," *Latin America Political Report* (June 11, 1976).

53. Ibid.

54. "Guatemala: Reign of Terror," *Latin America Political Report* (July 23, 1976).

55. As quoted in Richard Barnet, *Intervention & Revolution* (New York: Mentor Paperback, New American Library, 1972), reproduced in "Dominican Republic: Oppression and Struggle" (Washington, D.C.: Quisqueya Task Force, EPICA), p. 3.

56. Norman Gall, excerpts from "Santo Domingo: The Politics of Terror," *New York Review of Books* (July 22, 1971), reproduced in "Dominican Republic: Oppression and Struggle," op. cit. (n.p.).

57. *La Banda* (Toronto: Latin American Working Group, Fall 1971), pp. 1–76; also *"Revelan Trama," El Nacional* (Santo Domingo, June 7, 1971).

58. Gall, op. cit.

59. A. Kent MacDougall, "In Dominican Republic, Political Murders Rise, and So Does Poverty," *Wall Street Journal* (Sept. 7, 1971).

60. Michael Klare and Nancy Stein, "Police Terrorism in Latin America," *Latin America Documentation* (Washington, D.C.: U. S. Catholic Conference, June 1974), pp. 22, 26.

61. Miami *Herald* (July 24, 1970).

62. Philip Agee, *Inside the Company: CIA Diary* (London: Penguin Books, 1975), p. 604.

63. "Uruguay Police Agent Exposes U.S. Advisers," NACLA's *Latin American Report* (July–Aug. 1972).

64. "Brazil: Fortress Amerika," *Latin America* (London, Mar. 7, 1975).

65. *Brazilian Information Bulletin,* No. 16 (Berkeley, Winter 1975), pp. 5–6.

66. "Uruguay Police Agent Exposes U.S. Advisers," op. cit.

67. Raul Ampuero, *The Military Counter-Revolution in Latin America* (Rome: Russell Tribune II, Jan. 1976), pp. 1–15.

68. Taylor Branch, "*¿Quién Mató a Letelier?*" Spanish translation of New York *Times Magazine* article in *El Espectador* (Bogotá: Sunday magazine, Sept. 3, 1978), pp. 1–11.

69. Timothy S. Robinson and Stephen J. Lynton, "Evidence Links Letelier Death to Anti-Castro Unit," Washington *Post* (Feb. 1, 1977).

70. John Dinges, "Cuban Exile-Chile Link Under Examination," *Latinamerica Press* (Lima, Oct. 19, 1978).

71. Ibid.

72. Ibid.

73. John Dinges, "Pinochet Against Wall in Letelier Investigation," *Latinamerica Press* (Lima, Mar. 16, 1978).

74. Robinson Rojas Sandford, *The Murder of Allende* (New York: Harper & Row, 1975), pp. 159, 250.

75. "Pinochet Against Wall . . . ," op. cit.

76. Ibid.

77. Ibid.; also Rojas Sandford, op. cit., pp. 159, 250.

78. Branch, op. cit. Also *"M. Townley, vinculado con otros atentados"* (Washington, D.C.: Associated Press, Oct. 24, 1978).

79. Ibid.

80. "Chile: Playing It Cool," *Latin America Political Report* (Sept. 29, 1978).

81. *"M. Townley . . . ,"* op. cit.

82. Laurie Nadel and Hesh Wiener, "Would You Sell Computers to Hitler?," *Computer Decisions* (Feb. 1977), pp. 22–26.

83. "U.S. Computers: Weapons of Repression," *Outreach* (New York: Argentine Information Office, May–June 1977), pp. 6–7.

84. Ibid.

85. Ibid.

86. Nadel and Wiener, op. cit., p. 23. Also Michael Klare, "Secretary Kreps Won't Talk," *The Nation* (June 4, 1977), pp. 678–79.

87. Nadel and Wiener, op. cit., p. 25.

88. *Outreach,* op. cit.

89. Klare, "Secretary Kreps . . . ," op. cit., p. 679.

90. Alan Howard, "The Real Latin American Policy," *The Nation* (Oct. 15, 1977), pp. 365–70.

91. Stein, op. cit.

92. *The Americas in a Changing World: A Report of the Commission on United States–Latin American Relations, with a Preface by Sol M. Linowitz* (New York: The New York Times Book Company, 1975), pp. 1–248.

93. Author's interviews, Brazil (1976).

Notes—Chapter VII

1. "United Fruit Is Not Chiquita" (North American Congress on Latin America, Oct. 1971), p. 7.

2. Marcos Arruda, Herbert de Souza, and Carlos Alfonso, *Multinationals and Brazil* (Toronto: Latin American Research United, 1975), pp. 45–56.

3. Quoted in Simon Hanson, *Five Years of the Alliance for Progress* (Washington: Inter-American Affairs Press, 1967), p. 188.

4. Washington *Post* (Nov. 2, 1971).

5. AID, Proposed Economic Assistance Program (FY 1967).

6. "U.S. Grain Arsenal," NACLA's *Latin America & Empire Report* (Oct. 1975), p. 12.

7. "U.S. Confirms Food for Peace Halt to Chile," *Latinamerica Press* (Mar. 26, 1971); Sergio Prenafeta, "Who Is Affected in Food for Peace Halt?," *Latinamerica Press* (Mar. 30, 1971); and James T. Cotter, "U.S. Missioners Ask Nixon to Cooperate with Allende Government," *Latinamerica Press* (July 16, 1971).

8. Hanson, op. cit., p. 57.

9. *Barron's* (Oct. 2, 1967).

10. As quoted in Robert J. Ledogar, *Hungry for Profits* (New York: IDOC/ North America, 1975), p. 61.

11. Ibid., p. 61.

12. Simon Hanson, "The Alliance for Progress: The Sixth Year," *Inter-American Economic Affairs* (Winter 1968), p. 58.

13. *"Las corporaciones multinacionales en el desarrollo mundial"* (New York: United Nations, 1973), p. 34.

14. Fred Hirsch, "An Analysis of Our AFL-CIO Role in Latin America" (San Jose, Calif.: Emergency Committee to Defend Democracy in Chile, 1974), pp. 23–24; also Victor Marchetti and John D. Marks, *The CIA and the Cult of Intelligence* (New York: Dell Publishing Company, 1974), pp. 70, 373; and Clarence Moore, "Council Told: 'Let Labor Do Its Thing,'" *Times of the Americas* (Washington, D.C., Dec. 13, 1978).

15. Philip Agee, *Inside the Company: CIA Diary* (London: Penguin Books, 1975), p. 606.

16. Susanne Bodenheimer, "U.S. Labor's Conservative Role in Latin America," *Progressive* (Nov. 1967), reproduced in "Dominican Republic: Oppression and Struggle" (Washington, D.C.: EPICA).

17. Ibid.

18. Arruda, Souza, and Alfonso, op. cit., p. 17.

19. Hirsch, op. cit., pp. 14–16.

20. Thomas Braden, "I'm Glad the CIA Is Immoral," *Saturday Evening Post* (May 20, 1967), pp. 10–12.

21. *"Estrategin para el desarrollo de los años 70"* (Santiago: Comisión Económica para América Latina [CEPAL], United Nations, 1969).

22. *Primer Seminario Latinoamericano de Vivienda para Trabajadores* (First Latin American Seminar on Workers' Housing) (Bogotá, May 1974).

23. Peter Stalker, "The Detectives," *New Internationalist,* No. 37 (Mar. 1976), pp. 27–28. See also *"Las Corporaciones multinacionales . . . ,"* op. cit., pp. 32–34.

24. Richard J. Barnet and Ronald E. Muller, *Global Reach* (New York: Simon and Schuster, 1974), pp. 160–61.

25. As quoted in "Yanqui Dollar" (North American Congress on Latin America, 1971), p. 19; see also *Major Issues in Transfer of Technology to Developing Countries: A Case Study of the Pharmaceutical Industry* (United Nations, Oct. 8, 1975), pp. 28–29.

26. Mauricio de María y Campos, *"La industria farmacéutica en México,"* *Revista del Banco Nacional de Comercio Exterior,* Vol. 27, No. 8 (Mexico, Aug. 1977), p. 901.

27. Ibid., p. 899. Also *Major issues . . . ,* op. cit., p. 27.

28. *"Sección Nacional,"* *Revista del Banco Nacional de Comercio Exterior,* op. cit., pp. 914–17. Also *Major issues . . . ,* op. cit., pp. 26–28.

29. *"Demanda a 3 Laboratorios en Brasil por 'Bebés Talidomida' "* (Porto Alegre, Brazil: United Press International, Oct. 27, 1976).

30. Ledogar, op. cit., p. 46.

31. Ibid., pp. 47–49.

32. *Major issues . . . ,* op. cit., p. 47.

33. Ledogar, op. cit., pp. 32–34.

34. Samples obtained by author without prescription in Colombian drugstores (Sept. 1978).

35. Ledogar, op. cit., p. 63; also *Major issues* . . . , op. cit., pp. 21–22.

36. Daniel Chudnovsky, *Empresas multinacionales y ganancias monopólicas* (Buenos Aires: Siglo Veintiuno Editores, S.A., Oct. 1974), p. 124.

37. "Yanqui Dollar," op. cit., p. 58.

38. Ledogar, op. cit., pp. 65–67.

39. de María y Campos, op. cit., p. 907.

40. Barnet and Muller, op. cit., p. 168.

41. *"Las compañías transnacionales en Brasil y México,"* SIC (Caracas, July 8, 1976), pp. 329–36.

42. *"Las corporaciones multinacionales . . . ,"* op. cit., pp. 33–34; also Barnet and Muller, op. cit., p. 139.

43. *"Las corporaciones multinacionales . . . ,"* op. cit., pp. 33–34. Barnet and Muller, op. cit., pp. 153, 157.

44. Osny Duarte Pereira, *Multinacionais no Brasil* (Rio de Janeiro: Civilização Brasileira, 1975), p. 61.

45. "By the Way: United States," *Latin America Political Report* (Oct. 7, 1977); *"Dinero de Marlboro a Balaguer"* (New York: Associated Press, Dec. 28, 1976); Angel Romero, *"Investigador del caso Lockheed hace llamado a Congreso de E.U.,"* *El Tiempo* (Bogotá, Feb. 18, 1976); *"Denuncia sobornos en la compra de aviones,"* *El Tiempo* (Bogotá, Feb. 8, 1976); *"Preso Venezolano que Cobró Comisión a 'Boeing' "* (Caracas: Latin, Jan. 15, 1977); *"Destituído presidente de 'Viasa' "* (Caracas: EFE, Feb. 1, 1977); *"Boeing Desmiente caso de sobornos"* (Buenos Aires: EFE, Jan. 13, 1977); John F. Berry, "Extensive Bribery Charged to GTE," Washington *Post* (Jan. 28, 1977).

46. "By the Way: Canada," *Latin America Political Report* (Dec. 3, 1976).

47. *"Sofasa Licencia Parte del Personal Francés,"* *El Espectador* (Bogotá, June 15, 1976); *"Renault: Infatigable evasora de impuestos,"* *Alternativa* (Bogotá, Nov. 1975), pp. 14–15; *"Multada la Sofasa con 43 Millones,"* *Periodistas Asociados* (Bogotá, Feb. 28, 1977); *"Investigan cuantiosas violaciones cambiarias,"* *El Tiempo* (Dec. 3, 1976) and *El Tiempo* (July 23, 1976).

48. Al Gedicks, "Kennecott Copper Corporation and Mining Development in Wisconsin" (Madison, Wis.: Community Action on Latin America, 1973), p. 191; also "Latin America: A Study Course for Small Groups" (London: The United Society for the Propagation of the Gospel and the

Methodist Missionary Society, 1976); also "Statement by the U. S. Missionaries' Committee on International Awareness," *Latinamerica Press* (Nov. 24, 1972).

49. "Bolivia: The War Goes On," NACLA's *Latin America & Empire Report,* Vol. VIII, No. 2 (Feb. 1974), p. 17; also Darryl Hunt, "The Cross of Tin," *Maryknoll* (Jan. 1978), pp. 15–18.

50. "Bolivia: The War Goes On," op. cit., p. 30.

51. Eugene M. Rooney, "The Kennecott Copper Swindle," *Latinamerica Press* (Nov. 24, 1972).

52. "Amazing Grace," NACLA's *Latin America & Empire Report,* Vol. X, No. 3 (Mar. 1976), pp. 12, 25.

53. Interviews with author, Lima (1969–70).

54. Charles T. Goodsell, *American Corporations and Peruvian Politics* (Cambridge, Mass.: Harvard University Press, 1974), pp. 45, 57–58, 67.

55. "Amazing Grace," op. cit., p. 25.

56. "To the People in the Struggle for Their Rights," document of ONIS Priests Movement, National Executive Committee (Lima, Sept. 8, 1977).

57. Penny Lernoux, "Brazil: The Church of Tomorrow," *Alicia Patterson Foundation Newsletter* (New York, Mar. 15, 1977).

58. Interview with author, Bogotá (Nov. 1977).

59. José Comblin, "The Church and the National Security System," *Latin America Documentation* (Washington, D.C.: U. S. Catholic Conference, May–June 1976), pp. 1–26.

60. Father James Gardiner, "Church Told to Take Economics Seriously" (New York: National Catholic News Service, Mar. 4, 1975).

61. "Rosario Dominicana," *Latin American and Caribbean Inside Report,* Vol. 1, No. 1 (Ontario, May 1977), pp. 2–3.

62. *"Estiman Hombre del Campo Vive Situación de Miseria,"* El Caribe (Dominican Republic, July 3, 1977).

63. *"Obispo Denuncia Penurias Desalojados zonas Mineras,"* El Caribe (Dominican Republic, July 7, 1977).

64. "Rosario Dominicana," op. cit.

65. Ibid.; also Robert Sisselman, "Hispaniola: An Island with a Mining Future," *Engineering & Mining Journal* (Nov. 1977), pp. 135–45.

66. *"Obispo . . . ,"* El Caribe, op. cit.

67. "Death of Farmworkers' Organizer Condemned in Dominican Republic" (Santo Domingo: National Catholic News Service, Dec. 26, 1974).

68. Juan Miguel Pérez, "Watching a Revolution Come to the Boil," *Latin America Documentation* (Washington, D.C.: U. S. Catholic Conference, Apr. 1974), pp. 9–14.

69. Barnet and Muller, op. cit., p. 240.

70. "*¿Quién es Cyrus Vance?*" *Diálogo Social* (Panama, Feb. 3, 1977), pp. 42–43; also "Cyrus Vance," NACLA's *Latin America & Empire Report* (Jan. 1977).

71. Ibid.

72. "Smoldering Conflict: Dominican Republic, 1965–1975," NACLA's *Latin America & Empire Report* (Apr. 1975), p. 24.

73. Ibid. Ledogar, op. cit., pp. 80–81.

74. Ibid., "Smoldering Conflict . . ." and Ledogar.

75. "Smoldering Conflict . . . ," op. cit.

76. London *Financial Times* (Oct. 10, 1974).

77. Ledogar, op. cit., p. 77.

78. Ibid., p. 77.

79. Ibid., p. 78.

80. Pérez, op. cit.

81. Ledogar, op. cit., p. 85.

82. "Bad Land Distribution Brings Hunger to Dominicans, Study Shows" (Santo Domingo: National Catholic News Service, Sept. 25, 1975).

83. Pérez, op. cit.

84. "New Charges of Repression in the Dominican Republic," *Latinamerica Press* (Lima, Nov. 28, 1974).

85. "Priests Favored in Encounter with Dominican Landholders," *Latinamerica Press* (June 2, 1977).

86. Pérez, op. cit.

87. "Immovable Mountains," *Fortune* (Apr. 1965).

88. "LAWG Letter," Vol. IV, No. 2 (Toronto: Latin American Working Group, Dec. 1976), p. 6.

89. *Latin America and Caribbean Inside Report*, Vol. 1, No. 2 (Toronto, May 1976).

90. Edie Black and Fred Goff, "The Hanna Industrial Complex" (North American Congress on Latin America, 1969), pp. 4, 13.

91. Black and Goff, op. cit., p. 3, quoting *Time* (Dec. 16, 1966).

92. Paulo R. Schilling, "Brazil: The Rebellion of the Downtrodden," *Latin America Documentation* (Washington, D.C.: U. S. Catholic Conference, Nov. 1971), pp. ii, 9b: 1–4.

93. *Latin America Economic Report* (London: Jan. 9, 1976).

94. Arruda, Souza, and Alfonso, op. cit., pp. 31–33.

95. Ibid., p. 33.

96. Ibid., p. 35.

97. Ibid., p. 18.

98. Ibid., p. 17.

99. Ibid., p. 19.

100. Duarte Pereira, op. cit., p. 171.

101. Survey in 1967 by the Instituto Brasileiro de Reforma Agraria.

102. " '*Fríjoles Negros' Ganó Elecciones en Brasil*" (Rio de Janeiro: United Press International, Nov. 19, 1976).

103. Ledogar, op. cit., p. 114.

104. Lernoux, op. cit.

105. Duarte Pereira, op. cit., pp. 117–20.

106. "*O dominio das multinacionais na agricultura de exportação*," *Cadernos do CEAS* (Centro de Estudos e Açao Social), No. 44 (Salvador, Bahia: July–Aug. 1976), pp. 53–63.

107. "A Letter of Resignation Addressed to the President of Brazil," Keyhold Series, *Latin America Documentation* (Washington, D.C.: U. S. Catholic Conference, Oct. 1973), pp. 22–24.

108. Duarte Pereira, op. cit., p. 76.

109. "*Marginación de un Pueblo*," *Revista del Centro de Investigación Social*, No. 233 (Buenos Aires, June 1974), pp. 3–36.

110. Arruda, Souza, and Alfonso, op. cit., p. 160.

111. *Annals* from the Brazilian Institute for Geography and Statistics and Survey by Brazilian Institute for Agrarian Reform.

112. "*Marginación de un Pueblo*," op. cit., p. 20.

113. "Brazilian Bishop Defends Rights of Farm Workers," *Latinamerica Press* (April 29, 1976).

114. Arruda, Souza, and Alfonso, op. cit., p. 183.

115. Ibid., p. 176.

116. "Brazil: Law of the Jungle," *Latin America* (London, July 16, 1976); also Arruda, Souza, and Alfonso, op. cit., pp. 85–86, 167.

117. "Brazil: Law of . . . ," op. cit.; also author's interview with Bishop Pedro Casaldáliga (Vitória, Brazil, July 1976).

118. "A Survey of Mineral Resource Extraction in Brazil" (Toronto: Latin American Working Group, 1976), pp. 1–54.

119. Ben Muneta, "Brazilian Indian Massacre 1963–1973," *Indigena* (Berkeley, Calif., June 1973), mimeograph copy, pp. 1–5.

120. "A Survey of Mineral Resource Extraction . . . ," op. cit.

121. Ibid. Also Arruda, Souza, and Alfonso, op. cit., p. 174.

122. "LAWG Letter" (Toronto: Latin American Working Group, Dec. 1976).

123. "Tribes of the Amazon Basin in Brazil, 1972" (London: Aborigines Protection Society Report, 1973).

124. "Colombia Mounts Major Study of Excessive Pesticide Use," *World Environment Report* (New York, Jan. 15, 1979), p. 4; Gloria Moreno de Castro, *"Peligrosa herbicida usan en Colombia,"* El Tiempo (Bogotá, May 20, 1979); *"Niños Deformes por Fumigación Aérea,"* El Espectador (Bogotá, Aug. 3, 1978).

125. "By the Way: Brazil," *Latin America* (London, Aug. 6, 1976), and "Charge American Billionaire with Misuse of Chemicals," *World Environment Report* (New York, Apr. 10, 1978).

126. "By the Way: Brazil," *Latin America,* op. cit.

127. *Fortune* (Aug. 1974).

128. *"Una Iglesia encarnada en la justicia y la esperanza,"* Sendero (newspaper of the Paraguayan Bishops' Conference) (Asunción, July 23–Aug. 6, 1976).

129. Cover story, *Veja* (São Paulo, Dec. 29, 1976).

130. Los Angeles *Times* (June 17, 1973).

131. Document signed by Bishop Pedro Casaldáliga and Father François Jentel, vicar of Santa Terezinha (Brasília, Mar. 6, 1972), mimeograph.

132. Ibid.

133. *Brazilian Information Bulletin* (Berkeley, Calif., Fall 1973); also *Latinamerica Press* (June 25, 1974).

134. Document signed by Bishop Pedro Casaldáliga (São Paulo, May 30, 1973), mimeograph.

135. Extract of document signed by Judge Plinio Barbosa Martins, sentence condemning Father François Jentel, Military Tribunal (Campo Grande, May 28, 1973), mimeograph.

136. Document signed by Bishop Pedro Casaldáliga (Goiânia, Apr. 28, 1972), mimeograph.

137. Document signed by Bishop Pedro Casaldáliga (São Félix, June 7, 1973), mimeograph.

138. Ibid.

139. Ibid.

140. *Veja,* op. cit.

141. *Jornal de Bahia* (Salvador, Oct. 12, 1975).

142. "Brazil: Church Militant," *Latin America* (London, Dec. 19, 1975).

143. *Veja,* op. cit.

144. Speech by Ralph Nader at Nov. 8, 1974, Conference on "Indian Policy in Brazil: The Need for International Action and Concern," at the Brookings Institute, Washington, D.C., sponsored by *Indigena*.

145. "Covert Action in Chile, 1963–1973," Staff Report of the Select Committee to Study Governmental Operations with Respect to Intelligence Activities, U. S. Senate (Washington, D.C., Dec. 18, 1975), pp. 11–13, 21.

146. "Interfaith Group Warns GM Against Helping Chilean Regime" (Toronto: National Catholic News Service, Aug. 18, 1975).

147. Barnet and Muller, op. cit., p. 59.

Notes—Chapter VIII

1. According to Uruguayan Church sources.

2. Philip Agee, *Inside the Company: CIA Diary* (London: Penguin Books, 1975), pp. 466–67, 623.

3. "Uruguay: Won the Battle but Lost the War," *Latin America* (London, June 18, 1976).

4. Author's interviews with Uruguayan Church representatives, Montevideo (1976).

5. Ibid.

6. Leonardo Guerra, "Uruguayan 'TFP' Finding Communism in the Church," *Latinamerica Press* (Lima, Apr. 21, 1977).

7. Gary MacEoin, "U.S. Mission Efforts Threatened by CIA 'Dirty Tricks,'" *St. Anthony Messenger* (Mar. 1975), pp. 33–37.

8. John D. Marks, "The CIA's Church Connection: Missionaries as Informants" (National Catholic News Service: July 18, 1975).

9. MacEoin, op. cit.

10. Author's interview with O'Brien (Cartagena, Colombia, Jan. 1978); letter to author from Maryknoll Provisional John Breen (Petén, Guatemala, Apr. 11, 1978).

11. Richard Rashke, "CIA Funded, Manipulated Missionaries," *National Catholic Reporter* (Aug. 1, 1975).

12. Marks, op. cit.

13. Arthur J. Moore, "Missionaries and the CIA," *Christianity and Crisis* (Mar. 15, 1976), pp. 42–43.

14. MacEoin, op. cit.

15. Norman Kempster, "'I Got $5 Million Covert,' Jesuit Priest Reported," Washington *Star* (July 23, 1975).

16. Agee, op. cit., p. 229.

17. Marks, op. cit.

18. Stefan A. Musto and collaborators, *"Los medios de comunicación social al servicio del desarrollo rural,"* Instituto Alemán de Desarrollo (Bogotá: Editorial Andes, 1971), pp. 45–68 and 148–51.

19. Richard Rashke, "Chile Connection: White House, Church, CIA," *National Catholic Reporter* (July 29, 1977).

20. Ibid.

21. Ibid.

22. Ibid.

23. Washington *Star*, op. cit.

24. Robinson Rojas Sandford, *The Murder of Allende* (New York: Harper & Row, 1975), p. 112.

25. "Covert Action in Chile, 1963–1973," Staff Report of the Select Committee to Study Governmental Operations with Respect to Intelligence Activities, U. S. Senate (Washington, D.C., Dec. 18, 1975), pp. 24, 31.

26. Author's interviews, Santiago (1973).

27. Rojas Sandford, op. cit., pp. 101–2; also Marlise Simons, "Whose Coup?" *Brazilian Information Bulletin*, No. 12 (Berkeley, Calif.: American Friends of Brazil, Winter, 1974), pp. 7–9.

28. "Covert Action in Chile," op. cit., p. 31.

29. Thomas G. Sanders, "Military Government in Chile, Part II: The New Regime" (New York: American Universities Field Staff, 1975), 12 pp.

30. "Opus Dei Accused of Involvement with CIA in Chile," *Latinamerica Press* (Dec. 5, 1974).

31. Fred Hirsch, "Our AFL-CIO Role in Latin America" (San Jose, Calif., 1974), p. 39.

32. Rojas Sandford, op. cit., pp. 96, 113, 126, 161.

33. "Covert Action in Chile," op. cit., pp. 8, 13, 22, 24, 29.

34. Ramón Marsano, "Blast by Conservative Group Draws Return Fire of Chilean Hierarchy and Nuncio," *Latinamerica Press* (Mar. 25, 1976).

35. Ibid.

36. "LP Interview with Cardinal Silva of Chile: 'I Want to Be Objective. I Am Not Optimistic,'" *Latinamerica Press* (Apr. 8, 1976).

37. "Sanción ejemplarizadora," *La Segunda* (Santiago, Aug. 17, 1976).

38. *"Vaticano Sigue de Cerca Acusación contra Prelados"* (Rio de Janeiro: EFE, Mar. 15, 1977).

39. "Sigaud versus Casaldáliga and Balduino," *Latin America Documentation* (Washington, D.C.: U. S. Catholic Conference, Jan.–Feb. 1978), pp. 15–28.

40. Ibid.

41. Ibid.

42. Ibid.

43. Interview with author.

44. "Protesting a Campaign Against Liberation Theology: A Memorandum from Theologians in West Germany" (Dec. 26, 1977), mimeograph.

45. Ibid.

46. Agee, op. cit., pp. 205, 604, 620.

47. Author's interviews, Ecuador (1975).

Notes—Chapter IX

1. Charles Antoine, *Church and Power in Brazil* (New York: Orbis Books, 1973), pp. 161–64.

2. "Pastoral Letter," Bishop Pedro Casaldáliga (São Félix, Oct. 25, 1976), mimeograph.

3. *"Asesinato de Padre João Bosco Penido Burnier,"* *Mensaje* (Santiago, Jan. 2, 1977), pp. 38–39.

4. "Villagers Raze Brazilian Jail: Church-State Tension Grows," *Latinamerica Press* (Lima, Nov. 4, 1976).

5. Ibid.

6. "Pastoral Communication to the People of God," National Conference of Brazilian Bishops (Rio de Janeiro, Oct. 25, 1976), mimeograph in Portuguese.

7. *"Entrevista com D. Adriano,"* *Editora Vozes,* Serviço de Documentação (official documentation service of the National Conference of Brazilian Bishops) (Rio de Janeiro, May 1977), pp. 1213–15.

8. Jean Luis Weil, Joseph Comblin, and Judge Senese, "The Repressive State," *Brazilian Studies* (Toronto, Aug. 16, 1977), pp. 95–96.

9. "Brazil: Emerging Press," *Latin America Political Report* (London, Mar. 24, 1978).

10. "Documentation: Letter from a Brazilian Prison," *Latin America Documentation* (Washington, D.C.: U. S. Catholic Conference, June 1970), pp. i, 2.

11. "Report on Allegations of Torture in Brazil" (London: Amnesty International, 1976), pp. 58–60.

12. *Le Monde* (Jan. 23, 1974).

13. "Report on Allegations of Torture," op. cit.

14. "Brazil," *Latin America Political Report* (Mar. 11, 1977); "The Trials of Delegado Fleury," *Latin America Political Report* (Oct. 14, 1977); "Brazil," *Latin America Political Report* (Mar. 3, 1978); "Fleury Free to Kill and Torture," *Brazilian Information Bulletin* (Berkeley, Calif., Winter, 1974), p. 4.

15. Ibid., *Latin America Political Report* (Mar. 11, 1977; Oct. 14, 1977; Mar. 3, 1978) and "Fleury Free . . ."

16. *Visão* (Nov. 12, 1973).

17. Ibid.

18. João de Andrade, "Brazil: Police Links to Death Squad Cause Touchy Situation," *Latinamerica Press* (Lima, June 25, 1971).

19. *Noticias* (news bulletin of the National Conference of Brazilian Bishops) (Rio de Janeiro, Feb. 23, 1973).

20. Thomas C. Bruneau, *O Catolocismo Brasileiro em Epoca de Transição* (São Paulo: Edicoes Loyola, 1974), p. 374.

21. Ibid., pp. 374–75.

22. *"Brazil: Continua La Represión," Diálogo Social* (Panama, Aug. 1976), p. 7. Also "Communiqué" from Committee of Women Exiled in Chile (Santiago, June 1, 1972), published in *Brazilian Information Bulletin* (Berkeley, Calif.: American Friends of Brazil, Jan. 1973).

23. "Brazil," *Latin America* (London, Oct. 2, 1976).

24. Ralph della Cava, "Torture in Brazil," *Commonweal* (Apr. 24, 1970).

25. "Brazil: God Shall Be the Judge," *Latin America* (Apr. 20, 1973).

26. "Interview with Dom Paulo," *Latinamerica Press* (May 15, 1975).

27. "Brazil: 'Don't Let Them Die on the Table,'" *Latin America* (Jan. 30, 1976). Also *"Geisel ordena relevar comandante de São Paulo"* (São Paulo: Associated Press, Jan. 20, 1976).

28. "Argentina: A Monopoly of Force," *Time* (Oct. 18, 1976).

29. "More About General Ibérico Saint Jean," *Latin America Political Report* (June 17, 1977); also quoted in *Congressional Record*, U. S. Senate (June 15, 1974), p. S9890, citing New York *Times*.

30. Penny Lernoux, "Military Repression Angers Argentine Church," *Alicia Patterson Foundation Newsletter* (New York, Feb. 24, 1977); also *Alternativa* (Bogotá, Oct. 1976), p. 25.

31. Editorial, *Mensaje* (Santiago, Aug. 1976).

32. "Argentina: Cracks in the Façade," *Latin America Political Report* (Sept. 2, 1977).

33. "Testimony: The Murder of a Family," *Outreach* (May–June 1977), pp. 16–17.

34. Author's interviews, Buenos Aires (1976).

35. Author's interviews, Buenos Aires (1969).

36. "U.S. Narcotics Enforcement Assistance to Latin America" (Washing-

ton, D.C.: Argentine Commission for Human Rights, Mar. 10, 1977), 13 pp.

37. "Argentina: The Politics of Cocaine in America," *Latin America* (Dec. 19, 1975).

38. Ibid.

39. Ibid.

40. "Argentina: What Went Wrong?" *Latinamerica Press* (Nov. 4, 1976).

41. Harry Maurer, "Anti-Semitism in Argentina," *The Nation* (Feb. 12, 1977), pp. 170–73.

42. Scott Lubcek, "Specter of Nazism Once Again Stalks Argentina," *Times of the Americas* (Washington, D.C., Nov. 10, 1976).

43. Maurer, op. cit.

44. "Human Rights in Argentina," Hearings before the Subcommittee on International Organizations of the Committee on International Relations, U. S. House of Representatives (Washington, D.C., 1976), pp. 59–60.

45. Ibid., p. 5.

46. Guendolyn Holden, "Rightists Combine Extremism and Profit in Argentina," *Latinamerica Press* (Oct. 28, 1976).

47. "Argentina: Obscure and Pogromist Forces," *Latin America Political Report* (Aug. 5, 1977).

48. *"Cae nazi sátiro, mano derecha de A. Eichmann"* (Buenos Aires: Associated Press, Dec. 10, 1976) and *"Libre sátiro amigo de Eichmann"* (Buenos Aires: Associated Press, Dec. 17, 1976).

49. "Death and Violence in Argentina," compiled by a group of priests in Argentina (London: Catholic Institute for International Relations, Oct. 18, 1976), p. 4.

50. Author's interviews, Buenos Aires (July 1976).

51. Arturo Paoli, *"Golpearé al Pastor: ¿Quién Asesinó al Obispo Angelelli?,"* *SIC* (Caracas, Jan. 21, 1977), pp. 75–78.

52. Ibid.

53. "Death and Violence in Argentina," op. cit., pp. 7–8.

54. *"Alarmante Aumento de la Criminalidad en México"* (Mexico City: United Press International, Jan. 9, 1977).

55. Ibid.

56. *Bulletin No. 6* (Rome: International Documentation and Communication Center [IDOC], June 1977).

57. *"México en la 'olla' económica"* (Mexico City: Agencia France Presse, May 2, 1977).

58. "Bishops Ask Halt to Student, Campesino Violence in Mexico" (Mexico City: National Catholic News Service, May 6, 1976).

59. "U.S. Agribusiness Reaps Mexican Harvest of Anger," *Latinamerica Press* (Oct. 21, 1976).

60. Author's interview with Bishop Samuel Ruiz, of Chiapas, Mexico (July 1976).

61. *"México: terror en el campo oaxaqueño,"* *CENCOS* (Centro Nacional de Comunicación) (Mexico, Mar. 1977), p. 39.

62. Ibid.

63. "Pastoral Letter," Bishop Arturo Lona Reyes, of Tehuantepec, Oaz. (Jan. 26, 1977).

64. *"Mas de 200,000 Indígenas Peligran Morir de Hambre"* (Guerrero: EFE, Aug. 17, 1976).

65. "Bishop Threatened with Death," *Latinamerica Press* (Nov. 15, 1973)

66 "The Provincial of the Marist Priests Protests Torture in Mexico," *Latin America Documentation* (Washington, D.C.: U. S. Catholic Conference, Jan. 1973), pp. iii, 19.

67. IDOC, op. cit.

68. "Police Raid Ecumenical Center in Mexico," *Latinamerica Press* (July 28, 1977).

Notes—Chapter X

1. Alceu Amoroso Lima, "My Passionate Conviction," *Latin America Documentation* (Washington, D.C.: U. S. Catholic Conference, Dec. 1974), pp. 7–9.

2. Robert McAfee Brown, "Reflections on 'Liberation Theology,'" *Religion in Life* (1974), pp. 269–81.

3. Philip Scharper, "A Theology of Liberation," *World Parish* (Jan. 1973).

4. Ibid.

5. Dom Helder Cámara, *The Desert Is Fertile* (New York: Orbis Books, 1974), p. 24.

6. Paulo Freire. Second of three-part series in Nicaraguan monthly *Servicio de Investigación y Documentación* (SID) (Managua, Aug.–Oct. 1974).

7. Felipe Berryman, "Popular Catholicism in Latin America," *Cross Currents* (Summer 1971), pp. 284–301.

8. José Miguez Bonino, *"La Piedad Popular en América Latina,"* *Cristianismo y Sociedad*, No. 47 (Buenos Aires, 1976), pp. 31–38.

9. "Indian Towns Want Indian Priests," *Latin America Documentation* (Washington, D.C.: U. S. Catholic Conference, Oct. 1971), pp. ii, 7:1–6.

10. "A Patronizing 'No' to Optional Celibacy?," *Latinamerica Press* (Lima, Nov. 8, 1973).

11. "Canadian Bishop Sees Socialism Developing in Latin America," *Latinamerica Press* (July 10, 1975).

12. LADOC Keyhole Series: "Basic Christian Communities" (Washington, D.C.: U. S. Catholic Conference, 1976), p. 23.

13. Ibid., p. 25.

14. Ibid., pp. 41–44.

15. Ibid., p. 18.

16. Father Alfredo Schnuettgen, "The 'Leme' Movement of Fishermen in Brazil," *Latin America Documentation* (Washington, D.C.: U. S. Catholic Conference, Apr. 1975), pp. 29–37.

17. León Urrezti J., *"Compartiendo la Pobreza,"* *Mensaje* (Santiago, July 1976), pp. 287–89.

18. Ibid.

19. Ibid.

20. Penny Lernoux, "Popular Religiosity Forms New Social Conscience in Latin America," *Alicia Patterson Foundation Newsletter* (New York, Dec. 13, 1976).

21. *Mensaje* (Santiago, Mar. 1977).

22. Howard Handelman, "The Political Mobilization of Urban Squatter Settlements," *Latin American Research Review*, Latin American Studies Association (Oct. 2, 1975).

Notes—Chapter XI

1. "Christian Socialism Praised," *Latinamerica Press* (Lima, April 19, 1973).

2. "Cardinal Cautions about Socialism," *Latinamerica Press* (Nov. 30, 1973).

3. José de Broucker, *The Violence of a Peacemaker* (New York: Orbis Books, 1970), pp. 89–91.

4. *Latinamerica Press* (Nov. 30, 1973), op. cit.

5. Interviews with author: Bogotá (1974–77); Lima, Rio de Janeiro, Caracas, and Brussels (1976); Puebla (1979).

6. Interview with author, Bogotá (Dec. 1974).

7. Mark Winiarski, "Exclusive: Dom Helder tells *NCR* he was under ban; blasts U.S. as 'torture exporter,'" *National Catholic Reporter* (Mar. 21, 1978).

8. Ibid.

9. *Documento de consulta a las Conferencias Episcopales*, III (Bogotá: CELAM, n.d.), p. 130.

10. Author's interviews, Bogotá (July–Aug. 1978).

11. Ibid. and author's interviews, Puebla (Jan.–Feb. 1979).

12. Luis G. del Valle, *"Puebla, Proceso y Tensiones"* (Mexico City, Jan. 10, 1979), mimeograph.

13. "'Rightwingers' Added to CELAM list," *National Catholic Reporter* (Dec. 15, 1978).

14. Carlos Fazio and Francisco Ortiz, *"Puebla Relega al Pueblo de Dios,"* *Proceso* (Mexico City, Feb. 5, 1979).

15. Author's interviews, Puebla (Jan.–Feb. 1979).

16. *"Derechos Humanos en América Latina"* (London: Amnesty International, Aug. 1978), p. 3.

17. Author's interview, Puebla (Jan. 1979).

18. Enrique Santos Calderón, *"Puebla: El difícil arte del malabarismo,"* *El Tiempo* (Bogotá, Feb. 18, 1979).

19. "The Pope's Impact on Mexico," *Latin America Political Report* (London, Feb. 6, 1979).

20. Pope John Paul II, *"Discurso de Juan Pablo II"* (Zapopan Sanctuary, Guadalajara, Jan. 31, 1979).

21. Pope John Paul II, *"Discurso del Santo Padre al Inaugurar los Trabajos de la III Conferencia General del Episcopado Latinoamericano"* (Puebla, Jan. 28, 1979).

22. "El Papa en Puebla," *Boletín de la Confederación Latinoamericana de Religiosos* (CLAR) (Bogotá, Feb. 1979).

23. Pope John Paul II, *"Saludo del Santo Padre a los Indios de Oaxaca y Chiapas"* (Culipán, Oaxaca, Jan. 29, 1979).

24. Pope John Paul II, *"El Trabajo, Una Vocación para Cambiar al Mundo"* (Jalisco Stadium, Jan. 31, 1979).

25. Pope John Paul II, *"Encuentro del Santo Padre con los Sacerdotes y Religiosos de México"* (Guadalupe Basilica, Mexico City, Jan. 27, 1979).

26. *"Elogió Pinochet la visita del Papa a México porque impugnó los métodos marxistas en América Latina"* (Santiago: Associated Press, Feb. 6, 1979).

27. "Pope Backs Liberation Theology," *National Catholic Reporter* (Mar. 2, 1979).

28. Author's interview, Puebla (Jan. 1979).

29. Cardinal Aloisio Lorscheider, *"Relación Introductora a los Trabajos de la III Conferencia General del Episcopado Latinoamericano"* (Puebla, Jan. 29, 1979).

30. Author's interviews, Puebla (Feb. 1979).

31. *"Documento Confidencial: Presionaron en el CELAM para que fuera invitado el superior general de los jesuitas: López Trujillo,"* Uno más Uno (Mexico City, Feb. 1, 1979).

32. Miguel López Saucedo, *"Nuevas protestas de periodistas,"* Uno más Uno (Mexico City, Feb. 2, 1979).

33. *La Evangelización en el Presente y en el Futuro de América Latina* (Puebla: CELAM, Feb. 13, 1979), pp. 1–232.

34. *"Documento Confidencial . . . ,"* op. cit.

35. Penny Lernoux and Mark Winiarski, "CIA Ordered to Survey Latin American Church," *National Catholic Reporter* (Feb. 16, 1979).

36. Author's interviews, Puebla (Feb. 1979).

37. "Puebla Vignettes," *National Catholic Reporter* (Feb. 23, 1979).

38. "Preaching 'Economic Democracy' to the Pope," *NACLA Report* (Sept./Oct. 1978), p. 43.

39. *La Evangelización en el Presente . . . ,"* op. cit., p. 50.

40. Ibid., p. ii.

Notes—Chapter XII

1. Dom Helder Cámara, *The Desert Is Fertile* (New York: Orbis Books, 1974), p. 19.